# A Solomon Island Society

KINSHIP AND LEADERSHIP AMONG THE SIUAI OF BOUGAINVILLE

# *A Solomon Island Society*

KINSHIP AND LEADERSHIP AMONG
THE SIUAI OF BOUGAINVILLE

*DOUGLAS L. OLIVER*

*Beacon Press, Boston*

*Copyright, 1955, by the President and Fellows of Harvard College*

First published as a Beacon Paperback in 1967
by arrangement with Harvard University Press and the author.

Published simultaneously in Canada by Saunders of Toronto, Ltd.

Beacon Press books are published under the auspices of the
Unitarian Universalist Association

*All rights reserved*

Printed in the United States of America

*To the memory of*
**EARNEST ALBERT HOOTON**

# Preface

This book is a report based on field work carried out by the writer in southern Bougainville. It was written with two general objectives in mind. First, it attempts to describe all important phases of the culture of the natives studied; and secondly, it makes an effort to highlight the workings of the native institution of leadership.

My effort to summarize the whole culture of the Siuai in one book is based on a theoretical tenet and on a pedagogical need. In connection with the former, it seems to me that the Functionalists' dogma concerning trait and pattern interdependence does not require further belaboring; what has to be done now is to devise a methodology for analyzing and portraying *all* of the dominant patterns of a culture in a single morphological frame. Of course, I have fallen far short of success in this ambitious task, but my efforts have at least convinced me that the goal is eminently worth reaching for and that it will some day be reached. In connection with the pedagogical need referred to, as a teacher of cultural anthropology I am continually faced with the problem of assigning descriptive reading to elementary and intermediate classes of students. Highly desirable as it may be, it is simply not practicable to require such students to read enough of the many excellent descriptive works on such cultures as Tikopia, Nuer, Tallensi, Trobriand, Arapesh, and Tswana, to ensure that they will gain comprehensive and balanced views of all important aspects of these cultures. Fortunately we do possess some fine single-monograph and nearly whole-culture studies for assignment, including classics on such peoples as the Bemba, Crow, Lepcha, Navaho, Andamanese, Murngin, and Thonga, but there is a pedagogical need for many more.

My second objective in writing this book was to devote special attention to the political institutions of a "stateless"[1] nonliterate people, a department of anthropological inquiry which lags far behind the study of kinship, religion, and language. In connection with a description of Siuai culture this highlighting of native political institutions is not entirely arbitrary, as this book will indicate.

It should be emphasized that this report is intended to be primarily *descriptive*. In 1938, when I embarked on the field study on which this book is based,

---

[1] M. Fortes and E. E. Evans-Pritchard, *African Political Systems* (Oxford, 1940).

I was not intent upon testing a theory or solving a scientific problem. Quite honestly, my purpose was to gain some practical experience which would help me to become an anthropologist; and I suspect that I am not the only anthropologist who has undertaken his first field study in this way! Moreover, except in a few minor asides, in the writing of this book I have not attempted to recast my notes and memory about Siuai in order to test and document some general theory learned about since leaving the field. True, in the course of analyzing and organizing the data for presentation I have ventured to utilize some methodological concepts which are not entirely unoriginal; and I have stated some conclusions which may have implications reaching beyond the borders of Siuai. But I must repeat that the book is intended to be primarily descriptive, and it should be judged on that basis.

Carrying out the field work and writing the book has proved to be an enlightening and on the whole enjoyable experience. But now, with the job done, I must say that I would be reluctant to undertake another field study which is not explicitly related to theory formation. But this is a matter of personal preference, and I hope that some anthropologists will continue to produce descriptive ethnographies and thereby increase the store of raw materials of social science.

D. L. O.

Cambridge, Massachusetts
April 1953

## *Acknowledgment*

Some day a Siuai native may read this book; if so, I hope he will accept my gratitude to his people for the part they played in making the book possible. Some of them, like Peuru of Mi'kahna, came to see and describe their institutions with clarity and objectivity. Others were too deeply immersed for such perspective and served rather as unwitting bearers of the culture's norms and modes. Even those few who resented our presence provided us with useful insights.

Eleanor McClennen (formerly Eleanor Schirmer Oliver) contributed most towards carrying out the field work. With the help of Manao, our wonderful Muschu Island helper, she kept our "expedition" alive and healthy, and, in addition, she gathered masses of information on aspects of native life beyond my time or ability to learn about.

Cornelius Crane of Ipswich, Massachusetts, made our trip to New Guinea possible. Donald Scott, then Director of Harvard's Peabody Museum, the late Earnest Hooton, then Professor of Anthropology at Harvard, and Louis Pierre Ledoux of New York, provided us with financial and institutional support while we were in the field.

In Australia, Dr. H. Ian Hogbin of the University of Sydney rendered us many services, including the pleasure of his companionship. In New Guinea, Messrs. Stanley, Eve, and Marshall of Oil Search, Ltd., placed their time and other resources at our disposal; E. W. P. Chinnery and Robert Melrose, senior officials of the Administration, gave us every possible assistance; while Margaret Mead and Gregory Bateson provided us with the luxuries for what otherwise would have been an empty Christmas.

While we were studying the Siuai, the burden of living in a remote and harsh environment was immeasurably lightened by the friendliness shown us by Dr. and Mrs. A. V. Price, Mr. and Mrs. Alec Scott, District Officer J. E. Merryless, Patrol Officer and Mrs. K. Bilston, and by Bishop Thomas Wade and Father Joseph Schlieker of the Marist Mission.

Back home, I must express my gratitude to many Harvard and Radcliffe students who sat through my classes, with either interest or resignation, and thus gave me opportunity to try out much of the material recorded in this book. For the onerous task of typing the manuscript, or seeing it through the press while I luxuriate in another field study, I acknowledge with appreciation the assistance of Miss Maria von Mering, Miss Gwen Wolsted, Mrs. Natalie Stoddard, and Mrs. Martha Smith. But most of all, I am profoundly grateful to my wife, Sheila Mitchell Oliver, who patiently fed me and even encouraged me throughout the trying months of trying to put the Siuai on paper.

D. L. O.

# CONTENTS

## I. A SURVEY OF SIUAI LIFE

1. **Physical Adaptation**     3

   BOUGAINVILLE ISLAND, 3. THE SIUAI AREA, 8. THE SIUAI PEOPLE, 9. RAW MATERIALS AND TOOLS, 11. CONTAINERS, 13. SETTLEMENTS, 15. SHELTER, CLOTHING, AND GROOMING, 19. AGRICULTURE, 22. COLLECTING, HUNTING, AND FISHING, 30. ANIMAL HUSBANDRY, 32. COOKING AND EATING, 34. ART AND AMUSEMENT, 35. ECOLOGICAL TIME, 37.

2. **Some Beliefs about Nature and Man**     39

   THE AGE OF CREATION, 39. CLASSIFICATION OF ENTITIES, 62. RELATIONSHIPS AMONG ENTITIES, 80. TIME, SPACE, AND NUMBER, 96.

3. **Social Units**     102

   DEFINITIONS, 102. "TRIBE," 103. GROUPS, 104. MATRILINEAL UNITS, 107.

## II. SOCIAL RELATIONS

4. **Households**     125

   THE DWELLING HOUSE, 125. THE GARDEN, 129. THE DAILY MEAL, 135. HOUSEHOLD PERSONNEL, 138.

5. **Developmental Cycle of the Nuclear Family**     140

   INCENTIVES FOR MARRYING, 140. REGULATION OF MARRIAGE, 151. ARRANGING THE MARRIAGE, 154. NUPTIALS, 158. SETTING UP THE HOUSEHOLD, 163. PREGNANCY AND CHILDBIRTH, 169. BAPTISM, 177. INFANCY, 182. CHILDHOOD, 187. DIVORCE, 198. YOUTH, 201. OLD AGE AND DEATH, 208. SECONDARY MARRIAGES, 220. FAMILY STRUCTURE, 226.

6. **Hamlets**     236

   COMPOSITION, 236. ACTIVITIES, 238. AUTHORITY, 238. "TRUE-OWNERS" AND "ATTACHERS," 239.

## 7. Outline of Kin Relations — 247

KIN PAIR RELATIONS, 249. THE EXPRESSION OF KINSHIP "EMOTION" IN DIRGES, 275. RELATIONS BETWEEN KINSHIP GROUPS, 282. KINSHIP, 288.

## 8. Associations — 295

RELATIONSHIPS BASED ON TRADE IN ECONOMIC COMMODITIES, 295. RELATIONSHIPS BASED ON SALE OF SERVICES AND MAGICAL COMMODITIES, 301. RELATIONSHIPS BETWEEN CREDITORS AND DEBTORS, 307. PRODUCTION TEAMS, 309. CONGREGATIONS, 313. ADMINISTRATIVE GROUPS, 318. MEN'S SOCIETIES, 329. FRIENDSHIP, 332. NEIGHBORHOODS, 333.

# III. LEADERSHIP

## 9. Accumulating Capital — 335

SHELL MONEY AND ECONOMIC VALUE, 339. SURPLUS DURABLE AND CONSUMPTION GOODS, 346. PIGS, 348. SELLING SERVICES AND LENDING CAPITAL, 354. THE MAGICAL COMPONENT IN ACCUMULATING AND SAFEGUARDING MATERIAL RESOURCES, 356.

## 10. Acquiring Renown — 361

WEALTH AND PRESTIGE, 361. FOOD IN SIUAI LIFE, 363. FEASTS, 364. CLUB-HOUSES, 372. WOODEN SLIT-GONGS, 379. COMPETITIVE "GIVING," 386. THE COMPETITIVE FEAST, 390.

## 11. The Rewards and Burdens of Leadership — 396

BELIEFS ABOUT A LEADER'S PERSONALITY, 396. PRAISE OF A LEADER'S ATTAINMENTS, 399. RESPECT FOR A LEADER'S NAME AND PERSON, 399. AUTHORITY IN LOCAL AFFAIRS, 404. INFLUENCE BEYOND THE NEIGHBORHOOD, 407. THE BURDENS OF LEADERSHIP, 408.

## 12. Leadership and Warfare — 411

ORGANIZED WARFARE, 412. WAR LEADERS, 419.

## 13. A Leader in Action — 422

HISTORICAL SETTING, 422. THE RISE OF SONGI, 423. TURUNGOM VILLAGE, 426. SONGI THE MAN, 428. SONGI'S MUMINAI FEAST, 429.

14. *Analysis of Leadership and its Effects* 440

ESSENTIALS FOR LEADERSHIP, 440. LEADERSHIP AND SOCIAL RELATIONS, 441. LEADERSHIP AND RELIGION, 444. LEADERSHIP AND ECONOMICS, 446.

## IV. GENERALIZATIONS, CONJECTURES, AND QUESTIONS

15. *Integration* 451

KINSHIP IDEOLOGY, 452. RANK IDEOLOGY, 456. ADMINISTRATION IDEOLOGY, 458. MISSION IDEOLOGY, 461. OTHER CHARACTERISTICS OF SIUAI CULTURAL SYSTEMS, 464. COHERENCE? 465.

16. *Explanation* 467

ENVIRONMENTAL, 467. CO-VARIABLE, 468. HISTORICAL, 469. PSYCHOLOGICAL, 471.

17. *Evaluation* 473

SOCIETAL CONTINUITY, 473. SATISFACTION OF THE INDIVIDUAL'S NEEDS, 478. UTILIZATON OF HUMAN POTENTIALS, 486.

*Notes* 489

*Subject Index* 529

*Author Index* 535

# ILLUSTRATIONS

*(following page 10)*

1. A "line" village in northeast Siuai.
2. Turuŋom village. The ethnographer's hut is in the right foreground.
3. A hamlet in northeast Siuai.
4. High noon at the taro garden.
5. Women carrying taro and firewood.
6. Some of the taro corms are the main part of the principal daily meal; the pigs are fed what is left over.
7. Offspring and shell money are goals of most Siuai.
8. Pigs serve as pets, capital goods, and food delicacies.
9. Rolling twine for making a net bag like the one hanging from the craftsman's shoulder.
10. Plaiting a large carrying pouch.
11. Searching for fish and prawns. The youths have bows and spears to shoot at fish too fast to be caught by hand.
12. An artist displays the decorated baking frames he has made for a feast.
13. Trying out a new panpipe. Siuai males have plenty of time for recreation.
14. Roasting pork for a public meal. Women cook the everyday household meals but men take over when cooking delicacies for a feast.
15. Wedding ceremony. Ritual ablutions over bride, groom, and bridesmaid.
16. Wedding ceremony. Coconut oil is applied to legs of bride and groom. A male helper strangles the feast pig.
17. Baptism ceremony. At right is a live opossum scapegoat.
18. Baptism of an older child, who stands on a pig while magicians rub consecrated oil over his body.
19. Clearing the ground for a new garden.
20. Learning to walk.
21. The closest bond.
22. An ancient comforts his grandson.
23. Siuai women dancing.
24. Children try to imitate the dance of the women shown above.
25, 26. Small boys' greatest joy is permission to beat a wooden slit-gong as their elders do.

# ILLUSTRATIONS

27. One wife is enough for most men. Having many wives is in itself not particularly desirable.
28. The leader Moŋko, his eight wives, and one child. Women's skills and services are needed for accumulating capital.
29. Old women sometimes become magicians, as did the growth-magic specialists shown here.
30. Old men while away their last years dozing and chewing pre-ground betel mixture.
31. When death comes, relatives paint mourning marks on their faces and attend the corpse until it is cremated.
32. Kinsmen build a pyre for the cremation of a relative.
33. Men's world. A throng of youths and men wait for a feast to begin in a leader's club-house.
34. Accumulating capital for acquiring renown is a full-time occupation. Some make and sell pots.
35. Others accumulate capital by raising and selling pigs. Three men confer on the terms of a purchase.
36. A magician (right) helps his client gain rapport with a ghost, whose image is believed to be reflected in a cup of coconut oil.
37. Magicians sit on either side of a sick man and try to bring rapport between him and the demon who has caused his illness.
38. Carrying a new wooden slit-gong to install it in its owner's club-house.
39. A magician rides atop a new gong to lighten its weight.
40. A large wooden slit-gong in place across the front of a club-house.
41. Making a pudding for the feast. The leader, Soŋi, wearing a conical hat, holds open a leaf container as helpers pour a mixture of sago and almond into a wooden baking frame.
42. Wrapping up the pudding before baking it in an earth oven.
43. Bringing home a large sow. The most important step in preparing for a feast is the collection of live pigs for distribution among the guests.
44. At the pigpen. Pigs awaiting distribution at a feast are centers of public interest.
45. A composer tries out a new melody he has created for a feast.
46. A magician is assigned the job of protecting the hosts at a feast, by watching out for acts of sorcery on the part of envious guests.
47. Dress rehearsal. Natives fully ornamented for a feast practice dance steps while blowing on their panpipes and large wooden trumpets.
48. Feast in full swing. Natives dance and pipe in front of the host's club-house. In foreground is the display platform laden with food delicacies and decorated with coconuts.

49. Crucial moment. The guests estimate the value of the pigs given them at a feast.
50. Speech of presentation. Spokesmen for the host present the gift to the guest of honor at a feast. Strings of shell money, part of the gift, are laid out over a log in front of the spokesmen.
51. Leader, Siuai style. The prominent leader, Soŋi, poses for a picture with his favorite son.
52. Officials, new style. The Paramount Chief, Tomo (left), and his executive officer, 'Uta.
53. Signs of change. Methodists compete with Catholics in a Bible-knowledge bee. Catechists write Biblical names on the blackboard for the opposing congregations to identify.
54. The new order in government. Village headmen salute their Paramount Chief.

# Introduction

The Siuai [1] are a black-skinned Papuan-speaking people of some 4700 individuals living in the rain forests of southwest Bougainville. Their homeland is relatively isolated from the white settlements which are scattered along Bougainville's northern and eastern coasts.[2] Kangu, the nearest administrative outpost, is on the coast a long day's walk away; near Kangu are also mission stations and a Chinese trade store. The only white outpost in Siuai itself is a small Catholic mission station. Once a year the Australian Administration's subdistrict Patrol Officer tours Siuai to record census changes and collect head-taxes, and less frequently a white medical officer inspects the population. Now and then the Methodist missionary stationed at the coast looks over his Siuai congregations, and nearly every year Siuai natives catch fleeting glimpses of one or two planters recruiting laborers for their coastal plantations. Other than these, few whites ever visit the Siuai's peaceful scattered settlements and bountiful gardens and groves. This is not to imply that the influence of the West has been meager or unimportant. Actually, iron tools have long since replaced those of stone and bamboo, and every native past early childhood now wears a trade-store calico around his or her loins. In fact, it may be said that the Siuai are already well along into the *second* phase of westernization. The initial phase began some sixty to seventy years ago with the import of the first western goods and ideas, brought first by native traders from other islands and then by a few adventurous white traders themselves. This traffic in traits of culture continues today; missionaries account for some of the innovations, but Siuai natives themselves bring in many more on their return from working on whites' plantations and ships.

The second phase of westernization began for the Siuai about 1915, when the first officials toured the area and started the process of introducing the Pax Australianus. Peace did not come overnight, but the white men's rifles ultimately convinced the Siuai that a new and irresistible kind of power had entered their universe. Embodying this power was a new officialdom capable of applying physical force, including the ultimate sanction of death. In establishing this new officialdom the Australians outlawed warfare and other uses of physical force by *native* authorities, and in so doing they destroyed two of the most important foundations of the indigenous Siuai form of government.

Nevertheless, an indigenous form of leadership, altered but still vital, continues to exist alongside or even in conflict with the alien form of government. *The main task of this monograph will be to describe this indigenous leadership institution within the context of the total Siuai culture*: to identify and observe its holders of authority; to describe the locus and sources of their power; and to relate their statuses to those of other persons of authority, of influence, and of prestige, in this society of forest-dwelling gardeners and pig-breeders.[3]

To begin with, just to identify the holders of authority in the indigenous political hierarchies is not a simple matter. They wear no special insignia. Their standards of living are not markedly different from other men's. And in the presence of white visitors many of them tend to be purposefully unobtrusive.

When my wife and I first arrived in Siuai we were met at the Mivo River by a work-party of some forty natives waiting to carry our gear to the next rest-house. A Paramount Chief, carrying his staff of office, met us at the river's edge and smartly saluted. With him were five or six others clothed like himself in neat calicoes and wearing peaked officers' hats on their bushy mops of hair. All these were District and Village Officials, appointed by the Australian Administration; we had seen many of their counterparts as we traveled northwest from the coast. After learning our purposes and destination the Paramount Chief gave instructions to his subordinates, and these shouted orders to the crowd of hatless and unkempt natives squatting about on the ground. Quickly the latter picked up our boxes and started out, ourselves and the hat-wearing officials walking empty-handed behind. No mistaking the holders of authority in *this* hierarchy! But did the authority of these men carry over into other situations in Siuai life? "No," said one talkative native who stayed to look us over as we made camp for the night, "they are merely officials ('Hat-men nothing'); they only carry out the white man's business. The men whose talk we listen to in *our* affairs are our *mumis*."

The word *mumi* turned up often during the following days. Here is one of the earliest entries in my diary: "At about nine in the evening a neighbor rushed into the hut and excitedly told me that he had just seen a light shoot through the air and had heard something crash to the ground near the village of Hinna. 'That is a sign that some mumi is about to die,' he said."

On the following day an informant gave me this additional information: "A mumi is an important man — just like the Patrol Officer. When a mumi is about to die his soul changes into fire, rushes through the air, and falls onto ground sanctified by his sib ancestress. Not every man's soul acts in this way; only that of a mumi."

Who then are these mumis, and how do they become so?

In northeast Siuai, where we settled down to work, several informants recited to me lists of men whom they considered to be mumis. No two lists agreed. It transpired that every informant had produced a list made up largely of names of some of his own relatives; yet it was clear from other contexts that the word mumi is not a kinship term. When I read off Informant A's list to Informant B, the latter laughed scornfully at some of the inclusions, saying: "Why, so-and-so is not a real mumi; he's A's uncle, and that's why A included him in his list."

Of course, the very fact that each list was biased in this manner provided insight into one aspect of kinship, and this point was dutifully recorded. But I had not progressed very far in my search beyond noting that some men appeared on *all* lists.

One day I was discussing these findings with a neighbor when he brightened up and said: "Why, your question is not difficult. A mumi is simply a man who is the *peki* of former mumis."

Since *peki* is the kinship term for "their-offspring," the questions became: *Who* were the mumis a generation ago, and which of their offspring have succeeded them? Typical answers to the first question went like this: "You ask, which of our ancestors were mumis? Why, all of them were mumis. In those days all men were mumis. Conditions were different then. Everyone had lots of things, plenty of wealth and crops and land. It was not as it is today, when we children have nothing."

Answers like this convinced me that I had to rephrase the question and ask: "Which men used to be the highest-ranking mumis?" Responses to this question were less ambiguous, and a list of eighteen men was generally agreed upon. This finding led to the second question: "Who, then, are the peki of those former high-ranking mumis; and have these peki retained the rank of their predecessors?"

The term *peki* means literally: "their (personal possessive prefix)-son." But in a classificatory kinship system like this one, every term has a number of referents, and each particular meaning must be derived from its context. In the case of *peki* the primary meaning is: a male referred to through his own mother and father. Accordingly, I questioned my informants concerning the titles of sons of the men whom they had all called mumis. The answers were confusing. Only two of the eighteen outstanding mumis of the preceding generation had produced sons who now rank as high as their fathers did. Furthermore, some of those outstanding mumis of the preceding generation were known to have been the sons of non-mumis.

"Then why do you say that a mumi must be the offspring of a mumi?" I asked.

"You do not comprehend," I was told. "So-and-so had *many* fathers and mothers, and they all helped him become a mumi."

By this time it was obvious that my line of inquiry had become senseless. In the process, however, I did succeed in recording the names of certain living men whom all informants agreed to be mumis. For example, there was no disagreement about the mumi status of contemporaries like Soŋi of Turuŋom, Kaopa of Noronai, Kirisu of Novei, and a few more. How, then, did these mumis reach their positions?

When informants were asked this they were fairly well agreed that all these men were mumis because they own large tracts of land, lots of crops, plentiful supplies of wealth, and club-houses filled with wooden gongs; and, they added, "*any* man who owns these things is indisputably a mumi."

Thus equipped with these highly concrete suggestions I set about early in the course of field work to test these criteria against observations and inventories. The results were most enlightening. Although they did not bear out my informants' assertions that material possessions and status are directly correlated, they provided some working hypotheses that led me far along the road to an understanding of Siuai culture.

Active field work began during mid-February 1938, when our small party composed of Eleanor Schirmer Oliver, Manao — an indentured servant from Muschu Island — and the writer arrived by launch on the southern coast of Bougainville. From that point we traveled by foot to the village of Mataras in northeast Siuai. We remained in and around Mataras until late August of that year, at which time my wife developed an attack of appendicitis which forced us to return to Kieta for medical care. I went back to Siuai, but rejoined my wife a few weeks later and carried out linguistic and anthropometric investigations on the peoples living around Kieta. Then we resumed our study in Siuai in early October, and remained there until February 1939. Between February and April we visited other ethnic areas in central, western, and northern Bougainville, and then went to Australia, for rehabilitation. Restored to good health by a few weeks in Sydney, we sailed back to Bougainville and resumed field work in Siuai in July. Then, in November, we revisited Kieta, finished our anthropometric and linguistic survey of the east-central coast, and finally set sail for home on November 21, 1939.

Our intensive study of northeast Siuai was carried out according to conventional anthropological procedures: by prolonged residence in native villages, by learning and using the native language, by intensive use of several strategically placed informants, by observation of natives' behavior, and by limited participation in their activities. In Mataras village we lived in a resthouse opposite a men's club-house and about 100 yards away from native dwellings. In Turuŋom village, where we dwelt the longest, we occupied two houses, one facing a club-house and one in the midst of the village, the latter about fifteen feet from the nearest native dwelling. For the privacy we lost by actually living in the village, we were amply repaid: few domestic quarrels inside a village dwelling escaped our notice.

After we became established in Siuai I think it is safe to say that we were at no time identified either with Administration or Mission, and were accepted by the natives as whites without known status who wanted to learn their language and customs and record their land boundaries. I was called *kakotova*, "cockatoo (white)-like" rather than *master*, the usual term for a white man. Although we were the first of our kind and calling to visit them, and certainly the first whites to live semi-native lives, the Siuai were not particularly mystified by our presence and our announced objectives (after all, *everything* about whites is so odd and unpredictable; our behavior excited little additional curiosity), and soon they began to take no special notice of us. Yet, we were never assimilated to most native ways of life: we did not dress (or undress) in native fashion, concluded no trade-partnerships, were not adopted by any families, and remained dry-eyed throughout their cremations. On the other hand, we added many of their foodstuffs to our diet, lived in houses like theirs, treated their ailments, gave presents and received them, opened our houses to them and visited them in theirs, and achieved something of a social triumph by being told that I might possibly have become a mumi had I been born a Siuai and had I possessed more resources!

We arrived in Siuai fortified with a knowledge of pidgin English, and found several plantation- and mission-trained natives with whom we could converse, but I began immediately to record and learn *Motuna*.

Motuna is the Papuan language spoken by the Siuai. It had been previously recorded only in the *Solomon Islands School Exercises: English-Motuna*, a slight 21-page dictionary and phrase book published by the Methodist Mission for use in native schools, and having little value as a grammar. I did, however, gain some insight into Motuna syntax through study of a manuscript grammar of the related *Rugara* language, prepared by the Reverend B. Poncelet of the Marist Mission of Bougainville. Even with this assistance, I found Motuna to be an extremely difficult language. Recording and translating texts and explanations proved simple enough in time, but following normal conversations never became easy for me. As for my own speaking, I substituted more and more Motuna for pidgin as time went by, and after ten months could carry on a fairly lengthy conversation in the language. Toward the end of our stay I achieved a fair degree of fluency but never succeeded in speaking with entire grammatical accuracy. For example, Motuna contains over forty [4] classes of nouns in terms of the forms of numerical adjectives used with them; to avoid a difficult memorizing task I learned only three sets of numerical adjectives and used them to qualify all nouns when I spoke. Natives used to smile tolerantly at my mistakes but I believe they usually understood my meaning.

I am not a linguist and am not now in a position to set down a full and systematic descriptive grammar of Motuna which would satisfy the standards set by such anthropological linguists as Sapir, Lee, Hoijer, and Lounsbury. Partly for that reason and partly for reasons of space I shall not attempt here to outline such a grammar.[5] Because of this omission I feel that it would be premature for me to speak in general and systematic terms about the relationships between non-linguistic culture patterns and the large-scale patterns of the language. This is a regrettable omission but one that cannot be helped without delaying the publication of this study much longer. Of course, I use linguistic data throughout this book in many ways, but in view of the omission of a full-scale grammar I feel that it would be somewhat gratuitous (and very expensive!) to reproduce native statements in Motuna. Accordingly, I have set down whole utterances in Motuna only for the purpose of illustrating songs, magic formulae, and the like. For purposes of this book the following orthography will probably be found adequate:

|         | Labial | Apical | Dorsal | Glottal |
|---------|--------|--------|--------|---------|
| Stops   | p      | t      | k      | '       |
| Spirants| v      | s      | j      | h       |
| Nasals  | m      | n      | ŋ      |         |
|         |        | r      |        |         |

Vowels: a, e, i, o, u

The labial spirant is actually bilabial (i.e., $\beta$) but will be written $v$.

The dorsal spirant, normally written $X$ in phonetic alphabets, will be written $j$ throughout this book in order to conform to the orthography taught Siuai natives in mission schools.

$p, t, k, v, s, j,$ and $h$ are all slightly voiced, and might be properly termed intermediates.

All consonants are slightly aspirated.

$r$ most frequently occurs as an apical trill but is also heard allophonically as an apical lateral or a voiced apical stop.

A distinctly voiced dorsal stop, $g$, is occasionally heard in northeast Siuai, but in my opinion, only in connection with loan words from the neighboring Rugara language, wherein $g$ ordinarily replaces the Motuna $k$ in cognate forms.

# I

# A SURVEY OF SIUAI LIFE

CHAPTER 1

# Physical Adaptation

## BOUGAINVILLE ISLAND

The Solomon Islands extend from northwest to southeast in a double chain. At the northwest end lies Bougainville, the largest island of the whole group. Bougainville is about 130 miles long and averages 30 miles wide, with an area of about 3500 square miles; its axis is parallel to that of the whole Solomon chain and the approximate location of its center is 6 degrees south latitude and 155 degrees east longitude.

Like most other islands in the southwestern Pacific, Bougainville is probably a remnant of a Melanesian continent which extended as far eastward as Fiji — 1800 miles distant. Presence of metamorphic rocks throughout this area has been interpreted by geologists as meaning that such a Melanesian continent was built up by folded mountains during early geologic periods. Although continental in character, parts of it are said to have been covered by shallow seas at various times. The period of compression responsible for metamorphic rocks was probably followed by periods of tension and faulting. This faulting is thought to have resulted in the breakup of the Melanesian continent.[1]

Bougainville Island itself is composed chiefly of andesite (with some rhyolite and dacite), with evidence of older intrusive plutonics in the central region. Two great ranges, together with several lateral ridges, dominate the landscape. In the northern Emperor Range the active volcano, Balbi, rises to 10,171 feet; while the southern Crown Prince Range rises 9850 feet and contains Mount Bangana which is continually emitting clouds of steam and volcanic ash. Thick deposits of plutonic derivatives all over the Island are evidence of greater volcanic activity in the past; the occurrence in the north of marine deposits high up over the present sea level can mean that the Island has undergone recent upheavals.

Running across the Island from northeast to southwest between the two mountain ranges is a high trough which serves as a not insuperably difficult communication link for natives between east and west coasts.

Except where the mountains fall away steeply into the sea — as they do along the eastern and northern coasts — a moat of swamp encircles the lower slopes and isolates the beaches from habitable inland areas. An extensive alluvial plain slopes away gently south and southwest from the southern Crown Prince Range; it may aptly be called the Greater Buin Plain because it corresponds roughly to the Australian Administrative subdistrict of that name.[2] Less extensive alluvial plains slope away northeast from both ranges.

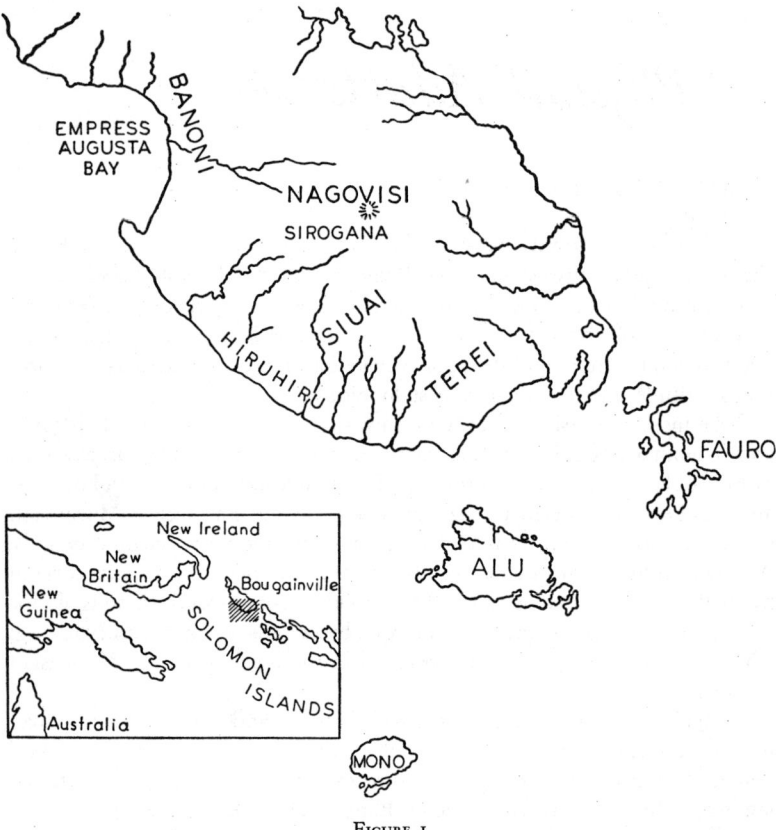

FIGURE 1

The native population of Bougainville is about 35,000. This figure is based partly upon actual census count and partly upon estimation. When the Australian officials took over Bougainville from Germany during the first World War they instituted a system of annual census patrols into the known, controlled areas, and started a systematic opening up of the uncontrolled areas by exploratory patrols. By the end of 1939 only a few isolated areas had not been visited, and either actual census figures or fairly reliable estimates were available for most of the Island. Still, even today in the well-controlled, frequently patrolled areas, new names are being added to the census every year, and it will be many years before a complete census figure can be compiled. The estimates shown on Figure 2 should, then, be considered as fairly reliable for coastal areas and for the whole southern part of the Island, but only approximately so for northern inland areas.

An estimated population of 35,000 for the whole Island would mean that there are about ten individuals per square mile; but, of course, natives are not distributed uniformly over all the land. There are several areas of population concentration, others with thin scatterings of people, and still others with no inhabitants at all. Figure 2 shows, among other things, how the natives are distributed over the Island; each dot represents fifty persons, but the positions of the dots are only approximate. Three kinds of areas of population concentration stand out: along the more or less swamp-free beach of the northern coast; along the Greater Buin Plain inland from the swamp belt; and along the intermediate mountain ridges and slopes of the higher ranges. The northern coast beaches are ideal for settlement because protecting reefs provide excellent fishing and safe transit for the slender plank canoes of the beach-dwellers. Elsewhere around the coast the beaches are unprotected from strong winds, and the coral falls away so steeply that fishing in canoes is hazardous and unrewarding. Then too, immediately behind most of the shallow beaches are swamps filled with mosquitoes which would make life miserable even for stoical natives.

In addition to these concentrations there are thin scatterings of natives along some of the eastern and southwestern beaches, other small settlements perch high up on the mountains, and still others spread out in the central transverse valley. There is evidence that three kinds of population movement have taken place recently. From fifty to sixty years ago several canoe-loads of Alu Islanders were driven out of their old homes by Mono Islanders, and finally succeeded in establishing settlements along the eastern Bougainville coast, where their descendants still remain. Another movement has been taking place in the southwest. There used to be large settlements of Melanesian-speakers along the southern and southwestern coasts, but when trading with Alu and Mono ceased, these beach-dwellers began moving inland, so that now there are only a few straggling hamlets on the coast. Still another movement is now taking place toward the eastern coast; with the cessation of head-hunting, brought about by Australian intervention, natives from several inland communities have moved timidly down to the coast and have built settlements there for themselves.

Figure 2 gives an impression that the Island is fairly densely populated: but that is due to the method of representation. Actually, even in the Greater Buin Plain area of population concentration, only a small fraction of the land is utilized by the natives. A traveler sailing along the eastern coast and looking inland can barely make out the tiny clearings which appear along the ridges; they look like specks of islands in an ocean of forest.

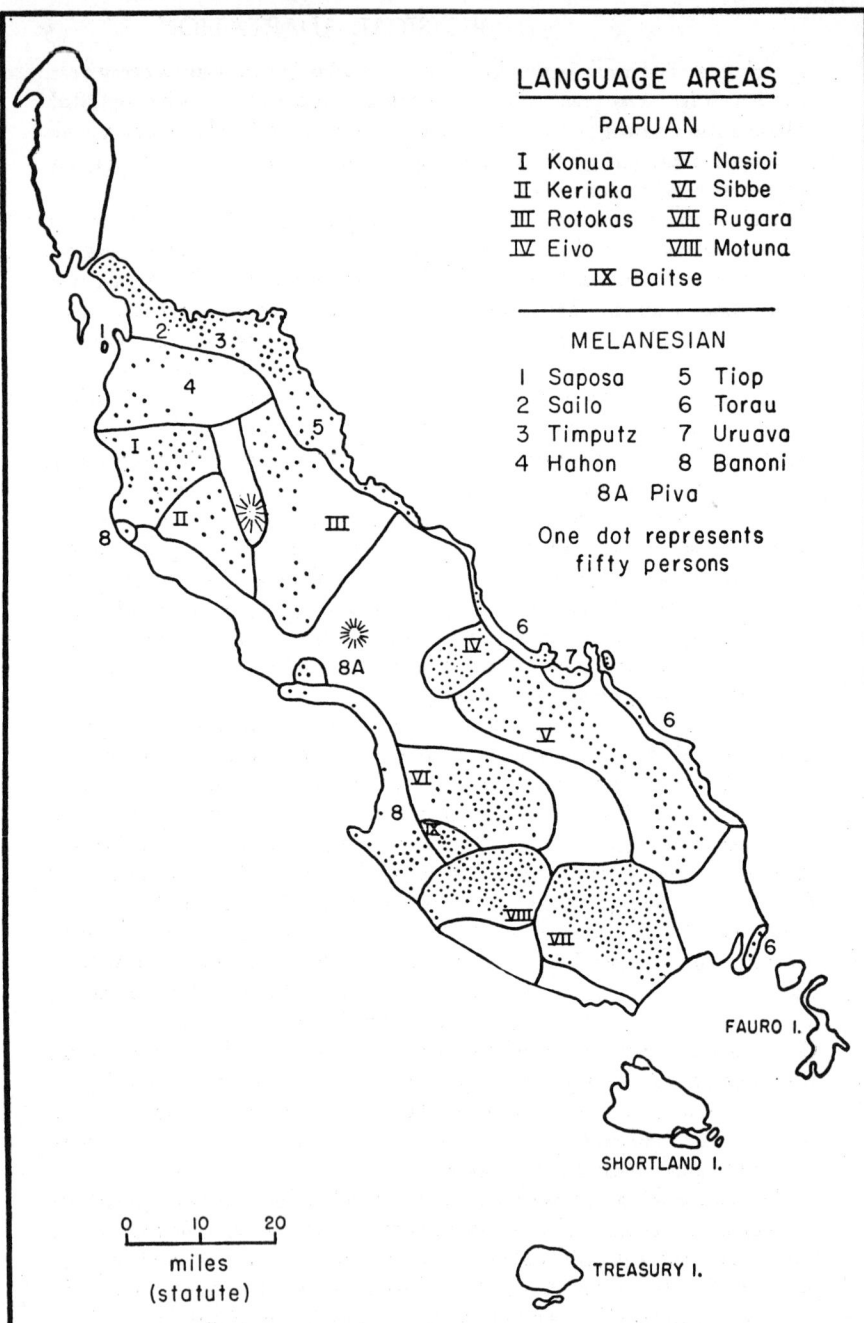

Figure 2

The different kinds of environment on the Island, together with the various techniques which natives use for adapting themselves to their local surroundings, have, naturally, very decisive effects upon social organization and symbolic paraphernalia, and contribute to the many local cultural differences. Even casual survey would reveal striking differences between coast-dwellers and plainsmen, and between plainsmen and mountain-dwellers.

Two types of languages are spoken on Bougainville: Melanesian and Papuan. Melanesian-type languages are also spoken by natives inhabiting the smaller islands and the coasts of the larger islands throughout Melanesia; Papuan-type languages are spoken by natives inhabiting the interior of New Guinea, New Britain, Vella-lavella, etc. The interrelationship of the various Melanesian languages is fairly generally recognized by linguists because of many similarities in vocabulary and structure. On the other hand, there is no such unity yet demonstrated for all Papuan-type languages; in fact, the word "Papuan" was coined to apply to all languages within the Melanesian area which differ strikingly from the Melanesian tongues. (Some writers have suggested "non-Melanesian" as a more appropriate label for Papuan languages.)

The sixteen languages so far discovered on Bougainville are shown in Figure 2.[3] *Nasioi*, *Sibbe* (the language spoken by the Nagovisi), *Rugara* (the language of the Terei), and *Motuna* are closely interrelated in vocabulary, morphology, and syntax.

Seen against the background of all Melanesia, Bougainville appears ethnographically uniform but on closer view several culture areas can be distinguished. The Melanesian speakers in the north use large plank canoes and practice elaborate initiation rites; culturally they resemble closely their neighbors on Buka Island.[4] Little is known of the northern Papuan speakers except that they live in very small hamlets scattered about the rugged mountainous terrain and still engage in warfare. Southern Bougainville is better known.[5] The speakers of *Uruava* and *Torau* migrated here, some of them very recently, from islands to the south. The *Banoni*-speakers probably also migrated from the south but have been settled on Bougainville for a much longer time. Some of them have moved inland and adopted many of the traits of their Papuan-speaking neighbors. The speakers of the four closely interrelated southern Papuan languages also have many cultural traits in common, although dissimilarities of emphasis serve to differentiate between the *mountaineers* (Nagovisi and Nasioi) and the *plainsmen* (Siuai and Terei). Some of these differences may be accounted for by differences in environment; others may be due to the proximity of the plainsmen to Alu and Mono islands whence came many cultural innovations.

Racially, all Bougainville natives are Negroid, being among the blackest and most frizzly-haired peoples in Oceania; however, the populations of the various language areas differ significantly from one another in some metrical and morphological features. For example, the Papuan-speaking, mountain-dwelling Nagovisi are shorter in stature than their plains-dwelling Siuai neighbors; and concave nasal profiles occur more frequently among southern inlanders than among the adjacent coastal peoples. The physical comparison of these populations and the relationships between somatic variation and ecological factors is the subject of another study.[6]

## THE SIUAI AREA

The word "siuai" originally applied to a cape on the southern shore of Bougainville, and later on was applied to a village of Mono Island immigrants who settled there to trade with the inland-dwelling Bougainville natives. European traders used to drop anchor there during the 1880's and 1890's and exchange European goods for copra; through them and Shortland Island natives the name "siuai" began to be applied to long stretches of coast on either side of the cape and to the hinterland extending north to the mountains. Most other natives of southern Bougainville refer to this region as "middle"; signifying, I presume, its location midway between mountains and coast. The inhabitants of this region are known as "middle-people," and their language is known locally as "middle talk" (*korokoro motuna*). In this account the word "Motuna" will be used when speaking of the language; but since the word "Siuai" has such wide acceptance among Europeans, it will be retained to apply to the natives who speak Motuna, to their culture, and to the territory in which they live.

The territory occupied by the Siuai is part of the Greater Buin Plain, which rises along the southern and southwestern borders of the Crown Prince Range, and slopes away gently to the sea. This Plain is dissected by numerous waterways; there is hardly an acre without a spring or stream of some sort, but, except during floods, none of the rivers exceeds 200 yards in width and a few feet in depth. Some streams flow directly into the sea; others debouch into a wide swamp belt which separates the pest-ridden blacksand beach from habitable inland areas. One characteristic of the landscape is the extent to which the streams have deepened their beds in the soft alluvium. The result is that there are many narrow, flat-topped interfluvial ridges running parallel to one another and sometimes extending for miles.

Most of the Plain is covered with rain forests. Untouched rain forest is an impressive sight. Each enormous buttressed tree-giant is a whole community of vegetation: numerous woody vines twine around the tree's aerial roots, and every limb is covered with luxuriant parasitic growth. So thick are the branches that very few shafts of sunlight penetrate, and ground-cluttering scrub growth is seldom encountered in the forests.

Inland from the coastal swamp there are only patches of marsh and these support small groves of sago palms. Along the banks of the larger streams there are narrow flood areas of sandy soil on which grow cane and scrub. Throughout the Plain, large areas have been cleared for settlements and gardens, but it does not require many years for the forest to reclaim a deserted hamlet or garden site.

The native mammals living on the Plain are wild pigs, opossums (*Phalanger orientalis breviceps Thomas*[7]), tree rats (*Unicomys ponceleti Troughton*), and many varieties of flying-fox (*Pteropus grandis Thomas, Pteralopex anceps. K. Anderson*, etc.), flying mice, and bats. Birds occur in great profusion: hornbills, eagles, hawks, herons, rails, ducks, starlings, parrots, owls, etc. Goannas, large and small lizards, frogs, eels, and snakes are common, but the streams contain few crustaceans or fish. Mosquitoes are a plague near the coast but are not unbearable a few miles inland.

The Plain is well within the equatorial climatic zone, but heat is rarely oppressive. Clear bright days are generally accompanied by light southeast breezes; and sultry overcast days are usually climaxed by freshening showers during midafternoon. Even if the day has been humid and cloudy and without showers there is always a cool night to look forward to. After sundown, mists roll off the mountains and send chilled natives into their warm, smoke-filled huts.

There is no such marked variation in seasons as obtains in many other Pacific areas; daily temperature variations greatly exceed those of means for different months;[8] and during the so-called "dry-season" (April–October) some rain fell during at least half the days.[9] Occasionally there are fierce cloudbursts preceded by violent electric storms. Once in a while rain clouds collect in the mountains and precipitate enormous quantities of water which then rush down the stream beds, increasing the normal water depths tenfold. These stream floods rush down with a roar, and sometimes drown natives who are unable to reach higher ground.

High winds occasionally sweep across the tops of the forest trees, but Bougainville is outside the hurricane belts, and no more serious damage occurs than a sheet of roof thatch blown away or someone hit by falling branches. Throughout most of the year the prevailing wind is southeast; from November to February there is an occasional shift to the southwest. In addition, during January and December there occur periods of strong northwest breezes. None of these changes, however, is great enough to allow one to speak of marked seasonal variations.

Earthquakes occur frequently, about once a week, and some of them are violent enough to topple houses and cause dangerous landslides.

The Siuai occupy the center of this Greater Buin Plain. The territory identified with them is roughly demarcated by the Mivo River on the east, the Torovera River on the west, the mountains on the north, and the swamps and sea at the south.

## THE SIUAI PEOPLE

The Siuai people numbered 4658 in October 1938 (2355 males, 2303 females). Recent censuses indicate that the size and sex ratio of the population is fairly stable, having gone through the critical initial contact period without suffering the customary decline. Although the land conventionally identified with the Siuai covers about 250 square miles, only some 80 square miles are habitually used by them for residential and agricultural purposes, the remainder being swamp and virgin rain forest.

In northeast Siuai, the site of my most intensive field work, the population numbered 1072 in October 1938. The dwellings of these natives were concentrated within an area of about eight and a quarter square miles. However, their garden lands extended over an area some four square miles larger, and the total area over which they resided, gardened, collected, and hunted covered some 32 square miles — giving a population density of about 34 persons per square mile. This population was distributed as follows:

|  | Males | Females |
|---|---|---|
| Under fourteen years old [10] | 195 | 191 |
| Fourteen and older | 349 | 337 |

The total population of this same area listed in the official census of 1937 [11] was 1015, representing a net increase of 57. Some of this increase may be accounted for by residence shifts from other areas and some by net increase of births over deaths, but the information available is not reliable enough to permit a more specific breakdown. Also, it is not possible for me to state the actual number of births and deaths that took place during this interval, since the Siuai often do not report births and infant deaths.

In connection with our anthropometric survey we estimated the ages of all Siuai males measured, but since these are only estimates and since the sample includes no seriously crippled or ill males, few pre-pubescent males, and no females, it cannot tell us much about age distribution and life expectancy.

Physically, the Siuai compare unfavorably with coast dwellers on Bougainville. The photographs in this book describe their physiques better than words can. One encounters many robust and apparently healthy individuals among them, but many more bear such obvious afflictions as hookworm, yaws, and tropical ulcers, along with a number of other ailments not so obvious. Malaria, pneumonia, and pulmonary tuberculosis are prevalent and seem to be the principal killing diseases, but dysentery and filariasis are also common. I also encountered indications of leprosy, but most of the advanced cases of leprosy are detected by Administration officials and the victims are sent to the Administration hospital at Kieta. Badly mended broken limbs are fairly common among adult males, and some of the older males show scars from wounds suffered in warfare.

During the rainy season common colds occur in nearly every household, and at all times many children appear to be suffering from conjunctivitis.

All in all, the Siuai give the impression of being an unhealthy people,

1. A "line" village in northeast Siuai.

2. Turuŋom village. The ethnographer's hut is in the right foreground.

3. A hamlet in northeast Siuai.

4. High noon at the taro garden.

5. Women carrying taro and firewood.

6. Some of the taro corms are the main part of the principal daily meal; the pigs are fed what is left over.

7. Offspring and shell money are goals of most Siuai.

8. Pigs serve as pets, capital goods, and food delicacies.

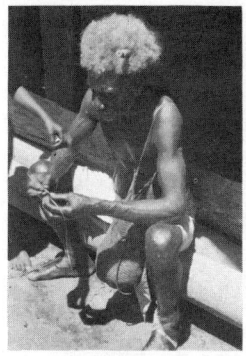  

9. Rolling twine for making a net bag like the one hanging from the craftsman's shoulder. 10. Plaiting a large carrying pouch. 11. Searching for fish and prawns. The youths have bows and spears to shoot at fish too fast to be caught by hand.

12. An artist displays the decorated baking frames he has made for a feast. 13. Trying out a new panpipe. Siuai males have plenty of time for recreation. 14. Roasting pork for a public meal. Women cook the everyday household meals but men take over when cooking delicacies for a feast.

15. Wedding ceremony. Ritual ablutions over bride, groom, and bridesmaid.

16. Wedding ceremony. Coconut oil is applied to legs of bride and groom. A male helper strangles the feast pig.

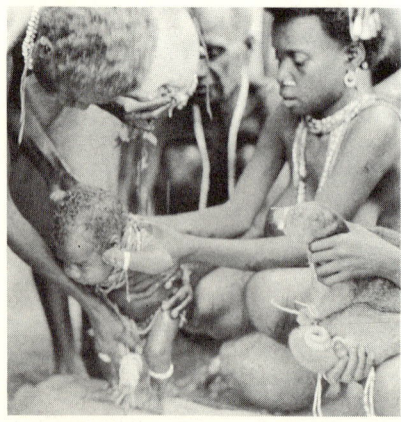

17. Baptism ceremony. At right is a live opossum scapegoat.

18. Baptism of an older child, who stands on a pig while magicians rub consecrated oil over his body.

19. Clearing the ground for a new garden.

20. Learning to walk.

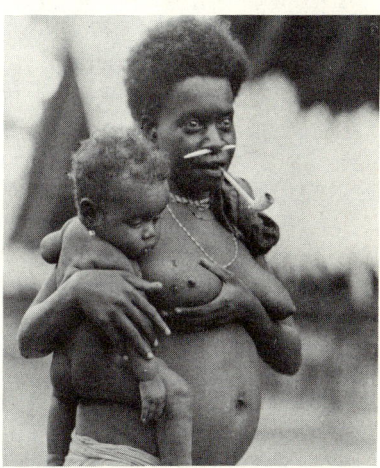
21. The closest bond.

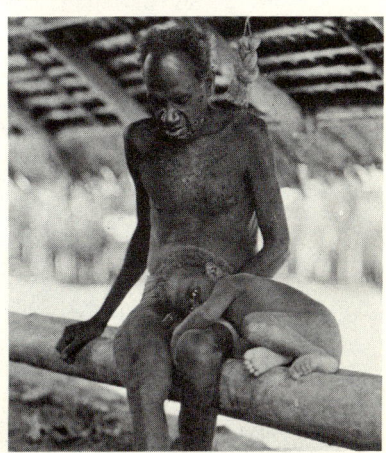
22. An ancient comforts his grandsons

23. Siuai women dancing.

24. Children try to imitate the dance of the women shown above.

25, 26. Small boys' greatest joy is permission to beat a wooden slit-gong as their elders do.

27. One wife is enough for most men. Having many wives is in itself not particularly desirable.

28. The leader Moŋko, his eight wives, and one child. Women's skills and services are needed for accumulating capital.

29. Old women sometimes become magicians, as did the growth-magic specialists shown here.

30. Old men while away their last years dozing and chewing pre-ground betel mixture.

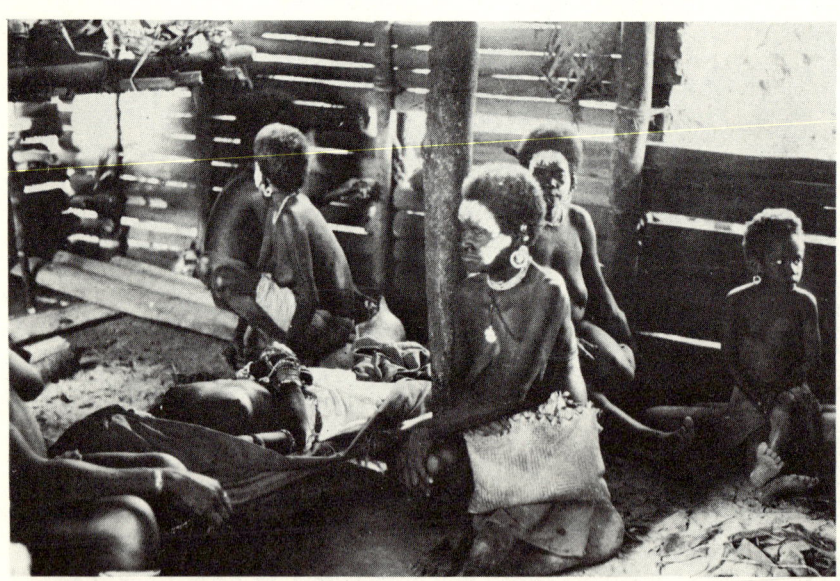

31. When death comes, relatives paint mourning marks on their faces and attend the corpse until it is cremated.

32. Kinsmen build a pyre for the cremation of a relative.

33. Men's world. A throng of youths and men wait for a feast to begin in a leader's club-house.

34. Accumulating capital for acquiring renown is a full-time occupation. Some make and sell pots.

35. Others accumulate capital by raising and selling pigs. Three men confer on the terms of a purchase.

36. A magician (right) helps his client gain rapport with a ghost whose image is believed to be reflected in a cup of coconut oil.

37. Magicians sit on either side of a sick man and try to bring rapport between him and the demon who has caused his illness.

38. Carrying a new wooden slit-gong to install it in its owner's club-house.

39. A magician rides atop a new gong to lighten its weight.

40. A large wooden slit-gong in place across the front of a club-house.

41. Making a pudding for the feast. The leader, Soŋi, wearing a conical hat, holds open a leaf container as helpers pour a mixture of sago and almond into a wooden baking frame.

42. Wrapping up the pudding before baking it in an earth oven.

43. Bringing home a large sow. The most important step in preparing for a feast is the collection of live pigs for distribution among the guests.

44. At the pigpen. Pigs awaiting distribution at a feast are centers of public interest.

45. A composer tries out a new melody he has created for a feast.

46. A magician is assigned the job of protecting the hosts at a feast, by watching out for acts of sorcery on the part of envious guests.

47. Dress rehearsal. Natives fully ornamented for a feast, practice dance steps while blowing on their panpipes and large wooden trumpets.

48. Feast in full swing. Natives dance and pipe in front of the host's club-house. In foreground is the display platform laden with food delicacies and decorated with coconuts.

49. Crucial moment. The guests estimate the value of the pigs given them at a feast.

50. Presentation of gift to guest of honor. Shell money, part of gift, displayed over a log.

51. Leader, Siuai style. The prominent leader, Soɲi, poses for a picture with his favorite son.

52. Officials, new style. The Paramount Chief, Tomo (left), and his executive officer, 'Uta.

53. Signs of change. Methodists compete with Catholics in a Bible-knowledge bee. Catechists write Biblical names on the blackboard for the opposing congregations to identify.

54. The new order in government. Village headmen salute their Paramount Chief.

## PHYSICAL ADAPTATION

holding their own but not much more. Some of their bodily difficulties may be laid at the door of their physical environment, but others are plainly the result of their own practices, which we now proceed to describe.

How have these Siuai adapted *physically* to their physical environment? Let us examine them against their physical setting and report on where they live and work, and how they utilize available materials to feed, shelter, and adjust themselves to the more tangible physical factors affecting human life in southern Bougainville. In later chapters the activities listed here will be treated in greater detail and in appropriate cultural contexts; the aim of this preliminary account is to provide one kind of framework for the descriptions that follow.

### RAW MATERIALS AND TOOLS

The Siuai utilize only a small proportion of the vast number of distinguishable [12] items found in their environment, but even so, their raw materials inventory numbers into the hundreds. Here are some of those items most commonly used.

They make use of soil for agriculture; red and black clay for pottery manufacture; white clay and red ocher for paints, cosmetics, and magic. Large boulders serve as shrines, grindstones, and anvils, small stones are used as hammers. They no longer manufacture or use stone axes and adzes but many natives remember using them, and scores are still being kept for eventual sale to whites.

Water is used for drinking, cooking, and bathing — a sharp distinction being made between drinking-water streams and those used for bathing and toilet purposes.

Here in this rank wilderness, where fence and house posts take root and keep on growing, native life is heavily dependent on plants. Besides the items grown for food (taro, yam, sweet potato, plantain, sago, coconut, almond, sugar cane, and many more), numerous other plants are collected in the forest for eating (leaves, ferns, flower buds, mushrooms, funguses, etc.). The natives mix areca nut and pepper catkin with lime for their betel-chewing mixture, and are inveterate smokers of their home-grown tobacco. All their houses are made of wood, held together with plant fibers and thatched with leaves. Most containers are of leaves, plant fibers, and coconut shells; all their furniture, most of their weapons and many of their tools and musical instruments are made of wood. Aside from recently acquired calico loincloths, all their clothing is made of leaves or bark. Most dyes, oils, adhesives, and many body ornaments come from plants or plant products; and their pharmacopoeia, too, is largely vegetable.

Animals and animal products are not nearly so extensively or variously utilized. The Siuai eat the flesh, heart, blood, and liver of pigs, and use pigs' long bones for tools and tusks for bracelets, but they ignore pig bristle and hide. They also capture opossums and eat their flesh and organs but discard hair and hide. They capture and eat tree-rats and eels but reject house rats, snakes, and lizards. Now and then they shoot or net flying foxes and some kinds of birds, but make little effort to exploit the forests' many other resources in edible flying things. They occasionally eat grubs and certain kinds of spiders and ants.

They engage in desultory attempts to catch the fish and prawns living in their creeks, and they travel to distant southern beaches to collect shells for making tools and lime, but do not trouble with fishing while there.

It appears then that the Siuai get most of their raw materials from plants; compared with such peoples as the Arunta or Pacific atoll-dwellers, they have not begun to utilize fully the other kinds of materials found around them.

Some of this selectivity may be because of the kinds of tools they possess or lack. Their native cutting tools consist of bamboo and shell knives, and stone adzes and axes. The stone adzes and axes have now been replaced by steel axes, machetes, hatchets, and adze blades, but large flat bivalve shells are still used for peeling things like taro; and bamboo knives, kept sharp by removing slivers, continue to be used in some cutting operations. Heavy steel axes are scarce and have not yet supplanted the small steel ax- and adze-hafted blades traded from the Germans twenty-five years ago.[13] The all-purpose cutting tool owned by nearly every youth and man is a ten- to twelve-inch machete; these knives are almost like appendages, as they are carried continually and used for purposes as varied as paring finger nails and felling trees. The casual rubbing against boulders they receive does not keep them very sharp, but it is difficult to imagine what this generation of Siuai natives would do without them. A new kind of tool among the recent imports is the small pocketknife now carried (but not in pockets!) by many men and used for carving with more precision than they found possible with native tools. There is no sex bar to use of cutting tools but in general the heavier ones, including steel, are wielded by males.

Bone is also used for tools. Small pointed bones are employed to pierce shells and to split fibers for weaving; a sharpened pig's femur is used for splitting areca nuts as well as for separating coconut meat from its shell. Scraping is done with sharp-edged bivalves; shredding with tooth-edged ones. Stone tools used to be polished and sharpened by grinding against boulders. Hammering is done with fist-sized pebbles; digging with pointed sticks. A rough-surfaced leaf is employed for smoothing wooden surfaces and an oily nut for polishing them.

All these tools are used to make end-products or other implements and hence might appropriately be named primary tools. Some end-products, to be sure, are made without tools: an effective umbrella is produced simply by ripping off a large banana leaf and holding it over the head, and an adequate container can be quickly made from a coconut frond entirely by hand. In a number of instances, moreover, tools are devised on the spot: a handful of

## PHYSICAL ADAPTATION

leaves is the most common brushing and wiping implement, and saplings are used as levers and carrying poles. Most end-products, however, require the use of primary tools in their manufacture; rather than list all end-products here according to their component raw materials or their process of manufacture, it will serve our purposes better to consider them in due course in connection with the kinds of activity for which they are used.

The Siuai are frugal and skillful in their utilization of fire; they use it rather like a precision tool, keeping it in narrow bounds and applying it specifically. Except for cremations and pottery-baking, one rarely sees a large blaze; even trash-burning fires in the gardens are kept within narrow bounds. Cooking fires are small, houses are kept warm and mosquito-free at night by a continual smolder of radially arranged sticks rather than by a lively blaze: as one informant expressed it, "one can get *nearer* to a small fire." Nor is the hearth a focal point; natives do not sit facing it. (One of the most difficult adaptations I had to make was to sit through long, cold, and pitch-black night wakes or dances with no fire save a smoking ash bed to light pipes from, and able to distinguish my mat-black companions only by their voices.) On the other hand, fire is used to fell trees; to straighten bamboo arrows; to harden digging-sticks, spears, and other tool points; to ring-bark trees; to preserve food and dry tobacco; to incise designs on objects and scarify skins; to soften fibers; to burn lime for betel-chewing; and to perform numerous other operations. A careful householder keeps a smolder going continually, and if it does go out, secures a live coal from a neighbor. Natives can and sometimes do make fire, by the plow method, but it is considered a long and strenuous job, and I have seen individuals give up in exhaustion and disgust before obtaining a spark. The few boxes of inferior trade-store matches that drift in from the coast are quickly used up. When traveling, natives carry a lighted chunk of wood or a bundle of smoldering twigs bound together with fibers.

### CONTAINERS

The Siuai possess a wide variety of containers and carrying methods and show considerable ingenuity in devising new ones. Clay pots, which are used for cooking, all have the same general round-bottomed, wide-mouthed shape, but vary in size from about eight inches in diameter and ten inches in height to eighteen inches in diameter and forty inches in height, the latter being used at club-houses for feasts. The best pottery clay is located in northeast Siuai which is the center of pot-making. Pots are manufactured by molding short strips of coil onto a hand-molded bowl-shaped base. A small wooden paddle is now and then used to thin and smooth the sides but most of the shaping is done by hands alone, kept wet by frequent dipping into a coconut-shell bowl full of water. The pot is fired in an open blaze, and this completes the process — no glazing, no painting, and only occasionally a few incised lines for decoration. Cracking is frequent during firing and the life of a pot is short. Nowadays every cook tries to obtain a more durable pot of iron from the coastal trade-store, but so far only about one household in ten owns one.

Green vegetables are often steamed in bamboo containers, and water is carried and stored in bamboo as well as in coconut-shell bottles stoppered with leaves. Coconut shell also is used to make bowls, cups, and ladles. Gourds sometimes serve as liquid containers but their principal use is for carrying betel-chewing lime. Food-mashing pestles are made of wood and have pointed bases to allow them to stand up in the ground; mortars are also of wood, as are some types of bowls and trays. But for every one of all these other kinds of containers found in any household there will be two or three baskets or woven trays. Basketry containers range widely in size, shape, and technique, from enormous five-foot-long coil-woven trays used for feasts to the tiny purses carried in men's net bags. Some of these take several days to make and require rare fibers, but a usable basket or tray can be improvised in a few minutes out of the wealth of leaves and common fibers always within reach. An examination of the photographs in this book will indicate the extensive and varied uses these Siuai make of plant-fiber weaving. In some cases a specific kind of container and a concrete use are fixedly linked, for example, the large satchels made by women and used by them to carry potatoes and taro corms; while in other instances one use will be served by a number of different kinds of containers, with fashions continually changing. When we first arrived in Siuai the place had the appearance of a pouch factory; nearly every man and youth was making a soft and finely woven pouch, about eight inches long by five wide, to be carried in their net bags. Whenever natives stopped chopping wood or eating or mixing betel, out would come the partly finished baskets from their net bags — reminiscent of a group of American women knitting in wartime. If one Siuai put his handiwork down for a few moments to do something else, as likely as not an unengaged companion would pick it up and weave a few rows. Later on the fashion in carrying bags changed and men went back to larger and cruder pouches which were carried by means of a shoulder strap.

Because of the wide variety of weaving materials and the uses made of dyes — indigenous vegetable dyes and trade-store imports — Siuai natives have wide scope for devising new forms and for imitating alien ones, and they are particularly receptive to innovations coming from the islands to the south.

Net containers are less varied in form and use, the chief one being the shoulder-strap bag carried or rather *worn* by nearly every male with anything to carry. In these bags one invariably finds a small gourd filled with lime, a few areca nuts, a leaf packet of pepper catkins, a piercing tool fashioned from a pig's femur, a bamboo box full of tobacco leaf, a packet or two of magical ingredients, and, perhaps, a few spans of shell money.

Australian shillings have holes through the center, thoughtfully coined in this form by a practical-minded government, and are ordinarily carried — on the infrequent occasions when they are carried — strung onto a cord which is passed through a pierced ear-lobe.

Woman's principal carrying device is a tumpline strap fashioned of bark fiber; in this she places her pouches of taro or potatoes, leaf packets of greens or relishes, her cape, firewood, betel mixture, and anything else, all usually topped by a small child. Bent over as she usually is with such burdens, her digging stick serves as a useful staff to help her up and down slippery paths. Men do not like to encumber themselves with burdens, and when they do have to transport heavy loads they attach them to a pole carried across one shoulder.

## SETTLEMENTS

A bird's-eye view of Siuai would reveal islands of cleared or scrub-overgrown land surrounded by a sea of dense forest growth (see Figure 3). In these clearings the Siuai natives dwell and work, only occasionally penetrating the surrounding forests to hunt or to journey to another settlement.

Figure 3 illustrates how the 1938 population was distributed throughout the main part of the tribal area. (Not shown are a few settlements to the southwest, and a deserted village on the coast.) This map records population by village, and as such introduces a distortion. Aboriginal settlements consist of small, one- to nine-house hamlets scattered about the scrub. When the Australian Administration began to bring this region under control during the early 1920's, it was part of the policy of patrolling officers to consolidate smaller hamlets into larger villages in order to simplify control, improve public health, and "bring about friendlier relations among the natives."

These villages — "lines" the Siuai call them — are usually located on top of interfluvial ridges, near springs (for drinking water) and large streams (for bathing and sanitation). A few villages are located directly on the sandy banks of streams to avoid the continual climbing back and forth to water, although natives recognize the hazard of this kind of location because of the danger from floods.

Each married man is required by the Administration to own a house in a village and these houses are usually built on piles — the officials' theory being that pile dwellings are healthier. Every village is kept clean of weeds and rubbish, and is surrounded by a sturdy fence designed to keep out pigs. There are from ten to twenty-five houses in each village, the average number of houses to a village in northeast Siuai being thirteen.

In nearly every case the Siuai have retained their older-type hamlet settlements so that now most households possess two houses each — one in the village and one in the hamlet. The hamlet or bush houses — "pig-food"

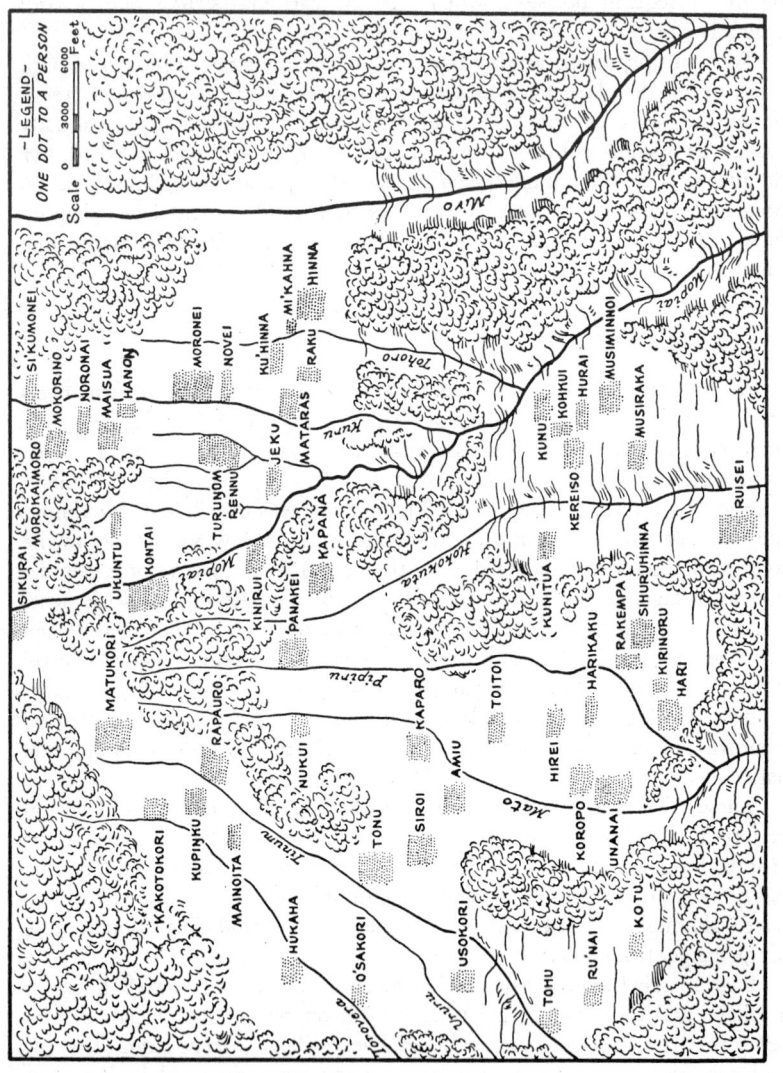

FIGURE 3

[ 16 ]

(*hurupao*), they are aptly called — are generally built directly on the ground. Figure 4 illustrates the distribution of villages and hamlets in a part of northeast Siuai. It reveals that hamlet houses are generally built nearer streams — at stream level, in many instances. Usually these hamlet houses are off the main paths and shielded from village clearings by trees.

Some natives reside in their hamlet houses all the time and keep their village houses in repair merely to satisfy Administration requirements. Others divide their time between village and hamlet houses. Still others eat and sleep in their village dwellings and retire to the hamlet houses only to feed the pigs and secure privacy.

Besides village and hamlet houses, there are other kinds of structures found in Siuai settlements. The most important of these are the men's club-houses (*kaposo*), where men meet together to gossip, beat slit gongs, and hold feasts. Generally, most club-houses are built beside important paths — a significant contrast to villages, which are usually separated from main paths by screens of vegetation, and in even sharper contrast to hamlets, which are completely hidden away.

In many settlements there are work-sheds (*aurui*), small replicas of club-houses but without slit gongs. Pottery-making takes place in the work-shed, which is also a center for gossip; women are not barred from it as they are from club-houses.

Finally, there are the *pari*, smaller sheds hastily constructed in the gardens to serve as shelters against rain and midday sun, and sometimes, when the garden is far away from home, as a place for sleeping. The typical distribution of dwellings, club-houses, and work-sheds is shown on Figure 4.

In spite of the lack of good fishing and suitable gardening land, and the presence of mosquito-ridden swamps and crocodile-infested lagoons along the southwestern Bougainville coast, there formerly were several Siuai settlements there. This is attested by traditions of the natives themselves and by accounts of Europeans who visited this region in the early twentieth century and shortly before.[14] At that time there was a lively trade between Mono and Alu Islanders and the Buin Plainsmen; and whole communities of trade middlemen settled along the coast. When Bougainville was severed politically from Alu and Mono and brought into the Territory of New Guinea, a customs barrier was interposed between the Territory and the Solomon Islands Protectorate and as a result native trade between Bougainville and Alu-Mono ceased. Consequently most of the coastal settlements of the Siuai were deserted, and the inhabitants moved inland to healthier, more productive land. In 1939 the last community on the Siuai coast withdrew three miles inland and built a new village at a place called Morokintu ("Flying-fox-Creek").

The area of land actually under cultivation in Siuai at any one time is not great (see Figure 4), but by constant rotation very extensive tracts are kept permanently cleared of large timber. The extent of these "cleared"

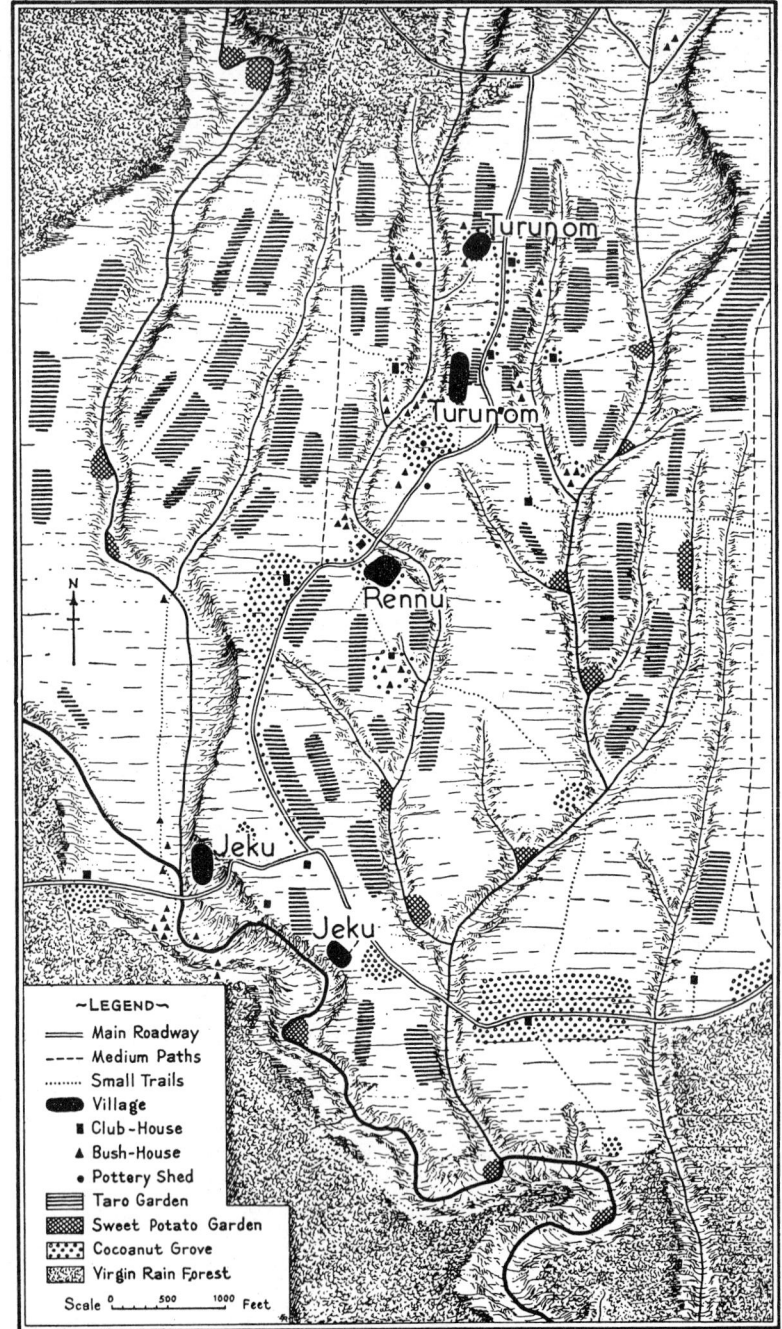

FIGURE 4

areas can be seen on Figures 3 and 4. Of course, clumps of virgin forest remain scattered through the "cleared" areas, and secondary growth is allowed to grow to considerable size before again being cut away for gardens; but in contrast with the majestic rain forests, the "cleared" secondary-growth areas are like open fields.

Besides utilizing land for cultivating the staple taro and sweet potato crops, Siuai natives plant groves of coconut and areca-nut palms. And they hunt in the forests, fish in the streams, and clear paths between settlements. Hunting and fishing activities do not transform the landscape; I have no record of any natural area set aside solely for hunting, nor did I discover that the periodic damming of rivers for fish drives had any permanent effect on the course of the rivers.

Pathways vary greatly in width: from faint trails through regions of secondary growth to eight-foot-wide roads — highways, actually — along which the Administration officials travel during their periodic census and tax-collecting expeditions. But width is no indication of the amount of traffic — the beautfully repaired "Government Road" might remain untraveled for days on end, whereas the tiny track leading from village to spring will be in constant use. Real transformation of the landscape by roads has occurred in only those places where rival leaders have vied with one another to see who could clear the widest roadway.

## SHELTER, CLOTHING, AND GROOMING

Protection against sun and rain appears to be a determining factor affecting when and how the Siuai erect shelters. They are not indulging in poesy when they speak of the *angry* (*iro*) sun; despite their bushy coiffures and black skins they are subject to mild sunstroke and burning. Hence they behave perfectly rationally and try to stay out of the midday sun. Rain they also avoid, and with good reason. Light showers are not disliked, but these usually give way to stinging, drenching, and chilling downpours which set them to shivering and, they believe, help bring on sickness. Consequently, on starting to work on a new garden site one of the first things they do is to build the sun and rain shelter already mentioned. This is usually a lean-to based against the fence or a simple four-posted shed, both types being thatched with sheets of sago leaves. When men spend several days in the forests hunting for opossum they usually build a rough lean-to covered with big leaves as protection against drenching, the sun being no hazard there.

Additional physical factors enter into the construction of dwellings. It is considered essential that houses be tight and sturdy enough to keep out cold night air and hungry pigs. (In former times of feuding it was also essential for walls to be sufficiently thick to ward off the arrows and spears of enemies.) Besides these physical factors there are other considerations which affect the forms of dwellings; these include the desire for privacy and need for space. Size requirements vary greatly, depending upon the numbers to be housed and the ambitions of the household head; on the other hand, what we might call *aesthetic* considerations play little part in house construction.

Some dwellings are on piles, others are built directly on the ground; still others combine both features by extending forward the verandah overhang of a pile-built house and by walling-in the whole structure. Materials and techniques are standardized but no two dwellings are of exactly the same size and form. The illustrations show more clearly than words what dwellings are like, but it will be helpful to list a few structural principles. The frame is nearly always made of peeled but otherwise unshaped poles of medium-hard wood. The roof is supported by posts thrust directly into the ground; in a pile-dwelling the raised floor rests on a separate set of posts and is only weakly attached to the roof supports. There is very little shaping of timbers to make fitted joints except at the tops of the ridge posts, which are occasionally gouged out to support the ridgepole. Rattan is used for all tying and binding. The floors of pile houses are made of split but otherwise unshaped lengths of tough areca-like palm. The lower parts of some walls are made of horizontal timbers, otherwise both walls and roofs are made by overlapping sheets of sago leaf. These sheets are as important to the Siuai as shingles used to be to a Cape Codder; they are the building cover par excellence and a supply of them is usually kept on hand for repairs or for trade. Industrious men and women can often be seen constructing them when they have nothing more pressing to do. They are made with sago or nipa palm leaves folded over and fastened to a double or triple span long lath.

The open-sided work-sheds are somewhat larger than most ground dwellings but structurally similar except for lack of walls. These huts serve the purpose of workshops; people sit in them to manufacture pottery and large baskets and to restring shell money. Also similar in structure but usually much larger and more elaborately built are the men's club-houses found near every settlement. In these, the rattan lashings may be neater, the roofs thicker, and some attention paid to decorative detail; but even including these structures Siuai architecture is makeshift and unadorned according to some Melanesian standards. On the other hand, their buildings do constitute fairly satisfactory adjustments to the southern Bougainville environment. They protect from sun and shed rain admirably. The open-sided structures, which are usually occupied only during daylight, permit free air circulation and are cool on the hottest of days. The hamlet dwellings, which are built directly on the ground, effectively close out cold, and smoldering fires keep them dry and mosquito-proof — although a less-hardened mortal might prefer to be chilled and bitten rather than be suffocated in the smoky atmosphere. Moreover, these dwellings keep hungry pigs away from infants and provide an impenetrable screen for privacy.

The pile dwellings, which the Administration has encouraged natives to build in the villages, may be more sanitary from some points of view, but they are much more drafty.

There is adaptive efficiency even in the flimsiness of Siuai buildings. Although the sedentary life of the natives makes permanency feasible, the readily available building materials and the climate limit narrowly the durability of anything they build. Termites and rot dissolve most frames within a decade, and the average roof has to be renewed after three or four years. Why, therefore, invest extra effort in strengthening and embellishing structures which in any case cannot endure?

In the matter of adjusting their own bodies to the environment the Siuai have been less successful. Nowadays every native past five or six years old wears a span-length of trade-store calico wrapped around the waist and reaching below the knees. For males this is the only garment, but women carry a kind of short, hooded cape (*soroma*), made by sewing together strips of specially cured palm leaves. This they use as rain-cape, sun-shade, and sitting mat. Some men wear fine conical hats (*ohkuna* or *iropira*) made of dried pandanus leaves, or rough cylinder-shaped ones (*kukutu*) made of wild banana leaves; physically speaking, both these hair coverings are of more nuisance than value because of low-roofed houses and narrow, tangled trails. The women's capes, and the ready availability of leaf umbrellas, provide protection from rain, but otherwise natives are fully exposed to mosquitoes, to cold and, in the case of males, to sun. Before the days of calico most men went completely naked throughout life except for a bark-fiber belt (*kurumira*) for carrying knives, and females donned a small pubic apron only upon marriage. There is, of course, a credit side to nudity in a wet tropical setting; except directly in the sun, exposed bodies are cooler and dry more quickly after drenchings. And in this sense, on rainy days and cool nights calico is likely to be damp, and may be a health hazard.

Infants are bathed in cold water poured out of coconut-shell containers, while all other natives past toddler age bathe in streams. Coconut oil is rubbed over the skin to make it glisten, and bamboo combs are used to untangle the frizzly hair and leave it bushy. Some men remove face hair with small bivalve shell depilators; those with heavier beards let them grow or occasionally shave them with trade-store blades. Delousing is a familiar scene wherever natives congregate.

Careful grooming is linked with age. People lavish tender care upon infants and toddlers — bathing, oiling, combing, and delousing them; but children past that stage are left for days covered with dust and ashes before being taken to the stream and forced to bathe. Natives again show interest in grooming themselves when sexual activity begins, and this fastidiousness continues until shortly after marriage, when most men and women revert to the comfortable squalor of childhood except on festive occasions.[15]

Red ocher and white riverine clay are used for body paints. Young dandies trim their mops of hair into many shapes and sometimes bleach it with lime or trade-store peroxide; others use lamp soot to color their hair a more uniform black. Women wear plaited fiber arm bands around the biceps, men wear theirs higher up. Both men and women wear nose plugs, ear plugs, *sieruma* [16] bracelets, and *kesi* [17] pendants made of tridacna shell; and on special occasions they deck themselves out with shell or dog-tooth necklaces, feathers, flowers, and scented leaves. Scar patterns are made on the body by cutting or burning and rubbing ash into the wounds.[18]

The Siuai use innumerable materials and techniques for dealing with bodily ailments, and while most of these depend upon magic for effectiveness there are also several of a more or less rational kind, including purges, emetics, unguents, and poultices. Surgery is rarely practiced, and then only for lancing boils or removing splinters, but bone-setting without surgery is in lively demand during the season when males climb the high almond trees to collect nuts.

## AGRICULTURE

More than half of an adult Siuai's working hours are taken up with food — with producing, collecting, processing, and consuming it. This is an average, for women spend about ten hours daily at it and men generally much less. These natives eat a wide variety of comestibles; but when one of them speaks of "food" (*pao*) he is usually referring to taro. In monthlong records I kept of meals eaten by representative households taro constituted some 80 per cent by weight of everything eaten. Informants told of having eaten a few "wild" taro during straitened times, otherwise all taro consumed is grown in their gardens.

Taro gardens are laid out on well-drained terrain where the soil is deep and free of sand. Another technical requirement is that gardens be located in areas of secondary growth; I did not see a single instance of primary forest being cleared for gardens. Natives say that it is too difficult even with metal axes to cut down and remove the huge trees; but there are other reasons why new gardens are located on old garden sites.

Taro gardens are laid out in patches fenced in to keep out pigs. These patches are rectangular and a single patch varies from one to five thousand square yards in area. Very rarely does one see isolated patches; they are generally arranged in sequence, as shown in Figure 5. Taro is ready for harvesting after about four months' growth, and planting is a continuous process without perceptible seasonal differences in growth and yield. Added to this is the fact that the Siuai do not know how to preserve taro and hence must consume it within a few days after harvesting it. As soon as the plants are harvested from a matured garden the corms are cut off just below the stalks, for eating, and the stalks are replanted in another site after their leaves have begun to rot. The gardener's ideal is to have several contiguous patches in various stages of growth. Figure 5 illustrates the technique. Patch A is completely harvested and overgrown with reeds and small trees; most of its fence timbers have already been used for firewood and those remaining are scattered and rotting. Patch B has been completely harvested of taro and now contains only a few banana and plantain trees still in bearing. Patch C contains growing taro some of which is ready for harvest. Patch D contains unripe taro in various stages of growth. Patch E has been wholly prepared for planting and contains a few plots of new taro shoots. Patch F is in process of being cleared and fenced; some trees have been felled and split for fence timbers, others have been laid on the ground to mark off plots, while still others have been strip-barked and left standing. The remaining plant rubbish is being piled and burned and the ashes scattered over the patch to enrich the soil.

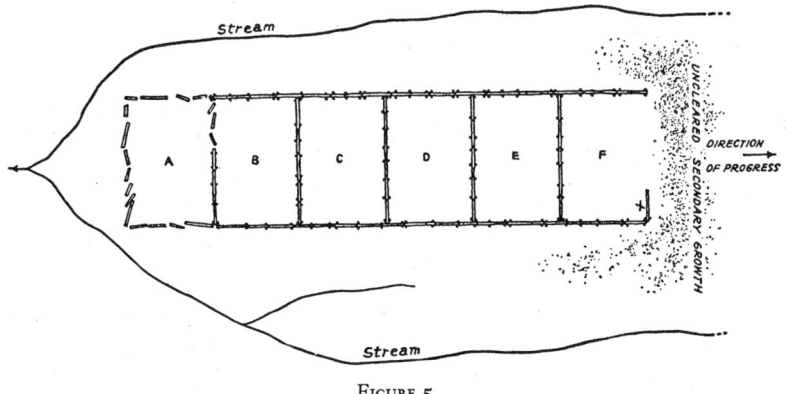

FIGURE 5

While Patch F is being cleared and fenced most efforts will be concentrated upon finishing that job; but on all other days the workers spend most of their time weeding and removing insects from Patches C and D. On all gardening days, however, before returning home a few plants are harvested from Patch C and their stalks piled up in Patch E ready for planting within the next day or so. Then natives load up with firewood by dismembering the fences or chopping up the dried trees left standing in Patch B.

Ideally this sequence will be continued as long as there is any suitable land adjoining the existing patches, and until an old patch is ready for reclaiming and planting. In hilly northeast Siuai, where suitable land is limited to the long and rather narrow interfluvial ridges, gardeners attempt to extend the patch-sequence in one direction until the old end-patch is ready for replanting (Fig. 6A). On more level terrain of central and southern Siuai the sequence follows a different pattern (Fig. 6B). In either case, natives judge that a place has lain fallow long enough when the trees on it are of a convenient size for fence-building (an interim of about six years). Their judgment might be a rationalization based upon convenience: it involves much less effort to clear land after six years than it does after three or seven or eight or more because there will be neither jungle undergrowth nor overlarge timbers to deal with, nor will there be a necessity for finding fence wood elsewhere. On the other hand, the natives' conception of the period of soil-replenishment might be empirically arrived at (I recorded several reports of crop failure due — according to informants — to gardeners not allowing land to remain idle long enough). Probably both of these factors are behind the native theory.

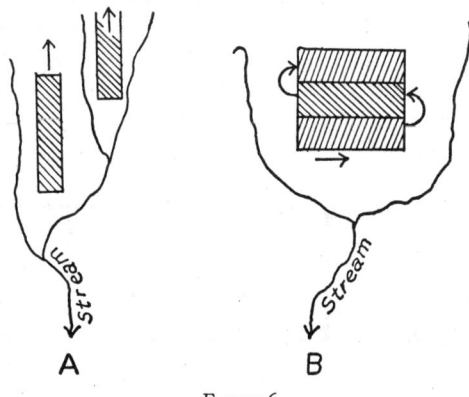

Figure 6

The *ideal* technique, in the northeast region, is to progress in one direction for about six years and then return to the starting point and begin again. For such a process each family would require a continuous strip of fertile land about 100 feet wide and about ¼ mile long. A mapping survey of northeast Siuai indicated that such an ideal is seldom realized. Some kind of barrier — either another household's garden or an effective natural or cultural boundary — usually gets in the way.

What sometimes happens is that each household has three or four gardens, as in Figure 7.

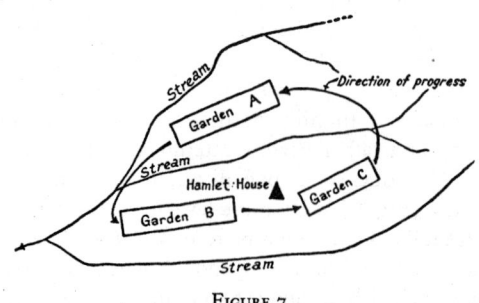

Figure 7

Garden A has been deserted for three or four years; it will be replanted when Garden C is completely cultivated.

Garden B is partly harvested (at the southwest), and there is a stand of ripe taro at the northeastern end.

Garden C is being cleared and fenced in now; the gardeners plant the stalks from Garden B in the southern end of Garden C.

Firewood is collected from the southwestern end of Garden B.

I spent many days in Siuai taro patches and became deeply impressed with the rhythmic efficiency of sequence-gardening. Given their implements — ax, machete, wooden rake, and digging stick — it would be difficult to devise a more efficient procedure which would also satisfy the need for strong fences. A steel-bladed hoe would probably speed up weeding, but more complex tools and chemical insecticides would not be feasible in terms of the present economy.[19] I learned to appreciate the labor-saving economy of sequence-gardening particularly after watching the preparation of a patch out of sequence. It happened, as it not infrequently does, that a patch was prepared at an isolated site covered with jungle past the customary growth stage. Many of the larger trees on the site had to be felled and laboriously dragged clear of the patch to avoid shading the garden excessively, and many of the fence posts and some of the horizontal fence timbers had to be brought from elsewhere since trees of the proper size were not to be found on the site. Fence building in any case is hard work, but when heavy timbers must be carried long distances it is back-breaking, and natives so regard it. Nor do they risk failure by attempting to replant prematurely an old garden site; the thorny tangle of vines and bushes is difficult to clear and the resulting taro crop is likely to be anemic.

Fences vary in height and in thickness according to the location of the garden. Those bordering much-traveled paths are made high enough to block out the stares of strangers; those within a few hundred yards of bush-houses have to be built unusually thick and sturdy to withstand hungry domestic pigs — wild pigs being smaller and easier to fence out. It would therefore appear easier for men, who build the fences, to locate gardens farther away from settlements to permit easier fence construction. However, women have much to say about the location of gardens, and they try to avoid walking over-long distances laden, as they usually are, with crushing loads of firewood. Other factors affecting garden location will be described later on.

The taro patch is divided into plots (*nopu*) two spans wide by nine spans long (10 by 45 feet), with pathways left clear along the fences and between every two or three plots (Figure 8). These plots are marked off with logs laid on the ground, and have a number of functions. All the taro in any one plot (an average of 102 plants) is at very nearly the same stage of growth, and on the rare occasions when taro is sold the sale unit is the plotfull, which therefore provides a convenient and fairly uniform unit. Furthermore when pigs break into a patch and root up the growing plants the number of plots molested supplies a basis for indemnification — although an additional tort payment is nearly always assessed. Sociological purposes are also served by the plot layout (see below, page 264); and I am tempted to point out — although it was never rationalized to me in these terms — that delineating plots with logs cut when clearing a patch saves having to drag the logs clear of the planting.

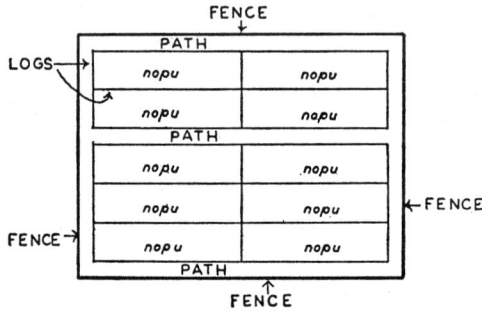

FIGURE 8

Taro occupies so prominent a place in Siuai life that one might appropriately go on for pages describing the numerous varieties grown;[20] the exact details of planting, weeding, and harvesting; the high value placed upon it as *the* vegetable food; the feelings of deprivation natives express when they must go without it; the frequency with which it enters into conversation; the numerous metaphors for it and its use in ritual; etc. Some of this will be reported in later chapters; but rather than burden the reader with a long technical account, however justified that may be by the importance of the topic, I merely ask him to remember that Siuai natives spend more hours growing taro than in any other enterprise, that the plant comprises 80 per cent of their diet, and that it is the basis of their subsistence economy generally. If that is forgotten during consideration of more dramatic activities, then true perspective on Siuai life will have been lost.

In most taro patches natives also grow some tobacco, a dozen or so plantain and banana plants, and several yam and gourd vines trained up along the fences. Now and then one comes across a patch containing a few stalks of maize, some tomatoes, and a bush of tiny red peppers which are used as condiments. Few Siuai have yet acquired tastes for the recently introduced maize and tomatoes. Yams sometimes reach lengths of three and four feet and are pointed out as curiosities, but no special effort is made to produce or display them; because of their coarse, fibrous texture they are not rated highly as a food. Being easily roasted however they, along with plantains, are occasionally cooked and eaten as snacks by natives working in the gardens or lazing in the club-houses.

Sweet potatoes are second only to taro in Siuai diets. As their native name, *peteita*, indicates, they are of recent introduction, assertedly from Alu, but their use is expanding and even during our short stay potato acreages increased. Older people express some contempt for them, calling them pap: "children's food; not solid, strength-giving food like taro." In fact, they figure importantly only in the diets of households with mission-trained members. As a food crop sweet potatoes have several advantages: they will grow on sandy soil unsuited to taro, they require little care after planting, and they produce a higher yield per area. On the other hand they are more tempting to pigs and require sturdier fences than taro gardens do; it is said that pigs will exert greater effort to break into a sweet potato garden. Consequently natives do not waste labor by planting taro and potato in the same enclosure; in fact, they usually locate potato gardens in flood-plain valleys far away from settlements. Here, out of reach of domestic pigs, there is less danger of marauding; and if the gardener wishes to take the extra precaution of building a fence he has only to build on the landward side of a creek bend (Figure 9). Furthermore natives claim that the sandy alluvial soil is ideal for sweet potatoes.

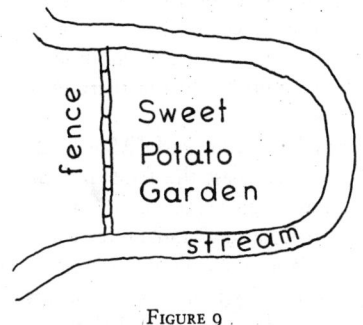

FIGURE 9.

No Siuai meal is complete without a few slivers of coconut meat or a portion of coconut oil poured over the vegetables. For special feast dishes it is indispensable — being shredded and baked with sago or mixed with boiled taro, or used to "grease" food generally, and in other ways. But far more important is the coconut's everyday use as a light repast or thirst-quencher; except for water and broth it is a Siuai's only drink. One of the compensations for anthropologizing in coconut-land is the drink of cool, slightly sweet, tangy liquid from an unripe coconut; it is not only superbly refreshing but nutritious and energy-producing. For a combination meal and drink the Siuai prefer a nut in which meat has begun to form; after cracking it and allowing the liquid to guzzle down their throats they separate the two halves and scrape out slivers of soft meat. For a more solid snack they obtain a completely dry nut and eat not only the half-inch-thick layer of meat but the spongy kernel as well. There are no sex-bound restrictions on collecting coconuts, but young boys are the ones usually sent scurrying up a palm for them. When climbing a high palm they slip a short loop of light rope around both insteps and, using that to grip the trunk, pull themselves upward with their hands by means of short hops. Coconuts are husked by jabbing them against a pointed stick stuck into the ground. Nut shredders are made of a shell or metal saw-toothed shredding blade attached to a wooden frame.

It is quite possible that some coconut palms might have "escaped" from cultivation and grown wild in parts of southern Bougainville; most of those we saw were clearly derived from native planting. If a few old palms are found standing in the wilderness, a little more searching or inquiry will establish that the place was formerly a settlement. Most palms are found near dwellings or immediately around club-houses, and show that not much thought has been given to spacing; but here and there one sees small and orderly groves. Indications are that new plantings are on the increase — stimulated partly by the Administration prescript that ten palms be planted for every newborn child, and partly by the ideas acquired at whites' plantations. There is no cash-income trade in coconuts — the only potential purchaser being a Chinese trader located on the coast one day's walk away; but judging by the frequency with which ambitious natives have to taboo their groves to accumulate nuts for feasts there is still an unfulfilled subsistence need for coconuts.[21]

The breadfruit season lasts from early May to the middle of June and while it is in progress natives roast the fruit and eat it as a staple. It rots so quickly that it is usually eaten on the same day picked. Siuai distinguish between a large and a small variety, and prefer the latter. Most households own a few breadfruit trees and the fruit is eaten with evident enjoyment during the first few days of the season; soon however the novelty wears off and natives return to their favorite, taro. Informants tell of certain trees having been purposefully planted in past years, but I did not learn of any new plantings during our stay.

Canarium almonds leave a deeper impress on Siuai life. When they ripen, in late July and August, even garden work is forsaken for a few days to allow time for collecting nuts and extracting the kernels. Almond trees grow to heights of 100 feet or more and the nuts cluster on the outermost branches, with the result that picking them is a hazardous undertaking. Poles and ropes are used to climb the long distance to the first limbs, and then natives have to edge out to the branch ends to cut or twist loose the clusters of nuts. Now and then someone will fall, and this occasionally proves fatal.

The skill required and the danger involved add a zest to almond collecting which these usually phlegmatic natives seem to enjoy. Numbers of them will gather around a tree and yelp with admiration when a climber breaks off and drops a cluster from a topmost limb.

The kernel of a ripe canarium almond is about the size and shape of the Jordan almond. It is covered with a hard shell encased in a purplish fleshy hull. (Pigeons often eat the hull and discard the rest, littering the ground with the nuts which natives then collect.) Kernels are extracted by holding the nut on one stone and cracking it open with another. Then the kernels are either eaten whole and raw or mashed in a mortar and added to sago and taro puddings, or they may be smoked and packed away in bamboo or leaf containers for future eating or trade.

The seasonal growth of almonds, which constitute an indispensable ingredient for most special feast delicacies, results in the holding of most feasts in the months immediately succeeding nut-ripening. There is nothing inevitable about this feast cycling since properly smoked nuts will last a full year or more, but it is customary to consume the nuts within a few months after picking.

The Siuai seldom plant almond trees. They carefully avoid injuring them when clearing jungle, and build small protective fences around young trees, but the long interval between planting and fruiting appears to discourage systematic cultivation. Men will however plant a new tree to replace an old one that has to be cut to make way for a Government road.

Compared with the vast areas of sago palms found in New Guinea, the few small groves scattered around the marshy places of southern Bougainville appear quite insignificant. Nevertheless, these antediluvian, giant fern-like plants do have a number of important uses for the Siuai. The starch obtained from the pith of the trunk is a substitute food staple, fronds are the principal thatching material, the broad bases of branches are used as troughs, and rotting palm stumps crawl with choice edible grubs. Sago flour is obtained by felling the palm, stripping off its outer hull, shredding the pithy center, and washing out its starch into a wooden standing-trough. A bamboo-edged adze is the shredding tool; one of the tree's own branch bases and its vegetable matting serve as washing-tough and strainer. After starch has settled in the standing-trough the water is drained off and the flour packed into cylindrical-shaped leaf containers for storage.

I could not learn whether the Siuai purposely plant sago palms, and suspect not, but I have seen them erect a crude fence around a new plant to protect it from being crushed by pigs crowding around to devour grubs and gleanings of sour sago in old stumps.

During periods of mourning, when the Siuai forego gardening, or during times of continuous rainfall, when they do not like to go to their garden because of the danger of crossing swollen creeks or the difficulty of walking along slippery paths or the cold discomfort of working in wet and mud, they reluctantly fall back upon sago for their staple; otherwise they reserve that food for their travels because of the ease of carrying and roasting it.

## COLLECTING, HUNTING, AND FISHING

In addition to the plants the Siuai grow or encourage to grow for food, they collect *hari* nuts, and many kinds of edible leaves, nuts, ferns, mushrooms, and fungi from the forest.[22] Some of these wild foods are ordinary fare, others have special uses: for example, one kind of wild yam is a rare delicacy; "pig's-wife" fern is eaten only with pork; the leaf of the *surasia* tree is a delicacy used in invalids' broth. All such foods are used as relishes — not being "solid" like taro; they constitute only a small proportion (about 2 per cent by weight) of any ordinary meal.

When food staples become scarce as a result of crop failure and sago shortage, natives ward off starvation by collecting "wild" sago,[23] wild yams, and wild taro, but such times are infrequent and only one such "Big Hunger" was recalled by my informants, who attributed it to a prolonged drought.

Salty condiments are used extensively and are considered indispensable for the domestic meal. Natives nearer the coast make a salt by evaporating salt water; those farther inland utilize the ashes of several plants.[24] Salt ash is kept on the smoke rack over the hearth to increase its pungency.

Collecting edible insects is only an incidental activity — if natives see them they may try to catch them; there are no special implements involved. In addition to the sago grubs, which are regarded as a delicacy, the Siuai like to eat beetles, white ants — large and small — and certain kinds of spiders.

Hunting is less haphazard. Hunting for wild pigs is in fact a serious undertaking requiring skill, persistence, and some courage. Many Siuai take sporting pleasure in hunting, even though the booty is usually small. Wild pigs and opossums are the chief quarries, but natives will shoot at tree-rats, flying foxes, and birds if they see them reasonably close.

In southern Siuai natives may go for a year or more without eating wild pig, and during my fifteen-week residence in one northern village only two wild pigs were killed by my neighbors. In villages bordering the unbroken rain forests, however, pigs are hunted more frequently and successfully, and some residents keep packs of starving dogs for the purpose. One native I knew spent about a fifth of his working time in hunting and managed to bring in a pig or two a month.

The customary hunting method is for one man to start off with dogs and roam through the forest until the dogs find and run down an animal which is then killed by a long throwing spear made of hard limbum palm with either a plain fire-hardened point or a point of razor-sharp bamboo. (The more elaborate bone-pointed and decorated "fighting" spears are now reserved for mock battles and feasts.) Until recent years wild-pig drives involved up to a hundred men. A stockade was constructed ("like a garden fence, but not so strong"), then the hunters would unleash their dogs, form a wide circle, and converge on the stockade, rustling bushes, shouting and blowing on conch shells. Pigs driven into the stockade were then speared. Very large-scale and successful drives are said to have netted up to thirty pigs. If old tuskers were cornered they would usually attack their tormentors, and now and then a hunter or a dog would be maimed or even killed.

Opossum hunting is an adventurous outing. Two or more boys or men equip themselves with "camping" provisions — packets of sago and large quantities of betel-chewing supplies — and remain for two or three days in the forest capturing the little marsupials. After one is treed, sometimes with the help of dogs, a younger native will climb the tree and shake down the opossum while his companions wait on the ground to pounce on the stunned animal. Occasionally a live animal is brought home for a ceremony but more usually the animals are killed, eviscerated, cleaned, and smoked soon after capture. Liver, heart, and blood are promptly eaten, while the smoked carcass is usually put aside for some feast. Opossum hunters appear not to mind the short rations and rough living of the chase, but the Siuais' characteristic uneasiness about tree-climbing is apparent despite the climbers' bravado. The Siuai also set ingenious but rarely successful traps for opossum by rigging a trip-noose over an "opossum trail," a thick vine stretched between two likely trees.

Tree-rats are occasionally captured for food but I discovered few natives who had actually done so or eaten any caught by others. Soups made from flying foxes and flying mice are favorite though infrequent fare, and natives spend hours manufacturing the special four-pronged barbed arrows used in hunting these creatures. They also value their wing bones for making spear and arrow barbs.

Fishing is also an occasional pastime with many Siuai but does not add significantly to their diets. One often sees a solitary male searching for fish and eels with his bow and arrow up and down a stream, hopeful but rarely successful. Or, once a fortnight or so, women and girls will spend a few hours wading in a stream searching by hand for prawns that may hide under ledges and roots. Almost everywhere large and small basket-traps are manufactured and left in likely spots — nearly every two or three hundred feet of a stream's course will harbor one; but these remain empty for weeks at a time, and word of a catch becomes a lively conversation topic in the neighborhood. In addition to these individual and spasmodic attempts to catch fish, natives sometimes — as often as two or three times a year in communities bordering large creeks — engage in coöperative fish drives. One technique is to select a spot where the creek divides around an island, divert the water from one stream by damming, and then proceed to shoot or capture the fish and prawns left floundering in pools in the dry stream bed. In one such fish drive I witnessed, about eighty natives took part and about two hundred pounds of fish plus several hundred prawns were caught. A second large-scale fishing technique involves the use of a long seine-net carried through the wider river pools by a score or more men. Seines are made from dried and shredded bark, and are usually manufactured by several specialists working together. There were only three of these large seine-nets in all northeast Siuai during my stay, and not a single seine-drive took place.

## ANIMAL HUSBANDRY

Pig-raising is vastly more important than hunting and fishing in Siuai economy. Nearly every household owns at least one pig, and most average three or four.

Domesticated pigs are fed once a day, during the late afternoon, and the rest of the time they are allowed to run free and forage. According to natives' belief, based apparently on experience, a full-grown pig must be given five to six pounds of food daily in order for it to remain properly domesticated. If fed less it will break through the strongest of fences and devour garden produce, or wander farther from home and invade the less protected potato gardens, or, worse still, it will run wild altogether in the forest. A proper diet for pigs, the Siuai consider, must be balanced and cooked like their own: a boiled taro or potato base, a portion of cooked greens, and some coconut meat. When preparing their own meals natives usually remove thick slices of peeling from taro or potatoes and cook the peel along with some taro tips for their pigs, but sometimes they feed them whole corms or tubers. This feeding is carried out with painstaking care, every animal receiving its portion on a separate basket-tray. Fully domesticated pigs do not have to be called for their daily meal; they return to the dwelling in midafternoon and clamor for it, and often remain nearby all night.

No attempt is made to pen grown pigs until they are held awaiting slaughter. At home, although the larger animals are kept outside the house, they are encouraged to stay nearby, this of course being possible only in the scattered hamlet residences, the "pig-food" houses, and not in the palisaded line villages prescribed by the Administration.

Some care is given to breeding, and a good boar is considered a very valuable resource. Sows usually farrow in thickets near their owners' dwellings; when that happens the owners close all paths to the spot and take the precaution of barring dogs. Young pigs are kept in pens alongside the dwellings; until the animals are domesticated enough to remain near home and large enough to fend for themselves, their owners believe it necessary to stay nearby at least part of each day; otherwise young animals become "lonely," natives say. During the first few months of their lives young pigs are cared for like the pets they are; their food is cooked in the pot along with their owners', and one often sees women premasticate a lump of taro or potato for sickly young animals.

It will be described later on how pigs are ritually named, "baptized," and magically treated for ailments. Here it should merely be noted that young male shoats are gelded without ceremony, as a purely practical measure — "to make them grow." Gelding is carried out with a knife (formerly with a splinter of bamboo) by splitting open the scrotum and removing the testicles. Natives take great interest in this operation and even children are allowed to try it. Pigs are also "branded" by cutting chips out of their ears; this is not an ownership mark but does serve to distinguish domestic from wild pigs (see p. 359). Additional ways of distinguishing between wild and domestic pigs are known to nearly all natives. Wild pigs are smaller, thinner, quicker, more malodorous, pure "razorback"; domesticated pigs are the result of mixing native with European breeds, the latter having been introduced within recent decades by laborers returning home from white colonists' coconut plantations. Before the introduction of European strains, wild pigs were probably not very different from domestic ones — thinner and tougher, perhaps, but probably the same breed. Later on, when Siuai youths finished their terms of indenture on whites' plantations, many of them invested their earnings in European pigs and proudly carried them back home. Older natives recall those times with feeling: how great was the excitement that prevailed upon first sight of the superior animals and how longingly every adult tried to obtain one of its offspring. Disdain for the native breed, including the wild pigs, became so marked that hunting was thereby discouraged. It is certainly obvious that the new mix-breed animal is a great improvement in size and succulence over the old; but it is not all gain, for natives also state that the domesticated native pig stayed nearer home, hence did not menace gardens located farther away than a few hundred yards. It is even claimed by some older informants that during their fathers' childhoods gardens did not require fencing. Whether that be true or not, and I suspect not, the new mixed breeds possibly do rove farther afield and, being larger, probably do require sturdier garden fencing.

Killing and butchering a pig is man's work and most men can butcher quite skillfully. Some men prefer to kill an animal by strangling it — by bending its head to one side to cut off respiration. This is the tidier and more economical method because there is less loss of blood; it is used in killing a pig while a ceremony is going on. At other times the animal is killed by having its lungs caved in and heart crushed with a few hard blows of an ax-butt; this is the quicker method. When the animal is dead — or thought to be near enough dead — it is fastened to a pole and hung over a fire for singeing. After this, soot and burnt hair are scraped away with a knife and the butcher sets to work cutting the animal into twelve longitudinal strips. During the butchering the gullet is knotted near the head in order to prevent the contents of the stomach from spilling over the animal. Blood is highly valued, and is scooped up from the body cavity and placed in containers — either to be drunk at once or made into a pudding. The heart is roasted and is regarded as a great delicacy. Belly fat is also carefully saved, mixed with blood, and cooked in a pot. No attempt however is made to retain stomach or intestines.

Every settlement contains a few fowl, which fend for themselves by stealing food leavings and catching insects. They hide their eggs in the scrub, but most natives do not care for eggs anyway. Only on rare occasions do the Siuai kill and eat one of these athletic birds.

Dogs are also to be found in every settlement — almost in every house. A few of these wretched rail-thin creatures are used in hunting but the rest serve only as pets, if that is the proper word to describe the lot of these half-starved, continually kicked animals. Some households also keep a cat or two for rat-catching and for the amusement of children, and now and then natives capture and keep a cockatoo.

## COOKING AND EATING

The Siuai domestic meal, the one full meal of the day, seldom varies in its main outlines: for each individual past early childhood a basic portion of three or four pounds of taro or sweet potato, along with a helping of cooked greens flavored with salt or coconut oil and, now and then, some small taste of relish — meat, fish, grubs, or other delicacy. Sometimes plantains or yams are substituted as staples for taro and sweet potato, but as already indicated they are regarded as second best, most adults insisting that taro alone gives them the feeling of stuffed satiation which should accompany every satisfactory meal. Sago is another substitute, usually eaten with the domestic meal only when some other staple is not available. Invalids are usually given vegetable or meat soups.

The Siuai vary their cooking methods with the occasion. Working in the gardens, hunting in the forests, or traveling far from home, they assuage hunger by simply roasting a plantain, a yam, or a leaf packet of sago on an open hearth. On special occasions they wrap their vegetables and relishes in leaves and bake them by covering them with hot coals. Or more elaborately, they dig a pit and place in it packets of leaf-wrapped food surrounded by hot stones; this is the favorite manner of cooking but it is laborious and hence used only for feasts. The daily meal of the household is cooked by steaming and boiling. A clay pot is wedged upright between stones on the hearth and into the pot are poured a few inches of water. Then it is filled to the brim with chunks of taro and potatoes, unpeeled plantains, small packets of greens, and any other supplement available; a covering of large leaves is fixed tightly over the top; and the pot is allowed to boil and steam until the starchy staples have reached a consistency which most Americans would find slightly underdone. This means that any meat cooked in the same pot is far tougher than stone-baked meat, and the Siuai recognize its inferiority, but the morsels of home-cooked meat are usually so minute that, natives reason, they are hardly worth while baking. Cooks sometimes use pointed sticks to test whether food is properly cooked, but usually they gauge — or more frequently misgauge — the time by some measure I was unable to fathom and proceed to spear out the food into basket trays. Onto each tray are placed several chunks of starchy staple, a plantain or two, a helping of greens mixed with oil, a few slivers of coconut meat, and a tidbit of the day's special relish. The solid food is then eaten by hand and washed down by drinks of broth or coconut milk. Then, after eating, comes the betel-chewing and the pipe of tobacco.

Siuai natives chew the betel mixture frequently and smoke almost continually. The betel mixture consists of areca nuts, collected from purposefully planted palms, along with catkins taken from a pepper tree, and lime obtained by burning shells collected on the southern beaches. One variety of areca nut is said to be strongly narcotic but I never noticed any native visibly affected. The Siuai say that betel-chewing staves off hunger, but they also chew it immediately after meals just for its pleasant taste. Native tobacco is smoked in trade-store pipes. It is grown in their gardens along the fences, and although some of it is sun- and smoke-dried before use, these inveterate and hardy smokers often pick a green leaf, "cure" it over a smoky fire for a minute or two, and smoke it forthwith.

## ART AND AMUSEMENT

To what extent do the Siuai embellish the things they use and the physical things they do?

Compared with many Oceanic cultures possessing similar or even fewer physical resources, Siuai is poor in architecture and in graphic and plastic arts. To begin with, most Siuai structures are built for service rather than for show; it is only occasionally and in connection with some club-houses and high tree-houses that extra effort is put into producing patterned lashings or smooth and uniform timbers. It cannot be inferred that these natives are entirely deficient in their appreciation of architectural symmetry, etc., or in the skills required for building handsome structures, it is just that their interests are focused upon other matters.

Except for the body ornamentation mentioned above, most Siuai graphic art is confined to the decoration of objects of everyday use. Bamboo cylinders used for carrying tobacco are covered with many kinds of highly conventionalized designs, incised with a knife and blackened with vegetable dyes. (Bamboo combs are also decorated in this manner.) Lime-gourd stoppers are woven about with fine, black-, red-, and yellow-dyed fibers from an orchid plant — the same materials and techniques being employed to decorate weapons used in dancing (spears, clubs, bows and arrows). Some plaited baskets have interwoven designs of fibers dyed red or black; coil-woven baskets and trays have designs produced by bleaching the fibers to different shades of brown.

Large conventionalized wooden human figures carved in the round are used in certain kinds of sorcery; the same kind of figure is sometimes carved into the shafts of decorated spears and dance ornaments. Some club-houses have conventionalized carved wooden hornbills tenoned into a mortise cut out of their forward-projecting ridgepoles and purlins. Other than these objects Siuai wood designs are all carved in low relief and most are filled in with mineral or vegetable pigment. Such designs are used to decorate pudding-baking frames and large wooden trumpets.

Small shell discs of white, red, and black are strung together in span-long lengths and serve principally as money, but they are sometimes combined to form geometrically patterned bead belts or squares and as such are worn as body decorations or are simply exhibited as articles of value and beauty.

The Siuai devote more time to music than to graphic and plastic art. Every club-house contains several wooden slit gongs, ranging in size from fifteen feet long by five feet in diameter to three feet long by one foot in diameter. These gongs are sounded with vertically held wooden beaters struck against the lip of the slit, and they are used both for signaling and for making music. The gong played by women consists of a single wooden board laid in a waist-deep hole dug in the ground. Two or three females stand in the hole and jump on the board in unison to mark the tempo for their companions' dancing and singing around the hole.

Flute-playing in concert by large numbers of men and boys accompanies many feasts and ceremonies, but individuals also play on the flute by themselves for their own diversion. Flutes are of many sizes and are made of bamboo; they vary in number of units from one to ten. The Siuai also play large trumpets made by attaching a half coconut-shell mouthpiece to one end of a hollow wooden cylinder. Children sometimes amuse themselves by playing on small musical bows, but young men prefer the trade-store jew's harp.

Singing is highly popular and accompanies many kinds of occasions. Parents sing lullabies to their children and use songs to teach them new words. Lovers compose boastful songs about their adventures, and relatives express their grief in moving laments. Even wailing follows a conventional musical pattern. Most dramatic of all however is the harmonized singing of large numbers of men and boys, which takes place at some feasts.

Dancing is a ritual as well as a diversion. As ritual it accompanies many feasts and nearly all life-crisis ceremonies, and is often combined with singing and flute-playing. Siuai adults also like to perform masques on the occasion of large feasts. Children amuse themselves with string-figures, toy bows and arrows, etc., and especially enjoy play-imitations of the activities of their elders. Otherwise the Siuai possess no competitive game-like diversions save the recent import of football.

For everyday amusement Siuai adults — and especially the males — like best to talk: telling stories, recounting experiences, reporting gossip, and boasting about plans. Judging by the interminable length and the consciously

## PHYSICAL ADAPTATION

rhythmic quality of their utterances, and the metaphor-rich style of their diction, it is probably not incorrect to say that such aesthetic talents as they have find highest expression in *vocal* performance — in song and in speech. Using words, with or without music, is the Siuai's finest art and their most enjoyable amusement.

### ECOLOGICAL TIME

*When* do all these activities take place?

If a western observer remained long enough, he would note how the sameness of the southern Bougainville climate is reflected in the sameness of Siuai life. To a visitor from the temperate zone the light breezes and clear sunny days of May–September are a welcome change from the continuous rains of October–November and the still, humid overcasts of December–April; but even if the Siuai themselves share this reaction they do not comment upon it, and in most respects it does not cause them to change their daily routines. Taro, their all-important food staple, is planted and harvested continuously so there is no basis for the agricultural cycling which structures time for so many peoples. It is true that continuous rainy spells slow down garden work and reduce natives to eating poorer and less. And it is also probably true that the mosquito-plagued days of December–April bring on more fever and hence result in less constructive work. But neither of these kinds of change has marked culture-wide ramifications. In fact, only the ripening of breadfruit and of canarium almonds provide any kind of general annual cycle. Breadfruit ripens in May–June and while its short season lasts it furnishes a welcome but quantitatively unimportant addition to the daily menu. This is also the case with almonds, which ripen in late July, but some natives forego eating this delicacy with their daily meals and use it only for feasts, and this has the effect of concentrating feasting within the few months immediately after almond picking.

The phasing of the moon is explained animistically, the new moon is greeted with ritual gestures, and bright moonlight keeps people gossiping and playing outside their huts long after nightfall; otherwise, lunar time has only minor effect on Siuai economic life. Not so with the sun. In this place of brief dawns and dusks and of ineffective man-made lighting, the rising and setting of the sun mark the start and the stopping of most activities having to do with getting a living; and throughout daylight the sun's position sets a rough kind of schedule for working and eating. But there is nothing very precise about this — the Siuai are slow starters and dawdlers, by bustling western standards. On the average day natives emerge sluggishly from their smoky huts at sunup and stand shivering and hugging themselves in shafts of sunlight for many minutes before picking their way down to a creek to bathe and make toilet. Back again at the hut, the cold remnants of yesterday's meal are divided among the children while the adults assuage hunger and sweeten breath with a chew of betel mixture followed by the first of the day's almost continuous pipe smokes. Then, some two hours after sunrise they set out for work.

Most mornings women and children go to the gardens, which are usually within a mile of the dwelling, and remain there working until midafternoon. Men and boys also go to the gardens some days but except when they are clearing a new garden site and building fences they seldom remain there as long as the women and girls. More often they will spend their working day building, repairing, manufacturing, trading, litigating, conversing, or, commonly, merely dozing. Around noontime natives eat a snack, a roasted plantain or yam if they are in the gardens, the milk and meat of a coconut, if not. Midafternoon they return home to prepare and eat the day's principal meal and feed their pigs; then they converse and visit until dark and retire into their huts to sleep.

Once in a long while this routine will be interrupted by daytime feasts and ceremonies and by all-night wakes and cremations. Or, if death strikes nearby, most work may cease for days at a time. Again, in settlements located near mission stations or possessing influential native teachers, the Sunday morning service, and sometimes even the daily one, will draw together several converts to drone out a mechanical prayer and sing a few hymns. In Methodist communities, especially, Sundays are marked by pious idleness and, consequently, frugal meals. The annual "karisimasi" (pidgin, for "Christmas") cycle and numerous Christian anniversaries have not brought about any marked change in the established flow of native activities, but the regular recurrence of "sande" is beginning to influence when and how natives do things.

Summarizing, it can be said that the annual cycle, manifested in the ripening of almonds, has some effect upon feasting; that the lunar cycle has some slight ritual and social significance; that the imported, artificial weekly cycle is beginning to have at least a negative effect on work habits; but that the main time marker is the diurnal cycle, it being divided into the period of darkness and sleep, the period of morning and early afternoon working. and the period of late afternoon eating and socializing. So much could any observer note about *when* Siuai activities take place.

CHAPTER 2

# Some Beliefs About Nature and Man

Empiricism plainly underlies much of Siuai technology, and it also forms a basis for much of their social behavior, as later chapters in this book will indicate. On the other hand, there are innumerable aspects of Siuai behavior which are not intelligible in terms of western canons of empiricism — behavior which can become comprehensible to a western reader only in terms of a set of assumptions and beliefs indigenously and peculiarly Siuai.[1] The aim of the present chapter is to describe some of the more explicit beliefs of the Siuai about themselves and their universe in order to provide the reader with a second kind of framework for comprehending Siuai life.

Since our knowledge of a very large part of Siuai beliefs reaches us by means of the spoken word, it would be desirable to begin this account with a full description of their language, bearing in mind that language is not merely a means of communication but also that "an accepted pattern of using words is often prior to certain lines of thinking and forms of behavior, —"[2] or, in other words, that Siuai formulations about "reality" are in some measure conditioned by their language. However, for reasons previously given[3] it is not practicable to include a full grammar in this work, and in the account that follows only indirect use will be made of the canons of logic and other conceptions of "reality" embedded in the structures of the language itself.

## THE AGE OF CREATION

*Creation Myths.*[4] While the world was still incomplete, when things were not yet "straight," manlike supernatural beings walked about performing wonderful feats of creation and discovery. These were the *kupunas*.[5] They came from the islands to the south and the mountains to the north. How they were created, or whether they had always existed, no Siuai knows; just because there were sibling pairs among them does not signify that even these kupunas had parents.[6]

Here in Siuai, it is said, the kupunas moved about from place to place, clearing land, cutting out river beds, inventing food plants, marrying and having offspring — including spirits as well as the first Siuai natives. How long they kept up these labors is not known, but eventually they turned over their handiwork to their human descendants and withdrew from direct participation in mundane affairs. Some of them withdrew so completely that only their names are faintly remembered. Others transformed themselves into demons and continue to haunt the settlements of the living. Still others turned into stone [7] and now serve as animated shrines for their matrilineal descendants.

Natives' knowledge about the wondrous careers of the kupunas derives from several sources. First there are the great creation myths, widely known accounts which string together series of episodes into epic proportions. Second, there are the additions and embellishments to these made by individuals who have picked up different versions on their travels beyond Siuai; myth characters and themes are similar in many respects throughout southern Bougainville and the adjacent islands, and borrowing was formerly even more active than now.[8] A third source of knowledge about the kupunas consists of myth anecdotes, short explanations of the occurrence of phenomena which have only local interest. An example of this is the account given by the inhabitants of Hinna village about the origin of the large stone, Kataku, now resting on the nearby tract of that name. Kataku is a demon, it is said, and was created by kupunas. Some kupunas saw the stone and decided to cut a hole in it and use it as a gong. Later, when the kupunas withdrew, Kataku became a demon which now has the power of moving about and eating taro from the gardens of men who are "Near-death." [9] Nowadays, when a native of Hinna discovers some of his taro uprooted and eaten, he first searches for evidence of thieving pigs; then seeing no pig tracks he concludes that Kataku was the thief and thus realizes that his own life is near its end.

A fourth source of knowledge about the kupunas and their exploits comes from philosophically minded natives who, reasoning from what is known about these extraordinary Beings, attribute to them the creation of other things and circumstances requiring explanation. This applies particularly to the culture hero, Orphan (Panaŋa), who by an increasing number of new myth anecdotes is being built into something of a super-kupuna. Many of these stories of local interest and of recent improvisation have probably been grafted onto the great creation myths, and the process is undoubtedly still going on, with the result that it is impossible to determine what is canonical and what apocryphal — not that such a distinction has any direct bearing on the content of current Siuai beliefs.[10]

The great creation myths are of two kinds: those concerned mainly with the discovery or creation of items and practices pertaining to all Siuai mankind, and those concerned mainly with the genesis of matri-sibs. This is not a rigid distinction because some of the matri-sib genesis myths contain epi-

## BELIEFS ABOUT NATURE AND MAN

sodes of universal application, for example, the invention of warfare credited to kupunas of the Parrot sib.[11] And conversely, some versions identify even the "universal" kupunas with specific sibs.

There is nothing esoteric about any of these myths; most natives delight in telling them whenever there is a willing audience; and this is particularly so when a myth contains salacious episodes, as is the case with many of them. The telling is usually done without solemnity and the listeners display no more respectfulness or interest than they do upon hearing neighborhood gossip — except in connection with litigation and when the myth touches upon the "history" of the listeners' own sib or neighborhood; then people follow alertly to detect and refute versions different from their own. Unlike the myths of many other peoples, those of the Siuai are seldom related to teach children manners or morals.

*The Creation of Universal Siuai Customs.* The principal universal Siuai kupunas are Maker (Tantanu), Hoŋing,[12] and Orphan (Panaŋa). Maker is credited with the creation of food plants. Hoŋing originated Paradise (Ru'no'no') and is headman of that realm. Orphan taught humans many useful techniques. There are a few other kupuna creators and originators not closely identified with specific sibs, including Food-maker (Paopiahe), who invented some kinds of food, and the brothers Komarara and Komakiki, who first fashioned rivers and streams by excavating channels; but judged on the basis of the scale and number of their exploits these kupunas are not nearly so important as Maker, Hoŋing, and Orphan.

Maker created the more important food plants:

> In kupuna times Maker and Food-maker dwelt together on the beach far to the west until Maker did something that made Food-maker exceedingly angry. The thing that Maker did was this: he promised his grandchildren to teach them how to cause work to be done without physical exertion — to cause trees to be felled, brush to be cleared, and food plants to grow merely by telling them to do so. This manner of doing things so displeased Food-maker that he drove Maker away, telling him:
> 
> "That is a wicked thing you promise your grandchildren; I won't dwell with you any longer. Leave here at once and do not stop going until I can no longer see you."
> 
> With this, Maker left and went westward along the beach. After a while he stopped to rest, but Food-maker shouted:
> 
> "Keep going. I can still see you."
> 
> This time, as Maker went along he bent the trees behind him to conceal himself from Food-maker;[13] but in spite of this, when he next tried to stop and rest, Food-maker shouted:
> 
> "Keep going. I can still see you. You will not be safe from me until you are completely out of my sight."
> 
> Maker kept going until noon, when he arrived at the place called Siuai,[14] where he saw some children.

"Who lives here?" he asked them.

"We do," they replied.

"Then where have your parents gone?" he asked them.

"They have gone into the forest to fetch some food," they answered.

"What kind of food?" he demanded.

"Wild plants," they told him. "That is the food we are accustomed to eat."

At this, Maker ordered them to take down a cooking pot from the smoke rack and put it on the cooking hearth.

"Now," he instructed them, "put me in the pot, cover me over with leaves, pour in some water, and then build a fire under the pot."

As they were doing this, Maker defecated in the pot and then slipped out of it unseen and went to the river where he bathed and combed his hair. Then he returned to the children, who were amazed to see him.

"Why, who are you?" they asked. "You look just like the one we are cooking in the pot."

"Not me," he told them. "That was *food* you put in the pot. Why don't you take out some of it and eat it. Fill up all of your baskets with this food."

While they were doing this, Maker hid himself and waited. Soon the children's parents returned and inquired: "What are you eating?"

"Good things," they replied. "When you left us to collect wild food our grandfather, Maker, came up and gave us some taro, yams, bananas, and other good things to eat, telling us to throw away our own food and eat these new things."

This was the origin of all our good-tasting food.[15] People came from all over to try the new food, and Maker gave them plants to take home and grow in their own gardens. Today taro, yams, sago, and other plants grow wild in that place, Siuai.[16]

Like all other Siuai myths, this one about Maker and the origin of food plants has several versions. One of the most popular has Maker causing food trees (sago, almond, and coconut) to grow to help hide him as he trudges along the beach escaping from Food-maker.

Siuai myths do not relate how Maker fared after this. Some informants explain that he "went up to the sky, where he now remains," but this concept is a transparent Christian innovation. For one thing, the "sky" has no place in indigenous Siuai cosmology. Moreover, both the Methodist and Catholic missions in Siuai translate "God" to "Tantanu Mekusim" (Maker True) in the native texts of catechisms, in sermons, and in prayers, with the effect that native beliefs about Maker have been reinforced and augmented by Christian myths even more spectacular than the Siuai ones.

Honjing went to the land of Paradise (Lake Ru'no'no) in this manner:

A long time ago the kupuna, Namaru, prepared a feast and invited several other kupunas, including Honjing, Konopia, and Pinos; then Namaru went visiting to Alu (Shortland Island). While he was away the guests arrived at the feast, war-dancing and blowing their panpipes. Honjing went to see the pigs penned up awaiting distribution and spat betel-nut juice on the back of the largest one, thereby marking it for his own. Then, after the dancing and piping had finished, Hoŋing went to the pen to claim his pig, but he found that Konopia and Pinos had already taken it out for themselves. At that Hoŋing became infuriated and started a brawl which ended in demolishing the pigpen and driving all the pigs into the forest. All the other guests were so angered at missing a pork banquet that they drove Hoŋing north into the mountains. He went on and on until he arrived at Lake Ru'no'no'.

So prosaic was the origin of Paradise!

Orphan (Panaŋa) is the favorite myth character of most Siuai. On the one hand, Orphan is represented as the originator of many useful objects and practices, and as the hero who destroys evil men and demons. In other stories, he delights in tormenting stupid people and is himself not above lying, adultery, and incest. Many of the exploits identified with other beings in the myths of neighboring cultures (Mono, Alu, Torau, etc.[17]) are credited to Orphan by the Siuai, who recount his adventures with obvious affection and humor. Often he is described as carrying out his exploits amid the skepticism and insults of his contemporaries, and despite his social handicap of orphanage — most myth tellers carefully point out that he had no living parents.

Some of the myths about Orphan's exploits as an originator are short:

> *Sago.* Formerly, when people were processing sago, they washed out the starch into a trough [18] and carried home the trough full of water and starch before the starch had settled out, thereby causing much of the liquid to spill out on the road. But when Orphan washed his sago he allowed the solution to stand for a time so that the flour settled out; then he poured off the clear water, wrapped the flour in leaf containers, and carried these home, thereby wasting none of the starch. When others saw what he was doing they were angry with him for a while [because his method was better than theirs]; but later on they followed his example.
>
> *Almonds.* Formerly, people ate almonds nut, hull, and all. Orphan showed them how much better it was to remove the nut and eat that only.
>
> *Slit gongs.* Formerly, people tried to signal by hitting sticks against stones; Orphan showed them how to hollow out logs and beat on them.

Similarly, Orphan invented improved hunting and fishing techniques, and he was the first to suggest that people sleep inside rather than on top of their houses. Orphan also originated sexual intercourse in its present form:

> Formerly Orphan lived near his older brother and the latter's wife. One day the older brother sent his wife and Orphan after areca nuts and betel-pepper. When Orphan and his sister-in-law reached the areca grove, Orphan told her to climb the palm and throw down some nuts. The woman hesitated for a while, explaining that people might look up at her genitals, but finally, after repeated urgings from Orphan, she climbed the palm and began throwing down clusters of areca nuts. Orphan stood underneath her and looked up at her genitals, and to prolong this diversion he kept urging her to remain on the palm until all the nuts were picked. Then when she descended he caught and

held on to her genitals; whereupon the woman exclaimed: "Hey! what are you doing with this thing that you are holding? Your brother says it's a sore."

Orphan then told her, "Well, let's try it out." And he had intercourse with her.

"Hey! that's good," she exclaimed. "When your brother does that he uses my arm pit and not my 'sore.' Your way is better."

After trying the new way again they returned home, and there the woman sat down on the ground and kept her legs tightly pressed together to hide the blood that flowed from her vagina. In spite of this, her husband saw the blood and was angry.

"Why are you angry?" she complained. "Your younger brother has merely cured this thing that you call a sore. Why don't you see for yourself?"

Whereupon her husband tried it, and admitted that it was a good thing Orphan has discovered. Nevertheless he remained angry with Orphan and plotted his destruction. The opportunity finally came one day when the two brothers were paddling their canoes far out to sea. The elder brother slipped two coconuts they were carrying into the sea and asked Orphan to retrieve them. Then while the latter was swimming after the coconuts, the elder brother paddled away, leaving Orphan to drown. Orphan implored him to return but the older brother kept on, shouting:

"In curing my wife's sore, you stole her good thing from me. You committed adultery."

Left alone, Orphan swam and swam until he finally reached a small island on which grew a single tree. He climbed the tree to learn where he was, and some ashes drifted by him.

Orphan inquired, "Where do you come from?"

"From fire," Ashes replied.

"In that case," Orphan said, "Go and collect all the [wild] things you can find around here, and I shall cook them in the fire and eat them."

In this manner Orphan originated the fine custom of cooking food.

One day his elder brother paddled over to the lone island to savor his revenge by looking at the bones of his younger brother [whom he assumed had died of starvation]. When he saw the bones of all the animals and birds that Orphan had eaten he thought they were Orphan's bones, and gloated:

"Excellent! Now you are truly dead, from having stolen the good thing of my wife."

At that he climbed the tree to look around. As he climbed, Orphan slipped down the other side of the tree and made off with the canoe, shouting back:

"Now it's your turn. You didn't kill me after all."

Orphan was deaf to his brother's cries and he paddled away, returning to his former home where he married his brother's widow. Later on his wife's belly became large, and when labor pains began all the people thereabouts hurried to her with bamboo knives, intending to split open her belly to take out the infant — in those times this was the way with all births. Orphan, however, barred their way into the house, telling them:

"Let's wait a while and see if the infant will be born without cutting open it's mother's belly."

They were all angry with Orphan, but after a while the infant was born

## BELIEFS ABOUT NATURE AND MAN

and only the umbilicus had to be cut. Then the people praised Orphan for discovering this new method of birth. Later on Orphan prepared a feast and caused the infant to be brought out of the home and baptized. This was the beginning of baptism.

Adding still more to his luster, Orphan is believed to have originated warfare wherein men are able to kill their enemies with finality and not merely render them temporarily unconscious. It was by means of this power that he made an end to the wickedness and depredation of several maleficent demons and evil men. In all these episodes Orphan overwhelms his enemies by use of clever stratagems rather than brute force. Typical is the manner in which Orphan brought about the destruction of the evil Ikuraka:

> One day Orphan killed some ants and cooked them at his house. Ikuraka came along and was given a taste.
> "Brother-in-law," Ikuraka said, "this is exceedingly good-tasting food. But how did you manage to catch these ants without being bitten by them?"
> "That's not difficult," Orphan answered. "I collect only the big ones, and I always take them out of their nest with my hand; never do I use a stick."
> Thereupon, Ikuraka went hunting for big ants. He did not take the small ones and looked only for big ones. When he saw some very big biting ones he started to reach for them with his hand, but one of his companions shouted:
> "Hey! watch out! Kill them with a stick first. They will bite your hand."
> But Ikuraka persisted, saying, "What you say is not true. Orphan told me to catch big ants only with my hand."
> Ikuraka thrust his hand into the nest and was severely bitten. In great pain, he took along his companions and went to Orphan's house to kill him. But when he arrived there he saw Orphan cooking centipedes, and he forgot his anger so curious was he to taste this new food.

Again, Orphan deceived Ikuraka into trying to capture centipedes barehanded, with inevitable and painful results. In similar wise Orphan caused his stupid enemy to be stung, bitten, defecated on, etc., by various vicious insects and animals. He even succeeded in inducing Ikuraka to jump from the top of a tall palm with a coconut clutched in his hand — having explained to him that this was the accepted manner of cracking open coconuts. Finally, Orphan made an end to Ikuraka by inducing him to try to capture singlehanded a large man-eating crocodile.

Orphan also delighted in playing harmless tricks upon his naïve contemporaries. In one typical episode, people saw him using a rattan fiber for tying purposes and asked where he obtained it. He directed them to a pool of water on whose surface they saw reflected a rattan vine. On his advice they dug for many days before finally realizing that the actual vine was hanging overhead. Tales like this are retold by the Siuai zestfully, frequently, and with countless additions and embellishments. Throughout all these myths and tales the narrators emphasized to the recording ethnographer the peculiar circumstances surrounding Orphan's adventures: he was without parents or other helpful relatives and was subjected to all manner of scorn and insults by his contemporaries; yet in spite of this he surpassed everyone else in cleverness and finally gained for himself a position of high rank and wide authority.

*The Founding of Sibs.* Far more numerous among the creation myths are those having to do with the exploits of the various kupunas who originated Siuai mankind and at the same time established the matri-sibs into which all Siuai mankind is subdivided. These myths have much more social significance than those just described, for not only do they "explain" important social relations and practices but they also enjoin and canonize them. In fact, these myths are such important ethnographic documents that several principal versions are given below, in abridged form. They are presented here as natives repeat them, the narrative being interrupted from time to time with explanations about how certain myth characters and incidents are now preserved as shrines, practices, injunctions, etc. If the reader becomes annoyed at the listing of large numbers of place names, he should bear in mind that the enshrining of a place name in a creation myth serves the Siuai as a title deed for land ownership.

*Origin of the Giant Tree-rat-people.* The natives give us the following account of the origin of the Giant Tree-rat-people:

When the land was young and human beings had not yet been born, two kupuna sisters, Noiha and Korina, lived to the east in a place called Sariai (a stream south of Mamoromina in central Terei). They had no relatives and no totemic taboos at first. They found some high-value shell money in a cave and called it *sariai* after the place where they found it. Then they invented *maru* (magic for the promotion of health, growth, and prosperity).

After a time the two sisters married two kupuna males, Hukasa and Raimoro, who took them west to Tuhuhroru (between Kimohu and Kanaoru, in Terei) and thence to Rotunoua (on the Kuru creek just east of Moronei village, in Siuai). While living there, the elder sister gave birth to a child which was small and covered with fur. She kept it hidden in a cave and sent her husband to fetch food for a feast. First she sent him for a pig, but when he brought one she did not like it because it was partly white so she sent him back for a completely black one. Then she sent him to fetch an opossum, and when he had brought one she sent him for coconuts. Her husband became wearied and annoyed at all this work thrust upon him so that he cut off his own penis.

With all the food the husband had brought they prepared a feast and brought the infant out of hiding. As they were combing its hair and repeating maru over it, the infant scuttled over to a vine and ran up it to the top of a tree and from there announced to the amazed onlookers: "I am your sacred Giant Tree-rat; it's forbidden to look at me."

At that, all the kupunas became frightened and ran away, leaving the pig and all the other food that had been prepared for the feast. (The partly cut pig has become a large stone and is now a shrine at Rotunoua. The original Giant Tree-rat lives in its cave at Rotunoua and is the sacred sib-mate of all members of this matri-sib. Tree-rat people are afraid to visit Rotunoua for fear of seeing their sacred Giant Tree-rat, for if they did, they would become Near-death and would quickly die. Nor may any Tree-rat person kill or eat any other giant tree-rats, because they are all sibmates.)

From Rotunoua the kupuna sisters and their husbands moved to Motuna (between Mataras and Jeku villages). One day their husbands gave them a pig which they had killed in the forest, and the sisters prepared to cook it. After it was butchered the younger sister, Korina, took the pig's liver to a creek to wash it, and while she was gone the elder sister, Noiha, selfishly ate all the fat from the pig's belly. When younger sister returned and discovered this she became greatly piqued and vowed never again to eat pig's belly-fat (*kurommi*). Then they parted, younger sister going north to Rukruk (near Ukuntu village) and elder sister staying behind. At Motuna, the place where this episode took place, there is a stone also called Motuna.

Younger sister settled at Rukruk, reared a large family — of human beings, this time — and eventually turned into a stone. Her descendants became known as Belly-fats because they respect the taboo of their ancestress toward that delicacy. Now, if any of these people happen by accident to eat some fat from a pig's belly they will become seriously ill unless they perform an antidotal rite. The stone into which the younger sister ossified has a hole in it; this is the vagina of the kupuna and it is claimed that menstrual blood flows from it at regular intervals. Also, whenever a Belly-fat is born the stone can be heard to moan in pain. Blood will issue from the hole if one pushes a stick into it; even the Methodist teacher at Morokaimoro village tried this and it actually happened. This kupuna used to use *irisia* leaves to wipe away her menstrual blood, and that is why these leaves are red and why no Tree-rat person may touch them.

Meanwhile the elder sister remained around Motuna and gave birth to several human offspring at a nearby place called Kiaman and eventually disappeared into a cave there. Her descendants became known as Left-behinds (*Si'nomui*), because their ancestress stayed behind when her younger sister went north. Left-behinds do not taboo pigs' belly-fat. Elder sister still inhabits the cave at Kiaman and Left-behinds are afraid to go there lest they become Near-death. If a Left-behind must go to Kiaman to procure some water from the sacred spring there, for use in performing maru, he can counteract the deadly effects of his close contact with this dangerously sacred place by carrying out an antidotal rite.[19] The descendants of the elder sister scattered over all the land between the Mivo and the Mopiai rivers; they were the first to occupy this land and in those times it all belonged to them. Eventually they divided into these branches [Note: The Siuai use a tree-branching metaphor when explaining this process]: the Kakahaiia, with its center near Mataras village; the Harukamuanai, with its center north of Tupopisao and east of the Mivo River, hence in Terei; the Honironai, with its center near Morokaimoro village; the Kuhunkurunai, with its center near Morokaimoro village. And in addition there is the disappearing remnant of the Mokakarui, who resemble the Left-behinds and whose special center is Kiaman itself.

For a while Rukruk was the only home of the Belly-fats, but later on men from neighboring settlements married Belly-fat women and took them to their own homes. One woman, Monai, moved to Korikunu in central Siuai, and

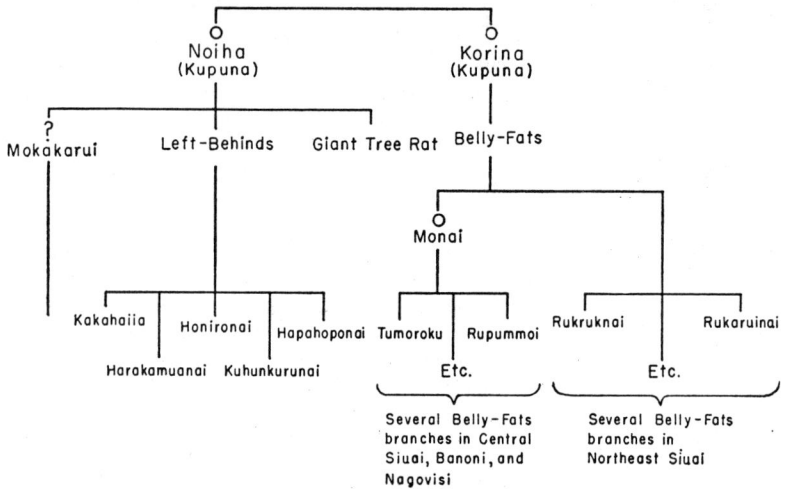

FIGURE 10. Mythical Genealogy of the Tree-rat People.

from her descendants several branches developed: the Tumoroku, whose center is at Korikunu itself; the Rupommoi, whose center is near Siuruhinna; the Pokuonoku, whose center is near Siuruhinna; the Ringriŋku, whose center is near Ruhuaku; the Rurarui, whose center is near Ruhuaku; the Kupunaŋ, whose center is northwest of Morokentu village; the Ramoi, whose center is in Ruhuaku.

Members of all these branches preserve the taboo on pig belly-fat with these exceptions: only males of the Rupommoi and Pokuonoku branches need regard the taboo, but this means that a pregnant female member must also avoid eating it because of the possibility that the infant in her womb might be a male. Other small branches of this central Siuai line have become established in Banoni and Nagovisi, through women having married and gone to live there.

Most Belly-fat women remained in northeast Siuai, where they eventually established the following branches: Rukruknai, whose center is near Ukuntu village, at the site of the Rukruk stone shrine of all Belly-fats; Rukaruinai, near Morokaimoro village; Hanuŋnai, near Hanuŋ village; Kukumihnonai, whose center is the Kukumih kupuna stone on Kuru creek, just west of Novei village; Motunanai, between Mataras and Jeku villages; Itonahupanai, south of Jeku; Kurananai, west of Mataras; O'sonnai, north of Turuŋom; Usahai, central Siuai; Kopusinai, north of Kontai.

The branching of the Rukaruinai and the Kukumihnonai from the other Belly-fats took place in the following manner:

Long ago two Belly-fat "sisters" used to walk about along the banks of the Kuru creek. The younger sister filled up her carrying basket with coils of the *kukumih* vine, believing it to be money. One day her older sister looked into the basket and seeing only vine there, exclaimed: "Alas, younger sister, someone has deceived you into thinking that you have lots of money, when actually all you possess is vine." With this she threw out the vine and gave her younger sister some real high-value shell money, and then went to Rukarui to live, leaving younger sister at the place where the vine was thrown away (*Kukumihno*, "at-the-place-of-the-kukumih-vine"). The elder sister owned large quantities of high-value shell money and her descendants became rich and powerful.

From such beginnings as these the Tree-rat people became numerous and spread throughout the land. The name for all of them is *Ta*.

*Origin of the Hornbill-people.* Here is the story of this sib:

During kupuna times there lived a sister, Sipikai, and two brothers, Kaokurumum and Orphan, at a place called Mamaruho on the island of Aosarara (shoals some miles south of Bougainville). Orphan seduced the wife of Kaokurumum, and the latter attempted to do away with Orphan, without success.[20]

Later, Sipikai went ashore on the Siuai beach at a place also called Mamaruha. There she married and gave birth to a crocodile (*uraivo*), a hornbill (*huhu*), a female kupuna named Uka, and a male kupuna named Nonun. Nonun remained at the beach; no one has seen him since. Hornbill and her descendants became the totem of all of Sipikai's other descendants. Crocodile also became a totem, and this is what happened to him:

When Sipikai gave birth to Crocodile she told her husband to fetch a pig. He found one and brought it to her, but she would not accept it because one of its legs was white. Then the husband brought a solid black one and that was all right. Sipikai then sent her husband after wood to make a bed for Crocodile to lie on. When he brought some wood, she would not accept it because it was too short. Then the husband brought some longer pieces and she made a bed and placed Crocodile upon it. After this Sipikai wanted to go to the stream to bathe, so she told her husband: "You remain here and guard the Hidden-one (an infant not yet baptized and hence restricted to the house), but do not go inside the house to look at it, for that is forbidden." After Sipikai had left, her husband said to himself: "What sort of infant is this that I should wear myself out working for?" Whereupon he took his ax, went into the house, and hacked it to pieces; then he ran away and hid. When Sipikai returned from the stream and saw what had happened she wept and joined Crocodile together again. Then she carried it to the river and left it there in the water, telling it: "You must stay here in the river and not go into the forest. Then one day when your father wishes to go to a feast I shall cause him to decorate himself with red flowers, and when you see a man with red flowers crossing the river you can kill him." Later on it happened as Sipikai had said. When Crocodile killed his father the latter's companions shouted: "Hey! Crocodile has caught him." Before this occurred Crocodile had no name, but when he killed his father people called him Crocodile; that became his name. After that it was forbidden for any of Sipikai's descendants to kill or eat crocodiles. It was also forbidden for them to eat the (red) *kanarao* fish, which formed out of the blood flowing from Crocodile's wounds.

When Sipikai's daughter, Uku, became an adult and was walking along the shore she came across a leaf of the *kiŋkirisu* palm and another one of the ficus tree. Being curious to see the trees from which these leaves had come, she carried them and walked inland along the banks of the Mopiai river. After searching for a long time she finally matched the leaves with trees growing on a place called Totokahao. She settled down there, married a kupuna named Nohun, and gave birth to five offspring. One of these was a pair of demons joined together at the back. This pair now roves about tracts of land associated with Hornbill people; sometimes it transforms itself into a stone by the name of Hokuhko, which is located near Kapana village. Uku's second offspring was the demon Pakao, which now inhabits the forest around Mataras village and is the most powerful demon there. The third offspring was the female demon Paivo, who used to dwell with Pakao until he killed her. (One day Pakao wanted to kill a flying fox which was sitting on top of a wild banana flower. Paivo drove away the flying fox to save its life and Pakao killed her in anger. Neighboring kupuna were about to cremate her near Mataras, at Pimonna, but Pakao was still angry and drove them west, first to Jeku, then to Kinirui, and finally to Tohu at the extreme western border of Siuai, where they succeeded in cremating her.)

Uku's other two offspring were female human beings, and from them were descended all the Hornbill people. The elder of these two sisters gave birth and had a pig slaughtered for a feast to accompany the infant's baptismal ritual. She then sent her younger sister to the stream to fetch drinking water and while she was gone ate all the pig. When the younger sister returned and discovered how she had been deceived she wept and vowed never to eat pig again. She kept on weeping at the thought of never again eating pig, until she conceived of the idea of performing a *Climbing* ceremony (*kinamo*) wherewith to remove the taboo on eating pork. She constructed a high platform, climbed to the top of it, and ate some pork while repeating a magic formula (*korona*), and this removed the taboo. She carried out this Climbing at a place called Pookai, east of Konga; this was the first Climbing and it was invented by this ancestress of the Hornbill people. (Members of other matri-sibs followed her example and adopted Climbing as a means of removing taboos that are not too strong. Since that time many other Hornbills must taboo eating pork until they have performed Climbing.) After the younger sister had performed Climbing she set out in search of canarium almonds, and having discovered some at Paramoni and at Rukarui she settled down there, eventually turning into the stone Paramoni.

From these beginnings the Hornbills proliferated and scattered throughout Siuai; but before tracing their steps it should be mentioned that the above version of their earliest adventures is not considered entirely authentic by all living Hornbills. For example, one sage old Hornbill man of Kinirui village does not accept the incident about Orphan and Kaokurumum as having anything to do with the Hornbills. "Orphan," he stated, "is a kupuna of all the Siuai and not just the Hornbills." And this same dissenter believes that the kupuna ancestress of all Hornbills came originally from Miheru and Pakuram (Nagovisi) and not from the Shoals of Aosarara; and further, that the original Hornbill totem was born at the mouth of the Honorai River, many miles to the west of the mouth of the Mopiai River. There are still other versions extant in other parts of Siuai, and while they agree with respect to some of the main incidents, they differ considerably with respect to names and places.

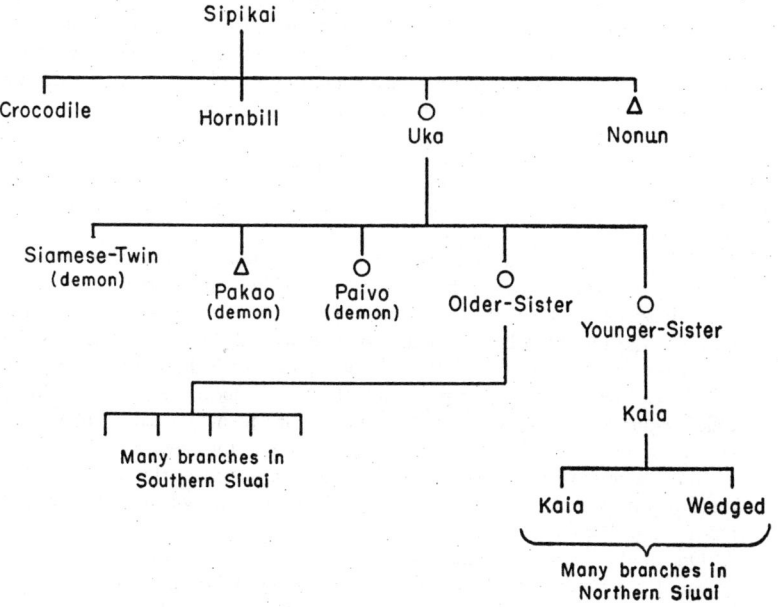

FIGURE 11. Mythical Genealogy of the Hornbill-People, according to the Most Popular Versions.

From the younger sister who settled at Paramoni and Rukarui there developed the Kaia branch of the Hornbills; the descendants of the older sister are called Kurava. The Kaia established settlements throughout northern Siuai, especially at the place called Moon-reflection-on-water (Tumonohinjo) near Sikurai village. One Kaia woman who lived in northeast Siuai was so pregnant that she had to crawl along the ground. On one occasion she became wedged (*pata*) between two stones, hence all her descendants were known as Wedged.

*Origin of the Parrot-people.* The Parrot-people were the first to arrive at the place called Romihino. They taboo the parrot (*pirihi, Eos cardinalis*

*Gray*), the white-bellied gray bird (*uiya, Graucalus papuensis perpallidus*), the coconut-lory [21] (*tonri, Trichoglossus haematodus aberrens*), and a bird called *sese*, which I am unable to identify. Parrot-people say they do not know where their original kupuna ancestresses came from, but reason that it must have been from the east, from Terei, since the magic formulae of their rituals are in the Rugara language. Also, nearly all Parrot-people now live in Terei or in northeast Siuai bordering Terei. Although the myths of the Parrot-people do not explain their ultimate origins, they do describe how their kupunas originated two important things: warfare and death.

Long ago when the kupunas of the Parrot-people were living in the south some stranger kupunas visited their hamlet one day while the parents were away. When the strangers asked the children where their parents were they were told that the fathers were hunting opossums and the mothers catching fish. At that the strangers sang this ditty to the children:

"Tun tututu e tum
Noi tooki noi teje"

(Free: "When they give the fish and possum to you, you must hold some in one hand while eating from the other.")

This visit was repeated day after day until finally the parents became annoyed at it and decided to kill the strangers. They dug a pit trap and built a bench on top of it. Later when the strangers returned they sat on the bench and fell into the pit, whereupon the parents covered them up. After this the Parrot-people moved to the north and built houses with thick walls at a place called Pisuruvao. For further protection they made spears covered with lime, called *supusupugu*, as well as a bow and a club; then they said: "If anyone attacks us here we shall kill them with the spear, the bow, and the club." Thus were originated all the things having to do with warfare. Before that there was no warfare. These same Parrot kupunas had two stone pigs, called Siromai and Poromai.

On another occasion some Parrot kupunas were celebrating the baptism of one of their newborn. When the infant was brought outside the house of hiding everyone became excited, climbed onto the house and began throwing down all kinds of food for people to eat. It was a very merry occasion and people danced around wildly so that they made their shell ornaments rattle. Nearby sat Frog and Sese-bird enjoying the spectacle. Suddenly, Sese stretched out her legs and died. As she was dying she said to Frog: "Ultimately all of you will do what I am now doing. Never mind, I enjoyed watching everyone dancing and rattling their shells." With this action Sese invented death. Before that no one had died.

Eventually the Parrot-people separated into many branches including the Hauonnai (around Romihino), the Tuparunai (east of the Mivo), the Kuuape of central Terei, the Incestuous-Parrot-people of Terei, and others not known to the Siuai.

*Origin Myth of the Crane-people.* The natives explain the origin of the Crane-people by the following story:

## BELIEFS ABOUT NATURE AND MAN

A kupuna woman living near Sireno (on Potommo creek, which flows into the Mopiai river) gave birth to three children. One of them was the first crane (*kou, Nycticorax caledonicus mandabularis*), the other two were female kupunas, one of whom was named Banana (*ruvinai*). One day Banana and her sister went to the stream to fill their water bottles and they happened to see in the water a reflection of some very fine shell money (*kurakanikana*) which was hanging from a tree growing on the bank of the stream. They kept admiring the reflection for a long while until their mother finally went to look for them. She found them gazing at the water and explained to them that it was merely a reflection. Then she cut down the real shell money and gave it to them. When their neighbors saw all this wealth they exclaimed to the sisters: "This is a wonderful thing you have discovered; you will both be wealthy." And so it was: the money increased in quantity and remained in the possession of the two sisters and their descendants, who became known as the Crane-people (or the *Sireno* people).

Later on Banana married a kupuna named Mikopui. One day the couple went to pick almonds. Mikopui climbed the tree and began throwing down nuts but very soon he became hot and thirsty so he sent Banana for some water. While she was at the stream a demon caused the bank to cave in over her and she was trapped in the hole. The demon then made herself to look like Banana and went to where Mikopui was collecting almonds. When he asked for the water she urinated in a shell and handed that up to him to drink. Mikopui recognized its odor and realized that the woman was a demon. As he was climbing down the tree to escape, the demon stuffed almonds up her anus in order to appear pregnant, like Mikopui's wife. Mikopui induced the demon to take the longer path back to his settlement, and by the time she arrived he and his kinsmen had constructed a trap for her. They dug a hole, filled it with hot stones, and erected a flimsy bench over it. Mikopui then invited the demon to sit upon the bench, whereupon she broke it and fell into the pit and was killed. Mikopui then went into mourning for his lost wife and in memory of her he planted a banana plant in his garden.

While Banana was inside the hole caused by the cave-in she gave birth to two sons. One day a River Kingfisher (*sim, Alcedo athis solomonensis*) dug a hole in which to lay its eggs and in doing so made a passage down to Banana and her two sons; another day a lizard went down the hole and discovered them there. (Thereafter all river kingfishers and lizards became taboo to Crane-people because of their good deed in making a passage out of the hole.) When the two boys were older their mother sent them up the passage to look around. The passage led them to Mikopui's garden, and when they saw the banana tree growing there they threw stones at it.

When Mikopui discovered that someone had been throwing stones at his bananas he hid nearby to catch the culprits. Next day when he saw them and realized that they were his sons he caught them and had them lead him to Banana. With the family now reunited Mikopui decided to present his two sons to all his neighbors in a fitting manner. He constructed a Climbing platform, the first one, and invited all his neighbors to partake of a feast. Then he led the two boys to the top of the platform and took off the bark-cloth covering which he used to hide them. When all the women saw the handsome youths they fought among themselves for the privilege of getting them as husbands for their own daughters. Finally the youths married Legs-apart girls, using the kurakanikana money belonging to their sib for betrothal gifts; that is how the fine money of the Crane-people came into possession of the Legs-aparts.

Thereafter, when Crane-people celebrate the Climbing ceremony in order to remove their taboo upon eating bananas, lizards and river kingfishers, they play at throwing stones at a banana tree in memory of that episode in their myth. Also, old Crane women dramatize another myth episode by stuffing almonds up one another's anuses.

*Origin of the Kingfisher-people.* The Kingfisher-people originated in the following way, according to the natives' account:

> Long ago the kupuna, Kohka, dwelt at Pakoram (Nagovisi), but whenever she gave birth, a demon there would destroy the infant's soul by piercing its fontanel (*ura*) with her fingernails. [Note: In Motuna, "soul" and "fontanel" are identical.] For this reason Kohka's people did not increase in number. One day, when Kohka left her offspring and went to the gardens, the demon tried to persuade them to dwell with her rather than with Kohka: "With Kohka you will be weak; with me you will be strong." Then she shot them with spears made from flying-fox wing bones. She was killing the last one when Kohka came up and asked her to fetch some water from the stream in a shell container. Kohka gave her a container with a hole in it, so that the demon was not able to keep it filled and remained a long time at the stream. This gave Kohka and her sisters a chance to escape, and they went south and east. On the trail they passed by a demon, Thunder, who was standing on top of a *ka'jaka* tree eating fruit. Kohka warned him that the Pakoram demon was following, so that Thunder was prepared. When the Pakoram demon arrived at the *ka'jaka* tree she asked Thunder for some fruit, intending to catch him off-guard and kill him. He threw down a few to her from the top of the tree where he was standing but she refused them, saying: "I do not eat the fruit at the top of the tree; I eat only that from the lowest limbs." Thunder guessed what her intentions were and became afraid. He climbed down to the lower limbs, and before she could catch him hurled lightning at her. She shielded herself from that with her hand so that the only way he could kill her was to fall on her himself. This he did, so that Kohka and her offspring escaped.[22]
> 
> Kohka and her sisters finally arrived at Koŋa and settled down there. Still grieving for her slain offspring she tabooed eating white pig, opossum, eel, sorghum cane, *ruvinai* bananas, and sugar cane. Then, in order to end the mourning and remove the taboo, she constructed a platform and climbed onto it to eat the food ceremonially. This was the first Climbing.[23] When Kohka left Pakoram she carried with her some water from the Pakoram stream, and when she arrived at Koŋa she deposited it in a spring there. This is the water in which she cooked all the tabooed foods eaten by her at the Climbing. (Now, before a Climbing, Kohka's descendants, the Kingfisher-people, go to Koŋa, dam the spring's runoff with a mat made of shell money, and obtain

## BELIEFS ABOUT NATURE AND MAN

some of the water in a bamboo for use in cooking all the tabooed foods to be eaten ceremonially at the Climbing. The only other occasion when Kingfisher-people may go to Koŋa without fear of becoming Near-death is at the time when Kingfisher children are taken there for their first view of the sacred spring.)

After Kohka had been at Koŋa for a while she gave birth to Kingfisher (*Halcyon bougainvillei*). As soon as it was born, Kingfisher dug a hole in the ground and hid inside it. When Kohka looked into the hole she discovered that she had borne Kingfisher and not a kupuna like herself. Later she gave birth to a kupuna daughter and instructed her never to kill or eat a kingfisher, since that bird is a true sibling.

Kohka was not the first of the Kingfisher-people who left Pakoram and went to the east. Even before her time some kupuna relatives went from Pakoram to Moon-reflection-on-water (Tumonohinjo) and thence to a spot on the Mopiai River just south of Jeku. They settled down there and became known as *Urimaino*.

Kohka and one of her sisters were at Koŋa one day cooking a prawn on a hot stone. When the prawn was half-cooked it jumped into the stream and swam away. The two kupunas were very surprised at this. One of them rolled her eyes in amazement; thenceforth her descendants became known as Eye-rollers (*rura*). The other sister continued sitting on the ground with her legs apart (*ke-tai*); thenceforth her descendants became known as Legs-aparts (*kehno*). The Legs-aparts remained at Koŋa, but the Eye-rollers went to Akuno near Koropo village.

One day four Legs-apart kupuna women were walking along a trail. The second of them whistled as she walked, and thenceforth all of her descendants became known as Whistlers (*urariŋ*). The third stopped for a moment to blow her nose, and thenceforth her descendants became known as Nose-blowers (*susavai*). The fourth one in line fell behind the others, and when night came she went to sleep at the base of the *kirakira* tree; henceforth her descendants became known as the Kira-people. All the descendants of the first Legs-apart in the line retained the name Legs-apart.

Another sister of Kohka's left Koŋa and went to Romihino (on the Kuru creek, just east of Novei village). There she dwelt alongside the kupunas of the Parrot-people and out of friendship with them she also tabooed parrots. One day she and one of her neighbors constructed a trap at Ane near Romihino in order to catch an opossum. Instead, it trapped a *rikrikmorova*, an animal-demon that is part eel, part opossum, part snake, and part lizard. When it was ensnared it sang this song:

*Kuŋ kuŋ kuŋ tuiama tui*

*Huro riri'me, huro kuku'me*
Come set me free, come cut me loose.

*Huro rimiroteme*
Come free me so that you can eat me.

*rokonara tamanara*
    your    fiber rope

*pai ru rerekui*
Who told you to make this trap?

*pai tama rerukui*
Who told you to make this rope?

*Kuŋ kuŋ kuŋ*

As the two kupunas were approaching the trap they heard this ditty and were afraid. They climbed onto it, saying: "raru raru komma, raru raru komma."

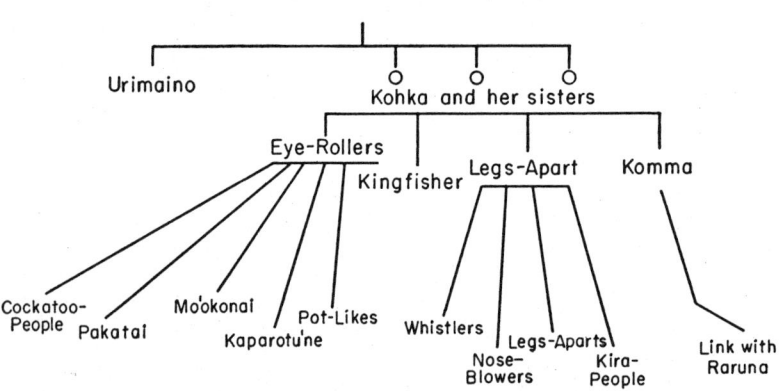

FIGURE 12. Mythical Genealogy of the Kingfisher-People, according to the Most Popular Versions.

This is how the two kupuna women received their names; the one from Koŋa became known as "Komma," and the other one "Raruna." The Komma kupuna ran away to the east and settled down at Kimaoto near the Mivo river. The Parrot kupuna remained at Romihino after killing and eating the Rikrikmorova. The bamboo knife with which she killed it is still at Ane, as is the blood and urine of the Rikrikmorova.[24]

Komma remained at her place near the Mivo River and had many descendants. All of them continued to taboo kingfishers, keets, and a new totem subsequently acquired, the megapode. In addition, all Komma women are forbidden to eat all other kinds of birds as well as flying-foxes; the reason being that women cannot shoot birds so why should they eat them? Their place near the Mivo became known as Forbidden (Kimahuti) because of the custom forbidding any man who marries a Komma woman to acquire a second wife. Now there is a bamboo thicket on Forbidden containing one cane for every living Komma. A new cane begins to grow as soon as an infant is conceived in the womb of a Komma woman.

The origin of dancing, instead of wailing, at the funeral of an old person took place among the Komma at Forbidden. Once an old kupuna woman there died and kupunas came from Terei, Siuai, and Nagovisi; but instead of weeping they danced so violently that the ground broke.

## BELIEFS ABOUT NATURE AND MAN

Meanwhile, the Eye-rollers were moving about and settling the central and southwestern parts of Siuai. One of them remained at their place between Koropo and Amiu while four others went in different directions. The one who stayed behind said: "I remain here, sitting still just like a pot (*hiuvo*)." Her descendants became known as the Pot-likes. Another went southwest to a place near Kotu village. While on the way she became feverish and thirsty, and cried out: "Alas, if I only had a green coconut to drink!" A cockatoo heard her and dropped one beside her, whereupon the kupuna exclaimed gratefully: "From now on you are my sibmate, and none of my people will kill or eat you." She established her new home and called it Place-of-the-Cockatoo, and her descendants thenceforth became known as Cockatoo-people. Another Eye-roller went to Uso and her descendants became known as Pakatai. Another went to Hukaha and Tonu, and her descendants became known as Moo-kunai. And the fifth went to a place near the present villages of Kaparo and Siroi; her descendants became known as Kaparotu'ne.

*Origin of the Eagle-people.*[25] The Eagle-people have two versions of their origin:

(Version A.) The Eagle-people originated at a place on the beach near Hiruhiru, called Mitahu. There were four original kupunas: Horomorun and Konopia, both males, Hurry-up (Osooso) and Makunai, both females.

On one occasion Horomorun prepared a feast in honor of the kupuna, Food-maker (Paopiahe), but he set aside one red pig for himself to eat. Food-maker arrived at the feast and took everything in sight, including the red pig; then he carried all this food back to his home at Sariai (Terei). Horomorun was angered by Food-maker's greediness and vowed not to eat red pig until he had done so at a Climbing.

From Mitahu several Eagle kupuna sisters went to central Siuai and had a feast at the stone named Nukui. Instead of a pig they butchered and cooked a frog. One kupuna ate the head (*puri*) of the frog and settled down near Kupiŋku village; her descendants became known as Head-people (*Purinnai*). Another kupuna ate the middle (*motu*) of the frog and settled down near the present villages of Sikurai, Kontai, and Kinirui; her descendants became known as the Middle-people (*Motunoŋ*). The third kupuna ate the legs and settled at Hari village; her descendants became the Legs-people (*Hipanopo*). A fourth kupuna took one look at the roasted frog and became afraid and ran away; she settled at Tokunotu and her descendants are the Run-aways (*Moruŋoŋ*, I ran away). Since *morokiŋ* (flying-fox) sounds much like *moruŋoŋ*, the Run-aways decided to taboo flying-foxes in addition to their original totems of eagles and frigate birds (*ķerai*). Another kupuna had never seen a roasted frog before and asked: "What is it called? (*ua toŋunom*)." She settled in eastern Siuai and in Terei and her descendants are known as the What-is-it-called people (*Toŋuno*). Another kupuna arrived after the frog had been eaten, and complained: "If I had only been here! (*nuķui*)." She remained weeping at the site of the feast and her descendants settled there, becoming known as the If-I'd-been-here people (*Nuķui*). The kupuna who arrived last of all at the feast got nothing and went to live at Korikunu and

Kaparo. Her descendants are known as the Late-arrivals (*Romotaku*, since-she-arrived-afterwards).

Several other Eagle kupunas did not attend the feast but went directly to the places where they established their branches: the Eagle-*mika* to Kotu and the territory south of Unanai, the *ŋinovo* to a place west of Tohu, the Mokiriku to a place near Kapana village, the Ruhoniku and the Ruvoroku to western and southwestern Siuai.

Most of these kupunas took along some of the water from Mitahu and deposited it at their new homes. The sacred water (*tu mikisa*) of the Middle-people, for example, is the Iku creek near Ukuntu village. When any of these people wish to perform a maru ritual they collect some of the sacred water in a bamboo container decorated with their high-value shell money, and use the water in the ritual. If one of the Middle-people goes there at any other time he would become Near-death.

The What-is-it-called people went to the east. One of their sacred places is Puriŋanai (near Hinna village). The demon-animal Reraŋ, who looks like a fowl, was born at the same time and place as the What-is-it-called kupuna of Puriŋanai. Reraŋ remains in the forest at Puriŋanai now, and when a What-is-it-called dies, Reraŋ attends the cremation with its face painted white for mourning. When the people walk around the pyre weeping, Reraŋ does the same, and many men are able to see it. Also, if a What-is-it-called man is Near-death, Reraŋ lays an egg in the man's club-house.

When the kupunas of the What-is-it-calleds gave birth to the first human What-is-it-called, they also gave birth to the yellow-throated white-eye [26] (*sihuru, Zosterops metcalfei exigua*), the midget-bird (*ti'tipi, Dicaeum aeneum aeneum Pucheran*), and the large green locust (*hakuhaku*). The What-is-it-called people spread through Terei and eastern Siuai. Later on members of the branch in southeast Siuai began to taboo eating the lizard (*mera*) and gave up the What-is-it-called custom of using the *unnaku* leaf for covering the openings of pots while cooking in them.

When all the Eagle kupunas had established human lines they withdrew from mundane living. Some of them disappeared completely while others transformed themselves into demons and still haunt the sacred places of their descendants. One of the original Eagle kupunas, Horomorun, remains in western Siuai; but Konopia and Hurry-up gave birth to many other demons like themselves, so that there now is a Konopia and a Hurry-up at nearly every Eagle sacred place.

(Version B.) In the time of the kupunas one of them by the name of Namaru prepared a feast at Mitahu and invited many other kupunas, including Hoŋing, Konopia, and Pinos. Then just before the feast he left Mitahu and paddled across to Alu Island. All the kupunas arrived, engaged in a mock battle, and then played their panpipes. After this Hoŋing went to get the pig he had marked for himself by spitting betel mixture on its back, but Konopia and Pinos had already taken it. Hoŋing then started a fight with them and broke down the pigpen so that all the other pigs ran away. The other guests were very angry with Hoŋing and drove him north to Ru'no'no' lake. And there he remains, the leader of all the ghosts who go to Ru'no'no'. Later, when

Namaru returned from Alu they killed and butchered him, distributing the cuts among all the guests, as substitute for the pigs they had not received. They gave the head to one kupuna, whose descendants became the Head-people; the middle to another, whose descendants became the Middle-people; etc. And thus all the Eagle people had their beginnings.

*Sib Origin Myth Themes.* The myth summaries just given were for the most part collected from informants living in the northern half of Siuai; and although the full narratives "explain" or at least touch on the origins of all the Siuai sibs, they provide more detail for those sibs principally represented in the north, e.g., the Tree-rat-people, and sketch in only broad outlines for those centered in the south, e.g., the southern branches of the Eagle-people. Moreover even the data presented on the northern sibs represent only part of the material collected; in every settlement where, say, Whistler-people have been living for a generation or more, new myth anecdotes about Whistler kupunas and totems become locally current. When I began collecting sib myths I entertained the illusion that if I collected widely and assiduously the many episodes would eventually fit together into an internally consistent account, a kind of comprehensive Siuai totemic epic. That, of course, was a naïve hope, and had to be abandoned because of numerous contradictions and ambiguities (which, incidentally, troubled my native informants not at all). On the other hand, although the narrative contents of the various sib myths cannot be made to fit together into a single comprehensive Siuai myth cycle, certain myth *themes* and attendant practices recur with striking consistency; the most significant of these are given below:

1. Each kupuna ancestress gave birth to certain demons, human beings, and animal archetypes, thereby linking them by special (i.e., totemic) ties.

2. Although the kupunas withdrew from mundane living, most of them remained near the scenes of their earthly activities, in the form of stone-demons or bush-demons; and in such transformations they are more dangerous than beneficent to their human descendants.

3. Primary totems — that is, descendants of the animal archetype siblings — require kindly treatment. Above all they must not be eaten by their human relatives; anyone breaking this taboo invites certain, automatic death, there being no magic antidote to save him.

4. Secondary totems — those acquired by other than genealogical means — are not as stringently protected from eating or handling.

5. The kupunas of several separate sibs independently invented: (a) a sacramental ceremony (Climbing) for the express purpose of lifting secondary totemic taboos; and (b) magical rites (maru) to insure the health, growth, and well-being of sib members.

6. The kupunas of several sibs also discovered and acquired sacred hoards of high-value shell money (*tomui, pata*) which they passed on to their human descendants for use in ceremonies.

7. During their wanderings around Siuai the kupunas tarried at certain places long enough to consecrate them in some manner; for example, at some of these shrines (*urinno*) the kupunas deposited sacred water from their homes, for use in connection with sib ceremonies, while others were consecrated through the continued presence of the kupunas in the form of stone-demons or bush-demons. These shrines are dangerously sacred (mikisa) to associated sib members, who may safely visit them only on certain occasions.

8. All the myths relate how the "scattering" of the kupunas and their early human descendants resulted in the fission of the sibs. Conversely, the myths of some sibs contain implications that parts of certain sibs became linked with parts of others.

The myths also contain themes which *may* reflect what natives consider to be the proto-typical pattern of intra-family relationships in their matrilineally biased society. One such is the mother's affection for her offspring as contrasted with the father's jealousy and hostility (there are exceptions here). Again, without giving too much weight to this structural analogy, the process of sib fission described by the myths is partly associated with the situations of conflict between siblings which the myths also describe. And finally, the myths provide clues about what the Siuai consider to be proto-typical reactions in situations of gratitude, resentment, and grief. But important as these myths may be for purposes of anthropological analysis, they are also highly important to the Siuai in the conduct of their lives, as we shall later on see.

*Miscellaneous Origin Tales.* The discoveries and creations of Maker, Hoŋing, Orphan, and the numerous sib kupunas, important though they are, account for only a small proportion of the aspects of the Siuai universe. A few other aspects of Siuai-wide significance became established through the exploits of some less versatile supernaturals; for example, all rivers and streams were created by Hoŋing's two brothers, Komarara and Komakiki, who dug channels for rain water to flow into (before that, rain soaked into the ground where it fell); the ocean grew out of the rotting and savory flesh of the snake-demon, Mavo, after he had been hacked to pieces by his enemies; etc. The account of how Moon lost its fullness is typical of this class of myths:

> A long time ago when Moon used to be big all the time, it used to climb down to earth on a vine and kill children. After this had been going on for a long time, Masa (an insect) urged all the people to kill Moon and put an end to the slaying of children. They agreed, and when Moon next descended to earth they cut down the vine and caught and killed him. Then they cooked Moon and began to eat him, but as they were eating, Hisa (an insect) thought to himself: "How will I be able to pick almonds at night if there is no Moon?" So he spit a small piece of Moon back into the sky.

A number of other tales relate how animals came to be as they are today. For example, the *si'iḳai* bird (not identified) has a very small bill and the

## BELIEFS ABOUT NATURE AND MAN

Hornbill a very large one because one of the latter stole the bill of one of the former while they were swimming one day. In another tale, Dog lost his ability to speak after spying on an unmarried couple as they fornicated; they fastened heavy stones to his snout so that he would not tattle. Then, there is a long tale about Dog's efforts to learn what his name was; he was piqued that people referred only to the man with whom he used to walk about.

Still another tale concerns the origin of lying: formerly all people could only speak truthfully, and if someone stole anything and was asked about his guilt he had to admit it. Then, one day a kupuna stole some food from his companions and lied to them about it, and that was the beginning of lying. In this connection it should be noted that Siuai stories contain numbers of episodes involving deceit, trickery, adultery, feuds, and violence, whereas altruism is rarely displayed.

Revealing of the cognitive side of Siuai culture as these miscellaneous tales may be, they have little direct effect upon present native life. Far more important in this respect are beliefs about the origins of certain dangerously sacred (mikisa) animals, places, and practices. For example, the stream called Poruro became sacred in the following way:

> A long time ago some men captured an eel, cut it into small pieces and put it into a pot to cook. But the eel slid out of this pot, which was too small, and into a larger one. Soon it also outgrew this pot, broke it and went into a larger one. This too it broke, and it went from pot to pot and from club-house to club-house trying out pots and breaking them all because they were too small to contain its increasing size. Then, the eel tried to hide in a river but the water was too shallow to cover its enormous size, so that it went to Poruru and excavated a pool deep enough to hide in, and there it remains.

If a man happens to be near this pool and sees the eel he will die shortly after returning home. Also there are usually three bamboos growing on the bank of this pool, but if someone nearby is about to die a fourth bamboo can be seen there and people know that someone is approaching death. If an opossum hunter sees an ant near Poruru pool he recognizes it as the eel's soul, and takes care to climb only smaller trees, knowing that the soul is moving about and likely to cause him to fall from any larger trees he might climb. And finally, some human sorcerers living nearby use this eel as an accomplice: they throw their victim's exuviae (hair, food, etc.) into the pool for the eel to eat, thereby bringing about the death of the victim.

The Siuai landscape is liberally spotted with such places and creatures associated with supernatural danger. Eels and their shadowy pools are commonly so endowed, but supernatural associations are also claimed for caves, odd-shaped boulders, swampy and snake-infested glades, and most other unusual features of the landscape. Tales about how these associations came about usually begin with the phrase "A long time ago; when the kupunas were walking about." On the other hand, some of these developments have taken place within the memory of living natives, and a few such occurred even during my stay; so that in this sense the Age of Creation is a continuing phase of time.

There is another kind of myth which absorbs much of the interest and motivates much of the behavior of the Siuai. It includes myths about their own recent past — stories about a pre-European age of nearly continuous feuding, dominated by the ambitions and rivalries of fierce leaders (*mumis*). By most of my adult male informants that era is described as a Golden Age, when heroic subordinates fought and feasted for the greater glory of their powerful and venerated leaders. We shall examine the content of these myths in a later chapter; here it is sufficient to take note of their existence and their decisive influence over the attitudes and actions of present-day Siuai males.

## THE CLASSIFICATION OF ENTITIES

*Principles of Categorizing.* After the kupunas had made things tolerably "straight," entities [27] and relationships among entities were more or less fixed.[28] Just how the Siuai categorize the entities within their universe is, however, difficult to comprehend, there being no native Aristotles to aid the ethnographer in this task, nor are there any priestly repositories of cosmological knowledge.

It might appear that the language itself provides one kind of meaningful taxonomy: a feature of Motuna is its forty or so noun classes,[29] the nouns of each class being distinguished by use of a separate set of numerical adjectives. Thus, areca nuts, shell beads, and other solid and more or less round objects are counted: one (*nori*), two (*kiriko*), three (*perih*), four (*korinakui*), et cetera; while containers or collections of items are counted: one (*navaki*), two (*kivakiro*), three (*pevaki*), four (*korivaki*), et cetera.[30] The most common items in each noun class are herewith listed:[31]

1. Male persons or spirits.
2. Female persons or spirits.
3. Animals (including birds and insects).
4. Limbs of persons, spirits, pigs, and fowls.
5. Limbs of all other animals.
6. Coconuts.
7. Shell money discs, areca nuts, wooden slit gongs, eggs.
8. Stones.
9. Metal and stone axes and adzes, knives, mirrors, smoking pipes.
10. Spears.
11. Arrows, jew's-harps.
12. Bows.
13. Trees, bamboos, cane stalks, reeds, flutes.
14. Women's capes, strips of pork.
15. Pots, women's fish nets, net bags, fish traps (basketry).
16. Baskets of shell money.

# BELIEFS ABOUT NATURE AND MAN

17. Rope, cord.
18. Canoe, raft, large basket-pouch, platform, base of sago branch.
19. Piles of things covered with leaves, pots of food, baskets of fish.
20. Taro.
21. Pepper catkins for betel-chewing.
22. Yams, sweet potatoes, other tubers.
23. Banana plants.
24. Single bananas, "hands" of bananas.
25. Breadfruit.
26. Leaves of sago palm, taro leaves.
27. All other leaves.
28. Wooden floor planks.
29. Wall- and roof-sheet ribs.
30. Shelves, benches.
31. Shelters (houses, sheds, etc.).
32. Settlements.
33. Roads, paths.
34. Garden plots.
35. Forests.
36. Tracts of land.
37. Water, spring, stream.
38. Day, night.
39. Moon (lunar cycle).
40. Canarium almond cycle (year).

It should be noted that the class membership and accompanying numerical adjective of many commonly used or talked-about items (e.g., people, shell money, pigs, nuts, pots, days, etc.) is so well known that these items are often referred to by means of their numerical adjectives only.[32] On the other hand, in connection with several items I found some disagreement even among adults concerning their class membership, and noted people making many "mistakes" when I systematically tested their usages in this respect.

What insight into Siuai categorizing does this noun class system provide? Do these natives really conceive — explicitly or implicitly — of the content of the Universe in terms of "small-round," "leafy," etc.? Or do the implications of this taxonomy provide no more fundamental a view of Siuai cosmology than does gender provide insight into the present-day cosmologies of English-speakers? I cannot answer this question on the basis of my data. All I can say is that noun class distinctions are suggestive, and add that other kinds of evidence suggest that the Siuai categorize the contents of their universe in several ways. For example, there is some ground for asserting that the Siuai, either explicitly or implicitly, make distinctions between the created and the spontaneously developed, between the animate and the inanimate, the self-animate and the animatable, the harmless and the supernaturally dangerous, etc., but I can go no further than this on the basis of my knowledge. I feel almost certain that longer study of the Siuai would reveal the existence of a few "logical" principles underlying what now appears to me to be a rather unsystematized collection of cosmological beliefs. Perhaps some readers may see in the data premises which have escaped me.[33] Unfortunately, then, the following survey of entities in the Siuai universe is more in the nature of a descriptive guidebook for western readers; it does not pretend to represent the formulations of a hypothetical native Aristotle, nor even the consciously held knowledge of the average Siuai adult. In fact, no Siuai could draw up such a guide — indeed, this kind of generalizing would strike him as senseless. In this connection I recall how I fared on one occasion in trying to piece together odd beliefs and practices into some kind of integrated picture. On this brilliantly moonlit night some little girls were dancing about in the cleared space between their house and mine, and singing a plaintive little ditty to the moon:

| | |
|---|---|
| Tai Tai to | Tra la la |
| Hekia, tai tai to | Moonlight, tra la la |
| Hinjo, tai tai to | Moon, tra la la |

As I sat with my friends, listening and smoking, one of them told me, for the fourth or fifth time, the story of the killing of Moon (see above, page 60).

"Just what is Moon, then?" I asked Siham, the oldest and wisest of my neighbors.

"Why, Moon is just Moon," he answered.

"But in the story," I reminded him, "Moon was like a demon. And the story is true, isn't it?"

"Of course the story is true," he said patiently. "And Moon may act like a demon, but in reality Moon is just Moon."

"Well, is it made of fire? I ask this because it shines like fire."

"No, no. Moon is not fire. Fire is fire and Moon is Moon."

"Then who made Moon?" I pressed him.

"No one made Moon," he answered. "Moon was always Moon."

Then a little later, after Siham had climbed into his house to sleep, a younger man, a worldly wise mission convert and ex-plantation laborer, confided to me that "the old people don't know much about such matters, and that, in reality, Maker had created Moon. Furthermore Moon works like a Coleman kerosene pressure lantern, waning, as the lantern does, when the pressure gives out."

The Siuai do not express beliefs about the size, shape, or nature of the earth. During recent years of European contact there has developed a general awareness that they live on a large island, one of many such (including, especially, New Britain, New Guinea, and Australia); before that they knew well about the existence of smaller islands to the south (Fauro, Alu, and Mono), but they were probably not aware that their larger land mass was also insular. Indeed, judging from their present disinterest, it is unlikely that they were curious about such matters. As for their own world-island as a

## BELIEFS ABOUT NATURE AND MAN

whole, it is not now — and probably was not in the past — conceived of as being anything other than various kinds of soil, rocks, and water. Of course, parts and aspects of this natural setting are variously animated or saturated with special supernatural qualities, but the base as a whole has no such noteworthy characteristics.

Certain areas of land and water are consecrated either as the haunts of spirits or as the settings where supernaturally charged materials are to be found. Among the first type [34] are the caves, the swamps, the pools, etc., where spirits dwell; these are usually dangerous places for unprotected humans. Also of this type are the places hallowed by association with sib spirits; the "gardens" of wild taro and yams planted by Maker; and the gardens, groves, and fishing areas tabooed to use — i.e., placed under surveillance of a spirit — in memory of a deceased relative. A second type consists of such places as the groves of supernaturally dangerous bamboo, whose splotchy internodes *look* like leprous skin and hence can cause leprosy.

Other aspects of the universe are like territory in this respect: they are either *natural*, like ordinary winds, and the vast majority of flora, fauna, and inorganic materials; or they possess supernatural qualities, either through identification or association with specific spirits, or through some intrinsic characteristic of color, smell, action, etc. For example, most innocuous insects such as house flies and potato bugs are regarded only as annoying pests. On the other hand, a maggot found in the ashes of a cremation pyre may be identified as the ghost of the deceased or the demon-familiar of his slayer, and stinging insects such as centipedes, ants, scorpions — i.e., intrinsically dangerous ones, those with anger (*iro*) — will be collected by sorcerers and mixed with their potions to increase their magical deadliness. To be sure, most entities in the universe can be pressed into service by spirits, or by humans having control over spirits, but until this occurs they are normally passive. Rain, for example, is not normally animated nor intrinsically potent, but there are individuals who possess the magical power to keep it away, thus causing droughts, or to increase its fall, thus bringing floods. Coldness also lacks magical quality, being an inevitable accompaniment to night, but there are certain Siuai specialists who can increase its intensity so that their enemies chill and sicken in their drafty huts. On the other hand, although earthquakes are *caused* by spirits, thunder-and-lightning *are* actual transformations of spirits; and while some stars are merely stars, others are large fireflies, and still others are demons.

The fact of the matter is, these uncurious Siuai are cognoscent of vast numbers of entities in their universe — of many kinds of rain and wind, hundreds of living things, numerous sorts of materials, etc. — but they have not troubled to fit these entities together into an all-embracing, neatly ordered explicit belief system. With the exception of those entities possessing noteworthily intrinsic characteristics, such as the stinging insects, the poisonous plants, the dangerous sinksands, and the like, their universe remains essentially passive until activated by specific spirits, so it is to these active elements, these demons and totems and ghosts, that we must turn for a better understanding of Siuai cosmology.

*Supernatural Beings.* The generic Siuai term for supernatural being is *mara* (spirit),[35] and the Siuai universe contains thousands of these spirits. In a nonsystematic but suggestive survey I found that all adults questioned could name and describe at least a hundred spirits. On the basis of such descriptions the ethnographer can classify them into several categories — although it should be noted that the Siuai themselves do not trouble with such generalizing. Upon having it pointed out to them, Siuai informants agreed that it is possible to make general distinctions among spirits according to whether they are "universal" or associated with specific places or social units, whether they dwell in the forests or at settlements, whether they were once ghosts of actual humans or not, etc., but they appeared disinterested in this kind of classifying. Moreover, informants disagreed about the nature of several spirits, hence the following classification is not absolute:

1. "Universal" culture-hero beings, especially Maker (Tantanu), Orphan (Panaŋa), Food-maker (Paopiahe), and Hoŋing. Of these only the last remains actively concerned in the affairs of humans; he is master at Ru'no'no', the afterworld where fortunate ghosts go. The others exist only in myths.

2. Spirits associated with sibs or segments of sibs, including otiose kupunas, active demon-kupunas, and the active totemic animals. With respect to the first, some sib kupunas exist only in myths and do not enter actively into human affairs. If asked directly about them, natives will either admit ignorance or rationalize their present whereabouts and activities in terms of better known demon-kupunas.

Other kupunas transformed themselves into demons of giant size, and as such inhabit the forests around the sib shrines. Some of these show themselves only to human sib-mates, and the sight of them usually brings on Near-death. Others have widened their baleful influence so as to inflict all human beings unfortunate enough to meet them. Still others have borne demon offspring and distributed them throughout Siuai, one to each of the sacred places of its sib; one of these is Konopia, a kupuna of the Eagle-people. The original Konopia is now a demon-kupuna restricted to the territory around the shrine where the Eagle kupunas held their frog feast (see above), but she has subsequently borne many smaller konopias who are scattered around Siuai. A generation ago there were no konopias in northeast Siuai until one of the Eagle-people living there secured one from a sib-mate living near the frog-feast shrine and brought her in a basket to Turuŋum village. Now, this konopia inhabits the groves around Turuŋum and sometimes assumes the form of a handsome woman in order to seduce men and thereby render them Near-death.[36] She and her demon mate have peopled this area with their demon offspring, who are small and rather ineffective duplicates of herself. Sometimes the Turuŋum konopia assumes the form of Hurry-up, the demoness of suicides. If any persons in the vicinity contemplate suicide, Hurry-up knows about it and encourages them; she appears to them and urges: "Hurry, hurry (*osooso*)," until they hang themselves.

The mate of the Turuŋum konopia is Ikaipakai, a demon-kupuna of the Tree-rat-people, who has also extended his influence beyond the lives of his human totem-mates and now visits misfortune upon anyone who happens to cross his trail around Turuŋum. Ikaipakai's special form of malignancy consists in killing people who have unwittingly eaten poison. The poisonous substance is hidden in the victim's food by an enemy, and when the poison reaches the stomach Ikaipakai smells it and attacks the victim. (See below.)

Another widely known demon is Horomorun, who is identified in the myth (above, p. 57) as a kupuna of the Eagle-people. There is a Horomorun demon-kupuna still haunting the area around Hiruhiru, the place on the coast where this sib is believed to have originated. In western Siuai, where Eagle-people and shrines are plentiful, this Horomorun plays an important supernatural role. When an Eagle man or woman is married, water is fetched from Hiruhiru for the ceremony; performance of this act assures the blessing of Horomorun, omission of it brings down his wrath. At Hiruhiru Horomorun appears to visitors — but only to Eagle-people — in the form of an enormous *Boiga* snake, and on occasion Horomorun can transform himself into thunder-and-lightning. Among these Eagle-people of western Siuai, Horomorun is a single dangerous sib-demon enforcing sib rules (exogamy, food taboos, etc.) with deadly effectiveness. In eastern Siuai Horomorun plays no such role; in fact, there is no single sib-demon Horomorun here at all.[37] Easterners know about this Horomorun but to them he is more or less otiose. On the other hand, distributed throughout Siuai are numbers of a whole class of lesser horomoruns, each one identified with specific territories — or better, with the club-house of the highest ranking leader in each territory. These horomoruns serve as the demon-familiars of native leaders, guarding their lives and property, etc. They will be described in detail later on, but for the moment it is worth noting that natives even in western Siuai differentiate precisely between Horomorun and horomoruns. Homonymy meant little to my informants: these are said to be entirely different kinds of supernaturals which *happen* to have the same name! In this connection I met natives in eastern Siuai who professed to know of konopias and ikaipakais only as *territorial* demons, knowing nothing of their derivation from sib kupunas.

Some demon-kupunas have transformed themselves into stones (*mara kupuri*), while retaining their powers of moving about in various animal or demon guises. It is fairly safe for human sib-mates to visit their stone demon-kupunas while they are inactive, and many of them do so out of pride and curiosity, but Near-death can result if one sees this kind of demon moving about in any of its other transformations.

In many cases the archetype totem animals of sibs and segments of sibs play active roles in the affairs of human relatives. For example, Reraŋ the Fowl, a secondary totem of the What-is-it-calleds, attends cremations of human relatives, etc. (see above). However, for most of the ordinary totemic animals, which are usually considered to be descendants of the totemic archetypes, the Siuai claim no special supernatural attributes other than the fact of totemic relationship.

3. Non-sib spirits associated with specific territories. In this category are hundreds of nameless common "bush" spirits (*mara muhni*) which haunt swamps, dark glades, caves, and similar places. If a Siuai must walk by such places he is certain to identify any animal he sees or hears there as a spirit, and such accounts have the cumulative effect of making these places feared and avoided. Especially during the nighttime are such places avoided, for it is then that spirits are most active.

In addition to these nameless bush spirits there are numerous named localized demons not associated with sibs. Some of these are believed to be ghosts, others have always been demons. Their transformations are varied, including part-time stones, eels, large snakes, and iguanas, and they are usually dangerous to all humans, regardless of sib affiliation. Along with the localized demon-kupunas they remain more or less within fixed boundaries and do not invade other territories. In fact, their jurisdictions are so well defined that I was able to plot generally acceptable [38] boundary lines on the map.

One noteworthy aspect of many of these localized demons is that they are intermarried and are frequently thought of as having demon offspring, smaller versions of themselves.

4. Functionally specialized non-sib spirits. In this category are included the familiars of diviners, magicians, sorcerers, and leaders. Some of these familiars are ghosts of relatives, others are spirits that have always been demons. Again, some of these are active in establishing their relationships with humans — and this is the case with nearly all the ghosts in this category, while others wait for a native to acquire their services, usually by purchase from another native.

5. Personalized natural phenomena. Moon, some stars, meteors, swamp phosphorescence, and similar aspects of nature are sometimes discussed as if they too were spirits, but I could not obtain unequivocal and comprehensive notions about their places in Siuai cosmology. For example, stars and fireflies are both called *ḳeva*, and keva are believed to hover in the vicinity of death. Some informants, when asked, said that keva were spirits and actually caused death; others denied this and said they were simply keva. Further, some informants described star constellations (*iruhŋum*, from *iruh*, a bush rat which is usually seen only in packs) as groups of spirits doing familiar things, e.g., going to a cremation carrying a pig. Again, meteors are sometimes alluded to as rapidly moving keva, but there is also a widespread belief

that they are the souls of dying high-ranking humans returning to their sib shrines (see Introduction).

Against this background of beliefs about the surrounding universe we are now in a position to consider how the Siuai distinguish and categorize the various aspects of man and mankind.

*Mankind.* The Siuai's knowledge of anatomy is quite detailed; they distinguish and name over a hundred parts of the body's exterior, including such aspects as molars, elbows, and palm lines, and they also distinguish such organs as heart, lungs, stomach, and intestines. In addition, each living individual is believed to have a soul (*ura*), which in one sense permeates the whole body and may appear as the shadow, but usually resides in the heart and may also be seen in the pupil. The soul has the power of wandering about during sleep; what it sees and experiences constitutes dreams (*ruroto*). Each normal adult also possesses vitality (*rumaruma*), which includes physical strength, sexual vigor, and robust health, and which may also be partly identified with normal breathing (*ruma*).

Food is one of the prerequisites of continued vitality. After food is chewed and swallowed it goes into the stomach where some of it turns into blood; the rest of it decays and enters the intestines for eventual evacuation. The new food-blood remains in the stomach until more food is eaten, thus pushing it out into the blood vessels which conduct it to the rest of the body, chiefly to the muscles. If any of this food-blood is lost the individual will become emaciated. Too much eating will force some of the food-blood into the intestines and be evacuated, hence there is no sense in eating gluttonously. Certain kinds of food eaten to excess, and certain kinds of magic, can cause an individual to defecate all his blood and die (i.e., dysentery, which is a common affliction).

There is believed to be some interdependency between soul, vitality, and breathing, the exact nature of which I could not discover.

Beliefs concerning the physiology of reproduction are compounded of many bizarre fancies and some near-truths. The Siuai's opinions about embryology probably derive from the former practice, growing out of curiosity, of opening up the belly of any pregnant woman slain by them in a raid. They know the location and shape of the womb and placenta, as well as the appearance of fetuses (*pooki*, the-one-inside) at various stages of growth. They also recognize that there is a relationship between conception and cessation of menstruation, but in other respects although their ideas about process may be highly consistent they are partly erroneous. The fetus, they believe, is formed out of the sexual fluids (*kosi*) of both mother and genitor. A man's fluid is stored inside his penis until emitted; it contains some of his *strength* (*itikaivo*) along with some of the material which goes into making his blood. Too much sexual intercourse weakens a man and can even cause [39] him to become thin and bony, but it is possible to refill and regain strength by eating coconuts and raw almonds. A woman's sexual fluid is stored in her womb; like a man's, it has the appearance of fluid from a partly dry coconut, until menstruation, when it changes into blood and is nearly all discharged. During sexual intercourse the man's fluid enters the womb and mingles with the woman's. If the same man repeats the act for about ten to fifteen times within one menstrual cycle, his deposit of fluid, mixed with that of the woman, is then large enough to start a fetus, whereupon the mingled fluids change into blood and become a nuclear heart.

Only one male at a time can precipitate the formation of a fetus. If two or more men have intercourse with a woman during her menstrual cycle no child can be conceived since the child contains the fluid of the genitor, and the fluids of different men cannot combine to form a child, "for," reason the Siuai, "how would such a child look and act?"

A woman knows when enough fluid has been piled up in her womb to form the child, and when that point is reached she refuses any further intercourse, believing that more fluid will only injure the fetus, perhaps fatally. After that her menstruation ceases and her fluid goes instead into increasing the size of the child and helping its parts differentiate.

The child subsequently born is therefore a true product both of mother and genitor, formed of materials from both their bodies: of blood-building substance, of strength-essence, of appearance, and presumably, of personality.

The human fetus (the-one-inside) is of little concern. If miscarried it is not cremated or mourned; in fact, most informants could not even agree that it had a soul, and probably had not thought about the matter prior to my questioning. The few natives who did entertain vague beliefs about a fetus' soul obviously received them from missions. The only unmistakably native ideas on this subject that I could discover were inferential: among the members of a certain sub-sib no male may eat pork from a white pig until he has removed the taboo at a Climbing ceremony. Now this taboo does not apply to female members, except to one who is pregnant, whose fetus *may* be a male — the implication being, or so I deduce, that the fetus has already begun to acquire some of the spiritual (i.e., totemic) affiliations of the ordinary Siuai.

Not only is an infant's body weak and its soul fragile, but the link between its body and soul is exceedingly tenuous. This results in a vulnerability not only to supernatural agents of destruction but to more mundane afflictions as well. Frambesical sores, for example, along with other common infirmities, are considered inescapable aspects of infancy and childhood, exacerbated, on occasion, by supernatural agencies, but otherwise as inevitable as cutting teeth. Because of this weakness infants may not eat "strong" foods, such as pork and opossum; and because of their spiritual vulnerability they may not eat "angry" insects or any food prepared at a club-house or in connection with rituals involving demons. The accompanying table represents the Siuai's conception of an individual's growth and change in time.

RECOGNIZED AGE CHANGES

| | | Male | | Female | |
|---|---|---|---|---|---|
| | | Pooki | "The-one-Inside" | | Pooki |
| Fetus | | 1. karakara, pu'utei | newborn, unbaptized | | karakara, pu'utei |
| | | 2. monika'kuɲ | "his-(her) skin-is-firm" | | monika'kana |
| | | 3. ku'tunutunupum | "he-(she) has-straightened-his-neck" | | ku'tunutunupuina |
| | | 4. uɲkahoɲu'koɲ | ? | | uɲkahoɲu'kana |
| Infant | ⎧ | 5. maɲkom | "he-(she) sits-up" | | maɲkana |
| (Tutu) | ⎨ | 6. kevi moikaɲ | "his-(her) teeth-appear" | | kevi moikana |
| | | 7. kokopa'kaɲ | "he-(she) crawls" | | kokopa'kana |
| | ⎩ | 8. rukuɲu'kaɲ | "he-(she) is caused-to-stand-up" | | rukuɲu'ukana |
| | | 9. tatovokori kopi'kaɲ | "he-(she) stands-holding a post" | | tatovokori kopi'kana |
| | | 10. koɲkoɲ hanahanavorokaɲ | "he-(she) attempts walking" | | koɲkoɲ hanahanavorokana |
| | | 11. koɲkoɲkuɲ | "he-(she) walks" | | koɲkoɲkuina |
| Child | ⎧ | ku'kai nakukoɲ | "he-searches-for small-insects" | | |
| (Kitoria) | ⎨ | mosi ɲokoɲ | "he-climbs areca-palms" | akanovoi kopi'kana | "she-walks-carrying a-basket" |
| | ⎩ | moi kokoɲ | "he-climbs almond-trees" | nunokaijori'kana | "her-breasts-have-come-up" |
| | | — | (begins to work and copulate) | — | (too young to copulate) |
| | | Honna "adult," "big" | | nunokuɲuroina | "her-breasts-are-big" |
| | | Nimaotu "handsome young man" | | nunoa'voina | "her-breasts-have-fallen" |
| | | Hoɲoponori rivorim | "he-has-become 'old'" | nunomorokevuina | "her-breasts-have-emptied" |

[ 71 ]

It will be noted on the table that in infancy sex distinctions receive linguistic expression solely through the agency of verb endings, and "age" differences are expressed in terms of physical change and activities and not in terms of measured time sequence.

During childhood — that is, while the individual is a "child" (*kitoria*), no longer an infant (*tutu*) but not yet able to copulate — both body and soul become stronger and more firmly linked, but some of the weaknesses and vulnerabilities of infancy remain until the end of the period. On the other hand, this is the stage when most proscriptions on eating and movement are lifted, either through performance of taboo-ending rituals or through noting of physical signs of growth. As in infancy, "age" distinctions are expressed in terms of activities and physical change, but, unlike in infancy, sex differences receive full linguistic expression. Towards the end of this period most boys and girls begin to experiment sexually and to assume some of the work habits of adults, and these things, rather than any perceptible physiological change, form a boundary between the stage of childhood and the stage of youth or maidenhood. The Siuai believe that a girl cannot bear children until menstruation, but they also believe that this can occur only after she has begun to copulate; and none of these circumstances is ritualized or otherwise marked. And similarly with a boy, there is no emphasis on "puberty" either as a physiological event or a social milestone; one boy-child will begin doing a youth's work before his playmates do — and that is a matter for approbation; while another will try copulating before his penis can harden — and that is a matter for jest.

When a youth is as large as other adult men and does an adult's work, he *is* an adult (*honna*), and from this time onward until he reaches and passes the crest of his physical powers, that is, until he becomes an "old man," his role in life depends on economic and social factors rather than on physical aging. During this period he has "vitality" and there remains enough youthfulness in this quality to render him vulnerable to the more dangerous agents of death and destruction, hence he must avoid contact with the materials used for those forms of vengeance-sorcery against which there is no effective insulation. For "old men" there is no such risk, having less vitality they are immune to this form of danger; but there is another kind of threat to their survival, that of "Near-death." "Old-man" is a literal translation of the Siuai term *hoŋoponari*, but more than agedness is implied; the term is also applied to men whom we would call "middle aged," who are by no means senile, i.e., those who have reached a plateau of living — with their offspring well past childhood, their food supply adequate, and their wisdom — but not necessarily their influence — broad. Nevertheless, the plateau does slope downward, however slight the incline, and old-men are never very far removed from death. Even though they are relatively immune to "angry" magical ingredients and to the danger-laden materials of vengeance-sorcery, which can destroy the vitality of younger men, old-men are assailed by numerous other spirits of the kind that hasten death.

Later on we shall chart another kind of progression in time in which Siuai men are carried along: one involving expanding economic activity and increasing renown. And although the crest of this development is reached only by adult males, there is otherwise no necessary inter-gearing of the two kinds of progression. Men gain wealth and renown because of what they do over and beyond subsistence activity, and not because of their vitality, their economic solidity, their general knowledge, or their "age." "Agedness," as a manifestation of progressive physical changes, receives little respect for itself in Siuai: some grayheads are loved, some are feared, and some are held to be troublesome old fools. But just as there is no inherent advantage in age, there is also no clinging to youth and vitality; the only suggestion of vitality-renewal I could discover was the information that men sometimes eat coconut and almonds to increase their supply of semen, and when I told them of the rejuvenescence magic of other peoples they were amused and somewhat scandalized.

After females have begun to copulate and to menstruate their life progression is expressed in terms of the form of their breasts, which is the Siuai manner of stating whether and how well a woman can nurse children. Menopause is of course noted but is in no way signalized, and it is generally believed — by men at least — that women cease childbearing before menopause is reached (although I could never obtain a rationalization for this in "physiological" terms). At least, by the time menopause is reached the breasts have already become totally flat and apparently without milk, and this, to the Siuai, is the main characteristic of the "old-woman" (*hoŋonari*).

Although there are Motuna terms for "male" (*raŋuriva*) and "female" (*moni'imo*), applicable to humans as well as to animals and spirits, there is no explicit native formulation of a concept of "maleness" or "femaleness" as such; nevertheless, it would appear inferentially that old-women have lost some of the "femaleness" that characterizes younger ones since they participate more in activities ordinarily reserved for males past childhood, and I do not believe that this can be explained away wholly in terms of their diminished sexual desirability.

Females, like males, possess the quality of vitality, but the component of physical strength (*itikaivo*) occurs to only a moderate degree — "weak as a woman" is frequently on the male's lips. Moreover, like a male's, a female's vitality also ebbs and eventually disappears, bringing on death. But most males are cut off before then; and old-men are particularly assailable. But the dangerous time for females is during their child-bearing stage; and as old-women they are quite likely to live out their decline unaffected by supernatural agents of death, such as sorcery.

As an individual approaches senility his (or her) vitality begins to diminish rapidly — *how* could not be explained — and the soul's attachment to the body weakens so that it leaves it more often and stays away longer. Under these circumstances the individual becomes increasingly vulnerable to certain kinds of destructive actions, and his soul is more easily lured away and captured. But even without such outside dangers a point is reached at which the ebb of vitality and the absences of the soul leave the individual in a state of "Near-death" (*mohkoru*).

Near-death refers partly to the individual's susceptibility to death brought about by a diminishing of vitality and by excessive absences of the soul from the body; in other words, it is a state wherein the essentials for continued living are lacking. But this state also has a positive facet: it can be detected by sight or smell by many spirits. Of course, the wandering soul can also be seen by some humans, and any child can tell when an aged person's vitality has waned, but that is not the point. Some supernaturals can detect the state of Near-death by its positive features even when these other signs are not readily apparent.

Some individuals reach the point of Near-death with senility, as the natural concomitant of aging. Others reach it prematurely, usually as a result of seeing certain ghosts and demons who transform themselves into visible or audible animals — eels, snakes, birds, etc. — just for the purpose, it would seem, of appearing to or being heard by older natives, thereby causing them to be Near-death sooner than would normally occur. There are large numbers of these spirits whose sole function is this. There are also many other supernaturals, including nearly all of the more powerful demons, who perform this function along with many others. And in addition there are other spirits who can detect Near-death without being able to cause it; their function is to make known the presence of Near-death in an individual. In the first category is the fabulous duck-like Koko bird, which dwells at Paradise (*Ru'no'no'*); it kidnaps a human's soul, takes it to Paradise, and feeds it on a certain forbidden food (*piakori*), then returns it to earth in a state of Near-death.[40] Included in the second category are horomorun demons in their snake transformation, numerous other territorial demons in snake and human transformations, and many sinister ghosts transformed into giant eels. The third category includes spirits who specialize in announcing the Near-death of persons of affluence, others who are specifically affiliated with certain sibs, and still others, like the Kurukuru bird, who function as general death omens. The Kurukuru bird, for example, detects a Near-death person and accompanies him everywhere he goes calling out its characteristic cry, which other people recognize as a foreboding. The demon, Umiai, is the death omen of the affluent; it appears in the form of a bolide, with all the drama appropriate to its superior mission.[41]

In some instances the soul of the Near-death person itself advertises his state. This soul transforms itself into a *ripo* (swamp phosphorescence?) and flies through the night to the Near-death person's garden where it ignites a banana tree. Then it returns to the sleeping person's house and moves about over the roof, so that people will see it and discern its message.

The Siuai's religious beliefs are so replete with omens of Near-death that one might be tempted to characterize them as a death-conscious people.

The soul of a Near-death person is compelled to do many things which, in turn, may serve to hasten death. For example, it is irresistibly drawn to a cremation pyre, hence before any pyre is lighted a magician causes his spirit-familiar to drive away all the souls sitting on it so that they, and consequently their human owners, will not be destroyed. It is also believed that persons in a state of Near-death do not prevaricate, although this does not automatically transform them into seers.

The expiring of vitality, manifested chiefly in the cessation of breathing (*ruma*), is the more critical factor in "normal" dying. When this happens the soul leaves the body altogether; but before that the soul appears capable of leaving for varying lengths of time without causing death. It leaves during sleep, for example, and during certain kinds of illnesses; and if it is merely held captive elsewhere for an extended period the owner may become demented (*poŋosere*). (On the other hand, if the soul is captured and injured through dirt sorcery this may bring about the owner's death, hence in "unnatural" deaths vitality may not always be the critical factor.) There is a threshold between life and normal death when vitality is no longer visible and the soul apparently absent; this state of coma is usually diagnosed as a kind of "preliminary" death if the person resumes consciousness, and under such circumstances it is concluded that vitality has temporarily revived. This revival is spoken of as *poŋororo*; it may sometimes be brought about through placing a certain pungent plant under the comatose person's nostrils, thereby causing a restorative sneeze. For the aged any such revival can only be temporary, but for younger persons who have died unnatural deaths the revival of vitality might have become a permanent condition but for an unfortunate occurrence in the legendary past.

> Once a man died, and after he died they cremated him and tabooed eating taro. Unable to eat taro, which was the only thing growing in her garden, the deceased's mother took some plantains which the deceased had planted, and ate these. She did this for several days until all the plantains were gone. Then her son came to life again and walked about the country playing on his flute. When his mother heard the flute-playing she asked, "Who could this be playing a flute just the way my son used to play?" Then the son walked into the settlement and revealed himself. His mother embraced him and wept, saying, "Oh my son! You died and we cremated you, and now you are alive again." Whereupon the son answered, "Yes, I am alive again. Whenever any of us dies he will come back to life and live without dying again. That's the way it will be."
> 
> One day the son was walking about the gardens and came upon his plantain tree, with all the plantains gone. He was very angry and stormed around trying to find out who had stolen his plantains. Finally he went to his mother and she told him what she had done. He was still angry but he could not kill his mother, so he decided to die again. He went down into the ground through a hole made by the rotting away of a wild banana plant, and he remained

underneath. As he went down he told all the people, "Later on, when you die you will remain dead as I am going to be. If you had not eaten my plantains no one need have remained dead."

The Siuai recognize that everyone must eventually *die* — that is, ultimately the body loses completely and irrevocably all vitality and begins to rot (*hiŋhaku-*). When that occurs the body is cremated and any remaining bits of charred bone are sifted from the ashes and thrown onto the nearest Place-of-bones (*ko'onakori*). (There is one of these ossuaries near every large hamlet, and it is an exceedingly dangerous and tabooed place, often inhabited by malevolent demons and ghosts, a setting for the sinister acts of sorcerers and avoided by all other persons.) Meanwhile, at the time of death, the soul permanently leaves the body and starts out for the abodes of ghosts.

There are three of these abodes. Paradise (*Ru'no'no'*) is a lake in the uninhabited mountains northeast of Siuai, an actual lake which is reported to have been visited by some fearless natives in the past; this is the abode of fortunate ghosts, whose deaths have been widely mourned and whose mourners have been suitably rewarded. At Ru'no'no' ghosts enjoy easy and joyful existences, with dancing and feasting on a plentiful food supply that requires no labor to produce. *Kaopiri* is another lake, a legendary one in the north, to which must go those ghosts who have not been suitably mourned, or whose mourners have not been adequately rewarded. Kaopiri is a lake of fire and blood and its ghostly inhabitants suffer everlasting hunger.[42] Judgment concerning whether a ghost goes to Paradise or to Kaopiri rests with Hoŋing, the principal kupuna of the afterworld. Hoŋing stands astride the path along which the new ghost travels north and intercepts it with a question: "How many pigs are following you?" (That is, "How many pigs were distributed among the people who mourned for you?") If the answer indicates that the mourners were generously rewarded — what "generous" means will be discussed later — the ghost is allowed to proceed to Paradise; otherwise Hoŋing cuts off its nose and shoves it into Kaopiri.

Blood-place (*Irinoru*), the third abode, is reserved for persons killed in fighting; some natives say that it is a lake, others that it is a dark valley.[43] The ghosts there neither feast nor starve; their chief characteristic is their anger at having been slain, and this leaves them restless and unsatisfied. Some informants say that the ghosts of suicides also inhabit Blood-place; while others claim that they go either to Ru'no'no' or Kaopiri, according to the decision of Hoŋing.

A ghost does not proceed direct to its afterworld abode. Immediately after death and until its mortuary feast has been held it tarries in Memory-house (*kiŋkiŋnapa*). Then, if it is admitted to Paradise, it dwells in Forgotten-house, that is, people no longer think about it.

Assignment to a ghost's abode does not bind the ghost to remain there all the time. Some of them return to the land of the living for long or short

## BELIEFS ABOUT NATURE AND MAN 77

visits; in fact, a few of them remain at their mortal abodes so continuously that some natives suggest that every Siuai must have two souls and hence two ghosts. Some of these returned ghosts transform themselves into large eels (*kamaŋu*) and assist dirt-sorcerers with their evil practices. Others change into snakes with powers of inflicting Near-death. Still others become the spirit-familiars of surviving relatives and assist them in their enterprises.

Other ghosts become memorialized in magical formulae (*korona*, see below, page 85); but except for these few, and the relatively small number that return as ghosts to participate directly and explicitly in human affairs, all souls of the dead are forgotten after three or four generations. They do not re-enter new infants [44] and are not revered in any special way.

All the foregoing is introductory, and will be expanded and documented as this account proceeds, but even these few abbreviations suggest certain general points:

Neither in belief nor in everyday practice is a Siuai's progression through life absolutely coördinated with physical aging, and, reflecting this, except at birth and death there is no ritualizing of physiological change. Moreover, although the life span of every person consists of a sequence of recognized stages (infancy, childhood, youth, etc.), these stages are not separated from each other by sharp thresholds. In other words, the individual Siuai moves into, through, and out of life by a slow and fairly continuous walk rather than by a series of jumps.

From these and other data it is possible to record certain of the Siuai's beliefs and premises regarding the more significant socially differentiating human attributes.

*Sex.* Beginning in later childhood sharp distinctions are made between the sexes in connection with many economic and social activities. For example, women are barred from participating in, or even from observing, the exciting activities of men at the club-houses; whereas men are free to watch their female relatives doing comparable things. Nevertheless those physical aspects of womanhood such as menstrual blood and sexual fluid appear to have no intrinsic quality of "femaleness" of the kind found among some Oceanic peoples, where they are thought of as exercising a harmful influence on the enterprises of men. In Siuai the menstruating woman is somewhat ashamed of her flowing blood and its odor, but she is not segregated or otherwise avoided. Again, sexual intercourse does not disable men from participating in rituals or any other activity, there being no concept of ritual impurity caused by sexual contact. On the other hand, there is some evidence which suggests that the sex act has a deleterious effect upon growth — of infants and of garden crops.

*Age.* The greater magical vulnerability of the young places certain restrictions on their activities, but otherwise the Siuai do not hold that there are serious disabilities associated with youth. Such estimable attributes as special skills, ambition, and industriousness are not thought to be the inevitable concomitants of advanced age;[45] and natives recognize that socio-political achievement is not reserved for graybeards alone.

*Kinship.* From the point of view of one person regarding another, one of the latter's most important attributes is the nature of the shared kinship tie, if any.

*Acquaintanceship.* Being acquainted means living nearby, and if a person is an acquaintance he differs from *strangers*, most of whom are potential enemies.

*Normalcy.* In the Motuna language, *poŋosere* is applied to all kinds of mental malfunctioning: to deafness and dumbness, to insanity and even to clear cases of slow-wittedness. Persons become poŋosere through the actions of spirits, either by sorcery or by the breaking of taboos. Victims are regarded as being unfortunate and may be joked with and teased, but they are usually well cared for by solicitous relatives. "Normal" persons (*nommai kuka*) are also accused of being poŋosere when they do something stupidly, hence the adjective "kuka" might be translated as "intelligent," except for the fact that no overt recognition is given to degrees of intelligence in the sense of more or less mental agility and wisdom. In Siuai terms, if two individuals are normal (kuka) and of the same sex and the same broad age category, any superiority one of them may have over the other is due, not to his having more of the attribute of normalcy, but rather to his having special skills, more industriousness, greater "goodness," or stronger motivation.

*Skill.* Technical skill (*tana*) is believed to account for some of the differences between persons — skill in gardening, in craftsmanship, in magical techniques, in accumulating capital, etc. Skill consists of technical knowledge plus practice in using it. The knowledge may be acquired in various ways but it has to be applied in constant practice before the person is truly skilled. Nearly every adult possesses at least one kind of skill, and some possess several. A skill, unlike "normalcy," is a praiseworthy attribute, and some skills such as successful healing, highly productive gardening, and expert musicianship, bring their possessors admiration and respect.

*Industriousness.* The Siuai consider industriousness a prime virtue, whether or not it is wedded to skill; and they disapprove of a lazy adult no matter how esteemed his other attributes may be. (On the other hand, they regard Paradise as a place where no one has to work.)

*Goodness.* Although the Siuai have separate terms for "generosity," "cooperativeness," "morality" (that is, rule abiding), and "geniality," I believe that they consider all these to be closely interrelated aspects of the same attribute of goodness (*nommai mirahu*). A person cannot be deficient in one of these aspects without being deficient in all of them. And, of course, if he excels in these virtues he is liked even though he may not be admired. Conversely, "selfishness," "noncoöperativeness," "immorality," and "uncongeniality" are heartily disliked, and the individual so characterized (*nommai kirahao*) is sometimes believed to be a crypto-sorcerer. A person is born "good" — or at least with a positive disposition for normal development of "goodness," badness being acquired through exceptional circumstances.

*Ambition.* The Siuai consider ambition (*haokom*) to be a positive attribute and probably an inborn one. It is the desire for *renown* (*potu*) and for the power that renown brings. Persons differ in the amount of ambition they possess, and some are almost entirely deficient in it. Ambition alone is not a virtue in the sense that goodness is; in fact, unless ambition is wedded to industriousness, skills, and goodness, it may become a vice. Without it, however, industriousness leads to nothing beyond self-sufficiency, and goodness to mere popularity. Conversely, deficiency in ambition is not considered to be a fault of character even though enculturation techniques do emphasize the desirability of having some of it. Adults say they can discern ambition in an individual as early as childhood.

Most of the attributes just listed are independent variables. For example, a man may be a kinsman without being "good," or he may become wealthy by dishonest means and without being industrious. Or he may be industrious and good, but unless he is also ambitious he cannot gain renown.

The Siuai also recognize qualities of human beings other than these — including handsomeness, wrathfulness, aggressiveness in warfare, and sacredness, but these and other qualities do not figure as importantly for social differentiation as do the attributes just listed.

Concerning sacredness (*mikisa*), it is a condition of any place, activity, thing, or person associated directly with dangerous supernaturals. For example, the abode of a dangerous spirit is mikisa, as are the actions and magical implements of a sorcerer, or the person of a magician possessed by a dangerous spirit-familiar. However, no person is continually mikisa; in fact the condition is too dangerous to be sustained for long, and magicians usually perform rites to remove the condition when the occasion for using magic has ended.

All the above attributes have to do with the Siuai themselves, with natives born into Siuai society, speaking Motuna and participating in Siuai activities. The Siuai are aware of cultural differences between themselves and their ethnic neighbors, and believe that even sharper differences separate them from natives further removed geographically and racially. Under the term "customs" (*onoono*) the Siuai include techniques — agricultural, magical, etc., and customary interpersonal behavior patterns. Informants say that most of their customs were established by the kupunas and continue unchanged. Some customs are said to be intrinsically right (*onoono mirahu*) for the Siuai, and should be followed by all Siuai. But even bad customs (*onoono kirahao*) were established by these kupunas, and although their practice was enjoined by kupunas, some of the kupunas themselves were guilty of practicing them (for example, incest, lying).

In general, most Siuai natives consider Siuai customs best, and they sometimes express contempt for their ethnic neighbors' customs. On the other hand, the Siuai are not aggressively chauvinistic, and even in the past permitted some outsiders (from Banoni, Nagovisi, Terei, and Mono Island) to settle among them. Moreover, they have been quick and even eager to adopt many traits from their neighbors, including songs, magical techniques, stories, and some kinds of material items. This kind of qualified "cultural relativism" is exemplified in another way: they do not explicitly claim world universality for their culture creators, the kupunas. In fact, they do not even speculate about such matters.

All these generalizations refer to *indigenous* premises and beliefs. As previously stated (see note 1 of this chapter) there are many Siuai who hold beliefs, etc., derived from alien sources, which will be treated later on.

## RELATIONSHIPS AMONG ENTITIES

*Relations among Spirits.* In the realm of the spirits there is no over-all hierarchic arrangement of beings, although there are specific instances of some spirits being subordinate to others. Hoŋjing, for example, is master of all souls admitted to Paradise, and he also has some control over which ones go there. Again, among the demons associated with each "spirit" territory one or two appear to be supreme, at least in the sense of being most powerful and dangerous. Also, each club-house demon (*horomorun*) is leader of all smaller horomoruns in its jurisdiction. And it should also be mentioned that some demons are related by marital ties, such as Konopia and her spouse Ikaipakai (see above), or by ties of matrilineal descent. Otherwise, the various kinds of active spirits are not interrelated or ranked, and accounts of their actions leave one with the impression that the Siuai believe them to behave according to individual caprice, within the bounds of certain patterns, of course, but not according to a comprehensive and ordered scheme.

*Relations among Humans.* According to explicit Siuai beliefs,[46] or to inferences which can be drawn from much of their behavior, the attributes listed above serve to order social relations in the following ways:

Kinship. It will be recalled (see above) that in the Siuai theory of procreation an embryo can only be conceived through the actions of a single genitor and mother. Both their sexual fluids intermingle and turn into blood and body-building substance; and both parents are essential. Similarly, consanguinity is recognized as applying bilaterally. Each person is of course unique — there being no belief in reincarnation; on the other hand, each person inherits some part of its being from each parent: blood, appearance, strength, and temperament.

The forebears of both parents are called "ancestors" (*rapi*), and inasmuch as the soul of every deceased person survives indefinitely, all the ancestral souls of each native would seem to be potential intervenors in his everyday life. In Siuai belief, however, only a few out of the total aggregate of any native's ancestral souls play active roles in his life. Natives do not even refer to "the ancestors" in the sense of their constituting any kind of social or functional aggregate. Similarly, any living person with whom one can trace or assume genealogical ties is a relative, to whom one can apply the appropriate kinship term of address or reference; but *all* such relatives do not constitute a group. Natives draw clear-cut distinctions between *close* (*meŋ*) and *distant* (*turumai*) relatives, both in conversation and in practice. They also distinguish sharply between their matrilateral relatives and all other people.

The Siuai consider all persons interrelated by actual or putative matrilateral ties to be sib-mates (*imo*, my-sib-mate) and to constitute a sib (*noroukuru*).⁴⁷ We have already given an account of the mythical origins of this kind of relationship: in Siuai terms, the reason why these natives emphasize matrilineal over other kinds of descent is that the kupunas so established it. As we have already seen, all members of a sib believe themselves descended matrilineally from certain kupunas, who in some cases still exercise influence over the lives of their matrilineal descendants. Sib-mates also believe themselves related to one or more species of primary animal totems, which they must not eat and should not harm. Among themselves, sib-mates should behave in certain well-defined ways.

Although matrilineal descent is much more highly conceptualized and institutionalized, the Siuai do not overlook the importance of the tie with and through the father. It is manifested, for example, in the practice wherein an eldest child respects his father's primary totem as well as his own. The major structural difference between the two kinds of ties is, of course, the genealogical shallowness of the patrilateral tie: an individual, his (or her) father, paternal grandfather, etc., do not constitute any kind of symbolic aggregate — in other words, there is no symbolically significant temporal continuity to the agnatic tie.⁴⁸

The Siuais' conception of the nature of consanguinity, quite apart from the matrilineal tie, is vividly expressed in a statement which they use to describe how closely related they are to consanguineous kin other than sib-mates. Here is the expression applied by a man to his own offspring and to those of his brother and his mother's brother: "Our blood is identical; our blood flows from the same belly." The reasons why this expression is not also used to refer to sib-mates was given to be: "the *noroukuru* relationship is self-evidently close and does not require any other explanation."

Siuai should and sometimes do marry an actual cross-cousin; and marriage between distant, classificatory cross-cousins is even more frequent. In fact, the web of kinship reticulates all Siuai so finely that no native can escape marrying a relative of some degree of consanguinity.⁴⁹ It would even appear that the norms of behavior between certain pairs of consanguineous kin are shaped by the presumption that the individuals will eventually become actual affinal relatives.

In any case affinity is regarded as a very important kind of tie, involving special kinds of rights and obligations.

Male-Female. The social relations between the sexes are colored by the widely held belief that males are superior to females in strength, in "goodness," and in ambition. Moreover, the skills associated with males are technically more complex and estimable; and whereas men sometimes acquire female skills (for example, garden cultivating, domestic cookery, and certain kinds of plaiting), women are barred from practicing many male skills. Nevertheless, most males would admit that females are essential in the realm of subsistence even though they play unimportant roles in socio-political activities.

In sexual intercourse males and females are believed to be more evenly matched. Rape is practically nonexistent, it being considered slightly improper to apply any form of coercion to force women into unwilling sexual relationships. In fact, many men assert that females are more aggressive than males in sexual matters. In this connection it should be noted that sexual intercourse is regarded as wrong only when it is incestuous, adulterous, or carried out by an adult male with a very young girl. Even adultery arouses disapproval only from persons directly affected; others usually consider it a fine joke.

Older-Younger. The Siuai distinguish terminologically between older and younger siblings of the same sex, and numerous maxims express the belief that younger siblings should respect and obey older ones. Moreover, the first-born, male or female, is specially designated *First-born* (*simiri*) and, in theory at least, exercises decisive authority over the affairs and belongings of his (or her) siblings. The belief in the primacy of the First-born and the super-ordination of older over younger family siblings carries over into other groups based on sibling-like ties of relationships. For example, the eldest female and male of a matrilineage should also be called First-born of that group, with all the attendant prerogatives. The fact that actual behavior does not always correspond to these norms is another matter.

Locality. Native moralists assert that neighbors should be friendly and mutually trustful, whereas people from far-off are dangerous and unworthy of morally just consideration. For example, natives lay great stress on honesty in transactions involving neighbors while holding that trade with strangers may be guided by *caveat emptor*. In days past, the Siuai were suspicious of strangers and sometimes killed them on sight; nowadays, they remain suspicious of them but must be content with merely avoiding them or injuring them by magic. In present-day Siuai, neighbors are nearly always interrelated by fairly close kinship ties, hence the factor of neighborliness per se is difficult to isolate and describe. Nevertheless the belief in space [50] relationship as a social determinant is an important Siuai concept.

Socio-political Rank. Siuai men conceive of themselves as members of a comprehensive Siuai-wide, hierarchic social system consisting of several layers, with mumis [51] at the top and "legs" (*moŋo*)[52] at the bottom. Moreover they express fairly explicit ideas about the rights and obligations associated with rank, and they appear convinced that high rank depends partly on birth and partly on achievement, resulting from a combination of ambition, skills, industriousness, and "goodness." Later on we shall examine those beliefs in detail; but whether or not they correspond with observable behavior, they occupy a central place in Siuai ideology. The desire for high rank in this socio-political rank system is so powerful and widespread that many men devote their lives trying to achieve it.

*Relations between Spirits and Humans.* Among the "universal" kupunas only Hoŋing has any continuing relations with humans. It is said that if Hoŋing is ill, then all people are ill; if he is hungry, all people are hungry. Numerous tales are told of natives' encounters with this kupuna; the following one is typical:

> Once when several men were in the forest hunting opossum one of them drifted away from his companions and climbed a tree some distance away. In the topmost branches he saw an opossum, and he called out for his companions to stand under the tree so that he could dislodge the animal and throw it down to them. He called and called but his companions were too far away. Hoŋing happened to be nearby and he heard and told the man to throw down the opossum. When that had been done Hoŋing picked it up and ate it raw. The man climbed down the tree and became angry when he learned that the opossum had already been eaten. "Never mind," said Hoŋing, "we'll get another one." So they kept on hunting together and captured several opossum; Hoŋing would eat one of them, and would give the next to the man. Meanwhile they went farther and farther into the forest until they arrived finally at Hoŋing's place. Once there Hoŋing showed the man a fire, a pot, and some taro, bananas, and yams, telling him to prepare his food as he would at home. The man cooked all his food in the pot and told Hoŋing to try some. Hoŋing did so and exclaimed, "Hey, that's good. We spirits usually eat ours uncooked."
>
> The two of them remained at Hoŋing's for some time, eating cooked food and talking, but finally Hoŋing told him, "Now you must return home, and I'll take you part of the way to show you the path. And when you return to your place you must chew this medicine (*kuna*) with your betel — otherwise you will be ill because of having visited in our sacrosanct (mikisa) place."
>
> So the man returned home, chewed the medicine and was all right.

In these and in other accounts of Hoŋing he is represented as having a benevolent interest in mankind. Even in his role as judge of the afterworld his standards of "justice," that is, rewarding the affluent and properly mourned, and condemning the poor (see above, page 76) are, after all, faithful reflections of Siuai concepts of equity.

From his side, the Siuai native makes no effort to communicate with or control any of the universal kupunas, there being no prayers, sacrifices, or any other rituals carried out on their behalf — unless of course one could term the telling of myths "oral rites." [53]

A more active relationship obtains between a Siuai and the spirits associated with his noroukuru. It will be recalled that some of the sib kupunas are otiose, appearing only in myths and not interacting with mankind. Other kupunas, however, have become demons and in various kinds of transformations — stones, animals, and monsters — they haunt places identified with their sibs and are in general more dangerous than otherwise, to human sib-mates as well as to other natives. Numerous stories recount how they waylay humans, cheating them, seducing them, smiting them deaf and dumb, making them demented, afflicting them with various gruesome ailments, and almost invariably rendering them Near-death. Natives do not attempt to communicate with such sib demons or to control them in any way; but curiosity, mixed with some pride, leads many individuals to visit shrines where their sib demons may be seen in ossified form. And even these unbenign beings may manifest some measure of sympathy for their human sib-mates by moaning in simulated pain every time a sib woman gives birth.

Totemic animal archetypes are more actively friendly. They are sometimes seen attending births or marriages or deaths of their human sib-mates, and many informants attest to having seen them at cremations, where they wail and dance with vigor. They also appear as death-omens to human sib-mates, not as perpetrators but as prophets. Otherwise, they neither aid nor harm their human sib-mates, and are not supplicated in any way.

As for the animal descendants of these primary totem archetypes, the only relationship between them and their human sib-mates is a negative one, an injunction forbidding humans to kill or eat their totems. But even here, a native of, say, the Eagle sib will watch with unconcern as other natives shoot an eagle, although he himself will not join in the hunt. As previously mentioned, any human guilty of killing or eating his primary totem animal invites certain and automatic death — a rare instance of an automatic supernatural sanction [54] in Siuai, and no magical antidote can save such a person. Taboos respecting secondary totems are however not so stringently enforced; anyone breaking them can ward off disaster by means of magical antidotes, and some of these taboos may be lifted altogether by participation in the sacrament of Climbing. The archetypes of some secondary totemic animals also function as death-omens and co-celebrants at life crises ceremonies.

As previously noted, only a few of the total aggregate of any Siuai's ancestral ghosts, including those of his matrilineal predecessors, play any role, direct or indirect, in his life. One of them may become his ghost-familiar — but for that matter *any* demon or ghost may become the familiar of any person it chooses to assist. Otherwise, only a few matrilineal ghosts guard over noroukuru heirlooms and become memorialized in noroukuru rituals.

The heirlooms (*tomui*) of high-value shell money identified with a noroukuru (see above, page 59) are believed to be guarded over by some ghosts — *which* ones are not specified — of deceased members of the noroukuru, and these guardians inflict Near-death on any human guardian who uses them improperly, that is, for individual personal advantage.

Maru rituals were invented by noroukuru kupunas for the purpose of promoting the welfare of matrilineal descendants. (See above, page 59.) Maru is performed on the occasion of the infant's debut to its community — about one month after birth, and again at weddings. It is also a basic part of the Climbing ceremony. (See below.) Maru is performed by specialists — usually old women but occasionally men, who learned the procedures from their noroukuru elders. The rituals involve the use of noroukuru heirlooms, sacred water from one of the noroukuru shrines, areca nuts from the noroukuru's own sacred grove, ritual gestures (see below), and verbal formulae (korona). Each noroukuru has its own formulae, but the pattern of all is similar, consisting of a recital of the names of matrilineal predecessors who performed the ritual in the past, together with suggestive words like "strength," "health," etc., and a metaphoric phrase such as, "You will be like the palm, which the hurricane bends but cannot break." Informants assured me repeatedly that maru is not a request to the ghosts to intervene actively; the performer does not call out: "You Ghosts, come make this child grow," but rather, "You Ghosts who were maru performers of our noroukuru, formerly you used to perform this ritual [with success], so now we do the same." On the other hand, there is some suggestion of at least indirect intervention by noroukuru spirits in connection with maru ritual. For example, the areca nut used in the ritual must be obtained from the sacred areca palm grove maintained by each noroukuru for exclusive use of its own members. The maru practitioners of each noroukuru look after this grove, which is guarded supernaturally by the ghosts of former noroukuru practitioners and, some informants claimed, by the kupunas of the noroukuru as well. If any nonmember were to eat any of these consecrated nuts he would become demented.

The Climbing (kinamo) ritual is carried out periodically for the purpose of lifting taboos against eating secondary totems and other foods forbidden as a result of illnesses. The members of one branch of a sib act as host and invite all their neighbors and relatives. The kinamo itself is a large platform, similar to the *raoku* platform used for feasts; on it are placed samples of all the kinds of tabooed food to be tasted. Maru specialists from the various participating sib branches stand at the bottom of the platform and repeat magical formulae over co-members as the latter climb up the platform and eat bits of the previously tabooed foods.[55] The only rationale offered for this ritual is the usual, "the kupunas did it this way."

Most of the spirits of purely local affiliation — some malevolent ghosts and those demons which are not associated with noroukuru — behave very like noroukuru demons towards natives unfortunate enough to cross their paths. Here is a typical story:

> Formerly a native of Hinna named Soŋka saw a handsome woman in the forest and married her. He thought he had married a human, when he had

actually married the demon, Piroma, sister of ŋomoŋomoi, the demon residing in Pakai's club-house at Mi'kahna. Soŋka and Piroma lived together for a short time and then Piroma killed her husband. A magician took a closer look at Piroma and recognized her to be a demon. Soon after that Piroma disappeared.

Not all these spirits win out in their encounters with humans. Miheru, a native of Hanoŋ village, was widely known for having bested the demon Konopia.

One day Miheru was picking breadfruit when Konopia, in the form of a woman, saw him and asked him to throw down some breadfruit for her. He did so, but he threw some for her far off to one side of the tree and those for himself to the other side. He suspected that it was Konopia, and not a real woman. Before he descended he broke off a thick breadfruit stem and hid it in his carrying pouch. He climbed down as Konopia was collecting her breadfruit, but she saw him and urged him to stop for a while and "chew betel-nut." Miheru knew what she meant, for when spirits say "chew betel-nut" they really mean copulation. Anyway, he agreed, and when she lay down he secretly took out the breadfruit stem and poked it far up her vagina. When he had done this and was running away, Konopia threw off all pretense and shouted: "Did the burning of my fire feel good?" (Actual copulation with a spirit will kill a human.) Then Miheru shouted back at her: "Good enough. And how did the poke of my breadfruit stem feel?"

Other spirits are notorious kidnappers of children; still others steal fire from hearths at night to light their pipes. The Siuai are not excessively fearful of all these spirits — some of them are, in fact, quite curious to get a look at them — but not many natives care to walk about alone at night in places known to be haunted.

There are numerous other spirits — demons and ghosts — who enter into the service of certain humans, either voluntarily or through magical compulsion. All such spirit-familiars perform faithfully only so long as they are fed, and inflict Near-death on their masters if food is not given them regularly.

Horomoruns are the demons associated with men's club-houses. When its human master dies a horomorun remains nearby until another man begins to emerge as leader of that locality. Then the horomorun afflicts the new leader with a sickness, as a sign of his choice. After the real cause of the illness has been divined, a magician helps the leader to formalize the relationship. After that the horomorun resides in the leader's club-house and protects his person and property so long as he is fed. A horomorun's food consists of the essence of pig's blood, and the more blood he is given the more powerful and effective he becomes. But woe to any man who neglects his horomorun, for before the latter becomes a starving wraith and forsakes the club-house he inflicts Near-death upon his faithless master.

## BELIEFS ABOUT NATURE AND MAN

Ghosts often attach themselves to human relatives and in return for food sacrifices, small tidbits set aside at meal times, afford some protection against other spirits as well as some assistance in practical enterprises, including the protection of the master's property from thieves and vandals. As in the case of the leader and his horomorun, the elected native is first inflicted with illness, and rapport has to be obtained with the help of a magician. In some cases a native's ghost-familiar perches on his shoulder, and man and ghost converse in a private language of grunts and whistles. Other natives carve conventionalized human figures (*poripai*) of wood and induce their spirit-familiars to reside in them.

In addition to all the foregoing, about one in every four Siuai adult males, and a smaller proportion of adult females, practices specialized techniques of magic concerned with afflicting or curing bodily ills. These techniques may be divided into a number of categories on the basis of function; for example, important analytical distinctions may be drawn between, say, the magical act performed by an owner to protect his property, and that used by an envious neighbor to kill his successful political rival. And both of these have different social meanings from, say, the magical attempt to cure a victim of sorcery or to revenge a sorcery killing. These various uses of magic will be described later in proper context, but for the present the emphasis will be upon the magical principles underlying these techniques and the light they throw on Siuai beliefs about relationships between humans and spirits. Let us consider first those magical techniques which might be termed "destructive"; six types may be differentiated:[56]

1. Spirit-attracting poisons (*koona*). These poisons (plant materials, insects, clays, etc., or compounds of these) are injected into the victim either through his food, by blowing the poison's essence (*ruma*, also means *breath*) towards him from the point of an arrow, or by "pointing" — that is, causing the shadow of the poison to touch him,[57] or by arranging to have the victim's shadow fall on the poison. Spirits, attracted by the smell of the poison, then enter the victim's body and proceed to sever his windpipe and blood vessels. *Naraipu* is a slight variant on this koona technique; the spirit-attracting poison is hidden near a hamlet and this by itself is sufficient to attract spirits and cause them to attack *all* inhabitants of the hamlet.

2. Intrinsic poisons. Intrinsically dangerous poisons become injected into the victim and bring about his death or illness by means of their own deadly properties. These poisons consist of certain "hot" or "angry" (iro) items (for example, stinging insects, nettles, irritating plant juices, etc.) or of items that appear similar to the effect desired (e.g., a bamboo with leprous-like surface markings is used for causing leprosy; a plant with a particularly noxious odor produces stinking ulcers; etc.). These poisons may be purposefully injected, as in the case of spirit-attracting poisons; or the victim may receive the deadly contact by unknowingly going near the poisons, this being

the action of many magical devices concerned with the protection of property. For most intrinsic poisons there are specific magical antidotes.

3. Consecrated poisons. Ghost-consecrated poisons are injected into the victim and subject him to attack by those ghosts identified with the poisons. The methods of injection are the same as for spirit-attracting and intrinsic poisons. The ingredients are similar to the intrinsically dangerous ones, and in addition these ingredients are linked with the ghosts of former practitioners of this magic in such a way that the latter add their destructive powers to those of the poisons.

4. Homicidal familiars. Some magicians are affiliated with demons or ghosts which specialize in maiming or destroying victims by direct physical attack or by soul capture. These magicians keep their familiars "domesticated" by means of frequent food offerings, and order them to carry out missions by issuing simple commands. Homicidal familiars transfer their allegiance to other magicians if not properly fed.

5. The curse (*horihoriko*). If an adult curses a child with sufficient vehemence (i.e., saying, "May the spirits kill you"), any spirit hearing the curse will oblige. Adults are not so physically vulnerable to mere verbally inspired attack; if anyone wishes to curse one of them he must enlist the aid of those "angry" ghosts of individuals who have died violently either in fighting or by sorcery. Special places (*peteikori*) are set aside to serve as haunts for these "angry" ghosts, and they are induced to remain in these haunts by placing some of their ashes there after cremation.[58] The person wishing to curse an enemy goes to an Ash-place, cuts off a limb from a tree growing there, and calls on the resident ghosts to kill his enemy along with all the latter's matrilineage mates. The ghosts then lure the victims' souls to the Ash-place, and this in itself is sufficient to afflict those souls and bring about the death of their human receptacles.

6. "Dirt" magic. A magician captures part of his victim's soul and destroys it by any one of a number of ways. Any part of the victim or anything touched by the victim will serve the purpose: a hair, a fingernail, a piece of his clothing or ornament, remains of food partly eaten by him, dirt from his footprint, etc. The most common methods of destroying the captured soul are to feed the victim's exuviae to an eel-demon, or to imprison it under the bark of a growing tree, or to place it in a demon-ridden spot. Another variant is to plant a wild taro in the victim's footprint; then when the taro plant matures, the magician makes cuts in stalk and leaves, thereby causing sores to form on his victim.

Magical countermeasures are also varied; they may be differentiated according to function (i.e., what they purport to do) and technique.

*Protection.* There are numerous techniques used for warding off danger. Some of these involve the aid of a specific spirit-familiar, either ghost or demon, which stands guard over its human associate against malicious spirits or humans. Each spirit-familiar is effective, of course, only in so far as it is more powerful than its opponents. Other protective techniques operate by using protective medicines (kuna) consecrated to the ghosts of former practitioners of the particular medicine involved — the ghosts being expected to afford protection.

Life-prolonging magic may be employed to prolong temporarily the life of a dying person. The magician fastens the soul of the patient by knotting a cord held over the patient's head; the cord is then kept knotted so long as it is desired to keep the patient alive.

There are also men who own certain plants, etc., which if chewed bestow the magical power to see poisons in the possession of other men. This magic (*tesi*) is widely used at large gatherings (dances, court hearings, cremations) to provide warnings for the owner and his relatives and friends against strangers and other potential enemies.

*Diagnosis and Divination.* In most cases the symptoms of the misfortune provide the clue to the nature of the agent: for example, any woman who dies in childbirth is unmistakably the victim of *tao* (sorcery employing a ghost-consecrated object); or anyone suffering from a grossly distended abdomen is believed to be afflicted by *marejahupa* (intrinsically dangerous water from a certain sacred spring near Kakarakiro village); etc. In some instances the agent of death becomes known after death or after cremation: for example, if part of what is believed to be the deceased's heart remains unburnt in the ashes it is assumed that the deceased was a victim of *tomoni* (sorcery employing certain ghost-consecrated poisons). Sometimes the victim of sorcery announces the cause of illness and the identity of the evil-doer just before expiring; the soul of a dying individual is believed to be acutely perceptive. In other instances a specialist will be called in to diagnose the cause of misfortune, these magicians usually depending upon their spirit-familiars to discover the cause.

Learning the identity of the evil-doer calls for a separate operation in most cases. With the kind of divination known as *tuki*, for example, the practitioner burns food sacrifices and white clay to his ghost-familiars (i.e., the ghosts of former tuki practitioners) which then lead the way to the guilty sorcerer; this divination is believed to be particularly reliable in cases of tao sorcery (i.e., death in childbirth). General practitioners of magic (*mikai*) also practice *tupunamu* divination as part of their stock-in-trade; their spirit-familiars capture the souls of guilty persons and hold them for their own masters to see and identify. In cases of theft the victim may wish to have divination combined with revenge; he does this by employing a specialist who orders his spirit-familiar to capture the thief's soul which he then proceeds to imprison in a miniature house, thereby killing the thief. This technique is known as *tukuveroro*.

Another widely practiced method of divination is *mirina*. Just before the cremation of a sorcery victim a stick of rattan (*povata*) is rubbed with ghost-attracting clay (*hiku*) and is run through his mouth while the magician calls upon his own familiars — ghosts of former mirina-magicians — to aid in discovering the identity of the killer. Then, after the sorcery victim and the rattan have been cremated together, the mirina-magician burns in the ashes some soul-attracting medicines along with a food sacrifice to his familiars, and sends the latter in search of the sorcerer. The familiars now know the identity of the sorcerer, having learned it from the victim's soul by means of the rattan episode, and they search out and force the soul of the guilty sorcerer to go to the bed of ashes where the mirina-magician keeps his vigil. Innocent souls also flock to the ashes — the medicines burnt there are powerfully attractive — but the magician knows them to be innocent because of the unfaltering manner of their approach. The guilty soul betrays itself to the mirina-magician by its dragging, faltering steps.[59]

In connection with all diagnosis involving the use of spirit-familiars, the success of the practitioner depends largely upon the strength of his familiar; but no matter how powerful the familiar may be it will not perform for a practitioner who does not feed it frequently and plentifully.

*Treatment.* The Siuai practice many kinds of treatment for illnesses and other physical disabilities. Some treatments are more or less "scientific" and consist of bone-setting or of the administration of emetics, purges, and soothing unguents. Others involve the use of medicines believed to be "intrinsically" curative; while still other treatments depend upon the assistance of supernatural beings acting by themselves or through the medium of "consecrated" medicines.

For most ailments there are specific cures which are owned by individuals, who practice for fees except when the patient is a close relative. Individuals may acquire the capacity to practice curing either by gift or by purchase. If the cure consists merely of the use of intrinsically potent medicines, then it is only necessary to acquire knowledge of the ingredients. But if the cure involves the aid of "consecrated" medicines, then the novice must be brought into rapport with the ghosts of specialists who formerly practiced the cure in question. These ghosts may then be expected to render more effective the "consecrated" medicines with which the patient is treated.

If a victim is found to have poison in his body a magician is called in to extract and neutralize it. If it is a spirit-attracting poison the magician will first drive away any attacking spirit by bespitting it with a betel and medicine mixture. Then, while the magician's own spirit-familiar works from the inside of the victim's body, the magician himself massages or fans the body to bring the offending poison to the surface, where he picks it off and neutralizes it. Plain poisons can be neutralized by mixing them with water, with spittle, or with ashes, but ghost-consecrated poisons require powerful medicines (*hurx*) to neutralize them. In the case of a ghost-consecrated poison hidden nearby but not actually inside the victim (*naraipu, rakana,* etc.), the countermeasure consists in finding the offending poison and then neutralizing it. The magician called in to do this is led to the hiding place by his own spirit-familiar.

Victims of "dirt" sorcery may be cured only by rescuing their captured exuviae and disposing of it in a neutralizing place, such as ashes, fresh water, etc. However, if the exuviae have been fed to an eel-demon (*kamaŋu*) then there is no way of retrieving it.

Against some other afflictions there is likewise no treatment. For example, if a person fishes in a pool tabooed by its owner with leprosy-bamboo (*rohku*), nothing can stay the course of the resulting illness. Even if the owner himself forgets and fishes there without first removing the bamboo, he too will succumb. Again, if a man pledges by any spirit to abide by a contract (e.g., to repay a debt) and then fails to live up to the contract, nothing can stop the spirit from killing him.

*Vengeance.* The Siuai are seldom content to leave a magical attack unavenged, so that vengeance magic is the almost invariable accompaniment to diagnosis and treatment of such an attack. Vengeance techniques are based on the principles underlying "cursing" and "dirt" magic (see above). For example, if a pig is found dead its owner may employ mandible-magic (*kanapuru*) to destroy its killer. He will deposit the pig's jawbone at a place made dangerous by "angry" ghosts (i.e., the ghosts of slain warriors and sorcery victims) and these ghosts will lure the soul of the pig's killer, together with those of his matrilineage mates, to the deadly place, thereby destroying the culprit and his matrilateral relatives. The same technique is sometimes used with jawbones of humans believed killed by sorcery.

"Dirt" sorcery may be used to avenge theft of a pig. Every domesticated pig is marked by cutting a piece out of its ear; this is not an ownership brand but rather a warning to thieves. The portion of the ear is kept by the owner and if his pig is stolen he will feed the portion to an eel-demon, with the result that the thief eventually dies.

In the case of death by sorcery, mirina magic may be used for vengeance as well as for divination (see above). The mirina-magician's familiars not only single out the sorcerer but they overcome his soul as well. This is also true of the theft-divination magic called tukuveroro (see above).

One feature common to most techniques of vengeance magic is that they destroy not only the culprit but his matrilineage mates as well, and usually the actual culprit is the last one to die.

Nearly every one of the many magical techniques just described has its specialist practitioners. Some natives, for example, specialize only in discovering the identity of sorcerers, others cure specific ailments, still others drive away malicious demons; nearly all of these practitioners base their powers upon control of functionally specialized spirits. The mikai, on the other hand, is something of a general practitioner of magic. Each mikai has a spirit-familiar — usually the ghost of a relative — which helps him to divine the causes of misfortune, restore captured souls, remove poisons from victims' bodies, trap and destroy the souls of thieves, etc. In all these enterprises the technique is quite simple: the mikai merely bids his familiar to carry out the task. His success depends upon the effectiveness of his familiar and the amount of control he is able to exercise over it. The ghost of a successful mikai makes the most effective kind of familiar, but such a creature demands frequent food offerings from his master.

How do these various magical specialists acquire their controls over spirits or supernaturally charged materials and actions? Here are the main sources of their powers:

1. A ghost or demon selects some native to associate with, or a native purchases a familiar from another magician. The familiar remains faithful to its human associate so long as the latter "sacrifices" to it (*tuputupu-* is the verb root for this kind of spirit-feeding).

2. A would-be "dirt" sorcerer selects some localized and malevolent ghost or demon and binds it to service by sacrificing to it (*kamukamu-* is the verb root for this kind of spirit-feeding).

3. A native who wishes to become a specialist in the use of ghost-consecrated materials (including matrilineage growth magic, maru) first acquires knowledge of the techniques and the ingredients from an expert practitioner — by purchase or otherwise. Sometimes some of the ingredients themselves are transferred to the novice, thereby providing a physical identity of ingredients among all practitioners of the technique, living and dead. Then the expert secures rapport between the novice and the ghosts identified with the ingredients by placing the ingredients in the novice's hand and popping his finger joints, meanwhile calling upon the ghosts to serve the new master. In some cases the potency of the rapport is so strong as to be dangerous to the practitioner if maintained continuously; he consequently breaks contact after each performance and resumes it only when he wishes to perform again. There are numerous methods of resuming rapport, including finger-joint popping, or tapping on ingredients with a special stone adze; and these gestures are usually accompanied by repetition of a verbal formula. Conversely, breaking contact is accomplished by washing the hands in a neutralizing solution (water, ashes, etc.) or by "head-rounding." Head-rounding (*k̯i'isaku*) is performed by circling the head with an areca nut which is then broken open and thrown away; the participating ghosts are thereby released from the body of the native and scattered along with the areca nut.

4. A native who wishes to employ intrinsically potent materials or actions purchases them or the knowledge of how to use them from successful practitioners. Occasionally natives "discover" new practices of this nature, either as a result of dreams or of alleged communication with spirits, but most such practices are considered to have been invented by the kupunas or are said to have been introduced from neighboring peoples.

## BELIEFS ABOUT NATURE AND MAN

Up to now we have been mainly describing magical practices having to do with bodily welfare or bodily adversity. There are also whole complexes of magic aimed at achieving success in economic enterprises and in social relations, including love affairs; and there are almost as many magical techniques for frustrating the enterprises of rivals and enemies without causing them actual bodily harm. However, the magical principles involved in all these practices are the same as those just listed. For example, garden magic (*maki*) consists of the use of ghost-consecrated ingredients planted in the sacred corner of the taro patch. The life of a failing pig may be prolonged like the life of a dying human, by the intrinsically potent means of magical knot-tying (see above, page 89). Hunting spears may be rendered deadly by rubbing their points with intrinsically dangerous items, with "angry" insects and nettles, et cetera. Conversely, an adversary's garden may be ruined by inducing a spirit-familiar to shrivel the plants growing there. An enemy's pigs may be driven feral — i.e., into the forest — by feeding them roots found in the heart of the forest. A rival's feast may be rained out by placing a rainstick under water. These and numerous other magical techniques used by the Siuai for controlling their natural and social universe will be described in chapters to follow, but enough has been said above to indicate the kind of logic underlying all such beliefs and practices. Summarizing, here are some of the more important canons of this logic:

1. Entities having similar appearances, sounds, tastes, odors, and actions *are* identical in some respects and produce identical effects. (This is the well-known magical principle of Association.)

2. The essential essence of an entity may be present in all its parts, and any effect produced in a part may affect the whole.

3. An entity and its name are identical in some respects, and utterance of a name can in some instances produce effects in the entity named.

4. Effects can be produced in an entity by bringing it into contact (real or imagined) with another entity.

5. Unusual, exceptional entities and actions are particularly efficacious.

6. "After this, therefore an account of it." (*Post hoc, ergo propter hoc.*)

Anyone acquainted with ethnographic literature will recognize these canons as being well-nigh universal; it is only the whole content of the derivative beliefs and practices that is peculiarly Siuai.

In closing this section we should not leave the impression that the Siuai are entirely magic-ridden. It is true that many of their beliefs and actions are based on premises that scientifically minded westerners would term "illogical"; but it is also true that they use the logic of empiricism in much of their thinking and acting. For one thing, they regard many mishaps as having natural causation; and in case of some misfortunes, while recognizing both natural and supernatural causation, they pay little heed to the latter and proceed to set things right by using rational measures.

*Property.* Siuai natives live on land, use scarce material objects, perform services, learn and utilize certain esoteric kinds of knowledge, acquire certain valued action-prerogatives, compete for renown, and so on; and the relations between Siuai natives and these and other *scarce goods*[60] can be considered from many points of view — technological, ecological, etc. For the moment, however, our focus will be on Siuai beliefs about their nature as *property*, i.e., entities in which one kind of social unit is recognized as holding "quasi-exclusive and limiting connections" vis-à-vis other social units.[61]

The first question to arise is: what kinds of entities are considered to be *property*? According to Siuai beliefs and practices, all territory is property, including the deepest forests and the most uninviting swamps. Along the eastern and western borders of Siuai the territories of Motuna-speaking natives abut directly on those of *Rugara, Banoni,* and *Siri* speakers, there being no no-man's land between. Even toward the northern forests that extend uninhabited for many miles up to the mountain settlements of the eastern Nagovisi and the Nasioi, Siuai natives assert claims of ownership. It is only the ocean, in the south, that is not owned in one way or another.

Similarly, nearly all corporeal objects constitute property — soil, fresh water, and things resting or living on or in them; and, of course, all useful or potentially useful objects are very explicitly owned. Ownership may even be asserted toward such harmful objects as snakes and nettles — I recorded one instance of a man bringing suit against a neighbor for cutting down some nettles growing in his territory; the plaintiff agreed that the nettles were useless but added that, "they are nevertheless mine." (I did not, however, note any landowner objecting to a visitor killing mosquitoes or flies!)

The Siuai resemble many other Pacific Islanders in their conception of separable property units. Distinctions are made between territory and improvements; for example, a native may have full title to a coconut palm or a house on territory in which he enjoys only provisional rights of occupation or access. Similarly, the owner of a territory may transfer provisional rights to another to garden on his territory while retaining full title to an edible bird killed by the tenant in his garden.

With respect to *knowledge*, only that having to do with the performance of certain magical rituals is regarded as *property* in the sense used herein; these include growth magic (maru), which is normally performed only by members of the owning sib, and all those magical rites learned and practiced for personal advantage or profit. Myths, even including sib myths, are not owned in any exclusive manner, and the same is true of the knowledge of technological skills. Anyone may recount any myths; and the skilled ropemaker, gardener, etc., is usually pleased to explain his superior techniques to whoever will bother to listen.

## BELIEFS ABOUT NATURE AND MAN 95

Entire persons are not conceived as being single property units — no Siuai has exclusive rights over all of his own functions nor does any social unit possess exclusive rights over all of the functions of any person — but many separable functions of persons (and spirits!) are conceived to be property, subject to recognized forms of transactions and social restrictions on use. For example, husband and wife own more or less exclusive use-rights in each other's sexual activities, normatively at least; and at marriage they also contract to perform certain other services on each other's behalf. Or, a specialist sells his services like any other commodity. Or again, ambitious men go to great lengths to obtain recognition from their fellows in the form of a certain kind of *praise* which in Siuai is most definitely a scarce good, varying in value according to the rank of the praiser.

Other nonmaterial entities also figure as property. For example, the right to the title of mumi — i.e., a man of *renown* (potu), a leader — is accorded to very few men, and these men work hard to guard and enhance the value of their title, as they do with regard to any other highly valued possession.

The list of entities conceived by the Siuai to be property will be extended and amplified in later chapters, where some attention will also be devoted to the subject of equivalences in valuation, but enough has been said for the moment to indicate that Siuai beliefs are highly specific concerning the nature of property and very broad concerning the range of property entities.

Type of ownership [62] is varied. In addition to individuals, every kind of group and nearly every kind of culturally meaningful aggregate [63] of persons in Siuai owns property. The most notable exception is the aggregate composed of *all* Siuai, there being no item of property which all of them together own exclusively. Even neighborhoods are owning entities in at least the one respect that all the members of any one of them share tacit rights to use paths within the neighborhood territory; the reality of these neighborhood rights becomes very clear when viewed against the attitude toward trespass by outsiders.

Social units of course vary widely in the relative importance attached to their property-owning aspect, with neighborhoods having the least and matrilineages the most exclusive and explicitly recognized property-owning characteristics.

The Siuai implicitly recognize three types of title — *full, residual,* and *provisional.* The rights, privileges, etc., associated with each type of title vary with the kind of property and, in certain cases, with the type of transaction which gave rise to the title. These matters will be treated later on in detail in appropriate contexts; for the present it should be sufficient to point out that while *full* title obtains frequently with respect to movable material items it rarely applies to the ownership of land.

Another circumstance which should be mentioned in this introductory account of property is the internal differentiation of property rights among members of any property-owning social unit. While it is true that some of these units may function as *corporations*[64] when dealing with outsiders in property matters, among the members themselves property rights differ according to status.

These many fine distinctions in ownership are reflected scarcely at all in specific linguistic forms. In Motuna, ownership is expressed either by use of pronominal prefixes or by use of separate possessive pronouns usually standing before the word for the entity owned. The pronominal prefix is invariably used in connection with kinship and quasi-kinship terms,[65] and frequently in connection with words meaning place, e.g., "home" (*uri*), "garden" (*koh*). In all other instances the separate possessive pronoun is used:

| Singular | Plural |
|---|---|
| *ŋom* = my, mine (male speaking) | *nonnikom* = our, ours (exclusive) |
| *ŋana* = my, mine (female speaking) | *nekom* = our, ours (inclusive) |
| *rokom* = thy, thine | *rekom* = your, yours |
| *pokom* = his, her, its | *pekom* = their, theirs |

## TIME, SPACE, AND NUMBER

Time itself does not "pass" for the Siuai; there is no concept of an independent and inexorable ticking away of moments. Events rather than clocks and calendars provide sequential frames of reference for these natives.

One such frame we have called "ecological time." As previously noted the only seasonal phenomenon which is importantly reflected in Siuai habits and expressions is the annual ripening of canarium almonds. It will be recalled that almonds are indispensable ingredients in the fine puddings prepared for feasts, hence feast-giving tends to increase during the three or four months after almond harvesting. It is these considerations that have led the Siuai to translate the pidgin term *Karisimasi* (i.e., "Christmas" or "Year") as *moi* (canarium almond). The more westernized natives now occasionally use *moi* when referring to someone's age or to some event in the past, but I feel reasonably certain that it is a new concept. Like the Christian "week" (*sande*), however, it is coming to have more influence in Siuai lives.

The appearance of the new moon is greeted with the beating of slit gongs throughout Siuai, but this is done to discourage that sharp-pointed demon from ruining growing coconuts[66] rather than to herald the beginning of a new time cycle. The Siuai do recognize some kind of relationship between lunar and menstrual cycles — a menstruating female is described as "going to the moon" — but they do not reckon time in moons; in fact, informants differed widely in their estimate of the number of days in a lunar cycle. Nevertheless, the moon is something of a time-marker; now and then natives say that such-and-such an event will take place "when the moon is full" or "when the moon is new."

The day (*ru*) is the most important time unit, and each day is divided into several periods:

## BELIEFS ABOUT NATURE AND MAN

*kiakia*, dawn
*kurivakumui*, sunrise, "it-begins-to-be-hot"
*koŋkoŋno*, midmorning, "time-for-walking-about," (i.e., for going to gardens, etc.)
*ra rera*, midday, "sun overhead"
*ra pirukori*, midafternoon, "sun turns-to-(go) downwards"
*ri'inunno*, late afternoon
*huruŋi ohkuna tokinoku*, sunset, "the spirit, Huru, is-drying (his) hat"
*motumo*, darkness, night.

Formerly, say the Siuai, there was no night:

> A long time ago there was only day in Siuai; there was no night and people used to eat continually. When two leaders noticed this they became concerned and said to their followers:
> "Hey, all of you. If we have only day we'll eat all the time and soon use up all our food. So you four over there go to Tupi and buy some darkness for us. [Tupi is a land to the north, high up on the slopes of the mountains in the territory of the Nasioi; viewed from Siuai this point on the horizon frequently appears dark and threatening, which may explain its link with night-darkness.] Then we can set aside a special time for eating and not go on eating continually."
> The four sent on this mission were Lightning-bug, Frog, Coconut-beetle, and Rera, a man-like kupuna. Arriving in Tupi they purchased a leaf package of darkness and started out on the long journey towards home, with Lightning-bug carrying the package. As they walked along the other three became curious to see what manner of thing darkness is, and they urged Lightning-bug to open the package.
> "No," he told them, "If we open the package darkness will cover everything and we won't be able to see our way home."
> But the others kept urging Lightning-bug and he finally gave in and untied the package. At that, darkness escaped and spread over the ground. Being unable to see anything Frog hopped about until he broke off his ears against a bush and became lost in the forest, and that is why frogs have no ears and remain hidden in the forest today. Coconut-beetle also flew about in panic and became lost after breaking off his nose on a hillside, and that is why coconut-beetles have broken noses today. Rera became lost but finally sat down to rest and turned into a stone, which now sits near the village of Morokaimoro. Lightning-bug, however, safely found his way home because he carried a light on his tail. And that was the way night was brought to Siuai.

The introduction of night may have helped the Siuai to fix upon a time to eat and sleep but it did not succeed in regulating all their other activities so strictly! It is true that most natives spend at least part of the forenoon at some constructive labor, but the time for beginning (*koŋkoŋno*) ranges from seven to eleven, depending upon the task and the individual. Also, throughout the day they nap whenever opportunity arises and make haste almost never at all. Times for the beginning of work-bees or feasts or ceremonies may sometimes be announced as "very early" (*kiakia meŋ*, dawn true) or "at noon itself" (*ra rera meŋ*, sun is exactly overhead), etc., but this attempt at precision has little effect on times of arrival, which usually straggle out over three or four hours. Either the language as constituted cannot be made explicit with respect to time, or the Siuai have so little awareness of the passage of time, and place so little value on time regularity, that no amount of precise comprehension could make them punctual; I suspect that all three of these factors enter in. With respect to their lack of time-awareness, I noted many occasions of individuals setting out on enterprises without rational consideration of the time element involved. For example, men would set out on journeys to known places too late in the day and would be placed in the fearful circumstance of having to walk in darkness. Or again, in connection with cremations the ideal is that the last embers of the burning pyre will die out just as dawn appears; but even using the morning star as a guide for lighting the pyre, according to my observations they were never able to cause the two events to coincide.

Towards the whole day as a unit, however, the Siuai have learned to express more precision, with the aid of a tally (*mitamita*). In setting a date for, say, a feast, the host sends to each of his principal guests a palm frond having a number of leaves equal to the number of days before the feast. Thereafter, the host and his guests tear off one leaf each day to mark the passage of time before the feast.

One aspect of "ecological time" which deserves special comment is the gardening cycle.[67] The method used by gardeners to replant a plot approximately every six years was described above. However, the Siuai do not measure the elapsed time; in fact, they do not describe the duration of the interval in terms of time. The criterion for replanting an old garden site is rather the size of the secondary growth there.

"History" provides a sense of time, a sequential frame of reference, for many peoples, but the Siuais' concept of history has little resemblance to that of the western historian. Their cosmogonic myths refer to an epoch when the kupunas walked about creating things, but there is no conceptualization of how long ago these events took place beyond dating them as *u'kisa*, "a long time ago." In one sense this epoch may be thought of as extending into the present, inasmuch as acts of creation are still taking place. On the other hand, most Siuai conceive of the age of creation as having had a definite ending, if not a beginning; and after the close of that epoch things were more or less "straight" — for a while, at least. The present epoch, that of mankind, followed the age of creation, although some human beings were already present when the kupunas were walking about. Some missionized individuals now speak of a Judgment Day, which will mark the end of the present epoch, but there is no concept of this sort in native Siuai belief.

With respect to actual events Siuai memories are quite short. A few exceptional old people are able to recall the names of lineal and collateral relatives six generations back, but most natives can extend their genealogies only four generations and even then they remember only matrilineal kin that far removed in time.⁶⁸ Each maru (growth-magic) formula contains a long list of former sib, sub-sib, or matrilineage members who used to perform the ritual, but these names are not considered to be linked in any specific genealogical manner.

Many elderly Siuai are able to describe events said to have taken place as far back as the childhood of their parents. The kinds of incidents best remembered had to do with warfare, epidemics, and contacts with aliens. Beyond that, however, the historic past is a blank.

A third kind of sequential frame of reference which might conceivably have led the Siuai to adopt some time scale is the individual's life cycle. But here again there is no regular measure, since age is phrased in terms of activity and physical criteria and not of years. Moreover, even physically evaluated age-progression is not formalized in terms of age-grade institutions, nor is socio-political rank closely correlated with age.

Turning now to language, the Siuai express temporal sequence by the use of adverbs and verb tense. U'kisa means "a long time ago," while "later" or "in the future" is expressed by romokisa; these, then, express relative sequence only. Rirokisa, on the other hand, specifically means "present" (or "new"). There are also special terms for "yesterday," "today," "tomorrow"; for "two (or three, four, etc.) days hence" and "two (or three, four, etc.) days ago" — however, I did not once hear a Siuai date events in terms of moons, and only rarely in terms of the new concept of "year."

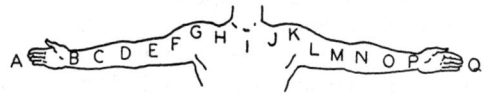

FIGURE 13

The distance A to B is called *kumoputo*
"        "        A to C   "     *hoŋomirumiru*
"        "        A to D   "     *ho'rorime*
"        "        A to E   "     *monikoŋ hoŋomaku*, "(the place where a) female (wears her) arm-band"
"        "        A to F   "     *hoŋomaku*, "(the place where a) male (wears his) arm-band"
"        "        A to G   "     *ukurahano*, "place for carrying things"
"        "        A to H   "     *kuiukonoui*, "place for carrying timber"
"        "        A to I   "     *tusinni*
"        "        A to J   "     *ku'kurua*
"        "        A to K   "     *mukonna*
"        "        A to L   "     *morokeŋkuho*
"        "        A to M   "     *monikoŋ hoŋomakuruho*
"        "        A to N   "     *ho'rorimeruho*
"        "        A to O   "     *hoŋomirumiruruho*
"        "        A to P   "     *kumoputoruho*
"        "        A to Q   "     *nori*

Verb tense permits the Motuna-speaker to be more precise. A Motuna verb consists of a bound morpheme base (indicating kind of action) plus bound affixes specifying, when appropriate: mode, tense, voice, person, number, and gender of subject and complement. Tense may be *remote past, recent past, present,* and *future;* and aspect may be action either *completed, habitual,* or *durative.*

The Siuai measure some kinds of distances much more precisely than they measure time. The span is the unit of measure, and it is used to lay out garden plots, floor plans, timber dimensions, etc. When purchasing goods worth less than one span of shell money or when measuring the girth of a pig, fractions of a span can be designated as shown in the accompanying illustration (Figure 13).

However, the span is used only for measuring lengths of garden-plot size or smaller; there are no unit measures applied to greater lengths and distances. Beyond the scope of span measurement, expressions about proximity and distance are bound up with sociological factors; for example, natives tend to judge their distance from another settlement by the nature of their relationships with people living there.

There is no evidence that a Siuai's feeling of personal security is dependent upon his ability to maintain directional orientation (as, for example, is reported for the Balinese), but *directions* do play an important part in communication. "North" (*rano*), "east" (*poŋo*), "south" (*ronno*), and "west" (*rino*) are widely used in all conversations and narrations—for example: "You-to-the-north come here-to-the-south"; "Leave it over-here-westwards"; "Tie that northward-lying thatch to that eastward-stretching rafter." And because of the location of Siuai, "north" and "south" have also the meaning of "upstream" and "downstream," respectively.

*Number* receives extraordinary proliferation in Motuna. As noted, verbs may be affixed to express number (singular, dual, plural) of both subject and complement, and other linguistic form classes are also inflected according to number, for example, my-father, thy-and-my-mothers (plural), their (plural)-two-elder-brothers, your (plural)-place, my-places, etc. In the absence of an abstract numeration system the form class which most nearly resembles nouns in the English language may be divided into some forty sub-classes on the basis of the forms of numerical adjectives which are used to qualify them.[69] However, the *pattern* of numeration is the same in nearly all cases:

1. *one*
2. *two*
3. *three*
4. *four*
5. *five* (*aŋumuka,* "hand-like," for nearly all sub-classes)
6. *one-towards-ten*
7. *two-towards-ten*

8. *three-towards-ten*
9. *four-towards-ten*
10. *ten*
11. *one-towards-twenty*
12. *two-towards-twenty*, et cetera
16. *one-towards-ten-towards-twenty*, et cetera
20. *twenty*, et cetera
50. *fifty*
60. *ten-towards-one-hundred*
61. *one-towards-ten-towards-one-hundred*, et cetera
100. *one-hundred* (same form for nearly all sub-classes)
101. *one-(and) one-hundred*, et cetera
106. *one-towards-ten-(and) one-hundred*, et cetera
200. *two-hundred* (same form for nearly all sub-classes), et cetera
1000. *one-thousand* ("one-chicken")

In nearly all cases, each set of numerical adjectives may be used for cardinal and ordinal numeration.

Potentially, then, it is possible for a Siuai to talk precisely in terms of, say, the 22nd house, 178 coconut palms, or 1000 leaves. In actual usage, however, these natives seldom number most items past *ten*, the general qualifier "many" (*ponna*) is specific enough for most uses, except for such entities as pigs, sheets of thatch, shell money, and other items which are commonly utilized in large numbers. Because of frequent use as a general standard of value, the set of numerical adjectives used to qualify spans of shell money occurs very frequently in utterances; and the set used to qualify certain hard and roundish items (shell-money discs, areca nuts, etc.) functions almost as an abstract numeration system because of the frequency of talk about large numbers of such items.

CHAPTER 3

# *Social Units*

## DEFINITIONS

Let us now look at Siuai from another vantage point, and survey the more important kinds of social units found there. To begin with, it will be useful to differentiate three kinds of social units: *group, gathering,* and *aggregate.*

*Group*: a combination of individuals who interact with one another face-to-face, with some frequency over a period of time, according to hierarchic patterns of interaction and as a discrete unit (i.e., while they are thus interacting with each other, the events involving each other have a more frequent occurrence than events with other individuals outside the combination).[1] This is the sociologists' "primary group," and refers of course to the smaller face-to-face social units of most societies. For the sake of terminological precision we might reserve the term "secondary" group for those larger social units like the United States Navy or the American Anthropological Association, *all* of whose members never interact with one another face-to-face, but who are nevertheless interrelated in hierarchic patterns of interaction. In this sense, there are no secondary groups in Siuai, so we can safely and unambiguously drop the qualifying term "primary" when characterizing Siuai "groups."

*Gathering*: a combination of individuals interacting face-to-face but non-recurrently. An example from American society would be four talkative strangers accidentally placed at the same table in a crowded restaurant. Situations like this occur much less frequently in Siuai than in the United States. In Siuai one could describe as a *gathering* the large numbers of people from near and far who troop to an important court hearing; some are of course directly concerned but others are present out of idle curiosity, and the most apparent factor which interrelates all of them is their chance gathering and interaction in the club-house where the case is argued.

*Aggregate*: a social unit composed of individuals sharing characteristics believed to link them together into a culturally significant unit, but not necessarily interrelated by hierarchic interaction patterns which include *all* of them and *only* them. An example of an *aggregate* in United States society would be "Veterans": they all share the characteristic of having served in the armed forces at one time or another and they are a culturally significant category to advertisers and politicians; but all of them do not participate in face-to-face interaction. Nor do they all together constitute any kind of separate organization — neither the American Legion nor the Veterans of Foreign Wars includes all American veterans in its membership. Siuai society also contains *aggregates*, and it is important to distinguish them from other kinds of social units.

It will be apparent that two entirely different kinds of operations have been used to differentiate these three types of social units: gatherings and groups being defined in terms of interaction data, and aggregates in terms of symbolic data. However, groups differ from gatherings in terms of both quantity and pattern of interaction.

*Social dyads* also constitute important elements in a cultural anthropologist's data universe. For this writer's purposes, a social dyad is defined as a combination of two persons who interact in a patterned manner. Some dyads constitute whole *groups* (e.g., a childless married couple) or parts of groups (e.g., a pair of brothers in a family), while other dyads may not (e.g., a pair of friends from separate families and villages, or a pair of allied chiefs of separate political units).

Anthropologists are more often concerned with dyads, groups, and aggregates than with gatherings. Oceanists in particular have to do with aggregates (e.g., fictitious kin units consisting of persons claiming common descent), but their main concern is with dyads and with primary face-to-face groups rather than with the larger secondary groups characteristic of many African societies.

We are now in a position to list and briefly characterize the principal kinds of Siuai *groups* and *aggregates*. Consider first of all the Siuai people as a whole: what kind of unit do they constitute?

## "TRIBE"

Their possession of a common language might lead one to expect that *all* Motuna speakers are bound together in a tribal organization. This however is not the case. They do not all together coöperate with one another in any kind of common enterprise, nor are they united in any sort of separate hierarchy.

Moreover, all Siuai do not act together to utilize the land; nor as far as I know did they ever fight together to defend tribal borders. In fact, among the natives themselves there is a fuzziness about the boundaries of Siuai. Inhabitants of northeast Siuai refer to the Mivo River as being the boundary between Siuai and Terei; but this is a mere convenience of speech. The fact is that there was until recently a community of Terei living at Mokuropa (Mogurova, in the language of the Terei) about a mile and a half west of the river. Further, Siuai and Terei natives from "border" villages intermarry freely, and most of them are bilingual. In the past it was not at all unusual for a Siuai and a Terei community to band together to raid and lay waste another Siuai settlement. And elsewhere, in the southwestern part of the Motuna language area, the Siuai living there interact more freely with their Banoni-speaking neighbors and share more interests with them than they do with people from other parts of Siuai.

All this, however, does not preclude the possibility that there may some day develop a tribal political organization accompanied by explicitly expressed identification between tribe and territory. There is some evidence that such a development is now taking place.

When young men go away to work on plantations, they are brought into contact with natives from all parts of the Island, but they associate as much as possible with their "one-talks" (pidgin, for *language-mates*); and some plantation managers intensify this by housing all Siuai in one dormitory, all Terei in another, etc. Consequently, there develops an appreciation of cultural unity and a consciousness of kind which is hardly possible at home.

The nearest approach to an expression of sentiment about "tribal" land which I heard was contributed by a returned laborer. He had been employed in the gold fields of New Guinea and on the Sepik River, and told me how happy he had been to return home — away from all the miserable upland grass plains and the soggy, mosquito-ridden swamps: "Our own Siuai forests are good — the source of all desirable things: of food and game and building materials. Only madmen would choose to live elsewhere!"

There is a possibility that some energetic native may some day outrank all other Siuai by winning out in the feast competitions now going on (see below). If and when that does take place, something akin to "tribal" political organization may emerge; at the present time, however, the Siuai all together constitute an aggregate and not a group.

## GROUPS

*Households* are the most important kind of Siuai group from the standpoint of quantity of interaction. The household is the principal residential and subsistence unit. Members sleep together in their own house and preserve a high degree of privacy. Most households also act separately to produce and consume their own food and many other basic economic essentials. The number of individuals in households varies from a lone bachelor or widower to a married couple with several offspring and one or two other adherent relatives; in other words, most households correspond to the *nuclear family*, at some stage or other in its cyclical development. There are no separate Motuna terms for "household" or "nuclear family"; in fact the symbolic aspects of these groupings are relatively undeveloped. Yet, from the standpoint of the individual, the family-household is far and away the most influential kind of group in his life; in it most of his biological needs are satisfied and his personality largely shaped.

The Siuai *hamlet* is a residence community made up of from two to nine households all of which are within a quarter of a mile of each other and easily accessible by paths — that is to say, they are not separated by difficult barriers such as large rivers, cliffs, or swamps. This is not an arbitrary definition: hamlets are interaction *groups*, in the sense of the definition given above; and the Siuai themselves recognize the existence of hamlets and give all of them names or such identifying marks as "the houses on such and such a tract of land." In some instances, the members of a hamlet coöperate in producing food and in other work activities. Invariably, the members congregate to talk and play, and they usually rally to one another's side in times of crisis. There are usually one or two persons of authority in each hamlet, but further generalizations about relations among hamlet members are not possible at this stage since the membership patterns of hamlets are so widely variable.[2]

*Work teams* constitute another kind of Siuai group: in many places natives habitually and voluntarily unite with neighbors and relatives to engage in coördinated production and construction enterprises such as land clearing (for gardening), sago processing, almond gathering, fishing, hunting, and house building. There is little technological necessity for work teams; most households can and do independently satisfy their own subsistent needs, or they may unite with other households in their own hamlet for such purposes. It is only in the case of large-scale fish or game drives that the efforts of numbers of individuals — more than can be found in a single household or hamlet — must be coördinated to carry out properly the traditional economic techniques. Even the largest club-house *could* be constructed by members of a single hamlet working alone.

Work teams vary greatly in size, in frequency of operation, and in degree of coördination; and they are much more characteristic of some neighborhoods than of others — for reasons which will be discussed in later chapters.

Siuai males also associate to prepare feasts, and by frequent repetition of such events the participants develop customary ways of interacting and some consciousness of group unity. Spatial contiguity is one basis for membership in this kind of unit, but such a unit is more than an aggregation of males who happen to be neighbors; it is an organized group, a hierarchy of leader and followers. Unlike many men's societies in Melanesia, this one requires no formal initiation; as soon as a boy leaves women's company and begins to frequent club-houses and participate in activities there, he is accepted as a member. Male exclusiveness is emphasized in many ways; for example, the club-house demon kills any female who goes too near.

Leadership in a men's society depends upon an individual's ability to mobilize his relatives, friends, and neighbors to help him give feasts. In this fashion the leader establishes and reinforces his *effective authority*[3] over members of his men's society and at the same time acquires public renown (potu) through his largesse. In former days leadership in a men's society probably also depended upon the leader's ability to organize and conduct raids, but now the emphasis is on feasts.

The leader has certain rights and obligations. His house is frequently larger than average, but his diet is no better. He is relieved of the onerous tasks of climbing palms and carrying heavy burdens, but he continues to work in his garden. He is treated with respect and deference wherever he goes, but in return must be a generous host. He frequently calls upon his followers to labor for him, but should repay their efforts with pork meals. Nowadays, he has no armed force to back up his orders, but he can control the opinions of most of his followers and thereby make life fairly unpleasant for a disobedient one. And, on top of all this, he has some supernatural sanction for his position.

Mention was made in Chapter 1 of the action taken by the Australian authorities in consolidating hamlets into "line villages," to simplify administrative control, improve public health, and "bring about friendlier relations among the natives" (see page 15). The authorities selected one man from each village to be headman, another to be official interpreter, and a third to be medical orderly. The headman is responsible to the Administration for maintaining "public order"[4] in his village, for keeping the village clean and adequately fenced (against pigs), for maintaining a section of the Administration trail, for providing porters to carry officials' baggage, and for assembling village residents for the annual census-taking and head-tax collection. The interpreter acts as the headman's assistant and interpreter, and the medical orderly, after some training in first aid, doles out Administration quinine, cough medicine, bandages, etc. For more effective control the Australian Administration divided Siuai into three administrative districts and placed a Paramount Chief and a Head Interpreter in charge of each district, with direct authority over the village officials.

Behind all of these native administrative officials ("Hat-men") stands the full power of the Australian Administration as personified by the white Patrol Officer stationed at Kangu, some twenty miles by road from the southeast boundary of Siuai, and in charge of all of southern Bougainville. Backed by a squad of native police constables, the Patrol Officer has the authority to jail and fine natives; while his superior, the Bougainville District Officer, headquartered at Kieta, has the authority to decide and mete out capital punishment. Hence, the native officials at the village level stand in positions to exercise some control over all natives in their villages. In some cases the Administration has had insight or good fortune enough to appoint actual *leaders* to the posts of headman. Elsewhere natives have been appointed headmen because of their knowledge of pidgin, their neat appearance, or their alacrity in carrying out whites' instructions, with the result that they do not command their subordinates' respect and are consequently either ineffective or tyrannical.

In 1902 the Roman Catholic Society of Mary set up a mission headquarters at Kieta, on Bougainville's east coast. Since then missionary priests of this Order have penetrated to every part of the Island and have established numerous mission stations including one in Siuai.[5] The Methodist mission has also been active, and for a number of years maintained a station in Siuai.

From these centers mission influence has spread throughout Siuai and most of the native population has been "converted." In nearly every village there is either a Catholic or a Methodist chapel and a native catechist trained at mission headquarters to conduct simple services. In some places both denominations are represented, resulting in competition and even strife.

In addition to belonging to households, hamlets, work teams, men's societies, line villages, and mission congregations, Siuai natives maintain more or less institutionalized pair relationships in the form of trade partnerships, political alliances and rivalries, magician-client connections, and, of course, numerous kinds of kinship and friendship relationships not subsumed under membership in groups. Most households consist of a nuclear family, in some stage of development; and the members of each hamlet group may in most cases be said to constitute a *composite* family in the sense that they are all interrelated by familial ties of one sort or another — otherwise, natives who share extended-family kinship ties but who do not reside together do not constitute a separate group. There is however another kind of social unit which is enormously important in Siuai life; this is the noroukuru.

## MATRILINEAL UNITS

*Sib Fission.* Chapter 2 described the peculiar importance which the Siuai attach to the matrilateral tie. People believed to be so related are members of the same sib and as such share certain taboos, shrines, and rituals, along with special totemic relationships with certain spirits, animals, and plants; in addition, sib-mates are bound by special rules of conduct toward each other. An account was also given of the myths which "explain" how these beliefs and practices came about, thereby enshrining them as dogma. These same myths also "explain" how the sibs came to be ramified into the many branches existing today — the Siuai themselves use the tree-branching metaphor when describing this process. For illustration of this process let us return to the origin myth of the Tree-rat people.[6] In it we learned how two kupuna sisters originated this sib and how they eventually separated, one to become the ancestress of the Belly-fats branch and the other of the Left-behinds. The myth then relates how the Belly-fats became established at Rukruk and the Left-behinds at Kiaman, and how eventually their descendants scattered and founded new branches throughout Siuai. (The Siuai apply the same term, noroukuru, to a whole sib as well as to all its subdivisions. As previously stated, throughout this monograph noroukuru will be used only when it is not possible to speak precisely of sib, sub-sib, or matrilineage.) How do these various subdivisions fit into the social framework of Siuai? Or, to begin with, what kind of social unit is this sib which includes all Tree-rat people? Let us review its characteristics.

All members of this sib regard the giant tree-rat as their primary totem; if one of them should kill or eat one of these animals, even unwittingly, retribution will be swift and automatic in the form of death, there being no effective antidote or penance. All Tree-rats believe themselves interrelated through matrilineal descent from either of the kupuna sisters, Noiha and Korina, who however are not worshiped or prayed to in any way. All of them regard the stones, Rotunoua and Motuna, to be peculiarly associated with their sib history. In addition, all of them consider their kupunas' earlier homes, Sariai and Tuhuhroru, as places of interest, although few have bothered to visit there. All of them also consider one kind of maru magic to be exclusively theirs, the belief being that it was invented by their kupuna ancestresses. Actually the magic formulae which form an essential part of this maru contain references to the sib's mythical history. Further, only Tree-rat magicians can perform Tree-rat maru. All Tree-rat members may refer to one another as imo ("my-sib-mate") in lieu of some more specific kinship term, and they think of themselves as having distinctive palm lines on their hands. No Tree-rat member should have sexual relations with another, and the penalty of death follows automatically unless an antidotal ritual is quickly performed. In one respect only is there, however, any form of coordinated action among Tree-rats as Tree-rats, regardless of other affiliations: every three or four years some influential man will sponsor a Climbing festival for the removal of secondary food restrictions (see above), and on such occasions all those Tree-rats present tend to ascend the eating platform together. Otherwise *all* or even most Tree-rats never congregate and interact. Despite their pious sentiments on the subject of affection and coöperation among sib-mates, they used to kill one another in feuds, and now have no compunctions about competing politically or battling legally among themselves. In other words, all Tree-rat people together constitute an *aggregate* and not a *group*. Following the practice standardized by Murdock, we shall call this kind of aggregate a *matri-sib*.[7]

The major division of the Tree-rat matri-sib is into Belly-fats and Left-behinds; what kind of social units are these?

All Belly-fats believe themselves to be specifically descended from the younger kupuna sister and all Left-behinds from the elder. Further, all

Belly-fats regard the stone, Rukruk, as their special shrine, the ossified embodiment of their original ancestress; Left-behinds, on the other hand, show only polite interest in Rukruk; their special shrine is the cave, Kiaman, where the elder sister disappeared. And finally, all Belly-fats are prohibited from eating fat from the underside of a pig until they have removed the restriction by eating some ceremonially at a Climbing festival; the Left-behinds are not bound by this restriction. This is the extent of the differentiation between these sub-sibs. Furthermore in terms of interaction neither of them constitutes a separate group; and I could discern no community of interests among members of either subdivision beyond the items just mentioned. Again, following Murdock's usage, these divisions of a matri-sib will henceforth be called sub-sibs.[8]

The Belly-fats sub-sib is more widely ramified than that of the Left-behinds, hence will serve our purposes better for illustrating sib branching. It will be recalled how the Belly-fats remained at Rukruk for a while; and later how men from neighboring communities married Belly-fat women and took them to their own homes, thereby bringing about the establishment of numerous branches with locality names: the Rukaruinai, Tumoroku, Ramoi, etc. The members of each of these branches possess a shrine of their own, which usually figures in their performances of the maru ritual; and it is considered desirable although not imperative that maru rituals of, say, a Tumoroku should be performed by a Tumoroku magician. Some of these branches also have supplementary food restrictions, from which members can free themselves only by partaking of the food at Climbing. As for interaction, I noticed that members of each of these branches tend to be present at one another's funerals with more regularity than mere neighborliness would prescribe, but neither on these nor on other occasions do they interact as a separate *group*. Moreover, they themselves express no special sentiment of common interests, and some of the most violent personal feuds I uncovered took place between members of this same kind of *aggregate*. In the case of none of these branches can its members trace their common relationships through remembered genealogical links; hence in the interests of consistency we shall call this order of sib branching a sub-sub-sib rather than a lineage[9] — for reasons which may be understood if not forgiven!

What are the relations between these various sub-sub-sib aggregates?

Among the surviving sub-sub-sib branches of the Belly-fats is one whose members call themselves Rukruknai, and on the basis of the mythological evidence this branch would appear to be older than other Belly-fats branches from the generational point of view (See Chapter 2, page 47); otherwise there are neither mythological nor genealogical indications of generational differences among the surviving branches of Belly-fats or the surviving branches of Left-behinds. Nor is the Rukruknais' alleged "seniority" manifested in any other way; it is true that the stone called Rukruk, which is the ossified ancestress of all Belly-fats, is located on land narrowly identified with the Rukruknai people living in that vicinity, but that circumstance gives the Rukruknai people no special rights or duties.

Where Siuai myth leaves off and history begins is of course impossible to discover, and it is also irrelevant in the present context. Here, the important consideration is that generational differences have little or no effect upon the relations among sub-sib and sub-sub-sib segments of the Tree-rat sib. In other words, the relations could be described diagrammatically as shown in Figure 14.

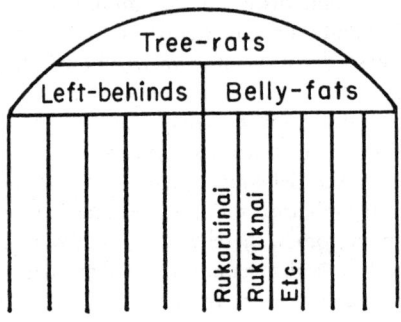

FIGURE 14

Now it is obvious that, as in any society emphasizing unilineal descent, lineage ramification is continually taking place whether it has any cultural significance or not. In Siuai this ramification does have cultural significance up to a point. To use the case of the Rukaruinai sub-sub-sib, which is well known to me: several generations ago two Rukaruinai sisters moved to Mi'kahna to live — but let one of their great-great (matrilineal) grandsons tell the story:

> A long time ago this land was owned by people of the What-is-it-called noroukuru (Eagle sib). These were rich, warlike people, and their land extended from Tohoro Creek to the Mivo River, and from Imarukei to Sipana. One of the What-is-it-calleds, Koura, married my ancestress, Puiri, who lived at Rukarui, and took her to Mi'kahna and reared a family, and when Koura died, Puiri — not wishing to return to Rukarui — induced her sister, Kuhai, to join her at Mi'kahna, and the two of them paid Koura's sub-sib-mates 2000 spans of shell money for full title to Mi'kahna. This transaction was a kind of purchase; just like buying tobacco at a trade store.

Since that day the region has remained in possession of the direct matrilineal descendants of the two sisters except for one short interlude when some What-is-it-called people drove them out and occupied the land. Later on the two sisters' descendants were able to regain it by force of arms, and have held on to it ever since in spite of their encirclement by occasionally unfriendly What-is-it-calleds. Frequently, Mi'kahna Rukanuinai people have

## SOCIAL UNITS

married What-is-it-calleds, but this has not resulted in alienation of their land. These *Mi'kahnanai*, for so they are sometimes called, can trace their interrelationships by remembered genealogical ties; they constitute a *matrilineage*.

Again, generations ago another Rukaruinai woman from Rukarui married a man living at the place now called Turuŋum and went there to live; many of her direct matrilineal descendants are still there, having subsequently acquired large tracts of land and considerable local influence. They are beginning to be referred to as Turuŋonai, and they are able to trace actual genealogical ties with one another.[10] Now neither the Mi'kahnanai nor the Turuŋonai can trace specific genealogical ties between their two branches nor between themselves and any other Rukaruinai; they are, then, separate *matrilineages*, though subdivisions of the same sub-sub-sib. The remaining members of this sub-sub-sib are scattered over the northern part of northeast Siuai and are likewise divided into a number of separate matrilineages, although none of these has yet received a separate name.

Among the Tree-rats a distinct *group* crystallizes at this matrilineage order of segmentation, and matrilineage mates can trace specific genealogical ties to one another through an ancestress usually less than four generations earlier than the oldest living generation. In few cases do all members of any one Tree-rat matrilineage reside in the same hamlet or village — some usually move to other settlements upon marriage — yet they all assemble on occasions to celebrate a maru ritual for one of them, or to gossip together, or mourn. Whenever one of them, or the spouse or offspring of one of them, is seriously ill, other members are sure to be present. They usually assist one another in economic and political enterprises, and seldom compete for renown. Matrilineage mates are considered responsible for one another's welfare in this life and in the next, and it is they who try to compel the family survivors of a deceased member to provide an adequate funeral (see below). The intimate relations among matrilineage mates is symbolized in the belief that if a sorcerer attacks one of them, all the rest will die; in the days of feuding, vengeance wreaked upon the matrilineage mate of an enemy was often as satisfactory as death of the enemy himself.

Nearly every matrilineage possesses its own tomui,[11] the heirlooms of high-value shell money used as accessories and ornaments at rituals and feasts, and disposed of, a handful at a time, in the blazing cremation pyres of deceased members. The heirlooms are guarded by the First-born (Simiri) of the matrilineage, usually the biologically oldest female member, who doles them out for use on ritual and festive occasions and who decides how much may be destroyed at a member's cremation. The origin myth of the Tree-rats contains an account of the manner in which this sib's kupuna ancestresses acquired heirlooms; but today there are no specific heirlooms associated with the whole Tree-rat sib, or with any subdivision larger than a matrilineage; and each matrilineage believes its own heirlooms part of the original hoard.

Heirlooms should not be alienated; any First-born who does so risks death through the active intervention of the ghosts of matrilineage ancestors — one of the few occasions when these spirits as a unit concern themselves in mortal affairs. So closely is a matrilineage's heirloom identified with it that the First-born should bury it rather than allow it to pass into the hands of another group, and this is said to be carried out when the matrilineage contains no more potentially childbearing females.

Even at this order of sib segmentation significant generational differences do not appear between different matrilineages of the same sub-sub-sib. For example, neither the Mi'kahnanai nor the Turuŋonai nor any other Rukarui matrilineage possesses its own separate shrine. Consequently, when a maru ritual is carried out for any matrilineage member, the maru magicians have to obtain some sanctified water from the Rukarui shrine itself. Moreover if one of these matrilineages does not count a maru magician among its own members, one belonging to the matrilineage residing nearest Rukarui is asked to officiate — not, however, as a representative of a "senior" matrilineage but solely as an individual professional who is perhaps more proficient on account of her residence nearer the shrine.

A factor of great importance is the link between matrilineage and land. Shrines and rights of access to them are shared by members of any sib, sub-sib, and sub-sub-sib, but none of those aggregates owns economically valuable land as does the matrilineage group. Every Tree-rat matrilineage corporately owns full or residual title to tracts of arable land, and most matrilineages can also claim such title to forest hunting grounds, sago swamps, and fishing streams. Natives have a sentimental attachment to their matrilineage land, and many insist on dwelling and gardening on it. There are various ways in which matrilineages have come to be identified with specific tracts of land; the account of the Mi'kahnanai (above) provides one example.

My informant, Peuru, one of the Mi'kahnanai, spoke with noticeable pride as he told about episodes which illustrate the cohesion of the little Mi'kahna matrilineage and its close association with their corporately owned land. Every portion of the region means something personal to him and his matrilineage mates: "that is the place where our maternal grandfather saw a snake demon"; "that tree marks the spot where our ancestor speared a trespasser," etc. And their land is not subdivided into individually owned tracts. Each of its matrilineage owners claims joint-ownership of *all* the land. Once when Peuru had a quarrel with his younger brother, U'ta, the latter threatened to divide the land and keep part of it himself; but that threat never materialized, and their landholdings remained undifferentiated.

At the present time Peuru and most of his matrilineage mates — together with their spouses and offspring — dwell on their land, garden on it, take fish from its streams, collect coconuts from its palms, nuts from its almond trees, and sago from its marshes.

The land tenure situation of the Turuŋonai matrilineage differs somewhat. The land identified corporately with this matrilineage is not a large compact region made up of several contiguous tracts, as is the case of the Mi'kahnanai, but consists of several scattered tracts, most of them near the village of Turuŋom. All members of the matrilineage corporately hold full title in these scattered tracts and use them in a manner that amounts to *joint-tenancy*: all members can garden, fish, hunt, or collect nuts in any of these tracts. Also, acting jointly, they can taboo these tracts against all entry and use, and can dispose of them at will; this form of use and disposal constitutes what amounts to the closest approximation to full land title known to the Siuai.

All this land of the Turuŋonai belongs to the matrilineal descendants of Nirai and Parai (Fig. 30, p. 488) but each tract was acquired separately. Nakisi was acquired by a maternal uncle of Soŋi's, Siham's, and Arapa's from the Kopusinnai (Belly-fats) matrilineage in return for providing pigs at the mortuary feast of a prominent Kopusinnai member. Turuŋom tract used to belong to some Left-behinds, but a wealthy Rukaruinai man (not a member of the Turuŋonai matrilineage) by the name of Koiri purchased the tract from them for 1000 spans of shell money, and Turuŋom thus passed to Koiri's matrilineage. Later on, when Opisa, a member of Koiri's matrilineage, was killed by sorcery, the present Turuŋonai member, Soŋi, contributed pigs to his mortuary feast and also killed the sorcerer. In return for this, Opisa's grateful matrilineage mates presented the tract to Soŋi, who in turn explicitly added it to other Turuŋonai holdings. When I questioned Soŋi as to his reason for not keeping the land to himself, he seemed scandalized and replied: "Land is not to be placed in a dark corner of a house like money or almonds; it is property of the matrilineage."

Mitapukori, Mitakunno, and Siŋkunoveino (Fig. 28, p. 485) were acquired by Soŋi and turned over to his matrilineage in much the same fashion.

Kiŋori used to belong to a Legs-apart matrilineage, but was acquired by Siham by contributing pigs to the mortuary feast of a prominent Legs-apart owner, and then added to the Turuŋonai holdings.

Pirui used to belong to a matrilineage of the Kingfisher sib. Soŋi married a woman from that group, and when she died he gave such an overwhelmingly large mortuary feast for her that her matrilineage mates presented Pirui to him, and he then turned it over to his matrilineage.

Northwest Rukarui is a large tract of virgin forest far north of Turuŋom. The Turuŋonai claim full title to it through matrilineage ancestors and now go there to hunt opossums.

Scattered about as these tracts are, the Turuŋonai dwell on some of them part of the time, and they garden, plant coconut palms, and hunt on them. Moreover they do all this *together*. They interact among themselves as do the Mi'kahnanai; and, like the latter, they corporately claim full title to *all* the tracts together and do not differentiate between the various tracts except to describe the several ways in which they were acquired.

It is important to comment on the oft-repeated statement of Soŋi and Siham that all this land will pass intact to their matrilineage descendants. "Why," I asked, "will not other matrilineages acquire portions of it when you die just as you acquired tracts when former owners died?"

"The difference is that *we* are wealthy," they answered. "We are able to provide generous mortuary feasts for ourselves, and need not call upon other matrilineages to contribute; therefore we do not have to throw away our land."

In contrast with these examples of flourishing matrilineages is the case of Nonroki, of Jeku village, who is the sole survivor of a once powerful Tree-rat matrilineage called Itonahupanai. About twenty years ago a head-hunting party annihilated all of Nonroki's matrilineage mates, so that now he alone owns full or residual title to the extensive tracts of Itonahupanai land, on which there are several shrines, extensive palm groves, and many almond trees. When Nonroki dies, his lineage will disappear forever, and the land will pass into other hands, probably his children's.

Tree-rat matrilineages vary in size from one to thirty members, with the mode being 12–20. In all but the smallest ones it is possible to discern even finer social subdivisions consisting of individuals of two or more generations related to one another through actual uterine ties, the simplest and smallest pattern being uterine siblings and the offspring of one of them. A typical *sub-matrilineage* is exemplified by a small sub-group of the Turuŋonai. (In Figure 30 members of this sub-matrilineage are shown thus ▶, ●.) Although members of this sub-matrilineage interact as a separate social unit on occasion and hence constitute what we call a group, there is no separate name for them; in fact most natives do not think of them as constituting a separate social entity. Nevertheless, several important criteria set them apart. For one thing they corporately own some tracts of land separately from the other members of their matrilineage. Members of this sub-matrilineage also share separately other kinds of materials and services. For example, when Hopuhopu was baptized, both Siham and Tamaŋ contributed pigs to the baptism feast without any apparent expectation of repayment; To'osi also provided a pig bought with some of his plantation earnings, but Pitaino was expected to repay that. When Tamaŋ's illness dragged on for months, Siham brought in a diviner to learn the cause and paid the fee himself. Other instances could be cited to indicate the distinctive nature of the relations among relatives linked as closely as these are, and these kinds of transactions ordinarily take place only among members of a nuclear family.

We summarized on Figure 10 (page 49) the data concerning the process of sib segmentation, as exemplified in the case of some segments of the Tree-rat sib. The diagram is a representation of the actual and traditional relationships between members of the various segments described;[12] it should be kept in mind, however, that generational level, although theoretically indicating closer or remoter genealogical distance from the sib founders, is not reflected in the relations among members of the various segments.

The structural principles illustrated in the case of the Tree-rat people apply also to the other Siuai sibs, although no two sibs are exactly alike in *span* or in *depth* of segmentation. The Kingfisher people, for example, offer a more complex case. Referring to the mythical "genealogical" chart of this sib,[13] it will be noted that the first subdivision is into the Urimaina sub-sib and the sub-sib made up of the descendants of the kupuna, Kohka. Further, the Kohka descendants are divided into three sub-sub-sibs: Eye-rollers, Legs-apart, and Komma; and these are still further subdivided into Kaparotu'ne, Pot-likes, Whistlers, Cockatoo-people, Nose-blowers, etc. But of these latter, only the Kaparotu'ne constitute a matrilineage; the others have further ramified into smaller segments that *are* matrilineages, hence I am compelled to commit another terminological atrocity and call the Cockatoo-people, Whistlers, etc., *sub-sub-sub-sibs* (or third-order sub-sibs). But here is a further complication: all the surviving members of the Urimaina sub-sib can trace their common relationship through "a specific series of remembered genealogical links"[14] hence they also constitute a separate matrilineage, withal one of very great depth.[15]

Obviously then the rate of sib ramification is not regular; sibs and sib segments vary widely in span and in depth. Differences of span and depth at or above the matrilineage order of segmentation have, however, few practical consequences for social relations between matrilineages[16] — and rarely are sub-sibs or sub-sub-sibs social groups. Generational differences between sub-matrilineages may be exemplified in social and jural relations, but at or above the matrilineage order of segmentation such differences are reflected only in totemic taboos and in beliefs about shrine ownership.[17]

*All* matrilineages in Siuai resemble those of the Tree-rat sib in some respects: no matter how scattered they may be (and members of some matrilineages are very widely scattered): matrilineage mates manifest their group unity through frequent interaction, expressions of strong sentimental attachment, and corporate ownership of property. However, not all matrilineages possess their own heirlooms, and there is wide variation in the manner in which they utilize corporately owned land. As a matter of fact, there is at least one matrilineage, the Iquana of Hinna village, which possesses no land of its own.

Several generations ago women of this group married Hinna men and left their Terei homes to go to Siuai and live. Their matrilineal descendants increased in numbers and became wealthy and influential, but they never acquired land. Even during their years of greatest influence they domiciled and gardened on land identified with their spouses' matrilineages. In the meantime their old landholdings in Terei became alienated.

The If-I'd-been-here matrilineages are also quite land poor. In explanation of their situation they refer to the Eagle sib myth, in which their sub-sib kupuna ancestress is said to have arrived too late on the Siuai scene (see Chapter 2, p. 57).

There are other instances of matrilineages owning larger tracts of land than they can use. For example, members of a Crane matrilineage living at Jeku village do not own full or residual title to the land on which they dwell and garden; their main holding is at Tupainoro, a mile south of Jeku. On Tupainoro is their shrine, a cave in which their matrilineage treasure was discovered by a kupuna ancestress. A few generations ago all the Tupainoro Cranes died except for the descendants of one woman who had married and gone to live in Jeku. Now her descendants remain at Jeku and do not even bother to plant on Tupainoro in spite of the fact that the land there is an ideal site for a potato garden since it is far away from all dwellings and thus escapes the ravages of domestic pigs. Moreover these Cranes do not allow others to plant on Tupainoro — an exception to the usual practice of not arbitrarily excluding others from using one's land. Kaŋku, the Firstborn of this matrilineage, brought vigorous legal action against an outsider who had innocently started a cultivation on Tupainoro, demanding that the trespasser leave Tupainoro as soon as he had harvested. When it was pointed out to him that he and his matrilineage mates never planted on the land — apparently had no use for it — he shrugged and said: "Nevertheless, it is ours. I would rather my pot be empty than full of the food of another man."

Land use is a decisive factor in sib fission. So long as matrilineage mates make joint use of their corporately owned land the continued unity of their group is assured. Let the women of a matrilineage begin to scatter, however, then fission becomes inevitable. The out-marrying women and their children acquire provisional rights in tracts where they reside, and ultimately acquire full title to such lands — thereby establishing the nucleus of sub-matrilineages, which will in time become separate matrilineages when memories of the more remote genealogical ties fade.

The extent to which change of residence can affect sib fission is exemplified in the case of the Eagle sib. My first contact with the Eagle-people took place in northeast Siuai, where of all the Eagle sub-sibs only the What-is-it-called is numerously represented. When first listing their totems my What-is-it-called informants did not even mention the eagle. In fact I first learned of the existence of the Eagle sib from informants in central Siuai, who, in relating the origin myth reproduced in Chapter 2, "explained" the origin of the term *What-is-it-called* (*Toŋuno*) in connection with the frog feast of the Eagle-people's kupunas. Later, when I confronted my What-is-it-called informants of northeast Siuai with this account of their mythical origins, some of them claimed ignorance of it, while others admitted that it was "possibly true," adding, "things are not straight with us Siuai; when we move away from our shrines (*urinno*) we neglect to carry out the proper customs." They all agreed, however, that even though they no longer regard eagles as their primary totem, to marry a member of the Eagle sib would be incestuous —

not that there is much likelihood of such a marriage, since most What-is-it-called people dwell three or four miles from the nearest center of other Eagle people. Of course it is quite possible that the What-is-it-called people are, in fact, not genealogically related to the Eagle-people of Central Siuai, and that the myth has no relation to genealogical reality. Name coincidence, as we shall see, is not unusual in Siuai. On the other hand, in support of the relationship which the myth purports to explain, is the circumstance that descendants of What-is-it-called ancestors of people of *southeast* Siuai, from whom those in northeast Siuai claim descent, do respect the Eagle totem and acknowledge direct relationship with Eagle-people in Central Siuai.

*Sib Fusion.* A different kind of problem is presented by the assertions or implications of informants that some sibs are *related* to others. When I was inquiring about sib exogamy there came to light many instances of marriage prohibition between individuals belonging to different sibs. Three different kinds of explanation were offered for this surprising circumstance:

1. "Formerly our noroukuru used to be the same."
2. "We both taboo the same totem."
3. "One of our ancestors bound us together."

Exemplifying the first explanation is the fact that Hornbills should not intermarry with Tree-rats, Eye-rollers, or Cranes. No further reasons are given other than: "Formerly we used to be the same noroukuru." These sibs share no totems, not even secondary ones; and even my most imaginative informants, who were rarely at a loss to invent mythical rationalizations, could not go beyond the bare statement just given. Similar marriage prohibitions obtain between several other sibs or segments of separate sibs. Following the common practice,[18] we might call these larger aggregations *phratries*, while bearing in mind that phratries may link whole sibs, or subdivisions of separate sibs, or a whole sib and a subdivision of another sib. In several cases, phratry exogamy is beginning to break down as a result of mission-induced skepticism and natives' cognizance that many instances of "incest" between phratry-linked individuals have not produced the expected dire consequences.

Marriage prohibition between persons who respect the same totem is more easily comprehended in terms of explicit Siuai beliefs. For example, Eagle-people and Whistlers, though belonging to different sibs, may not intermarry — the eagle being a secondary totem of the latter. Nor may a Raruna marry a Komma, the parrot being the primary totem of the former and a secondary totem of the latter; in this case the link receives additional "documentation" from the origin myth which associates the kupuna of the Parrot sib with the kupuna of the Komma subdivision of the Kingfisher sib in the incident involving the fabulous rikrikmorova.[19] "Incest" based on this kind of tie is rarely committed. Some natives go even a step further, and assert that *no* Kingfisher should marry a Parrot, while acknowledging that many Kingfishers (other than Kommas) do, and thereby commit incest. On the basis of my census of marriage unions, this particular kind of "incest" is very frequently committed, and the people involved seemed to have little fear of the consequences. However, in one case, when a partner of such a union mysteriously died, people generally agreed that "it was because of the incest." When I asked *why* no Kingfisher should marry a Parrot, some natives explained that *some* Kingfisher people (i.e., Komma) respect Parrot as a totem and consequently may not marry Parrot people, hence *all* Kingfisher people should do likewise. Others asserted that *all* Kingfishers probably respected the Parrot as a totem in former times, but that all but the Komma had in the course of time neglected the totem and the marriage restrictions. Still others explained simply that "formerly we used to be the same."

In another case of marriage restriction, the explanations were less ambiguous. It will be recalled that the Cockatoo segment of the Eye-rollers (Kingfisher sib) are said to have acquired the cockatoo as their secondary totem through a cockatoo's aid to a kupuna ancestress.[20] To my knowledge no natives attempt to link mythically this subdivision with the Cockatoo sib, some of whose members immigrated to northeast Siuai from Terei a few generations ago; but since members of both of these units respect the cockatoo as a totem they now avoid intermarriage; and I am tempted to speculate that generations hence, some native philosopher will "discover" mythical evidence linking the two units. (At this point, perhaps I should emphasize that in presenting these "explanations" I am not attempting to reconstruct Siuai sib history but rather to describe how natives account for present inter-sib relationships.)

The third kind of explanation natives give for marriage restrictions between separate sibs, or parts of separate sibs, is that the two units are joined by *nokihoro*. Nokihoro means "agglomeration," from *nosirihe-*, "to-place-unlike-things-together," e.g., yams with taro, a knife with an ax, or, as in this context, *women who belong to different sibs*.

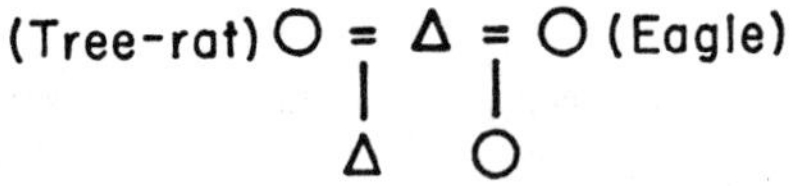

(Tree-rat) ○ = △ = ○ (Eagle)
           |     |
          △   ○

FIGURE 15

In this case, for example, when a man has two wives, either simultaneously or serially, and one belongs to the Tree-rat sib and the other to the Eagle, the offspring of these women are half-siblings, or, in *Motuna* terms, "brother and sister by nokihoro." The two cannot marry even though they belong to different sibs and respect different totems. This linkage continues into the next generation:

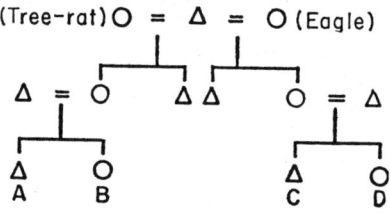

FIGURE 16

A and B cannot marry *any* Eagle-people, nor C and D *any* Tree-rats. This does not mean, of course, that *other* Tree-rats cannot marry *other* Eagles; the restriction applies only to the direct matrilineal descendants of the original "agglomerated" wives. The degree to which it applies even to these varies widely. For example, natives assert that members of the Legs-apart sub-sub-sib (Kingfisher sib) and members of the If-I'd-been-here sub-sib (Eagle sib) may not intermarry because some remote ancestor joined them by nokihoro. If their explanation for the marriage restriction were true, it might mean that the unknown ancestor was married to the common ancestress of *all* surviving Legs-apart and the common ancestors of *all* surviving If-I'd-been-heres. Or it might mean that at some point, the matrilineage mates of the direct matrilineal descendants of the "agglomerated" Legs-apart woman, had adopted the latters' taboo against marrying If-I'd-been heres, and that this matrilineage eventually ramified into the contemporary wider-spanned Legs-apart sub-sub-sib. This kind of fusion does in fact take place today: it sometimes happens that a man of low rank will attempt to enhance his position by stressing a tie with a high-ranking kinsman, as shown in Figure 17.

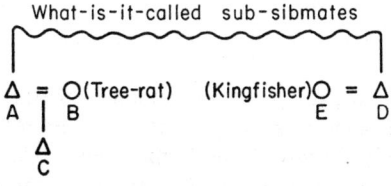

FIGURE 17

If C wishes to advertise his relationship to D, whom he calls "father" (because D and A are distant sub-sib mates), C will not only call E "mother" but will avoid marriage with *all* Kingfisher women, "because my 'father,' the great leader B, made them nokihoro." Moreover, the restriction can be made to extend, as shown in Figure 18. The result is that B's direct matrilineal descendants (G, H, etc.) will maintain the restriction against marrying any Kingfisher — or, what is more usual, some smaller subdivision of kingfishers.

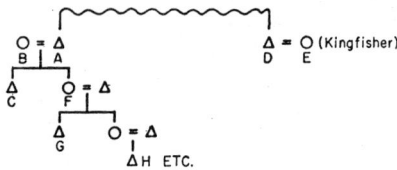

FIGURE 18

Nokihoro ties are more likely to exist between neighboring social units, since individuals tend to choose mates from nearby. In this way, if the "field" of a neighborhood's nokihoro's relationships were mapped, it would be found to encircle an area not much larger than the area from which spouses are usually chosen. The nokihoro field for Mi'kahna hamlet, for example, is as shown in Figure 19.

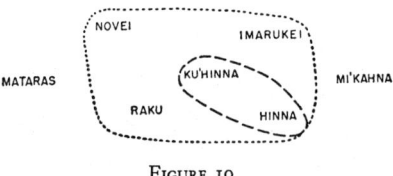

FIGURE 19

The entire Mi'kahnanai matrilineage (a subdivision of the Rukaruinai sub-sub-sib, Belly-fats sub-sib) is nokihoro with a Matuku matrilineage centered in Hinna and with a Kingfisher matrilineage centered in Ku'hinna. In addition, certain individual residents of Mi'kahna are linked by nokihoro with individuals or sib subdivisions in Novei, Imarukei, and Raku. If nokihoro relationships were similarly charted for other Siuai neighborhoods, the resulting map would look like chain mail made up of rings of various sizes and shapes.

Within this general pattern the application of the nokihoro principle is extremely flexible. It appears to be absolutely binding in the case of a man's own offspring by different wives; even if these wives belong to different sibs, their offspring may not intermarry. Furthermore, none of these offspring would marry matrilineage mates of their half-siblings, although I noted many instances of individuals marrying outside the matrilineage but within the sub-sib or sib of a half-sibling. In other words, the matrilineage is in this respect as in many others, the *effective* kinship unit. Beyond the matrilineage limits, however, nokihoro appears to operate according to variables of interaction, political values, and individual belief.

If members of two nokihoro-linked units which have ramified beyond the matrilineage span happen to live side by side there is more likelihood that the marriage restriction between them will break down: some individuals will commit "incest," and if nothing untoward happens to them, others will follow suit until that nokihoro link is universally ignored ("after all, we do not share totems") and ultimately forgotten. In other words, the same spatial proximity which *favored* marriage and nokihoro in the distant past may eventually contribute to the breakdown of that nokihoro.

In connection with rank, the nokihoro tie is more likely to be asserted and maintained if it bestows even reflected renown. In this sense, snobbery has the effect of restricting the choice of mate, but it is a price which many renown-hungry Siuai gladly pay.

And finally, individual belief—or rather, disbelief—has much to do with respecting or rejecting the restriction imposed by nokihoro. Some natives of skeptical bent purposefully break the taboo and thereby create a precedent which others will follow if the iconoclasts suffer no dire consequences.

Every Siuai has some nokihoro relationships, but it is obvious that application of the nokihoro principle calls for flexibility if Siuai kinship institutions are to persist in present form; otherwise, in the words of one informant, "there would soon be no one left to marry."

Now, having provided a framework for the description of Siuai social life, we can proceed to fill it in.

# II

## SOCIAL RELATIONS

CHAPTER 4

# *Households*

## THE DWELLING HOUSE

The labor recruiter or government official touring Siuai and keeping to the main paths finds most line villages excessively neat — and surprisingly empty. Visitors see one or two orderly lines of pile-houses surrounded by a stockade-like fence, all trees nearby hacked down, the ground cleared of every blade of grass and swept clean, and the whole place baked dry and dead by a relentless sun. More often than not, visitors see no smoking fires or other tell-tales of human occupancy, and many puzzled travelers are led to conclude that the Siuai do not *reside* in their villages. As a matter of statistical fact many of them do not. Few travelers see the dwellings where the Siuai reside most of the time, for strangers are not welcome at these secluded *house-pigs*.

"House-pig" is the pidgin word applied to the pre-European style of Siuai residence, and it is a particularly apt term, for the Motuna word is hurupao "(the dwelling where) pigs (get their) food." The house-pig, or hamlet house, differs from the *house-line*, or village house, in location, in use, and frequently in architecture.

Most village houses are constructed on four- to five-foot piles, so designed, by Government order, to be more healthful — to raise native living off the ground, to provide freer air circulation, cleaner disposal of waste, and surer insulation from household animals. What the well-meaning Administration overlooks is that the Siuai *like* the ground they live on, that they *want* their animals nearby, and that they are chilled and sickened from the night air that creeps in through wide cracks in pile-dwelling floors. For these and for other reasons to be mentioned later on, most Siuai regard the mandate to construct and reside in a village house a senseless imposition, an *onoono kakotoua*, another one of the inexplicable "white man's customs."

Hamlet houses vary considerably in architectural details but part at least of the living space of most of them is directly on the ground. Some are simple one-room, one-story, ground-level huts walled in on all sides. Others have higher ceilings, with a five- or six-foot high "mezzanine" platform stretching across the rear half of the structure, for sleeping and storage. Still others consist of a pile-house with a very long front overhang, which is either walled in completely or left partly open. In some cases the eaves on one side are extended to form an open-sided sitting place.

Except in the case of the *kakanoni*, an unusually high pile-dwelling commonly regarded as an oddity — there were only six in all northeast Siuai — the Siuai invest no special effort to make their hamlet houses anything but serviceable. They build them only large enough for their needs of the moment, adding to them or rebuilding as new needs arise, and they lavish no more materials and care in their construction than is required for warmth, shade, weather protection, and privacy. Several examples are shown in the illustrations; those could be multiplied for there are no two houses of exactly the same size and arrangement, although all of them possess the following features.

All hamlet houses are in whole or in part walled in for privacy and for keeping out large pigs. No one minds having fowl or dogs or small pigs underfoot, but a fully grown pig is a nuisance and a potential danger to infants. Before warfare was outlawed by the Australian Administration these walls were made of four- to six-inch-thick wooden boards built like garden fences for protection against enemies' spears and arrows. Today with this danger past, the upper parts of the walls are made of palm-leaf sheets.

Near the center of every hamlet house is an open hearth, a bed of ashes and stones, for cooking and for warmth. A vent is provided between roof and end walls, but smoke usually fills the house before it begins to seep out. (I never lost my amazement at the capacity of the Siuai for working, eating, talking, and dozing in heavy smoke. So accustomed to it are they and so indifferent to it even when their eyes run and their mouths choke, that they often sit in a direct stream of smoke without bothering to move aside.) Over the hearth there hangs suspended from the rafters a large rectangular wooden rack (*kurikurihai*) on which are stored cooking pots, dried carcasses of opossum, strings of shell money, and food left-overs, all of which, like walls and ceiling, are smoke-blackened.

Some beds consist of low platforms made of five or six lengths of split palm fixed against the side walls; others are of planks laid out on the ground nearer the hearth. In neither case are the planks shaped in any way: a Siuai native can sleep in apparent comfort flat on his back and with no extra headrest, on three narrow rounded planks. These beds are used also as benches, and in addition natives sit on single logs or sit and squat directly on the ground.

Along the walls of every house-pig there are shelves (*patapata*) on which are stored coconut-shell water bottles, the more valuable and ornamental kinds of shell money owned by the household, calico loincloths, and other tools and personal items that cannot conveniently be hung from the rafters, stuck into the walls, or piled in a corner. Nowadays most houses will have a small hurricane lamp with or without a precious little hoarding of kerosene, and a few dwellings will contain a smoke-blackened and battered suitcase or wooden chest, a relic of some householder's employment at a white's plantation.

Neither the hamlet house nor its fixed furnishings represents much of a labor investment for the Siuai. I witnessed the building of one of average size and recorded that two adult males and four females completed the whole project in about 120 man-hours, including searching for timbers, felling trees, manufacturing sago-leaf sheets, along with the actual labor of construction. The job was done desultorily, with little emphasis on workmanship and little apparent pride in the completed job.

The more usual house-building procedure is for a man to build his own house-pig in his spare time, assisted now and then by a kinsman and sometimes drawing out the process for several weeks. Very rarely does a native solicit the aid of a number of his neighbors in an organized house-raising; but when that is done, the job is usually completed by midafternoon and the workers are rewarded with a pork feast.

Despite the ease of house construction, the Siuai prefer and keep their grimy old dwellings as long as they can be patched up and kept rain-proof.

The yard immediately around a hamlet house shows little of the scrupulous tidiness and bareness of ground found in the villages. Pigs eat much of the household refuse, but scraps of discarded baskets, pieces of broken pots, husks of coconut and areca nut, along with weeds and bushes, announce that — whereas the village house may be under the surveillance of an exacting Administration — the hamlet house is a Siuai's own castle.

Jungle-shrouded privacy is a major factor in the location of hamlet houses. Proximity to drinking water is a practical requirement but that is no problem in this rain-drenched region of innumerable springs and streams. There are of course certain sociological factors which enter into the choice of residence, but within these limits the Siuai tries to locate his hamlet house away from main paths, villages, men's club-houses, and all other places frequented by strangers and mere acquaintances. Usually hamlet houses are clustered together in tiny hamlets of close relatives, but even so, nearly every household maintains a degree of isolation by means of a wide house yard and screens of shrubbery.

Another factor reinforcing the isolation of the hamlet house is the technique of pig raising. The dominant importance of pigs in Siuai life will be made clear as this account proceeds; their relevance at this point lies in the fact that although most pigs are exchanged and consumed for economic, political, and ceremonial purposes not directly related to activities of the household, pig *raising*, no less than gardening, is a household industry. As stated above,[1] nearly every household in Siuai has at least one pig; the average number per household is three to four.[2] Very rarely however does a household waste such an important resource by killing and eating one of its pigs just for food; pigs are indispensable for the feasts that accompany life crises and social advancement, and are used extensively in trade. Moreover, a pig raised from birth becomes so much of a pet that few owners could bring themselves to kill and eat it merely to satisfy hunger.

Feeding pigs is one of the household's principal activities, and all members assist. The householders provide part of their pigs' diet from their gardens, but expect that the animals will supplement this food by foraging for roots and tender plants in the woods. Unless there is some woodland close to the hamlet house, the animals in their hunger will either break through garden fences or roam within reach of some unscrupulous and pork-hungry neighbor or, worst of all, stray deep into the forest and go wild. This requirement for foraging space around each dwelling or small cluster of dwellings militates against full-time residence in the more populous and concentrated village settlements, where in fact pigs are forbidden inside the village fence by Administration regulation. There are of course no physical reasons why the Siuai cannot pen their pigs, feed them entirely from their gardens, and reside full-time in the villages, as the Administration wishes them to do; there are however so many traditional reasons, including the preference for privacy and the desire to be with their pigs, as to make the suggestion appear wholly unreasonable to them.

How often I used to recall with envy ethnographic accounts of lively beach villages and crowded open-sided native dwellings, and wished that the Siuai were less intent upon spending so much of their time out of sight in their own isolated, tight-walled dwellings. On fair days most members of the household trudge to the gardens after sunup and return home in mid-afternoon, and from that hour onwards all the women and children and many of the men remain at the hamlet house — cooking, eating, feeding pigs, nursing babies, playing, making things, dozing, or sleeping. Separated by a hundred feet, or by several hundred yards, another household lives a similar existence. Late afternoons, youths and men occasionally stroll to their favorite club-house to chew betel and share talk for an hour or so but even they return to their separate houses by dark and remain there until morning. Many, many days were spent by us at these hamlet houses, interviewing and observing, but such was the exclusiveness of each of these dwelling units that our visits invariably created an unnatural situation. In the villages it was a different matter. There our house was crowded among the others and in time our presence became accepted and even ignored. Even in the case of those few Siuai who reside as often in the gregariousness of their village houses as in the isolation of their "house-pigs," the latter retain their aura of privacy wherein mere acquaintances are unwelcome and strangers forbidden.

Siuai is a quiet place, but now and then the stillness is shattered by a woman shrilling at some male stranger who wittingly or not trespasses too near a hamlet house. Even male acquaintances are suspect and are likely to be screamed at: "Snake. Demon. You worthless one. You stranger. Go take your penis elsewhere."

It is assumed that most unannounced visitors to a hamlet house, whether strangers or acquaintances, are up to no good, intent either upon harming the male residents magically or spying upon and seducing females. Except among the closest of kinsmen and the most intimate of friends, all social and business visiting among males takes place in club-houses or villages. When a distant acquaintance wishes to consult with some man he goes to the latter's club-house, if he has one, signals by slit gong for the owner to come, and waits for him there. When some kinsman visits another at the latter's hamlet house and finds no one at home, he leaves a sign (*kokoua*), so that the returning owner, upon noticing marks of a visit, will know that the identity and intent of the visitor was friendly.

Assured thus of privacy by spatial isolation and social proscription the occupants of each separate hamlet house constitute a distinct, closed social group for several hours each day. In addition to the seven or eight hours of sleeping together in one small house; they share a breakfast snack of leftovers before beginning the day's activities; they very often spend the forenoon and early afternoon together at the garden; they nearly always re-form as a group in the late afternoon to prepare and eat the day's principal meal, and remain together between nightfall and retiring to sleep.

There is another aspect to this household exclusiveness. It sometimes happens that a household's hamlet house will be built on land to which none of the householders can claim ownership by any means other than occupancy — and this happens even more frequently in connection with village houses. Nevertheless, after the house has been built and occupied, all other persons, including the residual titleholders of the land, respect the occupancy rights of the household. I recorded no instance of a household being forced to vacate or remove their house. Warnings are sometimes issued to the occupants by the residual owners of the house site, but as long as the house is occupied the occupants appear to enjoy more or less inviolable *rights of occupancy*.

There is also a magical aspect of household unity. If some sorcerer places a deadly poison in the thatch of a house in order to bring about the death of one of its occupants, it is believed that all other regular occupants will also be affected.

## *THE GARDEN*

Between morning and midafternoon and on all but very rainy and windy days the center of Siuai activity shifts from dwelling to garden, and, fortunately for the ethnographer, the Siuai householder is not nearly so reluctant to show off his taro plots as he is to invite inspection of his house. In two respects, though, the garden is similar to the hamlet house: usually the members of a household maintain their separate identity in gardening, and in both settings women are the principal technicians.

In Chapter 1 were described the technical aspects of gardening — where gardens are located; how old garden sites are cleaned, fenced, planted, cultivated, and harvested; and how the whole process moves along with easy efficiency and results in an orderly sequence of gardening in one direction. It now remains to describe who carries out these activities and what significance this has for social organization.

Because of their greater size and their peculiar requirements (i.e., for suitable soil and drainage), gardens cannot be located with the same strict regard for privacy as happens in the case of hamlet houses, but the ideal is carried out wherever possible. Very rarely are gardens located within sight of a club-house — a double-edged precaution, since females should not witness what goes on in a club-house. If it is possible only with great difficulty to keep gardens well away from main paths, then the fences next to the paths are built extra high to block out a stranger's view.

There is a high correspondence between occupants of household and of taro patch and patch-sequence.[3] In many instances two or more households occupy adjoining patches, but the otherwise nonfunctional[4] fences between these adjoining patches serve as visible reminders of the social distinctiveness of each patch-sequence.

The decision concerning when and where to start a new patch-sequence emerges gradually. Every adult gardener knows weeks in advance when the current patch-sequence is about to terminate at some natural or cultural barrier. If he is industrious and foresighted the head of a household visits some of his old garden sites to see which one is suitable for replanting; often, though, wives have to remind their husbands repeatedly before the latter bestir themselves.

For one thing, the site should be easily accessible to the hamlet house, no more than about three-quarters of a mile away and not separated from it by a formidable stream or swamp. Ideally, the proposed site should be identified with some member of the household through some substantial form of land title, although it frequently happens that a household will secure permission and garden on others' land if there are no suitable sites of its own within easy access. In any case, before the site is finally selected, the wife usually looks over the location with her husband and expresses her expert opinion about its suitability — all but the most autocratic husbands readily admit that women should have some say in this matter.

The first stage in ground preparation is man's work: cutting down the smaller trees, strip-barking the bigger ones, and building the fence. Usually this is done by a youth or man working alone at the job for five or six hours a day. While he is thus occupied the women in his household carry taro plantings to the new site and make thatch sheets for a garden shed. When one corner of the site has been cleared and the fence begun, the women start to rake the trash into piles ready for burning.

If the patch is small, that is, less than about twenty plots, burning is usually done after the fence is completed, and the men assist with this job; otherwise women do the burning alone while the men are still constructing the fence. Then, after fencing and burning are completed, men place logs on the ground to outline the plots, and the major portion of their gardening work is over, having been carried out speedily and energetically with the use of metal axes and machetes. Thereafter gardening becomes a woman's affair. Women work in the gardens four times as long as men.[5] Nearly every day the woman carries or leads her children to the patch and remains there until midafternoon, planting slips in holes formed by her digging stick, or weeding by hand, or removing destructive caterpillars from the tender new leaves. She stops now and then and escapes from the burning sun to the shade of the shed to nurse an infant or to rest. Sometimes she instructs her young female companions how to weed and find insects, and encourages them to work with her. Or, if her young son or her sister's son is along, she prompts him to frighten birds away by throwing reed spears or shooting reed arrows from a toy bow. Her work is methodical and her tempo unhurried. (It always seemed to me that most women regard gardening as a fixed part of every day's life routine, an end in itself; whereas for many men it is a rather onerous but necessary job to be completed as quickly as possible in order to move on to other activities — or lack of activities.)

At midafternoon women harvest enough taro for the day's principal meal and return home, going by way of an old garden plot, where they load up with firewood from the dried and dismantled fence. They cut off the edible corms of the taro and take them home, leaving the taro stalks piled up for subsequent planting.

Once during the planting time the male gardener may visit the taro garden at sunup to plant a cutting of his private stock of magically consecrated taro and recite maru in order to insure a successful crop; this is done in one corner (*mono*) of the patch.[6] Also, if his garden fence has been broken through by a marauding pig, the owner will spend a morning repairing the damage. Now and then his wife may report having been spied on by some unidentified male, and for a few days thereafter the husband will accompany her to the garden and remain with her throughout the day to protect her from the stares — or worse — of mischievous natives. This surveillance is seldom maintained beyond a few days at a stretch, except in the case of jealous husbands with handsome young wives — a situation which evokes much humorous and lewd comment from neighbors. Aside from such accidents or alarms as these, most men do not return to work in their taro gardens until their wives notify them that it is time to clear and fence the next patch in the sequence.

Potato gardens are usually located farther away from dwellings than are taro gardens. Also, since the ideal sites are sandy flood plains and since shorter fences are required, men do not have to work as hard initially as they do in connection with taro gardens. On the other hand, because of the greater distance of some potato gardens from dwellings, more men tend to accompany their wives when the latter go there to work.

Thus there is a distinct division of labor in garden work, wherein women, with their aboriginal tools and their heavier allotment of time-consuming hand work, toil far longer hours than men and become much more experienced in the growing of food plants. I was invariably referred to some elderly woman when I asked about the names and properties of cultivated plants. (Early in our stay, when I asked one old woman to name and describe the different varieties of taro, she embarked on her recitation with gusto and had passed the fiftieth variety when my male pidgin-speaking interpreter gave up and confessed to me that she was far too technical for him, adding that he himself could distinguish only four or five varieties.) In fact, most women are very proud of their industry, skill, and knowledge of gardening; and one of the most infuriating insults is one woman's taunt to another that she is a poor gardener, that she produces so little food that her husband must purchase taro from a neighbor or beg it from a relative.

The *ideal* of an industrious gardener also applies to males. It is generally said that men who spend very little time in the gardens, building only rickety fences and leaving some of the heavier clearing to women, are "lazy" (*na'aru*); and one youth can insult another by saying: "Thy father's hand is clean; not a thing does he plant; he has no wealth in crops." There are instances of industrious male gardeners who spend nearly as much time as women in the gardens and who are noted for their fine taro, their straight sturdy fences, and their carefully aligned patches. In some conversational contexts, especially when parents are lecturing children, such men are held up as paragons; but at other times when men are discussing economic and political matters such individuals are mentioned with the slight edge of contempt reserved for the misguided, like American schoolboy athletes discussing their more studious friends.

As in the case of house sites, there is a jural aspect to the relationship between a household and the land on which its members garden; we might call this "constellation of rights, privileges, and duties"[7] *provisional ownership, by cultivation.* Only the nearest of kin or the closest of friends would enter another's patch uninvited, and this especially applies if only women are working in the patch and the outsider is a youth or a man. Further, if there is no one working in the garden at the time, an outsider will be at pains to stay out of others' patches lest he be blamed for any subsequent theft or sorcery affecting the owners. As a result of this exclusiveness and privacy, a married couple's patch serves as a useful retreat for intimacy, and they occasionally camp there for a night of more uninhibited intercourse than is possible in the usually unpartitioned hamlet house. They do this in spite of the fact that some natives claim that copulation in the garden will kill the taro.[8]

The Siuai prefer to garden on land to which they have full or residual title, and nearly every Siuai can claim *some* land in this manner; nevertheless two out of five households raise taro on land in which they do not possess such titles. One reason for this situation lies in their standards regarding maximum labor output, which place narrow limits on the availability of labor resources.

For one thing, it is unusual even for industrious women to spend more than about seven hours a day at garden work, including the time spent going to and from the garden. For taro gardening, most natives consider about three-quarters of a mile the limit beyond which they will not go unless forced by circumstances. Women are particularly insistent about having garden sites near home, for they are the ones who must carry home the back-breaking loads of firewood every day. Nor will natives attempt to clear virgin rain forest just to plant on land to which they have full or residual title; this is far too difficult an undertaking even using steel tools. Consequently, to avoid gardening on distant sites or on virgin forest land, natives choose to garden on others' land nearer home.

Before laying out his garden on another's land, the household head usually asks and receives the owner's permission, but this is not always the case. For example, a household may encroach on others' land in the process of extending their patch-sequence along a narrow interfluvial ridge — some derive a great deal of satisfaction from extending their patches in one direction; they speak of it as "orderly progress," using the same terms applied to the technique of the skilled potter who builds up coil upon coil without flaws. When this occurs, the owners of the land across which the patch-sequence extends will usually raise no objections even if their permission has not been asked. Aware of the technical and aesthetic principles involved, most owners grant the trespassers the right of cultivation. Any adverse reaction on the part of the owners is usually phrased: "*After* you have harvested, you must withdraw from my land."

Theoretically, allowing others to use one's land is regarded as a loan, and the residual owners are privileged to charge the gardeners a rent (*muhni ukum*, "of the landowner") consisting of about one-tenth of the garden's produce, i.e., one basket of taro — about ten corms — from each plot. However, this rent is charged only infrequently.[9]

Provisional title, by cultivation, involves strict limitations. The titleholders are not privileged to use the fruit of trees growing there — such as almonds, coconuts, and breadfruit. They are in fact required to avoid damaging such trees under threat of penalty. On one occasion I saw the irate (residual) owner demand and receive three spans of shell money from a cultivator who had cut chunks out of the buttresses of an almond tree while clearing. Also, there is a time limitation to this kind of provisional ownership: the cultivators may harvest the crop and collect firewood from the dismantled fence, but they may not claim any rights to land which they have already used on the grounds that they intend to use it again after it has lain idle. Nor can they project their claims to land to which the direction of their progress will eventually lead them — however, in most cases the residual owners do not arbitrarily block such progress. In this connection, I witnessed a happy compromise to a situation which might have turned into a quarrel. The problem crystallized toward the end of our visit, and it was particularly interesting because I had foreseen it.

The geography of this situation is represented in Figure 20. When I mapped these tracts (central Rinsa) in April 1938, Soma and his household

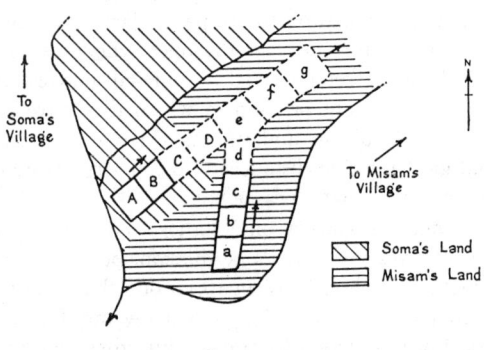

FIGURE 20

were clearing plot B while their taro was ripening on plot A. They were progressing northeastward. Misam and his household were clearing plot c and planting it in taro stalks harvested from plot a. At that time Soma's gardening was being carried out on land to which his matrilineage had full title, and the same was true of Misam. When I returned to this place fifteen months later, I found the two households working together in plot g. They had met at plot e, their wives had agreed to coöperate on Misam's land, and the two men had worked together to clear and fence off a large site. After clearing and fencing, they laid down marker logs across the center of plot e; Soma's wife weeded and planted the northern half, and Misam's the southern. They had repeated the operation in plot g.

These two households reside in different villages and are not interrelated by any important kinship ties. Moreover there is no question of Soma having no other land of his own, nor of Misam's inability to restrain Soma from planting on his soil; it was rather a case of a new relationship developing from application of the traditional technique of gardening.

Finally, the exclusiveness of the identity between household and garden patch is demonstrated by the practice of garden magic (maki). To anyone who has read of the elaborate communal rites of Trobriand garden magic, the Siuai equivalent seems a pale reflection indeed. Here there is no communal garden magician with an impressive stock of magical ingredients and formulae applicable to all the gardens in the community. Here it is up to each gardening unit, i.e., each household, to make its own arrangements for supernatural assistance. Many householders do nothing about it and rely on their wives' skill in producing good taro. Most of those who do employ garden magic use ghost-consecrated materials. For every variety of taro there is said to be a separate set of magical ingredients consecrated to a separate aggregate of ghosts of former practitioners. Some of these materials were purchased from the Terei along with the associated varieties of taro; others are believed to have been invented by kupunas and then given to humans. Nowadays it is customary for a practitioner to pass on his magic, along with slips of the associated taro, to his son and nephews; and in addition many practitioners sell slips and magic to neighbors.

Ghost-consecrated garden magic is performed in the following manner. In clearing a patch some of the trash is burned near the fence in one corner, and in the ashes the practitioner places his magic. He secures a cutting from the consecrated decorative shrub growing in the magical corner of an older patch and replants it in the new bed of ashes after reconsecrating it. Reconsecration consists of chewing some of the magical materials with betel mixture and spitting this on the shrub-cutting, while repeating a growth-magic (maru) phrase (e.g., "Let this taro be large and healthy, and able to survive drought or destructive magic") which begins with the naming of all the former practitioners. (This ritual is usually carried out early in the morning, before women have come to the garden.) Later, if this shrub is cut down it is believed that all taro growing in the patch will die. The first taro in the patch to ripen is made into a coconut-taro pudding and is eaten along with an opossum by older members of the gardening household, with a small portion of the banquet being offered to the garden-magic ghosts.

In a few instances men induce ordinary bush demons to take up residence in their gardens to guard the crops and help make them grow. This is done by sacrificing food in the garden to the demons.

A significant aspect of all these magical actions is that they are carried out by the lay gardener to benefit his own garden alone.[10] When told about other cultures possessing community magicians the Siuai remarked: "What stupid people!" and then went on to explain, "The garden is a man's own affair; why should a man help feed other people's pigs!"

## THE DAILY MEAL

The late afternoon meal is the climax of the Siuai's daily activities, and it is usually a household event. In some instances members of neighboring households will prepare their meal at the same outside hearth and may even cook their staples in the same pot, but even in these cases each household usually eats separately, within the privacy of its own dwelling.

Mealtime begins three to four hours after noon, when the women return from the gardens with their incredibly large burdens of food, firewood, and babies. Someone blows the smoldering fire into action and feeds it with kindling, and when this begins to blaze a younger woman or girl fetches water from the nearby drinking stream in coconut-shell bottles. Using a bivalve shell as a knife, the household's wife or mother removes thick slices of peeling from taro corms or sweet potatoes, cuts the cores into large chunks, and is ready to cook. Women are the chief contributors to this meal. Theirs has been the continuous work needed to produce healthy taro and other garden staples. It is also a woman's job to collect the greens and other wild plant foods needed for every balanced menu, and when she is trudging along to and from the gardens she will be continually on the lookout for them. In such matters women are the experts, knowing where wild plants are to be found and how they should be collected and prepared. Sometimes a woman may be fortunate enough to find edible mushrooms, funguses and flower buds, or snails, grubs, and white ants; all these she dutifully carries home for the household meal. She may, however, feast alone on any edible spiders she finds, or on the large white ant called "women's sing-sing," for males will sicken if they eat these insects. On days of light garden work a woman may also join company with a few kinswomen and spend a few pleasant hours searching underneath rocks in streams for the prawns which also are welcome additions to the usually monotonous menu.

Other household members do however add something to the daily meal. Boys scurry up a palm and twist loose the coconuts needed for "greasing" the food and it is usually an older man who shreds the meat and presses oil from it. Most members of the household help in the collection and processing of almonds, which occasionally appear on the menu. On the other hand, the most highly prized delicacies, that is, flesh from pig, opossum, and flying-fox, are usually supplied only by men. And although such items are rare, the few times they do appear on the daily menu are considered by everyone to balance the ledger of food responsibility. Fat pork from domestic pigs is, of course, the supreme food, but a household enjoys this treat only when one of its members brings home a cut from a feast or ceremony, or receives some as reward for attending a cremation.

The clear division of labor involved in the supplying of food for the household meal does not carry over so preceptively to preparation of food — there is no injunction forbidding men to prepare certain kinds of food and women others; nevertheless it is conventional for women to cook the domestic meal. Exceptions occur when flesh is available; men not only kill and butcher pigs as a matter of course, but they consider themselves more competent in the cooking of pork and other kinds of meat.

While the household's meal is steaming away in the pot, a separate pot of vegetable stew has been cooking for the pigs, which by this time have become clamorous. After scooping out some stew into trays, one for each animal, a few slivers of coconut meat are added and the trays are put on the ground. Then, the natives themselves are ready to eat. Small children are usually fed from their parents' trays, but everyone else past nursing receives a separate tray-full. Tray in hand, each person sits or squats apart and, using fingers for tools, eats his meal quickly and in silence.

While the meal is being prepared there is some visiting and gossiping between occupants of neighboring houses, but as soon as eating begins, visitors leave. Even children respect the convention that mealtime in the dwelling is the household's private affair. Thick-skinned as I became after continual prying into houses containing death and sickness, I never lost an uncomfortable sense of intrusion when observing a household at its principal meal.

Visiting is renewed after eating, the women and children gathering outside a neighbor's house and the men lolling in a nearby club-house. But just before dark they all return home and retire into their houses to smoke and sleep.

For women and girls this daily routine is almost invariable; a few nursing mothers and the sick and decrepit remain at home while the others work in the gardens, otherwise there are only occasional work-bees, gossip-fests, and ceremonies with relatives and neighbors to interrupt this routine. For men there is far more variety, especially during their working hours. Those who go to the gardens in the morning seldom remain very long, and the division of labor is such that many men can spend the working hours in other pursuits — in collecting nuts or hunting, or manufacturing or trading. For unmarried youths there is an even wider range of activities to separate them from other members of their household during the daylight hours; it is at this stage of life that young men gad about from one club-house to another, sometimes even eating the principal meal of the day with distant relatives and friends. However, notwithstanding these variations, no observer could fail to be impressed with the social distinctiveness of the household group.

As implied by the term I have given them, "pig-food" houses are usually clustered together into hamlets. This arrangement nearly always reflects close social interaction among occupants of the several houses: chatting, minding one another's babies, playing, hulling almonds, weaving roof sheets, sometimes even preparing and eating food together. Nightfall, however, nearly always signals the return to one's own household.

In some instances members of a household leave their hamlet house and reside in their village house for days or weeks at a time,[11] returning to the hamlet house each afternoon only to feed the pigs. Residing in the village provides more opportunities for interacting with members of other households, and this is especially significant for women and girls, who otherwise seldom see persons other than their hamlet neighbors. But even this more gregarious existence does not obscure the outline of each household grouping; the village houses offer less isolation and privacy but the household group continues to remain separate at mealtime and after nightfall.

## HOUSEHOLD PERSONNEL

The accompanying table shows the composition of the 273 households surveyed in northeast Siuai.

### Composition of Households

| Composition | No. of Households |
|---|---|
| A. Husband, wife, "offspring," and other dependents of same generation as husband and wife | 130 |
| B. Husband and wife only | 63 |
| C. Bachelors | 6 |
| D. Widowers, with or without resident offspring | 15 |
| E. Widows, with or without resident offspring | 4 |
| F. Wives of absent indentured-laborers, with or without offspring | 8 |
| G. Polygynous family households | 39 |
| H. Households including three generations | 8 |
| Total | 273 |

For the purpose of this survey no distinction is made regarding the genetic position of "offspring," whether they are recognized as being the actual offspring of both husband and wife, or of only one of them, or whether they are adopted; for most practical purposes of daily living all non-adults attached to a household are alike. A few of these households also contain dependent relatives of husband or wife, such as a younger sibling or cousin.

In Category B no distinction is made in the table between childless married couples and those whose living offspring are married and residing elsewhere.

Four of the bachelors listed in Category C are young men who will very likely marry in due course. The fifth is a lively old man who has his own hamlet house and garden and appears to lead an untroubled life. During his youth he is said to have been a skillful warrior and to have enjoyed many sexual affairs with both married and unmarried women. He is aware that he is something of a humorous curiosity to his neighbors, but reasons: "Why should I burden myself with a wife when I can grow my own food!"

The sixth bachelor is a moronic microcephal named Small-head (Ritung), who lives alone in a wreck of a house and works hard in the gardens of relatives in return for food.

Of the few single women past usual marriage age in northeast Siuai, all are physically deformed or mentally deficient, and all reside in the households of relatives.

The table suggests, what other data bear out, that elderly widows tend to remarry more consistently than do elderly widowers. It also suggests that some elderly people prefer to dwell alone even though they may garden with relatives.

Category F lists only some of the women whose husbands are absent working on white man's plantations and ships. During these absences, which last at least three years, many wives reside with their own parents or with their parents-in-law or other relatives.

In connection with Category G it should be noted that even though the co-wives occupy separate dwellings, each polygynous family counts as one household unit so long as these dwellings are located close together, for in all these cases the occupants of the adjoining dwellings work and eat together like a single household. However, there are a few unusual cases of co-wives residing and gardening in separate hamlets, thus constituting separate households.

The noteworthy fact about Category H is that there are so few cases of three-generation households, again bearing out the fact that elderly people prefer to live in their own dwellings and provide their own food so long as they are able. Younger married couples also prefer to live separate from parents and in-laws, but they share their dwellings and food supply with elderly relatives if the latter so desire.

The most important circumstance indicated by the foregoing is the high correspondence between household group and nuclear family. In fact, with the exception of two of the bachelor households, all the households surveyed exemplify different stages in the developmental cycle of the nuclear family. All the younger bachelors with separate households are laying the economic and social foundations for family life, and all the widows and widowers are survivors of former nuclear family groups. With this in mind we now turn to a consideration of that basic social unit.

CHAPTER 5

# *Developmental Cycle of the Nuclear Family*

## INCENTIVES FOR MARRYING

In Siuai the marital tie is the basis of all families and most households, but there are important differences between what might be called *primary* and *secondary* marriages. Most first marriages, for both spouses, are primary marriages. Secondary marriages include second unions of widowers or widows, and second, third, etc., unions of polygynous men; to the individual partners of these unions some of the incentives leading to secondary marriages may be no different from those of primary marriages, and even the most objective informants stated that the two kinds of union are the "same thing"; but only to primary marriages are applied the full ritual procedures of courtship, betrothal, and nuptials.

Why does a Siuai marry?[1]

First, both men and women marry for economic reasons. Here, in Siuai, custom ordains that households produce their own food; and the traditional division of labor involved in producing and preparing food calls for work by both males and females. Some men are quite capable of growing not only their own sweet potatoes but their taro as well; on the other hand, very rarely will they remain content to cook their meals day after day. Nor can they live like their contemporaries if they are bound to a daily routine of feeding their pigs. As for women, although they can supply most of their subsistence wants, they do require a man's help in felling large trees and constructing fences and dwellings. On the other hand, neither men nor women necessarily need a *spouse* to complement their subsistence labors; parents, siblings, or other relatives can and frequently do play these roles. Widows can usually depend upon male relatives for assistance with heavier work. Ambitious youths often secure a pig or two and entrust them to mother or sister for daily feeding, and widowers do the same. It must be noted, however, that a man who wishes to own several pigs must normally have a wife for this exacting job.

Secondly, men and women marry for a variety of reasons that might be summed up as "adult status." Full adult status usually comes only after marriage; signs of physical maturation are sometimes described in terms of "being ready for marriage," and there is an oft-expressed phrase to the effect that "so-and-so is old enough now, and *ought* to be married."

Third, most Siuai of both sexes are fond of children, and many of them show by words and actions that they desire to have offspring of their own.

Fourth, the parents of youths and girls add stimulus to the desires of their offspring to marry by attempting to arrange economically, socially, and politically useful alignments. In addition, a youth's fond parents often strain their resources to the limit to secure a wife for him and thereby discourage him from the restlessness which usully ends in his leaving Siuai for a three-year term of labor indenture. Once married, and satisfied with the arrangement, few men are disposed to "sign on" and leave a young wife behind as tempting prey to other men; many do, but age for age, proportionately more single men sign on than do married ones.

Can it be said that Siuai men and women also marry for sexual satisfaction?

In Siuai there is no vagueness about sex functions and sexual dichotomy, and little evidence of anything but strict heterosexuality.[2] During infancy, it is true, the distinction between the sexes is not emphasized, but as soon as the child begins to toddle it is conditioned for the sex role it will play in everyday occupations and in the sex act. By the time little boys try to climb palm trees and little girls walk about carrying toy baskets they sometimes enliven their game of "house" by pretending to copulate, imitating either parents or dogs, both of whom they have ample opportunity to observe in or around the hamlet house. However, their period of innocent sex play is not allowed to continue for long; their elders — although privately enjoying it as a great joke — put a stop to such antics with scowls and admonishments of "that's wicked" or "that's incestuous," so that the youngsters learn speedily that copulation is something important but must not be imitated in public, and particularly not with certain females. At that point, also, parents realize that they must in future be more circumspect in their own sex relations.

Thenceforth, throughout the rest of childhood, boys and girls separately continue to hear about coitus from companions of their own sex, but by their elders they are conditioned to regard sex differences less in terms of coitus than of their total occupational and social roles as males and females. These roles are sharply distinct. Something has already been said of the sexual division of labor in gardening; the full range of differences will emerge as this work proceeds, but it will be useful to note here some indications of their scope.

There is strict segregation of females from males outside the hamlets and gardens. Females should not walk along the main paths. Nor, at the risk of supernatural penalty, may they enter or even approach men's club-houses; so absolute is this sanction that females may not even eat food prepared there. Under most circumstances the mention of a woman's name in a club-house implies something derogatory about her — a device sometimes used for public censuring of a promiscuous or incestuous female.

When men and women assemble for coöperative fish-drives or for semi-public ceremonies such as cremations, the latter keep closely together and quite separate from men, who straggle about in ones and twos. In the case of young women it is especially censurable to walk about alone where male strangers are likely to be.

All this is a far cry indeed from the frequent and easy everyday contacts between males and females so characteristic of many Oceanic cultures.

By the time youths and girls are capable of effective sexual intercourse, they are thoroughly socialized regarding relationships between men and women. In a word, except with respect to certain relatives, the only imaginable kind of relationship between a virile man and a nubile woman is sexual. If such a pair is seen together at a secluded spot it is assumed that they are there to fornicate; no other interpretation is credible (native courts also take this view). Hence, nonrelated or distantly related men and women usually avoid one another unless they want sexual satisfaction. This prudishness is reinforced by the circumstance that extramarital sex adventures are also risky.

For nearly every woman there is at least one man concerned with preserving her chastity. To her own brother especially, and to all her sib brothers to some degree, she is sexually taboo: not only are they forbidden to have sexual intercourse with her, but they feel "humiliation" (*maio*) when any mention of coitus is made to them concerning or in the presence of their *sister*.[3] In the olden days, it is said, *brothers* thus humiliated might have killed both humiliator and seducer; today they salve their pride by accepting a token fine from the humiliator, but in case of a seduction the woman's own brother will exact a heavy fine of the seducer. Concern for a woman's virtue is greatly heightened if she is married or affianced; under these circumstances her father and her husband (or fiancé), along with the latter's relatives, become angrily and vengefully involved in her extramarital affairs, and the consequences for her seducer may be very serious, including a stiff fine and sometimes Administration jailing.

My informants recited the names of six persons now living in northeast Siuai and known to be illegitimate. From their accounts of these cases it is quite clear that a bastard child (*momoto*) suffers no social disabilities — in fact, it receives special consideration from its relatives, and in this matrilineal society it becomes at birth a full-fledged member of its mother's matrilineage. Its mother, however, is obligated to give her uterine brothers a "shame payment" (*numehu*) in order to alleviate their "embarrassment" and bring about a reconciliation with them. The genitor, if he can be identified, is also held blameworthy; and if the woman happens to be betrothed her brothers and her fiancé can be expected to seek indemnity from the culprit. The woman's father may prosecute the genitor in order to secure some money for purchasing a pig for the child's baptism feast, but few such cases succeed. Otherwise, the only case of illegitimacy which I heard generally censored involved a girl whose breasts had not yet filled; nearly everyone in the neighborhood joined her father in anger towards the genitor for his action in seducing a female "whose breasts were so young that she was unable to nurse the child."

The specific term for coitus is *ruru* but it is very seldom heard in ordinary conversation among men. Informants say that formerly it was rarely uttered under any circumstances; and even in the present "dissolute" age it is expressed, when absolutely necessary, through means of elaborate circumlocutions. Most times when I heard coitus discussed by men, and this was usually at my instigation, the talk was accompanied by tense, nervous titters and all-round embarrassment. Except for two standardized modes of expression, seduction songs (*jiŋje*) and masques (*mimmiŋ*), the prudish Siuai males keep their own sex experiences and fantasies to themselves, and laugh about such matters only when they concern the discomfiture of others.[4] Females, on the other hand, are less reticent; their scoldings and abuses are colored with rich and bizarre details of sex anatomy and copulation. In fact, among themselves they discuss sex matters openly, easily, and with Rabelaisian mirth.

All in all, sex adventuring is, for men at least, a hazardous pastime, and this may lessen its frequency in Siuai — according to some Oceanic standards; nevertheless it does not restrain most youths and girls from pursuing one another, surreptitiously, but avidly.

Through continuous association with older females from birth onwards girls learn their own occupational and other social roles earlier and more easily than boys, whose transition to the company of men takes place gradually and is not complete until well after puberty. Whether due to this circumstance, or to earlier (?) physical maturation, or to both, I do not know, nevertheless informants repeatedly stated that girls begin to copulate two or three years younger than do boys. As a result of frequent and open discussion among women, by the time a girl's nipples have begun to stand out she has learned secondhand many nuances of coitus and has developed a curiosity to experience it herself. However, until her breasts have filled out somewhat she should not copulate; otherwise, natives say, her nose will become mat-black and her breasts will never grow large and fall into the long pendulous shapes the Siuai admire. In due course, judging her readiness by her breasts, some young or middle-aged man will waylay her, usually while she is fetching water at the drinking stream, and will initiate her — without much resistance, informants say. From then on the girl is fair game, provided, of course, she is not closely related or betrothed to a leader. Some men prefer to wait until a girl's breasts have begun to fall before copulating with her — because, men say, the older girls' techniques are more skillful and their discretion more dependable.

A boy's sex initiation is more abrupt. In rare cases an older sib-mate will take him along to a rendezvous and allow him to look on or even test his ability; but most youths are too reticent for this. More often, and especially if the lad is handsome, a young woman will take the initiative and seduce him into beginning his sex career.[5] There is a certain hazard in this if the boy is "too young": it is believed that when a young boy copulates for the first time he must ejaculate two or three times to retrieve his penis, otherwise the woman's vagina will hold onto it and the boy will not grow to normal size and strength.[6] There remains, however, a large percentage of boys who make their own faltering beginnings, waiting sometimes until they are five and six years past puberty before an unmistakable opportunity presents itself. It is said that in the case of a very young boy his nipples will stand out after his first sex experience. When men at the club-house see that sign they put aside their usual reticence and josh the boy mercilessly. Older boys, "late starters," escape this good-natured but mortifying raillery. Once launched into sex life both youths and girls appear to avail themselves of every opportunity and, in the case of males at least, to go to rather far extremes to create opportunities. Formerly, it is said, contacts were not easy to establish, because most potential lovers dwelt in separate hamlets and had little chance for interaction. However, with the consolidation of several hamlets into villages, and with the establishment of missions, introducing common religious services for both sexes, contacts and arrangements for rendezvous were simplified; but even so, love affairs still have to be arranged and carried out in great secrecy.

Go-betweens — usually female sib-mates — are occasionally utilized by women, but most males, fearing possible indiscretions, will not entrust such missions to others. A male on the track of some girl or woman will sometimes signal to her by rolling his eyes when he sees her in a crowd, and if she does not frown back in complete repugnance he waylays her along one of her customary paths and the two either copulate on the spot or arrange to meet at a safer time and place. A less cautious person, male or female, will wait for a moonless night and slip into the lover's dwelling when the latter is alone; this of course being possible only in villages.

For reluctant or unknowing loved ones there is love magic. Some men possess magical materials to awaken desire, and use it to further their own amours as well as to earn money by selling it to others. One kind of love magic is "Pigeon-can't-eat-it" (*kuŋkuŋmenu*[7]), which was introduced into Siuai from Alu a generation ago. The principal ingredient is a variety of grass which grows in hot shadeless places. The courtier mixes this grass with coconut oil, rubs the preparation on his skin, and walks about near the home of his loved one. When she smells the fragrant mixture she becomes hot with desire and goes to him.[8]

*Vasim* magic is placed on a path along which the loved one frequently travels. Her inamorato then waits in hiding until she walks over the vasim, then he recovers it and cooks it at night in coconut oil. As the mixture heats, the sleeping female will become hot with desire and she will dream of the man and later go to him. Vasim also has the effect of causing a man to dream of copulating with the woman he has thus bespelled; this form of dream is "real" (*ruroto meŋ*) — people frequently dream of copulation without benefit of vasim, but such dreams are declared to be "meaningless" (*roruki ruroto*).

Vasim may also be mixed with coconut oil, some of it daubed surreptitiously on a woman's arm, and the rest placed in the sun. As the sun heats the mixture the vasim on the woman will make her hot and ill with desire and she will go to her lover.

According to my observations, women do not often require magic to awaken desire in the men they want, but now and then they do use such devices — though possibly not as frequently as men report. It is standard practice for men to blame their sex woes on women's love magic. To generalize from statements made by male defendants at seduction cases in court, most of Siuai would seem to be made up of passionate, aggressive females who continually wield love magic against unwilling but helpless males.[9] Actually, of the score of such cases I recorded, only one appeared to result from initiative being taken by a female; the others were clear cases of an initiating male and a not unwilling female. In this connection, male informants assert that actual physical rape no longer occurs, as it did during times of warfare, when raiders used to rape the enemies' women. Nowadays the nearest approach to rape would appear to be the kind of seduction tactic used by some men when they accost a woman working alone in a secluded garden. It is reported that such men wait in hiding until the woman starts out for home with a heavy load of firewood and produce on her back. The seducer then steals up behind her and topples her backward by pulling on the heavy load she carries. The woman's burden helps to keep her pinned to the ground so that the man has less difficulty in holding her. Moreover, all informants agree, "women who work alone in gardens don't dislike being accosted and don't fight very hard."

Hidden sandy stream banks are the favorite trysting spots; there the ground is clean and soft and bathing water conveniently near. On the other hand the Siuai do not pass up sexual opportunities just because the surroundings are not ideal; in fact they utilize any hiding spot available.

The sexual act itself is accomplished with little or no prior love-making. Siuai males emphasize this by contrasting their way with the customs of the Nasioi-speaking natives, with whose women they sometimes copulate while employed on plantations around Kieta. They relate that Nasioi natives waste much valuable time in senseless love-making, especially in rubbing noses. Nasioi men, they tell, visit a woman several times before actually copulating;

and for that reason, Nasioi women become annoyed with their Siuai visitors who invariably wish to copulate during the first visit and at once.

In Siuai the usual procedure is for the woman to lie on her back with knees up and legs apart while the man kneels on his knees between her legs with hands on the ground near her shoulders. Men say that most women are very passionate during coitus, urging more and more force and speed. In fact, men say, women lose all sense of the need for secrecy. As soon as the act is completed for the man they separate and sit or lie some distance apart. If there is time they may repeat the act; otherwise they bathe quickly — when water is available — and go their separate ways. We have no credible information from women on this point, but males say that females are very reluctant to terminate the trysts, urging their lovers to repeat the act.[10]

Except in the case of a young boy's seduction by an older woman, it is customary for the male to give a present to the female when she bestows her favors: a calico loincloth, an ornament, a few spans of shell money, or even a shilling or two serves the purpose. Some informants said this was "pay for services" (*pu*): "just like buying something at a trade store." Others vehemently denied that, and claimed "it is a gift (*o*): like the gift a man gives his trade partner." But even these latter added that "women are treating it more and more as a payment, which they demand." Also, there is a risk involved in the practice.

To a girl's parents or to a woman's husband and mother-in-law her few material possessions are familiar objects; and there is little space for secrets in a Siuai household. Consequently, when a new calico appears around her waist or an unaccountable coin or span of shell money turns up in her carrying basket, there can be only one answer, and the only thing left for her relatives to do then is to question her — which they invariably do — until she names a man. By the time the lawsuit is held before the Administration-appointed headman, the woman is ready and eager to join with her father or brother or husband in exacting a fine from her erstwhile lover. If she can produce the present he gave her and if she identifies the trysting place, the case is usually decided in her favor. Knowing all this, some men are reluctant to bestow gifts on their mistresses; on the other hand, if they are niggardly, they can almost certainly expect to be the subject of a seduction song (jiŋje).

When Siuai men or women are obsessed with desire for someone, instead of mooning about and composing poetry they make direct propositions or overcome reluctance by magic. The poetry comes after the act, and is as much an announcement of achievement as a profession of love. Seduction songs (*jinaje*, if sung by a male; *jiŋje* if sung by a female) are sung to describe a single tryst or a series of them. The following jinaje was sung by a youth gloating over his successful adventures:

| Je | pesi | jinaje |
|----|------|--------|
| —  | money | song. |

# CYCLE OF THE NUCLEAR FAMILY

*Monareko' amukori roko*
Path-at     border-of     your-at
Your trysting place was at the side of the path.

*Peukaki tiki monokikina*
Young-girl-with     there     you-saw-her
The one you seduced there was a young girl.

*No'kina rokom paro*
You-told-her:     "yours     calico"
You told her that her pay would be a calico.

*Je pesi jinaje*
— money song
*Je pesi jinaje*
— money song

*Ruhonori uiŋori roko*
Ruho-tree-at     base-at     your-at
Your trysting-place was at the base of a ruho tree.

*Rotiva tiki monokikina*
Married-woman     there     you-saw-her
The one you seduced there was a married woman.

*No'kina rokom kuriri*
You-told-her:     "yours     kuriri money"
You told her that her pay would be a span of kuriri money.

*Je pesi jinaje*
— money song.

*Munu rekom sirivi' maŋura*
Skin     your (pl.)     fragrant-grass     young (plant)
The skin of both of you smelled as sweet as fragrant new sirivi'.

*Munu rekom pano pira'*
Skin     your (pl.)     fragrant-leaves     young (plant)
The skin of both of you smelled as sweet as fragrant new pano,

*Maŋuraŋite koto kunaha*
New-growth-from     at-the-top     sweet-smelling
The sweet-smelling (pano) which grows at the top of the shrubs.

*Je pesi jinaje*
— money song.

*Kuru hisiakori roko*
Kuru-creek     bank-on     your-at
Your trysting-place was on the bank of Kuru creek.

*Norua tiki monokikina*
Widow     there     you-saw-her
The one you seduced there was a widow.

*No'kina rokom mani*
You-told-her:     "yours     'money.'"
You told her that her pay would be shillings.

*Je    pesi    jinaje*
—     money   song.

*Rekom         potoro       vaivai* [11]
Your (pl.)    "bottle"     fragrant oil
I am the perfume bottle of all of you women;

*Urini           tuuki     kunahurukom*
Settlements     all       they-perfume-themselves.
You come here from everywhere to copulate with me in order that your bodies will smell fragrant.

Speaking of himself in the second person plural, he describes three trysts he has had: one, at the side of a path, with a young girl whom he paid with a new calico; a second, at the foot of a *ruho* tree with a married woman whom he paid with valuable shell money (*kuriri*); and a third, on the bank of Kuru creek, with a widow whom he paid with shillings. In a standard poetic aside, he implies that these affairs were pleasant inasmuch as the bodies of his partners smelled like fragrant shrubs. In this case he was careful to preserve the anonymity of his conquests. If he had had no fear of consequences he might have named the women; some men do so out of spite or defiance; others do so simply out of the exuberance of conquest, but most women are wary of men so indiscreet.

Now and then jinaje are sung by men about other men as a form of ridicule; this is a favorite device for deflating self-righteous persons, particularly mission teachers.

Women compose and sing jiŋje less purposefully. Some of their jiŋje contain pleasant reminiscences, others light disparagement, especially of pompous males; but mostly, jiŋje are merely ditties sung by women as they work or nurse their babies. In the jiŋje below the girl, Tuvao, of Noronai village recalls some of her premarital trysts with well-known men of that neighborhood:

*Jiŋje    raoraovai    kikiriva'    no'osa*
Song     light rain    shower       small-part
My song is like a light rain, like a small shower.

*Noitaku             pimo        orahkom*
Another-place-to    it-goes     it-ends-quickly
which passes to another place. It is very short.

*Je    pesi    jiŋje*
—     money   song.

*Kupu    taŋuvamakori    roko*
Stone    straight-on     your-at
Your trysting-place was on the flat rock.

*Montoro    tiki     monokikina*
Montoro    there    he-saw-you
The one who seduced you there was Montoro.

| *No'kina* | *rokom* | *paro* |
|---|---|---|
| He-told-you: | "yours | calico" |

He told you that your pay would be a calico.

| *Je* | *pesi* | *jiŋje* |
|---|---|---|
| — | money | song. |

| *Je* | *pesi* | *jiŋje* |
|---|---|---|
| — | money | song. |

| *Peteita* | *uiŋori* | *roko* |
|---|---|---|
| "Potato" | base-at | your-at |

Your trysting place was at the base of the breadfruit tree called "Potato."

| *Kakantu* | *tiki* | *monokikina* |
|---|---|---|
| Kakantu | there | he-saw-you. |

The one who seduced you there was Kakantu.

| *No'kina* | *rokom* | *piri* |
|---|---|---|
| He-told-you: | "yours | 'beads.'" |

He told you that your pay would be beads.

| *Je* | *pesi* | *jiŋje* |
|---|---|---|
| — | money | song. |

| *Rekana* | *hoŋuŋori* | *makumaku* |
|---|---|---|
| Your | armband-in | fragrant shrub |

(All you men,) I am like the fragrant shrubs which you wear on your armbands, i.e., you "wear" (seduce) me so often.

Other women embellish their seduction-songs with vivid descriptions of the vanities and shortcomings of former lovers. For example, one song describes how a boastful headman was made temporarily impotent during a rendezvous because of his fear of being seen by others. Another tells how an importunate native catechist was reduced to an un-evangelical anger by the teasings of his coy mistress. In composing and singing seduction songs, as in other situations, Siuai females show far less restraint than males, and — informants complain — females seem to have little or no regard for the dignity and reputations of their lovers, nor for the troubles they bring about by their disclosures.

Hence, not the least of the hazards which men must face when they indulge their sexual desires is that the women might compose a jiŋje about them and thereby expose them to ridicule, or worse.

Institutionalized prostitution no longer exists in northeast Siuai. In former days influential men used to purchase or capture women from distant places and either sell their sexual services for shell money or bestow such services as incentives upon men assembled for a head-hunting foray. A separate house was set aside for this activity and, according to several informants, every prostitute had a very active trade. Otherwise the prostitute lived a normal life as part of her owner's household and eventually married and established her own household. Natives cited two women, now respectable grandmothers living in northeast Siuai, and I could detect no stigma attached to them because of their former activities. In this connection, prostitutes — like all other women who copulate with many different men within the same menstrual cycle — are believed to be unable to conceive.[12]

Both men and women assert that they have certain preferences in the kinds of lovers they select. Size, strength, or buxomness are not important factors, but smooth undiseased skin, cleanliness, and body "fragrance" are appreciated. Persons covered with ringworm or marred by yaws lesions are seldom the object of carefully planned seductions, nor are those with continually dirty skins and unkempt, lice-ridden hair. Particularly are young people somewhat fastidious in their choices. On the other hand, given the mood and the opportunity uncomplicated by fear of physical harm or social consequences, most fully adult Siuai are not very selective. None of my informants considered it unusual or amusing that Small-head, a moronic male microcephal, or Hopuvere, a filth-caked female epileptic, appear to be quite acceptable sex partners to many of their neighbors.

From all the foregoing it is probably correct to state that men and women do marry for sexual gratification uncomplicated by the restrictions and consequences which make extramarital copulation difficult and risky. Now, no informants ever stated the generalization in so many words; in fact, the general statement should probably be revised to read: men and women manifestly desire sexual gratification and, in Siuai, marriage is the most conventional means of satisfying the desire.

We recorded several instances of individuals attempting to marry primarily because of strong mutual attraction. The outstanding case within recent years involved a youth and his mistress who were distant sib-mates. They flaunted the convention against sib incest by openly living together for many months. Finally, though, their scandalized relatives and neighbors were so harsh and unremitting in their censure that the girl committed suicide by hanging and the youth left Siuai and worked on a plantation for three years. When I saw him after his return the case was still being discussed, as an interesting example of the power of love magic — it having been rationalized that such a strong and arbitrary attachment could only have come about through magic — an interpretation which the youth himself professed to accept.

During our stay in Siuai there were two well-publicized but short-lived instances of incestuous affairs between distant sib-mates, and informants were able to recall many more from the past.

Cases of actual marriages based principally on mutual attraction are harder to locate, not because they are taken for granted but because they do not obtrude upon public attention. I did however record several instances which seem to be explicable by no other reasons, and, by direct questioning, elicited from some men that they had, perhaps, been influenced in their choices by the "fragrant smelling skin" of their mates — all of which, according to the older men, is a modern and altogether deplorable situation: "— nowadays," they say, "our children forget the old customs; they seek after (satisfying) copulation rather than (correct) marriage." However, despite this gloomy view, Siuai marriage can hardly be termed a capricious affair.

## REGULATION OF MARRIAGE

The Siuai believe that a husband should be somewhat older than his wife but not more than about ten years.[13] For one thing, an old man married to a young woman invites trouble; natives say that he cannot copulate with her frequently enough, with the result that she will have many lovers and thereby become a source of friction in the neighborhood. The Siuai consider this as inevitable as night following day, and disinterested neighbors do not blame the woman for such actions, rather they jest about the cuckolded old fool, if he is not a man of influence, and usually join in the sport until the scandal reaches such proportions that the husband divorces his errant wife. Jealousy, as the Siuai know it, is not confined to old men married to young wives, but it is characteristic of them. An old man is apt to keep close watch over his young mate, even to the extent of locating his garden in an isolated place and of accompanying her when she goes to the toilet stream. In extreme cases such a man usually becomes a sorcerer, in fact as well as in public opinion, and he may even succeed in frightening off the neighbors pursuing his wife — until the death of one of them leads to his prosecution in court and the dissolution of his marriage. All these consequences of age-discrepant marriages are generally known, and actually serve to restrict the number of such marriages. But in addition, when a young woman has some voice in choosing a husband, she will select a young man, and preferably one with a healthy, unblemished skin, who bathes frequently, keeps his hair lice-free and combed, and wears a clean loincloth. Now, all these are characteristics of youth and are usually only to be found in young men and women, so that in a sense they are age factors and they influence men as well as women in their choice of mates, especially in their choice of a *primary* mate. On the sexual side, men do not concern themselves with a wife's vigor, but rather with her fertility and the size of her vagina, dislike being expressed for the larger flaccid organ associated with older women.

What might be called *idiosyncratic* factors also influence the choice of spouse. A slatternly woman, no matter how young, is not sought after for a wife, and usually becomes the neighborhood trollop until she is added to some older man's household as second or third wife, or until she becomes, by default, the spouse of someone utterly inconsequential. Similarly with disfigured, badly crippled, epileptic, or mentally defective women; epileptics are somewhat feared, others are fair game as mistresses but are shunned as wives. The only spinsters in northeast Siuai belong in this category. On the other hand, men similarly afflicted manage to get wives for themselves, although not desirable ones. Even the lunatic Kea, covered with ringworm and repulsively dirty by Siuai standards, had a wife until her recent demise; nor are male deaf-mutes or cripples condemned to bachelorhood.

On the positive side, the desire of both young men and young women for clean, good-smelling, well-groomed mates has already been mentioned, and I had ample evidence of its influence. Even after discounting some of his reports as conventional male boasting, it was apparent that Poroporo, our scrupulously clean and oil-perfumed seventeen-year-old servant, was pestered by young women wanting to marry him.[14] Immaruto, another cleanly and somewhat over-fastidious young man, was before his marriage in continual trouble because of the many young women who all too publicly invited his attentions. Although knotty muscles are not disfavored, emphasis is on cleanliness rather than on muscularity and strength; Siuai females expect their husbands to be capable of performing those economic tasks required of all adult males but place no special value upon brawn.

As for the requirement of chastity, Siuai men do not like to marry a wanton woman, but they neither expect nor value virginity in a bride; in fact, the question never arises.[15]

Overriding all other factors influencing choice of mate are those based on *kinship*. In the first place, marriage is absolutely forbidden between members of the same sib. Casual love affairs between distant sib-mates sometimes take place and are roundly condemned as being incestuous (*mo'oturu*), usually calling forth public censure, fines, and supernatural sanctions; and they never reach the stage of permanent union. One such affair, generally believed to have come about through someone's malicious application of love magic, reached the point where the young couple were expelled from their community and went on living together in an isolated homestead until the girl committed suicide.

Sexual relations are also disapproved of between members of certain pairs of sibs, as was described above,[16] but these prohibitions are occasionally flouted in love affairs and even marriages. In addition to sib-mates, all other kinship ties proscribing sexual relations also forbid marriage, but these vary in their degree of extension. For example, a man may not have sex relations with any of his father's wives nor marry any of his widows, and the prohibition is extended to those women's own sisters. These rules also extend to the wives and widows of a man's father's own brothers, but for extensions beyond this point the rules are relaxed somewhat in practice. Again, a man may not cohabit with or marry any of his own father's daughters, and the prohibition extends to all sib-mates of these women. The ramifications of this prohibition were discussed above in connection with the concept of nokihoro.[17]

# CYCLE OF THE NUCLEAR FAMILY

In terms of the effective operation of all these restrictions based on kinship, by a very rough kind of calculation it may be said that they reduce by about one-sixth the number of otherwise available women from among whom a man may select his spouse.

In contrast to the restrictions which some kinship ties exercise on choice of mate, certain other ties predispose relatives to marriage. Marriage with mother's brother's daughter is preferred to all other forms, and marriage with father's sister's daughter is only slightly less valued. When the girl occupies *both* statuses, as sometimes happens, then the marriage is pre-eminently "correct" and wins wide commendation. As we shall see later on,[18] some of the main features of kinship nomenclature reflect the expectation that cross-cousins intermarry. Customs of property inheritance also encourage cross-cousin marriage, land and other resources being thereby kept intact. Marriage between *classificatory* cross-cousins does not consolidate property holdings to the same extent but in other respects is looked upon with great favor. Instances of classificatory cross-cousin marriage occur frequently in neighborhoods dominated by two numerically strong matrilineages, most of whose members tend to maintain the tradition of intermarriage.

Widow inheritance, another preferential form of marriage in Siuai, will be described under a later section on "Secondary Marriage."

Men sometimes choose even a first wife on the basis of her industriousness and known success in gardening and swine husbandry. This applies particularly to men who have spent most of their youth away from Siuai working on plantations. Some of these, by the time they return home to settle down, have grown past the age when a shining fragrant skin counts for more than a productive garden and an increasing herd. Men in this category who also possess few rights in productive land are known to have selected women belonging to land-rich matrilineages; landownership is an important criterion for choosing second and third wives but it also holds for some primary marriages. *Economic* factors clearly lie behind this kind of wife selection, and these shade into *political* motives.

An ambitious and influential man tries to obtain for his heir, either son or sister's son, a wife from a large and wealthy matrilineage, not only for practical economic considerations but for reasons of status as well. Such "political" marriages usually result from a friendship alliance between two leaders and in some cases the couple become betrothed during infancy, or even pre-natally. (On the other hand, *friendship* also leads some men to betroth their children without concern for economic or political advantage.)

Coincidence may enter into choice of a mate. If a boy and a girl happen to be born in the same neighborhood a few hours or days apart, their parents may be so impressed with the circumstance that they will betroth the two.

Finally, location exercised an important influence on choice of mate in the past and continues to do so, though to a less extent. The ideal practice is to choose a spouse nearby; this practice acts like cross-cousin marriage to buttress existing kinship ties and to consolidate property holdings. Sentiment enters here too. Parents like their children to reside nearby, and unless political considerations dictate otherwise, try to arrange that their sons and daughters marry locally. During feuding days there was a practical side to this tendency towards local endogamy; the areas of common cause in warfare were so small that there was usually no opportunity for marrying any but a neighbor. With the outlaw of armed fighting this of course was altered, and on the evidence of genealogies it is clear that people now go farther away for their spouses. Not only is there less risk of marrying a potential enemy, but both men and women see more people and can be more selective than formerly. While unable to reverse this trend, old people nevertheless deplore it, saying: "A vagina from another place always looks better — just like areca nuts from another man's palm; but picking one leads to trouble."

## ARRANGING THE MARRIAGE

Formerly, as mentioned above, during raids on distant places, Siuai men used to spare and capture some young and middle-aged women and either install them in their households as secondary wives, or profit from their services as prostitutes, or sell them to native traders from Alu and Mono. In the case of prostitutes, their owners eventually sold them to neighbors to marry or gave them in marriage to followers; in neither case was the resultant marriage formalized by the usual ritual exchanges. A few such captured wives are still alive in Siuai; by force of personality and industry at least two of them I knew had become highly respected matrons despite their initial lack of property and influential relatives.

The Siuai equivalent of elopement sometimes takes place when a young woman goes to live in the household of her lover to escape having to marry her father's choice. According to our survey data, about one in fifteen of present marriages began this way — indicating, among other things, that romance does exist! Public opinion, at least in the husband's neighborhood, tends to support this action, holding that women should not be forced to marry against their wishes. But public opinion, including that of the husband's neighborhood, asserts that the marriage should be regularized by the usual exchange of property, and native courts support this attitude.

The ideal marriage arrangement involves an act of formal betrothal, a fairly lengthy betrothal period, a "payment" to the bride's guardian by the groom or his family, and a nuptial ceremony accompanied by a feast. Outside of marriage by capture (which no longer takes place) and elopement, all Siuai primary marriages include at least two of these elements and some of them add still another which might be termed preliminary betrothal.

If a girl is betrothed before she has begun to menstruate, the agreement between the parents of the betrothed couple is formalized with a preliminary betrothal gift, a "marker," a span of high-value shell money presented to the girl's father by the husband-to-be or by his father; it is eventually turned over to the girl to be added to the main betrothal gift. This "marker" establishes a kind of lien on the girl's potential sexual activities until either a formal betrothal payment be made or the agreement be broken off and the "marker" returned. This kind of agreement is more easily terminated than is a formal betrothal; the "marker" payment is relatively small, and fewer expectations will have been invested in the relationship. Moreover, most Siuai parents are sympathetic to their children's wishes and realize that they may grow to dislike a match which they had had no say in arranging.

Preliminary betrothal in its most extreme form takes place when the husbands of two pregnant women agree to betroth the expected offspring if one is a male and the other a female. This occurs not only between men seeking political or economic advantage from the future union, but between *brothers-in-law*, male cross-cousins, and friends ("because they like each other"). Shortly after the birth of the boy and girl, the father of the former presents a "marker" to the father of the girl.

An act of preliminary betrothal may also take place at the time of birth. Some woman present during parturition may claim the infant for one of her own young relatives — usually it is an infant girl who is claimed for the woman's grandson. The event is ritualized by calling out the name of the intended spouse while the infant's umbilicus is being severed, and in due course the "marker" is presented to the infant's father if it is a girl. Thereafter the young couple are said to be betrothed through "umbilicus cutting" (*hiuki tonnare*).

Formal betrothal is signalized when the youth's father or guardian presents to the girl's guardian a "gift" of high-value shell money worth from forty to one hundred spans of common shell money. The act represents a most serious undertaking on the part of both parties, with sincere expectation that it will lead to marriage. Formal betrothal cannot be broken off as easily as preliminary betrothal; any rupture usually results in bad feeling all around.

The distinction between preliminary and formal betrothal is reflected in language. Of the former, one says, "She is *marked* to be so-and-so's wife"; of the latter, "She *is* so-and-so's wife."

In the case of couples preliminarily betrothed and still willing to go through with the arrangement, formal betrothal takes place after the girl's breasts have begun to form (*nunokai'ori'kana*). With other young couples it takes place as soon as an agreement has been reached between their parents or guardians. This agreement may be arrived at through an understanding reached by the couple and subsequently approved by their parents or guardians; or it may be initiated — arranged — by the latter, with or, rarely, without the consent of the couple.

A thoughtful father will set about to find a fiancée for his son as soon as the latter has become "grown-up" (*honna*), that is, after he considers the boy to have begun to play an adult's role in subsistence activities (i.e., he is about fifteen years old). Most fathers do this on their own initiative, hoping thereby to forestall any less suitable selection the youth might make if left to make his own choice, and hoping to discourage him from leaving home to work on a white man's plantation. Most youths are totally dependent upon their father or father-surrogate to supply the shell money required to formalize betrothal and marriage. If the latter is slow to initiate a betrothal for his son the youth may reach an understanding with the girl of his choice and request his father to negotiate with the girl's parents. If the father disapproves the choice or cannot supply or obtain the necessary shell money, the youth can either set about to earn enough on his own — a process requiring several years, or, if he is less enterprising, he can hang about his home, disgruntled and listless, until he inherits some shell money or until some widow is bestowed upon him for a greatly reduced sum. One unkempt and shiftless youth I knew was at the age of about twenty-five still single and living in his father's household, and the neighbors blamed the father for not having secured a wife for him.

According to some informants, the modern trend towards more and easier social contacts has increased the number of matches resulting from sexual alliances. It is said that if the pair please each other they agree to marry, and the youth requests his father to negotiate with the girl's parents. (Many girls complain that boys often deceive them about their intentions and do nothing about formalizing the betrothal, leaving them to wait silently and in vain.)

Negotiating the formal betrothal is not always a simple matter even if both parents approve of the match, for there is usually some haggling over payments. In addition to agreeing on the amount of the betrothal "gift" (*akuno*), it is also necessary to agree on the actual marriage payment which must eventually be made before the marriage itself is formalized. This latter payment is in ordinary shell money, and it varies in amount from 100 to 200 spans, according to the rank of the girl's father. When agreement is reached on both these sums and when the betrothal gift has been presented, the formal betrothal period begins, ushering in important social changes. But before describing these changes a variant on betrothal-arranging should be mentioned.

Now and then ambitious men with younger sisters under their guardianship will agree to a mutual exchange and hence marry each other's sister, for the purpose of cementing a politically useful brother-in-law relationship. Whether or not such an exchange is formalized with betrothal gifts and marriage payments, such acts of "sister-trading" are considered reprehensible by most Siuai, and on two counts. First of all, people reason, women are not chattels to be traded like pigs and shell money. And secondly, it is most shameful for a man to concern himself with negotiations for sexual rights over his sister. Normally sensitive men feel great "shame" (maio) at the mere mention of sexual matters relating to a sister, and brothers-in-law in particular should avoid discussing such matters — or even hearing about any sexual matters in one another's presence ("they feel shame because of the sister"). Nevertheless, some men persist in sister-trading despite public opinion, and the scandal seems to wear away in time.

Here in Siuai it is the act of formal betrothal rather than the nuptial ceremony which establishes affinal relationships between the young couple and their closest in-laws; at the time of formal betrothal affinal kinship terms immediately begin to be used, along with corresponding patterns of behavior. For example, the avoidance relationship between the youth and the girl's mother enters into full force. They may not call each other's name or share food or sit near together. Also, the youth and his fiancée's brothers become full-fledged brothers-in-law in all their contacts with each other, assisting one another in various enterprises but avoiding boisterous jesting and all sexual references in one another's presence. Particularly should they avoid mentioning the fiancée in any context even remotely suggestive of sex.

For the girl, formal betrothal may change her life radically. Often she leaves her own family and goes to live in the household of her fiancé,[19] where she remains until the nuptials have been carried out or the marriage otherwise entered upon. She becomes a full-fledged member of her fiancé's household, working and living along with other females there and under the strict surveillance of his mother. During the betrothal period, although the couple do not call each other husband ($i\eta$) and wife (ina), and should not copulate or in fact touch each other, all other people refer to each of them as "so-and-so's spouse," and the fiancé assumes exclusive rights over the girl's sexual services even though he himself should not copulate with her until later. The Siuai believe that the mother of a girl's fiancé (or, in Siuai terms, her mother-in-law) is much more effective than her own mother in safeguarding the fiancé's sexual rights over her, and that is one of the reasons given for the girl's change in residence. Another reason given is the desirability of having the girl begin to provide food for her future husband.

It was our observation that a girl moves to her fiancé's household in about two out of three cases. Those who remain at home present something of a problem. Being of ideal age and usually of eager willingness for love affairs, they cause their parents and their fiancés great concern. Few Siuai parents are severe or watchful enough to keep them in line, so that the fiancé or his father may resort to assigning a scout, usually a young lad, to report on her activities. It was amusing to me as well as to many of the Siuai to see this small boy trailing after his charge; and it was considered a wonderful joke when word got around that one of these scouts turned out to be more mature than suspected! However, such goings-on are not amusing to the fiancé and his family. They often result in termination of the betrothal and, after much recrimination and argument over blame, in return of all or most of the betrothal gift. In other instances betrayed fiancés content themselves with exacting fines from their fiancées' seducers.

So disturbing to public peace can a lively and desirable young woman be that the community's leader sometimes steps in and tries to find a strong-willed fiancé for her if her parents cannot do so, taking care of course not to compel the girl into an utterly distasteful union, which is also recognized as containing seeds of strife. Particularly troublesome is the circumstance involving the fiancée of a youth who is away working on a plantation. The usual term of indenture is three years and that constitutes too difficult a test for the girl's fidelity or for her in-laws' watchfulness. Many young women are betrothed off and on several times before marrying — nor do their adventures cease there.

Betrothals may also be terminated for other reasons. There was, for example, the case of the young woman who, though remaining faithful to her fiancé and obedient to his mother, nevertheless became so disgusted with his pettishness that she returned home and prevailed upon her father to send back the betrothal gift. Or, somewhat more frequently, a young girl will be sent home if she proves indolent at gardening or household work. An almost certain break-off occurs when one of the couple slanders the other's relatives within hearing. Bitter quarrels and court cases nearly always develop out of all these types of rupture.

Most periods of betrothal lead into marriage upon transfer of marriage payment, building of a house, and celebration of nuptials; but it sometimes happens that a betrothed couple will drift into a state of marriage without further exchanges or formalities. This usually transpires, for example, when they flaunt the convention against sexual intercourse to the point of causing pregnancy. In such cases as these there would be no point to a nuptial ceremony and, according to the youth and his father, no necessity for a marriage payment. The girl's parents will usually agree about the inappropriateness of having nuptials under these circumstances, but they can be counted upon to litigate vigorously against the nonpayment. Whose point prevails depends upon the local and current meaning attached to the marriage payment, but in any case the marriage eventually receives wide enough sanction for all practical purposes.[20]

## NUPTIALS

The Siuai nuptial ceremony corresponds somewhat to a church wedding among urban, middle-class, Protestant Americans: it is a socially desirable way to formalize a marriage but it is performed for no secondary unions and for only some three out of five primary ones. As mentioned above, even in addition to unions involving elopement and, formerly, capture, some formal betrothals shade into a generally sanctioned state of marriage without further exchange of valuables. Family and matrilineage mates of the girl may protest such a situation but the effectiveness of their protest depends upon their influence; and if the girl likes the arrangement the husband's relatives and the public at large simply ignore the protests. In other cases, the two families may agree to forego the nuptial ceremony for reasons which will be mentioned below.

The ceremony itself consists of rites of ablution, unction, and union, followed by a feast and, in some cases, the formal carrying-off of the bride. In most cases it is not held until a home has been built for the couple.

The ceremony usually takes place at the residence of the bride's family, even if she has already been dwelling in her fiancé's residence in another hamlet. It is usually scheduled for midmorning, but ordinarily does not begin until midday, because of the inevitable Siuai delays in preparations. Both families attend in force, along with matrilineage mates and neighbors and the usual lot of idle male gadabouts (*avi'kura*, "swallow") who turn up at any special occasion where they are not specifically excluded by convention or by demand.

The rites of ablution take place in a nearby stream. Bride and groom sit facing downstream on a length of wood in the middle of the stream and between them sits a pre-pubescent girl, a young *sister* of the bride. All three are dressed in clean loincloths and ornamented with several spans of high-value shell money hung around their necks and shoulders. Behind each of them stands or squats an old woman, a growth-magic practitioner, who laves them with stream water by means of a bundle of leaves tied together with strings of high-value shell money. While the old women perform their ritual they repeat a growth-magic formula.

Like all maru,[21] these formulae are identified with single sibs. Ideally, in this matrilineal society, maru used for a nuptial ceremony should be that of the bride's sib, but if there is no one from the bride's sib available for performing the ritual, then a maru-magician from the groom's sib will substitute. Shell money ornamentation used to decorate the bridal party is also associated with sibs, each person wearing strands of his matrilineage's heirlooms (tomui), while the strands used to bind together the ablutionary leaves belong to the matrilineage of the performing maru-magicians.

Three explanations are offered for the presence of the "bridesmaid"; some natives say that every young girl should participate at least once in a nuptial ceremony in order to increase her own prospects for an early and fruitful marriage; others say that she participates because she would someday "assist" the bride, either as co-wife or, in the case of the bride's demise, as sororal substitute. Still other informants wave aside such explanations and account for her presence with the usual: "the kupunas performed it in this manner, so we do likewise."

The ablutions last a quarter of an hour or so and are anything but solemn. In those we witnessed the groom squirmed and frowned at the bother of it or relapsed into obvious boredom, while the bride tittered with her little companion, and the maru-magicians interrupted their performance to converse or to shout at some onlooker. Meanwhile, a few of the wedding guests looked on for a few moments, then lost interest and moved upstream to bathe. Children were allowed to frolic in the water nearby with nothing more than an ineffectual "Don't" tossed at them.

When ablutions are over the bridal party troops back to the hamlet for the rite of unction, which takes place in front of a dwelling house whose doorway is festooned with strands of shell money and branches of areca nuts. In front of the doorway a live pig lies on its side held down by cords staked to the ground. The groom, bridesmaid, and bride stand on unhusked coconuts a few feet from the house facing it and usually supporting themselves by leaning on stakes driven into the ground. The three maru-magicians squat behind them, lave them by hand with coconut oil dipped out of a coconut shell bowl, and repeat the maru formula said before. As in other maru rituals, the coconut props symbolize a plentiful food supply, but this may not be the whole explanation for usually the groom stands on or touches two coconuts to the bride's and bridesmaid's one each. (Why? "Because he himself has two," I was laughingly told.)

While this episode is in progress one or two men bend double the neck of the captive pig until it dies of slow strangulation or neck-break. This, far more than the ritual anointing, excites the interest of the onlookers, who stand around shouting suggestions and whooping with glee when the tortured animal wriggles. After twenty or thirty minutes of that even the sturdiest beast succumbs; whereupon the maru-magicians complete their performance by touching the genitals of bride and groom.

The third episode takes place in the house. Bride and groom, together with one of her old *mother's mothers* and one of his old *mother's mother's brothers* enter the house and seat themselves so that the young couple are in the middle. The bride is given a piece of uncooked pork which she hands to the groom while holding on to one end of it. The groom then cuts the pork in half; he hands his half to his old kinsman and his bride hands her part to her old kinswoman. (This action is usually accompanied by shyness and a show of reluctance on the part of the bride, the only such display of the whole nuptial ceremony.) Having received the pork, the older man, speaking for the groom, addresses the bride in this way:

"I shall make myself weary working industriously for this woman, and she will be like the *kurimpo* bird as it walks about a cleared space eating the worms." (Meaning, I shall be a good husband and work continually. I shall clear garden sites so thoroughly that she will have little more to do than to walk about it planting taro here and there.)

Then the older woman, speaking for the bride, replies:

"I shall work hard for this man, fetching water from the stream, carrying firewood, and cooking pork for him."

Meanwhile the guests outside wait in silence — for this is the climax of the ceremony, the real act of union. When the older pair leave the house upon completion of the pork-cutting episode, someone asks them: "Is it finished: have they held the pork?" The older pair answer affirmatively, and then everyone knows that the two young people are fully wed. No importance whatsoever is attached to actual sexual consummation: natives assume that it has already taken place before formal betrothal, or even during betrothal and despite the convention against it.

The pigs provided for the ceremony and not already butchered are now cut into strips and handed around to the guests, who take their portions home for cooking. (Bride's and groom's families are expected to furnish equivalent amounts of pork for the ceremony.) [22] If the newly married couple are to reside in the community where the wedding takes place, the ceremony is now complete. Otherwise, if they are to reside elsewhere the ceremony is completed by the carrying of the bride to the new abode. For this strenuous task the most robust *sister* of the bride's mother-in-law is selected, and they set off along the narrow, winding women's paths, looking like a mother with an overgrown child on her back, and accompanied by most of the women guests at the wedding. Natives do not attempt to rationalize this episode beyond attributing it to the kupunas.[23]

Upon completion of the nuptial ceremony bride and groom extend affinal kin terms, and appropriate behavior patterns, to each other's consanguineous relatives beyond the limits of the nuclear family, for example, the groom calls "brother-in-law" not only his wife's true brother, whom he began addressing thus upon betrothal, but many of his wife's male parallel cousins as well. In the case of marriages not formalized by nuptials affinal terms also come in time to be extended beyond the spouse's nuclear family, but it is a gradual development.

It used to be customary for women to remain naked throughout childhood and to don pubic aprons only after the nuptial ceremony; calico loincloths are now worn from early childhood onwards, so that this custom no longer holds. There still remains, however, some token respect for the norm prohibiting bodily contact between a betrothed couple until the pork-cutting rite; and that is why, some say, the bride becomes shy and reluctant during this stage of the ceremony: "she realizes that this man can now copulate with her."

A marriage formalized by nuptials is more difficult to dissolve than one otherwise constituted, but to comprehend this we must review and expand the information on property transactions associated with marriage.

Siuai distinguish sharply between the high-value shell money "gift" (akuno) made in connection with betrothal and the ordinary shell money paid just before marriage (pu). The former is turned over to the woman and is retained by her. If the engagement is broken off it should be returned to the fiancé; and although the girl's family may controvert this, the resulting litigation usually supports the fiancé's claim. If the fiancée dies the betrothal gift should also be returned, although part of it may be returned by the fiancé to help purchase a pig for the girl's mourners; this kind of gesture is praiseworthy but infrequent. If the fiancé is the one to die, and if relations between the two families are amicable, the fiancée may be allowed to retain some of the betrothal gift as her own, and the rest is returned to the fiancé's family in the form of pork for his mourners.

After marriage, the high-value shell money which constituted the betrothal gift remains in possession of the wife and, by convention, should be expended only for such special purposes as purchase of pork for mourners on the occasion of the death of one of her offspring. Most informants describe this betrothal gift as "payment" to the wife for her sexual services to her husband, and unless the death of either spouse takes place within a few months after marriage no repayment is made. On the other hand, if a man divorces his wife shortly after marriage he usually demands and gets back the betrothal gift, although some benign husbands may permit their estranged wives to retain some of it: "as payment for the food she contributed and the many times he copulated with her."

An entirely different meaning is attached to the payment (pu) in ordinary shell money made just prior to marriage. Most Siuai agree that this money should be used entirely by the bride's father or guardian to purchase pigs for the nuptial ceremony — with the groom's family providing an equivalent amount of pork. In other words, when used in this traditional manner, the payment results in no residue of obligation or liability on anyone's part, and no legitimate demand for restitution can be made by the husband in the case of divorce or death of his spouse. Latterly, however, some men are acting so as to transform this usage. Instead of using all the shell money to provide pigs for the nuptial ceremony, they hold back all or part of it, claiming that it is: "pay for the woman." The first few instances of this new practice were brought before the Hat-men by the outraged families of grooms, and native officials upheld the traditional usage. However, one stubborn father of a bride refused to comply and the case was brought before the white Patrol Officer; the latter reportedly upheld the defendant, presumably on the basis of some New Guinea practices. This decision added momentum to the trend, and now more and more men are attempting to derive profit from marriage exchanges. It has even reached the point where kinsmen of an orphaned girl are demanding payment for her nuptials-less marriage.

Most Siuai continue to regard this new practice as reprehensible, somewhat like simultaneous sister-exchange in its implication that women are chattels; and when marriage negotiations take place the youth's father usually demands assurances that the girl's father will abide by the traditional usage. However, there is now no direct physical sanction to prevent the girl's father from repudiating.[24] Some thoughtful informants say that the new practice results from a general modern trend wherein people think more and more in terms of money and less and less in terms of old customs. There is also a good possibility that some natives learned about the new practice on their travels beyond Siuai.

## SETTING UP THE HOUSEHOLD

Young couples in Siuai start off their married lives in their own houses, and in most instances these houses are located near the parents of one of them. Here are some figures derived from a survey of 270 primary unions among residents of northeast Siuai; the question asked was: "Where did the couple reside during the first few years (moi) after they began to live and copulate together?"[25] In listing these figures a distinction is made between line village and hamlet; for example, in 97 cases both husband wife resided in the same village prior to marriage and remained there after marriage, but of these only 9 couples resided in the same hamlet unit of the village both before and after marriage.

Using the village as the area of reference, virilocality can be said to have prevailed in 101 cases, uxorilocality in 55, neolocality in 3, and ambilocality in 14. "Virilocal" in the sense here used means that husband and wife resided in different villages before marriage (or before betrothal, in instances wherein the affianced girl changed residence during betrothal) and resided in the husband's village for the first years after marriage. The term is not meant to signify how the husband came to be in his village in the first place. "Uxorilocal" has a corresponding meaning, while "neolocal" means that the couple moved to an entirely new village after marriage. "Ambilocal" means that they alternated residences fairly regularly between his and her pre-marriage villages; it does not mean mere visiting.

In terms of the smaller hamlet unit of area, and in meanings corresponding to those just stated, virilocality prevailed in 176 cases, uxorilocality in 48, neolocality in 23, and ambilocality in 14. In 88 of all cases, the couple remained in their common pre-marital village, only changes in hamlet residence having been involved.

These statistics do not, of course, exhaust the subject of *residence*; they tell only where couples live in the years immediately after marriage.[26] Nevertheless, the early years of married life are crucial ones, and a young couple's first place of residence has important consequences for their everyday lives. The full significance of *residence* must await description of hamlet life for clarification; for the present it is enough to note the preponderance of virilocality and the very negligible number of couples that begin married life in relatively unfamiliar neighborhoods.

Siuai believe that every young married couple should reside in its own separate house, and relatives assist in building one for them if there is not an old one available. As previously mentioned, this is not a particularly large undertaking; if the couple is to live near the husband's home he usually builds most of it by himself, spreading the work over a number of weeks and receiving occasional help from relatives. For a house built in the girl's village her fiancé can always count on help from *brothers-in-law*, so that the construction goes faster.

Furnishing the house is a simple matter. Husband and wife provide their own tools, and parents donate the few utensils required for cooking and storage, there being no rigid prescription concerning who contributes what. Of much more concern to the newly weds are the first steps they take to produce their own food and raise their own pigs.

The Siuai ideal is for every married couple to produce its own food in its own separate garden patch, and it is the native belief — based on experience — that stable marriages are more likely if couples control their own food supply. Women, particularly, take pride in having their own gardens, and a bride complains if her husband does not begin a separate clearing soon after marriage. In fact, many young men begin to clear separate garden sites before marriage, utilizing some of the timbers for building their houses. It is assumed that the bride will work with kinswomen in their gardens until her own patch is producing; some continue to do this for reasons of sociability long after their own gardens are producing, and this holds especially for a bride co-gardening with her own consanguineous kin. Few brides, however, are content for long to work under supervision of a mother-in-law, continually reminded of a wife's duty to work hard and feed her husband well. Some brides even rebel under the circumstances, and one we knew returned to her own parents and succeeded in having the marriage annulled. From the standpoint of social stability one useful feature of cross-cousin marriage is the firm basis it provides for harmonious interaction among affinal kin and particularly between a bride and her co-gardeners during the first few months of married life.

Obtaining taro shoots for the new garden rarely presents a problem. Bride and groom take shoots from their parents' gardens, this being considered their privilege because of their previous labors there. I heard of only one case of a groom having to purchase all the shoots used in establishing his garden; he had just returned after six years of plantation labor, his parents were dead, and his bride came from a distant village.

One additional reason for a newly married couple's wanting an independent food supply is their desire for their own pigs. A slur aimed at a pompous man is: "He feeds his pig on others' taro."

To most Siuai, "settling down" to married life primarily means taking on the responsibility of raising pigs. One of the first acts of a couple after marriage is to acquire a small female pig. Usually the husband receives an animal from his father, or he may use his own or borrowed shell money to purchase a small pig from a neighbor. It sometimes happens that the bride contributes one she has tended in anticipation of marriage; or, in these modern times, youths now and then purchase pigs at the whites' plantations they work on and bring them home to be tended by mother or sister until they acquire a wife to do the job. For it is not a simple matter to feed and domesticate a young sow and bring it through its first farrowing.

The Siuai method of raising pigs requires the animal's owners to give it frequent feedings and constant care until it is properly domesticated. Hence a young couple usually retires to its new hamlet house and stays close by during the first few months of married life. The man builds a small pen alongside the house for the pig and cares for it lovingly, befitting the pet that it is. His wife cooks the pig's food in the common pot and tempts its appetite with delicacies all through the day. If the young animal refuses to eat in the new surroundings, the owners conclude that it needs a new name and proceed to name it somewhat in the same manner that human infants are named.[27] Food delicacies are placed on a platter and offered to the pig while calling off the names of prominent men and women now dead; the pig is then given the name being called when it begins to nibble at the food.

After a few weeks the animal is allowed out of its pen for increasing amounts of time, and after three or four months it may be relied on to stay near the house and fend for itself. When this is accomplished its owners feel freer to remain for longer periods away from home, taking care, however, to put in several appearances daily, "to keep the animal from becoming lonely" and running away. By the time the pig is eight to ten months old its owners can more or less rely on its domestication, and need thereafter to feed it only once a day.

Few couples are content with one pig, and most of them will acquire a series of them until one of their own sows farrows. With all this, and especially with the added responsibility of feeding and caring for a new litter, the man and his wife must work harder to enlarge their garden. For the woman all these new requirements of married life result merely in an intensification of labor, not a marked change in activities or routine. For the husband, however, they bring about a radical change in his everyday living. Young men, whether married or single, like to spend their days lounging in club-houses or gadding about like young peacocks in their clean calico loincloths with their bushy coiffures carefully bleached, combed, and perfumed. If they own a village house they prefer to sleep nights there, often affecting a fastidious distaste for the filth which invariably accumulates at a hamlet house. Tending a litter of pigs changes all that. Caring for a single animal can be a sport, even though it involves long stays at the hamlet house; but providing for a litter is another matter. Hungry squeals remind the young husband that more food will be required when the animals are larger; hence larger garden sites have to be cleared and extra supplies of taro shoots borrowed or purchased. There is less time for gossiping and visiting about, hence less purpose in grooming. His calico fades and tatters, and his coiffure becomes dirty and louse-ridden. Grimy and shabby as he is, he will be less likely to awaken desire in the young women who see him. Yet there are compensations in this new mode of living: older kinsmen and neighbors note with approval the youth's changed appearance, for it is a sure sign that he is no longer a mere dandy and has become a pig-raiser, a property owner, an associate in economic enterprises. He will now be more coöperative in neighborhood undertakings and will begin to join his voice with fellow property-owners when they critically discuss younger men: "Just see that lazy dandy walk about carrying all his property in his net bag!" Having acquired a taste for owning pigs and joining the councils of his elders, he will begin scheming to increase his herd and his influence in local affairs.

Meanwhile, everyday relations between the young husband and his wife are expected to develop in accord with Siuai standards regarding division of labor. As already described, man's work is to clear and fence the gardens, provide sago and food delicacies, and keep the house in repair; woman's job to plant, cultivate, and harvest the staple crops, collect wild foods, and prepare meals. They both have a hand in tending pigs, but as the novelty of a new litter wears off, the man usually leaves this work to his wife. On the other hand, it is the duty of the man to keep the herd restocked with new animals and to accumulate shell money for special occasions, including the hire of professional services for curing sickness and warding off catastrophes. Failure to carry out one's proper domestic role almost invariably results in friction.

The lazy bride is a familiar character in many Siuai tales and she usually ends up by being sent packing, in the tales no less than in real life. Siuai men expect less of young wives than of middle-aged ones; they observe and tolerate the circumstance that handsome young women do not automatically become drudges when married. Nevertheless, some things must be done if the domestic economy is to operate: food must be produced and prepared, firewood brought home and drinking water kept on hand. If a wife falls down on these chores, quarrels ensue and divorces sometimes result. For her part the wife expects as a minimum that her husband will clear and fence enough garden space, and if he fails to do that she may return to her home and break off the marriage; moreover, nearly everyone will applaud her action.

Extreme parsimony on the part of a man may also cause his young wife to leave him, and this too receives popular support. Men have to provide directly only a quantitatively small share of the family's food supply but when they fail in this, either through laziness or meanness, wives nearly always rebel. For example, one of our neighbors was something of a public joke when he continued to saunter elegantly about the countryside long after his marriage, but the jests turned into contempt when his wife left him, explaining that he alone ate the pork given them for mourning at cremations.

Another common source of friction is the bride's "homesickness." Some young women having to reside in their husband's settlement insist on making frequent visits to their parents' homes, either to escape intolerable conditions or because of genuinely strong attachments for their own consanguineous kin. Few husbands like this situation; it means irregular and inadequate meals and half-hungry pigs, and there is also the possibility of a lover lurking around the home of the wife's parents. But unless the husband has the sympathy and coöperation of his wife's family there is not much he can do short of divorce to stop the practice. And woe to the husband who attempts to restrain a young homesick wife! During our stay in northeast Siuai two young wives there committed suicide when forbidden to return to their parents' homes. In one of the cases the husband had ordered his wife to remain home because of the swollen creeks and the danger of drowning en route; the woman wept for a few hours and then made off to her father's garden where she hanged herself. In the process of documenting genealogies we noted that suicides from homesickness have occurred about twice a year during the past decade. It is quite possible, of course, that such cases as these are culminations of a series of dissensions; nevertheless they indicate the extent to which the "homesickness" of a young bride has become a standard expectation and a patterned device for resolving some of the difficulties of early married life.

Another common source of friction is infidelity. Some women, say the Siuai, become libertine as a result of desires awakened by affairs with too many men; others become uncontrollably so through the operation of passion-rousing magic secretly administered by some malicious ex-suitor. Whatever the cause may be, it is certainly true that there are numbers of such women — at least one well-known case in each village. As such women lose the buoyancy of youth — and Siuai women do so rapidly under their regimes of work and child-bearing — other men no longer find them so desirable and their husbands waste little jealousy on them and their occasional adventures. During their early married years, however, such women are a source of trouble not only to their husbands but to their neighbors as well. Some of them are married and divorced three and four times before they settle down with either a determined or an indifferent husband. Mairu, a pretty, coquettish, and lively young woman, was betrothed three times, and three times sent home by irate in-laws on account of her sharp tongue and roving eyes. After that no sensible youth would risk marrying her, so that the native headman of her father's village literally *assigned* her as fiancée to a slow-witted youth whose chances of getting a desirable wife would otherwise have been slight. Nuptials were omitted, and the young couple began married life in a house built by the youth and his father. After a month or so of frequent copulation interspersed with violent quarreling and not much gardening, Mairu wearied of her husband and returned to her old pastimes. When her father-in-law tried to control her by threatening to bring her before the headman for trial, she is said to have told him: "Do so; then the headman can put himself in jail along with all the rest of the village, for he too likes what I have."

Fortunately for the stability of marriages there are only some twenty to thirty women like Mairu in northeast Siuai; but there are few young wives who remain altogether faithful. Knowing this full well, most young husbands are continually suspicious, and often give vent to jealous anger. If wives return late from the garden they may be greeted with: "And who have you been copulating with this time, while I sit here without food?"

Young wives also taunt their husbands with infidelity now and then, and I recorded a few instances of jealous wives leaving their husbands for a few days; but such situations never lead to complete rupture and seldom even to continuous disharmony.

Probably all new marriages in Siuai contain some of each of the elements of friction listed above, and in addition there are other less dramatic factors which contribute to the relative instability of early married life. For example, in-laws sometimes interfere; in some virilocal families the husband's mother becomes assertive and critical even beyond the will of a Siuai wife to tolerate. Similarly, the wife's father and brother occasionally appear all too solicitous of her welfare and happiness, and may threaten the husband with annulment and fines if he does not mend his ways. Also the husband's father sometimes assumes the role of guarding his daughter-in-law's virtue.

Personal incompatibilities possibly lie at the base of all sharp breaks in young married life; more often, though, they show up in only minor explosions. This kind of episode occurs frequently and provides entertainment for the neighbors: Koura and his wife, Sinto, quarreled violently outside their village house one afternoon, she accusing him of putting in too little time at the garden, and he accusing her of general laziness. Koura became so enraged that he beat her shoulders with his fist, tore off her loincloth and tossed it onto the roof. Sinto retrieved her loincloth and ripped off his, tearing it in the process. At this point they became ashamed because of the crowd that had gathered, and retired inside the house to finish the quarrel. In another instance, Sinnui was sitting with some other women cracking almonds and she called out to her husband, Kakai, to build a rack so that the nuts could be smoked that evening. Kakai agreed to do so, but procrastinated and finally went to the club-house and slept. When all the nuts were cracked Sinnui and her companions carried them in baskets to the work-shed for smoking, but discovered that no rack had been built. Later that afternoon when Kakai returned home to eat he found an enraged Sinnui, who threw some husks at him, kicked over several baskets of almonds, and told him to go fill his belly and employ his penis elsewhere.

Few such episodes result in serious breaks; in fact, there is an institutionalized device which helps to insure that they will not. After a serious marital quarrel one of the couple usually leaves home and goes to live with parents or matrilineage-mates until a reconciliation token (*rakai*) has been presented. In the case of older couples and especially those with offspring, it is nearly always the husband who leaves home, and it is the wife who initiates the reconciliation by sending a rakai in the form of a new carrying-basket or a few spans of shell money. Whoever was at fault in such cases, the Siuai reason, it is the wife who has more to lose by a break, since she is no longer young enough to be desired by men. With younger couples, however, the husband is not above giving the rakai, especially if he is clearly at fault;[28] but usually there is an exchange of rakai.

It would of course be a distortion to imply that all or even most young marriages are characterized by disharmony, but it is certainly true that they involve a number of adjustments, some of them apparently difficult; and it is also an observable fact that older marriages are more stable than new ones. Time undoubtedly has something to do with this; another stabilizing circumstance is the arrival of offspring.

## PREGNANCY AND CHILDBIRTH

The Siuais' fondness of children and their desire for offspring of their own is evident in countless traits of their culture and in numerous everyday demonstrations of affection and concern.[29] We could discover no instance of a married man not wanting children; in fact, the mere suggestion that such could be possible brought protests from informants. Most women also want offspring,[30] although we did learn that some young married women try to avoid having children if they are dissatisfied with their husbands and repelled by their sexual advances. Also I was told by male informants that women now and then try to postpone having offspring[31] in order to hold off for a while the physical deterioration which seems always to accompany childbearing. However, for most women, as well as for men, having offspring is one of the main goals of married life.

Now and then I heard the wish for offspring put in terms of a desire for continuity. All Siuai are glad when one of their female matrilineage-mates gives birth to a girl, for that means the perpetuation of their matrilineage group with all that this implies. And men, especially, delight in the birth of a son, to whom they can transfer their earned wealth and perhaps aid in winning renown. Men also welcome the birth of a sister's son, a rightful co-owner of matrilineage property and a potential son-in-law. All in all, though, the impression remained with me that most Siuai parents want children mainly because they love them and enjoy them. The desire for continuity is certainly there but it is a very weak rationale in comparison with similar sentiments found elsewhere in many patrilineal societies. Moreover, in matrilineal Siuai, boys are as welcome as girls; differences in this respect may occur between man and wife and from family to family, but averaging these out leaves the assertion intact.

Siuai beliefs concerning the anatomy and physiology of reproduction have already been described.[32] It will be recalled that, according to native theories, sexual fluids from both mother and genitor go into the formation of the fetus, that several emissions from one genitor are required for conception, and that after the fetus has begun to form, intercourse should cease in order to avoid injuring it. The relationship between pregnancy and menstruation is known in a general way, but women say that they know when the fetus is formed even prior to the interruption of menstruation.

Promiscuous women are believed unable to conceive;[33] also, as just stated, it is believed that a woman can prevent conception from taking place. Natives say that older women become suspicious of a young wife if she does not become pregnant. They suspect that she is purposefully avoiding pregnancy by chewing contraception magic, which they seek to counteract by surreptitiously feeding her another magical compound. If on the other hand a woman wishes to conceive and cannot do so in spite of frequent intercourse with one man, plainly some malicious person has been secretly feeding her contraception magic, and she takes steps to neutralize this by eating its magical antidote. Husbands may also guard against barrenness by procuring a ghost-consecrated shrub and planting it beside the entrance of their hamlet houses; the guardian ghosts help to ward off the malicious attacks.

Despite their general knowledge of fetal development, the Siuai cannot estimate very accurately the period of gestation. A few assert that "nine months" is the period required, but this is information obviously acquired at plantations or missions, and is neither generally known nor used as a tally. Many women return to their parental homes to give birth just before they think the event due, and we noted that some of them miscalculate by two or three months, even granting the occurrence of actual physical delays. And of course, some men suspect their wives of deceptively anticipating the event in order to spend more time with their parents and avoid further garden work. For, most women ease up their working habits somewhat as pregnancy proceeds; about two-thirds along, for example, many of them reduce the size of loads of firewood — which still does not give them a life of ease! Husbands are expected to help them with their heavier tasks, and as the time draws near, to indulge their food fancies by providing more delicacies. But there is a limit to any husband's indulgence, as was indicated in the genesis myth of the Tree-rats in which Tree-rat's father cut off his own penis in annoyance at having to work so hard to satisfy his wife's whims.[34]

Pregnancy is a trying time to a husband in another way: he must either forego sexual intercourse altogether or find other partners, and that involves inconveniences and the hazards already described. Nevertheless most Siuai natives, including most wives, do not expect men to remain continent during a wife's pregnancy and I became amply convinced that they do not remain so. However, a husband must be circumspect in his adventures; most of all he must not allow word of them to reach his wife's brother. As mentioned above, a man is said to feel embarrassment or shame if he hears any *sister* of his mentioned in a context of sex or reproduction, and this applies to his own sister with such force that no one may announce to him the news of her pregnancy except the man most directly concerned, i.e., his sister's husband; and the husband must do so formally and accompany the announcement to his wife's brother with a gift (*numehu*) of at least ten spans of shell money to alleviate the latter's "embarrassment." On one occasion a native I knew demanded and got from his sister's husband double the amount of the usual numehu because he had learned of his sister's pregnancy through someone else. (In this connection, informants assured me that the main reason for a man wanting to learn the identity of an unbetrothed sister's seducer is to exact numehu from him.)

Meanwhile magical care must be taken of the pregnant woman to insure safe delivery and healthy offspring: "belly-washing" (*kipu u*) is a growth-magic ritual performed by a female magician once and sometimes twice during a pregnancy. Only the pregnant woman's husband and her parents and sisters look on while this short ritual is performed, and no feast accompanies it, the magician being remunerated, if at all, with a few spans of shell money.

Natives say that abortion is not practiced. We could not verify this, but it was evident from their horrified reactions to our inquiry that the idea is repugnant to them. Miscarriage itself is one of their abiding fears, and tao, the magic that induces miscarriage, stillbirth, and death in childbirth, is considered the most despicable kind of sorcery.

Tao sorcery is performed — or rather, it is believed to be performed — in utter secrecy; no man admits practicing it, although many are so charged. Natives say that the performer of tao does so out of revenge for having been denied a woman's favors by her or for having been refused by her parents when he sought to marry her. His reason is said to be: "if I cannot enter this woman with my penis then I shall do so with tao, and then no other man will have fruitful copulation with her." Tao is a small object, usually a short length of cane, consecrated by the ghosts of men who have successfully performed tao in the past. The sorcerer hides the tao in the center of a path customarily used by the victim, and then he hides nearby to wait for her. If other women walk by he whispers to the tao: "Not that one." But when the intended victim approaches he whispers to the tao: "That one. Enter that one's vagina. That one is your mother; remain in her womb. If a fetus forms there, kill it. But if the fetus grows, kill it and the mother at birth."

Some natives believe that tao remains active after birth, and can slay a woman and her infant until weaning is complete.[35]

If a miscarriage occurs or an infant dies, the husband summons a mikai magician [36] to discover the cause. The mikai peers around the victim's house to search out any demon that might be causing the trouble. If he sees one, he orders his own spirit-familiar to drive it away. If no demon is lurking about, the mikai knows that tao is the cause and advises the husband to employ tuki to prevent recurrences. Also, if a woman herself dies in childbirth, that is clear evidence of tao sorcery.

Tuki is a divinatory ritual which discovers the location of the tao and the identity of the sorcerer. Tuki specialists work in pairs. At the settlement of their client they set up a straight row of long sticks in the ground some ten feet apart; they presumably name each stick for a living or recently deceased male neighbor of the client, but do not divulge these names until later. Then they set up their tuki over a fire in which white clay and food tidbits are burning. The tuki itself is a small version of the stretcher used for carrying large pigs. While the smoke from the burning food-offerings rises around the tuki, the specialists address their tuki-ghosts, asking them to partake of the offering and sit on the stretcher. After a few moments of this, the specialists remove the sticks supporting the tuki and hold it themselves over the smoke. Then the tuki begins to shake, signifying that the ghosts have complied; the specialists assert that they are powerless to keep the stretcher from moving and usually invite onlookers to hold one end of the stretcher to see for themselves.

Gradually the tuki moves more and more violently, until it impels the specialists to run with it up and down the line of upright sticks. The climax is reached when the tuki causes itself to be thrust so violently against one of the uprights that it knocks it over. With this, the specialists shout out a name — the one they had presumably given this stick and hence the identity of the sorcerer. But that is not all. The tuki then causes its bearers to proceed at a run to the spot where the tao has been hidden, and the husband or father of the victimized woman destroys its effectiveness by throwing it into a stream, thereby removing the cause of misfortune.

Formerly the victim's relatives acted to revenge the misfortune by trying to spear and kill the person disclosed to have been the sorcerer. Now that such killing is outlawed there would normally be the alternatives of either legally prosecuting the sorcerer or using magical means to kill him, but neither course is followed. The Siuai know by experience that white Administration officials will dismiss any sorcery complaint in which the identity of the alleged sorcerer has been disclosed by divination, but that jail and fines await the native known to have practiced divination — as would be the case in connection with tuki. In fact, in some instances where tuki has been employed, the person disclosed as sorcerer caused the men who commissioned the divination (but not the professional diviners who performed it) to be prosecuted for slander and required to pay damages. Consequently many men now commission for only part of the tuki rite, the part which discovers the location of tao. In the two complete tuki rites I saw, divination disclosed two recently deceased men as having been the tao sorcerers! Even so, kinsmen of the two threatened libel actions.

Sickly children are sometimes thought to be stricken with tao; and if the father cannot afford to pay for a tuki he may call in a therapist, who has neither a spirit-familiar nor the knowledge of divination, who in other words cannot remove the cause of the affliction, but who employs ghost-consecrated magical ingredients — leaves, insects, unguents, etc. — to counteract the effects of tao. The therapist is not always effective but he is relatively inexpensive — only five to ten spans of shell money as compared with fifty or more for tuki; and if the local therapist happens to be otherwise respected, his neighbors will almost certainly call him in before summoning a tuki specialist.

I have no reliable statistics on miscarriages — nor, for that matter, on fertility, fecundity, or sterility — but it is my impression that nearly every Siuai woman has miscarried at least once. At any rate, miscarriage occurs frequently enough for there to be solid factual foundation for these natives' dread of it, but this dread is not transferred to the dead fetus, which is taken away by the woman's mother or sister and unceremoniously buried.

A Siuai woman is very dependent on her own mother or older sister immediately before, during, and after giving birth; distant *mothers* or *sisters* sometimes have to substitute but that is only second-best. Other female relatives, including mother- and sisters-in-law and co-wives, usually assist and remain with her during this period. No male except an infant in arms or an old magician may be present at the birth nor during the "hiding" period after birth. Most Siuai women like to return to their parental homes during their first and second confinements, but there are no magical consequences to giving birth elsewhere.

When labor begins, the assisting women warn all boys and men to keep away from the place of birth. As labor pains increase the woman is made to sit on a low bed or log and hold onto a rope tied to an overhead beam or tree; then when birth begins she is encouraged to assist by pulling on the rope. Her mother or sister kneels behind her and massages her abdomen with heavy downward motions. Women say that birth is very painful and there is much anguished crying by mothers during their first confinements. We could get no satisfactory information about the duration of labor; Siuai do not possess clocks! A difficult delivery, and especially one involving breech-presentation, is believed due either to tao or to a malicious demon; nothing can be done about the tao at this point, but a mikai-magician — preferably an old woman, but if none is available, an old man — is summoned to drive away the demon, if there is one, and to bespit the woman with kuna to keep any other demon from harming her.[37]

One of the older women present cuts the umbilicus with a splinter of bamboo; the end attached to the mother is tied around a small stick to keep it from drawing back into her womb and thereby killing her, but the end attached to the child is left untied and hanging. If necessary the woman continues to sit in the birth position and be massaged until the afterbirth (*kiroko*) comes away; if it does not discharge, natives say that the woman always dies, there being no known way to assist her, neither medical nor magical. When the afterbirth does come away properly it is wrapped in leaves and carried by one of the women to the bank of a stream and buried there so that some future high water will take it away without anyone's knowing, the object being to hide it lest some malicious person discover it and use it in the performance of "dirt" sorcery, either to kill the infant or inhibit its growth.[38]

If the house is too hot and too small to accommodate the many assistants, the birth may take place just outside; sometimes it takes place on a stream bank, for ease in disposing of afterbirth and blood. Immediately afterwards however the woman is helped back to the house, where she receives medical and magical treatment.[39] She is sponged with leaves which have been warmed and softened over a fire, and is made to sit astride two logs between which fire-heated stones are placed and continually renewed; the heat from the stones is believed to enter her womb and heal it. While this is taking place some intrinsically potent ingredients (kuna) [40] are placed on the stones so that their essence will fill the woman's womb and act as an antiseptic, neutralizing any harmful substances that may have touched the woman — e.g., such things as dried blood from women who previously died in childbirth in that place. Meanwhile a girdle of warmed leaves is kept wrapped around her abdomen, she is given a hot vegetable broth mixed with kuna to revive her strength, and her breasts are washed with kuna-water to make the milk flow.

An older woman, preferably a sister, wipes off the infant with warmed banana leaves — "to make its skin firm" — and holds it until the mother can nurse it — or if that is delayed too long any woman present who has milk nurses the child until the mother's milk begins to flow.[41]

Throughout confinement all these services are performed preferably by the *mothers* and *sisters* of the confined woman; other women present would not be prevented from assisting but, unlike sib-mates, would expect to receive gifts in return for their services.

There follows a period of four or five weeks of "hiding": the infant, "the hidden one," is kept in the house; its mother leaves it only to go to the toilet stream, and while outside keeps her head and torso hooded under her cape lest the sun shine on her and dry up her milk, and lest some youth or man see her, thereby bringing harm to the infant.[42] The other women also remain in and around the house, attending to the needs of the mother and infant, and, men say, relating their sex experiences. These women have no diet restrictions as does the infant's mother, who, in order to keep her milk from drying up, may eat only boiled leaves and one corm of boiled taro a day — no oils or other delicacies being permitted.[43] During the period of "hiding" no male past toddling age should enter the house; in fact, males are not even told the sex and name of the infant. Nor may males eat food or chew areca nut handled by any one of the females staying in the house of hiding; they usually eat at the household of an older brother or sister or mother's brother.

A few hours after birth is carried out the first of the series of growth-magic rituals which are performed at intervals during the child's early years. The confined woman's husband summons a maru-magician, preferably a matrilineage-mate of his wife, and provides her with a package of almonds, an areca nut, and a mature coconut. Then the maru-magician, accompanied by most of the women in "hiding," goes to a nearby jungle grove and locates a *ho'* tree big enough to provide firewood. While repeating a growth-magic formula, she taps slowly against the tree with the package of almonds, naming a former maru-magician with each tap. After the whole list has been named, she repeats the sequence with the areca nut, then with the coconut, and then with an ax decorated with some high-value shell money from her matrilineage heirloom hoard. After this, some male matrilineage-mate of the infant fells the ho' tree with the same ax and chops it into firewood, which female matrilineage-mates of the infant carry back to the house of "hiding." While these women eat the almonds and dance (*koija*) outside, the maru-magician returns to the infant, makes oil out of the coconut, and rubs this oil over its body while repeating the growth-magic formula.[44] This ritual is performed in order to clean the infant somewhat and to strengthen it enough for it to survive until the main rite of baptism can be carried out at the end of "hiding." The maru-magician and all the women who carried wood are given a small feast by the newborn's father, and the maru-magician herself is paid a fee of a few spans of shell money if she is not a matrilineage-mate of the infant.

A day or two after this, the infant's first and most important name is made known to the women in "hiding." It is held in its mother's lap and offered her breast while some older *sister* of the woman calls names of older or deceased matrilineage-mates. When the infant "hears" its own name it begins to suckle, and all those present then know it, too. In some instances a ghost of one of the infant's deceased matrilineage-mates bestows its name on the newborn and causes it to "recognize" the name. In other cases the name of a living matrilineage-mate will be bestowed, in this manner: an older *brother* (or *sister*) of a pregnant woman will say to her, "If the child is a boy (or a girl) you will name it after me." Then, when the list of names is being called out to the child it will recognize the name previously given it, and henceforth there will be a special (but undescribed) bond between the homonyms.[45] In no case may this name be announced outside the house during the period of "hiding."

When the umbilicus left hanging to the infant dries and drops off it is kept inside the house for a few days, lest a sore form at the infant's navel; then it is planted under a taro stalk in the household garden. After this taro ripens it is eaten by the infant's mother and other adult matrilineage-mates living nearby; it may not be eaten by a child, for the one who ate it would thereby capture some of the growing power of the infant and would grow quickly while the infant would remain undersized.⁴⁶

Clearly, then, the period of "hiding" is a dangerous one for the infant. Its skin and flesh are not yet firm enough to ward off dangerous substances, and its soul (ura) is weak and insecurely attached to its body at the fontanelle, where it can be seen faintly pulsating and highly vulnerable to attack and abduction by unfriendly spirits. Some protection is assured it by performance of the preliminary cleansing ritual above, but effective supernatural guardianship cannot be counted on until the full-scale baptism ceremony is performed four or five weeks after birth. Meanwhile, the safeguards of "hiding" help to ward off some of the more tangible dangers, such as dirt sorcery and any form of sorcery which depends upon the sorcerer actually seeing or obtaining some exuviae of the victim. All males past early childhood are excluded from the house of "hiding" and two reasons are given for this. First, it is dangerous for the males: to enter the home would make them liable to falling from a tree — by what *specific* factor ⁴⁷ I could not fathom. And secondly, it is dangerous for the infant "because of the horomorun," which we can surmise to mean that such males frequent club-houses and hence come into contact with these powerful demons which are inherently dangerous to all females and infant males. Why the name and sex of the infant should remain generally unknown is not so facilely rationalized; true, it would protect the infant against any form of malicious magic the effectiveness of which depends upon the magician knowing the name and sex of the victim, but the Siuai could offer no clue concerning the necessity of keeping uninformed such obviously non-malicious persons as the father and mother's brother.⁴⁸

Another question arises: why delay performance of the main baptism ritual for four or five crucial weeks, since this rite is believed to strengthen so effectively the infant's resistance to harmful influences? I was never able to secure explicit rationalizations for this practice, but one circumstance which may have a bearing on this matter is the high rate of infant mortality during the first few weeks after birth. Administration census figures do not reflect this because the Siuai seldom report births and deaths of infants who succumb before the main baptism ritual. In fact, they often remain officially silent about infants born after the preceding census and deceased before the current one, such infants being "not worth recording in the Government book." ⁴⁹

There is some support to the saying that an infant in "hiding" is "not worth reporting," for those dying during this period are neither cremated nor extensively mourned, except for the one whose mother dies too, in which case both mother and infant are cremated together. The women in "hiding" carry the little corpse to a nearby bone-burial place, dig a shallow grave and line it with leaves, place the body in it, and cover it with leaves and dirt. The mother sometimes weeps a little but the others do not, because "they are not very sorry." Its ghost is said to return to the womb to be reborn later on.⁵⁰

It is a different matter if the mother dies in childbirth or shortly afterwards; her female companions cover the body and her husband makes haste to cremate it on the night following the death. Young girls and women of childbearing age avoid touching and looking at the body because of its danger to themselves during their future confinements. In fact, throughout preparations and cremation the solemnity and display of grief which characterizes the usual death is partly replaced by a manifestation of fear among the survivors, and especially among women survivors.[51] The object appears to be to get the cremation over with as quickly as possible and with a minimum of overt mourning activity. Neighbors and distant relatives are discouraged from attending the cremation, and a magician is always present to dispel any dangerous spirits that may be lurking nearby. Also, the husband's grief is usually heavily charged with rage at the unknown *tao* sorcerer — that being assumed to have been the cause of death.

## BAPTISM

Natives give many reasons for carrying out the baptism ceremony (*uharei*, washing). It helps protect the child, weak and vulnerable as it is, from both inherently dangerous and malevolently directed influences abounding in the Siuai universe, and it helps to insure for it health and wealth. It also introduces the child to its relatives and neighbors, and restores its mother to normal everyday living.

Under normal circumstances the ceremony is held four to five weeks after birth; the schedule is set not by a tally of days but by physical readiness of infant and mother and by the time it takes the father to make preparations. The infant's skin should be "firm" and its behavior normal — in other words, it should be clear that the infant will survive and prosper; and the mother should be recuperated enough to resume her domestic labors. However, the crucial factor in preparing for the event is the father's ability to obtain pigs for the feast which must accompany the ceremony. Sometimes the ceremony is put ahead: one we witnessed was held fourteen days after birth; an aged kinswoman in the same hamlet was dying and the infant's father hurried preparations so that the baptism might be completed before death could take place and necessitate a long postponement. In other cases the baptism may be delayed for months and even years, depending upon the father's success in obtaining pigs. When this occurs the period of "hiding" is terminated without ceremony as soon as the mother has recuperated; but this situation is doubly perilous for the child. Not only is it thrust into the hazardous world with little or no supernatural sanction, but it is also liable to attack by some of the ghosts of its own matrilineage ancestors, who become angry if the baptism is unduly delayed and visit their wrath on the child (and not on the parents). Living matrilineage-mates of the child press a procrastinating father to speed up baptism, feeling some responsibility in the matter — but evidently not enough to move them to donate pigs of their own! Besides its spiritual vulnerability an unbaptized child suffers many tangible physical limitations: for example, it cannot enter a garden nor eat certain delicacies, nor can its name be made known. It must be called "Nameless" (Miruho) and in doing so people are continually reminded that it is the offspring of a man who is so poor that he cannot even finance the baptism of his own child. During our stay there were nearly a score of little "Namelesses" in northeast Siuai ranging in age from three or four months to six or seven years. In addition, three adults bore the name, but none of these appeared stigmatized nor disabled by the designation, having long since disregarded the associated injunctions and outlived the social disabilities.

Baptism is one of the more elaborate of Siuai rituals and employs a number of materials. One pig has to be provided for the ceremony and several more for the accompanying feast. In addition, there should be a live opossum; a green drinking-coconut consecrated by a matrilineage ghost; a cupful of coconut oil mixed with *kuna*; a stew made of taro, coconut oil, and edible greens (*uvahno*); a few areca nuts, almonds, and whole taro plants; a dagger-punch made of the femur of a pig; a woman's cloak; high-value shell money strung on spans and woven into mats; and several handfuls of leaves for bathing mother and infant. The green coconut used for laving the infant is consecrated prior to the ceremony by the officiating maru-magician; as she pierces out the eye of the nut with the bone punch she repeats a growth-magic formula. Likewise, she repeats another such formula when collecting the edible greens for the stew. And finally, the bath-leaves are selected for their intrinsic magical qualities: some are from large and sturdy trees (*kiŋiri, miru, morinaŋ, hana, tonnimo*), others from fragrant bushes (*tarirapito, neso*); all these are tied into brushes with strings of high-value shell money.

The officiating maru-magician, preferably a woman, should be a matrilineage-mate of the mother and infant. Assisting, as at the nuptial ceremony, is a younger *sister* of the mother; by her participation, it is said, she will be assured of an early and fruitful marriage. The child's father hovers in the background and prepares food for the feast that follows the ceremony. A matrilineage *brother* of the mother assists with the ceremony itself; other matrilineage-mates and neighbors make up most of the participant onlookers.

Baptism is woman's ceremony ("an affair of females," males somewhat contemptuously say) and takes place in the hamlet where the child was born. It begins in midmorning after the feast pigs have been butchered and after enough female guests have arrived to begin a dance. The dancers wear their best loincloths and shell ornaments, and paint their faces with dots of red ocher. They dance their stiff-bodied hop-and-jump steps either on the ground in front of the house of "hiding" or in and around a dance-hole, the "females' gong." As they dance they sing the women's song (koija):

*Ji kuku je;*          *rari koija*
*Ni ŋonokite*         *urinno*          *Tuhuhrorukite*

# CYCLE OF THE NUCLEAR FAMILY

I    my-place-from    settlement-at    Tuhuhroru-from
I come from our sib homeland at Tuhuhroru.[52]

*Nonni    taromorim        manniko sirojemaramum*
Us     you(pl.)-listen-to    place-at    we-sing-and-dance
Listen to the way we sing and dance at our place,

*Nonnikonoki    uri        Turuŋom*
Our-place-at   settlement   Turuŋom
At our place, Turuŋom

*Minniko    muma    riku*
Place-at    leaders   high-ranking
The place of high-ranking leaders.

*Tivuŋori       sinojemarame*
This-like    we-sing-and-dance
This is the way we sing and dance.

This is a koija composed and performed by members of a Tree-rat matrilineage residing at Turuŋom; the koijas of other Tree-rat matrilineages follow the same pattern. Each sib, and in some cases, each sub-sib, has its own koija pattern, which usually refers to some episode in the sib's mythical past, and often contains some exhortation to the sib totem — like this one of the Eagles: "You, Eagle who dwell by the sea, run quickly here and teach this infant how to walk."

After an hour or so of singing and dancing the mother and her companions-in-"hiding" emerge from the house, covered with shell ornaments and squinting at the unaccustomed glare, and troop off to the bathing stream accompanied by the maru-magicians and the dancers. At the stream the mother squats in the water while the maru-magician laves her with one of the prepared leaf brushes while repeating growth-magic. Meanwhile all the other women bathe themselves and reapply their face paints, and everyone returns to the hamlet. Back there the maru-magician lays out a large woman's mat on the ground in front of the house of "hiding" and alongside a live pig which the infant's father has staked to the ground. Next to the pig a covered pot is wedged upright, containing the taro stew, and on the mat are placed taro, almonds, areca, shell valuables, and bone dagger. When all is thus prepared the mother brings her newborn out of the house for the first time and squats with it at the side of the mat opposite the pig and pot of taro stew. On one side of her sits a younger *sister*, holding firmly onto the muzzled opossum; on the other is the maru-magician, holding the consecrated coconut in one hand and a brush of leaves in the other. Then, as the dancers return to their hopping and singing the maru-magician begins to lave the infant, pouring on a little of the coconut water and using the leaves to brush it down, repeating growth magic all the while. This continues for several minutes, until the formula is completed, all accompanied by the singing and dancing in the background. This done, the maru-magician puts aside the empty coconut, picks up the shell cup of oil and kuna, and begins to rub the oil over the infant's body to the accompaniment of more growth-magic formulae. After a minute or two of this she grunts an instruction to the mother, who places the infant's feet on the mat and walks it along, taking care that it touches the shell money and other materials spread on the mat. Then the infant's feet are touched against the pig and its head held close to the pot, now uncovered, so that some of the aroma of the taro stew reaches the infant's nostrils. Also, a little of the food is rubbed over the infant's gums. While this is proceeding, the maru-magician accompanies the pair across the mat, rubbing oil onto the infant and droning growth-magic. Here is the formula which belongs to the Legs-apart sub-sib, said when baptizing a Legs-apart child:

*Tana*;   *Koiki*
Skill;   Koi (subject of action)
Skill; (our ancestress) Koi (used to perform this rite)

*Tana*; *Ouaki*
Skill;   Oua (subject of action)
Skill; (our ancestress) Oua (used to perform this rite)
(Et cetera, — naming some twenty former Legs-apart growth-magicians, male and female)   .

*Rino   suhaŋ;    rino    sumoŋ*
West it-lights-up;  west  it-darkens
From daybreak to darkness,

*Kiŋkirisu       nomuŋori      manamana    hororopihini*
Kiŋkirisu palm    you-two       similar     let-you-two-compare
You two, mother and child, will be like the sturdy kiŋkirisu palm,

*Hiŋi              rino     poŋo     ahamoŋ*
The wind (subject of action)  west    east    it-bends.
which the wind bends back and forth (but does not break).

Then while the infant is held upright in the middle of the mat the maru-magician holds a large taro leaf over its head as she repeats the last of the formulae, the purpose of this being to permit the infant to be carried to the gardens without risking injury there. The baptism is now over but before the ceremony can end the maru-magician must sever contact between the principals and the participating ghosts; continuous rapport would be dangerous for the principals. First, she performs "head-rounding"[53] upon each of the principals (mother, infant, younger *sister*, and herself) using areca nuts from the mat for the rounding, and breaking them open with the pig-femur dagger, while saying the following:

My life (*ruma*) is in my head,
My essence is at the top of me,

> Remove yourselves from us so that I can continue to live —
> So that this infant and its mother can become strong.

Then the mother passes her newborn to the younger *sister* and places her hands into those of the maru-magician, who holds them over the pot of taro and cracks the joints, saying:

> I hold these hands over the pot so that near-death will be removed
>   from them —
> I stretch out these finger joints so that near-death will leave them.

Finally, as mother and infant retire into the house, the maru-magician snatches the mat into the air, scattering things on it in every direction and evoking shouts of laughter from the onlookers as she says:

> e     he   ui!
> I come from Tuhuhroru to
>   scatter this pile of valuables.[54]

Meanwhile, throughout the ceremony a *mother's brother* of the infant slowly strangles the pig, it being desirable though not essential that the animal expire just as the ritual ends. Then, immediately following, the infant's father slits open the opossum with a knife and pinches its heart out, so that little or no blood is lost; the opossum is later singed, boiled, and eaten by the infant's father, mother, and the latter's young aide; no one else may eat this meat. The pig is butchered and cut into strips, which are passed out among all those present at the ceremony who are matrilineage-mates of the mother and infant; all others, including the infant's father, receive pork from the other slaughtered pigs. The dancing goes on for an hour or so, and then the whole event ends by early afternoon.

No two baptisms are identical, but the episodes just described may be said to represent the *ideal* inventory of materials and events inasmuch as the given sequence corresponds to informant's ideas on what should take place. One baptism we witnessed was performed by two maru-magicians, with a third, a novice, looking on. Moreover on this same occasion a dead, smoked opossum was used ("too little time to capture a live one"); no sounding trench was provided for the dancers; the pig was strangled by three small boys, none of them sib-mates of the infant; and the edible greens cooked with the taro stew were the object of a separate rite, having been gathered by the maru-magician in a grove while the dancing women looked on and accompanied with a song.[55] At still another performance we witnessed, two children were simultaneously baptized, one boy of six and one a girl of a year and a half, both "Nameless." Growth-magic was performed over this pair as they stood on the trussed and expiring pig.

Such variations are typical of all Siuai ritual, and according to Siuai opinion they do not influence the effectiveness of the rite. Ceremonies differ from sib to sib, and even maru-magicians from the same sib differ among themselves in their performances. Variations which are *significant* — that is, significant to the Siuai — have to do not with the ritual itself but with the amount of pork distributed among those who attend the ritual, and the quantity of shell ornaments worn by the infant during the event. The baptism for a man's first-born child, male or female, requires more pigs than that for later children; the ratio may be as much as four to one. In addition, a man desiring to acquire or maintain renown must be more generous with pork than a man of no ambition; some of the former provide as many as ten animals and some of the latter only one. And finally, although some of the shell ornaments used to decorate the infant belong to the heirloom hoard of its matrilineage, the father himself is expected to provide the major share out of his earned capital. Thus, it is said pityingly of some infants:

"Poor child, with no valuables for ornament. Its kinsmen are so poverty-stricken that unconsecrated water has been used to baptize it." (I.e., the ghosts of former maru-magicians will not consecrate the coconut water used for baptizing the infant unless high-value shell money is used in the ceremony.)

## INFANCY

In Siuai usage the individual is an *infant* (tutu) from birth until it begins to walk steadily and is more or less weaned.[56] After the first few weeks of "hiding," this period of about three years is also something of a distinct stage in the life of its parents. For one thing, they are expected to remain sexually continent. Some of a pregnant woman's milk is believed to help nourish the fetus she carries, and that means less milk for the infant she may be nursing; hence intercourse between a nursing mother and her husband is considered thoughtless and wicked, and to result in undernourishment and illness for the nursing infant. For a different reason, which native informants were unable to explain, the father of a nursing infant is expected to refrain from sexual intercourse with all other females as well; and if he breaks this proscription, the infant will remain small and weak.[57] Another circumstance which distinguishes this period for the parents of the infant is the extent to which they lavish time and care upon it; even pigs become relegated, so preoccupied are the parents in feeding and playing with the new being. Fathers spend many hours daily at this pastime, but for mothers it is a full-time job, and this is reflected in many beliefs about the dependence of the infant upon its mother.

The infant's soul is only insecurely attached to its body, at the fontanelle, and clings to the mother much of the time. During the first few months of the infant's life, its soul is so closely dependent upon the mother that the latter should not leave her child for long, lest its soul follow her and perhaps become lost. When the mother of a young infant must leave it at home to go to the garden or the stream, she wears a small soul-rattle (*uraparapara*) made of shells; the infant's soul, which accompanies her, will then hear the sound made by the rattle and so will not become lost — otherwise it might stray too far from the mother and never be able to find its way home again, which of course would result in the death of the infant. So close indeed is the attachment between the infant's soul and its mother that measures have to be taken to separate it if and when the mother should die. Natives place a banana pod in the dead woman's hands in order to deceive her soul-ghost into believing that she holds her infant; otherwise her soul-ghost would take along the infant's soul when she departs for the afterworld. (This precaution is occasionally taken when an infant's older sibling dies — if the latter has been accustomed to tend the infant.)[58] In case of the mother's death it also becomes necessary to purge the infant of suck, which is thought to contain some of the mother's sickness. The widower employs the services of a kuna-doctor who feeds the infant a purgative called "orphan-defecate" (*panatoto*) and the sickness substance is thereby voided. If this were not done, the infant would remain undersized and sickly. Sometimes a maru-magician is called in to administer "orphan-defecate" and perform growth-magic as double insurance against harm.

Throughout infancy — more so than in later life — there is danger of the infant's soul straying or being kidnapped by a spirit. Such is the diagnosis when an infant cries more than usual, and a magician is employed to send his spirit-familiar to fetch the lost or stolen soul.

The infant's universe is very narrow in the beginning: first in the womb, then the house of "hiding," then the household, hamlet, and garden; the gradual widening of this universe is formalized in a series of simple *introduction-rites*. One of the first of these is moon-presenting (*hinjonai*), on which occasion the infant is "shown" to the new moon and thereby insured against persecution on the part of this demon. Occasionally the garden-admittance rite is omitted from the baptism ceremony and performed separately later on; particularly is this done in the case of an obviously sickly infant, whom the natives would consider too fragile to expose to the *anger* of the sun immediately after baptism. Still another infants' *introduction-rite* is the pudding-eating one performed at the end of the first three or four months. Most infants receive only mother's milk supplemented by a little coconut water until they are ritually fed some *kavo* pudding (taro and coconut oil), which has the effect of sanctioning the eating of solid foods. This rite (*kevisi*, teething) is similar to the pudding-tasting episode of baptism, but this time the infant is actually made to eat some of the pudding after it is rubbed against its gums.

The most elaborate of the little *introduction* rituals is shrine-presenting (*urinnonai*), which is required in the case of infant members of some sibs.[59]

Infancy is also the time for piercing a Siuai's nasal septum and ear lobe (and ear shell, in the case of females), for attaching ornaments; it is believed that "infants do not feel pain from such operations, whereas older individuals do." These operations are performed without ceremony, by knowledgeable relatives.

There follows a brief résumé of the *mechanics* of infant care. Comprehension of the social context in which this takes place must await description of the polygynous family and the broad network of kin relations, for no infant is insulated from some of these wider social influences.

Until the mother purposefully sets about weaning her infant the latter is fed on demand. As soon as an infant shows the slightest degree of restlessness the mother, or some other woman if the mother happens to be away, gives it the breast. Giving the breast is also used by women to comfort a frightened or hurt infant. A woman will nurse a very young infant from a sitting position by holding it across or between her knees and leaning forward. Or she may lie stretched out on a mat, with the infant beside her. When the infant is a bit older and can hold up its head it is held astraddle the woman's waist to feed. The infant usually feeds for ten to twelve minutes without cease, then stops of its own accord for a few minutes, and then returns to suckle again, repeating the process two or three times, so that a whole regular feeding period lasts nearly an hour. Since the infant is completely naked and the woman wears only a loincloth, there is direct bodily contact between the two. If the mother happens to be absent other women will nurse the infant, and it is considered most fitting that the mother's sisters or other matrilineage-mates do so; in the first place such measures are used to encourage the infant to recognize and behave appropriately towards all its *mothers*, and secondly, it is customary to pay a fee to any wet-nurse not of the infant's sib.

After the first three or four months the infant is fed small bits of taro, potato, sago, and coconut, all mashed or even pre-masticated; and more of these semisolids are given as time passes. It is also given husks of areca nut to chew on — "to strengthen the mouth." When a mother becomes pregnant again, she takes steps to hurry along the weaning of her nursing infant, and we recorded cases of pregnancies occurring within a year after giving birth; most natives consider this wicked, however, and assert that a woman should not allow herself to become pregnant until her nursing infant has begun to walk, at which time it should have been mostly weaned anyway — "mostly" is used advisedly, since it is not unusual for children of six and seven to cling to their mothers and suckle occasionally for asylum and comfort. Mothers complain good-naturedly that their offspring are very difficult to wean, and some of them have to resort to relatively harsh measures, such as rubbing nicotine juice from a pipe onto the nipple, or frightening the infant away from the breast by allowing a large insect or worm to crawl about on it.

Little attempt is made to toilet-train an infant. If one begins to urinate or defecate while being held the holder will hold it at arms' length, upright and feet on the ground, until it finishes; the infant is not moved violently or shouted at. Most women appear quite accustomed to being soiled and try only to avoid having their loincloths dirtied. After the infant has finished a woman will patiently collect a handful of leaves and wipe herself and the infant, and then clean up the worst of the mess made on the floor or the ground. Later, when the child begins to walk, it is taught to signal when it wishes to defecate, and is led to a refuse area just beyond the settlement's clearing. Little heed is paid to a child's urinating until it is five or six years old, and then it is told to step a few yards away to perform. At night even this formality is dispensed with, the only convention being that the child urinate outside the house, or, if inside a pile dwelling, that it urinate between the floor boards — a convention which we quickly learned to respect as one of the hazards of field work!

Very young infants are bathed about noon on every sunny day; otherwise they are cleaned by rubbing coconut oil over their whole bodies. Bathing is done by the mother or whoever may be tending the infant at the time, and the water is poured out of coconut-shell containers. It is not heated in any way, and invariably shocks the infant into shudders and screams, with no apparent concern at all from the persons bathing it — the only kind of instance witnessed in which an infant's cries are ignored and no steps taken to stop them. Later on during infancy, bathing may be overlooked for days at a time, and is resumed as a regular daily event only during late childhood, if indeed then.

An infant usually sleeps at night alongside its mother, and at most other times during day and night it is in direct physical contact with someone. During the day it may be placed on a mat after it falls to sleep, but is picked up again immediately upon waking. Or occasionally the infant may be allowed to sit on the ground by itself for a few moments at a time, but there is always someone hovering near to pick it up again at the first sign of displeasure. A cry from the infant usually brings an immediate response from its nurse or someone else nearby, and a mother who allows her infant to cry is regarded as worthless.

Infants are carefully watched over at all times, never being left alone. If the mother must be absent, then some other female relative will substitute. A father may also tend his infant, and fathers do not appear to object to spending long hours at this pastime; however, a male always likes to have a nursing woman nearby so that the child can be fed at the first sign of hunger. Young and old like to fondle infants, by jogging them or rocking them in their arms while singing little ditties.

As the infant acquires new traits, such as playing with its toes or kicking its feet, it receives warm encouragement from everyone around; and nearly every speech-like sound it makes is repeated by its nurses in an effort to encourage it to talk. Also, when the infant is resting beside its reclining mother, the latter sings to it little songs made up of family terms: "thy-mother, thy-mother; thy-father, thy-father; thy-sister, thy-sister; etc."

Crawling is not punished but it is not encouraged in any way, and as soon as the infant begins to crawl it is taught to stand and walk. For this purpose a stick is planted in the ground and the infant assisted in holding onto it, first from a sitting then from a standing position. Then, later on, with an audience of admiring relatives it is urged to take a step toward its mother. Soon it is taking short steps from stick to person and from person to person, and then a railing is constructed for it to walk along, and in this manner it begins to toddle at the earliest possible stage. However, toddling does not mark any change in the care with which the little one is treated; relatives continue to give the closest attention to its needs and moods, and nursing and fondling continue as before.

Beginning with the birth of their first offspring, husband and wife undergo a gradual change in the nature of their relationship. The fact that sexual intercourse between them is traditionally discountenanced does not altogether stop its taking place, but it is certain to result in a more complex relationship. Even though the husband remains at home for many hours every day he interacts less frequently with his wife, and less in terms of their direct interrelationship than of the needs, moods, and activities of the infant. The jealousy which a young husband usually evinces becomes much less apparent; if the wife remains away from home over-long during this stage her husband is more likely to chide her for deserting the infant than to accuse her of having had a love tryst. Aside from his concern for the infant this may reflect an actual situation, viz., I heard of no instances of a woman with a young infant having lovers. As already noted, the infant's father should also remain completely continent, lest the infant remain undersized and weakly, but informants generally agreed that all men occasionally transgress. Wives also appear to consider this inevitable and take their husbands to task for it — not, however, phrased as a manifestation of jealousy but rather as a display of concern for the infant's welfare.

Quarreling between spouses by no means disappears upon arrival of the infant but it does not lead as frequently to divorce nor to the point requiring formal reconciliation (rakai). In this connection, it is symptomatic of the changing relationship between spouses that after the woman has a child it is practically always the man who leaves home after a serious quarrel and who must be enticed home again by a reconciliation token from his wife.

Occasionally a man finds home life so burdensome at this stage that he escapes and goes to a plantation to work. The picture presented by the wife and infant of such a man is quite pathetic, the situation being so well known that it is reflected in song — as, for example, in this one composed by a young wife left in this predicament:

>    Oh husband, you are far away.
>    Where can I leave this crying child?

> I am weary of her continual crying
>   and am ready to hang myself.
> Her father has left her and me.
> Just show me another place where a
>   woman has to dwell alone.
> I grieve — for who is there to call me a pretty bird,
>   now that you are gone.
> Where can I leave this crying child so
>   that I can go to be with you?

The presence of the infant undoubtedly accounts for some of the increased harmony of marriage during this stage, but we cannot leave out of account other and possibly more important circumstances, such as the progressive accommodation in interaction taking place between the spouses and becoming buttressed by each one's adjustments to the other's relatives. For clearer understanding of these factors, however, we must wait for the description of other kinship relations.

## CHILDHOOD

Weaning and walking do not always coincide but together they constitute fairly distinctive criteria of the beginning of childhood for most young Siuai. (As, similarly, the ability to copulate and perform the same kinds of jobs as adults — though not necessarily the same *amount* of work — helps mark the gradual transition to adulthood.) "Childhood" is not an arbitrary designation; the Siuai differentiate clearly between the child (*kitori*) and the infant (*tutu*), and the child and the youth (*honna*) or maiden (*nunokuŋ-uroina*) — although it should be kept in mind that the thresholds between these age categories are defined broadly and more in terms of what the individual does than what he is. Some infants are propelled into "childhood" earlier than others because their mothers conceive sooner. Others remain "infants" in everything but walking until they are four or five; this applies particularly to the last child of an older woman. The upper time limit of childhood also varies from individual to individual, with some beginning to work or to have sex adventures earlier than others, there being no age-grading institutions to specify precisely when activities should change.

From the standpoint of the activities and relationships of the parents, "childhood" is not as distinctive a stage as "infancy." For the mother there is often a new infant to tend, so that her life remains about the same. For the father, however, there is less preoccupation with offspring and more with economic and political matters. The marriage is somewhat more stable in the sense that divorce is more infrequent; and it is during this stage that some men acquire a second wife. But before enlarging on this let us return to the activities of the child.

The Siuai regard childhood as a period during which the boy or girl suffers various unavoidable — or rather, indispensable — maladies preliminary to growing up. Chief among these are frambesical sores: *novum*, which form all over the body, and *taruru*, which cover particularly the mouth. When these persist "too long" (*how* long I could not discover) it is believed that they will stunt the child's growth, and a therapist is called in to rub kuna over the child and prescribe certain food taboos. Otherwise these sores are regarded as a perfectly normal manifestation of child growth. Sores (*musai*) also form on the scalps of children as a result of lice bites; some parents react to this by delousing the child more thoroughly, while others ignore such sores as being inevitable. Certain other maladies are considered to be typical of childhood, but inevitable only if proper protective measures are not taken. Among these is enlarged spleen, believed to be caused by the eating of sago (infants but not children may eat it). Then there are a number of items which children are forbidden to eat, or in some cases touch, until they have participated in a Climbing ritual.[60] The list of restrictions is long: red banana (ruvinai) causes the skin to be covered with red sores; pork from a white pig causes white sores to develop and the legs to be crippled; kuriru banana causes the legs to be bone-thin; the smaller variety of tree-rat (*kamari*) causes sores to form on the head; etc. As many as three or four years elapse between Climbing ceremonies (none was held during our visit) so that some individuals have to retain these restrictions past childhood; a few middle-aged men I knew were still unable to eat these delicacies because of having been absent or incapacitated when Climbings were held. These taboos apply generally throughout Siuai; they were invented by kupunas but are not associated with any particular sib, although members of several sibs assert that their own kupunas invented the Climbing ritual and thereby made it possible to remove the taboos.

All the above restrictions are regarded as inherent in the growing process. In addition, children who have been treated with kuna to cure specific maladies, such as tao-inflicted ones, are forbidden by the therapists to eat certain kinds of foods, like pork and eel, as essential parts of the therapy.

The child's inherent weakness, coupled with its unknowing way of living, renders it particularly vulnerable to "dirt" sorcery. Having little knowledge or anxiety about such matters, children carelessly throw away banana skins and other food refuse, or leave their footprints in soft earth, thus providing malicious people with dangerous implements.

Despite all these weaknesses — or as the Siuai would reason, along with these weaknesses — children are believed to be less sensitive to pain than adults are, hence childhood is the best time for decorative scarifying of the body and for enlarging the holes punched during infancy in nasal septum and ears. Infants are said to feel even less pain than children, but their skins are not yet "strong" enough for scarifying. Some scarification is continued into adolescence but many individuals of that age object to the ordeal. Also, as another sign of increasing hardiness, the fontanelle ceases to pulsate, signifying that the soul has now moved its principal location to the eye.

All age-inherent weaknesses disappear in time if the child is normally healthy (*rumaruha*), which in Siuai terms means: lacking in obvious physical deformities and in such behavioral abnormalities as dumbness, deafness, epileptic seizures, imbecility, and other disorders. If, however, the apparently healthy child does not outgrow the weaknesses, or if it lags far behind other children in growing taller or in acquiring expected habits and skills, it is said to be *kotipaka*. But more of this later.

The widening of the child's horizons is formalized in a series of *introduction* rites similar in technique to those carried out in infancy, with the difference that some of them are performed only for the boy-child of a leader.

Dance-hole-showing (*rominai*) is performed for all girl-children on the first occasion, after they have begun to walk, that they are taken to a woman's sing-sing. The rite is simple; they are lowered into the hole and encouraged to jump on the sounding-board while the older females dance around the hole and a maru-magician utters a growth-magic formula.

Both girl- and boy-children are ceremonially shown the first stockade-type pig pen (*huhu*) constructed in their neighborhood after they have begun to walk. The huhu is strongest and most carefully fitted of all stockades and is constructed only on the occasion of an important competitive feast, being designed to hold only large pigs. The growth-magic formula repeated for children on the occasion of their first view of the huhu stresses the hope that they too will someday be affluent enough to fill such a stockade with prize pigs.

Most fathers will attempt to arrange for at least their eldest sons to become initiated to opossum hunting with ceremony. This is accomplished merely by sending the boy on an opossum hunt and then feasting the hunters on pork afterwards. Some other *introduction*-rites are reserved for the eldest sons of men who are able to mobilize enough resources to provide large feasts. Club-house showing (*kapasonai*) takes place when a father invites a number of his neighbors to attend a feast at his club-house for the purpose of introducing them to his eldest son; the guests acclaim the son as a future leader and are repaid for their flattery with a generous pork banquet. Sing-sing showing (*orinai*) takes place on the occasion when a father permits his eldest son to attend the first sing-sing given at his club-house; guests signalize the event by lifting the boy on their shoulders and carrying him around the dance ground as they sing and play their pipes. Debut to fighting (*haraŋi-tutu*) occurs when a leader's neighbors take his eldest son to the coast to show him the sea for the first time. On their return they are intercepted by men from a nearby settlement, who engage in a mock battle with the boy's companions and thereby introduce him to "warfare." Later, the boy's father must reward all the participants with a pork feast.

What do young Siuai do during childhood? With patient, systematic observation of children's activities over a long period of time it should be possible to predict much about the behavior of adults — or at least to "explain" partially why adults behave the way they do. Unfortunately, during our all too short visit to Siuai most of our attentions were focused on the adult's world, and our observations on children were incidental and unsystematic.[61] Here, however, are some general statements which are suggestive and reliable as far as they go — which admittedly is not very far!

For the first half of childhood boys and girls remain together in the woman's group and do the same things. They delight in imitating adult dances, both men's and women's; but even at this early age it is evident that men's dances evoke greater excitement, and it is not long before boys will scorn to dance the woman's koija and will no longer tolerate the dancing of men's dances by their girl playmates. Children also play at "family," with boys and girls taking appropriate sex roles. In such circumstances little girls soon learn to sit primly with their legs stretched out together in front of them, the woman's manner of sitting, while little boys sit or squat with legs apart, like men. If play becomes excited and a little girl begins to roughhouse, her elders warn her to quiet down: "Bush demon, do you want to grow a penis?"

Organized games are, however, seldom played. During most of early childhood both boys and girls remain close to mothers and their companions, with rarely more than five or six children to a group, whiling away the time in dozing, munching left-overs, coddling infants, torturing little animals, delousing one another, and sometimes quarreling. They always appeared to us to be a listless crew; and this impression was heightened in retrospect when we later visited the coastal villages of the Melanesian-speaking Torau people and saw their youngsters frolicking hour after hour in the water, paddling their miniature canoes, and in every respect living spiritedly in a children's world of their own.

When the very young Siuai children do fight it is usually with sticks and stones, with very little hand-to-hand wrestling. Friendly horseplay never remains so for long, invariably and quickly developing into angry scrapping following the pattern of hit-and-run, or be-hit-cry-and-run, with the criers seeking to involve their parents — who became very easily involved! Despite our efforts to remain objective and avoid stereotyping small Siuai children, we could not escape the feeling that most of them are both bullies and cry-babies, depending upon the strength of their antagonists of the moment.

Much of the listlessness disappears when children are a little older and begin to accompany their mothers or fathers as they work. Little girls put on a carrying strap and go along to the garden where they work alongside their elders picking insects off taro leaves or piling bits of trash in heaps for burning. Returning home they are usually given a minute load to carry, and quickly simulate the stiff-legged trudge of older women even without the heavy burdens borne by the latter. Little boys begin to drift away from women's groups when they are four or five. They disdain searching for insects and prefer to shoot at birds with tiny bows and arrows; or, they remain with father and perform little chores for him. Now and then they edge their way into a nearby club-house, and despite the shouts of "Out," "Go away," "Demon," they usually persist until their presence is taken for granted and finally ignored. Later on, they will earn the privilege of associating with older males by performing all sorts of little chores — climbing palms for coconuts or areca nut, fetching drinking water, handing around pipe-lighting embers, and the like. To record another *impression* (in lieu of better data): it appeared to us that Siuai children do not know how to play for long among themselves and do not especially enjoy doing so, preferring rather to be with adults and to do as adults do. At this point we may inquire: what behavior do adults *expect* of children?

In the first place, it is believed that infants are born *good* (*mirahu*), in the sense that they are not predisposed to evil ways, but only acquire morally reprehensible (*kirahao*) characteristics as they grow and begin to talk. Most children still retain this pristine innocence but adults assert that the child who does not share delicacies has taken the first step towards evil ways. There is however no speculation concerning how the first step came to be taken, and in fact there is not much interest in the matter.

Similarly, distinctions are made between industrious and lazy children, between the manly little fellow who stays with men and the timid and fearful one who remains with women, and between the quiet and modest little girl and the shrill tomboy.

Although manliness in boys and modesty in girls, and industry in both, are valued and sometimes rewarded, none of these traits evokes adult interest to the extent that *ambition* (haokom) or the lack of it does. Men say that they can discern this characteristic in a small boy even before he is able to work industriously. He must be rumaruha, that is, physically normal and up to average expectations in skills and habits, but in addition he must be quiet though not fearful, and above all, intent and serious about whatever he is doing. I spent much time eliciting opinions on this subject from natives because of their obvious importance for understanding Siuai political statuses, and the above description is a reliable condensation of the consensus; it certainly applies quite admirably to the few male children my informants singled out as possessing the qualities they described. To drive home their meaning they invariably added: "That one can be a leader (mumi) some day."

How are skills, habits, norms, and beliefs transmitted to the Siuai child? Without attempting a full exposé of this subject — indeed, I do not have adequate material for one — I can however record a few impressions.[62]

Skills are acquired mainly by imitation. There is of course ample opportunity for children to watch objects being made and work performed, since they remain nearly all the time with parents and other adults. Now and then we saw a woman interrupt her weaving or a man his rope-making, etc., to explain technique to a small onlooker, placing the object in the child's hands and guiding the movements. Parents and other adult relatives react with delight when a child displays dexterity and serious interest, and take special pains to instruct and praise. But such situations are unusual, and most of the time there is little direct inculcation of technical skills and no rigid expectations concerning technical proficiencies which children *ought* to have.

It is much the same with eating, cleanliness, and toilet habits. The child who clamors to suckle long after the normal weaning period is mildly scolded but usually permitted, and I received the impression that mothers are not at all displeased by this demonstration of dependence. On the basis of the few family meals actually witnessed, I feel that there is little direct pressure applied to initiate children in the eating of new foods; they watch their elders and then experiment with little morsels of their own. One informant stated that he wanted to eat new foods even before he was allowed to do so, and that his desire came from seeing adults eat them and hearing descriptions of how delicious they were.

Siuai adults believe that children should use the creeks for defecation by the time they can run and climb trees, and this habit is learned when the children accompany their parents to the creek every morning. On the other hand, children who persist in defecating too near the houses are yelled at ("For shame; demon take you") but otherwise not punished. If however the practice persists on into late childhood the child is considered to be a kotipaka, i.e., generally backward and probably afflicted supernaturally. Urinating by children is considered offensive only when it is done within a few yards of a group of sitting people. The only violent reaction to it I saw occurred when a boy of seven or eight cut loose against a slit gong in a clubhouse; he was cuffed by an older sib-mate and sent home crying, with warnings to stay away. (He returned the following day and was jokingly referred to as "the Pisser," which again sent him home in tears.) Training in cleanliness can hardly be said to exist. As already noted, infants are bathed with some regularity, but as they grow older they are left to acquire gray patinas of dirt, and this situation often lasts until sex activity begins. Since skin maladies are considered inherent anyway, ordinary bathing is not resorted to as a preventive or cure. Later on in childhood some children like to accompany their parents to the creek to bathe or to fish because of the adventure involved, and in this way they rid themselves of some of the grime.

Sex training was described briefly in another context;[63] older companions rather than parents take it upon themselves to teach the proper techniques.

Language training is not consciously fostered after infancy. Here again the reader is asked to rely on very slender evidence, but in talking with children and listening to them talk among themselves, I formed the impression that they proceed very slowly in enlarging their vocabularies and in mastering the intricacies of Motuna morphology. In fact, it seemed to me that the capacity for uttering the long, involved, and metaphorically rich paragraphs which Siuai men, especially, delight in, is acquired some time after childhood and is less an adaptation to the exigencies of everyday communication than to the requirements of club-house palaver. Obscenity on the part of children is sometimes reproved, but just as often it causes mirth among adults.

Social norms, far more so than technical skills and personal habits, are purposefully inculcated in children by adults. Children are forever being reminded by adults that so-and-so is a *mother* or *father's-sister*, etc., and hence requiring special kinds of behavior. More on the content of this behavior will be described in a later section; here it is sufficient to note that most children by the age of six or seven are able to designate correctly all the individuals in their hamlet and even village. Except in the case of strangers, whenever a new face appears parents solemnly introduce the person to their children, calling him by the appropriate kinship term and hinting how the children should behave toward him: "That is your *mother*; go to her"; "here is your male cross-cousin; give him some of your banana"; or "that one is your paternal aunt; do not trouble her"; etc. But even more purposeful is the respect for leaders inculcated in children: "Be quiet; the mumi is walking by," is frequently and ominously uttered, as is: "Do not strike him; his father is a mumi."

Fear of darkness and of spirits is inculcated in every Siuai child at a very early age by a continual stream of admonitions: "Stay inside here; the night is outside"; "don't do that; the demons will steal you"; and hosts of others. All this is more deeply engraved by the constant telling and retelling of tales concerning the terrors of night and the forest and the malevolence and treachery of demons. The effect of all this is to restrain children from adventuring and to keep them close to and dependent on the parents — which I honestly believe to be the latters' unconscious intent! For, although industriousness and display of skills receive high praise from parents and other relatives, exploration and adventuring on one's own is discouraged.

And speaking of praise, that is the principal form of reward offered by Siuai adults to deserving children. "Well now! (*akai!*) just see what a heavy log Soiri is carrying! Just like a man," adults will exclaim in semi-earnestness. Or, if little Manihui catches a prawn while fishing with her mother, she will bask that evening in effusive praise, which some member of her family may even commit into a ditty. It was clearly evident that children enjoy praise and quickly learn what actions of theirs will earn it. They discover, for instance, that the "show-off" is laughed at and the over-imaginative mildly reproved, whereas the quietly industrious is approved and the food-sharer volubly lauded. They also learn that praise from an outsider must be paid for: for, if a friend of father or mother sees a child for the first time and expresses admiration for its appearance and conduct the parents must give that friend "praise-pay" (*pavaru*) consisting of a few spans of shell money. It is even said that some leaders delay longer than usual taking their young sons along to feasts and dances to avoid having to give praise-pay to all the acquaintances there who insist on expressing effusive admiration for the boys.

Punishment, like reward, is usually verbal; but verbal abuse coming from parents alone is not very effective. For one thing, parents seldom follow up threats with action; also, the children hear such a continual stream of "demon," "go away," "stop that," all day long that they appear to become insensitive to them, ignoring them quite blandly. But just let someone other than parents or near-relatives shout at or threaten them, and tears begin to flow as they make for home. But not even threats from outsiders are as effective as mass ridicule in reducing the child to tears. I have seen troops of three and four children send a neighbor's child whimpering homewards with a few sing-song jibes at his appearance or his family.

In nearly all cases children are treated with affectionate indulgence by their parents. Disciplining is ineffective not only because the verbal warnings are not followed up with action, but also because parents do not present a "united front." If one parent threatens and hardens, the other one can be counted on to relent and offer comfort. Sinu, one of my more objective informants, and himself a father, summed it up thus:

> A child knows his father too well to be afraid and consequently doesn't bother to obey him. His father will scold him continually but will not display real anger. Often at mealtimes both father and mother will punish the child by offering him no food, telling him to go find his food somewhere else; but they always relent and fill his platter. The child knows that this will happen, so does not bother to obey. No father would turn out his son, because he knows that the child would run away and work on a white man's plantation.

By way of illustration Sinu described the case of his brother-in-law, Seima, of Kapana village:

> Seima has absolutely no control over his children. If he asks them to do something for him, they tell him to do it himself, and stalk away. One day Seima was preparing some food for a small feast he was giving to the men who built his house, when Seima told one of his young sons to fetch a basket of taro from his house. The child answered: "Do it yourself." Seima became angry this time and beat the boy soundly; if there had been no other men present he would probably have done nothing about it, but this time he became embarrassed and his shame turned into anger. As he beat his son he told him not to return home again. The boy sobbed for a while, and when the time came for Seima to return home the boy went along with him, with nothing more being said about the matter.

Other informants considered Seima overindulgent; on the other hand they regarded Hera as being altogether too harsh. Hera is the native catechist at Kapana village: "His children live in mortal fear of him and instantly obey him. While they were still very young he used to beat them at the slightest provocation. He learned this custom when he worked for a white family. Now his children obey him, but when he is not with them they disobey everyone else."

To continue Sinu's views on family discipline:

> Usually it is the child's mother's brother and his own elder brother whom he obeys. He does not mind being scolded by his father because he knows that the latter will change his mind. But he is afraid of his mother's brother — not because his parents tell him to be so but because that individual is stern with him.

The mode probably lies much nearer to Seima than to Hera, and if anything, mothers are even more indulgent than fathers. But children do not receive such pampering from all members of the family; there are siblings to reckon with.

When I mentioned to our native friends that among some peoples can be found evidence of jealousy and strife between father and son, they were amused and somewhat shocked, stating that such a situation could not develop in Siuai,[64] then adding that with them the conflict is between older and younger brothers. As indeed it is. Every man I questioned could reel off numbers of instances wherein brothers have quarreled, seduced one another's wives, litigated over jointly held property, and even wounded one another in violent fighting. The causes of strife between adult brothers are varied and most of these can be traced to situations developing after childhood, but sibling jealousy *during* childhood is also an important factor in family relations. Before turning to this subject, let us consider the extent to which birth order has become institutionalized.

A man's first-born (or rather first-surviving male or female child), his *simiri*, occupies a special position among his offspring. Its baptism ceremony is more elaborate and is celebrated with the largest provision of pork and other feast foods; and all its other *introduction* rites are more carefully observed. It is most likely to receive more care and affection from its parents, and especially from its father, during infancy. It is popularly accorded a position of authority over all its siblings if it is a male — or over all its female siblings, if a female; this is not rigidly adhered to, as we shall see, but in matters concerning the use or disposal of jointly held property the *First-born* usually has the final say.

Certain kinds of proscriptions apply only to the first-born child of a man, for example, all persons must respect the totemic regulations of their mother's sib — which is of course their own sib, but in addition the *First-born* is forbidden to kill or eat the primary totem of its father. Moreover, if he is first-born, a male infant or child must avoid all physical contact with his father's sister, but this taboo is relaxed considerably if he is later born.

The last-born child of a man (but not the last born of each wife) is also specially designated (*romokekero* "The Last One"), but being *Last-born* carries no special privileges or limitations, nor does birth sequence in general, other than primogeniture.

The act of weaning cannot itself exercise a direct effect on sibling jealousy; should a nursing mother become pregnant, she begins to wean her infant months before giving birth. Nursing, however, is only one element in the infant's relationship with its mother, — let us record how a native put it:

> If a new infant arrives while the first one still wants milk we turn the older one over to its mother's sister to suckle; but the small one does not like that and cries to be with its mother. It is not yet old and wise enough to realize that the other woman is also its *mother*. Its soul stays with its true mother and that makes the infant cry.

Because of the continual intimate contact between an infant and its mother from birth on into late childhood we may be permitted to assume that the infant's feelings of deprivation are generalized and profound. Moreover, other situations during childhood serve to increase the jealousy between siblings. Again, in Sinu's words:

> They tell me that when I was very small my brother, Puipui, used to fight me because I always received the choicest food. He would see a good morsel and take it, then someone older would take it away from him, saying: "You may not eat that; it's for the infant." That made Puipui very angry, and as I became older he used to beat me. And that's the way it is with all children.

One need not subscribe wholly to Sinu's generalization, for we knew many sibling pairs of children who were evidently fond of each other and usually at peace; still, sibling jealousy and strife are so prevalent that presumably true-life stories about older brother-younger brother or older sister-younger sister rivalries and conflicts are numerous and intelligible.

A similar theme of sibling conflict occurs in the origin myth of the Tree-rat [65] sib and in the story of Orphan and his elder brother.[66] It should be noted that all these accounts of sibling conflict, both true-life and legendary, concern siblings of the same sex. The relationship between brother and sister is of a different, more complex nature. Whatever potential conflict there may be in it is subordinated to the more important factor of sex, and brothers and sisters are separated by the most rigid of all sex prohibitions. Any contact between the two even suggestive of sexual relations is forbidden. They may not sit on each other's bed, nor bathe in the creek close to one another. If one small boy hurls at another, "Go copulate with a dog," it will bring forth a reply like "Go eat semen." But if it is "Go copulate with your sister," a quarrel will start which may end by involving the parents in litigation.

Now, there is little to suggest these restraints in the interaction of a very young brother and sister pair; the older one tends the younger regardless of sex, and little girls often can be seen carrying infant brothers on their backs, and little boys carrying infant sisters. In fact, during these early years there is the closest kind of affectionate companionship between the two, and this continues throughout life; but the restraints involving sex are immediately evident if, for example, a dog is seen mounting a bitch, or if a companion tells a story about copulation. In such instances, the elder of the pair will usually leave the scene. If there is any jealousy between the two it does not often manifest itself in physical conflict, for not only is it unseemly for a boy to strike a female, but it is doubly wrong for a brother to strike a sister.

In the course of this summary of children's life there has begun to emerge some picture about the way their parents live during this third stage of their married life. For one thing, they have become less preoccupied with each other. Jealousy is less evident, and the man who persists in keeping jealous vigil over his wife of such long standing is something of a joke. Here is the way one native at this stage of marriage described his marital life:

> My wife and I get along fine. I do not trouble myself about her, nor she about me. She can watch out for her skin, and I for mine. I do not accompany her to the gardens nor bother always to return home at night. I don't worry about whether she copulates with others or not. She's a quiet one, and the only way I could learn would be to follow her all the time, and that's too much bother. And besides I don't care too much. Also, she provides plenty of taro, and I don't beat her. And even when I do not bring home meat she does not berate me. It is a good marriage and I do not want another wife.

But not all marriages are so tranquil. Some wives are by no means tolerant of a lazy husband: for example, the following song from central Siuai found popular acceptance among women in the northeast, and is sung on many occasions (the song is directed by a long-suffering wife at her lazy husband):

> During famine times you forsake us —
> You who call yourself a *leader*, but whose buttocks are as thin as an insect's.
> During famine times you forsake me,
> But if I have food you call me *wife*.

Some wives accept their lot with patience and silence — this is the way things *should* be, according to male informants. However, there are many women who make life miserable for indolent or quarrelsome husbands. Nearly every settlement contains one or two cases of strong-willed and shrill-tongued wives. Some even fall upon their husbands with sticks and beat them roundly. Such situations are greatly deplored by other males, who label the hen-pecked husbands, weaklings ("like a woman"), and assert that such a thing could never happen to them!

It is at this stage of married life that men usually leave home after a quarrel and wait to return until the wife has sent a reconciliation token — most women realizing themselves to be no longer as desirable as before.

If the marital relationship becomes intolerable for the wife there is the alternative of suicide — and a few actually do kill themselves; but for the man who finds a marriage intolerable, as well as for women who do not wish to escape through suicide, there is always the possibility of divorce.

## DIVORCE

It is appropriate to consider divorce at this point in our developing account of family life because if a Siuai man and woman remain wedded until their first offspring reaches "adolescence" there is a very strong probability that they will always remain so. Separations occur with decreasing frequency after children are born and grow up; the statistics I gathered, although admittedly not highly reliable, indicate that for every fifty marriages concluded, about twenty break up during the period after nuptials or its equivalent and prior to the arrival of surviving offspring; five during the infancy period; three during the childhood period; and only one after this.

There is no single word for "divorce" in the Motuna language; if a man wishes to be rid of his wife, he "turns her out" (*asi'imana*), whereas if she wishes to terminate the marriage, she "runs away from him" (*omoreumanna*). It is not always as simple and neat an action as this in real life, but the Motuna phrases do offer some insight into Siuai thought on the matter, it being considered abnormal to suppose that a woman could physically expel her husband from their household, and just as abnormal to suppose that he would weakly give up house, pigs, and garden to a mere woman. Plainly, neither of these phrases fits the situation, which occasionally does develop, wherein a man residing in his wife's settlement "turns her out" by declaring the marriage dissolved and by returning to his former home. And even in the extreme situation created by the wife's kinsmen expelling the husband from the uxorilocal residence and causing her to dissolve the marriage, the fiction of "he turned her out" is maintained. Situations like this occur when the uxorilocal husband is continually ill-tempered and non-coöperative; moreover such a man is usually the one to be accused of sorcery if any deaths take place in his wife's settlement. (In this connection, a break serious enough to lead to divorce is not to be confused with the kind of domestic quarrel which sometimes provokes the husband to leave home temporarily; informants say that such men leave home to "punish" their wives and not to get rid of them.)

We have already considered most of the circumstances leading up to divorce; it now remains to describe how the break is formalized and what effects it has upon the offspring of the divorced couple.

If divorce terminates a marriage based on the traditional exchange practices, the only complication likely to result involves disposal of the high-value shell money previously given by the groom or his parents to formalize the betrothal, since the ordinary shell money paid over by the groom will already have been reciprocated by the bride's father in the form of pigs provided for the nuptial ceremony. If the divorce has come about through the man's having turned out the woman, the man usually demands total repayment of the betrothal gift, although some benign individuals may permit the woman to retain part of it — "as payment for her work and copulation." Generally there is not much argument over the man's rights in such cases: a marriage requires a troublesome amount of effort to conclude, and Siuai men do not lightly turn out a wife unless she is flagrantly lazy or promiscuous or ill-tempered, and the characters of such women are so well known for miles around, and sympathy for the husband so marked, that her kinsmen do not press their claims very energetically. Litigation does however arise now and then; Kummai of Sikumonei village was involved in one of these cases. Just before our arrival in Siuai, Kummai married a girl from a nearby village, but the marriage did not fare well. The girl was chronically "homesick" and neglected her domestic duties so that Kummai finally turned her out, but not before she had become pregnant. Shortly after she returned home, she died. Kummai attempted to recover the betrothal gift he had paid for her but the girl's father returned only one of the two spans given, saying that the one he retained was "pay which Kummai owed to the girl (and her family) for having made her pregnant." The case was not without precedent, and there was some surprise voiced when the man who adjudicated the case required the father to return the rest of the gift; some natives felt that the case had been decided in Kummai's favor because he was a Hat-man, whereas the father was without authority or influence.

If the marriage dissolved by divorce happens to be one of those wherein the bride's father did not provide pigs for the nuptials, then there is bound to be a vigorous — and usually successful — effort made by the groom to recover both betrothal and marriage payments in full. This kind of marriage, in fact, would seem to contain a seed of contention and be rather more likely to dissolve in bitterness than would the traditional type.

As for disposing of other property associated with a marriage, the precedents are usually so clear that controversy seldom arises. A man has no claim on land identified with his ex-wife and her relatives, and she certainly has no claim to his. In fact, their only jointly held *real* properties are the house site and garden site, to which they together have title by occupancy and by cultivation, respectively. If either one of these happens to be on land identified with the wife and her relatives, as would be the case with a uxorilocal marriage, then the husband would assert no claim. In all other circumstances he would probably hold onto house (and house site), garden (not even allowing the woman access to the garden), pigs, and all house furnishings and utensils except those made by the woman herself or brought by her to the marriage.

The man's rights are also favored in connection with the retention of offspring. Very young nursing infants are usually left with the mother, but all other offspring can be kept by the father if he has any desire to keep them. This practice is inconsistent with the actual and conceptualized dependence of infant and child upon the mother, but the evidence I collected supports the assertion: when the father actually wants the offspring, he keeps them. Of course, theoretically this does not prejudice the children's rights to move in with their mother's relatives — who include, after all, their own matrilineage-mates — and some of them do so upon reaching maturity; but others of these children of divorce remain always closely identified in residence and in interest with their fathers' kin. The cases we collected cover almost every conceivable possibility.

Twenty years before our visit Siha of Raku turned out his wife and allowed her to take their three-year-old son, Maŋira, with her. The woman soon became the second wife of Korerua, of Mataras, and still lives there with him. Maŋira spent his childhood and youth in Mataras, but returned to his mother's birthplace and matrilineage landholding when he married, and he now spends most of his time there, with occasional long visits to Mataras. Maŋira has few or no contacts with his own father, Siha, whose dwelling is only one mile from his, and will inherit nothing of Siha's when the latter dies. On the other hand, Korerua, his stepfather, has promised him a portion of his personal accumulation of shell money when he dies — but none of his land, part of which will all go to Korerua's own son and part will revert to matrilineage mates.

At the other extreme is the case of Pakano of Rennu village; here is his story:

> I divorced the mother of my two boys; she didn't work hard enough in the garden, and was always having affairs with other men. She wanted to take the two boys with her, but I told her that she was no good and couldn't have them. Her matrilineage mates were very angry with me and tried to force me to release the boys but I defied them. Once the Patrol Officer came here and told me that he didn't approve of having children separated from their mothers; but I told him what a wicked woman the mother was, and also that I am capable of looking out for them, so he said he would give me a chance. Later on he returned here and admitted that I have fed them all right.
>
> Once the new husband of my former wife came here and stole the two boys, taking them back to their mother. When I discovered them gone, I went to the man and we nearly had a fight. He said he wouldn't return the children to me; and I told him that he obviously didn't realize what an important man I am, else he would not have talked that way. He said that I wasn't a *leader* and that he didn't have to do as I said. I told him to wait and see. Then I went to Kope (the highest ranking leader and the Paramount Chief of central Siuai) and told him what had happened. Kope told me to go back and take the children without further argument. When I reported Kope's words to my former wife's husband the latter said for me to go ahead and take the children, adding that he hadn't realized how important I am and that he was sorry for the way he had talked to me.
>
> Now I look out for the two boys, feeding them well and teaching them everything. I'm a man who really knows how to provide food delicacies. My new wife feeds the boys on lots of taro and I bring them lots of delicacies. Do you see how strong they are?

## YOUTH

After childhood all Siuai natives go through a stage of development, characterized by certain activities, experiences, grooming habits, etc., which is terminated by marriage for most of them. This stage could be called "adolescence," but because of many connotations of that term it will best be avoided in favor of the more neutral "youth." For precision, then, I shall speak of the period of "youth," of "young men" and "young women."

The beginning of "youth" coincides only partially and indirectly with the onset of physiological puberty. When a girl-child begins to have love affairs involving copulation, she becomes a "young woman." As stated above,[67] the Siuai believe that a female cannot bear children until menstruation, but they also believe that menses occur only after she has begun to copulate. Menstruation, then, is incidental and is not ritualized or otherwise signalized. The Siuai assume, what I noted to hold true, that by the time a female has reached the copulating stage she is usually doing adults' work, which also partially distinguishes her from the child. As for males, active copulation — and not just ability to copulate — distinguishes the young man from the child; but there are some males of twelve and thirteen who have not yet begun to copulate but who garden and carry weights like adults and are consequently considered to be no longer children. In any case, there is no ritualization of the transition.

For the parents of a young man or a young woman this stage is distinguished from the previous one in several respects. By this time most fathers are past the prime of their physical strength and vigor and are just reaching the climax, if any, of their social advance. And by now, mothers are usually past childbearing and have no more infants of their own to tend; hence they have more time and energy for such activities as visiting and prawn-fishing — in addition to the greater amount of time which must be spent in the gardens to produce the larger amounts of food needed to feed larger herds of pigs.

A sharp distinction has to be drawn between the lives of young men and young women. For one thing young women tend to marry earlier than young men; for another, their everyday activities are quite different.

Young men spend only a small part of their time working, the rest being taken up with strolling, playing, sex-adventuring, and schooling. Also, most of them spend the middle years of youth away from Siuai working on white men's plantations; while a few others attend distant mission schools for a year or two. Even before going away to plantations or to schools, young men begin to live in a manner that vexes their elders. They are capable of hard work but escape from it whenever possible. Their appetites are large but they disdain gardening. The time they spend in school is wasted time in the view of their parents, and they are altogether too preoccupied with keeping their loincloths unsoiled, their hair bleached, and their bodies clean. As far as they are able, they pattern their lives on those older young men who have recently returned from working on plantations.

Nearly all able-bodied young men past "fourteen" — the Australian Administration's lowest permissible age limit for employing native laborers — work a three-year term under contract at coastal plantations. Most of these work on Bougainville plantations; only a few go as far as New Britain or New Guinea. While so employed they see small glimpses of the white man's world, from a distance. A few may serve as house boys in the homes of plantation managers, but most of them live out their contract periods between the coconut groves or copra sheds they work in and the barracks where they eat and sleep surrounded by other natives. They see copra freighters come and go, they make petty purchases at the plantation commissary, they may even have brief opportunities to gawk at the civilized wonders of such colonial outposts as Kieta. But although white men manage the plantation world they live in, the main influence on Siuai youths working there comes from other natives — Siuai, Nagovisi, Nasioi, Terei, etc. They receive little or no direct indoctrination in white men's values except for rules about punctuality, "a full day's work," legally sanctioned contract obligations, and the like. At most plantations they have no access to native women, so except for the very few Siuai who succumb to sodomy practices, most must remain continent. Card playing is discouraged, gambling forbidden, and the murderous form of barefoot soccer played on some plantations does not attract many Siuai players. Their main pastime is strolling about the water front wearing clean loincloths and carefully combed and bleached coiffures. Under such circumstances nearly every Siuai laborer develops a very close friendship with another Siuai or two. Such pairs can be seen strolling around hand in hand acting like schoolgirl "crushes," but probably few if any of them reach the point of homosexual practices. In any case, this kind of relationship is characteristic of young men back in Siuai, and it may derive in part from the plantation experience.

While on plantations, Siuai natives acquire few or no skills that have any relevance to their lives at home. They return home with a few Australian pounds in accrued earnings, a small wooden suitcase filled with calico, tobacco, etc., and a somewhat cynical disdain for the "bush kanaka" [68] life of their elders. The Australian money goes toward paying the annual Administration capitation taxes of the young men and their near kinsmen who have not worked on plantations and hence possess no Australian currency. The goods in the suitcase are distributed among family members or are hoarded and used sparingly until they disintegrate or disappear. The attitude towards bush life and the other habits acquired on the plantation persist a little longer than the tangible souvenirs, and constitute something of a disruptive influence. Here, briefly, is the situation.

Despite the limitations of plantation life it is a *different* life, and young men return home somewhat contemptuous of the provincialism of Siuai beliefs and practices. On the plantations they are somewhat timid, remain with their Siuai "one-talks" and speak Motuna whenever possible. Back home, however, they show off their new sophistication by speaking pidgin among themselves and by relating the wonders of the civilized world. They prefer sleeping in village houses off the ground and away from the pigs, and avoid garden work. Their strolling habits continue, and young women welcome their attentions. For a while their parents encourage their conceit, so pathetically pleased are they to welcome the young men back home. Soon, however, trouble begins. Fathers tire of their indolence and fastidiousness. Parents of young women complain about their visits to settlements where they have no business to transact. Men in club-houses speak disparagingly about their dandified ways and old men resent their disrespectful conduct. The "revolt," however, is not entirely successful.

As has already been implied, Siuai society is certainly no gerontocracy. On the other hand, marrying, remaining healthy, and advancing socially all require expenditures of *native* forms of wealth, especially pigs and shell money; and young men are largely dependent upon their elders for these. The few pounds of Australian currency which young men bring home from plantations would not amount to much even if they could all be exchanged for native wealth, which is not the case. Even should a young man disdain other Siuai values, he cannot contract a marriage without some native wealth, and for this he is primarily dependent upon his father. Furthermore, he is dependent upon his family for most of the food he eats; he could theoretically produce and prepare his own meals, but few Siuai males choose to do so. And, being a Siuai, he cannot remain forever aloof from the activities in the club-house nor, consequently, be insensitive to the opinions of the older men there. The period of recalcitrance, then, is a temporary one, ending in most cases a few months after marriage. There are however some notable exceptions, and some men retain the characteristics of the rebellious young dandy long into married life.

For young Siuai women, adventure does not consist of strange places and alien ideas but rather of early adaptation to sex life and betrothal. Even so, the adaptation does not have to be made abruptly. Most Siuai girls learn about the realities of sexual life and marriage long before they begin to have affairs of their own, and menstruation is no mystery to them. From early childhood on they realize that most women periodically "go to the moon" (*hinjoki pina*), which they know to be the euphemism for menstruation. Despite this knowledge, however, all Siuai females past early childhood feel *shame* (*maijo*) at the sight of menstrual blood and never refer to menstruation except euphemistically. It is the same with Siuai males, who are not embarrassed to state that some woman has "gone to the moon" but who avoid any direct reference to menstrual blood — like "copulate" (ruru) it is too "strong" (*itikai*) a word for polite conversation. Indeed, if a male speaks of a woman's menstrual blood, other males are embarrassed and call him an immoral (kirahao) man, adding that he spends too much of his time with females otherwise he would not know about such things. Yet, Siuai shame of menstrual blood does not extend to the setting aside of special menstrual huts; during their periods women remain inactive in their hamlet houses and try to dry up the flow by holding heated leaves against their abdomen. They try to avoid standing or walking lest the blood run down their legs and be seen, thereby bringing them great embarrassment. Menstrual blood itself is not considered dangerous; the reason most men do not copulate with a menstruating woman is "because of her disagreeable odor, and because some of the blood might get on the man thereby causing him to have *shame* (*maio*, which in this context seems better translated as *disgust* or *repugnance*).

Notwithstanding all this embarrassment and repugnance generated by the sight of menstrual blood and by direct references to it, the euphemism appears to satisfy all the requirements of prudery, for there is no hesitancy about stating that "so-and-so has gone to the moon," or that "she must be carrying a Hidden-one in her belly since she no longer goes to the moon." In fact, when the moon is full and red, natives can be heard to exclaim: "Just look there! Some woman is going to the moon, for it is red."

When a girl begins to menstruate, it is said that her shame is so great that she hides herself and has to be comforted by mother and sisters. Noting her tears and chagrin other persons will conclude that she has begun to "go to the moon" and from that will infer that she has already started having sex affairs and is therefore no longer a *child*. All this will stimulate talk about her availability for betrothal, and so gradually relatives and neighbors will begin to evaluate her in a new set of terms, including her diligence, her beauty, and her conduct.

Henceforth the young woman must avoid all boisterous play and, in fact, all companionship with males her age or older — except, of course, her nearer relatives. When she goes anywhere she walks with another female; to walk alone suggests trysting. She must work harder than before; even the most indulgent of parents require that. And, of course, all these new standards are applied with extra stringency when she goes to live in the home of her fiancé. At the same time, these new standards do not require her to hide her beauty; to the extent that grooming does not interfere with working, she is expected to have clean and glisteningly oiled skin, combed and lice-free hair, and reasonably unsoiled loincloths. If her skin becomes disfigured with ringworm, it is no longer attributed to the "natural" diseases of childhood but more often to her own unsanitary habits. In Siuai words, she must be as industrious as the ant and as pretty and fragrant as the hibiscus blossom. But while her male contemporaries are still at the peak of their youthfulness, she becomes a wife and mother and so enters another phase of her life.

# CYCLE OF THE NUCLEAR FAMILY 205

What more can be said about relationships among family members at this stage of development? Let us begin with father and son, a relationship in which ethnographers of some cultures see the whole social order writ small. We have already described the indulgence with which most fathers treat their children, the usual ineffectiveness of their discipline, and the pride they evince in a son's little accomplishments. Quarrels, angry bursts of temper, and blows sometimes break out between fathers and sons during the latter's childhood, but I could find no evidence of enduring irritation or bitterness. Later on, though, a change takes place. When young men return from plantations, or when they begin to ape those who have returned, there is almost sure to be some dissension. Some friction is avoided through building a separate sleeping house for the son, usually in the line village, but this does not resolve the other causes of conflict. Many of these derive from the aftermath of youths' sojourns away from home; but some develop out of situations which probably antedate white man's influences. There is, for example, the kind of situation created by the maturing of the young man in a family relationship system which does not ordinarily stress the father's absolute authority over everyday conduct but which gives the father strong control over family resources, including those needed to acquire a wife for the young man. Added to this is the complication resulting from structural causes. For example, when Nensa of Turuŋum died, I noticed that his son, Pinoko, did not show any signs of grief. He managed the cremation quite properly and distributed most of his father's earned wealth in order to obtain pigs for the mourners, but his mourning was perfunctory and dry-eyed. When I queried a neighbor of his about this the latter explained that Pinoko and Nensa had not been on good terms for more than a year. When Nensa had married Pinoko's mother she brought along a few spans of high-value shell money which she had inherited from her mother. Later, when Pinoko's mother died, Nensa quickly remarried, and instead of reserving the shell money for Pinoko he gave it to his second wife. This angered and embittered Pinoko, because ultimately the child of the second wife will inherit the shell money; however, Pinoko did not bring suit to obtain the money, saying, "One cannot take legal action against one's own father."

Hence, the behavior of a son is not always the precipitating cause for father-son conflict. In fact the Wicked Father is a character in several Siuai tales, of which the following is typical:

> A long time ago a woman gave birth to two males. When they were young men their father said to them: "Let us go to the garden to build a fence." They started out together but the father left them at the edge of the clearing and returned home; the two youths went on to the garden and worked hard all day. Meanwhile the father returned home alone and told his wife that the two youths had gone strolling in the forest and had not worked in the garden. To punish them the woman dug up some wild taro and cooked it for their evening meal. Later, when the two youths returned home wearied and hungry from

their labors they tasted the food set out for them. The bitter wild taro caused their mouths to pucker and they had to go hungry. The younger one wept but the elder brother comforted him, saying: "Tomorrow perhaps it will be different." But the following day the same thing occurred, and again on the third day. Finally the two youths ran away.

They made their way to a distant settlement, and there two women saw them and claimed them for husbands. The married couples settled down in adjoining houses and prospered. Then after a few years the two brothers decided to visit their parents. When they arrived home, they discovered that their father had died of hunger and that their mother was near death from the same cause. They revived her with sugar-cane juice and coconut water, and then brought her back to health with taro and delicacies. Then they took her back to their new homes where she remained. When they arrived there the brothers told her of the deception their father had practiced, and this caused the woman to weep, because she had believed the lies of her husband about her children.

Whatever the causes, dissension between father and son becomes manifest in several ways. When the son is totally lacking in spirit and initiative, as in the case of Koiai of Turuŋum, he lapses into sullen slothfulness and goes on living in his father's house; quarrels break out now and then, but usually the two simply avoid talking to each other. In other cases a separate house is a partial solution until the young man marries and sets up his own household. Or, it frequently happens that young men will make their way to plantations and sign three-year contracts to escape from an unhappy family situation and to spite their fathers. Again, if the young man has already served his plantation indenture and does not wish to go again, he may leave his father's household and live elsewhere with relatives, usually with his mother's people. In this connection, dissension between father and son sometimes influences the latter's choice of residence after marriage.

It would be erroneous to suppose that all or even most young men remain at loggerheads with their fathers, for such is not the case. Much more frequently [69] one sees the pair working together amicably and obviously fond of each other. Nevertheless, dissension is potential in the relationship, and if it remains only potential that is strong evidence of the pair's mutual affection and forbearance.

The relationship between a young man and his mother is characterized by mutual affection, and is not threatened by conflicts over authority or property. Mothers are known to become vexed with their sons' indolence but they seldom erupt into anger as their husbands do, nor are they in the habit of instructing their sons what to do and how to do it — after middle childhood such instructions to the son come from male relatives. As for property, most of that which belongs to the mother belongs jointly to her offspring by reason of their common membership in a matrilineage; in fact one of the factors which reinforces the tie between mother and children is their joint-ownership interests in land and in other matrilineage valuables. I heard of no instances of serious dissension between a young man and his mother; on the contrary, mothers often side with sons in the latter's quarrels with fathers. I saw women show touching affection and admiration for thoroughly worthless sons. On one occasion, for example, I was walking about mapping garden sites with a guide who was a notorious thief and trouble-maker, the only known sodomist in northeast Siuai;[70] and when we reached the new garden patch where his mother was burning the trash which he should have cleared away, she walked over to him and touched him lovingly and then turned to me and, clutching her breasts in both hands, explained that "the handsome flower of a man with you is my own son and used to suckle at these very breasts."

Informants were horrified even at my suggestion that incestuous relations might take place between mother and son, and certainly no instances of it were reported. One young man did acknowledge that he had once dreamed of copulating with his mother, stating that the dream was not "real" but that he had nevertheless felt great shame as a result of it.

Something has already been said in this chapter of the relationship of a young woman and her mother.[71] This is probably the most affectionate of all Siuai relations. The two spend nearly all their time together before the daughter moves to her fiancé's home. They have identical and non-competing interests in matrilineage property, and as far as I could determine, the daughter's status is in no way improved by her mother's death. Nor could I detect any signs of jealousy between the two with respect to father-husband or brother-son — which is not to say that it does not exist but merely that it was not accessible to my investigations. However, despite the lack of more or less institutionalized bases for dissension, it would be surprising if all mother-daughter relations were harmonious; incompatibilities resulting from personality differences must surely be expected with such intimate everyday contact. But if they occur, and they probably do, at least they are not serious enough to have been noticed by myself or to have been commented on by informants.

The relation between a young woman and her father is also an affectionate one, but it is lacking in the identity of activity and in the continuous everyday interaction of mother and daughter. Also, the relation is complicated by the reticence of the two to discuss sexual matters in each other's presence — less so than in the case of brother and sister but a factor just the same. Added to this is the father's concern that his daughter become and remain advantageously betrothed, which requires guarding her against her own inclinations as well as against would-be seducers. This last circumstance sometimes causes angry flare-ups between father and daughter which now and then lead to the daughter's going to live with other relatives until the inevitable reconciliation takes place.

Some of the jealousies and conflicts between siblings of the same sex which occur in childhood presumably carry over into youth, but I received the strong impression that most pairs of youthful brothers were very closely linked by ties of affection and of common interests and activities. In fact, there is less basis for dissension during youth than during infancy and childhood, after parents have relaxed the exaggerated solicitude they show towards the younger infant and child. Brothers in their teens are constant companions, and there seems to be an absence of the kind of situation, familiar to us, wherein the elder becomes plagued by the younger's tagging along. They sometimes make a point of serving their plantation indentures together, and I recorded one instance of an older brother, who had already completed one three-year contract, staying on for another term "to look out for his younger brother," who had meanwhile signed on. Serious conflicts between brothers only begin to develop after the father dies, when quarrels over property may ensue; or after the brothers marry, when strife between their wives may also involve them.

During their youth the sexual taboos between brother and sister harden into a rigid code of conduct. Any reference to sex organs or to the sex act in their presence will arouse a show of shame in both of them — as well as anger in the young man. At the same time each shows great concern over the other's welfare; the sister sees to it that her brother is well fed, and the brother, while not usually entering into the negotiations leading up to his sister's betrothal and marriage, which would be shameful, nevertheless makes certain that her fiancé is a worthy one and that all other males keep well away. As a measure of his respect and of the strength of the taboo, the most inviolate oath a brother can express is, "by the bed of my sister."

What was said of the trend of the relationship between father and mother of children past infancy is even more applicable here.[72] By this time marriages are almost completely stable in that they very rarely dissolve in divorce. The man's preoccupation with extra-family matters continues, and his wife exercises even stronger management over the domestic economy. If anything, quarrels occur less frequently, and the wife seldom has to employ a reconciliation token to bring a sulking husband home, knowing full well that his days of divorcing are past.

In searching through my memory of the numerous married couples I knew, those monogamous pairs at this stage and age of life stand out as the most companionable.

## OLD AGE AND DEATH

In Chapter 4 it was pointed out that the household is a basic social unit in Siuai and that most households consist of a nuclear family, at some stage of its cyclical development. We then proceeded to trace the formation and proliferation of a typical family, carrying it up to the stage when its young members begin to disperse to form new nuclear families. In Siuai, however, this dispersion does not obliterate the original family-household unit; husband and wife continue to live together and maintain their separate house-

## CYCLE OF THE NUCLEAR FAMILY 209

hold after all their offspring have moved elsewhere. "Elsewhere" may be only a few meters away, but even when the offspring marry into distant settlements, usually the original family ties are maintained by frequent visiting. And if anything, visiting becomes more frequent as the father and mother approach senility.

While age by itself does not command great respect in Siuai, the offspring are usually tenderly affectionate toward aging parents, demonstrating by word and deed that they feel an obligation for their welfare. If the parents occupy the same hamlet or neighboring hamlets the son or daughter will ofttimes perform much of the work of clearing and cultivating their parents' garden. Or if they live too far apart for that they will usually take along baskets of food when they return for visits. As it is explained: "When we were children they fed and cared for us well; and now that they are aged we repay by giving food to them. For, if we did not, they would surely starve."

In time the aging couple may become completely dependent upon their offspring and other relatives for food, but they persist in occupying their separate house until one of them dies. How, then, does this natural and inevitable event affect the survivors?

"Natural and inevitable" describes accurately the way most Siuai look upon the death of an aged person. It is generally believed that younger people die only as a result of supernatural contrivance, but aged people may die simply because their vitality has expired.[73] When an aged person dies there is not much mourning, and the funeral includes several unique features — but before discussing these it will be useful to describe the practices observed in connection with other deaths.[74] These events include wake, cremation, rewarding of the funeral guests, and a mourning period of two or more phases. As a basis for describing these practices let us consider the course of events which follow upon the death of an aging but not yet senile man whose socio-political rank is about modal for men of his age; we can call him Maimoi.

When Maimoi dies his nearest of kin, including his widow, his offspring, his widow's brother, his own brother, and his uterine nephew crowd around his corpse for an hour or so and cry with some vigor. Then the males withdraw from the hut and begin to prepare for the funeral, leaving room for more females — distant kinswomen and neighbors — to continue the weeping. The death took place in the forenoon; Maimoi's son, a youth of about eighteen, and his widow decide to have the cremation on the night of the following day. Meanwhile the principal female mourners have painted their faces with white clay, and the men have tied mourning bands of cord fiber around their upper arms.

The deceased's son now must estimate how large a funeral can be afforded. He consults with his mother and the two of them decide that of the six hundred spans' worth of shell money belonging to the family, four hundred shall be used for the funeral, along with one of the deceased's own pigs. In addition, Maimoi's son takes from the family savings high-value shell money worth fifty spans and gives this to his father's brother and uterine nephew. This is a "breath-die" gift (*rumapui*), given to a deceased's male matrilineage-mates, who usually do, but are not obliged to, repay it in the form of pigs for the funeral. The other four hundred spans' worth of money are call *nori* and are distributed among the deceased's relatives and friends, being used by them to secure pigs — either their own or purchased from others — for the funeral. *Breath-die* is presented shortly after the death and before the funeral; nori may not be actually distributed until after the funeral, but within a few hours after the death the deceased's son and matrilineage-mates are agreed among themselves concerning how the money will be distributed and how many pigs it will bring in. At the same time it is decided what settlements will be permitted to attend the funeral en masse — since everyone who attends and mourns must be rewarded with enough pork for a meal, the number invited must depend upon the number of pigs to be provided. In the present instance all communities comprising three neighboring villages are given general invitations; these are the settlements of the deceased's nearest consanguinal and affinal kin. In addition, it is assumed that individual relatives and close friends from other places will also attend. All these negotiations are carried out in brisk, businesslike fashion by the deceased's son, brother, and uterine nephew, and they are completed by nightfall of the first day.

While the negotiations are in progress, the women's weeping continues vigorously. After every group of female visitors leaves, the principal mourners withdraw from the house where Maimoi lies and sit around outside smoking and chewing betel, tear-stained but no longer weeping. Then, when a new lot of visitors arrives the principal mourners usher them into the house and lead off in a renewed session of wailing, which lasts for an hour or so.

There is not much sleeping during the night following the death. Natives sit around in quiet little clumps smoking and chewing betel, now and then retiring into the deceased's hut to weep. Maimoi's widow is the most faithful of the mourners, and her characteristic cry, which has now become a short, song-like refrain repeated over and over again in a high-pitched nasal whine, is heard when everyone else is silent. Since the time of the death none of the principal mourners has done any regular work nor prepared a solid meal; the eating of taro is forbidden, and hunger is satisfied with snacks of sago, plantain, and yam.

On the day of the cremation, Maimoi's son and matrilineage-mates construct the pyre. They fell enough barked and standing *koropoi* trees in Maimoi's garden and carry them back to the hamlet, where they cut and split them into pieces about nine feet long. A railing is built a few feet out from the pyre, and over this are hung whole taro plants taken from Maimoi's garden. Then Maimoi's son constructs a stretcher out of laths of an areca-like palm, for carrying his father's body from the house to the pyre.

By nightfall some of the visitors have begun to arrive, the women in clusters and carrying their infants, the men singly or in pairs. Upon arrival each cluster of women joins Maimoi's widow and other close female kin in his house for a few minutes of weeping, and then withdraws to make way for the next arrivals. By this time speculation over the cause of Maimoi's death has been quieted by general acceptance of one neighbor's story: Maimoi had told him on the day before his death that he, Maimoi, had seen a large *haŋoro* snake (*Boiga irregularis*) near one of the settlement's taboo places, and obviously that snake had been a Near-death-causing demon. No one suggests sorcery as the cause, because, as everyone knows, Maimoi was not a *leader* or himself a sorcerer, and was in fact, a harmless man with no known enemies.

Within four or five hours after sunset all of the visitors have arrived and contributed their voices in a weeping chorus or two, and the tired and sleepy natives sit around in quiet clusters; some of them succumb to sleep but they are wakened if their snores are too loud: it is not seemly to appear too indifferent to this solemn event. Maimoi's son now begins to scan the eastern heavens for a sign of Panoi, the star whose rising is the signal for the cremation. Some man suggests in a loud voice that the cremation should begin, but a woman — one of Maimoi's distant sib-mates — objects, pointing out that one should not hurry up a cremation. At any rate, this exchange stirs the mourners into renewed weeping, and Maimoi's son decides to proceed with the cremation even without the star: "my father has been dead for a long time," he explains, "and will begin to rot and stink if we delay any longer."

The essential thing is that the body be reduced to ashes by dawn. I could discover no other reason for utilizing Panoi as a signal than the fact that the interval between its rising and dawn is known by experience to correspond roughly to the time usually required to cremate a body. Children and infants require smaller pyres and cremate more rapidly than an adult, so that their pyres are lighted some time after Panoi rises.

Maimoi's son and brother then carry the corpse outside on the stretcher, all to the accompaniment of greatly increased wailing. Then they carry it to the edge of the clearing and pour water over it and rub on coconut oil, "to remove the stench of death." After this they wrap calico loincloths around the corpse and carry it to the pyre where they deposit it in the trough formed at the top. The stretcher is then laid on top of the corpse, more wood over that, and Maimoi's son lights the pyre in several places. While this is taking place one of the magicians present runs several times around the pyre rustling a branch of leaves and shouting to the souls of Near-death individuals to leave or be burnt.[75] As the fire begins to blaze the wailing increases, and Maimoi's nearest kin stand close to the pyre holding to the uprights and sobbing. Other relatives stand in a wider circle around the pyre and weep loudly, while farther back stand little clumps of visitors who perform with dry-eyed and sing-song wailing. Every adult present half-weeps, half-sings a mourning refrain, addressed to the deceased according to the relationship with him.[76]

At one point the First-born of the deceased's matrilineage throws into the pyre a small quantity of the matrilineage high-value shell money heirloom. This funeral offering (*hikuhiku*) varies in quantity according to the wealth of the matrilineage and the socio-political rank of the deceased, but it is never more than a small handful.

The blazing pyre soon forces back the inner circle of mourners, although widow, son, brother, and nephew hold onto the uprights as long as they can bear the heat. When they retire a few feet a distant matrilineage *brother* of the deceased begins to circle the pyre, singing and half-dancing as he goes. Others join in and soon there are some ten or twelve slowly hop-stepping in a line, while the son and widow remain standing and sobbing out their laments near the pyre. A crescendo is reached when the part of the pyre holding the corpse blazes forth, after that the wailing begins to subside and the dancers fall back. After an hour or so only the nearest relatives remain near the pyre crying; all others stand or sit further back and leave off wailing save for an occasional perfunctory whine. Gradually visitors drift back into the darkness to smoke or sleep, and during the hour or so before dawn even the widow and son sit and watch the dying fire, the son quietly and the widow with only an occasional wail.

By dawn most of the female visitors have returned home, and only a handful of male visitors remains. When it is completely light Maimoi's son and widow walk over to the ashes and pick out all bits of unconsumed bone, which they carry to the nearby Place-of-bones and scatter there. Returning to the house they wash their hands thoroughly to rid them of the aura of death, and this marks the end of the funeral.

There is no rigidity about who performs the various actions at the funeral, but the spouse and the son, if he is old enough, always play central roles, while the deceased's siblings invariably take assisting parts. If the deceased is young, then his or her parents are usually the principals. Generally speaking, members of the deceased's nuclear families — both *orientation* and *procreation* — are the leading actors.

The period of mourning has various phases of different intensities, which differ according to the mourners' relationship to the deceased. In the case of a man like Maimoi there will be a first phase, lasting for one or two weeks, which affect his widow and offspring, his own siblings, his uterine nephews and nieces, and all other persons who dwell in his hamlet. During this phase little work will be done. Women mourners other than his widow will go to the gardens only to harvest enough plantains and yams for Spartan meals.[77] Males will stay at home and do nothing; females will not remove the white clay paint from their faces and will periodically sing-song their mourning laments. No one bathes or puts on clean loincloths. Even the pigs are fed only enough to keep them domesticated. As this first phase draws to an end the adult males go to the forest and capture a few opossums for a small feast. While these are roasting, nearly all members of this inner circle of mourners visit the deceased's garden and obtain some taro which they carry home and cook before placing on the bed of ashes remaining from the cremation. No person may eat this taro nor replant the stalks, it is called *hoŋona* and is believed to be eaten by the ghost of the deceased. After this the opossums are eaten with sago, plantains, and yams, and the first mourning phase is thereby ended. The mourners may now resume their normal activities, although they are still prohibited from eating taro. They all bathe and remove all signs of mourning; in fact the women replace the white paint of mourning with the red paint of rejoicing.

The second phase of mourning ends a few weeks later, when all the men who received shell money from Maimoi's son and widow carry the pigs so purchased to Maimoi's hamlet. There the pigs are slaughtered and butchered, and strips sent to each hamlet represented at the funeral. This is the feast of *Cutting*; the principal mourners cook and eat their portions of pork with taro, thereby ending the taboo on eating taro and terminating all mourning for everyone but the widow. Her mourning is not completely ended until another complete almond cycle has passed; until then she should not remarry nor have sexual intercourse.

Had Maimoi been more influential one or more of his brothers, brothers-in-law, political adherents, or trade partners (*taovu*) would very likely impose additional mourning taboos on themselves by uttering an oath at the funeral not to eat, say, taro-and-almond pudding until after holding a feast in honor of the deceased. In return for this gesture the deceased's son is expected to give each one of them an extra pig, as a reward for this manifestation of *sympathy* (*piapiare*). Or, if it had been Maimoi's wife who had died, and not Maimoi, the widower would not be obliged to wait for a year before marrying, but he would very likely impose severe restrictions on his activities and eating habits for several months as a sign of deep mourning. Many widowers, in fact, remain secluded in their hamlets for months following the death of a wife, until some kinsman or friend presents them with a Bringing-out gift (*ruhoto*), usually a pig or fifty or so spans of shell money, this "gift" being eventually repaid. Fathers also go into seclusion after death of a favorite son or daughter, and this must also be terminated by a Bringing-out gift.

In the case of death of a man of high rank a taboo on land-use may be imposed by his kinsmen or adherents. If, for example, several men are cultivating a tract of land at the time of the death of their leader or matrilineage First-born they all agree to taboo the land to all future work — except harvesting the crops already planted — until a memorial feast has been prepared for the deceased. Such land is called *set-aside* (*parepare*, or *maŋana*); and it is not unusual for large tracts of economically valuable land to be set-aside in this manner.

*Setting-aside* usually consists in issuing a verbal invitation to the ghost of the deceased, along with some of his matrilineage ghosts, to visit misfortune upon any individual who breaks the taboo. It is usually removed by holding a feast in honor of the deceased, whose ghost partakes of the essence of the food consumed at the feast. Setting-aside may also include areas of forest, which may not be hunted, or stretches of river, which may not be fished. In the latter instance restoration of the river to use also involves providing a food offering to the ghosts of expert fishermen who formerly fished at the place.

Sometimes the exigencies of everyday affairs bring about an indefinite postponement of the ceremony and its accompanying feast. For example, on the east bank of Kuru creek, immediately south of Mataras village, is a plot of land which was set-aside — as nearly as I could estimate — in about 1922. All close relatives of the deceased have since died, and there is no one willing to provide an expensive feast merely to restore the land to use. Consequently, it remains taboo even though it is fertile and conveniently located. Its original name has been discarded and forgotten, and it is now called "Set-aside."[78]

In our hypothetical case of Maimoi we assumed that he was an aging but not yet senile man. Had he been the latter his funeral would have differed significantly. (As the Siuai put it: "When a very old man dies we sing more than we weep, for he has reached his time (*poti*) and we are not too sorrowful. But if a younger person dies we grieve, because that one's time has not yet arrived.") To begin with, his son would have issued invitations to the cremation by sending thirty to fifty spans of shell money to each settlement invited, signifying that each one should arrive at the funeral bearing a pig, worth the value of the shell money sent with the invitation, and prepared to sing and dance in honor of the deceased. The funeral itself does not differ markedly from the one described above,[79] until the cremation fire has burnt out. Most of the guests remain throughout the cremating and when dawn comes each settlement group present brings in the pig it has left outside the hamlet, hands it over to be butchered, and proceeds to dance and sing a song composed specially for the occasion. These songs contain first a salute to the deceased, and then proceed to air a grievance which the composers hold against some other persons present, including even the survivors of the deceased! By midmorning all the participants begin to wilt, and they return home carrying strips of pork distributed by the deceased's son. After such funerals mourning is less strict, and usually does not involve taboos on eating taro or working.

The death of a child or young person concerns fewer people and occasions smaller funerals, and an infant's dying is usually a matter for near relatives alone. On the other hand, the death of a high-ranking leader gives rise to a more elaborate train of events and the funeral may be attended by hundreds of persons.[80] Special practices also characterize the funerals of suicides, of women who die in childbirth, men who are killed by falling from trees, and persons believed killed by sorcery.[81] All women avoid looking at any woman who has died in childbirth, lest the same fate befall them. At the cremation of a man killed falling from a tree, all males at the funeral leave the scene as soon as the pyre has been lighted, lest the smoke touch them and thereby make them liable to the same fate. They retire to a nearby club-house and beat the wooden gongs all during the cremation in order to drive away the ghost of the deceased and the spirit that caused him to fall from the tree. (It would appear that the ghosts of tree-fallers are compelled by their fate to return and cause other men to fall.)

We began this account of mortuary practices with a query: How does death affect the surviving members of a family? The foregoing description indicates how family survivors carry out the conventional funeral and mourning practices, so the question now is: What permanent changes, if any, in family organization, residence, property, etc., result from the death of a member? For some general answers to this question we can continue consideration of the hypothetical case of Maimoi.

Assuming that Maimoi's widow does not remarry — and this is the case with many aging widows — she can keep on residing where she is, with her unmarried offspring, if there are any, or alone if there are none; or she can join forces with a married son or daughter and their offspring, either she moving to their household or they to hers.[82] If the widow and any of her offspring reside in different households in the same hamlet, she is most likely to keep on occupying the same house while merging all her other activities with theirs, including gardening, cooking, and eating. I recorded no instance of a widow living entirely alone and maintaining a separate domestic economy.

Any change in residence of the deceased's son depends in some measure on the disposition he makes of his patrimony.

Every married couple owns an accumulation, large or small, of valuables. This property, known as *pure*, consists mainly of shell money and comes from several kinds of sources: some of it is money remaining from that inherited by the husband from *his* father, some is money (known as *aŋupi*) earned by the husband, or by the wife after her marriage, by sale of foodstuffs, pigs, manufactured articles, etc. Family pure does not include the high-value shell money paid over to the wife's father at the time of her betrothal and now held by her; nor does it include any other money owned by her prior to her marriage, nor any matrilineage-identified property of either spouse. Natives disagree as to whether money earned by offspring before their marriage and through their own individual efforts (e.g., plantation wages) should be lumped in with the family's pure; and this disagreement often leads to disputes and litigation. There is also disagreement as to whether the family's pigs should be classed with pure.

While the husband is still alive he has final authority over disposal of any of the family pure, but he usually consults with his wife and older sons before doing so. When he dies the pure remains in the possession of his widow and offspring; theoretically, his widow (first wife), his eldest son, and his oldest daughter, if she is the family *First-born*, should exercise control over its disposal, but sometimes — depending upon personality — his other widows and offspring also have a decisive say in the matter.

In the case of Maimoi the family pure amounted to six hundred spans' worth of shell money, part of it consisting of ordinary mussel shell (*mauai*) and part of high-value denominations (*koso*). Of this, fifty spans were given to the deceased's male matrilineage-mates for the Breath-die payment, and four hundred more were distributed among relatives and friends to provide pigs for the mourners' reward (that is, literally, to pay for their service), leaving only 150 spans for the family survivors. Most Siuai consider this a fully adequate funeral expenditure in terms of Maimoi's rank and the total amount of his family pure. It is certain to ensure his ghost's safe reception in Paradise, hence it completely satisfies his surviving matrilineage-mates who — implicitly, at least — bear responsibility for his welfare in life and in death. Since it does satisfy them, they permit Maimoi's widow and offspring to assume full title to Maimoi's share of their corporately owned matrilineage land. If Maimoi's survivors had *not* made what his matrilineage-mates consider an adequate funeral expenditure, and hence jeopardized his ghost's fate hereafter, they would deny all use of their land to Maimoi's widow and offspring. However, few Siuai would be so hard-hearted and impractical as to withhold pure and thereby endanger a husband's or father's fate as well as forfeit ownership of valuable land. These are the considerations which dominate the discussions about pig buying which take place immediately after death; and if the son and widow appear niggardly about how much pure to distribute, Maimoi's brother, his uterine nephew, and any other matrilineage-mates present may be counted on to become angry and threatening. If the widow and son remain unmoved, then Maimoi's matrilineage-mates retire sullenly and summon all their male matrilineage-mates within reach for an anger demonstration (*mih*). They deck themselves out for war, wearing both the white paint of mourning and the red paint of battle, take up their spears, and return to Maimoi's hamlet. Just before reaching the clearing, they form an attack line and rush up to the house of mourning, shouting and thrusting defiantly with their spears. After a few minutes of this they leave, and their frightening demonstration usually has the desired effect — although some individuals hold out even against such threats and are consequently barred from all use of their husband's and father's matrilineage land. In this connection, it is interesting to note that *nori*, the term for

## CYCLE OF THE NUCLEAR FAMILY 217

the payment made by family survivors to buy pigs for the funeral of a deceased family member, is also the term for certain kinds of indemnity.

If Maimoi and his family had been residing and gardening on land identified with Maimoi's matrilineage, then it is necessary for his widow and offspring to satisfy Maimoi's matrilineage-mates in the matter of the nori payment if they wish to continue residing and gardening there. But even if a man's family survivors do not wish to utilize his land — for example, if they are already established elsewhere — they cannot avoid at least the moral obligation to provide enough nori to ensure the deceased's welfare in the hereafter.

It is clear, then, that the use made of family pure by the deceased's survivors may affect where they reside and work. As for Maimoi's personal effects — his tools, weapons, etc. — these are turned over to his eldest son; but this is a minor matter, since among these Siuai such personal effects are so few and inconsequential, few of them having much exchange or symbolic value. But before leaving the subject of inheritance and nori payments it will be useful to speculate concerning what might have happened if there had been no accumulation of pure in Maimoi's family to provide him with a proper send-off, this being a not uncommon occurrence. If Maimoi had been a generous and congenial individual, on good terms with all his relatives and neighbors, then his nearest matrilineage-mates, including his *siblings* and uterine nephews, might themselves provide a pig or two to reward the mourners invited to the cremation; and if they are satisfied that Maimoi's family survivors possess no valuables and are at the same time congenial and coöperative, they will give them provisional title to some of their matrilineage land, including the right to reside and garden on it. Back of this generosity lies the expectation that Maimoi's sons will eventually earn enough to contribute pigs for the funerals of Maimoi's *siblings* or other matrilineage-mates; and these delayed payments will then entitle the sons to full title to some of Maimoi's matrilineage's land.

It sometimes happens that in a household which does not own a pure the wife has a separate stock of shell money directly inherited from her parents. Here is the way one informant described such a situation:

> When my mother married my father and went to live on his matrilineage land, she took along many baskets filled with shell money which she had inherited from her mother and father when they died earlier. Her family was wealthy, but my father's owned nothing but land. Nevertheless while my father lived he used as much of *our* money as he wished: he was our mother's husband and our own father, and that is a firm tie. He used whatever he wished of ours, and we denied him nothing nor were we angry about it. Later, when he died, he left no pure of his own, but my mother and my siblings used 400 spans of *our* money to buy pigs for the funeral. This was not my father's money; it was ours, but he was our father, and that is something true. Because of this we remained on his land. Later on, when my other

*fathers* died, we again used some of our own money to buy funeral pigs, and for that we were given larger pieces of land in this district.

This record shows how a virilocal family's residence may be rendered secure for the survivors even though they possess no *family* pure. However, more importantly, it provides a glimpse of one aspect of family structure which until now has been only indirectly suggested, and that is the component unit consisting only of mother and offspring. In the account above, this kind of unit stands out quite clearly, mainly because of the source of the family's money, but also because of the fact that the father was dead. In the case of monogamous families where both parents are alive it is more difficult to detect this separate social unit, but it is nevertheless there.

Now, sub-units of this nature are probably to be found in some families in all societies; they result from interaction patterns, which in turn derive from techniques, personality idiosyncracies, etc. For example, if the father's occupation requires him to be away from home most of the time, thereby leaving wife and offspring together, these latter constitute a distinctly separate unit with respect to interaction, i.e., they constitute a family sub-unit. In most monogamous Siuai families this kind of sub-unit is not very distinct in terms of interaction patterns alone, but because of the matrilineal sib institution it is extraordinarily important from a structural point of view, inasmuch as each family sub-unit potentially constitutes the nucleus of a new matrilineage. This is especially true of virilocal families but it may also apply to those uxorilocal families owning large quantities of valuables.

The death of a husband and father does not always remove his influence from the lives of his family survivors. His ghost occasionally returns and becomes the familiar of one of his sons and helps the latter to acquire wealth and influence. In that case the son makes periodic food offerings to the ghost; otherwise there is no parental ancestor-worship or any other attempt to secure the intervention of a deceased parent *qua* parent, in mortal affairs.

Suppose, now, that Maimoi's wife and not he were the one to die: what changes would this event bring about in the lives of her family survivors?

If Maimoi had no living offspring, or if all of them were married and residing elsewhere, he might well remain alone in his own house for the rest of his days, joining with relatives or neighbors to produce and prepare food but otherwise retaining his separate residence. Such a situation is not unusual; eight such households were recorded in northeast Siuai. These old men value highly their independence, and only one of them has to my knowledge become a burden on his relatives and neighbors. One of them is the ancient Kuipuru, who despite his near-blindness proudly takes care of all but his food needs quite alone. In seven other recorded cases, widowers are residing with unmarried offspring in more or less independent households. Of these, three are still in their prime and have stated their intentions of remarrying; they have young children to care for and are obviously finding the responsibilities burdensome. The other four are older and have older sons and daughters who provide for their fathers as well as for themselves; these are quite normal households in every sense except for the absence of a wife-mother. In two other cases the widowers, both of them approaching senility, dwell in households with married sons, who themselves have offspring. One of these old men is still an energetic gardener and man of affairs; the other spends his time happily nursing his grandchildren. In addition to all these instances there are in northeast Siuai six widowers of various ages who have no regular abodes; drifters and spongers, they go from one relative to another for their meals, and sleep in club-houses. They are certain to appear at all feasts and important rituals, and are humorously tolerated by most people.

Most widowers not yet senile remarry after a few months of mourning, and such were the plans of several younger men we knew whose wives had died shortly before or during our visit. None of these tries to maintain an independent household; they sleep at home but attach themselves and their children to neighboring households for food. Those with infants turn them over to the latters' matrilineage-mates to nurse, and in some instances it appears that the "adoption" will remain permanently.

If both parents die within a short period their younger orphans will be cared for by the formers' married siblings or other matrilineage-mates, there being no formal rite of adoption. Nearly every hamlet has one or two of these orphans. If anything, adults are more solicitous about them than about other children, and take special pride in their accomplishments: "Just see how industrious that one is — and he only an orphan at that!" One orphan boy living at Jeku is the darling of the village. He eats when and where he likes and is exhibited as if he were some prized possession; and this is not an exceptional situation. *Pananjas*, truly parentless orphans, suffer no institutional disabilities in Siuai; there are classificatory *mothers* and *fathers* aplenty to care for them, and if need be they can depend on matrilineage mates for material assistance. Reflecting these circumstances is the admiration and affection which the Siuai have for the legendary Orphan (Pananj). Stories about Orphan's feats and inventions are countless,[83] with new ones continually developing; most of these legends contain the theme of this parentless Culture Hero overcoming numerous obstacles to achieve personal success and bring benefits to mankind.

To complete our inquiry: What effect does the death of an infant or child or young man or woman have upon their family? In a word, no fundamental changes take place in family life except in the very rare cases wherein the grief-stricken mother of the deceased infant or child commits suicide. If a family suffers the loss of two or three infants then the father may decide to move to another place to try and avoid the *tao* sorcery which is believed responsible. But otherwise the death of an unmarried son or daughter, despite the obviously deep grief it causes, does not break up the family or change its mode of living.

Consideration can now be given to the cases of those widows and widowers who remarry.

## SECONDARY MARRIAGES

Up to now the discussion has been focused on *primary* marriages and the monogamous families resulting from them. However, by the time Siuai men and women reach senility most of them will have been married more than once, their earlier marriages having been terminated either by divorce or by the death of the spouse. If the earlier marriage had produced no issue, then the second marriage differs in no important respect from the model we have been describing, except that the arrangements for the second one are simpler and the nuptial ceremony is usually omitted, especially if it is the woman's second marriage.

As in many other societies, Siuai remarriages sometimes involve a special preferential choice of mate — that is, except after divorces. When a couple dissolve their marriage through divorce it is quite certain that neither will remarry a close relative of the other; the bitterness usually engendered by a divorce serves therefore to restrict rather than determine the choice. After death of a husband, however, there is some sentiment in favor of the widow's remarrying one of the deceased's *brothers* — not necessarily his actual brother but at least one of his matrilineage mates. This *brother* may be of the same generation as the deceased, or of that of his grandson; neither his maternal *uncles* nor his *sister's sons* being eligible. During our stay in Siuai I did not hear of any cases of a widow marrying her deceased spouse's brother, and informants could recall only six having occurred there during the preceding decade, but there were large numbers of instances of remarriage to other matrilineage-mates of the deceased.

The Siuai give three reasons for favoring this form of widow remarriage. First of all, the woman is already closely related to the members of her deceased husband's matrilineage. Perhaps some of them actually helped the deceased's father collect enough money for the betrothal and marriage payments; this, however, does not lead the Siuai to assert explicit "ownership" of the woman's person or functions (here in Siuai there is little if any similarity to the common African institution wherein members of a husband's corporate unit consider his wife — or functions of her — to belong to all of them). Secondly, if she has been married a long while and is congenial and coöperative with her deceased husband's relatives, they like to keep her among them and insure that she is well cared for in her approaching old age. And third, only a fraction of the normal marriage payment is required to remarry her — a bargain price for the services of a productive gardener and pig-raiser. This practice may be called the "levirate" although it is not a case of the second husband "raising up seed" for the first. Nor is it a clear case of widow inheritance; it is necessary to make some payment for the woman, and her own consanguinous kin are within their rights to refuse the price offered and encourage her to marry elsewhere. Here, as with a primary marriage, the woman herself usually has the final say in the matter, and the choice she makes usually depends upon her relations with her affinal kin. A description of a few actual cases will indicate some of the complexities involved.

Maŋira's younger brother married a young woman while Maŋira was working on a plantation and, their father being dead, used some of Maŋira's own money to pay the betrothal and marriage payments, intending to help Maŋira secure a wife for himself after he returned. While Maŋira was still away the brother died, leaving the woman pregnant. Upon Maŋira's return he decided to marry the widow ("she was already there and had no husband"), and she agreed. To formalize the matter he gave her high-value shell money worth forty spans — her father was dead and she had no brothers, and they settled down together without further ceremony.

The leader Kapika died leaving a widow, Kurusaki, in her mid-thirties, and their two offspring, both infants, in addition to some of his adult offspring by a first marriage. Kapika's eldest son together with his uterine nephew and his sister's daughter's son decided that the widow Kurusaki would be better off remarried to a member of Kapika's matrilineage, and as she herself had no objections and no close consanguineal kin who had to be consulted, they fixed her marriage price at twenty spans — "it would have been less but for the fact that her deceased husband had been a leader." They also decided that the brideprice would be used to reimburse Kapika's oldest son for buying pork for Kapika's funeral feast. When the year of mourning had passed, it turned out that Kapika's sister's daughter's son himself married her, paying only ten spans for her and that direct to Kapika's eldest son. The nephew's decision to marry her was based on his desire to enlarge his gardens and increase his herd of pigs; he was Tomu, the Administration-appointed Paramount Chief of most of northeast Siuai, and he was anxious to start giving feasts in order to achieve high rank in the native political hierarchy as well.

In another situation, when Opisa of Turuŋum decided to acquire a second wife in order to increase his herd of pigs, he arranged with some of his father's matrilineage-mates in Imarukei to marry the aged widow of one of them who had died five or six years previously. Opisa paid the woman's son and her actual brother five spans of shell money for her — which they turned over to her — and she remained in Imarukei several miles from Opisa's residence at Turuŋum. Opisa left four new shoats with her to feed and visited her every week or so to see how they were developing, and that was the extent of their marriage. The arrangement suited the woman because her son wished it and because Opisa was a man of some influence.

Some informants claim that widow remarriage to a brother of the deceased is the only "correct" form; that such was invariably the practice in the old days and that formerly it was not even necessary to pay for her, it having been sufficient merely to give the woman a small gift for herself. Nowadays, these informants state, the fathers and brothers of widows are insisting on direct and large payments to them in return for their consent. This latter circumstance may well be so; it coincides with the increasing emphasis on the purchase aspect of the marriage payment which was noted above.[84] On the other hand, genealogies suggest that marriage to the deceased spouse's matrilineage-mate or sib-mate was not much more prevalent in the past than it is now. There is another factor of relevance here. The sentiment in favor of cross-cousin marriage, which has already been mentioned,[85] increases the likelihood of the widow's remarriage to a matrilineage-mate of the deceased; and without stopping here to speculate on cultural origins, it is conceivable that one of these practices might have developed out of or along with the other.

The sentiment favoring cross-cousin marriage and local endogamy also has the effect of promoting the sororate, which is the "rule favoring the marriage of a widower with the sister of his deceased wife,"[86] with *sister* being used here in the classificatory sense. Otherwise there is no conscious effort made on the part of the widower to marry his wife's actual sister. If a newly-wed woman should die it is more likely that her widower will attempt to recover part of the betrothal payment than to demand one of her sisters as substitute.

How do the offspring of the first marriage fare when one of their parents dies and the other remarries?

Consider first of all the case of the widow with infants or young children. When she remarries her husband addresses them as "stepson" (*nuri hamaovai*) or "stepdaughter" (*nuro hamaovai*), but they call him "father," and in those families I knew mutual adjustment appears to offer no special difficulties. Even if the husband has had offspring by another marriage, or if the marriage in question itself has produced issue, the husband does not seem to discriminate between sets of offspring insofar as everyday living is concerned. But this seemingly equitable situation does not always prevail when the step-offspring become young men and women, and especially when the young man reaches the point when he needs money for betrothal. If by then the stepfather has offspring of his own he may be reluctant to use up slender resources on a stepson. It is at this point that the young man, especially, depends heavily on matrilineage-mates, and particularly his maternal uncle, to provide the support normally expected of a father. By this time, in many cases, the young man will have left the household of his stepfather and gone to live with matrilineage-mates. Sinu's case is typical: Sinu's father died while Sinu was still a child and his mother married Kunnato. According to Sinu himself, he and his stepfather always remained on excellent terms, but when the time came for Sinu to marry he had to go to his mother's brother for money. And later on, when Sinu's infant son died, Kunnato provided some money to buy a pig for the funeral, but in due course Sinu had to repay this money. "Had Kunnato been my real father I would not have had to repay."

The remarriage of a widowed father of infants or young children creates different kinds of situations. If the offspring are still very young and dependent on a woman, their widowed father may relinquish them to their matrilineage-mates to nurse and guide through childhood. Or, the new wife may undertake to mother them, and this is usually the solution if she is a sib-mate of theirs. It was my impression that fathers of motherless children are especially solicitous of their welfare, and that very strong bonds of affection develop between them. In fact, such offspring, being somewhat pitied as "half-orphans," are doubly assured of affection and material support, from the father and his family, from the dead mother's family, and from their own matrilineage-mates.

If a Siuai widow is still youthful she may become the only wife of her second spouse, but marriages involving older widows are nearly always polygynous. At the time of my census there were in northeast Siuai 210 monogamous families, 26 families of two wives, and 8 of three or more; but there is hardly a Siuai who will not admit that polygyny is a deplorable institution. Sinu describes it as follows:

> There is never peace for long in a polygynous family. If the husband sleeps in the house of one wife the other one sulks all the next day. If the man is so stupid as to sleep two successive nights in the house of one wife, the other one will refuse to cook for him, saying: "So-and-so is your wife; go to her for food. Since I am not good enough for you to sleep with, then my food is not good enough for you to eat." Frequently the co-wives will quarrel and fight. Kaŋku (Sinu's maternal uncle) formerly had five wives at one time and the youngest one was always raging and fighting the others. Once she knocked an older wife senseless and then ran away and had to be forcibly returned. Since then all but one of those wives had died, and there is peace in Jeku — not a single polygynous family. Formerly there was no sleeping at night; the co-wives were continually shouting and throwing things at one another. Kaŋku had absolutely no control over them.

Such stories as this are commonly heard. But not all husbands are so passive; Kaopa of Noronai is also a polygynist and at one time he had four wives: "Kaopa's wives were frightened of him because he beat them when they quarreled. He beat one, his oldest and first wife, so severely that she was ill for a long time; he did so because she nagged at him for not sleeping in her house any more."

Some husbands who intervene in their wives' quarrels, or persist in showing favoritism, do so at the risk of poisoning or sorcery. Wives have ample opportunity to murder or frighten their husbands by feeding them poison or by collecting some of their exuviae for dirt sorcery. A few such women were pointed out to me as having actually killed their husbands. Nor were they censured generally for their deeds; other natives agreed that the murdered husbands bring upon themselves such trouble by having more than one wife. In another well-known case the following episode is said to have occurred:

The two wives of a resident of Mokorino quarreled continually and were dissatisfied with their life so they decided to poison their husband, even though he was a mild-mannered man and did not intervene in their fights. The women are reported to have agreed: "As long as we live together here we shall quarrel, and the only way we can become separated is through the death of our husband." So, they mixed some of their urine along with a demon-attracting poison into his food, which he ate and quickly died.

In another well-known case the husband hanged himself, so harassed he was by the jealousy and quarreling of his two wives.

Not all disputes between co-wives end so dramatically; usually they are able to patch up their quarrels with a reconciliation gift. In fact, many polygynous marriages appear superficially harmonious, and this is especially so when the co-wives are sib-mates. Nevertheless, the bases for conflict are always present, and cynical Siuai believe that conflict is inevitable. Why, then, do reasonable men acquire more than one wife at a time?

The leader Soŋi, whom I estimated to be about forty-five years old, the most renowned feast-giver in northeast Siuai and intensely ambitious to become even more eminent, gave these reasons for having more than one wife (only one of his wives now lives but he has had as many as three at a time in the past): "Having many wives does not add directly to a man's renown. A man acquires additional wives in order to produce more food and fatten more pigs for feasts. Also, each new wife adds another set of affinal kin to assist him economically and to be his friends and supporters."

Soŋi's explanation is the most current, but it is not the only one. Tomu's case comes to mind. Tomu, as already noted, is the Administration-appointed Paramount Chief for most of northeast Siuai, a handsome young man in mid-twenties and member of a wealthy matrilineage, although having little renown of his own. His first wife, the daughter of an influential leader, is a pretty but sullen and headstrong woman who is known to win her way in the frequent quarrels she and Tomu have. It was through her insistence that Tomu and she left their first residence, the center of his matrilineage territory and relatives, and moved to her family's home. Her marriage with Tomu was arranged by relatives while they were still children, and was obviously done for political reasons. During our visit Tomu caught sight of a young woman from northwest Siuai who happened to be visiting near his home. To hear him describe the occasion, it was a case of mutual love at first sight! After a few secret rendezvous with her he began to arrange their marriage. Being a Catholic convert he appealed to the Missionary Priest to relax the dictum against polygyny, stating that as Paramount Chief he needed to have more than one wife in order to increase his prestige; his corresponding numbers in central and northwest Siuai having four and eight wives respectively. Despite the missionary's opposition Tomu persisted and went through with the marriage — by this time having explained to everyone that it was his "duty" to have many wives because of his exalted Administration position. Still later, he acquired Kapika's widow, Kurusaki, as has already been reported;[87] and this marriage seems to have been a clear case of obtaining an additional woman for gardening and pig-raising.

There is much substance behind the explanation that men marry additional wives for economic reasons. The results of our property survey of 199 family households turned up the finding that polygynous families possess an average of 5 pigs each as against 3.6 for the monogamous ones.[88] And it is also a statistical fact that the higher-ranking men do tend to be polygynous.

From the woman's viewpoint a polygynous marriage is unsatisfactory, most women preferring to be the only, or at least the first, wife of a man. Traditionally, second wives are either widows or are so personally or socially undesirable that they do not obtain husbands readily. Reflecting this, the marriage payments for the latter are smaller and nuptial ceremonies are usually omitted. To the Siuai these factors bear weightily on status, and quarreling women can be expected to insult one another in these terms. Men tend to brush these factors aside as irrelevant, but I noted that prominent men would not betroth their daughters to men who already had wives. Even a first wife does not favor polygyny. Her work burden might be eased somewhat but at the same time she acquires a rival. Nor is her prestige enhanced or her authority respected — the Bantu Big Wife has no analogy in Siuai, where personality largely determines which wife will dominate.

Twenty-nine of the thirty-four polygynous families now living in northeast Siuai are *united* in the sense that co-wives of each family reside in the same hamlet and garden in the same patch-sequence. In a few such cases the wives dwell in the same house but more often they dwell in separate closely adjacent houses. Those with offspring tend to occupy separate houses and to prepare separate meals, but for all other purposes husband, co-wives, and offspring constitute single households. Five other of the thirty-four polygynous families form *split* households: that is, one wife from each of five families resides in a distant hamlet and gardens separately from her co-wives. These five are older women, remarried widows, whose marital duties seem to consist only of fattening pigs for their nonresident husbands.[89]

The membership patterns of these thirty-four polygynous families vary widely. At one extreme there is a husband with three wives, each with offspring and all his own offspring. At the other extreme is a husband with two remarried widows, both with offspring from former marriages but none by their present husband. And it is not unusual for a polygynous husband to have stepsons almost as old as himself. In keeping with these variations the internal organization of polygynous families differs a great deal.

It was noted earlier [90] how it is possible to detect the existence of a sub-unit, consisting of mother and offspring, even in the closely knit monogamous family. This sub-unit is much more distinct in a polygynous family, where, in fact, each may occupy a separate house, with the husband alternating between houses. If the co-wives happen to be matrilineage-mates, which occurs in neighborhoods favoring cross-cousin marriage, then the distinctiveness between each wife's sub-unit is not very marked. There is less likelihood of quarreling, and they may even pool their resources and cook together.

Distinctions between a man's different sets of offspring crystallize most clearly when he dies and leaves a large personal fortune (pure). In such cases it is traditionally his first wife and his eldest son, along with his eldest daughter, if she is the First-born, who decide on the distribution of the pure; but judging from the disputes which develop, tradition often competes with personal forcefulness, and the opinion of a younger and brighter son may win out. As already noted, this kind of controversy can arise only among the deceased's own offspring; any step-offspring he might have acquired have little or no say in the matter. At this point it should be pointed out that potential conflict over patrimony is mitigated by two circumstances: first, most of that inheritance usually goes towards financing the father's funeral, and secondly, most offspring can depend on another source, i.e., their matrilineage, for some forms of property.

Despite the distinctiveness of the sub-units making up a polygynous family, they all call one another by family terms, with the co-wives calling each other "older-sister" or "younger-sister," according to relative ages. And of course the brother-sister sex taboo prevails between step-siblings, the husband having conjoined them and their separate matrilineages — i.e., made them nokihoro — as a result of having wedded both their mothers.

## FAMILY STRUCTURE

I have endeavored to show that the Siuai household is none other than the nuclear family in some stage or other of development, and that each family-household is quite independent in matters of subsistence. Also, the observations recorded in this chapter indicate that the family-household is the principal social agency for the nurture of children; and it is between spouses, i.e., within the family, that most sexual intercourse takes place. The matrilineage displays some interest in what might be called its members' spiritual needs during and after life, but even in this sphere direct responsibility rests also with the family.

There is no distinctive word for "family" in Motuna and individual families are not named; however we have seen how the identity of each family is recognized and respected in connection with property ownership and household-garden privacy.

Attempts to summarize the social relations among family members inevitably run into the difficulty that these vary somewhat according to each family's stage of development and the relative ages of its members, as this chapter has shown. Nevertheless it will be useful to make certain broad generalizations about family relationships irrespective of stage and age, provided we keep in mind that our constructs are static and hence somewhat arbitrary.

Before proceeding with this summary of relationships among family members it may be useful to the reader if I list the analytical categories I make use of when describing a *relationship* of two or more persons in the social system under consideration: [91]

*Interaction*. Quantity (that is, frequency and duration of interaction events), direction (that is, which person initiates), and other purely quantitative aspects of communication events.[92]

*Transaction*. Kinds and amounts of scarce goods[93] passed to or used for or taken from one individual or social unit by another.

*Emotion*. Those sounds, gestures, and other kinds of social action associated with interpersonal behavior which are not primarily transactional and which I infer to be more or less directly expressive, or at least tacitly meant to be expressive, of internal states.[94]

In connection with all these dimensions of a relationship it is of course essential to distinguish between normative and behavioral modes; and it is important to know what sanctions help to enforce the norms. Also it is essential to record the context in which the interaction takes place, i.e., its time, location, and activity-setting (e.g., fishing, manufacturing, co-residing, etc.). And finally, certain primarily symbolic[95] aspects of the relationship (or set of relationships) should be described — such as relationship terms; myths about the relationship, including expressed awareness of "unity," "opposition," "enmity," and the like; and labels and scarce goods identified corporately with the related persons.[96]

Turning now to relationships among family members: in terms of *quantity* all of them should, and in fact do, interact together far more often and for much longer periods than do members of any other kind of group. Husbands who spend too much time away from home are subject to mild reproof from their wives and may even acquire the unenviable reputation of "gadabouts" (*avi'kura*, a swallow). Similarly, parents use all the moral suasion they can mobilize to keep their sons from leaving home to work on plantations. Even after their marriage it is expected that out-marrying sons and daughters will visit home occasionally.

In the opinion of most informants, interaction among family members ought to conform to a *direction*-pattern characterized by initiative of father over rest of family, of male over female, and of older over younger. In actual behavior, however, the pattern is not nearly so sharply delineated: the wife-mother exercises initiative in most events concerned with food, while personality often overrides sex or relative age in connection with the direction of interaction among siblings.

Before summarizing the *transactions* most characteristic among family members it will be useful to enumerate the principal kinds of transactions recognized explicitly or implicitly by the Siuai. But first, let us describe how property comes into being and how it becomes extinguished.[97]

*Creation.* Scarce goods brought into being by a social unit (person, group, or aggregate) are owned by that unit in full title,[98] provided the unit's labor is not owned by someone else. If, for example, a household gardens on territory belonging to a neighbor, that neighbor has no right to seize any of the produce from the garden; the tenants sometimes pay *rent* to the owner in the form of produce but that is a separate, though related, transaction.

Siuai beliefs and practices emphasize these full ownership rights of property creators. For example, most of the productive activity of a woman is absorbed in her regular duties as a member of a household; but if she manufactures a fine basket and sells it for money, no other person has a claim on that money — and woe to any husband who tries to assert such a claim! Again, if a household group gardens time after time on territory owned by some distant and disinterested owner, not only the produce of their gardens but full ownership of the territory itself eventually (i.e., after twenty or thirty years) becomes vested in the land-users for all practical purposes.[99]

*Extinction.* Much property becomes "extinguished" through consumption and wear; otherwise property is purposefully destroyed only on the occasion of death, when a few of the deceased's possessions may be demolished or burnt.

I have categorized Siuai transactions according to the following criteria:

1. The social units involved. (Is the transaction between members of the same social unit or between representative members of different social units?)

2. The direction of the transaction. (I.e., Who initiates it?)

3. The type of scarce goods transacted.

4. The technique of transaction. (Is it verbal? manual? etc.; and to what degree is the transaction ritualized and ceremonially embellished?)

5. The motivation for the transaction (expressed or implied). (That is, is it primarily "economic," i.e., is the desired end the scarce goods transacted? or primarily social-relational, i.e., is the desired end the establishment, maintenance, discontinuance, etc., of social relations between the principals?) Obviously, these types of motivation are not mutually exclusive.

The principal categories of Siuai transactions are as follows:

*Sharing.* Among the members of any Siuai group there is usually a well-understood division of labor which includes among other things regular contributions of goods and services from all members. It is based on a principle of equitable division of duties and rewards — "equitable" being explicitly or implicitly defined in terms of differences of age, sex, etc. When the items shared are services, we can speak of *coöperation*.[100]

*Sale* and *Barter* (*pu*). Food of all kinds and movable manufactured items are exchanged for money or for articles of equivalent value (in terms of shell money). Skilled services are also sold in this way. There may be other social implications involved in such transactions but the chief motivations of the parties are "economic" and prompt payment is usually expected.[101]

*Loan.* In loan transactions, distinctions are drawn in practice between productive and nonproductive property. Friends or relatives will lend to one another without interest such nonproductive items as hurricane lamps, cooking pots, knives or axes — with the expectation, however, of increasing one's right to borrow similar items when the need arises.

Productive property may also be lent without interest to a friend or relative, but on many occasions interest is explicitly demanded or tacitly expected. Men often lend money for interest (*totokai*) as a straight commercial transaction. They also "lend" young sows to relatives and friends with the expectation that the latter will repay with three or four shoats when the sow litters; this differs somewhat from the kind of transaction known as *aŋurara*, which contains an implication of *sharing*. (See Chapter 9.) Land, or rather soil, is also lent out for interest; the borrower pays the lender in produce (*muhni ukum*, "of the landowner"). In connection with most of these loan transactions the time of repayment is either specified or implied.

Services are also lent, and usually without implication of "interest."

*Gift.* While the same general term (*o*) is applied to all of them the Siuai distinguish in practice four kinds of "gift."

(1) Coercive: Natives give to one another purposefully and consciously to build up obligations, with tacit expectation of ultimate equivalent [102] returns. For example, an ambitious man will distribute pork among his neighbors with the hope that they will ultimately reciprocate by helping him in his enterprises. Sacrifices made to spirits come mainly under this heading, there being little or no implication of sharing, expiation, or atonement involved in such practices.

(2) Competitive: Men of high socio-political rank give presents of pigs and money to others in order to humiliate them. Such gifts are given purposefully to create unfulfillable obligations, the donor actually desiring that his gift will not be returned.[103]

(3) Betrothal "gift" (*akuno*): The high-value shell money presented to a female on behalf of her prospective husband and retained by her seemingly as partial compensation for her services — sexual and domestic — to him.

(4) *Nonreciprocable:* Gift-giving among close relatives over and beyond the normal expectations of sharing cannot entirely be reduced to conscious expectation of reciprocity. A father might rationalize the giving of tidbits to his son by explaining that he expected to be cared for by the latter in his old age, but I am convinced that some giving between, say, father and son does not involve any desire or expectation for reciprocation.[104]

*Exchange (ootu).* Male friends and distant relatives sometimes engage in a kind of reciprocal exchange transaction which is a combination of sale or barter and coercive gift-giving. The time for repayment is not specified but it should not be delayed more than a year or two. Also, each repayment is expected to equal or to exceed only slightly the value of the original item; it is felt that each partner's give and take should balance over a period of time. This kind of transaction takes place between trade-partners (*taovu*), including those who are political allies rather than rivals.

*Ceremonial Exchange.* Many kinds of property transactions are ceremonialized to some extent, but there are some exchanges which are primarily ritual in function.

*Inheritance.*[105] The general rule in Siuai is that title to property is inherited by the owner's own offspring. A foster parent may bestow gifts of property to adopted or stepchildren; otherwise own offspring inherit everything. This general rule of inheritance applies to owners whether they be single persons or larger property-owning social units. For example, if a matrilineage dies out, its property in land and other economically valuable resources [106] is inherited by its male members' offspring.[107] It is customary for the heirs to contribute death dues (nori) to the funeral feasts of their "parents" in order to validate the transaction,[108] but if none of these "parents" survive there are no social mechanisms for withholding this inheritance.

If a person dies leaving no offspring, his (or her) spouse or siblings will inherit the property, depending upon circumstances. In case of the death of a young person, what little property he or she may have acquired individual title to passes either to siblings or parents.

*Indemnity (rakai).* As described above, an aggrieved spouse is expected to be indemnified by his (or her) guilty mate before the marriage can return to normal. In other contexts, a leader assesses a fine (rakai) against fractious subjects, and native courts award damages (rakai) to aggrieved persons. *Numehu* is also probably to be understood as an indemnity with ritual overtones; it is the shame-alleviating money which a man has to pay his wife's brother when he announces his own wife's pregnancy.

*Nori.* The shell-money paid by a deceased male's family survivors to his matrilineage mates for the purpose of furnishing pigs for the funeral feast. Formerly the term was also applied to the indemnity paid by a war leader to the relatives of a warrior slain while fighting on behalf of the leader.

*Detraction.* Stealing or impairing goods, including effective assailing of established highly valued reputations.

*Forceful Seizure.* This no longer takes place in Siuai, and I found no evidence that it was extensively practiced even in the days of warfare. Enemies used to lay waste one another's houses and gardens and groves but large-scale looting and capture of territory and persons seems to have occurred only infrequently.[109]

Numerous measures exist to safeguard material property rights and punish infringements of them. The person who damages or destroys another's material goods, willfully or non-willfully, is subject to severe fines or deadly magic. Trespass may also be punished by fines and magic, including many publicly approved devices involving death-dealing ghosts and demons. Here in Siuai, where people's material goods are usually well known to all their neighbors, theft is not very prevalent. Nevertheless there exists a number of magical devices for guarding against theft and for detecting and killing an unknown thief. And, in addition, heavy fines are levied against known thieves.

Fines are also levied against provisional title-holders who do not carry out their obligations, and these include borrowers who do not return on time loans of material property. Against the man who infringes property rights by nonfulfillment of his obligations to repay an exchange (ootu) or a competitive gift, the sanctions are less concrete but just as effective.

Details of these and other sanctions which serve explicitly to enforce proper performance of transactions, including those respecting services and other secure goods, are given elsewhere throughout the text.

Returning now to transactions among family members as a whole, many kinds of data indicate that natives believe such relationships should be characterized by *sharing*, by nonreciprocable *giving*, and by *inheritance*, and it was my observation that actual behavior does conform fairly closely to these norms in most families. In most instances all family members share material resources according to a fairly explicit set of expectations. Moreover, there is little accounting kept between parents and young children or between young siblings, but this tends to change as children grow older. Between husband and wife the accounting is more strict, and serious defaults may lead to divorce. On the other hand, even the most cynical scrutiny will not permit us to reduce all transactions between older family members to conscious bookkeeping; the element of nonreciprocable giving which characterizes many of the interchanges between parents and children is also present in some of the interchanges between older siblings and between husband and wife.

What can be said in summary about the "emotional" dimension of relationships among family members? The Motuna language contains few words concerning internal states; for example, as far as I could discover, only one verb, *haru-*, signifies the emotions presumably felt between fond parent and child, devoted spouses, lovers, and friends, thus permitting little possibility for verbal expression of differences in kind or intensity of feeling. The word "iro" covers actions ranging from mild annoyance to violent anger and hatred, and also refers to heat and to the state of magical dangerousness. A few metaphors and similes are somewhat more specific in this respect, for example, "to cause someone to climb the *ru* tree" means "to embarrass," and "to treat someone like one's lackey (*hunu*)" carries an obvious meaning. Significantly, the words "pavaru" (praise, admiration) and "maio" (shame, embarrassment) enter everyday speech more prominently than any other words of this class — or so it seemed to me. The paucity of terms expressing "emotion" appears even more striking when this circumstance is compared with Motuna's rich and highly explicit vocabularies for objects and technical processes. Of course, this paucity of "affect" words is only suggestive; it does not mean that the Siuai do not distinguish among various kinds and degrees of, say, "affection" in their actual behavior.

In this connection, most Siuai adult males are not given to effusive display of "emotion" in their interaction with other adults. When men working together carry off some difficult task to their satisfaction they often shout and hop about, but in most other everyday situations they look askance at the person who expresses "emotion" exuberantly and excitedly. Most kinds of interpersonal behavior among men presumably expressive of "emotion"[110] are highly formalized, some to the point of ceremony. When relatives and friends meet after long absences there are no embraces or loud shouts of greeting; instead there is usually a limp and perfunctory hand-shake — a recent acquisition from the whites — followed by common betel-chewing and a few muted phrases of conversation. Youthful companions are occasionally seen strolling together holding hands, but older men seldom display so openly those feelings which presumably they have now and then. Among males, de-lousing expresses perhaps the most intimate and affectionate relations, and it is common to see adult brothers and matrilineage-mates thus engaged. Other than such patterned manifestations as these among close relatives and friends, most adult males eschew loud talk and physical contact. It used to be a constant source of entertainment to me to observe men as they met and then parted. For example, the club-house of the leader Soŋi was a popular destination when men had nothing more pressing to do than saunter about the countryside visiting and picking up gossip. There was nearly always some native at this club-house, stretched out on top of a slit gong, dozing, or repairing a tool or net bag. One after another, other natives would slip quietly into the club-house and squat on benches or gongs without saying a word. To me it always seemed that no notice whatsoever was taken of their presence for twenty or thirty minutes; then a little desultory conversation would start up, interrupted by long silences which were punctuated by occasional belches and snores. As many as ten or twenty men might "visit" together in this fashion for an hour or more, and then they would slip off one by one as quietly and unceremoniously as they had come. If an officious and unpopular Hat-man or catechist were among the visitors his departure would be followed by a general murmur of disapproval and a few mocking imitations of his manner of speaking. On ordinary occasions like these about the only event that could break the conventional calm was the arrival of the area's demented buffoon, Kea. Kea heralded his approach from afar by letting forth war whoops, and he usually entered the club-house shaking his spear and talking excitedly about his latest persecution and his plans for revenge. He was usually greeted with a chorus of half-amused, half-annoyed commands to shut up and go away; so that finally even Kea reduced his babble to mutters or left to find some more sympathetic audience.

Among themselves women also engage in formalized expressive behavior, including de-lousing and betel-exchange, but in addition they tend to be more informal and direct in their speech. Interaction among them is usually accompanied by much shrill and lively talk, and they are not timid about demonstrating approval or disapproval for one another's actions. Nor are older women timid about expressing what is presumed to be their affection for some of their younger male kinsmen, usually through pats on the arm and offerings of food or tobacco — all of which tend to cause the male visible embarrassment. Women are also much freer in displaying annoyance at males; it is really a lesson in eloquent obscenity to hear a Siuai woman berating some man she thinks is spying on her.

Although much of their emotion-expressing behavior has become formalized to the point of ceremony, the Siuai have elaborated few of these patterns in such a way that fine distinctions in kind or in intensity of feeling, etc., can be unmistakably expressed; for example, the etiquette of chewing betel together differs in no technical detail whether it takes place between uterine siblings or between political rivals.[111] Hence the observer cannot always infer the relations of persons by merely watching them interact. Even in connection with formal expressions of sex avoidance between, say, *brother* and *sister*, wherein native moralists, if hard pressed, will admit that the genealogical distance of the tie has a bearing on how rigidly the rules of conduct should be observed, gradations in behavior are not defined sharply enough, either in prescript or in practice, to indicate the exact genealogical nature of the tie. To describe adequately [112] any particular kind of institutionalized relationship it is necessary to do so in terms of emotion-expressing behavior patterns *and* interaction *and* transactions.

In view of all these complications it seems somewhat factitious to characterize the emotional dimension of relationships in terms of neat formulae; nevertheless, we can try, in an effort to generalize about Siuai culture and society. At least, the reader will have been warned about the limitations of such analysis. Here, then, is the way I group the more formalized and readily identifiable patterns of Siuai emotional behavior; the labels which I have given to the assemblages made of these patterns are italicized.[113]

*Affection*:[114] hand-holding; de-lousing; chewing betel together; vigorous mourning for each other's death; vocal support for each other at crises; embraces, etc.

*Repudiation*: purposeful and pointed break-off of interaction and renunciation of obligations, either one-sided or mutual; avoidance of interaction but usually no evidence of mutual fear.

*Amity*:[115] chewing betel together; eating together; mutual formal expressions of esteem; at least token mourning for each other's death.

*Enmity*: mutual disparagement; (by women) verbal abuse; litigation; sorcery (hence avoidance of contact, and caution with regard to eating in each other's presence); anger-signal beaten on a slit gong; mock spear-throwing; performance of anger-ritual (mih).[116] Formerly enmity was expressed also by fighting and murder.

*Constraint*: mutual abstention from discussion of sexual topics and from joking at each other's expense; some formality of address.

*Unconstraint*: free discussion of any topic; mutually permissive joking at each other's expense; absence of formality of address.

*Deference*: one-sided yielding of opinion, preference, and precedence.[117]

*Equality*: expressive behavior presumably indicative of lack of deference.

*Sexuality*: expressive behavior based on active or potentially active sexual relations.[118]

*Avoidance*: various degrees of incest- or adultery-avoidance, from patterns expressive of taboo on sexual intercourse to total absention from physical contact and mutual name-calling. (*Avoidance* and *affection* are not mutually exclusive; i.e., while it is true that a youth and his sister will usually avoid physical contact with each other, they will also display many signs of affection.)

To this list should be added the qualification that manifestations of "affection" between adults and infants or children are much more easily recognizable. In fact, there are few men, and certainly no women, who will not display protective and affectionate care for their little relatives.

We are now in a position to list the assemblages of emotional behavior patterns which characterize relationships among family members.

To begin with, relationships among all family members should — according to standards of Siuai morality — be characterized by *affection*, and they usually turn out to be so. Conflict among family members is by no means rare, and quarrels occasionally descend to physical fighting, but it is significant that intra-family conflicts are usually short-lived or, if they go too far they usually result in *repudiation* rather than active *enmity* between the principals.[119] (But see the cases of intra-family hostility described in the Creation myths.[120]) *Affection* among family members shows up most dramatically at times of sickness and death; it is usually not difficult to pick out family survivors of the deceased among the mourners because of the violence and what seems to be the authenticity of their weeping.

In addition to *affection* there are some other ways of describing the relations of specific pairs of family members. Between spouses there is of course the additional complex of emotion-expressing behavior patterns built up around legitimate and fairly frequent sexual intercourse (i.e., "sexuality"). Moralists also assert that a wife should show *deference* to her husband and some occasionally do, although most couples I knew behaved towards each other with *equality* and *unconstraint*.

Most natives assert that a son should show *deference* towards his father — although it is clear from observation that this rule is frequently violated by sons past youth.

A daughter ought to be and usually is *deferential* towards her father; in addition the relationship between father and daughter is slightly colored by the taboo on *sexuality*.

The relationship between mother and son is also colored by the taboo on *sexuality*, but *deference* is less in evidence. On the other hand, all daughters should and younger daughters usually do show *deference* to their mothers.

The basic complex of *affection* between brothers is complicated only by the rule that the younger brother show some degree of *deference* towards the older. This rule is occasionally honored in practice, but in the case of many brother pairs, deference is replaced by *equality* and *unconstraint*. These generalizations also apply to the relations of sisters.

The relations between brother and sister are highly colored by elaboration of the complex of *avoidance*.

Most of the sanctions explicitly supporting all these expressive behavior patterns have already been described and need not be reviewed here.[121]

At the beginning of this summary, mention was made of the *symbolic* aspect of the family as a whole. In this connection it will be interesting to review certain features of religious belief and practice which have a bearing on the place of the family in the wider social and cultural setting. Sib myths and rituals indicate some dependence upon and perhaps deference for remote matrilineal ancestresses, but ghosts of specific mothers rarely play supernatural roles in the lives of their family survivors. And while it is believed that a male ghost may occasionally become the familiar of his son, an institutionalized paternal ancestor-cult does not exist. However, in another symbolic respect the family does constitute an important unit: myths which refer to the very beginnings of humanity conceive of people as living in families practically identical with those of today — except insofar as hostility between fathers and sons and between siblings appears more marked in the archetypical family than in the families of today.[122]

CHAPTER 6

# *Hamlets*

Nearly every household in northeast Siuai is a separate social group in terms of interaction: its members sleep in a separate house, work in a separate garden patch, and partake of a separate common meal. In addition, the members of a household own certain kinds of property in common and share nuclear family kinship ties — actual or simulated. Some polygynous households may be divided into sub-units for purposes of sleeping and eating, but are otherwise interlinked. Now, a few of these households are not only "separate" in the meaning described above but are isolated from other households in other respects, including actual spatial distance, difficulty of communication and social interaction; but most households are clustered into *hamlets*.

As already noted, the Siuai hamlet is a residence community of two or more households located within a quarter mile of each other and easily accessible by path — that is to say, they are not separated by difficult physical barriers such as large creeks, cliffs, or swamps. This is not an arbitrary definition: the Siuai recognize the identity of hamlets and give all of them names or refer to them as "the houses on such-and-such a tract of land."

There is no fixed arrangement of houses within a hamlet. Location factors are, of course, the same as those previously mentioned for individual households, including proximity to drinking water and a bathing creek, insulation from main trails and club-houses, etc.

## COMPOSITION

Of the 273 households surveyed in northeast Siuai (comprising about 90 per cent of the total population of this area) thirty-seven reside all the time in line villages and do not possess hamlet-houses. Those possessing hamlet houses are distributed as follows: 30 isolated households; 24 two-household hamlets; 16 three-household hamlets; 9 four-household hamlets; 4 five-household hamlets; 5 six-household hamlets; and one each of a seven-, an eight-, and a nine-household hamlet.

In other words, members of over five-sixths of the northeast Siuai households reside at least part of the time in hamlets. Now, as urban apartment-dwellers know, co-residence may mean little in terms of interaction, shared symbols, etc., but that is not the case in Siuai, where co-residence in a hamlet betokens all these things and many more besides.

All persons residing in any one hamlet are usually interrelated by kinship ties, but the nature of these ties is extremely variable. The 24 two-household hamlets contain these combinations of heads of household (listed in order of numerical importance): father and son; brothers (uterine and half); *brothers-in-law* (actual and classificatory); paternal uncle and nephew; maternal uncle and nephew; male cross-cousins; widowed mother and son.

Siuai kinship norms and principles of land tenure are flexible enough to permit almost any residential combination. For example, in one of the cases of *brother-in-law* co-residence, the two-household heads could best be described as mere friends, living on land one of them had inherited from his father (better, land allotted to him by his father's matrilineage mates in return for the pigs he had contributed to reward his father's mourners). These two friends had met for the first time while working on the same coastal plantation, and one of them asked the other to live on his patrimonial estate. The only apparent kinship tie between them was this: a distant sib *sister* of one of them was married to a distant sib *brother* of the other, hence they were classificatory *brothers-in-law*. This is a standard device Siuai natives use for rationalizing and regularizing relationships which, like co-residence, conventionally fit into the category of kinship behavior.

The membership combinations of the 37 multi-household hamlets surveyed are even more variable; in terms of residence pattern, their order of numerical importance is: predominantly patrilocal; evenly mixed patrilocal and matrilocal; predominantly matrilocal; predominantly avunco-virilocal.[1]

It is obvious from these statistics that several factors enter into choice of residence. Here are the more important ones:

1. While a father is alive, his sons tend to set up their households in his hamlet.

2. If a man is wealthy and influential, both his sons and sons-in-law are likely to establish their households in his hamlet. In fact, the influential man exercises a strong pull on other relatives as well.

3. Upon a man's death, his co-resident sons and sons-in-law tend to move to their matrilineage centers, where their own maternal uncles may be residing, unless they acquire important rights in the deceased's landholdings.

4. A wealthy matrilineage or sub-matrilineage is also a magnet, resulting, in many instances, in matrilocal and avunco-virilocal residence.

5. Close friendship between kinsmen, especially between brothers and between classificatory *brothers-in-law*, frequently induces them to reside in the same hamlet.

## ACTIVITIES

In many cases all the households of a hamlet garden together to the extent that they coöperate in clearing and fencing adjoining patches; later on the women may assist one another in weeding their separate household patches. Some households even pool their food resources and cook around a common hearth, but even in such cases the households usually eat separately. The adjoining households also coöperate in building houses, in hulling almonds, in hunting, and in fishing. Many hamlets contain a work-shed which serves as a common center for making pottery, smoking almonds, weaving baskets, or for gossiping and playing; but even in those hamlets without a common work-shed, residents tend to congregate around one house for work or talk or tending children. Hamlet mates invariably attend one another's rituals and frequently are the only ones who do. For women the hamlet is even more important than for men; the latter range far and wide visiting distant club-houses, but women seldom travel beyond their own and their parents' hamlets except to go to the garden or the stream.

The residents of two-household hamlets are usually closely interrelated by family-like emotions, transactions, and interaction. The women and children of such households appear to spend nearly all their waking hours together, and an outside observer would find it difficult to distinguish between members of the separate households.

Even relationships as intimate as these, however, may suffer abrupt changes. Men claim that quarreling frequently breaks out between women, and that men have to move apart in order to keep the women from fighting. But these male paragons are also given to quarreling, generally over pigs or woman-seduction, and such quarrels may also lead to separation.

Multi-household hamlets are more numerous than two-household ones, and in general they are not quite so closely knit. Although residing together, the households may garden separately. Back at the hamlet, however, the women and children of these larger units spend much of their waking time together, gossiping, making baskets, and tending one another's offspring.

## AUTHORITY

In some hamlets it is not difficult to discern who exercises authority in common enterprises; some woman and man usually signal when common activities are to begin, or give directions about how things should be done. They are spoken of as "the Old-ones of such-and-such a place." As one native explained, "They remember all the customs of former days, and we *children* (kitoria) do as they say." While age is a factor in determining who these hamlet leaders will be, personality is just as important. Here are some of the ways the Old-ones assert leadership:

When residents of a hamlet attend a cremation it is customary for all the women and children to attend in a body, and on such occasions they remain close together under the watchful eye of their female Old-one, who sees to it that the younger women do not wander away from the others. Similarly, it is this Old-one who decides when they should return home. This same Old-one supervises other common activities among females and children of the hamlet, such as almond-hulling, thatch-sheet-making, and prawn-fishing.

The youths and men of a hamlet act more independently than do the females, but even they single out one elder as their Old-one, and defer to him in many matters affecting the whole hamlet. For example, it is this Old-one who usually settles minor disputes among hamlet residents, and it is he who decides to move the settlement in case of an epidemic. Also, it is usually this Old-one who acts to oust any *Attacher* who causes trouble in the hamlet.

## "TRUE-OWNERS" AND "ATTACHERS"

In every hamlet a distinction is made between *True-owners* (*ukunopo meŋ*; from *ukarei*, "to own"; *-nopo*, suffix of person, plural; *meŋ*, "true," "real," or *owners-true*) and *Attachers* (from, *hotu'urei*, "to-adhere-to-something," i.e., lichen *adheres* to rocks). True-owners are those residents of the hamlet who own, or whose parent or parents own, full or residual title to the land on which hamlet members reside and garden; Attachers own only unsubstantial *provisional* title to such lands, and their presence in the hamlet is usually to be accounted for by their marital ties with True-owners. In many instances the True-owners of a hamlet consist of all or part of a matrilineage or sub-matrilineage which has full or residual title to the hamlet's lands. These include hamlets made up of the following combinations: brothers, maternal uncle and nephew, widowed mother and son, and those multi-household hamlets that are predominantly matrilocal and avunco-virilocal in residence pattern. Those hamlets that are characterized by an evenly mixed patri- and matrilocal residence pattern are to be found in places dominated by two (cross-cousin) intermarrying matrilineages or sub-matrilineages. Since we have already described matrilineally aligned groups in some detail, including the nature of their ties with tracts of economically valuable land, we can pass on to consider those hamlets whose True-owners are related primarily by patrilateral ties, i.e., those whose heads of household are either father and son or paternal uncle and nephew, and those multi-household hamlets whose residence patterns are predominantly patrilocal.

Father-and-son hamlets are the most numerous of all two-household hamlets in northeast Siuai, and it is a living arrangement which most male Siuai prefer if they are on good terms with their fathers. In addition to the tie of sentiment between the two, many men feel some moral obligation to remain nearby and be of assistance to an aging father. In addition, the son realizes that he stands to inherit property from his father, either directly or after the payment of death dues (nori).

Hamlets made up of a man and his father's brother are also numerous, even more so than those consisting of a man and his mother's brother, which may appear surprising in this matrilineally biased society. However, in terms of the Siuai kinship system the father's brother is also called "father," and if the real father is dead his brother may assume some of the obligations of parenthood. Moreover, since many hamlets are made up of pairs of brothers there is ample opportunity for the development of intimate ties of affection between a youth and his paternal uncle. Also, since the custom of paying death-dues on behalf of a deceased father may be extended to classificatory *fathers* as well, it frequently happens that nephews "inherit" land from their paternal uncles.

Turning now to multi-household hamlets: those having a predominantly patrilocal residence pattern outnumber all other types in northeast Siuai. Typical of these patrilocally based hamlets is True-Moronei, one of several hamlet settlements which are associated in the line village also called Moronei. Manrai, the Old-one of this hamlet, was born there — as was his father before him — and has lived there all his life with his half-brother, Kapumansa. Their wives went there from other places; their offspring have all remained there even after marriage. In other words, for two generations offspring have remained at their fathers' residence, and have been thrown into closer contact with fathers' than with mothers' kin. Before them, the land around Moronei belonged to the matrilineage of the paternal grandfather of Manrai and Kapumansa, and their own father acquired full title to it by paying death dues when *his* father died. Consequently, Manrai and Kapumansa inherited it direct from their father, without payment of death-dues, and they will pass it on to their sons and daughters in like manner. This social unit made up of Manrai, Kapumansa, and their living descendants constitutes a corporate unit in view of the nature of the members' common ownership of land. They are the True-owners of True-Moronei hamlet land and all their spouses are Attachers.

There are several of these patrilineally structured landowning corporate units in northeast Siuai. In some cases the members all reside together and constitute the True-owners of a hamlet. In other cases the members may be somewhat dispersed, due usually to the marriage and change in residence of one or two daughters — male members of such corporate units do not as a rule change residence. It is possible that in some of these corporate units the entire membership occasionally interacts as a separate group, particularly in connection with matters relating to their landholdings; however, I did not witness any such group interaction, and informants were not very clear on this point. In any event, in none of these patrilineally aligned corporate units that I knew about have the ties among members become hypostasized to any significant degree. They are not named and have not yet acquired mythical or religious aspects worthy of note.[2]

In regard to Attachers, in a few cases the presence of a male Attacher in a settlement may be based primarily on his friendship with one of the True-owners; however, most adult [3] Attachers, male and female, base their residence rights on marital ties, and even the Attacher who is primarily a friend legitimatizes his position by means of a simulated *brother-in-law* relationship.[4]

When residence is uxorilocal, it brings about a profound change in social relations for the husband. He interacts with new people, becomes a member in a different hamlet group. He does not necessarily cease interacting altogether with members of his family of orientation or of his original hamlet group, and his own or his father's matrilineage. Indeed, he might visit his old home quite frequently and partly preserve his old relations, but it would be unrealistic to suppose that those old relations remain entirely unchanged. And it would be just as unrealistic to assume that the husband fits easily, without a hitch, into the new hamlet group. I encountered little of the open hostility toward a "stranger" husband which Fortune so vividly reported from Dobu, but the Siuai nevertheless call him an *Attacher* and, in theory at least, regard him as an outsider. This attitude is reflected in a quarrel which took place at Moronei village. One youth whose two parents had been born at Moronei, warned another youth, whose mother was a Moronei woman, but whose father had been an Attacher, saying:

"Son of a snake father, why don't you crawl back into the (distant) hole that he crawled out of."

There is little evidence of universal, pathological fear of sorcery among the Siuai, but the natives frequently account for misadventures by referring them to sorcerers. And suspicion is not limited to persons living *outside* the village. The unsociable man, the individual who prefers to build his hamlet house and tend his garden far away from those of his fellows, the suspicious husband who jealously watches over his wife and hides her from the eyes of other men — these are the potential sorcerers. And the same is true of an Attacher, at least until he demonstrates his ability to coöperate congenially. The case of Upasi illustrates the kinds of troubles that beset an unsociable Attacher. Upasi's birthplace and matrilineage territory is at Morokaimoro but when he married he moved to his wife's place near Mokorino. Upasi is about forty and his wife some fifteen years younger; the delay in his marrying came about through his having worked for a number of years on plantations. Upasi is now thin and tired and morose while his wife is still young-looking and apparently greatly desired by some of their neighbors, including Aisa, who first told me of Upasi's wicked ways. Here is Aisa's account:

> Upasi is a real sorcerer. He denies it, but we know he is one. A few days ago a neighbor of ours died, and as he was dying he was heard to murmur: "Upasi, what did you do to that banana we were eating a few days ago?" And this of course meant that Upasi had placed poison in the banana: a dying man doesn't lie. Upasi has actually killed many people by sorcery; in fact nearly everyone who dies around here now is probably killed by Upasi.

Once, two brothers went to Upasi's garden and were engaged in conversation with Upasi's wife when Upasi came up and warned them to stay away from her. They were both frightened and ran away to work on a plantation, and soon they both died — killed by Upasi's sorcery.

Once even I was threatened by him. I gave Upasi's wife some taro for her pigs and Upasi accused me of trying to seduce her. That was not my intention at all; everyone knows that the Patrol Officer says that men shouldn't steal other men's wives. (!)

So now, everything that goes wrong around here is probably due to Upasi; even his wife accuses him of sorcery, saying that he recently brought about the death of her mother.

When I asked Upasi about all these reports he agreed, with mountainous understatement, that "People appear not to like me here." Then he explained:

"When I was first married, my wife's brothers pleaded with me to live near them; but no sooner had I moved here but they began to slander me as an Attacher."

When residence is virilocal, the changes are not so violent. In many cases the bride has already had time to adjust to her husband's relatives during the period of betrothal. She is not ordinarily suspected of being a sorceress, for, as one informant pointed out, "Women are always talking; they aren't capable of keeping secrets. If one woman is a sorceress, all other women know it!"

Women belong to fewer groups than men; they interact with fewer people. On the other hand, by frequent visiting they preserve their old relationships long after changing residence at marriage. And woe to the husband who balks at such visiting.[5]

There are few cases of *strict* virilocality. Homma, married to Soŋi of Turuŋom, did not once visit her relatives in nearby Rennu village during our entire stay in Turuŋom. Instead, her father and mother used to visit her at her husband's home. This situation can be partly accounted for by explaining that Soŋi is a very important leader, and travels only when it is politically expedient.

Strict uxorilocality is likewise encountered in only a few exceptional cases. When To'osi married Nirai he moved to her hamlet at Turuŋom, built a house there, and entered immediately and effectively into the activities of Nirai's relatives. Now, he seldom visits his old village of Jeku — has even identified himself with Turuŋom villagers in quarrels with Jeku villagers.

Between those two extremes there are all degrees. After Maŋira of Ku'hinna had divorced his first wife he married a woman from Jeku. Now, he and his wife and children live part of the time in Ku'hinna and part in Jeku. Tomo formerly lived in Mataras village. He was wedded to a girl from Hinna village and took her to Mataras to live for a few years. Later she prevailed upon him to return to Hinna, where they are now living.

Polygyny introduces a complicating factor. The eight wives of Moŋko,

Paramount Chief of northwest Siuai, live with their wealthy and powerful husband at his settlement all the time. Opisa, on the other hand, with one wife in Turuŋom and another at Imarukei, resides most of the time at Turuŋom, but makes occasional visits to Imarukei. His Imarukei wife never visits Turuŋom.

What effect does the type of residence which characterizes a marriage have upon land tenure?

In the strictly virilocal case of Soŋi and Homma, Soŋi claims no part of Homma's matrilineage land at Rennu; he rarely interacts with Homma's kin and he does not garden on their soil. But Homma has become completely identified with her husband's land; she gardens it coöperatively with her affinal kin and alludes to it as "our land."

Most men insist upon usufruct rights in their wives' land. "When we buy the women, we buy her land." Of course, they do not "buy" the women; as already noted, the "brideprice" is usually reciprocated by the bride's father in the form of pork. Hence, the man does not *purchase* his wife's land, but — by implication — he does acquire the right to *use* that land as long as the marriage lasts. Soŋi with his extensive landholdings can afford to be casual about usufruct rights in his wife's land. Opisa, on the other hand, insists that both wives' territorial properties are partly his, but admits that he would not attempt to force the issue with the relatives of his Imarukei wife — the one whom he visits so rarely.

Maɲira, who resides part of the time in his Ku'hinna home and part in his wife's Jeku home, was uncertain of his status as a landowner in Jeku, but supposes that he could claim land there if he wanted it. An even more modest opinion was expressed by Puipui, who resides with one wife at his home in Jeku and merely visits a second wife living at Imarukei. He vigorously disclaimed all *ownership* of the latter's Imarukei land. "She gardens and uses the taro to feed my pigs, but her land is not mine."

Then, there is the case of Tahiŋ, a quiet, unassertive little man, married to a Turuŋom woman and residing on her matrilineage land. His own home is several miles away, and he is the only local representative of the *Kaia* sub-clan; he has neither wealth nor influence and is merely tolerated by Turuŋom villagers. He is not even treated with the fearful respect sometimes accorded a suspected sorcerer. And even though he does not claim ownership, he gardens on his wife's soil, and no one questions that right.

To'osi, from Jeku, is also married to a Turuŋom woman and lives on her land, but what a different story! It was noted above how closely he coöperates with his wife's kin. This situation is reflected in the land tenure: To'osi claims provisional ownership in his wife's matrilineage property and the original owners confirm his claim. So *persona grata* is he among his affinal kin that they raised no objections when he announced his intention of obtaining a second wife and bringing her to Turuŋom to share his first wife's land.

We can generalize from these cases and estimate the effect upon land tenure of the type of residence which characterizes a marriage: change of residence at marriage brings about changes in land tenure to the extent to which interaction changes. A spouse dwelling on land belonging to his or her affinal relatives, and engaging in correct social relations with them, comes in time to be associated with their land. That Attacher spouse *utilizes* it and might even claim provisional title to land identified with the spouse, and not only to the house and garden sites.[6] But, if a change of residence is *not* accompanied by far-reaching changes in social relations there is no effective transfer of land title. Opisa occasionally utilizes his Imarukei wife's land and in his more expansive moments claims ownership of it; that is his manner of speaking. His affinal relatives at Imarukei, with whom he rarely visits and never coöperates, laugh to scorn his unjustified claim.

Actually the marriage contract alone does not involve important change in land ownership. It merely bestows a right to utilize one another's land; but if that right is utilized, and if it is utilized in close coöperation and constant interaction with affinal relatives, then the Attacher spouse may claim more substantial provisional title to the spouse's land. The extent to which that claim is honored depends upon the kinds of relations that have been built up between the Attacher spouse and his or her affinal relatives.

A marriage followed by change of residence of one spouse produces really long term changes in land tenure only after children are born. On four separate occasions during our stay, virilocal marriages *without* issue were dissolved by death of the husbands. In three cases the widows returned to their own homes. The fourth widow was elderly, and had lived so long with her husband's kin that she did not even consider returning home.

A virilocal marriage *with* issue is quite a different matter. When the husband dies, his widow and offspring usually distribute nori to the deceased's matrilineage mates, remain in the deceased's hamlet, and assume full title to part of the deceased's matrilineage land. Many cases like this occurred during our stay in Siuai, and to them we were able to add the corroborative evidence derived from studying genealogies.

An uxorilocal marriage *without* issue would — I was informed — end in the widower's returning to his home in the event of the wife's death. I recorded two instances wherein this actually occurred, but I suspect that a man like To'osi, who, incidentally, is childless, would continue living in Turuŋom.

Finally, if the wife in an uxorilocal family *with* issue dies, her husband generally remains in her settlement and continues to utilize her matrilineage land. Rommai, living in Mataras on his wife's land, made no move to return to his own home at Ku'hinna after his wife's death. "Mataras is my children's land," he explained, "They sympathize with me, so it is also my land."

Let us consider the relationships brought about through cross-cousin marriage.

Assume, for example, that there is a tract of land owned by a Hornbill matrilineage to which A and B belong. There is a neighboring tract of land owned by members of an Eagle matrilineage to which C and D belong. A marries D; Eagle land passes automatically into the hands of their children G and H, who are Eagle members. C marries B, and Hornbill land passes automatically into the hands of their children E and F. Later on, the cross-cousins G and F, E and H intermarry, as indicated below. When A dies, his son G need not distribute all his money inheritance in the form of death-dues in order to secure possession of his father's Eagle matrilineage land,[7] because eventually that land will pass automatically into the hands of G's children, I and J. (See Figure 21.)

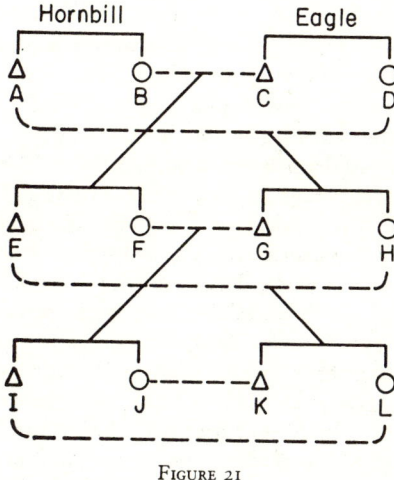

FIGURE 21

At any period the Eagle land is owned by members of the Eagle matrilineage, who share it with their Hornbill matrilineage spouses. By preserving the symmetry of this arrangement the land need never pass out of the hands of Eagle matrilineage mates so long as there are female members left to produce offspring.

Actually, after members of two matrilineages have continued to intermarry over a period of several generations, the tracts of land associated with them tend to become merged into one common property. This is then referred to as, say, "the land belonging to Eagles and Hornbills." By bringing about this kind of situation, cross-cousin marriage is an important factor for stabilization of the interrelationship of individuals, and of the relationship between people and land.

The process may even become reflected in myth. At Siuno, for example, title to the merged lands of two intermarrying matrilineages is explained in a myth wherein the kupunas of both matrilineages are described as having taken possession of the land at the same time and as having coöperated in the primeval tasks of cutting out river beds and building mountains.

Exogamy has the obvious advantage of fostering closer relationships among individuals of many different groups. But the wide ramifications in kinship groups brought about by wide choice of mates leads to frequent changes in land tenure. Cross-cousin marriage, on the other hand, keeps property intact and continuously associated with one or two groups, and litigation does not often arise in connection with land occupied in this manner for several generations. And, generally speaking, the people who own and occupy such land are wealthier than their neighbors, because of more stable relations.

As previously noted [8] there is a preference for local endogamy, quite apart from cross-cousin marriage; and this process is also a factor of conservatism because it necessitates less readjustment in personal relationships and fewer changes in land tenure. Old people shake their heads in disapproval when a youth marries a girl from another village.

Murukupe, for example, married a woman from Noronai village even though there were several eligible girls in his own villege of Moronei. His wife moved to Moronei but was never content to remain there for any length of time. Very frequently she returned to her relatives at Noronai; and there was talk of a divorce. Then she bore a child, and settled down for a while in her husband's place, and even began to assist her husband's relatives with their garden work. Then, as soon as her child was weaned, she renewed her frequent visits to Noronai — sometimes neglecting her child and remaining away for a day or two at a time. Finally the long-suffering Murukupe exploded and beat her, after which she made a vain attempt to hang herself, was beaten for a second time, and escaped to Noronai. Murukupe followed a day later and confronted her in her father's house. "You are wicked," he told her, "you do not serve my child nor till my soil. Consider my land to be like your mother's womb — do not return there!"

Having noted the roles of the Old-ones in hamlet social organization, and having described in general terms the basis of differentiation between True-owners and Attachers, we should now consider the relations among the individual residents in order to provide a full picture of hamlet social organization. However, since hamlets vary so much in membership pattern the reader will have to infer this picture from a survey of the entire kinship system.

CHAPTER 7

# *Outline of Kin Relations*

If we constructed a map showing the location of any Siuai person's primary and secondary relatives it would reveal clusters usually concentrated within an area about two miles in diameter; attitudes about cross-cousin marriage, local endogamy, strangers, etc., help to account for this circumstance. On the other hand, the Siuai recognize kinship as extending far beyond primary and secondary relatives, and in fact each individual's recognized [1] kinship ties extend throughout Siuai — or beyond it, for that matter, since natives living along the borders of the Motuna language area often marry across the border. In actual practice, sibship and the theoretically almost limitless extension of kinship ties permit a Siuai to apply a kinship term to any other Siuai he meets. For example, should he meet a total stranger and wish to establish some useful basis for interaction, all he needs to know is the stranger's primary totem or the totem of the latter's wife or father, and with that knowledge — added to the fact of the stranger's sex and relative age — he can call him or her by an appropriate kinship term. Or, he can resort to the device known throughout the Melanesian pidgin area as "helping": he can discover what kinship term some kinsman or kinswoman calls the stranger and go on from there. For example, when Peuru learns that a stranger calls one of Peuru's distant sib *mothers* by the term for *father's sister*, Peuru can then call the stranger "cross-cousin." Moreover, a native usually has a choice between two or more kinship terms he can apply to a total stranger — or even to some secondary relatives — so that the term he chooses to use depends upon the kind of relationship he wishes to emphasize. For, in Siuai as in other societies there is some degree of congruity between kinship term and behavior pattern. The present chapter will describe Siuai kinship in outline form and mainly in terms of the *transactional* behavior patterns between pairs of relatives.[2] It is not possible for me to generalize with the same degree of confidence about the dimensions of *interaction* or *emotion* in the cases of relatives outside the same nuclear family. It is a well-established fact that family members invariably interact a great deal, but the amount of interaction among relatives not related by family ties depends in large measure upon circumstances of residence; and as has been pointed out, residence patterns vary considerably.

These situational variations in amount of interaction show up mainly in connection with the assemblage of expressive behavior patterns which I have called *affection*, it being more or less true that some components of affection tend to exist where interaction is frequent.[3] Moreover, in Siuai at least, affection tends to remove some components of *deference* and *constraint*. On the other hand, higher rank and, to a less degree, greater age, tend to increase deference and constraint in relationships where these pattern assemblages already exist, or superpose them on relationships where they would not otherwise be. All these situational and status factors should be kept in mind in reading the following summaries.

It should also be recalled that despite their emphasis on matriliny the Siuai reckon kinship ties patrilaterally as well. And although they apply most kinship terms over a wide classificatory range, they can, if called upon to do so, and within the limits of their genealogical memories, justify the application of a particular term to a distant relative with *descriptive* precision. If, for example, a youth of normal intelligence is asked to tell why he calls a certain old woman *mama* he might reply "because she is the wife of the true brother of my own mother's own mother." It is true that their memories of genealogy do not usually extend further than four or five generations beyond the oldest living generation, so that they frequently have to fall back on classificatory explanations when justifying application of terms (e.g. "I call her *mama* because she is the wife of a sib *brother* of my own mother's own mother"). The fact remains, however, that their classificatory application of kinship terms is a matter of convention rather than a reflection of naiveté.

A second aspect of this problem of nomenclature and behavior was touched upon by my neighbor, Opisa, when describing how a person should behave toward his *mothers*: "We Siuai act the same toward *all* our mothers; but a child is not yet aware, and thinks of the woman who bore it as its *only* mother." Thus, from the Olympian heights of adult intelligence! But on other occasions this same Opisa was able to list the various applications of the term *eie* (*sibling* of opposite sex), explaining how the intensity of the relationship shades off by degrees so that a very distant *eie* may be seduced without running much supernatural risk. And again, when I chided Opisa for not attending the cremation of a man he called *umoka* (*father*), he explained that the deceased was after all only a *distant father*.

In the following summaries of behavior patterns, I have indicated for each dyad category how the intensity [4] of a particular class of relationship shades off with real or putative genealogical distance — and, where necessary, in terms of native opinions about how people *should* behave (normative gradations) as well as in terms of native's reports and my observations of *actual* behavior (behavioral gradations),[5] there being certain significant discrepancies in many instances between the results of these two methods of scaling.

## KIN PAIR RELATIONS

*Lateral Extension of Nuclear Family Kinship Ties.* The summary of Chapter 5 characterized the relations between pairs of members of the monogamous nuclear family. Eight such pairs can be isolated: husband-wife; mother-son; father-son; mother-daughter; father-daughter; older brother-younger brother; older sister-younger sister; brother-sister.

In fully developed polygynous families, these additional pair relationships obtain: co-wives; stepmother-stepson; stepmother-stepdaughter; half-brothers; half-sisters; half-brothers and sisters.

As we have seen, except for co-wives, nokihoro-derived relationships can be regarded as fairly close facsimiles of those among members of the monogamous family, both as regards norms and actual behavior. Even co-wives address one another as older or younger *sister*, and ideally should behave towards one another accordingly — although few Siuai really expect them to do so.

Except for the husband-wife (*iŋ:ina*) tie, which is peculiar to the nuclear family, nuclear family kinship terms are extended beyond the family, as the following outline will illustrate.

*nuka:nuri* (mother:son).[6] It is my belief that one's own biological mother is the primary meaning of the term *nuka*; when a Siuai adult now says "nuka," without any qualifiers, it is almost certain that he is referring to his own mother — and with the child this is even more probable. Moreover, the term appears to refer to a single class of relationships, with distinctions between one's many *mothers* being differences of degree rather than of kind. Native informants ranked the various degrees of "motherhood" about as follows:

*Normative Gradations*
1. own mother
2. own father's other wives
3. own mother's sisters, uterine and half
4. own mother's sib *sisters* (i.e., all other female sib-mates of mother in her own generation)
5. wives of any man ego calls *father*;[7] mother of anyone ego calls *sibling*

Etc. — the list being almost indefinitely extendible.

According to my own observations, the ranking would have to be revised, as follows:

*Behavioral Gradations*
1. own mother
2. own mother's sisters (with distinctions between real and half)
3. own mother's matrilineage *sisters*
4. own father's other wives
5. own mother's sib *sisters* (i.e., all female sib-mates of mother in her own generation)
6. wives of any man ego calls *father*; mother of anyone ego calls *sibling*.

Beyond this point, natives seldom attempt to trace or utilize the mother-son relation, although now and then this kind of situation occurs (in the words of one informant):

"Once when I was returning from the coast where I had traded some small pots for betel-mixture lime, I stopped off in a club-house in Kunnu (about fifteen miles away). As I sat resting I told some of the men there that I was hungry. They asked me about my totem, and when I told them it was hornbill they said: "Then go to that old woman over there, she's hornbill too; she's your *mother*." So I went to her and called out, "Hey, *mother*, I'm hungry." She took me to her home and gave me some sago, but it was sour and there wasn't much of it: she was only a distant *mother*."

Another native told this account of his experiences during fighting days:

"When raiders from Mono Island attacked our place and captured me, I was still a small child. They took me to Mono and were planning to kill me, until a woman there saw my palm lines and announced that she and I had the same totem. After that she fed me and I called her *mother*."

We have already characterized the amount and kind of interaction to be expected between most own mother-own son pairs, and indications of how much interaction takes place between a male and his other *mothers* may be inferred from a review of residence and work patterns. The fact is that unless a man resides or works near a kinswoman he does not frequently interact with her.[8]

Another criterion of "proximity" in this mother-son relation has to do with intensity of incest restrictions. Most natives would declare categorically that sexual relations with any woman called *mother* are incestuous and hence absolutely interdicted and punishable by the extreme supernatural sanction of automatic death. Case histories bring out, however, that effective dread of incest extends only through No. 3 on the list of behavioral gradations. There were a few cases of fornication with No. 4 and No. 5, and several flagrant instances of "incest," including actual marriage, with No. 6.

*umoka:nuri* (father:son).

*Normative Gradations*

1. own father
2. own father's brothers
3. own father's matrilineage *brothers*
4. own father's sib *brothers* (i.e., all other male sib-mates of own father in his own generation)
5. stepfather (if ego's own father is deceased)
6. husband of any woman ego calls *mother*; father of anyone ego calls "sibling."

*Behavioral Gradations*: Same as normative except for the following:
— own father's uterine brothers are closer than any half-brothers the father may have.
— the younger ego is at the time of the death of his father and the remarriage of his mother, the higher up the list will his stepfather be. But if ego

is past childhood when his mother remarries, or if ego's own father is still alive, ego will in all probability not call his stepfather "father."

Because of the prevalence of virilocality, many males will reside near and interact a great deal with their fathers' own and half-brothers, both before and after marriage. Other *brothers* of the father will, however, tend to be dispersed, and a man's interaction with these is limited to more formal occasions.

Relations between co-resident nephew and paternal uncle tend to be affectionate. In many instances the father's brother is even more indulgent than the father, and this is especially true if the older man has no son of his own. For example, Sinu's brother, Koŋkora, spent hours every day nursing Sinu's young son, teaching him crafts, feeding him tidbits, etc.; and this relationship was matched in a number of instances I knew, including some where the uncle also had a son of his own. In all such cases, the *father* showered services and little gifts on his *son* without demanding recompense other than the conventional: "When I am aged my *sons* will provide for me; and when I die they will furnish pigs for the mourners." Despite the prominence of the father-son conflict theme in myths (see Chapter 2), I could discover little evidence that the word "father" evokes images of hostility or stern authority or awed respect. In fact, about the only occasion when distant fathers — father's brothers and father's matrilineage mates in this case — exert forceful pressure on a *son* occurs after the death of the *son's* own father. It was previously described [9] how the *fathers* perform a warlike demonstration to coerce a reluctant *son* into contributing more liberally for his own father's funeral. It will also be recalled that a son may inherit a portion of his father's matrilineage land only through making such contributions, and how some *sons* will increase their landholdings by similar contributions to the funerals of other distant *fathers*. Ambitious men will go even beyond the limits of their own father's matrilineage and avail themselves of the material aid of more distant *fathers* in order to build up their resources for social-climbing feasts. In this sense, the Siuai term for "father's sib-mates" (*umanu*, my-fathers) connotes persons who can be turned to for aid. It is generally understood that this kind of aid is on a loan basis, but to a Siuai a potential lender is next best thing to a potential giver or sharer.

At this point we can state another generalization which applies more or less to all kinship relations: relatives ought at least to *lend* goods and services to one another, and many of them do.

Another significant terminological practice is a man's use of the word my-*sons* (*nuri'*) to refer to his wife's sib-mates as a body, even before his wife has borne him a son.

*nuka:nuro* (mother:daughter). It is my impression that the gradations in these behavior patterns, both normative and behavioral, closely parallel those of the father and son, but it must be confessed that more data might alter this opinion.[10] In attempting to reconstruct a female's relations with her *mothers* it should be recalled that many girls move to their fiancé's household shortly after puberty, but that until then the relationship with their own mother is continuous and extremely close. For one thing, there is no basis in property transactions which would lead to competition or conflict. Moreover, mothers are not usually strict disciplinarians with their own daughters; nor could I detect any signs of open conflict between them, in fact, the eagerness with which affianced or newly married girls return home as to a haven, strengthens my belief in the warm affective ties between mother and daughter, which, if anything, may be increased as result of contrast with the mother-in-law. In other words, we might say that the Siuai daughter's "mother image" is one of an affectionate and tolerant protectress, and this probably colors her relations with other *mothers*.

There would appear to be a particularly strong attachment between a female and her matrilineage *mothers*, including her mother's own sisters. These women assist at her birth — as later on they assist when she bears children; they serve as wet-nurses to her and her offspring; rear her if her own mother dies, teach her sib magic, etc., and all without tangible recompense. Such *mothers* particularly welcome and cherish *daughters*, who insure the continuity of the matrilineage.

The only evidence of conflict I personally witnessed between *mother* and *daughter* existed between a young unbetrothed woman, whose own mother was dead, and her father's second wife. The two continually bickered in the garden, with the older woman chiding the younger for her laziness and the younger becoming increasingly soured by her own dependency. Informants claimed that this is a familiar pattern. Another situation said to prevail in polygynous families is conflict between co-wives occasioned by one of them being harsh to the offspring of another.

*umoka:nuro* (father:daughter). Both normative and behavioral gradations are about the same for this kind of relationship as between *father* and *son*, although a female interacts less frequently with any *father* than with the corresponding *mother*.

The restrictions on sexual relations between a man and his own daughter extend to stepdaughters, but men occasionally fornicate with matrilineage *sisters* of their own daughters and some even marry their own daughters' distant sib-sisters. A few native moralists term all such relations "incestuous" but admit that the taboo is not generally honored, adding, "many practices of us Siuai are not straight." Despite those lapses, however, the taboo does have the effect of injecting an element of restraint into the otherwise friendly and open nature of this relationship.

As for the jural aspects, a female's distant *fathers* play hardly any role in a *daughter's* life until her own father dies. At that time, one of the latter's own brothers or matrilineage *brothers* may assert some interest in the girl's welfare; and recently some substitute *fathers* have taken upon themselves the duty of arranging their *daughters'* marriages, including retaining the brideprice for themselves! In these machinations they usually share dubious honors with the girls' maternal uncles.

*tata:naramoŋ* (older brother:younger brother, actually or putatively of same generation). Under this terminological reciprocal it is necessary to draw a fundamental distinction between *brothers* in ego's own generation and *brothers* in his second ascending generation; only the former will be considered here.

*Normative and Behavioral Gradations* (the chronologically older is *tata*)

1. own uterine brother: same father and same mother
2. half-brother: same mother but different father
3. half-brother: same father but different mother
4. male matrilineage-mate of same generation
5. male sib-mate of about same age
6. son of father's own brother
7. son of anyone [11] ego calls *father* or *mother*
8. husband of any woman ego calls *mama*

In the rank order of behavioral gradations matrilineage *brothers* would be "nearer" than half-brothers by different mothers, with respect to joint identification with matrilineage activities and property; otherwise the two scales are identical.

The data on residence [12] gives only a rough indication of the significance of ties of interaction between *brothers*. Parallel cousins, whether sib-mates or not, form very close relationships — working and playing together, sharing possessions, aiding one another's enterprises, and extending long-term loans in goods and services. Interacting pairs of *brothers*, real or classificatory, are such a commonplace that there is a special term, *monoŋo*, for two males thus related. Moreover, the Siuai have hit upon a very apt metaphor by describing two objects bound closely together as being "brothered"; e.g., an ax blade is "brothered" to its handle.

An example of the relationship between two distant sib-brothers is typified by an episode involving Kopisai and Samporo, both of Moronei village. Kopisai owned a small hurricane lamp, acquired at the plantation where he once worked, but Samporo had none. Samporo used to purchase kerosene with his own savings and give it to Kopisai. Once Samporo borrowed the lamp and managed to break the chimney. When he returned it with regrets, Kopisai's wife became very angry and called Samporo a clumsy fool, adding that he "probably broke the lamp in trying to copulate with it." Kopisai was so enraged by her insults at his sib-brother, that he beat her severely and tore up all her calicoes.

Occasionally, however, even uterine brothers break sharply apart — usually, natives claim, because of quarrels between their wives. In some cases I knew, these quarrels led to changes of residence and deep bitterness. One pair of matrilineage-brothers was in fact known to be trying to kill each other by sorcery.

Natives distinguish uterine brothers from others by explaining: "they drank from the same breast"; whereas they describe brothers with the same father but different mothers as being "aggregated" (nokihoro). Distinctions between matrilineage or sib *brothers* and all other *brothers* reflect the society's emphasis on the matrilineal tie, especially in symbolic matters.

*mama:naramana* (older sister:younger sister, actually or putatively of same generation).

*Normative Gradations*
1. own uterine sister: same father and same mother
2. half-sister: same mother but different father
3. half-sister: same father but different mother
4. female matrilineage-mate of same generation
5. female sib-mate of about same age
6. mother's brother's daughter; father's sister's daughter
7. co-wife
8. sister's husband's sisters
   Et cetera

Of all these, ego calls father's sister's daughter "older sister" (*mama*); whereas she calls any of the others "older" or "younger" (*naramana*) according to relative chronological age.

*Behavioral Gradations*
1. same
2. same
3. daughter of mother's sister
4. same
5. half-sister: same father but different mother
6. mother's brother's daughter
7. co-wife
8. father's sister's daughter
9. female sib-mate of about same age
   Et cetera

The difference in behavioral rank order takes account of the actualities of betrothal, residence, marriage, and women's generally restricted social lives. Betrothal, for example, separates most sisters early in life, and unless they have a common mother, different hamlet residences keep many of them effectively separated.[13] Co-wives, on the other hand, may interact frequently — all too frequently! — but their relationship is very often characterized by enmity. Also, despite common sib membership, unless a woman resides near a distant sib *sister* she has little opportunity to form warm affective ties with her.

I do not feel that the mythical prototype of heartless Older Sister and mistreated Younger Sister faithfully reflects present conditions.[14] Certainly, I heard of quarrels between *sisters*, but my impression is that except for many co-wives, *sisters* who live and work together are usually congenial and mutually generous with goods and services.[15] Linguistically, at least, the paired term "sisters" (*monoruko*) has about the same connotation of junction as *monoŋo* ("brothers").

EIE:*eie*[16] (brother:sister, actually or putatively of same generation).

*Normative Gradations*
1. sibling of opposite sex: same mother and father

# KIN RELATIONS 255

2. half-sibling of opposite sex: same mother but different father
3. member of own sib or aggregated sib, of opposite sex, and of about same age
4. half-sibling of opposite sex: same father but different mother
5. opposite-sex offspring of any man own father calls "brother"
6. female speaking: husband of any woman called *mama*
7. male speaking: wife of any man called *povoi*

Et cetera

*Behavioral Gradations*

1. same
2. same
3. opposite-sex offspring of mother's sister
4. matrilineage-mate of opposite sex and same generation
5. half-sibling of opposite sex: same father but different mother
6. sib-mate of opposite sex of about same age
7. member of aggregated sib of opposite sex and about same age
8. opposite-sex offspring of any man father calls "brother"
9. female speaking: husband of any woman called *mama*: male speaking: wife of any man called *povoi*

The normative pattern of behavior between opposite sex siblings of all gradations is friendly interaction and mutual generosity absolutely devoid of any suggestion of sexual intercourse. A Siuai male makes fundamental distinction between *eie* and all other females of his generation; as one of them put it:

"If a man sees a *sister* somewhere, he says to her: '*Sister*, give me some areca nut; I don't have any with me.' But if a man meets up with any other woman not yet senile the latter runs and hides; she must not talk with him."

It would appear, then, that the incest taboo, which applies with such effectiveness to real and half-siblings of opposite sex, is also counted upon to apply with equal effectiveness between all other opposite-sex *siblings*. But does it?

I recorded no cases of incest between *siblings* of opposite sex linked by matrilineage ties, but several between those linked only by sib ties and even more between those related only by phratry ties. In all such cases, supernatural sanctions are believed to apply: unless the incestuous pair perform the antidotal ritual they will automatically die. And even if they escape this doom, they usually face a scandalized public opinion, which is uncomfortable enough for the woman, but even more so for the man, whose sin is "talked about in the club-house" — that most effective form of humiliation a Siuai can experience. For some men the contempt and ridicule are so painful that they avoid going to club-houses for many months, until the talk dies down. One man I knew, who was not abnormally sensitive, became a virtual recluse on account of the publicity attending an incestuous affair he had during my visit; and natives told me of men and women committing suicide rather than live through the shame of having committed incest with a sib *sibling*.

"Incest" with an affinal *sibling*, although theoretically the same kind of sin, seems to be more like adultery in the social reaction it provokes. The injured spouse brings suit and the penalty usually consists of a fine and specific enmities rather than a general public reaction.

The sexual taboo between opposite-sex siblings also finds expression in the institution of numehu — "shame payment." It will be recalled that a husband with a newly pregnant wife must announce that fact to her brother with the accompaniment of a "shame payment" (see pp. 170–171). Some distant *brothers* will attempt to capitalize on a *sister's* pregnancy, but husbands usually draw the line to include only their spouse's matrilineage *brothers*, and even these receive only a token. On the other hand, if a woman commits incest or adultery, she herself is expected to give shame payments to at least all her matrilineage *brothers*.

*Other Kin of the Same or Successive Generations.*[17] Mention was made in earlier chapters of the Siuai preference for cross-cousin marriage. This preference is reflected in kinship terminology. For example, a male addresses his mother's brother's son, his father's sister's son, his wife's brother, and his sister's husband as *povoi*, and his actions toward all these contain some common elements of behavior. Theoretically, all these statuses may be centered in a single individual, and if all marriages conformed to the stated norm, then no distinctions would have to be made between different subclasses of povoi. Actually, however, a very small percentage of marriages — about 15 per cent — do so conform, and over and above the elements of behavior common to all subclasses of povoi, there are some significant behavioral differences between otherwise unrelated male cross-cousins on the one hand and brothers-in-law on the other. I know no way of determining which meaning of povoi is the primary one. If we knew which, if either, meaning had historical priority that would provide an interesting but not necessarily reliable clue concerning the present primary meaning. On the other hand, it seems to me unwarrantedly facile to assert that we are dealing in each case with separate words which happen to be homonymous.[18] Similar complications apply to *apu* (father's sister, mother's brother's wife, and mother-in-law), to *papa* (mother's brother, father's sister's husband, and husband's father), to opposite-sex cross-cousins, and to opposite-sex siblings-in-law.

The only kinship terms which are applicable to successive generations and which are distinctively affinal are *nura* (male speaking: *father-in-law, son-in-law*), and *ŋonum* (*wife's mother's brother*; male speaking: *sister's daughter's husband*).

Keeping these general remarks in mind, we can proceed with the outline.

*papa:nopum.* Here we must distinguish sharply between two classes of *papa*, consanguineal and affinal, as the Siuai themselves do.

## KIN RELATIONS

Class I. MOTHER'S BROTHER: SISTER'S SON

Normative and behavioral gradations
1. own mother's uterine brother
2. own mother's matrilineage *brother*
3. male sib-mate of first ascending generation
4. any other male ego's mother calls *brother*

In native theory as well as in actual practice, a male's mother's uterine brother is one of the most important relatives in his life. Some informants would in fact place this kinsman ahead of the father in many respects; but when the question arose, some native would invariably recall the following parable to demonstrate that the tie between father and son is, after all, the closer affective one:

Once a man climbed an almond tree in search of nuts and happened to catch a small bird that was nesting there. When he climbed down carrying the bird his sister's son saw it and said: "*Papa* (mother's brother), give the bird to me." But the man's son also saw the bird and said: "*Umoka* (father), give it to me." So the man gave the bird to his son.

In terms of residence, avunculocality is least prevalent of the four common types,[19] but it was my observation that visiting between mother's brother and sister's son occurs frequently and visits sometimes last for days.

The nature of the relationship between a mother's uterine brother and his sister's son appears to range between stern discipline and genial mutual dependence, but most informants agreed that all boys stand in some awe of their mother's brothers, and are more likely to obey them than their own fathers; I also found this to be the case. Moreover, own maternal uncles assert their authority frequently and forcefully, whether the nephew's father is present or not. During a boy's late childhood and early youth his maternal uncle will spend much time with him, teaching him crafts, encouraging his ambition, and giving him gifts. In return, the uncle expects certain services from his nephew, but these hardly balance his outlay in services and goods, the relationship being definitely complementary from the point of view of property transactions. In later life the nephew will look upon his mother's uterine brothers as his most dependable backers in political enterprises.

If the question is put to them directly some natives state that the tie with the mother's *eldest* uterine brother is "strongest" (*pooki*), but it was my observation that unless that individual is also the First-born of their common matrilineage, any behavioral differences obtaining between a male and his mother's several uterine brothers is influenced more by factors of residential proximity and personality than of the relative ages of the latter.

Factors of residence and personality also importantly influence the interaction and expressive behavior which takes place between a male and his mother's matrilineage *brothers* (as distinct from her own brothers). In fact, I recorded instances in which some of the former actually outweigh the genealogically closer maternal uncles in their influence over the nephews' lives. Matrilineage *uncles*, being older members of this important corporation, possess stronger control over the use and disposition of matrilineage property than do their sister's sons; and in the case of the *uncle* who is matrilineage First-born, the degree of control is even greater. Now, Siuai natives are heavily dependent upon their matrilineages to provide them with many of the material and supernatural resources of life, and for most natives a rupture with matrilineage mates, and especially with their more influential matrilineage *uncles*, is almost inconceivable. Even a break with one's own father brings less serious consequences — and occurs more frequently.

The close tie between a native and his matrilineage *uncles*, including of course his mother's uterine brothers, often survives after death, since the ghosts of the latter become the familiars of their nephews in more instances than they return to serve and be served by their sons.

Relations with a sib *papa*[20] who is not a matrilineage mate are not governed by considerations of common ownership of property or by explicit moral obligations. Circumstances of residence and common interest may bring the two into close contact, and in such cases it may be said that the fact of common sib membership provides a *disposition* for affection and reciprocal lending, but that is all. And in this connection it should be noted that this disposition is probably stronger the closer the genetic ties between their matrilineages are conceived to be; for example, among Tree-rat sib members a Belly-fat is closer to a Belly-fat than to a Left-behind.

The strength of the tie with any other putatively consanguineal maternal uncles (i.e., with any non-sibmate ego's mother calls *brother*: usually one of the mother's *half-brothers*, own or distant) depends almost entirely upon such considerations as residential proximity and chance common interest, there being little or no jural or moral basis to the relationship defined by the tie itself. This is also true of a native's mother's own half-brother (same father but different mother and different matrilineage).

Class II. FATHER'S SISTER'S HUSBAND : WIFE'S BROTHER'S SON

Normative and behavioral gradations

1. husband of own father's own sister (*apu*)
2. husband of anyone ego calls *apu* (except own father-in-law)

There is so little patterning in the relationship between a male and this affinal *papa*, such an absence of prescriptions and proscriptions, that it is somewhat misleading to speak of *status* in a normative sense. The generationally older of the pair possesses no authority over the younger and has no property to share with him. Moreover, there is no distinctive institutionalized basis for their interaction, and the actualities of residence do not encourage much everyday companionship or coöperation. The older man is of course a potential father-in-law of the younger, as indeed is the consanguineal *papa*, but in neither case could I discover that this theoretical possibility exercises any apparent effect upon the relationship. Perhaps the distinguishing feature of the relationship with an affinal *papa* lies in the very absence of distinctive norms, for, in fact, a male's father's sister's husband is the only close kinsman of the next older generation toward whom he has great freedom to act as he pleases and as circumstances dictate.

*nura:nura* (wife's father:daughter's husband). If a male Siuai is hard pressed to demonstrate a kinship tie with any male his wife calls *father* (or his *daughter* calls husband), he may call him *nura*; otherwise the term is usually restricted to wife's own father (or foster father) and to own daughter's husband. A native looking for a loan may search out any man of his wife's father's matrilineage or sib and pave the way by pointedly addressing him as *nura*, and vice versa.[21]

Save for complicating circumstances, the relations between father-in-law and son-in-law are actually characterized by reciprocal lending colored somewhat by constraint and by deference on the part of the younger man; and this according to native informants is what the relationship *should* be. Constraint between the two is exemplified in their avoidance of discussing sexual matters in one another's presence.[22] It is also expected that the survivor will lend a pig for the other's funeral feast, and that he will join in with the deceased's other kinsmen in avenging his death. Informants did not comment on this situation, but it was my observation that the arrival of offspring usually has the effect of buttressing the tie between the father and the mother's father by removing some of the constraint and by increasing the disposition for reciprocal interest-free lending. Also, common hamlet residence, when not complicated by conflict over property, usually leads to the development of close ties of amity. In fact, I knew of cases wherein a high-ranking leader had brought up a promising orphan youth and eventually married his daughter to him, in order to be in a better position to help support the youth's acquisition of renown.

On the other hand, a marriage which begins with any dissatisfaction over betrothal or wedding exchanges[23] is likely to result in continued coolness between son-in-law and father-in-law, and may even result in declared enmity — with possible repercussions on the marriage itself. Also, marital strife usually leads to trouble between son-in-law and father-in-law; the picture of the estranged wife being forcibly returned to her husband by her father does not yet fit into the Siuai scene.[24]

Another complicating factor in the relations between son-in-law and father-in-law is the relative socio-political rank of the two. Because of ordinarily greater age of the latter his rank is usually higher, and this may reinforce somewhat the complementary nature of their relationship. However, I knew of father- and son-in-law pairs in which the former ranked lower than the latter in the same men's society, and in fact were among the latter's most loyal and deferential supporters. In the case I knew best, the father-in-law of the very high-ranking leader, Soŋi, showed as much deference to Soŋi as the latter's humblest supporter, and received in return no special consideration that I could discern.

Polygyny, except of course the sororal variety, results in some men having more than one father-in-law. However, I found no evidence of institutionalized differential behavior based on marriage order.

When "correct" cross-cousin marriage leads to a man becoming the son-in-law of his consanguineal *papa* (mother's *brother*), the new composite relationship, which is recognized in the composite term, "father-in-law-onto-mother's-brother" (*papakorinura*), may develop into reinforced ties of sharing, nonreciprocable giving, and affection; or it may develop into a situation of role conflict, some seeds of strife being present in the affinal tie. I observed pair relationships at both extremes, but it was also evident that the consanguineal facet of this relationship served as a brake on serious conflict. In fact, this composite relationship is — and is recognized as being — a most satisfactory solution to the problems presented by *affinity* and by the rules of inheritance.[25] Young men often joke about their elders always trying to keep intact their family and matrilineage resources by arranging marriages between their own and their sisters' offspring.

Marriage with the daughter of one's affinal *papa* (*father's sister's* husband) can hardly be said to result in a composite relationship, since there is so little patterning in the affinal *papa-nopum* relationship to begin with.

*povoi:povoi.*

Class I. MOTHER'S BROTHER'S SON:FATHER'S SISTER'S SON

Normative and behavioral gradations

1. mother's brother's son
2. matrilineage *brother* of mother's brother's son
3. sib *brother* of mother's brother's son

Pairs of cross-cousins very often reside together in the same hamlet or in neighboring hamlets and interact frequently — playing, working, strolling, and lounging together. Even if they reside in separate villages they can be expected to visit each other's family from earliest childhood on.

In some instances a male's mother's brother's son and his father's sister's son are identical, but more frequently they are different individuals.

A dominant consideration in a male's relationship with his mother's brother's son is the fact that the rights he enjoys over the matrilineage land of the latter's father supersede any claims the latter may assert. We saw earlier how this advantage finds expression at the time of a man's death: his matrilineage survivors, including his sister's son, can deny his son access to a share of the deceased's matrilineage land. On the other hand, during a man's lifetime he will usually favor his son over his sister's son on nearly all occasions. Now, this division of rights is generally recognized, but there still remains enough margin for variation to permit conflicts between cross-cousins over their respective shares. For example, an especially doting father will sometimes attempt to individualize his share of matrilineage land in order to devise them directly to his son. Or, a high-ranking father will sometimes concentrate his efforts on helping his sister's son to win renown. Situations like these occasionally result in repudiation and even enmity between cross-cousins.

Under other circumstances cross-cousins are drawn close together by their rights and obligations respecting the property, commitments, etc., of their common uncle-father. For example, I heard of several cases where a deceased native's son and sister's son combined their resources to repay debts incurred by the deceased. And the numerous instances of co-resident or co-gardening cross-cousins attest to the element of amity potentially in this relationship: they are, as the Siuai put it, "of the same blood," i.e., descended from a common pair of grandparents even though their kinship is only partly matrilateral.

The obligations owed by a male to his father's sister's son extend in some respects to the matrilineage *brothers* of the latter; they too join in the anger-ritual staged to force a reluctant son to provide generously for his father's funeral. This however is only an occasional incident in the relationships between such distant cross-cousins; in many cases they reside in the same hamlet or village, and coöperate often in economic and political enterprises. As a general rule, the one who is "Resident-owner" has a jural advantage over his "Attacher" cross-cousin, but because of the wide variations in residence patterns this does not result in any society-wide advantage accruing to either father's sister's son or mother's brother's son vis-à-vis each other.

The offspring of a cross-cousin marriage are of course doubly interrelated, each povoi being both mother's brother's son and father's sister's son of the other. It is my impression that this type of kinship tie leads to greater identity of interests, less conflict, and closer affective ties.

Class II. WIFE'S BROTHER:SISTER'S HUSBAND

Normative and behavioral gradations

1. wife's uterine or half-brother, uterine or half-sister's husband
2. any male called *brother* by wife or by sister's husband
3. husband of any woman ego calls *sister*

The essence of the emotional tie between actual brothers-in-law is amity colored by constraint; the two are said to be drawn together "because of the woman," but since the latter is a sister of one of them, expressive behavior between them is characterized by constraint. Joking (mimmiŋ, "talk-play") of any sort should be avoided, and neither man should make or listen to any reference to the sexual act in the presence of the other. Mention has already been made of the shame-payment (numehu) demanded by a woman's brother of her husband when she conceives.[26] As mentioned earlier, most Siuai look with disfavor upon a simultaneous sister-exchange marriage (*apaapatu*), it having too much the appearance of a bartering of material goods. Moreover, it is considered doubly wrong for prospective brothers-in-law to negotiate with each other concerning sex rights over their sisters. On those rare occasions when two symmetrical cross-cousin marriages are arranged, the fathers should do the arranging.

The element of constraint between brothers-in-law moderates with genealogical distance, so that a man may drop nearly all pretense of constraint with the husband of a distant *sister* provided of course that the distant *brother-in-law* is not a high-ranking leader and hence deserving of respect referable to the rank rather than the kinship system.

*Brothers-in-law*, actual and distant, often reside together in the same hamlet and coöperate in all kinds of enterprises. My records of loan transactions emphasize how often they depend upon each other for financial assistance, and this is also frequently true of their support of each other during times of sickness, litigation, and feast-making. However, all is not congeniality and mutual helpfulness between *brothers-in-law*; some pairs I knew or heard about were anything but friendly. A man and his wife's own brother, especially, are apt to become cool or openly hostile in situations of trouble between the man and his wife. Another source of conflict is exemplified in the following tale:

"There was once an orphan whose only close relative was his older sister. He lived at the house of his sister and her husband and fared well because his sister always gave him the choice morsels of food. In fact, she favored him to such an extent that her husband became angered and plotted to do away with the boy. One day while the three of them worked together in their garden the husband bade his wife return home, telling her that he and the boy would remain in the garden for a while to enlarge the clearing. The woman left and the two brothers-in-law began cutting trees and brush. They disturbed a sleeping snake and captured it, tying it with vine. As they worked they captured many more snakes. Finally, after twenty snakes had been captured the older man held his young brother-in-law on the ground and forced all the snakes down his throat. The snakes thrashed around inside the boy so violently that the boy "died." Thereupon the older man returned home alone and told his wife that her brother had been lazy and now slept in the garden. His wife suspected him of lying and anxiously went to the garden to find her brother. She wept when she found him, but seeing a snake's tail hanging from his mouth she jumped up and down on his body, forcing him to vomit forth all the snakes. Conscious again, the boy cut a bamboo flute and played on it, so happy was he to be "alive" again. His sister then urged him to return home with her but he refused, telling her with regret that he would seek a new place to live. With that he started off, blowing his flute as he went and leaving his sister to grieve.

"After a while the boy sat down on a large stone and began to beat on it in time with the flute music he was playing. At that the stone spoke up, asking the boy not to beat on it so hard. The boy was greatly surprised to hear a stone speak and stopped his drumming. Then the stone instructed the boy to climb two nearby coconut palms and fetch a coconut from each. This having been done the stone told him to place the coconuts on the ground and cover them with leaves. After doing all these things the boy played some more on his flute and started out again on his travels, but as he was leaving, the stone bade him look under the leaves. The boy did so, and found instead of coconuts two handsome young women whom he forthwith married at the stone's behest.

"One day the boy's two wives went to fetch water from the creek and they dropped the stopper of their water flask into the stream. Far downstream the boy's sister spied the stopper floating past and went upstream in search of the persons who had lost it. When she came to the two young wives she asked them if they had seen her young brother, the one who had been filled with snakes by his wicked brother-in-law. In reply they led her to her young brother and they all returned to her house where they roasted a pig in a joyous reunion feast. But there was still the wicked brother-in-law to deal with.

"The boy's young wives sought the help of the stone and the latter agreed to do away with the brother-in-law. He instructed them to bring the brother-in-law to him, and when they did so the stone asked the brother-in-law to sit beside him. When the brother-in-law was seated the stone rolled over onto him and killed him."

If I had been sufficiently aware of structural problems at the time of field work I would have collected more data on the relationships created by the marriage of actual cross-cousins. The composite ties relating the two husbands contain elements which might lead either to increased amity or to conflict; unfortunately I do not have enough case history material for generalizing about the way this situation is usually resolved.[27]

Class III. FATHER OF SON'S WIFE:FATHER OF DAUGHTER'S HUSBAND

To the best of my knowledge this relationship has no extensions beyond the two men actually related by the marriage of their offspring. If there is no other close kinship tie between these two they do not often reside together nor have many opportunities for interaction within the context of kinship activities. Under these circumstances they remain friendly or become hostile according to the stability of the marriage of their offspring.

*apu:imiho.* Following the usage of the Siuai we can distinguish three classes of apu:imiho.

Class I. FATHER'S SISTER:BROTHER'S SON

Normative and behavioral gradations
1. an eldest son's own father's eldest uterine or half-sister
2. own father's uterine or half-sister
3. own father's matrilineage *sister*
4. sister of anyone called *father*

The most noteworthy feature of this relationship is *avoidance*: the two should not call each other's name nor touch each other nor handle items just touched by the other. In the case of distant *father's sisters*, avoidance behavior becomes greatly attenuated — so much, in fact, that I was often unable to distinguish between the behavior of a distant *father's sister* and that of a *mother's sister* toward a male infant or child. Informants even told me of certain well-known love affairs between distant apu:imiho pairs, although I heard of no instance of marriage between the two.

On the other hand, between a man's eldest sister and his eldest son the avoidance is very strict. In many instances the lad will spend his infancy and childhood in close proximity to this woman, and a deeply affectionate tie develops between the two; but this does not lead to a relaxation of the taboo against personal name-calling and physical contact. In fact, the name taboo is so strictly observed that neither may so much as utter the name of the other. If, for example, an eldest son addresses or refers to some female whose name is the same as his father's eldest sister's he calls her "Old Apu" or "Name-like-that-of-Apu." As for physical contact, I have many times seen a woman jerk away when a toddling brother's son touched against her, exclaiming: "Hey, don't touch me, *Imiho*! I'm your-Apu. It's forbidden." (Effective conditioning!) One informant confessed to me that it is easier to train a lad to *avoid* his father's sisters than to *accept* his co-mothers.

An affectionate father's sister may shower little gifts and services upon her brother's son when the latter is still young, but the most important transactional aspect of this relationship lies in the circumstance that the woman has some voice in deciding whether any of her matrilineage's land will be devised to her deceased brothers' offspring.

Class II. WIFE'S MOTHER:DAUGHTER'S HUSBAND

Normative and behavioral gradations
1. wife's mother
2. wife's mother's sisters, matrilineage *sisters*, and co-wives (provided, of course, that the co-wives are not sib-mates of ego)
3. mother-in-law of *sibling*

The patterns of behavior between a man and his wife's own mother closely resemble the avoidance relationship between father's eldest sister and brother's eldest son, with respect to taboos on personal name calling, on eating, and on physical contact (including sexual relations); if anything, the taboos are stricter. If, for example, a man marries and his wife's mother's name happens to be the same as his own sister's, he must henceforth call the latter by some other name. The taboo even extends to syllables contained in each other's name: for instance, the wife's mother of a man named Tomo cannot use the word *mo*, the common name for coconut; when she speaks of coconuts she uses a circumlocution, of which there are many in the language. However, avoidance of this kind extends only to a few much-used homonyms; otherwise excessive complications would be imposed upon many natives' speech — a fact which natives themselves recognize and comment upon.

If a man marries and then divorces a woman before she bears a child, he and his ex-mother-in-law are not required to taboo each other's names. Once a child is born, however, the taboo remains permanently effective; either one must maintain it even after the death of the other — if the survivor violates the rule it is said that the ghost of the deceased would wait for the ghost of the other to appear and beat it with a stick. I could not learn what tangible sanction, if any, applies to a name taboo-breaker while both principals are still alive.

Food for this pair may be harvested from the same plot and cooked in the same pot, but if they happen to eat parts of the same taro corm or banana, etc., it is believed that the teeth of both will drop out. To avoid this accident, identifying marks are cut on the corms or tubers or bananas intended for the woman when their food is cooked in the same pot.

The taboo on physical contact and proximity is also rigidly maintained, although by what manner of explicit sanction I could not discover — and indeed I am nearly convinced that the taboo is so thoroughly internalized that an explicit sanction, either in the form of public censure or supernatural penalty, is neither present nor necessary. The two do not sit nor stand near each other, nor do they directly hand things to each other. When walking along a path they keep several paces apart, and if possible, a third person walks between them. In the garden they do not work in the same plot at the same time; some informants explained the technique of laying out gardens into separate log-bounded plots as being based on the necessity of separating a man from his wife's mother while they work in the same patch.

There appears to be no "retroactive" embarrassment derived from becoming the son-in-law of a woman one has previously had sexual relations with. As one informant put it: "When I know that I am to marry the daughter of that woman, I begin immediately to taboo her name and do not think any more about wanting to copulate with her." My queries about sexual relations between a man and his wife's mother (and his wife's mother's sisters, matrilineage *sisters*, and co-wives) were met with such indignant denials that I am almost persuaded that this form of adultery does not exist!

In only one respect is the avoidance relationship with wife's mother less strict than that with father's sister: the prospective wife's mother of a child betrothed in infancy will avoid calling his name but will frequently touch him and hand him food tidbits until he has reached the age of six or seven. On the other hand, a male is taught to avoid physical contact with his father's eldest sister in all respects from earliest infancy on, "even" — and here is one informant's unelicited statement — "if it is known that the child will not marry the woman's daughter."

In practice, avoidance rules are greatly relaxed with respect to the wife's mother's sisters, matrilineage *sisters*, and co-wives, except in connection with sexual relations and, to a less extent, personal name-calling.

As for the mother-in-law of a distant *sibling* (either half-, matrilineage, or sib), the rules of avoidance become attenuated to the point of nonrecognition.

Class III. MOTHER'S BROTHER'S WIFE:HUSBAND'S SISTER'S SON

Normative and behavioral gradations
1. wife of mother's brother
2. wife of anyone called *papa*

Other than a mild taboo on personal name-calling and on sexual relations there is little patterning in the relationship of a male with women in the second category; but a male's relations with the wife of his own mother's brother is clearly defined. They may not use each other's name and they avoid sexual relations, but otherwise they might even treat each other with affectionate informality.

Earlier, I defined *avoidance* as consisting of some or all of the following behavior patterns: taboo on sexual intercourse, taboo on all physical contact, taboo on mutual name-calling, taboo on hearing sexual subjects discussed in each other's presence, etc. Thus, *avoidance* can be said to characterize the relationships of all pairs between whom sexual intercourse is forbidden, comprehending taboos on both incest and adultery. Now, it is obvious that *avoidance* behavior between a man and his father's sister (or mother-in-law) comprises certain behavior patterns (e.g., name-calling taboo) not called for in his relations with, say, his mother. In fact, in the interests of precision we should perhaps differentiate between incest-avoidance (mother, sister) and adultery-avoidance (wife's mother, sib-mate's wife). Furthermore, since a male's mother-in-law and his father's sister may be identical according to the Siuai kinship model of bilateral cross-cousin marriage, and since the behavior patterns respecting these two statuses are in fact nearly identical, I am inclined to describe this aspect of the father's sister: brother's son relationship as *adultery-avoidance*.

*apu:nonna.*

Class I. FATHER'S SISTER:BROTHER'S DAUGHTER

Behavioral gradations
1. own father's uterine or half-sister
2. sister of anyone called *father*

I could elicit few statements from natives about the way a female *should* behave towards her consanguineal apu but, on the basis of observation, the latter appeared to play the role of a strict and rather formal mother's sister. Also, the older woman usually has a voice in determining whether any of her matrilineage's land will be devised to her deceased *brothers'* daughters. As for relations with more distant consanguineal apus, I did not record any relevant observations other than the fact that the appropriate kinship terms are used.

Class II. HUSBAND'S MOTHER:SON'S WIFE

Normative and behavioral gradations
1. husband's own mother
2. husband's mother's sisters, matrilineage *sisters*, and co-wives (provided the latter are not ego's sib-mates)
3. mother-in-law of sibling

In view of the prevalence of patrilocal residence, interaction with a husband's mother and her co-wives is likely to be quite active and usually consists of *sharing* in connection with common household or hamlet enterprises. Something of the nature of the interaction was described in a previous chapter.[28] It will be recalled that the older woman usually receives respect and obedience from her daughter-in-law; in a few cases the relationship is marred by incompatibility, leading to change of residence or divorce; but more often it develops into warm mutual affection, and as the marriage becomes firmly stabilized, the older woman becomes almost a second mother.

Class III. WIFE OF MOTHER'S BROTHER:DAUGHTER OF HUSBAND'S SISTER

Behavioral gradations
1. wife of own mother's brother
2. wife of anyone called *papa*

I could not discover any distinctive norms concerning either of these pair relationships, but in those cases I did know a female's mother's brother's wife treated her as an overindulgent mother would. When the younger woman reaches maturity the relationship is usually characterized by informality and companionship. I have no record of actual interaction between a female and the wife of a distantly related *papa*.

*papa:nonna.* Following Siuai practice, it is necessary to distinguish three classes of papa:nonna.

Class I. MOTHER'S BROTHER:SISTER'S DAUGHTER

Normative gradations

1. own mother's uterine brother
2. own mother's matrilineage *brother*
3. male sib-mate of first ascending generation
4. any other male ego's mother calls *brother*

Behavioral gradations correspond to the normative except when common residence brings a female and any of her mother's half-brothers into close contact; in such a case the affective dimension of the tie betwen the two may counteract somewhat the absence of common matrilineage or sib membership.

I knew several pairs of mother's brother:sister's daughter, and can attest to the very close affectionate nature of the tie. Moreover, the relationship has much of the same transactional content as that of mother's brother:sister's son. To a somewhat less degree the same generalizations apply to the relationship between a female and her mother's matrilineage *brother*. In addition, in both cases sexual relations between the two are forbidden, but in the pairs I knew this issue did not obtrude, partly perhaps because of the age discrepancies involved. About the only normative element in the relationship between a female and her mother's sib *brother* is the taboo against sexual relations. As for the nature of the relationship with one of her mother's *brothers* by aggregation (nokihoro), I have no other information except that a mild incest taboo obtains.

Class II. FATHER'S SISTER'S HUSBAND:WIFE'S BROTHER'S DAUGHTER

Normative and behavioral gradations
1. husband of father's sister
2. husband of anyone ego calls *apu* (except own father-in-law)

As in the case of a male, there is little or no patterning involved in this relationship. It is true that sexual relations between the pair are proscribed, but in recording genealogies I came across a few marriages between distant affinal *papa* and *nonna*; and in retailing the sex adventures of other natives some of my informants recalled several instances of violation — it being quite apparent from their attitudes that the taboo has little weight.

Class III. HUSBAND'S FATHER:SON'S WIFE

Normative and behavioral gradations
1. husband's own father
2. husband's father's brother
3. anyone husband calls *father*
4. brother's wife's father

A woman's father-in-law plays an important role in her life, beginning at the time of her betrothal and terminating only at his death. It is mainly his resources that finance the betrothal and wedding, and not infrequently it is through his initiative that the marriage is arranged — from first negotiation to establishment of residence. In many cases a father actually selects his son's bride, and in most other instances he has some influence over the son's choice. As soon as the betrothal is formalized the girl and her fiancé's father call each other *papa* and *nonna*, and are expected to behave toward each other accordingly. The fiancé's father assumes direct interest in the young woman's conduct; he expects her to be industrious, modest, and chaste, and if she is not he may influence his son to break off the engagement. He is particularly concerned that the young woman preserve her sexual services for his son, and can be counted on to demand return of the betrothal gift if he hears of any lapses on her part. As it happens very often that his son's fiancée actually resides in his household, he can exercise close surveillance over her actions, and it was my observation that some prospective fathers-in-law do just that. One of my neighbors guarded his son's adventurous fiancée so jealously that she complained of not being able to visit the toilet stream without his spying or accusing her of trysting. Most other prospective fathers-in-law leave the actual surveillance to their wives but their concern is no less serious.

I did not hear of a single instance of an actual or prospective father-in-law seducing his daughter-in-law; in fact, informants were genuinely scandalized by my query. Relations between the two are characterized by avoidance of all signs of sexual intimacy, although this does not bar their discussing sexual matters — a father-in-law will not hesitate to confront his daughter-in-law with accusations of infidelity, and he openly chides her if she is slow to conceive after marriage or if she conceives while still nursing an infant.

If father-in-law and daughter-in-law continue to reside in the same hamlet, as is often the case, the strict surveillance and the formality usually give way to an easier and even affectionate relationship — still, however, colored by some degree of respect and obedience on the part of the woman. For example, in the village of Turuŋum I watched old Asinara on many occasions chatting and working with his daughters-in-law as well as his daughters, and the only distinction in behavior I could detect was that the former were more respectful and if anything more genuinely solicitous of Asinara's wishes.

When father-in-law and mother's brother are identical, then this individual will have an even stronger claim over the respect as well as the affection of his *nonna*.

There is little evidence of patterning in the relations between a female and the other kinsmen classed as *fathers-in-law*. Sexual relations are proscribed but the rules are often violated.

*tata:naramana.*

Class I. FATHER'S SISTER'S SON:MOTHER'S BROTHER'S DAUGHTER

A male's most eligible mate is his mother's brother's daughter, whom he also calls *ḵemuroi*. When the two reside in the same hamlet they have, as children, frequent opportunities for playing together, and their playmates as well as their elders continually remind them jokingly of their marriageability. Later on they tend to be shy when together, either carrying on a love affair in "secrecy" or avoiding each other altogether. Usually their parents will encourage a match between them, and although this sometimes results in mutual affection and marriage, it leads in some other instances to profound dislike. Young men often complained to me of their parents' efforts to mate them with undesirable cross-cousins, "just to keep things straight."

# KIN RELATIONS

These terms are extended to include all *sons* of a female's father's *sisters* (matrilineage and sib) and to all *daughters* of a male's mother's *brothers*; and along with this extension goes an emphasis on marital eligibility.

Class II. OLDER SISTER'S HUSBAND:WIFE'S YOUNGER SISTER
HUSBAND'S OLDER BROTHER:YOUNGER BROTHER'S WIFE

The principal feature of this relationship is the social sanction against any behavior suggestive of sexual intercourse. The brother- and sister-in-law pair are expected to be friendly and reciprocally helpful, but to avoid any sign of adultery. Notwithstanding that, adultery of this kind is not unusual — common residence providing many opportunities for it; and if it is discovered it usually leads to conflict between pairs of brothers or sisters.

Natives also assert that this sexual taboo extends to spouses of all one's sib-mates ("we have affection for all our sib-mates and do not steal their spouses"), but the numerous cases of "adultery" between such persons indicate what little respect is paid to the norm.

The terms applied between these affinal kin exemplify an important principle of Siuai kinship terminology. The primary meaning of tata is "older brother" (male speaking); the primary meaning of naramana is "younger sister" (female speaking). In calling his wife's younger sister "naramana" a man adopts the term for her used by his wife, and vice versa.[29] A similar device is used frequently by the Siuai for identifying and addressing or referring to distant affinal kin.

*naramoŋ:mama*

Class I. MOTHER'S BROTHER'S SON:FATHER'S SISTER'S DAUGHTER

Marriage between these two cross-cousins is also favored, but to a slightly less degree than that between father's sister's son and mother's brother's daughter. The stronger preference for the latter type is probably to be explained by the circumstance that some matrilineage property (land and other economically useful resources), although passed from one generation to the next along the female line, tends at any one time to be publicly identified with male members of the matrilineage, with respect to use and disposal. A son-in-law who is also a sister's son is a matrilineage mate to whom a man can safely entrust active proprietorship over matrilineage property, whereas a son-in-law who is merely a wife's brother's son may belong to a different matrilineage or sib.

It is probably no accident that love trysts between a youth and one of his father's sister's *daughters* outnumbered all others I heard about — partly perhaps as a consequence of the lesser amount of pressure upon them to become married. There being no sexual taboos to restrain them and fewer implicit obligations upon them to form a permanent union, an affair between these two cross-cousins is apt to be both pleasantly adventurous and uncomplicated.

We shall consider this point later on, but it should be noted in passing that terminologically a male's father's sister's daughter is "older" than his mother's brother's daughter. This may be a reflection of the actual circumstance that most men are somewhat older than their wives; other things being equal, this would result in the father's sister's daughter being actually older than the mother's brother's daughter, as shown on the accompanying diagram.

On the other hand, property considerations may be involved. Ego's father and ego's father's sister's daughter belong to the same matrilineage, hence the latter, theoretically at least, has a voice in determining whether any of her matrilineage's land will be bequeathed to ego. Hence ego might be expected to be somewhat deferential towards his father's sister, as to an "older" person, and informants did suggest the desirability of this — although I have no data about behavior of this kind based on actual observation.

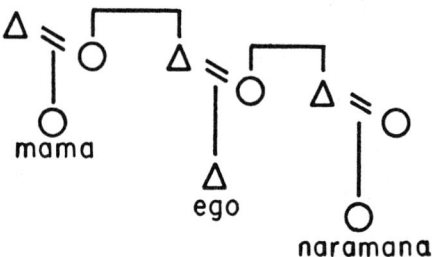

FIGURE 22

Class II. YOUNGER SISTER'S HUSBAND:WIFE'S OLDER SISTER
HUSBAND'S YOUNGER BROTHER:OLDER BROTHER'S WIFE

The rules governing this relationship are identical with those governing relations between affinal tata and naramana. I expected that adultery between a man and his *older* brother's wife or wife's *older* sister would be considered either less or more reprehensible, but after pointed inquiries I found this not to be the case. Moreover, among the many cases I recorded of adultery between affinal cross-cousins, neither type predominates to any significant degree.

It will be noted that the device of adopting the kinship term used by one's spouse also applies to this relationship.

*mama:mama* (father's sister's daughter:mother's brother's daughter). Although females related in this manner belong to different sibs, they would be difficult to distinguish from uterine sisters if they happen to dwell in the same hamlet, which is often the case. The fact that a man's sister's daughter has stronger claims on his matrilineage property than does his own daughter presumably introduces the possibility of tension between the two females, but I could uncover no instances of conflict resulting therefrom.

These usages of the term *mama* are widely extended to include sib *sisters* of both cross-cousins.

*poma:poma.*

Class I. BROTHER'S WIFE:HUSBAND'S SISTER

Like female cross-cousins, females related in this manner would be difficult to distinguish from sisters in terms of actual behavior. Because of betrothal customs and residence patterns they often live for a while in the same household and later on in the same hamlet. With a few exceptions, those pairs I knew were reciprocally affectionate and helpful. The exceptional cases involved older women who objected to the wanton ways of their brothers' younger wives and attempted to keep the latter in line.

In the event of a cross-cousin marriage the sisters-in-law may refer to one another as "sister-in-law-onto-cross-cousin" (*mamakoripoma*), but they usually continue to address one another as *mama*.

There are four other kinship terms commonly applied to affinal kin: *ŋonum:ŋonum* (wife's mother's brother:sister's daughter's husband); *kimaruko* (husband of wife's sister); *kimaru* (husband of daughter's daughter); and *eie nokihoro* ("sister by joining":wife of wife's brother). I could not discover any evidence of patterning in the relationships of the various relatives paired by these terms.

*Kin of Alternate Generations.* In Siuai the lives of alternate generations occasionally overlap by as much as some twenty years, and one frequently sees natives past puberty having one or more grandparents still living. The data on household and hamlet personnel, given elsewhere, show that many hamlets are made up of three generations of relatives, although households usually include only two.

Nephews are known to visit their mother's brothers for days at a time, but otherwise there is little large-scale or extended visiting — certainly there is nothing here comparable to the mass visiting of, say, the Samoans or the Orokolo. These circumstances increase the situational importance of common residence: the grandparents who live near a child will be the ones with whom he will interact most and develop strongest ties of affection. And this leads to another generalization about Siuai kinship: whatever the specific kinship connection may be, the relationship between relatives of alternate generations tends to exhibit mild deference on the part of the younger native, mixed with mutual affection;[30] and the more interaction there is, the more noticeable the affection becomes. Also, along with this affection usually goes mutual nonreciprocable[31] giving. Individuals differ, of course, and some grandparents, grandaunts, and granduncles may be feared or hated or despised because of individual traits and special situations, but these are exceptions. The transactional aspects of these relationships differ somewhat according to the specific kinship ties involved, but in observing everyday interaction I would have found it impossible to detect how pairs of individuals of alternate generation were actually related without having genealogical information, or without hearing the principals use kinship terms. The old man crooning to a child, or the old woman giving tidbits to a youth, could be anyone from a distant affinal granduncle or grandaunt to an actual grandparent. These generalizations about deference and the interdependence of interaction, affection, and nonreciprocable giving apply to all classes of relationships between close kin of alternate generations. Let us now see what qualifications, if any, have to be made about the behavior patterns of specific classes of pairs.

In presenting data on each of these classes only the primary meaning of each kinship term will be given. As in the case of the terms for "father" and "mother," the terms for relatives of alternate generations may be extended laterally by natives to almost any limit they desire. However, in the case of consanguineal kin of alternate generations the term is not usually extended in practice beyond the matrilineage of the individual through whom the relationship is traced, and, in the case of affinal kin of alternate generations the term is rarely extended beyond the articulating individual's own siblings.

Before commencing this list there is one further point to be made: in some cases sibling terms are used between kin of alternate generations, and there are innumerable instances of alternate generation kin having common interests, etc.; but otherwise the Siuai have not elaborated the ties between alternate generations into social units nor have they emphasized them in ritual activity.[32]

*teti*:NUPI (1) mother's mother:daughter's son;
(2) father's father's sister: brother's son's son.

The first pair belong to the same matrilineage, with all that that circumstance implies in the way of property ownership, mutual aid, ritual coöperation, taboo on sexual relations, etc. Also, the probability is that the woman called *teti* will be one of her matrilineage's First-borns, hence will hold some authority over the male she calls NUPI.

The only noteworthy aspect of the relationship of the second pair is the moral injunction against sexual intercourse. This requires no special sanction, because of the age discrepancy usually involved; and in the case of a more distantly related pair, when the taboo is occasionally broken the incident receives only mild disapproval. Insofar as I could determine, this taboo is not directly specific nor is it based on extension of any other specific kinship behavior pattern (e.g., *apu:imiho*); it is merely one application of the general injunction against sexual relations between most classes of close consanguineal relations.

*teti:nupi* (1) mother's mother:daughter's daughter;
(2) father's father's sister:brother's son's daughter.

As with teti:NUPI, the first pair belong to the same matrilineage, of which the older woman is usually a First-born.

There is no evidence of patterning specific to the relationship of the second pair.

*tata:naramoŋ* (1) mother's mother's brother:sister's daughter's son;
(2) father's father:son's son.

Being matrilineage mates the first pair are bound together closely by joint ownership of property, mutual obligations, ritual coöperation, etc.; and the elder man usually exercises greater control over the disposition of the common property. In the case of ego's own mother's mother's brother, the matrilineage tie is of course reinforced by the close tie both have with ego's mother.

In the case of the second pair it is unlikely that they will in common possess full or residual title to any property, although one of them may possess provisional rights to property held in residual title by the other. On the other hand, property owned by the older man may pass to the younger man's father and eventually to himself, through proper nori payments. Informants offered no generalizations on this point, but my few observations indicated to me that a native acts with more deference towards his father's father than towards his mother's mother's brother.

In instances where actual cross-cousin marriages have taken place, ego's father's father and his mother's mother's brother may, of course, be the same individual.

EIE:*eie* (1) mother's mother's brother:sister's daughter's daughter;
(2) father's father:son's daughter.

In connection with the first pair, the generalizations made about the mother's mother's brother:sister's daughter's son also apply, and in addition there prevails the sib incest taboo.

I could discover no evidence of additional patterning specific to the relationship of the second pair other than the injunction on sexual relations.

Occasionally a man applies the term "eie" to the wife of any man he calls NUPI, but there is no behavior pattern specific to this kind of relationship.

AIIA:NUPI (1) mother's father:daughter's son;
(2) father's mother's brother:sister's son's son.

There are no other distinctive behavior patterns characteristic of the relationship between mother's father and daughter's son. In connection with the second pair relationship, however, it will be recalled that a native's father's matrilineage mates, including his father's mother's brothers, have the power to deny him some of his "inheritance" unless he provides an adequate funeral feast for his father, their matrilineage mate. I found that this obligation of the younger man to his father's matrilineage mates also carried over into other transactions between such pairs, and in fact characterized most aspects of this kind of relationship.

AIIA:*nupi* (1) mother's father:daughter's daughter;
(2) father's mother's brother:sister's son's daughter.

The generalizations stated for the relationship AIIA:NUPI also apply here. In addition, sexual relations are tabooed between natives thus related — although I recorded several marriages between distant AIIA:*nupi*.

*aiia*:NUPI mother's father's sister:brother's daughter's son
*aiia*:*nupi* mother's father's sister:brother's daughter's daughter

Natives explain these uses of the term "aiia" by stating that a male (or female) simply extends the term applied to mother's father to all the latter's siblings. Aside from the taboo on sexual relations between aiia:NUPI, no special behavior patterning applies in either of these relationships.

*mama:naramana* (1) father's mother:son's daughter; (2) mother's mother's brother's wife:husband's sister's daughter's daughter

Natives do not specify norms for either of these two relationships; nor was I able to discover any actual behavior patterning specifically applicable.

*mama:naramoŋ* (1) father's mother:son's son; (2) mother's mother's brother's wife:husband's sister's daughter's son; (3) wife's mother's mother:daughter's daughter's husband.

It is interesting and perhaps significant that both males and females distinguish terminologically between their son's son (*naramoŋ*) and their son's daughter (eie, *naramana*), whereas they apply the same term, *nupi*, to both son and daughter of their daughters. It is not impossible that this may be an adaptation to the residence situation, i.e., the predominance of patrilocality and hence the practical necessity of differentiating between the male and female grandchildren with whom one frequently interacts.

The only other noteworthy feature of any of these pair relationships concerns the second: during my stay in northeast Siuai there occurred three instances of a man marrying a widow of his mother's mother's brother, and genealogies revealed several more. In each instance the woman became the man's second or third wife.[33] Terminologically, the woman is a *cross-cousin* of the generationally younger man, a fact which parallels the preference accorded this kind of marriage. (I find caution necessary here, because I cannot state with any assurance either that a man marries his mother's mother's brother's widow because he calls her *cross-cousin*, or that he calls her *cross-cousin* because of the desirability of this kind of marriage.) In this connection, it is interesting to note that a male's preferred mates among his kinswomen (i.e., his female cross-cousins) are to be found in his own generation and in the second ascending generation — but not in the second descending generation. In other words, the kinship system encourages men to marry into the ascending alternate generation but not into the descending one — a factor which would seem to promote the personal security of older widows as well as to lessen the likelihood that older men will monopolize young widows.

Kinship terms applied to the third ascending and descending generations are the same as those used for the first ascending and descending generations respectively, thus emphasizing the principle of identity of alternate generations, at least in a terminological sense. On the other hand, actual overlap between the life span of a native with that of his or her great-grandparents occurs rarely if at all. There was no case of such an overlap in northeast Siuai during my stay there, and my queries about relationship norms in hypothetical cases convinced me that natives have given no thought to this matter.

# KIN RELATIONS 275

In the course of recording genealogies I did discover a few cases of overlap between a native and one of his great-grandparent's sib *siblings*, but I could not discover whether kinship terms are normally used between such remotely related pairs.

## *THE EXPRESSION OF KINSHIP "EMOTION" IN DIRGES*

The visitor to Siuai may be able to infer the existence of affection, deference, etc., among relatives by merely observing their actions: the tenderness with which children are nurtured, the good-natured banter between matrilineage *brothers*, the companionable coöperation between most spouses, the innumerable instances of ungrudging helpfulness between all kinds of close relatives, and many other indications. Otherwise, in contrast to the readiness with which they advertise dislikes and enmities, the Siuai rarely verbalize or publicize the affection they may feel for one another. The one occasion on which natives give public and dramatic expression to affection and amity is a cremation. On these occasions nearly every guest who can talk joins in the lamentation with a dirge expressing some appropriate sentiment for the deceased. The dirge may be long or short, an original expression composed for the occasion or an old and well-known standardized lament. The longer dirges are sung either by close relatives as they circle the burning pyre, or, in the case of a funeral for a senile native, by distant relatives after the cremation fire has died down.[34] The shorter dirge phrases are intoned by distant relatives as they stand in a wide circle watching the burning pyre. The example on page 276 is of a short dirge as it is sung in Motuna by a distant sib *mother* at the cremation of a young boy.

Here are some other short, fairly standardized dirges, usually sung by distant relatives and with expression varying from racking sorrow to perfunctory woodenness. The lyrics closely resemble that of the example just given.

By a man for an elderly sib *sister*: "Oh my *sister*, valued as shell money." (That is, good as gold!)

By a woman for a young sib *son*: "My son, oh my little hornbill *son*. Your *mother* is unconsolable." (Note: the hornbill is known for its clean and unruffled feathers.)

By a man for a young sib nephew: "My *nephew*, oh my *nephew*. Where can I ever find you now?"

By a woman for a sib *brother*: "My *brother*, oh my *brother*. What form of ghost-animal will you become so that I can see you again?"

By a man for a male cross-cousin: "My cross-cousin, oh my friend, cross-cousin. You have gone away forever from the place that your father left to you, the place where you and I used to walk about together."

By a man for a sib *brother*: "My elder *brother*, oh my elder *brother*. Where have you gone, leaving me to walk about alone on the places our *fathers* left to us?"

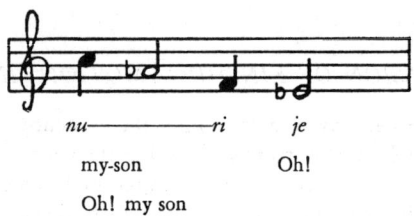

*nu———ri    je*
my-son      Oh!
Oh! my son

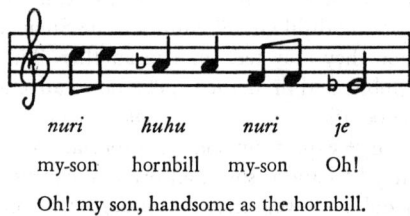

*nuri    huhu    nuri    je*
my-son   hornbill   my-son   Oh!
Oh! my son, handsome as the hornbill.

*rokuna    romanata         simmiŋ    nuri    je*
thy-mother  behind         thou-hast-left  my-son   Oh!
Oh! my son, you have gone away and left your mother

*nu———ri    je*
my-son      Oh!

By a woman for her brother's son: "My brother's son, oh my brother's son. You have gone away and I grieve for you."

By a man or woman for a *grandchild*: "My *grandchild* (nupi), little one. You who were like a small bird."

By a man or woman for a young *daughter*: "Oh my daughter, tender little plant seed."

In most cases the deceased is addressed as a kinsman or kinswoman, no matter how attenuated the tie, but occasionally other terms of address are used, as in the following:

By a man for a close friend: "My friend, I grieve for you. Our talk (companionship) used to give me pleasure, but now you are gone and I won't see you again."

By friends and neighbors for a high-ranking man: "Oh mumi, feast-giver, basket of shell-money."

Next is a longer lament as it is sung in Motuna by a matrilineage *brother* of a deceased man:

*tata        hikum              je*
Older-*brother*  invulnerable warrior  Oh!
Oh! older-*brother*, invulnerable warrior,

*ro   ne   kiuroi            poŋosere       je*
thou  oh!  bundle of shell money  demented one  Oh!
Oh! you valued one, you demented one,

*mamaka        itavotomim              je*
While-I-mourn  thou-makest-me-to-stand-up  Oh!
You have caused me to interrupt my mourning [for some other death]

*tata        hikum              je*
Older-*brother*  invulnerable warrior  Oh!
Oh! older-*brother*, invulnerable warrior,

*raramoŋi           vako    kunnamo       je*
thy-younger-*brother*  where?  stroll-about  Oh!
Where can your younger brother stroll about now?

*u'kisa     urukiŋ      hoŋoua'     je*
Long-ago   they-lived   old-ones    Oh!
In days gone by, when our old people were alive,

*toku   putakahŋum                je*
not    they-fenced-out-one-another  Oh!
They were considerate and helpful to one another.

*impa   nuiiom    kitoria    je*
Now    we-live   children   Oh!
Whereas in our times, we descendants of theirs

*putaputanuukom*
We-fence-out-one-another
We lead separate and selfish lives.

*tata       hikum       je*
older-*brother* invulnerable warrior  Oh!
Oh! older-*brother*, invulnerable warrior

*raraokaki      vaka      je*
Raraoka-on  garden-site  Oh!
Your garden site on Raraoka

*impa      rarauitum*
now      it-will-remain-unworked.
will now remain unworked.

*tapaŋi        moŋi        romo        sihin        je*
clearer-of-it  worker-of-it  behind  he-left-it  Oh!
Now that the one who cleared and worked it has left it

*ho ko raraokaki      rariŋ      je*
that   Raraoka      it-remains idle  Oh!
the place called Raraoka is now deserted.

*kinikiniroinoru*
when-thou-crashed-down-like-a-huge-tree

*oromonuro*
when-thou-left-it-shadeless

*pim*
thou-went-away
Your downfall [death], like the falling of a huge tree, left the area around it without protection.

*tui        erihitumoŋi        sihino        je*
when-thou-lived  thou-fenced-in-the-place  Oh!
Your being there protected the place like a strong fence.

*tata      hikum        je*
Older-*brother*  invulnerable warrior  Oh!
Oh! older-*brother*, invulnerable warrior.

These stanzas are sung to music like the accompanying example.

There follow a number of examples of longer dirges, usually sung by close relatives of the deceased. The musical settings of all of them closely resemble that of the example just given, with tempos varying from the dead-march singing around the burning pyre to the lively and cheerful dance-time delivery performed in the morning after cremation of a senile native. The following have been freely translated:

By a woman for her own daughter:

Oh my daughter, little daughter.
They said you must be taken eastward to the "house-sick,"[35] and I agreed, telling you that you would get well once you were there. But you did not get well, so now your mother (metaphorically) drinks your blood, oh little daughter.
We went along together to the "house-sick," and then something made you die, oh my daughter, so I had them carry you westward to our home where we could cremate you.
The kupunas caused you to be born unwell; they beset your birth with difficulties.
Oh my daughter, if only I could follow you.
As you lay sick you whispered to me: "Mother, I'll never get well. A great pain fills my chest."
Your *papa* (the singer's brother) wanted to have you carried to the "house-sick," and I agreed, thinking that the "doctor" there would make you well. But he did not make you well, and now I have lost my only spear (child).

By a man for his own son:

My son, oh little one, my son.
Now that you are stretched out in death your body has become long. When you and I used to walk about together you were not so long.
You, Miruho (the singer addresses his daughter), run to your sib-mates and tell them that Keia's (the singer's) son has died.
Oh my son, little one, my son.

In another dirge sung by a man for his son, the singer blames himself for having been the indirect cause of his son's death, and in voicing this sentiment presumably attempts to elicit additional sympathy for himself:

My son, oh hornbill, my son.
Many were the times when you and I clambered about the steep paths near our home, and never did you fall. How often we used to climb over the mountains without a mishap.
Then came that day when you fell (and died), just because your father (the singer) had a longing to eat baked meat, and took you along to hunt opossums. Now, instead of feasting on opossum your father eats (metaphorically) your rotting flesh. Oh hornbill, my son.
If the living could follow the dead I would follow you. I would leave the life of the living to be with you, oh hornbill son.

The following dirge was composed long ago by a woman whose husband was slain in a fight at the club-house of the leader, Soŋi, of Turuŋum:

> Oh my husband, you who were like the hornbill.
> Alas, none of your own people heard your cries as you were being killed at Runiŋkini (the name of the club-house).
> Oh my husband, hornbill husband.
> I, your wife, (metaphorically) drink your blood. I, your wife, eat your rotting flesh.
> When the almond and breadfruit seasons come around again I shall think of you with my first mouthful and with my last.
> I, your wife, am about to hang myself from sorrow, oh hornbill husband.

By a widow for her brother:

> Oh, my brother, you who are valued like fine shell money. Your sister has come to weep for you. The ku'utoŋ bird (a rail?) stays at home eating its fill, but I come here to mourn for you, oh my brother.
> If my husband were alive he would have brought a log for your pyre, and I would have contributed a pig for your funeral. But alas, I cannot, and I am ashamed. Your sister is ashamed. As it is, I am unable to show my sorrow (by deeds), and can only mourn with words. If only my husband were alive we could contribute a pig, as was always our custom.
> Oh my brother, where will I find you now?

In this dirge by a man for his wife's mother, the singer alludes to slander which has been directed against him, presumably in an effort to arouse sympathy for himself and shame his belittlers:

> Oh mother-in-law. You who are like a hornbill.
> Who do you think this is mourning for you? Do you not know that it is I, the one they call Yam-pole,[36] weeping for you? It is I, the one whom people belittle by calling "Yam-pole," who am mourning.
> Where shall I, your yam-pole son-in-law, be able to see you now? Where can I find you now?

By a man for his mother's father:

> Mother's father, man of renown: I say these words over and over; I repeat them again and again.
> I come to mourn for you at daybreak; I weep for you in the early dawn.[37]
> When I arrived at Sikurai (to attend your cremation), when I came up to this place also called Raisiku,[38] and was given only ten spans of shell money (for providing a pig for the funeral feast), only a mere handful of shell money, I nearly turned around to go home, but then I said to myself: "Never mind the money," and I remained, Oh mother's father, man of renown.
> Oh mother's father, who is there for me to walk about with now?
> Hey, all of you, (addressed to the other funeral guests) clear out of the

way so that I can perform my dance. My back is cold from standing still; my bones are cold from doing nothing.

Oh, mother's father, you were like the great ficus tree, like the walls of a big house; where you were you gave shelter and protection. And as it is when a great tree falls, your falling (death) has left the place empty, oh mother's father, renowned.

By a man for a distant cross-cousin:

Cross-cousin, oh my friend: I say these words over and over. I come to mourn for you at daybreak; I weep for you in the early dawn. Oh cross-cousin, my friend.

Cross-cousin, if I were not so close to you as a shelf is to its wall; if I were only loosely linked to you, I would not have dared to come (so far away from home) across the Hiri creek. I would not have dared to cross the Tohoro creek and enter the territory where I have killed so many people in times past.

And now you, my sib-mates (he addresses the relatives who accompanied him to the cremation), if others suddenly attack us while we are here, we must not throw down our spears and run. We must not be like some men who throw down their spears and run when attacked away from home.

Cross-cousin, oh my friend. Who can I visit with again?

By a man for one of his father's matrilineage mates:

My *father*, oh warrior father: I say these words over and over. I come to mourn for you at daybreak; I weep for you in the early dawn.

Tatoua said to me: "Where do you think you're going?"

Kerukeru asked me: "Why are you here? You don't usually mourn (contribute shell money or pigs for your relatives' funerals)."

In this manner did they defame me. But they lie when they claim that I am a stone-heart who does not mourn properly for his relatives; for here I come bringing one hundred spans of shell money, Oh *father*.

If any friend of mine asks me to contribute money for his funeral, naturally I will do so. Of course I will do so. When I go to funerals I always carry along pigs or shell money.

Oh *father*, where will I find you now?

By a man for an older sib *brother*:

Elder *brother*, invulnerable warrior. Where can your younger *brother* find you now?

When I arrived here at Piruvasi a stranger said to me: "Peu has died; why have you come?" Thus did a stranger speak to me, oh elder *brother*.

I replied, saying: "I have come to mourn and to remove ashes from the cremation fire." [39] Thus did I speak, oh warrior elder *brother*.

In the old days when you and I were close friends you made me a false promise, saying: "When I, your older *brother*, die they will give you a whole *kainoru*;[40] they will fill a basket with a kainoru and carry it to you (so that you can contribute a pig for my funeral)." But no one has brought a kainoru to me. You promised me falsely when you told me that they would bring one to me.

Oh elder *brother*, invulnerable warrior, where can your younger *brother* find you now?

The following dirge was composed and sung by a man who believed himself badly used by others in money matters, and who therefore wanted it plainly understood that he expected repayment for the money he contributed for this funeral.

Mother's *mother*, high ranking, handsome one.

When I returned to my home over there in the east and was told: "your mother's *mother* sleeps," I said: "I shall hurry and send along a *momoruta*[41] (to help buy pigs to reward the mourners at the funeral). If it is not repaid right away, then it can be repaid when my mother's *mother's* widower dies. But if it isn't repaid then, I will litigate for it.

The long dirges just given are representative in form and content of all those collected in the course of field work.[42] In very few instances were the dirges new in the sense of having been composed for the occasion on which I first heard them. The Siuai tend to use old dirges over and over again, only adapting them slightly to the situation at hand. Noteworthy features of dirge lyrics are the numerous stereotyped phrases, the repetition of lines, and the frequent use of simile and metaphor. Several features of the content in lyrics are also worth noting: nostalgic allusions to "the good old days" of firmer loyalties; eulogy phrased in terms of wealth and warfare; the attitude that mourning must be backed by a tangible exchange to be sincere; and the use of dirges to air grievances and elicit sympathies. Dirges also provide insight into eschatological beliefs, for example, they contain no allusions to a general reunion of relatives in the hereafter.[43]

There is one other point of significance about Siuai dirges: no matter how tenuous the tie may be, natives usually stress kinship above all other kinds of relationship on the occasion of death.

## RELATIONS BETWEEN KINSHIP GROUPS

Up to this point we have been looking at kinship mainly from the standpoint of intra-group and person-to-person relationships. Let us now shift our viewpoint and see what kinds of relations obtain *between* kinship groups. The question can be put in this way: On what occasions does a Siuai act as a representative of one kinship group towards representatives of other kinship groups?

To begin with, in the ordinary business of everyday living there are innumerable occasions on which an adult represents his household in dealings with representatives of other households. For example, a woman nursing a sick child and unable to go to the garden borrows taro from a neighboring household in order to feed her family. Or, a man complains to a neighbor about some mischief done by the latter's children. Also, representatives of the separate households composing a hamlet occasionally deal with the *Old-one* of the hamlet acting in his capacity as hamlet head.[44] On the other hand, there is little or no occasion for relations *between* hamlets *qua* hamlets.

There is much evidence of relationships between matrilineages, particularly in matters concerning ownership and transfer of land. Full or residual titles to most Siuai land rest with whole matrilineages, hence most disputes over landownership eventually broaden out into disputes between whole matrilineages, represented by their respective *First-borns*. In many instances negotiations concerning land transfer follow the same pattern.[45] Matrilineages also act towards other matrilineages in connection with the affairs of individual members. For example, serious quarrels over such matters as charges of theft or sorcery usually serve to mobilize the principals' matrilineages; and if a person's death is believed to have been caused by sorcery, then his matrilineage mates sometimes act as a group to bring about the magical annihilation of the suspected sorcerer and all his matrilineage-mates.

We have also considered situations in which matrilineage-mates act together with reference to other individuals or to family units — for example, in connection with relations between *true-owners* and *attachers*, and in connection with the hostile demonstration (mih) before the widow and offspring of a deceased matrilineage-mate.[46]

Summarizing, then, communication takes place between the following kinds of Siuai kinship groups: household-household, matrilineage-matrilineage, and household-matrilineage; and these communications involve many types of transactions and "emotional" expressions.

When generalizing about the relationships of individual relatives it was found useful to do so in terms of transactions and expressive-behavior patterns. Can we generalize with the same degree of precision and comprehensiveness about these dimensions of relationships between groups? I believe not. Precision is possible in the case of classes of individual relatives because their kinhip statuses vis à vis each other are fixed by birth and marriage. In contrast, matrilineages are not graded according to seniority,[47] nor are households — except insofar as a son's household is "junior" to his father's or to any other older male relative's. Moreover, it is not appropriate to describe matrilineages or households as having socio-political *rank*.

As we shall see, *rank* appertains most specifically to persons. Relatives and neighbors assist an individual to acquire rank; and they bask in his renown. Also, the close relatives of a high-ranking man enjoy privileged positions so long as he maintains his rank; but that is all. Some households and matrilineages possess more wealth than others, but wealth and rank are not synonymous in Siuai. It is only in a very limited sense, then, that we can speak of one kinship group as being "superior" to another. The privileges that go with this kind of limited superiority involve some show of deference on the part of members of the "inferior" group, but the relative positions of the two groups may change. Also, the relations between a pair of groups may be described as "hostile" at one time and "amicable" at another.

A similar situation prevails with respect to *transactions* between groups, but there is one question which may be raised in this connection. On the basis of comparative data (see especially *Les Structures élémentaires de la parenté*, by Claude Lévi-Strauss, published in Paris in 1949), a reasonable working hypothesis has been put forth to the effect that in a more or less "stable" society exchanges between two interacting kinship groups will be found to balance over a period of time. Now, in Siuai most kinds of transactions which take place between kinship groups involve scarce goods of such variable valuation that rather elaborate equations would be needed to test the hypothesis, and I do not have sufficient data to construct a thoroughly credible formula for all types of intergroup transactions. For one type of transaction, however, my information is fuller. I refer to that of *marriage*. Let us review our data on Siuai marriage and see what light it can throw on intergroup relations. This is a matter which has aroused great interest among anthropologists, and occupies a central position in discussions of kinship structure. We can best begin by asking: What are the social units involved in primary-marriage transactions?

In connection with most Siuai primary marriages it is nearly always the nuclear families of the two principals that appear at first sight to be most directly involved. In the case of youths without private accumulations of money — and this includes most of them — their fathers have to supply both betrothal gift and brideprice, and consequently play decisive roles in agreement and negotiation. Lacking a father, a youth may be aided in this enterprise by a maternal uncle or elder brother or any other close relative, but in all such cases the aid is usually considered to be a loan which has to be repaid. A few youths earn enough money on plantations to contract marriages — they must of course convert the Australian coin into native currency — and they are consequently relatively free agents in contracting their own marriages; moreover, this kind of independence is considered perfectly proper, even commendable.

At first sight, the other contracting party in a primary marriage would appear to be the female's family, represented by her father or, if she has none, by her stepfather or uterine brothers or any other close kinsman. Usually her maternal uncle is allowed a voice in the proceedings, but his views are given decisive weight only if he is a man of high rank.

Next, comes the question: What kinds of items are exchanged in connection with primary marriages, and what are the structural implications of these transactions?

It will be recalled that the betrothal gifts — both "marker" and the regular one — consist of a strand or two of high-value shell currency, and these are eventually turned over to the female to use and dispose of as she wishes. No part of this gift should be retained by her father or anyone else. The manner of disposing of this gift in the event of death or divorce [48] seems to bear out the natives' assertion that it is indeed a "payment" to the wife for some of the services, mainly sexual, which she renders her husband. The fact that the husband's father may actually provide the betrothal gift does not mean that he thereby acquires any part of the woman, services or otherwise. In helping his son he is merely *sharing*, that is, carrying out his obligation to his son within the context of their intra-family relationships.

Consider next the brideprice of common shell currency paid to the bride's father (or some other relative) by or on behalf of the groom. The reader will recall that this money should be and normally [49] is used to buy pigs for the wedding feast, an equal amount of pork being provided for the feast directly by the groom or his father. The upshot of these actions is that the groom (or his father) foots the entire bill for a wedding feast which *both* parties attend as co-hosts. Now, most Siuai feasts serve to enhance the host's prestige, but I have already recorded my impression [50] that weddings are largely women's affairs. I did not once hear a wedding feast specifically mentioned as a factor in anyone's quest for renown. Men regard the whole occasion as something to be gotten over with, and the groom usually looks upon it as a boring or painfully embarrassing affair. For women, however, and particularly for the bride and her companions, it is a thoroughly enjoyable festival.

In return for its expenditure on the wedding feast, what does the party of the husband acquire, other than the little amount of prestige enhancement that may possibly result from it?

This being a matrilineally biased society, it cannot reasonably be maintained that the brideprice "buys" the woman's offspring for the husband's party, as is the case in certain patrilineal societies. In fact, it should be made clear that it is usually the husband alone who receives direct compensation for the brideprice.[51] It is true that a youth's family receives the benefits of his fiancée's services when the latter moves to her fiancé's household before nuptials, but this does not occur in all instances, and in any case after the nuptial ceremony couples usually live and work on their own. Moreover, as in the case of the betrothal gift, the groom's father's contribution to the brideprice merely constitutes an instance of *sharing* within the context of intra-family relationships. Rephrased, then, the question becomes: What direct compensation does the husband receive in return for the brideprice?

First of all, there are the domestic and sexual services which the woman performs for him; and second, there are the provisional tenure rights which he secures in land identified with his wife. But let us look at these acquisitions a little closer.

Siuai marriage is based on the expectation of an *equitable* division of labor for man and wife, and according to Siuai evaluations the contributions of both spouses do in fact balance in most marriages. In terms of man-hours it is true that the wife works about four times as long as her husband in household subsistence activities, but this is theoretically balanced by the differential valuation placed by this culture upon male and female skills. As for a man's rights to land identified with his wife, this might appear to be a more substantial return for his brideprice — but for the fact that there is little jural basis to such claims. Moreover, the husband is left without either of these forms of "compensation" if his wife dies or if the marriage ends in divorce. No matter how soon after marriage either of these events takes place the brideprice cannot ordinarily be returned, it having usually been consumed at the wedding feast.

Even with all these qualifications, however, it would seem that the husband receives better compensation for his expenditures than does the wife's family, who in return for their loss of a daughter-sister seem to acquire only a little prestige, if that, at the time of the wedding. In fact, looked at from the viewpoint of the principals and their families, the transactions which validate a primary marriage do not appear to balance according to any Siuai evaluation criteria that I know of. It is true that there are some families which are linked by more or less balanced exchanges of women — or, rather, functions of women, and this is considered an ideal arrangement provided the brideprices are paid and the exchanges are not simultaneous; and provided someone other than the women's brothers carry out the negotiations.[52] However, such families are few in number, and I am reluctant to propose that they constitute the ideal model on which are based, consciously or unconsciously, all other Siuai marriage transactions. If we are to maintain the reasonable hypothesis that marriage exchanges involve *balanced* transactions, then it is my belief that we must look for an explanation of these transactions beyond the social units immediately involved.

The Siuai express preference for both matrilateral and patrilateral cross-cousin marriage, and it will be recalled that throughout Siuai many matrilineages tend to be paired with respect to intermarriage; there are some neighborhoods made up wholly of pairs of matrilineages whose members have been intermarrying for generations. Such marriages conform to the most "correct" Siuai mating norms, and have important implications for social "stability" — among other things, the intermarrying matrilineages become *local* descent groups. Now, in connection with such marriages, betrothal gifts and brideprices change hands and wedding feasts are held in the conventional manner, but the question of transactional "balance" takes on new meaning. For, over the years, the numbers of women (read: functions of women) exchanged between two such local descent groups do more or less balance; and from this point of view, the brideprice is quite superfluous to what might be considered the more basic transaction, an implicitly reciprocal exchange of women's functions between two local descent groups. From this it would appear that each such marriage may be viewed as *two* kinds of transactions. First, it is one of a series of reciprocal exchanges of women's functions between two local descent groups; and secondly, it is a more or less private contractual arrangement between the groom and the bride, as individuals.[53] In this light, I suggest that the fathers or other family representatives of the bride and groom are to be considered agents and not parties to the contract, and that the brideprice — or rather the festival provided by it — is best understood as a *ceremonial* gift given directly to the bride by or on behalf of the groom.[54]

I must hasten to add that Siuai society does not consist entirely of maritally discrete pairs of intermarrying matrilineages. It is true that such pairs do exist, but in the more typical situation, matrilineage A — while having most of its marital links with matrilineage B — will also have links with matrilineages C, D, etc.; the different sizes of matrilineages make this almost inevitable. In other words, in many specific instances the woman-exchange relationship between two matrilineages may not even approximate a balance over the years. Nevertheless, in all such instances the pattern of events and the kinds of goods exchanged are the same, so it could be held that the premise of reciprocity which underlies marriage between two continuously intermarrying local descent groups, also underlies, implicitly, every other primary marriage.[55]

I offer the above interpretation as one way of "explaining" the somewhat puzzling features of Siuai marriage transactions. Perhaps it is not the correct way; some readers may see implications in the data which I cannot see because of my too intense preoccupation with ethnographic details. Several alternative "explanations" might conceivably fit better than the one given. For example, it may well be that the working hypothesis I began with constitutes a false assumption; that is, it may *not* be safe to assume that transactions between two interacting kinship groups will be found to balance, or — what is more usual — to trend towards balance, since in reality social relationships are rarely ever static. In other words, this rather tedious argument may have been entirely gratuitous. For my part, however, I believe that comparative data lend so much weight to this working hypothesis that it cannot be altogether ignored.

Another conceivable "explanation" is that each marriage constitutes a balanced transaction: the functions of a woman for those of a man. It is well known that in some matrilineal societies the bride's relatives retain the offspring of a marriage and compensate the relatives of the groom for use of the latter's services.[56] Applying this arrangement to Siuai, we might then regard the woman's functions as being the "compensation" given to the man's relatives. Actually I do not believe that this explanation fits Siuai marriage. The woman's "group" (i.e., matrilineage) does "retain" her offspring, but only in the sense that the latter become members of their matrilineage. Moreover, as we have already seen, the woman's functions are not transferred to her husband's "group." There remains, however, some evidence which might be considered as supporting the "explanation" that a single marriage constitutes the balanced transaction: the functions of a woman for those of a man. I recorded several cases wherein a man prevailed upon a sister's son to reside near him by offering his daughter to the latter in marriage.

Before leaving the subject of marriage let us see whether rank has anything to do with marriage transactions. Informants told me that formerly only the son of a high-ranking mumi was permitted to marry another mumi's daughter, and that the latter could be taken only as a first wife. Today this ideal still prevails, but in actual practice it is partly ignored. Nowadays marriages take place between persons whose fathers are of widely different *rank*, and there is no consistency as to whether the bride's or the groom's father happens to rank higher. If the bride's father is high ranking, however, a higher brideprice is demanded, so that it usually transpires that the father of the groom must in such cases be wealthy if not high-ranking.

In any event, the larger brideprice merely goes towards cutting another pig for the wedding feast, and no one's prestige receives significant *enhancement* from the affair — although the convention of paying a higher brideprice for the daughter of a high-ranking man may be interpreted as serving to *maintain* the latter's status.

Rank does, however, have some implications regarding choice in residence. The high-ranking man who already has a wife does not ordinarily move his residence in connection with subsequent marriages. Also, youths with high-ranking fathers tend to reside near their fathers, but if one of these marries the daughter of a maternal uncle it is not unlikely that he will move to the latter's hamlet no matter what the latter's rank may be. Within certain limitations, men can acquire renown and raise themselves in rank wherever they may reside; and the disabilities connected with being an *Attacher* can easily be overcome.[57]

### KINSHIP

*Normative.* The logic underlying Siuai terminology for primarily consanguineal relatives is represented on Figures 23 and 24. This logic is, obviously, based on the assumption underlying the native kinship model that all marriages be "correct," that is, that they are between own cross-cousins. This terminological system may be extended vertically by the principle of the identity of alternate generations, laterally by the principle of the identity of siblings, and — in all directions — by use of the device known in pidgin as "helping." [58] Here are some other generalizations that can be made about kinship terminology:

1. Theoretically there is no limit to the possible extension of kinship terms, vertically or laterally.

## KIN RELATIONS

2. Kinship *distance*, vertical as well as lateral, is expressed by use of such qualifying terms as *meŋ* ("true" or "own"), *pooki* ("strong," "close"), and *turumai* ("distant"). However, there is not entire consistency in the use of such terms.

3. The *lumping* of relatives into broader categories (e.g., *imo*, "my-sibmate"; *nuri'*, "my-son's-(and my wife's) sib-mates") is a commonly used device. Other linguistic devices used for specifying relatives are:

*Pairing*: e.g., *monoŋo* (a pair of *brothers*), *monomaharo* (a pair of sisters-in-law).

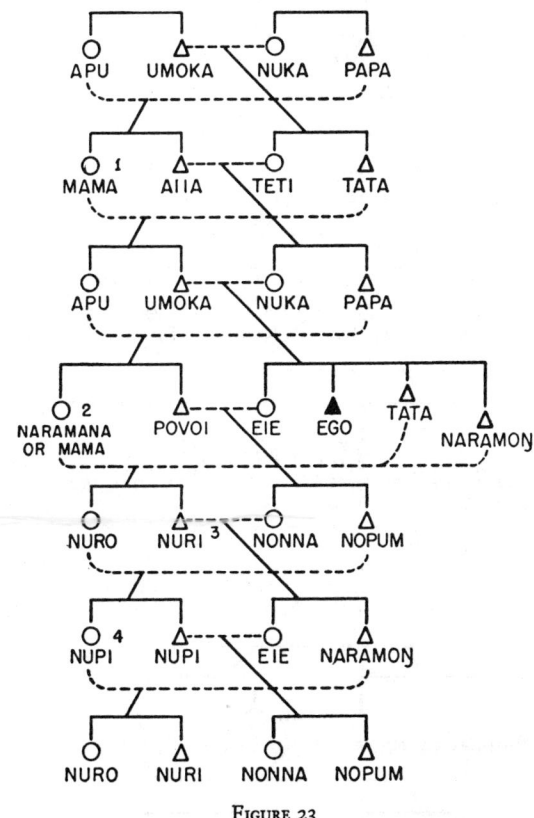

FIGURE 23

1. If this woman were not ego's father's mother or if she were not married to ego's mother's mother's brother, she would be "lumped" with her brother and called "aiia."

2. See pp. 268–269 to determine which term should be used here.

3. If ego's sister's daughter's husband is not ego's *son* he calls him "ŋonum" (reciprocally "ŋonum").

4. If this female is married to ego's son's son or sister's daughter's son, ego calls her "naramana."

## A SOLOMON ISLAND SOCIETY

*Joining* (*nokihoro*, "agglomeration"): e.g., *eie-nokihoro* ("my-opposite-sex-half-sibling").

*Compounding*: e.g., *tatakorinura* (male speaking: "my father-in-law-who-is-also-my-mother's-brother").

4. Age distinctions among same-sex siblings are specified only within ego's own generation. And in this connection it will be recalled that among cross-cousins, a father's sister's daughter is terminologically conceived to be "older" (i.e., *mama*) than is the mother's brother's daughter (i.e., *naramana*).

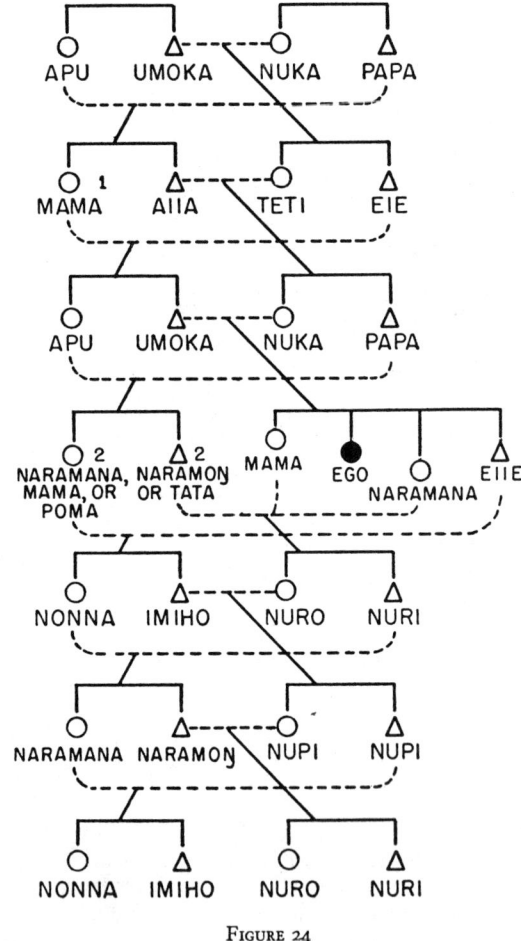

FIGURE 24

1. If this woman were not ego's father's mother or if she were not married to ego's mother's mother's brother, she would be "lumped" with her brother and called "aiia."
2. See pp. 268–270 to determine which term should be used here.

## KIN RELATIONS

5. With few exceptions kinship terms specify the sex of the referent, the exceptions being *eie, aiia,* and *nupi.*

6. Matrilaterally related relatives usually are more specifically differentiated than other consanguineal kin. Moreover, in the case of an individual who is related to another through two or more different genealogical routes, informants assert that matrilateral ties have more weight than other kinds in determining what kinship term is to be used.

7. Marriage results in some terminological changes for both spouses even when it is perfectly "correct": for example, *cross-cousin* is always changed to "husband" or "wife." Moreover, a husband sometimes adopts his wife's terminology towards certain of her close consanguineal kin (e.g., her older sister becomes *mama,* her younger sister *naramana*) regardless of what he called them before; a wife may do likewise, although she will continue to call her mother's brother *papa* even if he becomes her father-in-law.[59] If a marriage terminates in divorce most affinal relationships based on that marriage are considered nullified and the affinal kinship terms are no longer used.[60]

Turning now to behavioral norms among relatives, most Siuai would assert that kinship term and its associated behavior patterns *should be* congruous, although even the strictest moralists state that kinship distance permits an attenuation of rights and obligations within any one class of kinship dyad.

What other general conclusions may be drawn from our characterizations of the ways relatives *should* behave towards one another?

As previously stated, a few native moralists assert that *all* relatives should interact a lot and that their interaction should be characterized by nonreciprocable giving and by affection, these being the so-called "Utopian" norms,[61] which are to be distinguished from the more "typical" norms described in this chapter. Among these more "typical" norms are three which apply to nearly all kin relationships:

(1) In terms of biological age, and regardless of generation, a younger person should show deference to an older relative of the same sex; and a younger male should show some deference to an older female relative if she is "much" older (i.e., at least ten to fifteen years older).

(2) Unless a female is "much" older than a male she should show some deference towards him after he reaches manhood.

(3) A person should avoid behavior suggestive of sexual relations with all relatives except unbetrothed or unmarried cross-cousins (and, of course, one's own spouse).

In addition to these generally applicable norms there are others that apply more specifically to the relationships between a native and the members of his various constellations of relatives. In the case of a married male these constellations are as follows:

(1) Families of orientation and procreation: frequent interaction; non-reciprocable giving, sharing, and direct inheritance; affection.

(2) Other sib-mates: sharing; affection.

(3) Father's matrilineage mates: nori inheritance,[62] aŋurara, and loans; amity (with males).

(4) Affinal kin (spouse's family of orientation and sibling's spouse): aŋurara and loans; amity (with males) and constraint.

It occasions no great surprise that behavioral norms applicable to ego's sib-mates outside his family are identical in some respects (sharing, affection) with those applicable to his mother and family siblings. Nor is it surprising, in view of marriage preferences, that there is similarity approaching identity between norms applicable to his affinal kin and those applicable to his father's matrilineage mates. In other words, the formulated preference for cross-cousin marriage has the effect, theoretically at least, of aggregating ego's relatives terminologically into two mutually exclusive units: one containing his sib-mates and one containing his spouse's (and father's, cross-cousins', etc.) sib-mates. This is not to say that any Siuai native conceives of his society as being organized on an exogamous moiety basis. It is however true, as previously stated,[63] that there are many neighborhoods where intermarriage has taken place so consistently between two locally dominant matrilineages that the situation has the effect of creating a local exogamous moiety system.

*Behavioral.* On the basis of actual observation we have to revise our picture of Siuai kin relationships in several important respects. To begin with, despite the theoretical possibility of extending specific kinship terms indefinitely, the usual limits of extension tend to be rather narrow, seldom extending — in everyday usage — beyond ego's matrilineage, ego's father's matrilineage, ego's spouse's family and matrilineage, and the residents of ego's neighborhood. Beyond these limits, distant kin are lumped into broader terminological categories (e.g., "sib-mate," "son's sib-mate," etc.) or are called by non-kinship terms unless the need arises for precision, that is, unless there is a practical need for utilizing a specific kinship tie.[64] In this connection, notwithstanding the fact that matrilateral ties are asserted to be weightier than other kinds in determining what one should call a multi-linked relative, it was my experience that natives sometimes select that genealogical route, and use that term, which best suits the practical purpose in hand.

As for congruence between kinship term and associated behavior, it was my observation that the matching of a term and its associated normative behavior pattern is in some respects closer between residentially separated relatives than between many of those who live nearer together and interact more frequently. In the case of the latter, factors such as relative age and relative rank are often more overriding considerations than are specific kinship ties in determining actual behavior.[65]

## KIN RELATIONS 293

Few ethnographers would expect the facts of actual behavior among relatives to be wholly congruent with the norms, but among the Siuai the incongruence is particularly evident except in the case of family mates. I have indicated elsewhere how frequently natives flout rules regarding avoidance and deference; and how lax they often are in living up to other obligations. Also, my notebooks bulge with cases of conflict among close relatives: fighting and killing one another in feuds, practicing sorcery against one another, competing in political rivalries, and prosecuting one another in court. It is true that a death mobilizes the deceased's relatives, even some distant ones; and they flock to the funeral to express their sympathy in tearfully sung dirges. But even in such impressive manifestations of "solidarity" as these appear to be, many of the mourners often use the occasion for airing old grievances, and some of these so-called "rites of intensification" more nearly resemble verbal civil wars.

Many of these conflicts develop out of situations outside the context of kinship, but the kinship system itself contains elements of "structural strain." For example, the fact that a married woman is a wife-mother in her family of procreation and a daughter-sister in her family of orientation creates situations which can and do lead to conflict between, say, her father and her husband; and except for the quality of constraint which is believed to be fitting to the relationship between a woman's husband and her father there exist no social or ritual mechanisms for keeping the two men's paths from crossing or for keeping separate the two statuses of the woman, thereby formally avoiding situations of inherent strain.[66] The custom of paying numehu ("shame payment") might be looked upon as a mechanism for reducing tension between a man and his wife's brother, but judging by the many instances of brother-in-law conflict I recorded, this mechanism is not too effective. Even cross-cousin marriage, which in some ways promotes stability and harmony, also opens up new possibilities for tension: for example, male cross-cousins, already cool because of conflicting claims to property,[67] may become outright enemies as a result of the additional tensions engendered by their relations as brothers-in-law or by the marriage of the daughter of one of them to the son of the other. The Siuai have gone so far as to dramatize one common manifestation of tension among kinfolk: I refer to the anger ritual (mih) performed by the matrilineage mates of a deceased father in order to force funeral costs (nori) out of the latter's offspring and widow.

Obviously, then, actual behavior among many relatives falls far short of stated norms; and even the actual behavior between specific kinds of pairs of relatives is difficult to generalize about, because of the following complicating factors:

The frequent occurrence of "incorrect" marriages, and consequently the existence of cross-cutting genealogical links, which often serve to relate persons by two or more different kinship ties.

The facts of residence, which are themselves complicated and vari-patterned. Co-residence does not guarantee close interaction but it does promote it and thereby complicates relationships.

The existence of economic and socio-political relationships ofttimes overriding or complicating kin relationships.

The idiosyncrasies of individuals, in the sense that natives differ widely in their inter-personal adjustments, including the amount and content of their interaction with relatives.

We have already observed some of the complicating effects of the mixed residence patterns (i.e., "mixed" in the sense that residence is not consistently matrilocal, patrilocal, etc.). And by this time there should at least have been planted a suspicion that all Siuai personalities are not cast in the same mold! As for the complications introduced by economic and socio-political relationships, these will be described in the chapters that follow. But before proceeding to these matters, it is possible to make one more generalization about kinship relations on the basis of data already presented: out of the whole matrix of kin relationships only the nuclear family and the matrilineage emerge as sharply distinctive and consistently patterned *groups*; and important as these two kinds of groupings are for such activities as subsistence, child-rearing, spiritual welfare, etc., they are very small groups and do not possess enough of other kinds of resources, for example, wealth, control of supernatural power, etc., to give their authority-role holders extensive "political" power. Moreover, authority is not sufficiently centralized [68] in either family or matrilineage to have encouraged its use as a model for the highly centralized position occupied by the authority-role holder in each socio-political group.[69]

CHAPTER 8

# *Associations*

So far we have been considering relationships based primarily on *kinship* — on the facts of birth, child rearing, marriage, etc., and on the actions and beliefs associated therewith. We now turn to relationships based mainly on technical specialization, common residence, and common interest — economic, religious, and political. The two categories of relationships are of course not entirely distinct, it is rather a matter of emphasis. For example, all kinship relations involve common interest and some exchange of goods and services, and many of them involve common residence and technical specialization (as manifested in division of labor); but for the kinds of relationships we are now about to describe the factor of kinship is secondary to other considerations.

## RELATIONSHIPS BASED ON TRADE IN ECONOMIC COMMODITIES

In pre-white days a lively trade existed between Southern Bougainville and the islands to the south — Alu and Mono. According to Siuai informants, natives in western Terei and eastern Siuai traded with Alu and those in the west with Mono. For natives of eastern Siuai the coastal village of Riorio served as the trading center; they would walk or raft down the Mivo or Mopiai rivers and meet there the traders from Alu who traveled thence by canoe. For natives of central and western Siuai several coastal villages, including the village named Siuai, served as centers for their trade with Mono islanders. In fact, the now abandoned village of Siuai, from which all the Motuna area and people got its name, was at one time occupied by a colony of Mono islanders who served as middlemen in the interisland trade. As recorded in eye-witness accounts [1] the Siuai exchanged pigs, taro, smoked almonds, pottery, and decorated spears for shell money, fish, and lime. When European traders appeared on the scene after 1880 smoke-dried copra was added to the list of Siuai products, in return for which the Siuai received calico, machetes, and steel ax and adz blades. Now and then a venturesome white trader would anchor his schooner offshore and trade direct with the

Siuai, but most Siuai-white trade at that early period was carried out through Mono- or Alu-islander middlemen.

Occasionally the Mono and Alu islanders needed human beings as sacrifices or as menials or prostitutes, and their Siuai trade associates obliged by kidnaping and trading some defenseless fellow Siuai. I recorded several instances of natives who had been thus enslaved and exported but who had survived and returned to Siuai to finish out their lives. Needless to say, all these contacts and exchanges of goods resulted in transmission of nonmaterial culture traits as well — how much I cannot say, but the Motuna language contains numerous loan words presumably derived from Alu and Mono, and this is also the case with many characters and episodes of Siuai myths.[2]

When interisland trading flourished there seems to have been less active hostility between the associated areas, that is, Alu islanders engaged in little active aggression against eastern Siuai, and Mono islanders were more or less at peace with central and western Siuai. Occasionally, a hostile act would temporarily interrupt the trade peace; it must have required extraordinary self-control for these head-hunters to withstand the tantalizing temptation of having a go at each other. The remarkable thing is that peace of any duration obtained. What probably occurred was that the more numerous Siuai were matched by the better armed and better organized island visitors, and that each side badly wanted what the other had to offer; these considerations overrode appetites for bloodletting for more or less extensive periods of truce.

Some of this interisland trade went on between regular partners (taovu), and this was particularly the case with influential men. These pairs of taovu became so friendly in some cases that they respected the relationship even during times of general hostility. I recorded one instance of a marauding Mono islander having secured refuge in the household of a Siuai taovu when the rest of his party were ambushed and slain. Later on, after white rule made Mono and Alu safe for visitors, Siuai natives occasionally went there to trade and to visit relatives, victims of earlier kidnaping who had chosen to remain in the more westernized island communities; the taovu institution proved useful to such travelers.

As a result of the first World War, Bougainville became part of the Australian Mandated Territory of New Guinea and an international customs barrier was interposed between the Territory and the British Solomon Islands Protectorate, which includes Alu and Mono islands. Natives were forbidden to travel across the Bougainville Straits without first securing clearances at the official ports of exit and entry, Kieta (on Bougainville) and Faisi (on Shortland or Alv). This ruling effectively wiped out native interisland visiting and trade, and led to the abandonment of the coastal Siuai villages. With the passing of interisland trade the Siuai coast dwellers left the inhospitable mosquito- and crocodile-infested shores, where soil is poor, and moved their settlements inland to higher ground.[3]

The severance of trade relations with Mono and Alu by no means put a stop to all Siuai trade. If anything, internal trade is livelier today than in the past; the rational basis for this trading is to be found in the regional and individual specialization that obtains. With the exception af a few items nearly all Siuai households are materially self-sufficient, but those few items are important enough to foster a vigorous inter-household, inter-hamlet, and inter-regional trade.

Every Siuai household uses clay pots for cooking but pot-making is centered in northeast Siuai, partly because the best clay is to be found there and partly because it is customary for more men of that region to specialize in pot-making. There are, to be sure, a few potters scattered through the other regions of Siuai but even they purchase clay from the northeast. Not all men even in the northeast can make pots, however; I estimated that only about half of them can turn out a usable product and only about one in eight produces pots for sale.

An average household has to replace about three cooking pots a year, while a feast-giving leader may require as many as seven or eight. For residents of northeast Siuai it is a simple matter to make pots or purchase them locally as needed, but those living elsewhere have to undertake a buying expedition. Siuai craftsmen do not peddle their wares; they manufacture on commission or with the expectation that purchasers will seek them out. A few householders of less than average substance will, upon needing a new pot, spend a whole day walking around northeast Siuai looking for one to buy before he finds one which is ready for use and not reserved for some other customer. Most men, therefore, act with foresight and arrange for a regular source of supply, going to the same potter each time and thereby establishing a trade partnership. In the case of wealthy, influential men the relationship based on purchase of pottery may develop into a taovu partnership, involving exchange of other commodities as well as mutual lending of money and extension of credit. An important feast-giver will have up to five or six taovu partners scattered throughout Siuai, and the relations between such pairs involve mutual visiting, exchange of small (coercive) gifts, and friendly though formal give-and-take, somewhat in the pattern of the brother-in-law relationship. When preparing for a feast, an ambitious man will exploit his taovu partnership up to and sometimes beyond the limit of tolerance — I recorded instances of men breaking off the taovu relationship with partners who made too frequent demands; as one aggrieved native put it, "A man is not his taovu's subordinate."

A taovu can be counted on to attend his partner's funeral, and will usually demand shell money from the deceased's family in order to supply a pig for the mortuary feast. In the case of taovu partnerships between high-ranking leaders, their relationship will sometimes extend to all their followers with the result that whole communities will be taovu — this, however, does not involve a pairing off of natives from the allied communities.

Lime used for the betel mixture is another regionally specialized product which forms the basis for trade relationships. As previously described, lime is obtained by burning marine shells. Many natives of southern Siuai make a business of collecting shells for sale to northerners, either in the raw state or as powdered lime. Some northerners prefer to provide their own lime and travel to the coast two or three times a year to collect shells. Most, however, secure lime by purchase or barter, northern pots being exchanged for southern lime.

Ocher is found mainly in north Siuai, hence is also a stimulus to interregional trade relationships, although on a much smaller scale than pottery and lime. The northeast happens to be a center for the manufacture of woven arm-bands, which are popular throughout Siuai; one reason for this specialization is the greater abundance of fine fiber in the northern forests and another reason is the fact that the northeast is nearer to that part of Terei whence this craft has spread into Siuai.

Canarium almonds are also most plentiful in northeast Siuai, and some hamlets there specialize in smoking large quantities of nuts for sale or exchange. Much of this trade follows taovu channels, for almonds are an essential feast ingredient and active feast-givers have to arrange for supplies well in advance because of the shortness of the nut-ripening season, the large demand, and the relatively limited supply.

In addition to the regional specializations which help to stimulate wide-range trade relationships throughout Siuai, there is a complex network of trade relations based on individual specialization. Every normal household is capable of providing food and shelter adequate for its own survival, but there are numerous items whose manufacture requires knowledge and skills possessed only by specialists. The most important of these are cordage, wood carvings, plaited stoppers for lime gourds, ohkuna hats, ornamented or bone-pointed weapons, and bamboo boxes and combs. There is another class of objects which, to my mind at least, requires just as much skill in manufacture as those mentioned but which every man makes for himself; these include men's plaited carrying pouches, net bags, and, in northeast Siuai, fine plaited arm-bands. Siuai men work at these latter items as American women at their knitting. They carry unfinished pouches, etc., wherever they go and work away at them continually. If one man puts aside for a moment the object he is working on, a companion will pick it up and advance the plait or the design a bit further. With the specialized items, however, it is entirely different; most natives consider such handicrafts very difficult to master and leave their manufacture in the hands of experts, who turn out objects on commission and sell them for shell money. No individual native requires these kinds of objects frequently enough to lead to the establishment of a recognized taovu partnership between manufacturer-seller and purchaser; some customers will make a point of returning to the same manufacturer, but others will shop around for the best purchase they can make.

Taro becomes a trade item only under special circumstances: when a man is preparing for a feast he may purchase taro corms to feed his guests; or if he wishes to enlarge and improve his gardens he may purchase planting stock of specially good quality. Under ordinary circumstances it is considered improper for a householder to buy taro to feed his own dependents — the self-respecting Siuai should produce his own food supply; but the circumstances just noted provide permissible exceptions. There are a few householders who make a practice of producing surpluses of taro which they sell to neighboring feast-givers. For example, the variety of taro called *paike* is in wide demand by gardeners wishing to improve their production. Paike is said to have been discovered by the kupuna, Rerua, who also created the Kuru River which flows by Moronei and Mataras. Rerua bestowed his planting stock of paike to a human sib-mate named Tuvara, and along with it he gave Tuvara some spirit-consecrated plants to be planted in the taro patch to the accompaniment of the following formula:

"Hey! all you who have grown paike in the past, look out for this crop and make it grow plentifully. Make it so plentiful that men from all directions will come here to gape at my crop and offer much money to buy planting stock."

In due course Tuvara sold paike plantings and the accompanying magic to other men, and the latest to own both plantings and magic is Kukue of Moronei village who bought them from Ripa for thirty spans of shell money. Other natives of Moronei village bought the plantings without the magic so that their crops are only moderately successful. Kukue's taro is in wide demand, but he is reluctant to sell the magic because of the favored economic position its monopoly gives him.

The exchange transaction between taovu partners is distinguished from ordinary barter or purchase. For one thing, taovus should never haggle with each other. The pots or lime or pig brought by one of them to the other ought to be reciprocated by a return of equivalent [4] or slightly more than equivalent value; and the whole transaction is called *exchanging* (ootu).[5] In the words of one informant:

"Men who are taovu exchange gifts (*oourumum*) rather than make purchases (*puunum*). If one of them carries a gift of pots to the other, the latter will reciprocate with large quantities of lime and shell money. The visiting taovu will return home happy thinking 'My taovu is a fine and generous man.'"

Informants also stated that taovu do not insist on prompt or equivalent reciprocation — being beyond such petty considerations. This I found to be quite contrary to the facts; I witnessed two and heard about several more cases of litigation between taovu based on complaints of delayed or non-equivalent reciprocation of "gifts." And some of the most bitter political rivalries, including cases of outright enmity, involve former taovus. In fact, several successful natives I knew expressed cynicism about the taovu relationship, considering it a vehicle for fraud and trouble. One successful leader even boasted of his independence of taovu ties, implying that he at least among his compeers had acquired affluence honestly.

Ordinary purchase and barter, both called "pu," are carried out according to a system of exchange values fixed enough to permit only a narrow margin for bargaining. Nor do buyers and sellers haggle much over price in this context. Economically Siuai is a perpetual seller's market; it is nearly always the buyer who seeks out the potential seller and initiates the transaction. If the price seems unreasonable, the buyer will either search elsewhere, or he will make the purchase and then complain about it later. Most sellers I have observed seemed quite indifferent, pointing out to the grumbling buyers that *they* had no interest in making the sale anyway!

Most Siuai contend that purchase or barter negotiations should be backed by visible evidence of the buyer's intentions. Men who walk about claiming to be searching for something to buy but without goods to back up their talk are dubbed "swallows" (avi'kura), after those restless, continually moving birds that never seem to alight. The name is also applied to all men of little substance who gad about the countryside, with no apparent purpose other than curiosity and, natives suspect, a desire to spy on and seduce women. In the pidgin phrase, Siuai are contemptuous of men who "walk-about nothing," just as they speak slightingly of men who chatter to no purpose. These circumstances were vividly impressed upon me when I once heard a leader exhort his followers to arrive all together in the distant village whence they were bound for the purpose of buying a pig: "See to it," he warned them, "that the owner of the pig beholds the money before you discuss the purchase; otherwise he will think me a man of no account."

In order to provide some notion of the extent of trading, I asked four male informants, all of them married and heads of households, to attempt to recall the exchanges they had made during the preceding year, either with taovu or by barter or purchase; the results are rendered not altogether unreliable, on account of the Siuai's almost obsessive preoccupation with material goods. One of these was a well-known potter. He sold about thirty pots, mostly for shell money; three small pigs, for shell money; four lots [6] of smoked almonds, for shell money and lime; and he bought two lots of sago flour; and three calico loincloths, from a returned plantation laborer.

The other three men were not craft specialists: on an average each sold three small and two large pots, five lots of smoked almonds, and three lots of sago flour. Each bought, on an average, one lot of lime or lime-making shells, one special container (lime gourd or tobacco tube), two calico loincloths — all for shell money. None of these four men gave feasts during the year; had they done so their purchases would have been far more numerous. It is my impression that the trading activities of these four are about average for non-feast givers, but unfortunately I made no general survey of this matter. Active feast-giving stimulates trade — and hence both formal and informal trade relationships — to an extraordinary degree, as later chapters will describe.

## RELATIONSHIPS BASED ON SALE OF SERVICES AND MAGICAL COMMODITIES

Many Siuai possess specialized skills which they practice on other people's behalf in return for tangible recompense of one kind or another. Hence to our list of social relationships we have to add a category for *specialist-client* relations. Most of these have to do with magical practices.

In listing these kinds of specializations I have grouped them according to what the practitioner purports to do for his client rather than according to the mechanics or beliefs involved in his practices.[7]

*Purveyors of "economic" magic*: Under this heading come those persons who specialize in helping crops to grow — taro, sago, and almonds. There are very few of these specialists — here in Siuai every gardener is his own magician; and most specialists in this category, as in the case of Kukue cited above,[8] guard their trade secrets rather jealously and sell or give their magical knowledge and paraphernalia only to trusted friends and close relatives.

*Therapists*: In this class belong midwives, bone-setters, life-prolongers, and dispensers of magical liniments, emetics, and purgatives.

An earlier chapter [9] described the circumstances under which professional midwives are called in to assist with births, and the techniques they employ. It was also pointed out that these services are paid for only when the midwife is not closely related to the woman or her husband.

Bone-setters are usually old women; three were practicing this skill in northeast Siuai during our stay there. They use both splints and magical liniments, and are said to be very skillful in manipulating and binding bones back into place. Men are their principal patients, because of their habit of climbing — and falling from — trees. One native described to me his experience with a bone-setter: he fell from a lower limb of an almond tree and broke his jaw — "into such bits that it rattled when I moved my head." According to this informant, "The woman manipulated the pieces into place, then rubbed magic (kuna) over the face and applied splints and bandages. Before long I was chewing betel again. I paid her two spans of shell money; she asked for five but I reminded her that it was only a jaw and not an arm or leg!"

Life-prolongers are employed to prolong the life of a dying person whose death would interrupt some important event. If, for example, a leader has completed preparations for a feast and some member of his community appears to be near death, the leader summons a life-prolonging specialist to carry out *mitoi* (or *imatu*), a maru ritual, in order to restrain the sick one's soul from quitting his body until the feast is over. The life-prolonger squats beside the patient and brushes a ghost-consecrated leaf (*kupo*) over his head and shoulders while repeating a magical formula containing the names of previous life-prolonging magicians. Then the magician ties the leaf into a tight knot while holding it over the patient's head and repeating the formula. The knotted leaf may then be buried near the door of the patient's house, with a kupo shoot planted over it, or it may be kept on the smoke rack in his house. A person whose life is thus prolonged is said to "live by the knotted leaf" (*mitoikori turoŋ*). After the feast is over the leaf is recovered and untied and the magician is paid up to ten spans of shell money.[10]

General therapists (*kuna kuka*, medicine-expert) will be called in to treat nearly all kinds of illnesses except those known to be the result of soul loss. They work with ingredients such as herbs, leaves, vine sap, clays, etc., the exact formulae for which are jealously guarded secrets. The following is an account of the procedures of Opisa, a general therapist of Turuŋum village:

> If an infant is sickly and does not take nourishment, the parents carry a strand of high-value shell money to Opisa and ask him to try his hand at effecting a cure. Before he accepts the money Opisa consults a divination plant [11] to learn whether the infant is curable. If the answer is unfavorable Opisa will do nothing further; if favorable he will wrap the shell money around his wrist and go to the forest to collect kuna. Since the patient is a weakly infant, Opisa will collect the roots, sap, bark, and leaves of plants that are hardy and "strong." The money wrapped around his wrist attracts the ghosts of men who formerly used his particular kind of healing magic and these ghosts help him to locate the appropriate ingredients. (If the money is not sufficient they will not help and alone he will be unable to find enough efficacious plants.) After he has collected enough plants he leaves them in a container with the shell money for an hour or two, and then grinds the leaves, roots, bark, and sap, along with red clay (*ukura*) to form a mixture which he gives to the patient's mother to chew.[12] The woman then spits the mixture along with some of her saliva onto the infant's fontanelle.[13] After this, numerous taboos are imposed on mother and infant. The woman may not eat pork, opossum, sweet-smelling taro, or soup made of native spinach, until the infant appears to be eating normally. The patient, however, is forbidden to eat pork and other delicacies until later on in childhood. When the child's father has gathered together enough resources, he prepares a small feast to initiate the child into eating the tabooed pork, and at this time he will pay Opisa for his services.

During the time of his telling, eight children whom Opisa had treated were subject to the pork-eating taboo; all these lived in Opisa's own or in neighboring hamlets. Most of his neighbors, in fact, look upon Opisa as the community specialist for sickly children, because of his record of successful treatments; and most of them consult him in case of illness. He encourages their confidence by reminding them of his successes and by recalling the deaths that have occurred to persons he has not treated. Also he boasts of his honesty by pointing to the instances wherein he has been consulted and has turned down patients after negative responses from the divination — patients who ultimately died, as he had predicted, in spite of their treatment by other specialists. (The Siuai therapist, unlike his western counterpart, is not ethically bound to refrain from disparaging his colleagues!) Opisa's favorite story concerns his advice to Maimoi. Maimoi consulted Opisa about one of his offspring, a sickly infant still in "hiding." Opisa received a negative response from the divination plant and advised Maimoi not to waste any more money on a hopeless case. Maimoi disregarded the advice, provided a costly baptism ceremony for the infant, and paid a sorcery diviner to discover the cause of the illness. Nevertheless, the infant soon died, and Maimoi admitted to Opisa his error: "I wish I had taken your advice and saved myself all that money."

Opisa has a healthy respect for mikai-magicians,[14] and sometimes refers patients to them when they do not respond to his treatment even though his divination has established that they will live. He usually refers such patients to Koura, a distantly related neighbor. He stated that he did not ask a commission from Koura for this service, but I could see that my query aroused an interesting possibility in his mind.

Opisa learned his profession from his father, who initiated him into practice by popping his finger-joints and saying: "This thing (power) is now transferred to you so that you can administer the medicine." Opisa has announced that he will share his business by selling his professional secrets for seventy spans of shell money, that being the price his father's father originally paid for it.

Opisa is one of the more influential general therapists; there were only a half dozen or so in northeast Siuai with comparably successful practices and large clientele. On the other hand, there are forty to fifty persons, men and women, who have more specific therapeutic specialties and who practice only occasionally.

*Sorcerers, Counter-Sorcerers, and Diviners*: As previously stated, some Siuai natives actually practice sorcery. Of course, in innumerable instances of sickness and death natives assert the cause to be sorcery when actually black magic has not been performed; on the other hand, there are numerous individuals who engage in such practices more or less openly, and probably an even larger number who do so surreptitiously. Missions and Administration have tried to wipe out sorcery but if anything sorcery practices have probably increased under white rule, with an even larger proportion of performances now being carried out in secret than was formerly the case.

Sorcery involving "dirt," spirit-attracting poisons, most "intrinsic" poisons, and such spirit-consecrated poisons as infanticidal tao,[15] is usually carried out in utmost secrecy and against acquaintances for whom the sorcerer bears personal grudges. Under these circumstances such practices are considered to be "immoral" (kirahao) and public opinion condemns them. Certainly, few natives engage others to practice these forms of sorcery on their behalf, the chances for maintaining secrecy under such circumstances being remote. Persons wishing to practice these kinds of sorcery acquire the knowledge and the ingredients from matrilineage mates, who are less apt to inform on them, and then perform their own rites against personal enemies.

Sorcery involving homicidal-spirits, such "intrinsic" poisons as Nagovisi mara, such "consecrated" poisons as rakana and tomoni,[16] is usually directed against more or less common enemies living in distant places. Before Administration control became established, these practices were engaged in quite openly as instruments of public policy within the context of feuding. Nearly every political unit[17] contained at least one notorious sorcerer who performed his skills on behalf of his neighbors, and usually for fees. Today these practices continue, although less openly, because of fear of Administration reprisal.

When "destructive" magical techniques are employed as mechanisms to avenge deaths believed due to sorcery, public opinion backs the practice; because of Mission and Administration disapproval these rites are performed in some secrecy but word of them quickly gets around. Since vengeance magic is customarily carried out by one of the victim's relatives there is usually no fee involved.

Murderer-divining practices which do not include vengeance mechanisms are performed openly and for profit. The Missions disapprove of such rituals, and since the Administration also objects, native practitioners have to peddle their skills surreptitiously. During our stay in Siuai the most popular of these techniques was tuki, which was employed to locate the cause and identify the culprit behind "dirt" sorcery and the spirit-consecrated sorcery, tao.[18] This tao, which kills human infants, fetuses, and childbearing women, is held in such universal repugnance and dread that measures to combat it receive strong popular support. The most successful tuki-diviners of northeast Siuai were two brothers of Moronei village. They were much sought after and received fees of 30 to 50 spans for each performance; during the eight-month period that I followed their activities they performed seven times — and, of course, always successfully, that is, they always "located" suspicious-looking objects and, when called on to do so, pointed out plausible culprits.[19] Their fame was considerable enough for them to be consulted by natives living in central Siuai, nearly seven miles from their home base at Moronei, an unusually wide range for relationships based on sale of professional services.

General therapists and mikai-magicians also use divination techniques as part of their stock in trade, but with the growing fashion in specialized divination they are beginning to refer many such cases to the tuki-diviners.

Thief-divination also provides some specialists with occasional opportunities to expand their influence and income, but since these techniques (*minnaokari, horihoriko, tukveroro*) [20] include mechanisms for killing as well as identifying the thief, they are condemned by the Administration and hence must be practiced with more circumspection than other forms of divination.

The mikai, general practitioner of magic,[21] may come to exercise considerable influence over his neighbors. There are usually one or two of these specialists in every neighborhood, and natives tend to consult their local mikai on most matters of misfortune beyond the scope of the ordinary therapists. For example, during a six-months' period, Koura, the most influential mikai of Turuŋum, was called upon to divine the identity of a pig thief, recover the soul of a delirious woman, establish rapport between a man and his father's ghost, and diagnose the cause of a death. He received fees for all these cases, and so highly respected was his judgment that no complaints were heard against the amount of his fees — a rare, rare thing for Siuai! I gained the impression that the faith his neighbors have in Koura's abilities, buttressed of course by his confidence-lending personality, provides them with an additional sense of security against the supernatural dangers of their universe. Here certainly has developed something of a permanent specialist-client relationship system.

Not all mikais are as influential as Koura; in fact, some of them are reputed to be thoroughly ineffective, or too exorbitant in their fees. In such cases as these their neighbors tend to consult mikais in other neighborhoods.

Men become mikai in order to earn money and to gain influence, and a successful practice accomplishes both these goals.

Numerous other kinds of magic specialists ply their trades in Siuai — the sellers of love potions, the dispensers of property-protection poisons, etc. — but few of these persons succeed in building up a regular clientele. There are fads in magic just as there are fads in crafts and music. A particular variety of litigation-winning magic [22] may earn money and notoriety for its owner for a year or so, but a few unsuccessful episodes and the appearance of new magical fashions will transfer public interest elsewhere. Typical of this process was the tree-sprite fad.

When we first arrived in Siuai there was much talk about tree-sprites (*kuinoukere*); some men claimed to own individual sprites, and a few of them were actually sold by their owners. Some purchasers paid to acquire a sprite merely for the sake of possessing an interesting novelty; others bought them for assistance in their hunting of opossums, this being the specialty of these sprites. They are said to resemble human beings in all characters save their skins, which are covered with opossum hair, and this enables them to approach opossums without exciting fear. It appears that only a few tree-sprites are held in captivity by human beings; the rest dwell in the forests in a wild state, there being one tree-sprite for every large tree, with a new one born every time a new tree begins to grow. Wild tree-sprites live in the top branches of their tree homes and keep opossums as their pigs.

Tree-sprites were "discovered" by the Siuai only a year or so before our visit; before that the Siuai believed in the existence of demons attached to particularly large trees deep in the forest, but there was no general conception of a whole species of tree-sprites. Then, one day when a number of men were clearing land for a new garden, the spirit-familiar of one of them heard a whimpering cry coming from the branches of a felled tree. It was an infant tree-sprite deserted by its parents who had been frightened away from the area by the felling of the trees. The spirit-familiar adopted the tiny tree-sprite and took it along when he accompanied his master home. Later that evening the master heard the sprite crying, and seeing nothing (tree-sprites are invisible to human beings), was informed of its identity by his spirit-familiar. Every day after that the man gave daily offerings of coconut meat to the tree-sprite, who quickly grew to full size and began to accompany the man on opossum hunts, which turned out highly successful. Meanwhile the man used to converse openly with the sprite, the latter answering in scarcely audible whistles. The neighbors' curiosity was piqued by these goings-on and some of them offered to buy the tree-sprite. The owner then prevailed on his spirit-familiar to capture several more tree-sprites, which he then sold for five to ten spans of mauai each. Meanwhile other enterprising men in the neighborhood "discovered" and captured tree-sprites and there developed a lively trade in them. Quickly, however, they became commonplace; and by the time we left Siuai there was hardly any talk at all about tree-sprites, tuki-divination [23] having become the newest fad.

*Artists and Composers*: Several men in northeast Siuai are noted for their skills in composing songs or carving wood. Sometimes they are commissioned by others to produce a song for a feast or to carve designs on the wooden frames used for baking special puddings, and in such cases they are usually paid a few spans of shell money or a small pig. Just as often, however, they work gratis, using their skills as part of their contributions to the common enterprises of their men's societies.

*Census of Specialists*: Except for a few mental defectives nearly every Siuai adult, male and female, is a specialist of some kind. Even among the defectives there are some who have gained reputations for skill in divination or in other kinds of supernatural manipulations. Moreover, some individuals practice more than one specialty; for example, one man I knew was a successful mikai-magician, an expert wood-carver, and a noted rain-maker.

## RELATIONSHIPS BETWEEN CREDITORS AND DEBTORS

The subject of credit and indebtedness in Siuai is a very broad one; for example, one aspect of a son's relationship with his aging parents could be characterized as an indebtedness on his part, an obligation to repay their past care by ministering, in turn, to them. Also, the relations between a leader and his followers possess many of the characteristics of the creditor-debtor relations, as we shall later on describe.[24] Here, however, we are concerned only with the situation which arises when a man lends some valuable tangible object, such as a sum of shell money or a pig, to another man with the expectation of repayment in kind within some more or less specified period of time.[25] (This rules out of the present discussion, therefore, situations like those created by an individual borrowing an ax or a pot from a friend.)

Siuai natives have frequent occasion to borrow: when a pork meal must be provided to celebrate a ritual; when resources must be collected for a large renown-acquiring feast; when fines are levied or Administration head-taxes collected; when sickness occurs and specialists have to be paid; etc. Every man queried on the subject owed and was owed; most of them had five or six debtors as well as creditors, and an active feast-giver might be indebted to twenty or thirty individuals. (When I was engaged in making a property inventory of Siuai, many individuals complained that their actual possessions provided little indication of their true wealth, because of the large amounts of money and goods owed them.)

The borrower invariably seeks out the lender, who is usually a kinsman, a neighbor or a taovu; natives do not make a special business of lending — the returns are too risky and the "interest" is considered too small. The lender publicizes the transaction rather widely to insure that it will not be disowned. No definite interest rate is stipulated, but it is understood that the borrower will present the lender with a *totokai* when he makes repayment. This totokai should amount to about one-fourth of the value of the loan: that is, a totokai of ten or fifteen spans of shell money should accompany repayment of a loan valued at 50 spans, etc. If a smaller totokai than this is given the debtor is called a "stone-heart" (*mu'ukiŋ kupuri*); and if he persists in such practices he will not be able to find people to borrow money from. Some men noted for their generosity pay a totokai amounting to half the value of the loan. The time element does not appear to be a factor, since the expected totokai does not vary with the duration of the loan.

A loan repaid promptly and adequately *helps*, if anything, to solidify friendly relations between individuals; it does not appear to provide the mutual satisfactions evoked by spontaneously given gifts, but it is the next best thing. Many firm taovu partnerships are based as much on lending and borrowing as on trade. Conversely, tardiness in repayment usually leads to coolness and even enmity.

Creditors have various means of forcing repayment. They may, for example, resort to debt-transference (*kupurihe-*, "to transfer the stone"): if A borrows from B and fails to repay on time, B goes to a mutual acquaintance, C, collects from him the amount of the debt along with an additional amount to cover the expected totokai and asks C to collect this amount plus an additional amount of "shame-money" from A. The report of this transaction is widely circulated, and when it reaches A's ears he is greatly embarrassed by this publicity and makes every effort to recompense C the amount of the debt and the totokai plus the shame-money asked for by C (usually about one-quarter to one-half of the original debt). This is an effective form of debt collection, since nearly all Siuai are highly sensitive to this form of public embarrassment. Also, a creditor has no trouble finding someone to accept the debt — to "bear the weight of the stone" — because of the shame-money which the latter receives for his part in the transaction.

Kupurihe- is customarily used when the debtor is not very influential, since most natives would not court trouble by coöperating with a creditor to collect a debt from an influential leader. When the debtor is a leader his creditor resorts to more subtle pressures. If, say, the leader A owes B 100 spans of shell money, B will name a well-known palm tree "one hundred spans," and everyone will recognize the allusion. Men in club-houses will jest about A, "talk about his meanness" and thus "cause him to climb the ru tree." [26] Incestuous persons are also scornfully discussed in the club-houses and "caused to climb the ru tree"; but to a leader the contempt represented by "ru-tree-climbing" for debt may be dreaded more than the charge of incest, or even the threat of sorcery. The usual result is therefore that A will repay B immediately; he may even repay the sum many times over in order to shame B for his faithless action and in order to reëstablish his own reputation for honorable transactions. Also, such affairs as these generally result in mutual hostility and political feuds. Because of these complications, creditors will weigh carefully any decision to use this form of debt-collection against a debtor who is potentially a dangerous rival.

In these modern days of Administration control some natives will resort to litigation before Administration-appointed headmen to retrieve money and goods owed to them, and if a satisfactory settlement is not forthcoming a creditor can even appeal to the white Patrol Officer, who will either force the debtor to pay up or send him to jail for a few weeks. This kind of debt collection is usually practiced only in those places which lack influential leaders and which have gone farthest in adopting Administration concepts of law and order; elsewhere the more conservative natives scorn this new device.

If a man dies owing debts, his creditors have no way of forcing his relatives to pay, but usually these latter make earnest efforts to do so. Sometimes the deceased's matrilineage mates will make restitution by transferring some of their land to the creditor. In all such cases of voluntary restitution the individuals who make good the old debts receive wide acclaim.

## PRODUCTION TEAMS

As has been repeatedly stated, nearly all households are quite self-sufficient labor units with respect to the production of most of the necessities of living. Put another way, most Siuai production techniques do not require large numbers of persons simultaneously performing complementary jobs. It is true, as has been pointed out, that relatives living in the same or neighboring hamlets sometimes coöperate in gardening and other kinds of productive work, but these groupings result from circumstances and attitudes attributable to kinship and are not necessitated by the technology of the work. I also recorded instances of team production work carried out by individuals from several neighboring hamlets — individuals many of whom were related by kinship ties too remote to have provided a special basis for coöperation. The fact that they were neighbors contributed towards their working together but it was only one of a number of factors. The gardening team at Moronei provides some understanding of the workings of such voluntary production groups.

The Moronei gardening team was composed of fifteen youths and men drawn from its four hamlets (*True*-Moronei, Siuno, Tokei, and Novei), representing about half of the total adult male population of Moronei line village. The reasons given for the other males not joining in were: "They prefer to garden separately," "They are misanthropes," "They are too weak for such hard labor."

Formerly a powerful mumi named Moki lived in Moronei. He was wealthy, and a renowned warlord and feast-giver. In 1935 he died; his son Ripa distributed large sums of shell money among Moki's matrilineage-mates and set out to emulate his father. Shortly afterward, in 1936, Ripa also died and the remainder of his wealth passed to *his* son Tumare. Matrilineage-mates of Moki and Ripa *set-aside* (tabooed) [27] large tracts of land on Kiukiu south of Moronei, and carried on a minimum amount of gardening in small isolated patches north and east of the village. Then, after a year of mourning, Tumare reopened the *set-aside* land to gardening; in the words of one team member:

> Tumare summoned us and told us to leave off the mourning for the dead and to prepare the *set-aside* land for gardens. We *coöperators* ground our axes and set to work, ring-barking the larger trees and splitting the smaller ones for fence rails. After four days we had completed the work; it went effortlessly like children's play, so great was our zeal. *Coöperators* never tire; they whoop and sing and devise tests of strength and skill. *Lone-workers* are otherwise. They prepare gardens far away, and attempt to hide their women. *Lone-workers* like ——— (and here he named several men) did not aid us.

After the whole area had been cleared and fenced in, Tumare assigned separate patches to all these men, then their women took over and began the brushing and planting.

The essential feature of this particular coöperative enterprise was that the people who participated were not a single hamlet group nor were they the *whole* membership of several hamlets. The people of *True*-Moronei hamlet had separate garden sites about a mile to the north — there *all* of them took part in the activity; but here on Kiukiu only part of the *True*-Moronei residents participated. The same was true of the other hamlets. The principle of the association on Kiukiu was something other than kinship; the *coöperators* were relatives *and* neighbors and friends, all working together voluntarily in a joint enterprise.

All this occurred just before my visit in 1938. During my stay I witnessed a repetition of the activity: Tumare brought together the same men, plus two additional men, and invited them to clear a garden site on another of his tracts of land. In other words, a social group became crystallized. Furthermore several members of this new group had already begun to hypostasize the relationships and identify themselves with the land which they cleared. One member invented a name, *mamajenopo*, for himself and his co-workers. As far as I was able to learn, the term was a true innovation. *Mamajee* is a "heave-ho" term used by Siuai men; *nopo* is the plural personal suffix — together they became "heave-ho-people" or *coöperators*. This term vividly expresses the *esprit de corps* which develops out of communal labor like that undertaken by the Moronei men. The land on which they garden is most specifically identified with Tumare by virtue of the fact that he had distributed nori among his deceased father's matrilineage-mates, who had been the previous residual owners. But while the site was being cleared *and afterward*, several gardening team members referred to the land as *our land*. When I questioned Tumare about such presumption, he replied: "*My* land, it is true; but I share it among my coöperators."

Not every line village has its gardening team. In Hinna village, garden work is an enterprise of separate households or separate hamlets; gardens are scattered all around the area, providing a striking contrast to the clustered Moronei gardens.

A superficial glance at the land around Mataras would leave an impression that the garden work there also is *team* work; during the first half of 1938 most Mataras people were gardening on western Rinsa, south of the village. Actually, however, there was no team organization involved. Each household or hamlet cleared, fenced, and planted its own patch and did not coöperate with members of other households or hamlets. There was no leader who initiated the work, no talk about "We Mataras coöperators," and no permanent claim made to the land on which they worked. That land belongs principally to one old man who no longer gardens there; and not one of the gardeners on the land claims it in the manner of the team members at Moronei.

In northeast Siuai gardening teams are the exception rather than the rule. I recorded only two others that had developed into groups like the one at **Moronei.**

Sago work teams are more numerous. It is quite possible for one man to fell a sago palm, remove its bark, chop away the pith, reduce it to starch flour, and pack it away in leaf containers. Very frequently this labor is carried out by a pair of brothers, or by a father and his sons. In a few areas, however, there are sago teams, made up of men who join together at intervals to help one another prepare sago flour from individually owned palms. In such places there develop regular process-lines, divisions of labor wherein certain men become specialist choppers, shredders, washers, and packers.[28] Such a team can fell and completely process a sago palm in a single forenoon, whereas an individual working alone will be at the job constantly for eight to ten days. The owner of the sago palm worked by a team will reward them with a small banquet of taro and opossum rather than pay for their services with money or part of the sago.

Nutting teams have also developed into more or less fixed membership groups in several neighborhoods, with both sexes and nearly all ages participating. Youths carry out the hazardous work of stripping the almond trees, while boys and older men gather the fallen nuts, and women and children extract the kernels and package and smoke them. Here again, the tree owner rewards his helpers with a special meal rather than with money or a share of the almonds.

The wild-pig hunts of former days required scores of men to drive the animals into a stockade. Today, however, the only production requiring large-scale coöperative efforts is an occasional fish drive involving the diversion of streams or the use of huge seine-nets. As previously mentioned, I knew of only three of these seine-nets in northeast Siuai, and during our entire stay there they were used not once; informants did tell me, however, that certain skillful men always work together as a seining team when any of the nets is brought into use. The stream-diversion method of fishing was carried out several times during my stay; and in two instances the co-workers appeared to work smoothly and efficiently, evidence of their long association as fellow members. In other cases coördination was lacking, which indicated — what informants confirmed — that the participants were drawn haphazardly from many scattered hamlets and had not previously worked together as a team.

I soon discovered that activities in those neighborhoods with organized work *teams* were enlivened by much more *esprit de corps* than could be discovered in other neighborhoods. Furthermore, natives themselves recognize the difference. Members of work teams interact more frequently than they would under the ordinary circumstances of neighbor-proximity. They interact in the process of doing specific things associated with specific places. In other words, they are united in groups to exploit and utilize the land and the products of the land; and as one would reasonably expect, team members claim certain tenure rights to the land so exploited. It is not practicable to generalize about such tenure rights because situations vary so from place to place. For example, the opossum-hunting team at Turuŋum village is well organized and functions frequently; most of the hunting is done on land which belongs to one matrilineage, but all members refer freely to that land as "*our* bush," "*our* hunting ground," and "*our* opossums." Occasionally a single team member will hunger for meat and will spend a day or two hunting there: his booty will be his very own, without objections from the *True-owners*. But what a hue and cry such an action would arouse in, say, Hinna village, which has no team organization! There the outsider would be regarded as a poacher and would be vigorously prosecuted.

Owners of a tract of land or of a section of river will sometimes allow mere acquaintances to garden on the land or fish from the river in return for a share in the produce. This is a well-recognized custom. Yet when a team member gardens on land cleared by himself and his teammates, he does not pay rent to the real owners — except under circumstances noted below. The same is true of fishing.

Normally a teammate cannot pass on his provisional land-use rights to his children or other relatives. If these latter participate regularly in the teamwork, they are — *ipso facto* — team members, and as such have their own rights of usufruct.

The identification of team members with land was clearly brought out by an acculturation phenomenon. The Australian Administration has ruled that natives must improve the roads around their line village, this being done mainly to expedite the Patrol Officer's tax and census collection. The order specifies that each native must be responsible for the road which passes through or abuts on his own territory. Consider the case of Immarito. This native lives at Moronei line village but most of his real property is a mile and a half southwest of there on Hororoŋo, a tract inherited from his father. Moronei men team together to do their road work, near their village, and also assist Immarito repair the road which passes through Hororoŋo. As a consequence, Immarito has allowed his teammates the privilege of making gardens on Hororoŋo.

Similar situations exist throughout Siuai. Administration-sponsored road work and its emphasis upon teamwork is throwing open more and more land to more users. And, quite expectedly, those neighborhoods characterized by a long tradition of teamwork become adapted more easily to the change. Moronei villagers — particularly team members — have taken over the compulsory road labor in their stride; whereas among the Mataras people, where teamwork of any kind is unusual, the Administration-appointed headman has a great deal of trouble trying to compel his recalcitrant followers to improve the roads.

Summarizing: except for certain fishing methods, Siuai production techniques do not necessitate large-scale teamwork, and only a very small proportion of production comes from such teamwork. In fact, enterprises of this kind are carried out only in places where positive leadership now prevails or has prevailed in the recent past; in such places there is also to be found more than the usual amount of community spirit, along with freer land use rights among team members.

## CONGREGATIONS

Except for a few of the older men all Siuai natives are affiliated with either the Roman Catholic (*popi*) or the Methodist (*taratara*) missions. Degree of affiliation varies widely. At one extreme are a few paid native catechists who conduct daily services in their respective villages and who maintain 'close relationships with their white missionary superiors. At the other extreme are a large number of nominal converts who have learned and then forgotten a few rudiments of Christian doctrine but who otherwise participate in mission activities only to the extent of attending one or two services a year. In between are the majority, who attend services with some regularity and are able to repeat the simpler liturgies with mechanical precision.[29]

Even before Administration control was established, mission influence began to reach Siuai — indirectly, through natives returning home from residence or work on other islands, and directly, through the proselytizing activities of white and native missionaries, including some Siuai who had received training in the British Solomons. In time, the Roman Catholic Society of Mary established two stations in Siuai (later reduced to one), each manned by a priest and nuns. The Methodists also maintained a white missionary and his family in western Siuai for a number of years, but later withdrew to the southeast coast. From the very beginning mission rivalry was intense. The Government Anthropologist, who visited Siuai in early 1930 had this to report:

> The expansion of mission influence attracts considerable attention, especially as the competitive methods employed by the respective mission organizations in gaining converts wherever possible, leads the population into channels of excitement and strong feeling, such as have not been experienced, probably, since the days of inter-tribal warfare. So intense was this interest in some of the villages visited during my survey, that I was impelled to draw the attention of the administration to the position, and suggest an inquiry into the whole question of local mission expansion, with the object of inducing the rival organizations to come to some agreement as to their methods of competing for the control of villages. So keenly had some of the natives responded to the spirit of competitive religious expansion that was being sown, so I was told, by certain native evangelists of both sects, that seeds of conflict were actually on the point of germinating, and supporters of the rival Christian bodies were on the point of introducing spears into their sectarian discussions, placing law-abiding villagers living under the protection of the Government in a position of having to take one side or the other, when all they wanted was to be left in peace.[30]

Subsequently this rivalry flared up into actual hostilities, with both factions burning the other's village chapels, and an official investigation had to be undertaken to restore peace. By 1937, however, most natives had already been "converted" to one side or the other and the heat of rivalry had cooled, although each side continues its attempts to win supporters from the other's ranks.

Nearly every line village now has either a Methodist or a Catholic chapel (some have both), presided over by a native evangelist who conducts daily services for his local congregation. In addition, these native evangelists sometimes conduct short daily classes in rudimentary reading and writing for village children. Catholic natives who live near the central mission station usually go there for Sunday services, as occasionally do natives who live farther away. Also, the missionary priest visits all his native congregations quite regularly to conduct worship and rites of christening, marriage, and extreme unction. The Catholic mission station also maintains in Siuai an elementary school, a dispensary, and a nursery for motherless infants, and these provide additional points of contact with natives. The white Methodist missionary is less accessible to his flock. Now and then he tours Siuai but spends most of his time at his coastal station some forty miles southeast of the eastern border of Siuai; instead, his native assistants visit him at his station quite frequently. Also, he maintains a school at his station where nearly all the brighter Methodist boys from Siuai spend a year or two acquiring the rudiments of reading, writing, arithmetic, and western manual skills.

The contrasting doctrines of the Roman Catholics and the Methodists need not be described here. I cannot say how far the white missionaries go in expounding these doctrines to the Siuai; my only data on the subject concern what various natives say about the doctrines.

The Siuai kupuna, Maker (*Tantanu*), has been appropriated by both missions to designate "God," and although the divine attributes of the Christian "Maker" are considerably greater than those of the native version, the change has not proved too difficult of acceptance — at least by those few natives who do accept the new definition. As for the other major deities, Jesus and the Virgin Mary are of course new concepts to the Siuai, but the Holy Ghost (*Mara Mikisa*) fits easily into the native belief system in its familiar form of a supernatural bird. A Methodist convert characterized the differences between the beliefs of the two sects in these words: "The Popis talk a lot about Jesus' mother and a place called Roma, while we Taratara think mostly about Jesus Himself."

As for other supernatural beliefs, mission doctrines about souls and saints accommodate quite easily into native beliefs, and mission attacks on demons and magic have served only to stress what natives already know — that most demons *are* dangerous and that magic can be deadly. The Christian concept of *sin* is new and, according to my inquiries, not well understood by even the most sophisticated of native evangelists. On one occasion I succeeded in having three native evangelists — two Catholics and one Methodist — discuss the subject together, and they agreed on the following proposition: that *sin* accumulates within a person as he does evil things, forming a hard round object that lies in the stomach. Catholics can get rid of sin through taking Communion, but Methodists have no special means of ridding themselves of it and hence have to take special care to avoid doing evil things.

We could go on at great lengths describing in detail some of the interpretations of Christian doctrine given by Siuai informants, some of them highly entertaining and many of them adjusted to the traditional native belief systems; but in order to keep within the bounds of this general monograph it will be better to summarize this subject in the following terms:

1. In many superficial respects Christian and Siuai beliefs about supernaturals and related magical practices are enough alike to make accommodation an easy matter; but

2. Neither Motuna nor Pidgin English contains words suitable for communicating adequately to the Siuai such Christian concepts as *sin, divine justice,* and the like, with the result that such concepts have not begun to influence Siuai standards of morality and ethics, or their beliefs about salvation.

3. Contacts between white missionaries and native converts are so indirect and infrequent that literal and meaningful transfer of Christian ideology is out of the question, even if the conditions of Siuai life made such an eventuality possible.

In matters of belief, then, mission influence has made little impact upon most Siuai. Similarly, Christianity cannot be said to have changed many Siuai practices. It has caused some Methodists to give up productive work on Sundays, and it has encouraged many of the younger men, especially Methodists, to wear cleaner loincloths; but it has had little effect in curbing polygyny or in changing other sex mores. It has discouraged the practice of image-sorcery — the carved wooden figures (*poripai*) used in this sorcery are condemned by the missions as being "graven images" — but it has probably had little inhibiting effect on other kinds of magical practice. In fact, some zealous converts now use Bibles as magical aids in litigation, and most natives see no difference at all between Catholic Communion and Siuai "Climbing" or between christening and Siuai baptism. Some Methodists heed their missionary and inhume rather than cremate their dead relatives, but for most natives Christian rites of passage merely reinforce the native rituals.

More significant than their influence upon religious beliefs and practices have been the missions' effects on social structure. As a result of mission rivalry new lines of social cleavage have formed or old lines of cleavage crystallized. Catholics and Methodists no longer burn one another's chapels but many tensions continue to exist.

Catholics outnumber Methodists in Siuai, not because of differences in doctrine or practice but mainly because white Catholic missionaries have been at the job there longer and more continuously than their Methodist counterparts. Some villages are entirely Catholic, others entirely Methodist, depending usually upon which missionary began his work there first. Once the missionary had received consent from the highest ranking local leader to construct a chapel and install a native evangelist, most of the leader's followers moved into his fold. Troubles began only when overzealous native evangelists tried to set up rival chapels in places already nominally affiliated. Many of these efforts were frustrated but some of them succeeded, with the result that there are today many villages with both Catholic and Methodist congregations. In such cases the smaller congregation, usually representing the later mission to have become established, is nearly always identified with one or two hamlet units, conversion or transfer of affiliation having followed kinship lines. In most instances when a whole hamlet unit changed missions it did so at the behest of one of its more influential members. For example, one such unit became Methodist when its senior male member became piqued after being advised by his Catholic priest not to acquire a second wife. Another unit became Methodist after one of its brighter young men returned from indenture with glowing tales of the imagined practical advantages of learning arithmetic and bookkeeping, which Methodist schooling specializes in.

In some cases the division between Catholics and Methodists corresponds to long-standing political divisions, with whole neighborhoods having purposefully embraced the sect opposite to that of their traditional enemies. This also occurred with respect to minority enclaves; for example, the M'ikahnanai Tree-rats [31] have been more or less unfriendly with their neighbors ever since their ancestresses moved there five generations ago, and no one was surprised when they became Methodists after all their neighbors had embraced Catholicism.

The tendency towards sect-endogamy has some effect upon the maintenance of social cleavages between opposing congregations, but many intersect marriages take place, with one of the spouses usually joining the congregation of the other, depending upon the choice of residence. There are, however, a few steadfast mission members, usually men, who do not change sects when they move to the places of their spouses, and these account for most cases of scatterings of sect A members in villages belonging predominantly to sect B.

Lines of inter-sect division do not harden so long as a village's minority sect members do not band together into a definite congregational unit. Nor, in the case of present-day relations between separate villages of opposing sects, does the fact of different mission membership create new cleavages or add significantly to cleavages already present; active religious hostility between separate villages seems to have ended.[32] Today, social cleavage between sects is mainly manifested in villages having opposing congregations, each with its own chapel and native evangelist.

Novei is a case in point. Novei is a large Methodist hamlet in the predominantly Catholic village of Moronei, all of whose men used to owe allegiance to the great war-making mumi, Moki.[33] Several wealthy matrilineages are centered in Moronei, including a unit of Eagles, which forms the nucleus of Novei hamlet; but under Moki's strong leadership all these matrilineages are reported to have been friendly and coöperative among themselves.

Poroni, brightest and most ambitious of these Eagles, spent his youth and early manhood in the British Solomons where he became a zealous Methodist. Later he returned to his home as an evangelist, intent on converting his relatives and neighbors to Methodism and also ambitious to play a prominent role in political affairs. Being shrewd and persuasive he had little trouble winning over from Catholicism all but two of his Novei kinsmen, but most of his other Moronei neighbors rejected his advice and soon began to object openly to his aggressive insistence and his self-important and domineering ways. He gave two feasts in an effort to win some renown for himself, but could not mobilize enough assistance to continue an active renown-achieving career. Finally, when he announced his intention of erecting a Methodist chapel near the entrance to the Moronei line village on land he claimed for the Eagles most villagers united against him to contest his claim. The ensuing litigation reached such magnitude, and the issues involved were so important, that the white missionaries are reported to have intervened [34] and the whole matter had to be settled by the neutral Administration Patrol Officer. Poroni was obliged to build his chapel off the main road and at Novei hamlet itself, a visible sign of the frustration of his ambitious proselytizing plans.

After this, innumerable little incidents have occurred to keep alive the antagonism between the Methodists[35] and the rest of Moronei. The former like to show off their superior knowledge of writing and Biblical history, but are jeered at by the latter because of their attempts to ape white ways. Troubles between individual members of the two rival sects usually end up as factional disputes. For example, when Poroni's sister's son was discovered at a rendezvous with a Moronei married woman many otherwise unconcerned Moronei men took up the issue and tried to use it as grounds for jailing both the culprit and Poroni. Threats were hurled from both sides, and some of these gave warning of the intent to enlist the aid of the white Methodist pastor or the Catholic priest.

This case of Novei exemplifies several significant aspects of the mission institution in Siuai.

To begin with, it typifies the circumstances surrounding mission membership. At first the residents of Moronei were Catholic, because the Catholic missionary was first to work there, and all but a few old men consented to "believe" in the bizarre doctrine which formed part of the many novelties being introduced by the feared and incomprehensible whites. It was also a novelty, and probably a pleasant one, to discover that the white missionary took an interest in their personal welfare in a manner that Administration officials and labor recruiters did not. In the beginning everyone became "converted" — that is, took part in mission activities — except those otherwise preoccupied or too old to bestir themselves. It was not a case of believers versus nonbelievers, of Christians versus heathens; in Siuai that is not a basis of social cleavage even today.

Next, this case exemplifies the generally valid observation that ties of congregation often follow ties of kinship, thereby throwing additional light on why some natives are Catholics and some Methodists.

And finally, the Novei case, which is typical in this respect of a number of recorded instances, shows how ambitious men, unable to gain prominence by traditional techniques, try to use the mission institution — including the power of its white leaders — in efforts to gain influence and authority.

## ADMINISTRATIVE GROUPS

The system of relationships imposed upon the Siuai by the Australian Administration contains some elements that are quite familiar to these natives along with some that are completely alien. From the point of view of natives now living in northeast Siuai, here is the way this new regime entered their lives.[36]

Siuai natives were aware of the arrival of Europeans at the outer edges of their universe during the last three decades of the nineteenth century — perhaps farther back than that. By the turn of the century some had even seen and traded with whites along the coast; though, at that early time, the natives do not appear to have been overawed by the aliens. (As, indeed, they had little cause to be, since the tiny launches and schooners in which the whites arrived provided slight evidence of their technological superiority.) In time, however, a few Siuai males began to work for whites farther south in the Solomons, and the tales they brought home, when added to the steel implements, the cloth, and other materials secured by trade, began to have a strong cumulative effect. Even then, however, the reaction was not altogether one of awe and fear. White men's firearms were accorded great respect but white men themselves seem to have been respected or held in contempt according to their personal traits.[37] It is told of one mumi (Kaopa, of Tohomono) that he changed his name to "Mister Tinder" after a Shortland Island white trader of that name, who was liked and respected by natives there.

According to native accounts, the Germans did not attempt to consolidate their rule over the Siuai. At one point (1912?) a German warship stopped at the coast and sent an exploring party inland as far as the Mokakaru, but left no tokens of authority. Then, the story has it, after the Australians had ejected the Germans from New Guinea and Bougainville, two administrative officers toured with a troop of New Guinea native police constables (1915?). The white officers stopped in Boreburu (western Terei) and sent their native police to Mokakaru to round up Siuai youths and men and return them to Boreburu where head-tax was demanded of each of them. Those few natives who possessed any British currency paid and were released; the others were taken to an east coast plantation where they worked for two months, earned enough to pay off the head-tax, and were permitted to return home.[38] Some of the younger men were encouraged to continue to work on Bougainville plantations while others were given opportunities to go and work in Rabaul; after these men returned home they constituted a pidgin-speaking channel for further acculturation.

Meanwhile, the Australian officials appointed Aiŋkes, the leader of the coastal Terei village of Riorio, as Paramount Chief (*Luluai*) over all western Terei and eastern Siuai, and left with him the responsibility of maintaining the Pax Australis. Ariku was appointed Paramount Chief over the rest of Siuai. After Ariku died, Kope of Unanai became his successor for central and southern Siuai (Korikunu and Ruhuaku), while northwest and west Siuai (Tonu) were placed under the jurisdiction of Moŋko, of Kupiŋku. Kope and Moŋko continue in office, but several changes have taken place in eastern Siuai.

After the death of Aiŋkes (1933?), Konsei was appointed Paramount of all eastern Siuai under circumstances that are still resented bitterly by most residents of this area. Then, as now, the residents of Rataiku (the northern three-quarters of northeastern Siuai) shared more kinship and other relationships among themselves than they did with residents of Mokakaru. There was, in fact, a considerable amount of feuding between residents of the two regions. For one thing, the most influential men of Mokakaru belonged to two intrusive sibs, the What-is-it-called (Toŋuno, an Eagle sub-sib out of southern and western Siuai[39]) and the Iquana (out of Terei).[40] Among the Rataiku, on the other hand, most of the mumis were Tree-rats, and they used to band together on occasion to raid Mokakaru. The Mokakaruans, being nearer to the coast, were in closer contact with western influences than were the Rataikuans; some of the former had even worked for whites, and several spoke pidgin. One of these Mokakaru sophisticates was Konsei, who had actually been a native police constable in the Solomons. Konsei ingratiated himself with the official white visitors and also became a local leader by native standards. On one occasion he reported to an Australian official that the Rataiku were feuding among themselves, with the result that a punitive expedition was sent there. Several club-houses were burnt down, a few natives killed or wounded, many more imprisoned, and the area generally "pacified." Shortly afterwards (1934?), Aiŋkes having meanwhile died, Konsei was appointed to be his successor with jurisdiction over Rataiku and

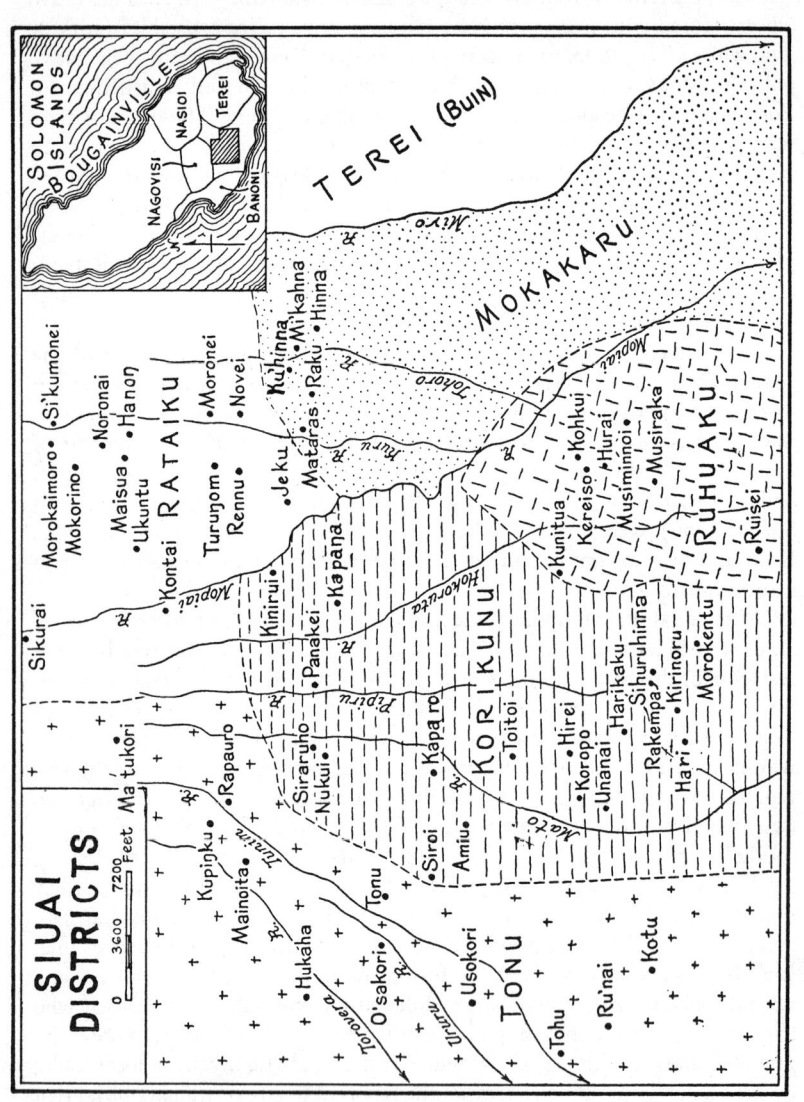

FIGURE 25

Mokakaru. It appears that the white officials actually held an election among the adult males to choose a man for this office, and Konsei was in fact the popular choice, partly because of his descent from the former mumi Kupiraki (who was his mother's father) and partly because of his own achievements. The only flaw in this otherwise admirably democratic procedure was the fact that only Mokakaruans voted in the election! Konsei remained Paramount Chief over Mokakaru and most of Rataiku [41] until his death in 1936. Meanwhile both Methodist and Catholic missions became established throughout Siuai, and so many youths had spent three-year terms working on plantations that nearly every hamlet contained at least one male who could speak pidgin.

After appointing Paramount Chiefs over all Siuai the Australian Administration continued to exert its influence, partly through the hierarchy of appointive native officials and partly through the more direct means of annual census and tax-collecting tours. The most visible evidence of this influence is to be found in the consolidated line villages,[42] the rest houses, and the network of wide paths that interlink the villages.

Although the settlement pattern represented by large fenced-in villages is an alien one to the Siuai, in many cases the residents of the hamlets which were forced to consolidate did share enough interrelationship to make the consolidation meaningful and palatable. For example, the several hamlets that were joined together to form the line village of Moronei had as their residents people who were close relatives, co-members of production teams, and supporters of a single mumi. In such cases as these the Administration-appointed village headman usually conformed to local choice. In other instances, however, the consolidations were arbitrarily made and the official appointments were unpopular with at least some factions.

Today, every Siuai native is required for official purposes to be affiliated with a line village, and in this sense the 1938 "population" of line villages in northeast Siuai ranged from 38 to 158, with the average around 70. In reality, however, there are many households which have very little to do with their officially designated line village. For example, many households reside only in their hamlet houses and do not even possess village houses. And an even larger number of households stay in their village houses only during the annual visit of the Patrol Officer. But whether or not a native resides and socializes with other members of his line village, he is compelled to submit to the authority of his village officials.

As previously mentioned, each village has three Administrative officials: the *kukerai* (headman),[43] the *tultul* (interpreter and deputy),[44] and the doctor-boy (medical tultul or orderly). All three of these officials are in fact appointed by the white Patrol Officer, although an effort is usually made to conform to popular choice at least in the naming of the kukerai.[45] In some cases a single native stands out so prominently that the choice offers no difficulty. Elsewhere there are rival factions and rival candidates, and the Patrol Officer must either count noses or resort to his own judgment by naming the man who appears best qualified from the Administration's point of view — which may or may not be pertinent. In still other instances the outstanding native leader of the village prefers not to hold Administration office and influences the appointment of some henchman.[46]

There is no fixed limit to tenure. By the time of my visit the institution had not been established long enough to allow for the surviving original incumbents to reach extreme senility — although there was some grumbling from young men that certain headmen were too old and bad tempered and ought to be replaced.

The lines of authority are theoretically simple: from Patrol Officer ("Kiap," in pidgin, from "Captain") to paramount chief to headman; the interpreters and medical orderlies should be aides to their headmen, but sometimes they usurp the latters' authority. The district interpreter usually serves as executive officer or as deputy to his paramount chief; in pidgin the latter is called "Number One" and the former "Boss-boy," which pretty well describes his activities. All these officials are exempted from paying the annual head-tax of ten shillings, and in addition each paramount chief receives an annual wage of sixty shillings. (This wage should be compared with the six to ten shillings per month, plus keep, earned by natives on plantations.) All native officials are given hats to wear when carrying out their Administration duties, and for this reason are referred to generally by other natives as "hat-men." They quickly learn to imitate the military bearing of the Patrol Officer's native police constables, and are expected to salute when reporting to their line superiors. (So sharply did some of them bring their heels together that mine nearly ached!) Despite Administration discouragement many of them insist on dignifying their official persons with western clothing.

Village headmen are officially responsible for helping the Patrol Officer to maintain law and order, being specifically charged to "arrest natives belonging to their tribes or villages whom they suspect to be guilty of wrongdoing or an offense," and to "bring them to the nearest court in the district, or before the district court, to be dealt with according to law."[47] The "courts" here specified refer to formal court sessions presided over by white officials. Theoretically, therefore, native officials should not[48] try cases or execute judgments; on the other hand, "wrong-doing," as defined by the Administration, covers an exceedingly wide variety of commissions and omissions, including gambling, sorcery and threats of sorcery, use of intoxicating liquor, "careless use of fire," the wearing (by males) of clothes over the upper part of the body, unsanitary practices, burying bodies too near to dwellings, keeping bodies too long before burial, etc. Here is one such regulation (Number 83): Any native who

(a) unlawfully lays hold of or strikes or uses violence towards any other person; or

(b) spreads false reports tending to give rise to trouble or ill-feeling amongst the people or between individuals; or

(c) uses threatening, abusive, insulting, or obscene language; or

(d) behaves in an indecent, offensive, threatening, or insulting manner towards any person; or

(e) behaves in a riotous manner,

shall be guilty of an offense. Penalty: Three pounds or imprisonment for six months, or both.

In addition, headmen have the authority to send natives under their jurisdictions to medical officers or hospitals for treatment or examination. Also, they are charged with maintaining order, keeping a record of vital statistics (births, deaths, individuals moving in and out of the village), for constructing and maintaining a fixed portion of the Administrative road, for supplying white travelers with porters along assigned stretches of road, and for various other duties assigned by their Paramount Chief and Patrol Officer. The village interpreter usually does the actual recording in the village book,[49] since the headman can seldom speak pidgin or write. Under the headman's general supervision the medical orderly is expected to see that the village is kept sanitary and its residents healthy; he ministers to minor coughs, fevers, and wounds with Administration-supplied cough syrup, quinine, aspirin, and bandages, and is required to report serious illnesses to the Patrol Officer. The Administration has of course regulated against abuse of authority: (Number 124)

Any luluai, kukerai, tul-tul, patrol medical tul-tul, medical tul-tul, or other native upon whom the Government has conferred authority, who uses such authority for the purpose of blackmail or wrongfully to get any property or benefit for himself or any other person or wrongfully to injure any other person shall be guilty of an offense. Penalty: Three pounds or six months imprisonment, or both.

But in this connection native officials who try to go beyond their powers are more effectively checked by *native* sanctions, including those applied by native leaders, than they are by a mere regulation.

We have already considered some of the effects of the village consolidation policy.[50] Periodically there spreads a rumor that the Patrol Officer means to enforce the policy rigidly, and this causes widespread consternation since natives realize what fundamental changes such a move would bring about (abandonment of the hamlet-house, modification of the present techniques of pig husbandry, etc.); but fortunately for Siuai life in its present form this rumor never materializes. Of all the other aspects of Administration, the Siuai most resent road work, portering, and taxes.

Native trails serve the purpose of foot travel but are narrow and circuitous. To facilitate patrolling, the Administration caused the Siuai to construct straight trails some nine feet wide and suitable wherever possible for bicycle travel. Bridges were ordered over the smaller streams, and these were required to be roofed over to prolong the life of the spans. Then at intervals along the road-network rest-houses were built to house Patrol Officers and other white travelers. The original construction of all these projects must have been a tremendous enterprise for the Siuai. Informants recall (or invent?) how garden clearing had to be laid aside for weeks and how food shortages resulted. The mandatory labor under alien pressure and for alien purposes must also have been extremely distasteful, as indeed it still is. Once completed, however, all these Administration projects would have required only a modicum of effort spent in maintenance but for the ambitions of some of the "hat-men." A few headmen and many interpreters seized upon Administration work as a means to lord it over their subordinates and curry favor with the Patrol Officer. They caused their stretches of road to be widened, graded, and smoothed far beyond necessity. Bridge timbers were shaped and planed as flat as a floor — really first-rate engineering, but hardly necessary for bare feet and a few bicycles a year.[51] The climax was reached with the rest-houses. A small two- or three-room affair would have served every possible contingency, and most rest-houses were so built; in some villages however the hat-men caused enormous barn-like structures to be built, up to ninety feet long and suitable for permanent residence on an expansive scale. The competitiveness which characterizes native politics is carried over into these new activities, and many hat-men endeavor to build better roads, bridges, and rest-houses than neighboring villages and districts. All this is highly rewarding for the hat-men, but for the ordinary villager it is time-consuming and onerous. Some of course share the satisfactions of the hat-men when their efforts result in praise from the Patrol Officer, but these are meager rewards; and because it is Administration work they receive neither wages nor the food, entertainment, and other satisfactions that accompany working for native objectives. In some villages one whole day a week is spent on Administration work and in others a half-day a month seems to suffice; the average is about one-half day a week. Yet no matter how much or how little the time so spent, most natives complain about it, saying that it leaves them no time for gardening — not a very plausible story in view of the relatively little time men normally spend in their gardens. A few headmen share their subordinates' views and do not impose any more work than a minimum, thereby earning their people's gratitude. Others are almost tyrannical in their demands and are roundly disliked. And there are a few who are too ineffective to secure either obedience from their villagers or support from the Patrol Officers.

Portering is another unpopular aspect of the new regime. Headmen are expected to supply porters for passing white travelers. For this work each porter receives an equivalent of one shilling a day (usually paid in twist tobacco), with each crew working about one-quarter day for one twist of tobacco. Even with this relatively high remuneration, plus the fact that most natives do not porter more than three or four times a year, the work is thoroughly distasteful to the Siuai.

A head-tax of ten shillings a year would appear at first glance to be a heavy burden upon natives with as little opportunity to earn Australian currency as these have, since their only important source of cash income comes from working on whites' plantations, at about 70 to 120 shillings a year. In reality, though, the exemptions are so numerous that the burden is spread quite thin; none of the following need pay: females, males under sixteen and over forty, fathers with four or more living children by one wife, village officials of the Administration, mission catechists, students at Administration or mission schools, natives serving in the constabulary[52] or under indenture, and men crippled, chronically ill, or invalided. For the whole adult male population of Siuai it turns out that only about one in three has to pay. Nevertheless, this does not help greatly to popularize the tax. The theory of "taxation for responsible citizenship" has been frequently expounded to them in pidgin English by sympathetic Patrol Officers, but even those few natives who comprehend the general theory feel that it hardly fits their case inasmuch as they do not elect the Patrol Officer or participate in making the rules he enforces. They admit to receiving some medical service and supplies, but why should not the rich and powerful Administration donate these? Moreover, it strikes many natives as being unjust and unreasonable that white officials, with their great treasures of money, should collect the natives' few hard-earned shillings — "they do not need our money, having so much of their own."

It may not be officially intended, I believe, that taxation will force natives to work on plantations, but it does have that effect (although taxation is not the only force operative).[53] When a youth returns from his three-year period of indenture he brings back with him some four to six pounds (Australian); such natives usually save a pound or two against future taxes, and lend or exchange the rest for native goods and currency. As a result there are several hundred pounds of Australian currency in circulation throughout Siuai, and natives in need of tax money usually experience no difficulty in obtaining some through trade or loan. The man who cannot or does not pay is usually jailed at the Patrol Officer's headquarters on the coast, where he is made to work off his indebtedness.

So far as I could learn, native officials are tacitly authorized to hold preliminary hearings on cases not involving death or serious bodily injury and the like, but in many instances these hearings contain all the elements of actual trials, with judgments being passed and executed by the presiding native officials.

Village "hearings" (*koti*, pidgin for "court") are usually held in the headmen's club-houses and are well attended by curiosity- or diversion-seekers. Sessions are highly informal and slow to begin, and litigants usually arm themselves with magical devices to add power to their speaking and to weaken their opponents. Since everyone present, including the presiding headman, has already formed his firm and unalterable opinion about the case, the headman's main task is to announce *his* judgment with as much show of impartiality as possible. The idea of compromise is quite alien, so that most judgments are clear-cut findings for one side. The loser theoretically enjoys the right of appeal to his paramount chief and beyond him to the Patrol Officer, but few natives will have the desire or the courage to antagonize their village headman in this manner, except in the case of large matters, which will ordinarily come up before the paramount chief or Patrol Officer in any case.

Litigation between residents of different villages is usually decided by the paramount chief. Such sessions are more formal, and attract audiences of thirty or more natives.

It would be almost safe to assert that in Siuai no case is *finally* settled in native supervised "courts." When a Patrol Officer makes a judgment it is usually accepted — with sullen acquiescence or with bewildered resignation, but with the realization that no one can change it. (The existence of village record books has finally discouraged natives from "testing" each successive Patrol Officer by renewing old lawsuits.) On the other hand, a loser before a hat-man can always bide his time and renew the suit on some more propitious occasion. During my stay, I witnessed cases involving land ownership which were at least three generations old and which had been many times "decided." In general, a headman who is also an influential leader is a more acceptable and effective judge than one who is not, but it is also a fact that in villages where the leader is headman litigation is less frequent.

Let us now consider how the Administration regime operates in a few typical villages.

The village of Moronei has already been described as being formed of several closely interrelated hamlets and as having a large and enthusiastic gardening team. Kakantu, the present headman of Moronei, is a figurehead, a popular and genial man of low political rank. The first headman was Moki, a greatly feared and respected mumi; his son, Ripa, did not long survive him. After that the local sentiment favored either Tumare, Ripa's son, or Manrai, one of Moki's chief supporters (*mouhe*). Tumare was trained in the Catholic school and became the native evangelist for his hamlet; he preferred to retain this post rather than become headman. Manrai also expressed little interest in becoming headman, so the villagers asked the Patrol Officer to appoint Kakantu. As far as I could discern most of the village was already so unified[54] that little positive leadership was required to enforce the carrying out of its obligations to the Administration. The favorite occupation of most of the male residents seems to consist in sitting around the local club-house and reminiscing about the greatness of the deceased Moki and the excitements that prevailed during his regime.

The small village of Jeku consists of a nucleus of Crane matrilineage-mates whose First-born, Kaŋku, is the local leader and headman. Jeku villagers are a closely knit group, and naming Kaŋku headman merely confirmed the authority he already possessed. Kaŋku has already passed his feast-giving prime and is in fact too ill to continue such activities, hence there is no noticeable *esprit* about the village — but neither is there much strife (at least, not since four of Kaŋku's five wives died!).

Mataras village provides a sharp contrast to Moronei and Jeku. It is composed of several comparatively unrelated hamlets, and possesses no outstanding leader. It was formerly held together by the mumi and Paramount Chief, Konsei (see above, page 319), but his nephew, the present headman, Sipara, is a silent and dull-witted man who prefers gardening to administrating, and who enforces Administration orders mechanically and tactlessly. His villagers continually complain about road work and are forever suing one another for real or imagined wrongs. For example, in the act of consolidating the village, the Patrol Officer caused the site to be located on land identified almost exclusively with members of one hamlet. This site contains many coconut and areca nut palms, and the owners are perpetually accusing their neighbors of stealing nuts.

Morokaimoro is another unhappy village. Most of the residents are closely enough interrelated by kinship and other ties, but the headman, Kummai, is suspicious, vindictive, and overbearing. He was appointed to the post by the Patrol Officer because of his command of pidgin and his ingratiating behavior towards Administration officials, after the local leader had refused the post. Kummai belongs to a small and uninfluential matrilineage, and apparently has decided that he can obtain more power through Administration channels than by the traditional route. His orders are peremptory and he is continually fining and threatening villagers for insubordination. (On one visit of a Patrol Officer he is said to have "courted" every youth and adult male in the village!) A few of his villagers and most men in neighboring villages are contemptuous of him, and his reaction to this is to practice sorcery and to threaten people with this instrument as well as with the Administration.[55]

The village of Turuŋom was formed by consolidating some fairly disparate hamlets, but so powerful a personality is its leader, Soŋi, that the village has held together as a highly effective political unit. Litigation is infrequent and appeals never go beyond the village. Soŋi at first caused his older matrilineage-mate Siham, to be appointed headman, partly out of respect for the latter's age and partly to avoid having any truck with the alien Administration; but Soŋi continued to dominate the village. We shall hear more about Turuŋom and Soŋi in the chapters that follow.

Turning now to the officials of the "tribal" Siuai Districts: Tomo is now Paramount Chief of Mokakaru and most of Rataiku, Kope of Korikunu and Ruhuaku, and Moŋko of Tonu. (See map, Siuai Districts, page 320.)

After the death of Konsei, a delegation of his matrilineage-mates succeeded in having the Patrol Officer appoint Konsei's sister's daughter's son, Tomo, the next Paramount Chief; again, the Rataiku were not consulted. Konsei's own sister's son, Sipara, now headman of Mataras, was considered for the post, but was rejected by his kinsmen because he did not speak pidgin and did not particularly want the job. At the time, Tomo was a handsome, bright, and ambitious youth who had had some mission schooling and "knew all about Government." He even showed promise of becoming a leader, so his kinsmen and Konsei's other loyal followers recommended his appointment.

Tomo himself is a well-intentioned young man, and he set about his job with a reformer's zeal to make his District "straight" according to mission and Administration models. The Rataiku were at first disposed to accept him since he lacked Konsei's vindictiveness; they even referred to him good-naturedly as "the pickaninny Number One." The difficulty lay with Tomo's district interpreter, U'ta, who was also Konsei's. U'ta is a smooth-tongued, ingratiating scoundrel, whose conceit and appetite for power are continually being increased through exercise of his Government authority. U'ta had hoped to succeed Konsei, and it was a blow to his pride to become subordinate to the younger Tomo. He immediately set about to undermine the latter and succeeded with all but a few of Tomo's close kinsmen — without, however, winning any support for himself, since most natives are contemptuous of him and his official airs. Relations between Tomo and U'ta became so strained that the Patrol Officer had to intervene and order them to hold a betel-chewing feast, a hatchet-burying type of ritual formerly carried out to end hostilities between two feuding mumis. Meanwhile, like most reformers, Tomo's zeal to make his District "straight" has led him to interfere more and more in the domestic affairs of his subordinates and he has become something of a self-righteous tyrant. The Rataiku, particularly, resent him and talk of trying to have him replaced. They boycott him as a judge, and take their inter-village quarrels to Soŋi, of Turuŋom, to adjudicate. During one period the Rataiku officials even put aside their Administration hats and wore native ones instead as a sign of protest against Tomo's regime.

Kope, the Paramount Chief of Ruhuaku and Korikunu, is an extraordinary man in several respects. He is one of the highest ranking leaders of all Siuai as well as a loyal friend of the Administration. He accepts the inevitability of westernization without rancor, and does not use his office opportunistically — as, indeed, he has no cause to since he has already achieved preëminence according to native Siuai standards. He is a courageous protector of his people against senseless Administration interference, but he is also a friend and interpreter of the Administration before his people. In his interpersonal relations he is solemn and usually benign, giving vent to anger only against opportunistic upstarts like U'ta. (In a word, he is one of the wisest and most admirable men I have met in any society.) Kope administers his District with restraint, with the result that his direct official influence is not as apparent as that of his fellow Paramount Chiefs.

Monko, the Paramount Chief of northwest Siuai (Tonu), is also something of a reformer like Tomo but in addition he is the highest ranking leader in his District and hence has the influence and authority to enforce his reforms. Unlike Kope he completely dominates his people, but few of them question his right to do so.

It is clear from the foregoing that status in the Administration hierarchy must be reinforced by status in the native political hierarchy in order to permit effective leadership, and this is true even though the hat-man has behind him the unlimited power of the Australian regime.

## MEN'S SOCIETIES

In an earlier chapter [56] men's societies were described as consisting of males past childhood who coöperate to prepare feasts not directly concerned with the exigencies of kinship. There are many men's societies in Siuai but not all Siuai males belong to such groups. In many instances the male residents of the unit of Administration, the line village, are the nucleus of a men's society. Elsewhere membership may be largely made up of males from neighboring hamlets which adhere to two or three different line villages. And in nearly all cases a men's society will have among its members one or more men who reside in distant hamlets and who are drawn into membership by ties of kinship or friendship; the numbers of these nonresident members tend to increase directly with the feast-making activities of the society and the *renown* of its leader. Some men's societies become quite inactive with respect to feast-making, so that the only factor which binds its members together is coöperative gardening, etc., reinforced by reminiscing about the active feast-giving days; such a men's society is to be found at Moronei village.[57] Other men's societies of former days have become completely inactive and have in fact disintegrated; such is the men's society at Mataras, which broke up after the death of Konsei. In still other instances, feast-making is carried on just often enough — about once every two or three years — to preserve the identity of the men's society. Elsewhere, feast-making and all the many enterprises associated with it take up a large part of men's time; in such instances as these the activities tend to follow an annual cycle, increasing with the advent of the almond season and letting off after the climax of the year's biggest feast three or four months later.

The average size of active men's societies ranges from some twenty to forty members, while the less active ones may have as few as fifteen.

The center of activity of a men's society is the club-house of its highest ranking leader, although occasionally events take place at club-houses belonging to some of his adherents; for example, in preparing certain kinds of choice puddings it may be necessary to have some of the ingredients cooked outside the main club-house because of limitations of space. (As previously noted, all club-houses are located away from residences, both to bar outsiders from seeing the women and to keep women from watching the proceedings in the club-houses.)

The large feast, always involving pigs, is the climax of activities of a men's society; it requires months of preparations — accumulating resources, repairing club-houses, cooking food, inviting guests, etc. Nor can these preparations be carried out in a haphazard manner; expert planning is demanded along with close timing and coördination. In other words, organization is required.

Native ideas about organization were summed up in the following statement:

"Men are either at the top or at the bottom or in the middle. If a man is a *mumi*, he is really on top; if he is a *mouhe*, he is not quite so high; if a *turaturana* or a *moŋo*, he is at the bottom. A mumi's *pokonopo* are in the middle."

The informants readily pointed out the metaphor involved in the use of the term mouhe: "Just as the mouhe (roof plates) support the thatch of a club-house, so do human mouhe support their mumi." "A mumi's pokonopo," they said, "are like the native police constables who accompany the white officer on patrol; they are not as high up as the mouhe." Moŋo means, literally, "leg"; and turaturana are "couriers" (derived from the verb root *tur* — "to send"). "These are the mumi's menials; they fetch and carry for him, procure his betel pepper, and cut open his drinking coconuts. They are below all the others."

Numerous other statements like these led me to believe that my informants were faithfully describing a complex and explicitly graded hierarchic system. Natives were agreed that the mumi was "truly on top," that the mouhe were "high up but below the mumi," that the mumi's pokonopo were "in the middle," and that moŋo and turaturana were "really below." They also stated that there was normally only one mumi, two or three mouhe, a few moŋo and turaturana, and many pokonopo in most places.

Equipped with this information, I started out to record the political hierarchy of each village, to learn the title of each man and thereby place him in his proper stratum.

This naïve hope persisted for about a week. Stratification there is, but it certainly does not conform to my construct. First of all, I discovered that the word pokonopo is compounded of the possessive pronominal prefix, *poko-* (his), and the plural form of the personal numerical suffix, *-nopo*; *ŋonosim*, the first person singular form of *pokonopo*, can be properly translated as "my friend." This term was frequently applied to mumis by their adherents, hence cannot be construed as meaning "underling."

"Then why do you call so-and-so 'ŋonosim'?" informants were asked. "Because he assists me and I assist him," was the reply.

"Explaining" native thought processes is usually a brash undertaking, but it is not difficult to account for this ambiguous use of the word pokonopo. When the Siuai speak of the members of a kinship group or of the inhabitants of a distant settlement, they refer to them through the name of some widely known individual in the group or settlement. Thus, Rovaro of Moronei village is a widely known tuki diviner (he is not a mumi); when men in distant villages refer to Moronei people they sometimes say, "Rovaro pokonopo" (Rovaro's people). It is logical to assume that the mumi with the widest reputation will be the point of reference when outsiders speak of the personnel of some region. Natives of northeast Siuai allude to the inhabitants of southeast Siuai as "Uremu pokonopo" even though Uremu, a prominent feast-giver, has no effective authority outside his own small village.

The words mouhe and turaturana would be useful rank designations were they not used interchangeably in practice. In every village there are a few men who use their own wealth to assist their mumi to prepare feasts and distribute property. They are, literally, "supporters." When the mumi needs a courier to go on some formal mission he usually sends a mouhe, who for that occasion becomes known as a turaturana. One informant persisted in his defense of my stratification construct but later on, during the same conversation, added: "When a big mumi sends out the invitations to a feast he chooses another mumi to act as courier (turaturana) and generally this other mumi is a supporter (mouhe) of his. 'Legs' (moŋo) are also *supporters* if they assist the mumi with their capital."

The explanation for the definition of "leg" as a "menial" probably should be sought in the social context of fighting times. The native, Piŋkei, of Jeku village is said to have been the "leg" of a mumi with whom he sought refuge. He tilled his mumi's soil for him, and in return was fed and provided with a wife. After fighting was outlawed, Piŋkei returned to his own village and resumed his activities as an independent man. Needless to say, today under the Australian Administration no native is compelled to remain a "leg" unless he wishes to.

Obviously, little dependence is to be placed on natives' generalized statements about the hierarchic structure of their men's societies, except that certain men, called mumi, are the leaders. It was necessary, then, for me to embark on an investigation of what actually happens among members of a men's society when they are engaged in coördinated activities. This required intensive observation and inquiry concerning who gives orders and who obeys them, a very tedious process but one that turned out to be richly rewarding, since it helped me to ascertain not only the structure of men's societies but also the process whereby individuals attain high rank in these societies.

In terms of the *direction* of interaction, each men's society is differentiated into those who characteristically give orders which are carried out by co-members, those who characteristically receive *and carry out* orders from co-members, and those who do both — in other words, each society is a hierarchy consisting of at least three levels. In some instances, the middle level may be further differentiated, as in the Maisua men's society:

| | |
|---|---|
| upper level: | Sipisoŋ |
| middle level: | a. Iroro<br>b. Tumari, Kumeruki, Nammito, Horona, Kutomai, Kunkei, etc. |
| lower level: | Tohui, Sarapana, Tokura |

In events involving several members of this society Sipisoŋ nearly always effectively originates action (commands, requests, suggestions, signals, etc.) to others, but very rarely does he join with the others in carrying out commands, etc., from anyone else. Iroro is also characteristically a successful action-originator to everyone else except Sipisoŋ, and he frequently carries out or transmits Sipisoŋ's orders to others.

As for titles, Sipisoŋ is always addressed and referred to as mumi, and for Iroro it is usually the same. Some of their co-members and other kinsmen and friends occasionally call Nammito and Kunkei by this title; and these two along with Tumari, Kutomai, and some others in the middle level are also described as *supporters* (mouhe) of Sipisoŋ. The title of *courier* (tura-turana) is applied on occasion to nearly everyone in the society except Sipisoŋ, but only Tohui, Sarapana, and Tokura are consistently referred to as "legs."

The process whereby individuals attain high rank in men's societies forms the subject matter of Part III, but before embarking on that description let us consider two more kinds of association — that based on *friendship* and that based on *vicinity*.

## FRIENDSHIP

In Siuai there is not much scope for the development of friendship ties separate from the other ties of kinship and association already listed. This is not to deny the existence of amicable and even affectionate interaction among persons not linked by ties of close kinship, etc.; it is merely intended to indicate that "friendship" as we know it in our own and in many other societies is not recognized by the Siuai as an important social category, bonds of "friendship" usually being rationalized and institutionalized in terms of kinship, taovu-partnership, work-teammate, etc. Natives sometimes use the word "ŋonosim" in a way that corresponds approximately to the English "my friend," but there are no mechanisms for formalizing such friendships, and in fact there is probably less emphasis on friendship in Siuai than in most societies.

For one thing, the wide dispersal of settlements does not encourage continuous interaction among persons living in separate hamlets; and work habits do not tend to bring such persons together frequently. Nor is age-grouping an important organizing principle with the Siuai. Children do not ordinarily flock together in large play groups or carry on a life of their own. Even in the few closely knit villages like Moronei, children are usually to be seen either working or playing near their older relatives. When play groups do form they are likely to include toddlers as well as near-youths. Similarly, later in life, the aged do not usually segregate themselves from the middle-aged at gatherings. In fact, coevality appears as a relatively strong relationship bond only among young unmarried men, and particularly among those who have just returned from terms of indenture. Pairs of such youths may be seen strolling together,[58] but not long after marriage most such friendships dissolve into casual acquaintanceships or become perpetuated in formalized taovu-partnerships. It is perhaps significant that the Siuai have turned to pidgin English to find a word (*peren*, friend) to describe these temporary friendship alliances of young unmarried males.

## NEIGHBORHOODS

We cannot tell much about neighborhood communities [59] solely by study of settlement maps. It is true that there are some such "communities" which correspond to the hamlet residents assigned to a single line village — Moronei is one of these, where with few exceptions the residents are all interrelated through ties of active, face-to-face interaction, based on closely interlinked kinship ties, membership in common work teams, and a great deal of daily visiting and conversing.[60] At the other pole there is the small hamlet of Mi'kahna [61] which is surrounded by people who are rather unfriendly and uncoöperative towards them; Mi'kahna's principal matrilateral relatives and associates reside at Maisua, some two miles to the north.

In other words, spatial contiguity is no guarantee of social interaction. A map showing bonds of interaction and interest would resemble a highly complex and disorderly network, with lines revealing especially heavy concentrations only in those areas where active men's societies prevail or used to prevail a few years ago.

Nevertheless, it is possible to speak of neighborhood communities in a sociological as well as in a spatial sense. Even in areas such as Mi'kahna and its surrounding hamlets there is inevitably some face-to-face interaction among all the residents, and this circumstance is reflected in their attitudes. For, however much the Mi'kahna people's neighbors may dislike them they do not term them "strangers"; [62] and except in times of active hostility both factions permit one another free *right of way* across their respective tracts of land. At the other extreme, among the most cohesive neighborhoods, these tacit rights of land-use reach a point where neighbors are more or less free to plant on one another's land, and even speak of the whole neighborhood area as "our land."

The sizes of Siuai neighborhoods vary from about six households to fifty; another feature of such neighborhoods is that nearly all of them overlap.

# III
LEADERSHIP

CHAPTER 9

# Accumulating Capital

Siuai natives attach much importance to possessing *manunu*. There is some difference of opinion among them concerning what constitutes manunu, but the root meaning comprises the following items: all shell money; all pigs; all other consumption and durable goods which are in excess of household consumption and which are convertible into pigs or shell money.

The word "surplus" approximately expresses the term manunu in so far as it applies to foodstuffs and durable goods. The Siuai *expect* a household to be able to provide adequately for its own minimal subsistence and ceremonial needs and to carry out its traditional social obligations. Natives do not praise others for their capacity to survive; they reserve their respect for those who accumulate surpluses, and express only contempt for those who do not work hard enough to sustain themselves properly.

Moreover, a Siuai does not attempt to produce surpluses to raise the level of his or her household consumption above that of a neighbor's; these natives are not given to gluttony or to the expression of conspicious waste in their household economy. No value is placed on having four pots for household use when three will do; and to produce for domestic consumption more taro, etc., than the average individual eats would strike them as foolish waste of effort. On the other hand, surplus pots manufactured for the purpose of exchanging for pigs or shell money, or surplus taro produced for the purpose of converting into pigs or of giving a renown-bringing feast — such items are valued as *manunu*.

The word "surplus" is less appropriate as a translation for manunu when this Motuna term is applied to pigs and shell money, since *all* these items are labeled manunu. It is true that neither shell money nor pigs is required for securing domestic food or housing, and very little money is required for clothing and tools. On the other hand, Siuai natives marry, have children, become sick, and die, and all these require the use of pigs or the expenditure of shell money; therefore it would seem that reserves of money and pigs for these inevitable crises can hardly be called surpluses.

Under these circumstances manunu might best be translated as *capital*,[1] and will be henceforth. In this connection, it is significant that Australian currency has not generally come to be regarded as manunu. The main reason for having any is to pay head-taxes and to purchase western trade goods; it has not yet entered widely into Siuai exchange transactions.[2]

The desirability of possessing manunu is explicitly expressed in three ways: in the high esteem usually expressed for the wealthy, in the prominence accorded manunu in ritual, and in the emphasis placed on acquiring manunu in connection with child conditioning.

Much admiration is expressed for the wealthy (*rurenopo*), provided they are not miserly;[3] whereas the fully adult male with no manunu may be contemptuously called a "nothing-man" (*roruki nommai*), unless there are extenuating circumstances to his poverty.[4] Males are not expected to begin acquiring manunu before marriage,[5] but the exceptional one who does so wins praise from his elders.

Respect for the wealthy is shown in a number of ways. They are never to be found among the lower levels of men's societies, being usually either leaders (mumis) or important supporters (mouhe) of leaders. In the planning of a feast, their advice is usually sought, since their riches may be required to help finance the feast. Even under ordinary circumstances most men will behave with deference towards the wealthy, against the day when a loan may be needed or against the possibility that they could become dangerous rivals or enemies. When wealthy men go visiting they are treated with courtesy and formal hospitality; being men of substance it is expected that they travel only for serious purposes. Some of these manifestations of respect are also shown for wealthy misers who are feared even though they are not liked or admired.

The acquisitive *skill* (*tana*)[6] of the self-made wealthy man[7] is believed to persist after death; and surviving kinsmen and friends try to obtain rapport with his ghost in order that it will aid them in their economic enterprises.

Some recognition is also accorded men on the road to becoming wealthy — in other words, men who are *effectively* industrious. The man who works and works merely to sustain life for himself and his household is looked upon with pity or disdain, according to his special situation; but the man who toils abnormally long hours producing taro or pots, etc., for sale is regarded with respect and wonderment, even though he may not be considered a potential leader.

Wealth symbolism figures importantly in Siuai ritual, especially in life-crises rites. We have already seen how concrete units of wealth form part of the ritual paraphernalia, and how the verbal formulae used on these occasions stress the desirability of wealth no less than health and longevity.[8] High-value shell money also enters prominently in myth, as in the case of the sib hoards (tomui).[9]

## SHELL MONEY AND ECONOMIC VALUE

To the Siuai shell money [10] is the most concrete form of capital. For some natives the accumulation of money is an end in itself, for others it is a means of facilitating trade, for still others it is merely a necessary instrument for carrying out kinship obligations. And, there are a few persons who possess practically none of it and hence make little or no use of it. But even to these latter, who barter goods for goods, shell money serves as a standard of valuation for the things they barter.

Siuai money consists of bits of marine shell pierced and strung on plant-fiber strings each a span long. As far as I can determine, none of the money now in use originated in Siuai; it was manufactured elsewhere, mainly in the islands to the south and east, and traded to the Siuai in return for local products.[11] There is no technical reason why the Siuai could not manufacture some of their own shell money, for marine shells are not altogether unobtainable; these natives often restring and rearrange the shell discs, but they make no effort to cut, pierce, and polish new discs.

*Pesi* is the general Motuna term for all native money, but it varies greatly in type of shell, as well as in color, diameter, and thickness of disc. The most common form is called *mauai*, one span [12] of which is the unit of all money value; mauai consists of bits of unpolished mussel shells. Generally, ten spans of mauai are fastened together in a bundle, and five of these bundles are packed into a basket and kept on the smoke rack.[13] *Kuriri* is also made of mussel shell but of much smaller fragments, one span of kuriri being equivalent to five of mauai. Both mauai and kuriri are said to have come from Alu. All other native money consists of small discs of mollusc, tridacna or spondylus shell ground down to various thicknesses; the generic name for these more valuable types is *koso*. All koso is evaluated in terms of one-span units of mauai, with denominations ranging from ten to one hundred and more, in units of ten. Size for size, red discs are worth about two and one half times the white ones.[14] Some spans of koso consist of all white or all red discs; others consist of two-inch strips of red discs (*mu'kapu*) interspersed among the white, thereby increasing the value of the span. The largest discs are about one-quarter inch in diameter and one-tenth inch in thickness, while the smallest have a diameter of about one-sixteenth inch and a thickness of one-thirtieth. The size of the disc, however, is the same throughout any single span. For valuation purposes there are two sizes of red discs and three of white. Here are the principal denominations and the values they possess in northeast Siuai:

> *Koso* is also the specific name applied to a span of the largest and least well-rounded white mollusc discs. It is said to come from Alu and its value is ten mauai.

*Sansai*, or *isaisa*, are white mollusc discs, thinner than koso; they come from Alu and Banoni and are valued at twenty mauai a span.

*Poponi* are the smallest white mollusc discs; they come from Banoni and have a value of sixty mauai a span.

*Sariai, momoru, runnaku.* These are red discs made from red-lipped spondylus. They are said to have been in Siuai for a very long time (since *u'kisanum*), and are believed to have come here originally from the place Sariai, in Buin.[15] Each span is valued at fifty spans of mauai.

*Mimis* is almost identical to sariai, momoru, and runnaku in color and size, but is said to have come here from Alu about 1900–1910; its value is fifty mauai.

*Kurakanikana* is made of very small red discs. It is believed to have been in Siuai for a very long time and to have come from Banoni.[16] Some spans are interspersed with a few discs of white poponi. Pure red kurakanikana is valued in excess of one hundred mauai.

*Karoni* consists of white koso containing one strip (*mu'kapu*) of red discs (mimis, sariai, etc.); its value is "a little more than ten mauai."

*Tomo* resembles karoni but has two or more strips of red discs, its value depending upon the number of red strips: one with two strips is worth twenty mauai, etc.

*Kurireu* consists of poponi with strips of very small red discs; each strip adds ten mauai to the poponi's value.[17]

Siuai natives themselves restring high-value shell money to obtain the denomination required, and they frequently accuse one another of skimping on red discs when they are making up composite spans. Because of this practice there is some disagreement about the values of composite spans. There is also disagreement about the value of kurakanikana. Those natives who own a span or two of this precious shell money claim for it a much higher value. One of these told me:

> I want to tell you the real value of kurakanikana. Mine is worth 500 mauai, although I would never use it to purchase pigs. I keep my two spans in my carrying-bag and take it wherever I go, because if I am traveling and become swept away in a swift river current, the kurakanikana should be lost with me. My wives also keep theirs with them for the same reason. It is the most valuable of all money; and nothing-men, who own none, always lie about its true value.

There is also some inconsistency involved in the equivalence of denominations; for example, a tomo which includes five strips of red discs alternating with intrinsically less valuable white is said to be worth fifty mauai, which is also the same value ascribed to an all-red span of mimis made up of the same size of disc. Natives tacitly recognize this difference; a man selling a pig worth fifty mauai will sometimes insist on being paid

## ACCUMULATING CAPITAL 341

with mimis rather than tomo, even though he will admit under questioning that "each is worth fifty mauai." A man who continually uses tomo instead of mimis in his transactions becomes unpopular in time, somewhat like the miser; natives say that such a man can become wealthy but never a leader.

All the above denominations may be properly called *money* in that they are used in payment for goods and services. Kurakanikana is ordinarily kept as part of a matrilineage's heirloom (tomui), but it is also occasionally acquired, held, and used like other high-value money. Other denominations of high-value money similarly serve as parts of matrilineage heirlooms but are more often used as currency.

For more strictly commercial purposes such as buying commodities and paying for expert services people generally use mauai and kuriri. Mauai and kuriri are also used in ritual payments, such as flattery-rewarding (pavaru), shame-payment (numehu), indemnification (rakai), competitive "gifts" to political rivals, etc., while betrothal "gifts" and the like are usually made in the form of high-value money.

Today few natives barter native goods for other native goods and services. Informants state that part of the former trade with Alu and Mono islanders was by barter; nowadays Siuai natives favor barter only to exchange northern pots for southern lime and to obtain European trade items, and otherwise prefer to pay or be paid in shell money.

In the list of comparative values represented below, one feature is characteristic: the *unit* equivalence of many of the items, i.e., *one* span of mauai = *one* bow, or *one* hunting spear, or *one* plot's yield of taro. (This in itself throws some light on what might have been one of the original price-fixing mechanisms.) The following list represents the current price of some of the most common items actually sold for shell money. One span of mauai buys:

One plot's yield of taro.[18]
Two *miŋkams* of almonds (a miŋkam is a cylindrical leaf container about two inches in diameter and two feet long — measured as portion of a human span from dactylon to mid-humerus).
Two *piŋa'* of sago flour (a piŋa' is a cylindrical leaf container about six inches in diameter and two feet long).
Twenty coconuts.
Two opossums.
One hunting bow.
One bundle ( = ten) plain hunting arrows.
One hunting spear.
One medium-sized pot.
One medium-sized net bag.
One large carrying-basket.
Two decorated arm-bands.

Ten spans of mauai buy a suckling pig, fifty a large sow — each pig being valued according to girth measurement in terms of fractions of a span.

The complete list of purchasable objects is very extensive.

For most purposes, the exchange values of the listed items are fairly stable. Deviations do, however, occur and are worth mentioning. One great advantage in being a leader lies in one's ability to buy things more cheaply. ("When a mumi sends out thirty spans of mauai to purchase a pig for a feast, the pig owner would be ashamed to send along a pig worth less than forty.") On the other hand, this commercial advantage of the leader is usually counterbalanced by the traditional exercise of *noblesse oblige*.[19] Also, some natives are continually trying to raise prices for selfish economic advantage. For example, during our stay one maker of bamboo tobacco-containers attempted to double the price of his products, but without success. I did, however, hear of several instances in which prices of items (pottery, combs, lime, etc.) had risen during the past decade.

It would not be possible to formulate any consistent labor-cost theory of value applicable to Siuai. The yield of a plot of taro, valued at one span, represents an incomparably larger amount of labor than does a pot worth one span. But here there enter other factors, such as supply and demand and specialization of skill: everyone plants taro and practically no one has to buy it, whereas pottery clay is scarce and expert pot-makers few in number.

The Siuai's penchant for evaluating goods in terms of mauai also extends to some services and other less tangible property. Fees of professionals vary quite directly with the practitioners' reputations. The relative amounts paid in fines and indemnities also provide some clue concerning the way the Siuai assess the seriousness of the crime or tort. For example, without attempting to draw general conclusions from the comparison, it is nevertheless interesting and possibly significant that the indemnity (*kujo*) paid to the relative of anyone killed in a brawl by the man who started it is only ten spans, which is also the amount of indemnity charged an individual who breaks a three-shilling machete.

Since land is such an all-important resource to the Siuai, and since it occasionally changes hands, I sought for some clue concerning its valuation. There are various methods which might be used to assess the value of land in terms of shell money. One of these is to compare the amount of land received in return for payment of nori. Another, the most obvious, is to learn the price paid for land by nori purchase. A third is to estimate rent, and a fourth is to evaluate produce.

The custom of paying nori has already been described in some detail.[20] Peruru and his brothers and sisters distributed 450 spans of mauai among matrilineage mates of their father, and received in return the tract Kokonom (*ca.* 73 acres) *plus* usufruct rights on Nanuno (see Figure 28, p. 485).

Tumare distributed the equivalent of 1065 spans of mauai among matrilineage mates and contemporaries of his father, and received western Siuno and a portion of northern Kiukiu (total of 91 acres). The discrepancy between these two sets of figures: 450 spans for 73 acres, and 1065 for 91 acres, illustrates the difficulty of evaluating land in this manner. Tumare's father was the leader, Ripa, and a man of great wealth besides. It was expected that Tumare would distribute a large proportion of his inheritance to provide his father with a fitting mortuary feast. Had Tumare given less, he would probably have been rebuked by his father's relatives and friends. Peuru's father, on the other hand, was neither very prominent nor wealthy. The 450 spans used to provide his mortuary feast belonged to Peuru's mother, and before her to her mother. When I questioned the surviving matrilineage mates of Peuru's father, they all agreed that under the circumstances Peuru's 450 spans had been a generous distribution.

As a matter of fact, the ratio, in Peuru's case, of 6.1 spans of mauai to each acre was quite near the average for all land "prices" estimated in this way. It is most important, however, to keep in mind the limitations involved in this estimation of "price." The transaction takes place among close relatives, with apparently little profit motive involved. The payment expected by the deceased's matrilineage mates depends partly upon the deceased's rank and the "purchaser's" patrimony. In one recorded case the deceased's land was handed over to his son without any payment, it being generally known that the deceased had exhausted his resources in feast-giving, and had left no *pure* to his son.

When we turn to slightly different cases of this kind of transaction, to cases in which a native pays nori on behalf of his father's brother or, better, father's remote sib-mate, we come nearer to the notion of "purchase." Also, there is a fairly general attitude concerning the proper "price" for land exchanged in this manner; for example, I attended two court cases in which the plaintiffs charged that they had not received enough land in return for nori payments they had made on behalf of distant *fathers*. Considering all the data collected on this kind of "nori purchase," an average of about 2.5 spans was paid for each acre. Compared with 6.1 spans which the son pays to "inherit" his own father's land, this 2.5 seems low. Why should a son pay more than a distant kinsman or friend? Well, he owes more to his father's ghost, natives would argue. Furthermore, he has first choice over his father's land, and almost invariably receives the most productive, the most centrally located tracts.

Outright land purchase is rare. Not one case occurred during my stay in Siuai, and I suspect that by "purchase" my informants meant a very attenuated form of "nori purchase." This, in spite of the fact that they assured me "true purchase is different from nori payments."

In Peuru's account,[21] his ancestresses were said to have paid 2000 spans for Mi'kahna, Parupa, Aura, and central Siromotuna, a total of about 150 acres. Soŋi purchased Mitakunno (about 30 acres) for 4000 spans. Koiri bought Turuŋorn (about 50 acres) for 1000 spans two generations ago. Poroni paid Kapumansa ten spans for the site (about one acre) on which Novei village is built. Obviously, these sets of figures are widely discrepant; and I could not discover any properties of the land involved which would account for such discrepancies, with the possible exception of *location*, of proximity to population centers. But even location did not invariably influence purchase price.

A third potential method of assessing the economic value of land is by estimating *rent* paid for use of another person's land. *De jure, True-owners* may exact rent (*muhni uḳum*, "of the landowner") from persons planting on their land. This rent consists of the first basket of taro (about ten corms) harvested from each plot, or about one-tenth of the total yield. The yield of an acre of taro has been estimated as being about 8670 corms; one-tenth of that — or 867, to be paid as rent — could be sold for some 8.5 spans (yield of one plot costs one span). In other words, if it were at all reasonable to reckon along these lines, cultivable land could be said to rent at 8.5 spans per acre; and if the economists' traditional rent-value ratio were to be applied (rent = 10 per cent of value), then cultivable land in northeast Siuai is worth 85 spans of mauai per acre. But such as estimate of land value in terms of rent is based on a slender theory. The fact is that rent on land is seldom exacted. People who are more or less equivalent in wealth and rank rarely require rent of one another. Nor does a commoner demand it of a leader. And in very few cases do leaders grow careless of their *noblesse* obligations and demand rent of commoners. This third method of estimating land value is, then, thoroughly artificial and quite useless.

There remains a fourth potential method of assessing the economic value of land: that is, by evaluating produce. There are obvious differences between arable and nonarable land. Whereas the ownership of arable land is often vigorously controverted, nonproductive swamplands are seldom quarreled about. Some arable land is, of course, more fertile than other; natives often recognize this and state quite sensibly: "His land is much better than ours; taro is plentiful there." But then in the next sentence they will usually add something like: "He owns a potent taro magic; and someone has probably bewitched our taro."

Although it is certain that natives recognize differences in land values, I saw no evidence of their *evaluating* those differences in terms of shell money or any other concrete unit of measure.

But what about fruit and nut trees growing on land? All these have standard values in terms of shell money (a bearing coconut palm is worth five spans, etc.); would it be possible to evaluate land on the basis of the value of trees growing on it? In a great many cases it might. A son, after paying nori, almost invariably receives the most productive part of his father's portion of matrilineage land. Included with this inheritance is nearly always the deceased father's coconut and sago groves, together with his almond trees. One native actually described the value of his patrimony in terms of the number of coconut palms growing on it. Yet, such a method of evaluation has only limited application. Frequently, trees may be owned quite independently of the land on which they grow. Furthermore, there are large tracts of cultivated land which have no valuable trees growing on them, and they are not for that reason "valueless."

From the foregoing, it seems necessary to conclude that Siuai culture provides no generally applicable method for assessing the economic value of land. Amount of nori payment, price of outright purchase, rental costs, evaluation of produce — all these criteria have but limited application. Land certainly *has* economic value to the Siuai; furthermore, there is a single factor — shell money — through which land values might conceivably be expressed. Yet, the Siuai do not make consistent use of that factor and as a result they cannot agree on the comparative economic value of separate tracts of land.

In the property survey I carried out in Siuai, I recorded a total amount of some 78,000 mauai units of shell money in circulation in northeast Siuai, this being in addition to the 41,000 mauai units of high-value shell "money" serving as matrilineage heirlooms and hence supposedly not used for currency.[22] Both currency and heirloom money are decreasing in quantity, the former through wear and breakage, the latter through funeral offerings;[23] and there is no chance for adequate replacement since the main source of supply has been cut off.

In view of the importance of money in Siuai culture it is not surprising to learn that there is an almost universal desire to possess more of it. How, then, do individuals acquire it?

Ownership of heirlooms (tomui) is vested in the whole matrilineage, although it is left in the keeping of the First-born, who is expected to preserve most of it for future generations. Members may secure small portions of it to finance life-crises ceremonies but not to satisfy domestic or sociopolitical needs.[24]

Inheritance of *pure* is a source of wealth, but in most cases the amounts inherited are not very large. It was described earlier [25] how most of an individual's shell money inheritance should be spent to provide pork for mourning. In a few cases I recorded, the deceased's family survivors hung on to all or most of the inheritance, but these were exceptional. Usually there is little left of a young man's inheritance after he has carried out his kinship obligations, and most men have to acquire through their own efforts what riches they want. And how do they acquire riches? Chiefly by raising pigs, by producing surpluses of goods and exchanging these for pigs or money, and by selling services.

## SURPLUS DURABLE AND CONSUMPTION GOODS

Every village contains specialist craftsmen of some description. Misam, the most expert cordage and rope-maker of northeast Siuai, resides in Mataras, and is visited three or four times a month by men from as far away as Ruhuvaku in search of a climbing rope or a ball of twine for making net bags. The best wood carver in the region lives at Jeku; nowadays he has little market for his products but formerly he conducted a lively business in carving and selling human figures for sorcery purposes. During our stay, it was the fashion to use incised bamboo boxes for carrying leaf tobacco, and a number of specialists spent most of their spare time manufacturing them on commission. None of these enterprises, however, earned much money for the craftsmen. Misam, for example, earned about six mauai a month through the sale of rope and cord; part of this he used to purchase lime and pots, part to convert into shillings to buy a steel ax; he did however, in time, manage to accumulate enough to buy a shoat. With most other craftsmen it is the same; they earn enough to supply their household with useful items, and save only enough to set aside for emergencies or to buy two or three shoats a year. Poor business, one might conclude; yet there is more to it than business. Craftsmen like Misam, and the many others who while away their time making boxes, combs, woven arm-bands, ohkuna hats, and ornamented weapons, do not seem to be feverishly engaged in acquiring capital. They leisurely work away at their crafts as if they were hobbies, with evident enjoyment in the activity and with satisfaction in the product.

With pot-making it is quite different, at least for those specialists who work at it intensively, that is, who devote about one out of every three or four days to it. With these men, pot-making is primarily a means of earning money. Even they seem to derive satisfaction from the good products they turn out but their tempo of working is faster than that of the man making a pot or two for his own use, and they appear more impersonal about the proceedings. (I am aware of the impressionistic nature of these statements but can offer nothing more concrete.)

Pot-making also differs from most other crafts in that, time for time, it is far more remunerative. One potter I knew made and sold on commission pots worth eighty mauai in a two months' period; another earned one hundred fifty in four months' time. These are large incomes when compared with the average capital of a household.[26] Why, then, do not more individuals engage in the business of making pots, since the work is so remunerative and since so much importance is attached to the possession of capital? "Because," informants replied, "men's desires differ, along with their qualifications and their capacity for work."

The Siuai do not make a business of manufacturing sago flour for exchange. An owner will occasionally sell some to a neighbor who is temporarily without taro and sweet potatoes, but most of it is kept in the household as a reserve or as provision for traveling. The feast-giver who wishes to serve his guests a special sago-almond pudding will usually secure the flour from his own palms, by individual or team labor. Only occasionally will he borrow or buy some from a kinsman or neighbor.

Sago palm leaves, on the other hand, are not infrequently made up into roof-thatching sheets for sale. Most of this work is done on a commission basis: if a man wishes to build a club-house he will usually commission neighbors and friends to manufacture most of the thatching. Up to 2000 sheets are required for a club-house and no individual owns enough sago palms or controls enough labor to manufacture so many sheets within the allotted time. (Natives could, of course, stock up on thatch by working many months ahead of actual construction; but the Siuai do not like to place old and dry thatching on a new roof.) Five sheets sell for only one mauai, so that no one can expect to earn more than a few mauai a year in this manner, even if commissions were continually forthcoming — which is by no means the case.

Coconuts are another potential source of cash income, but they are very seldom so used. Before the Administration interrupted interisland trade and before the Siuai began to obtain much-wanted knives, axes and calico from elsewhere, they used to carry coconuts and copra to their southern beaches to exchange with Mono and Alu Islanders and with the occasional European schooner that called there. Nowadays superior plantation hot-air dried copra has largely supplanted the inferior native smoke-dried product and the latter is no longer in demand on Bougainville. Also, the nearest trader, a Chinese storekeeper, is at Kangu, a full day's walk from Siuai, and the Siuai natives are no longer dependent on such trading for their imports; consequently, the sale of coconuts and copra to outsiders has ceased.

Nor do the Siuai sell coconuts to one another, except now and then to help a neighbor or kinsman prepare for a feast. In fact, even with the steadily increasing supply of palms,[27] no household ever seems to have enough available ripe coconuts for preparing the food delicacies the Siuai are so fond of, and most natives would be hard-pressed indeed to sell coconuts merely for tangible profit. Perhaps the main reason for this apparent shortage for domestic use is the increased consumption brought about by more frequent feasting. In any case, it is so difficult to purchase large quantities of coconuts that most active feast-givers try to enlarge their groves in order to supply their own needs. Coconuts are, then, a valuable form of wealth, but do not often enter trade.

The almond, more than any other Siuai economic plant, is purposefully harvested for sale. A portion of every tree-owner's crop is domestically consumed, and some households possessing only a single tree may keep all its crop for home consumption; but other owners will reserve large quantities of smoked nuts for sale. As noted above,[28] northeast Siuai is the center of almond-growing, and the demand is so lively that during the picking season natives from all parts of Siuai go to northeast Siuai in search of nuts to buy. So active is the demand at the height of the season that vendors often have to put up "sold out" signs [29] in order to discourage over-eager buyers. In every northeastern village can be found two or three men who specialize in collecting and selling nuts. Some of these may own only a single tree or so but will buy the privilege of stripping another man's tree. In one village for which I recorded this information, four such specialists sold altogether 350 mauai worth of almonds in one season — a substantial income indeed for a Siuai producer. As a rough estimate, I expect that some 3000–4000 mauai are earned in this manner each year by natives of northeast Siuai.

A taro begins to rot a few days after harvesting and it is not stored for future consumption or sale. Nor do these natives follow the practice of some Islanders of accumulating and merely displaying vegetable foods for prestige purposes. To the Siuai, spoiled food is a deplorable waste. Some natives do produce extra taro to serve as an accessory food at their own feasts or to sell to others for similar purposes,[30] but the main reason for growing surpluses is to feed more pigs.

The average household can feed one or two fully grown pigs from the culls and peelings of taro grown for household consumption, but to feed any pigs over that number requires additional production. Moreover, the additional production required to feed two or three more pigs cannot be accomplished without severe strain on the household's labor resources — at least, on the part of the women of the household, although not necessarily on the part of the male householder; but after that, the man who wants to raise more pigs must increase his supply of female helpers, because the amount of extra time he invests in gardening has to be matched by them in almost geometric proportions. The most direct way to raise more pigs, then, is to acquire another wife to produce more taro. And as has been previously noted,[31] this knowledge is explicitly recognized and purposefully acted upon by many ambitious Siuai men.

## PIGS

Throughout this account reference has been made to the uses the Siuai make of pigs. It was pointed out that pork is very seldom consumed in the household, and then only when a member brings some from a hunt, a feast, or a funeral distribution; usually Siuai natives do not slaughter their pigs for ordinary domestic consumption. On the other hand, data were presented to show that pigs are indispensable for ceremonies at birth and christening, at initiation into various economic enterprises, at marriage, and at death. In addition, pig-ownership is considered essential for adult socio-economic status. To shout at a person "You have no pigs" is to offer him an insult.[32]

Pigs also have utility in interregional trade; for some natives pig-raising and selling offer the only important means of obtaining desired goods. Also, distributing pigs at feasts is the conventional method for acquiring renown and influence, as we shall presently see. Then, there is another side to all this. When Siuai natives call their pigs by name, grin with pleasure as the beasts troop in squealing, carefully set out food for them in baskets and discuss their merits with noticeable pride, it becomes apparent to an observer that these people look upon their pigs as pets. There are times when an owner might discuss the money value of his beasts, but it is certain that not all incentives to possess the animals can be reduced to rational economic or social calculations.

Hunting pigs [33] is one potential way of supplying some of the desire for pork, but it is more for sport, and the booty is usually small. Pig-hunting seems to be on the decline. Before the introduction of European breeds, wild pigs were probably not very different from domestic ones — thinner and tougher, perhaps, but almost certainly the same breed. When natives were recruited for plantation labor they were brought into contact with larger, European-breed pigs. At the end of their period of indenture many natives used their accumulated wages to purchase these more desirable animals and carried them back home. Old natives have often reminisced to me about the early years when the first European-type pigs were introduced, and of the great excitement which prevailed: everyone wanted either to own one of the new beasts or to buy one of its offspring. It is obvious that the product is a great improvement in size and succulence over the old local variety. Most Siuai now disdain their native breed, and the difference between domesticated mixed-breed and wild pure-breed is great enough to discourage hunting.

Raising pigs is vastly more important for Siuai economy than hunting them. I have already described how intensely preoccupied natives are with caring for pigs and how the techniques employed influence other departments of their lives. And the end result of nearly all this activity is capital formation. In the first place, a thrifty Siuai would be very meat-hungry indeed before he would butcher a domesticated pig for himself and his family alone. His momentary gourmandizing pleasure would not offset his realization that he had sacrificed valuable capital and that by not inviting outsiders to the banquet he had wasted an opportunity for enhancing his prestige. But even granted that a man must occasionally butcher a pig to celebrate an event, he rarely ever uses a pig which he, himself, has raised. After years of looking after a beast, a native becomes fond of it. For example, Sinu of Jeku village invited a number of friends to help him build a house and promised them a pork banquet as a reward. When time came for killing his pig, he said, he couldn't bring himself to do it. Then someone suggested that he do what was ordinarily done: exchange his pig for that of someone else; he again demurred. Finally, he bought another pig outright and butchered it. He added, as a postscript: "I don't even like to kill my own fowls. When one has to be killed I get someone else to do it." Sinu was a more squeamish soul than most, but many natives share his sentiments. This being the case, if a man has to butcher a pig he generally secures one by purchase from some other native. On the other hand, he frequently has to supply others with pigs in order to fulfill ritual and social obligations, or in order to secure shell money capital so that he will have some resources on hand when he does actually have to secure a pig for butchering.

For purposes of sale, pigs are evaluated in terms of girth; and spans and fractions thereof are the common standards of measurement. A pig with a girth of or less than *kuiukunoui* (from dactylon to mid-clavicle, "place for carrying timber") is worth ten spans of mauai, and so on up to one with a full-span's girth, which is worth 100 or more mauai.[34] This standard of pig evaluation is common throughout Siuai, but that does not discourage some few individuals from bargaining. Nor are natives above taking advantage of one another's emergencies and raising prices on urgently needed animals. People who do this too frequently, however, soon acquire reputations for selfishness.

Informants told me that there were great fluctuations in prices when European pigs began to be introduced. For one thing, the European breeds and their progeny were larger, fatter animals than the native ones, hence by the standard girth measure evaluation they naturally brought higher prices. It is claimed that the native pure-breeds seldom exceeded *morokeŋkuho* in girth, whereas the mixed European-native breeds often reach a whole span in girth. But in addition, the early European pure-breeds used to fetch disproportionately higher prices; some of the more enterprising natives obtained as much as two or three times the standard value for animals brought in by them from coastal plantations.

It is not a simple matter to purchase a pig. Owners become fond of their beasts and are often loath to give them up. A would-be purchaser cannot merely let it be known that he is interested in buying, and then sit at home and await offers. He usually has to trudge from place to place seeking people out before he succeeds in finding a seller. After he locates a willing owner with a pig of the desired size he makes a down payment, and when the owner delivers the animal the purchaser completes payment. If the purchaser hasn't the full purchase price, he can often prevail upon the owner to wait a few months for full payment. But failure to complete the payment within the agreed time frequently leads to litigation and fines. The Siuai are cynical about deferred-payment purchases of pigs, and claim that they generally lead to lifelong enmity between the principals.

One situation was observed in which a hopeful purchaser visited a potential seller every day for nine days before finally concluding the transaction: all for a pig worth 20 spans of mauai! It is no wonder, then, that institutionalized arrangements have developed whereby acquiring pigs becomes simplified. One of these is the taovu relationship already described. For example,

Soŋi of Turuŋom village has an intimate taovu relationship with Sipum of Kaparo:

"When I hear that Sipum's sow has a new litter," Soŋi states, "I visit him and look them over. 'That pig will be mine,' I tell him; and later on when I wish to prepare a feast I send money along to buy the chosen pig."

Thus, an enterprising man like Soŋi always knows where he can go to buy pigs without having to search out and convince a prospective seller. This is a time- and labor-saving arrangement for a man who is continually giving feasts.

Economically, taovu is a fairly reciprocal relation; both partners may sell or purchase and the price paid for a pig should be near the traditional "open market" price. The aŋurara relation, on the other hand, is quite different.

After an ambitious man has established his influence over friends and relatives in his own neighborhood, and has begun to carry out social-climbing feast competitions with leaders from neighboring villages, he farms out pigs among his followers. When his sow farrows, he distributes the small pigs among his followers who retain and feed them until the owner has need of them. Then each follower returns the fully grown animal and receives about 10 spans of mauai as token compensation (aŋurara). Some leaders go beyond the limits of their own neighborhood and induce distant relatives to become their aŋurara-men (aŋuraranopo). One leader I knew chose his third wife from a distant village, "because her relatives were expert pig-raisers and might be induced to become aŋurara-men." An underlying assumption of this transaction is that the aŋurara-men will share in any renown accruing to the pig owner from the use he makes of the pig.[35]

Acquiring and raising pigs are, then, serious and laborious enterprises, not to be undertaken lightly. In addition, the mere ownership of them adds heavy responsibilities which impose more work. Pigs must be fed well. Hungry pigs will break through almost any garden fence, or they might leave home altogether and run away into the forest and remain there. Pigs that break into gardens cause continuous trouble for their owners; irate gardeners should not kill the beasts, but they may sue the owners for crop damage. This situation is an ever-present cause for strife among Siuai natives and accounts for half, at least, of all litigation. That is the reason why some cynical natives place the man with a large herd in the same category as the polygynist, saying that the rewards are not worth the effort and inevitable consequences.

A pig gone wild (huru pihoto) is a total loss, a greatly dreaded eventuality to these thrifty-minded natives. (There is a whole department of sorcery aimed at attacking an enemy by means of driving his pigs into the forest.) What's more, a man with many pigs lays himself constantly open to theft, and has to be continuously alert — to feed his pigs well and keep them near home out of reach of pork-hungry neighbors. In a place like Siuai it would not be possible for one man to steal another's pig and add it to his own herd: news of the theft would be broadcast, and the thief could not hide the stolen beast indefinitely. Consequently, the thief must kill and eat the pig, and the owner-victim uses magic to wreak vengeance on the thief rather than to recover his pig.

As previously mentioned, a full-grown pig requires a daily amount of five to six pounds of food, in addition to grazing, to keep it properly domesticated. The method of feeding pigs whereby much of the owners' food is sliced away with the peel and fed to the animals is such that about five taro (or the equivalent in sweet potatoes) are needed daily to feed each fullgrown animal. This means that three pigs (together with their householderowners) consume the contents of a garden plot in about seven days. Now, a man can clear a plot in a day and a half, but women's work of clearing and planting takes about three times as long, in addition to which she must weed and kill insects. There is, of course, no *physical* reason why this labor output could not be somewhat increased. There is no serious land shortage, and a labor "stretch-out" could be and often is undertaken. Siuai women work hard at their gardens but not nearly so hard as some women in other parts of Melanesia; it is conceivable that they could work longer and harder without doing themselves physical injury. That is to say, it is conceivable by *other* cultural standards of work habits.

Cultural rather than physical factors influence Siuai standards of "maximum working hours." Garden work is taboo for long periods following upon death of a relative or friend. Nursing mothers may spend but a few hours daily away from their babies, who, because of ritual restrictions, often may not be carried into the gardens. And aside from these ritual restrictions upon continuous garden work, there are certain other less spectacular limitations. It is conventional to cease working during even light showers; it is customary to start for the garden only after the sun is well up, and to leave for home in midafternoon. Now and then a married couple will remain on their garden site all night sleeping in a lean-to, but only the most ambitious and enterprising care to discomfort themselves thus.

One solution to this shortage-of-labor problem is polygyny. It is by no mere accident that polygynous households average more pigs than monogamous ones.[36] Informants stated explicitly that some men married second and third wives in order to enlarge their gardens and increase their herds. They laughed at the writer's suggestion that a man might become polygnous in order to increase his sexual enjoyment. ("Why pay the brideprice when for a handful of tobacco you can copulate with other women as often as you like!") Opisa of Turuŋom did not even trouble to move his second wife from her village to his own. She, a woman twenty years his senior, simply remained at her own home and tended two of his pigs.

Some of the wealthiest, most influential men had several wives; but when

# ACCUMULATING CAPITAL

it was suggested to informants that polygyny was a sign of renown, they vigorously denied it, stating that the main reason for the custom is to increase herds. Ethnologists are, of course, aware that such statements generally are unreliable rationalizations, and they are reported here merely for what they are worth. But whatever happen to be the motives back of polygyny, the fact remains that such families own more pigs than monogamous ones, and that this is brought about largely through their additional labor resources.

At this point it will be instructive to examine a concrete case of a single hamlet over a period of time; to record the numbers of pigs owned and the uses to which they were put.

Mi'kahna hamlet comprises six households, whose members are interrelated in a single extended family with kinship lines focusing on an old woman, Sahkui (Fig. 29, p. 488). There are other family members not permanently resident in Mi'kahna: Moio and Motoko are native constables stationed at a Police Post thirty miles away but keep houses at Mi'kahna and frequently visit there. In the beginning of May 1938, there were the following pigs in Mi'kahna:

|  |  | Worth in Mauai |
|---|---|---|
| Peuru | 1 | 30 |
| U'ta | 2 | 30, 30 |
| Kakai | 5 | 50, 30, 10, 10, and 10 |
| Motoko | 1 | 30 |
| Koura | 1 | 20 |

a total number of ten pigs, worth all together 250 spans of mauai. These figures show Mi'kahna natives to be poorer than average in the number of pigs owned,[37] but the proportion of needs to resources is fairly typical.

From May 1938 to February 1939, two of these pigs were disposed of. Once, Sahkui's brother, Sipisoŋ, living in Maisua village, gave a feast for which Peuru contributed his only pig. Peuru did this, he said, because "Sipisoŋ is my true mother's brother: I handed the pig to him without pay. Later on he will reciprocate." (In other words, a loan.)

U'ta is the Administration's chief interpreter (Boss-Boy) for all of northeast Siuai. Once during our stay he quarreled violently with his superior, Tomo, the Paramount Chief for this same area. News of the quarrel reached the Patrol Officer on the coast, who commanded the two native officials to hold a friendship-truce feast for which each had to contribute a pig.[38]

During this same period (May–February) another daughter of Sahkui's had begun to live with a native from another village, her second "marriage." This match was thoroughly disapproved of by her senior brother, Peuru, and was not sanctioned by any kind of property exchange.

In the meantime there had been no replacements of pigs; but U'ta's remaining animal had increased in value to 40 mauai, as Koura's had increased to 30. There was some question as to whether Kakai's three shoats had really increased enough in girth to be worth 20 mauai apiece; the consensus was that they had not. Therefore, at the end of the nine months, the inventory stood as follows:

|        |   | Worth in Mauai |
|--------|---|----------------|
| U'ta   | 1 | 40 |
| Kakai  | 5 | 50, 30, 10, 10, and 10 |
| Motoko | 1 | 30. (This pig was more of the smaller, native-unmixed variety, and would probably never grow much larger.) |
| Koura  | 1 | 30 |

thus making a total number of eight pigs worth all together 210 spans of mauai.

By February, Peuru's wife was obviously pregnant, and Peuru had begun talking with his uncle, Sipisoŋ, about furnishing a pig for a birth feast. U'ta was talking vaguely about acquiring a sow in order to begin accumulating pigs for some future renown-acquiring feast. He complained that he would have owned a large number of pigs if only Tomo would reciprocate the feast U'ta had previously given in honor of Tomo's now deceased mother's mother's brother. Kakai had bought a pig worth 30 mauai and given it to a kinsman in another village, who used it for a feast; the money was still owed to Kakai. None of the other natives in Mi'kahna had any outstanding debts or credits in pigs.

## SELLING SERVICES AND LENDING CAPITAL

Siuai natives do not hire themselves out to other natives as ordinary laborers. Specialists practice their skills for pay, but when natives perform manual labor for others, their motives are more complex. When members of a team assist one another in some productive enterprise, they are rewarded with a feast and not with wages or portions of the product. Likewise, if a man wishes a house built for himself he invites neighbors and friends to help him and then recompenses them with a feast. One reason, I feel certain, for the unpopularity of carrying cargo for European travelers is the method of reward. The wages natives are paid in stick tobacco or Australian currency are high compared with wages paid on plantations, but the payment of such wages is a poor substitute for the usual workers' reward of a feast — even though the "feast" provides each man with no more than a taste of pork or opossum.

Nor is it possible to discern a strong profit motive in the practicing of many specialists. The bone-setter, the life-prolonger, and the dispensers of emetics and purgatives take pride in their skills, practice them when called upon, and usually demand fees, but they make no obvious effort to extend their clientele, and judging by the infrequency of their practice and the small amount of their fees, they can hardly regard their labors as milestones to wealth. Such is also the case with composers and artists. Leaders sometimes commission composers to create the music and the lyrics for songs to be sung at feasts and pay them with pork or shell money, but just as often these composers voluntarily contribute their creations for the feasts of kinsmen or friends. And it is the same with artists, with men who carve designs on pudding frames or with men who create festive hair ornaments out of wood and feathers and paint.

There are, however, some kinds of specialties which persist in attracting men seriously intent on earning money. Chief among these are the general therapist (kunakuka) and the mikai. As described previously,[39] fashions in magic change quite frequently, and although fads like tuki-divination[40] and Nagovisi poison may provide some quick profits for men who speculate in practicing them, the professions of the general therapist and the mikai usually provide more enduring sources of income.

A general therapist like Opisa of Turuŋum village[41] may earn one to two hundred spans of shell money a year working at his profession. Opisa is quite candid about his motives, stating that he likes to "help" his relatives and neighbors, but that he expects them to pay for his services. ("After all, if I did not practice they would have to pay a comparative stranger for less effective treatment.") He practices therapy to earn money, and serves gratis only members of his family and their dependents. Opisa announced that he would share his trade secrets, for seventy spans, only with persons living outside Turuŋum, thus insuring against loss of his local clientele. He learned his skills from his own father, who purchased them from a Kontai village man for seventy spans; eventually Opisa will teach these skills to his own son. Opisa's attitude towards his profession is typical of most of the successful general therapists I encountered.

A successful mikai may earn even more in fees than a general therapist.[42] Throughout northeast Siuai I counted fifty-two men who claimed possession of the powers associated with this profession, six of them having acquired their powers during my stay. Of these fifty-two, only about half practice regularly; the professional records and reputations of the others are such that they attract few clients.

Nearly all men of high rank are mikai, and several of these boast of their magical powers in order to attract clients and earn fees. On the other hand, some of the highest ranking leaders are rather ineffective practitioners, as even their most loyal supporters would admit.

Mission teachers receive payment in shillings for their services, but the amounts are too small to add significantly to an individual's earnings. Motives other than money-making lead men to occupy these positions.

A previous section described the mechanics and the extent of borrowing money and goods.[43] As stated, the interest (totokai) is high by western standards, and borrowing is very lively, with nearly every household head deeply engaged. Despite this, lending — in contrast with aŋurara — is not purposefully engaged in as a means of increasing capital, nor for most individuals does it result in significant net gains. For, nearly every adult male is both creditor and borrower, and the interest his goods earn for him is usually offset by the interest he has to pay. The reasons for borrowing cannot be reduced entirely to economic need, and the reasons for lending have very little to do with the motives of the western moneylender, as we shall see later on. In the present context it is sufficient to note that lending capital, as practiced, is not an effective way of increasing it.

## THE MAGICAL COMPONENT IN ACCUMULATING AND SAFEGUARDING MATERIAL RESOURCES

The Siuai recognize perfectly clearly that prosperity depends mainly on hard work and intelligent enterprise, but they also seek supernatural aid in accumulating wealth. I was never able to obtain an explicit statement about the relative importance to prosperity of industry and wealth-magic, but formed the very firm impression that these hard-headed rationalists look upon the magical component in wealth accumulation as supplementary insurance. "We perform wealth-magic to increase our capital; it is an old custom with us."

All magic rituals having to do with insuring good crops (i.e., *maki*, garden magic [44]), healthy pigs (i.e., *hohosipa*, pig naming [45]), and healthy, *prosperous* children (i.e., *maru*, child baptizing [46]) relate to the increase of property; but there is one other ritual which is directly and exclusively concerned with accumulating capital. Wealth-magic (*sinapo*) involves the use of formulae which explicitly invoke supernatural aid in becoming wealthy, and it employs ghost-consecrated materials.

In general, the kinds of influence possessed by the wealthy in life remain with their ghosts after death; they continue to exert influence over mundane affairs. Other things being equal, people prefer that their spirit-familiars be ghosts of wealthy individuals. The sinapo ritual seeks to mobilize the ghosts of former wealthy natives to assist their matrilineal descendants in the latters' struggle for wealth. Each *noroukuru* has its own sinapo rite which can only be performed by and on behalf of members.[47] These rites are said to have been invented by noroukuru kupunas, and although no two rites are identical in detail, they all conform to the following pattern. In most cases [48] the rite is performed when a wealthy individual dies, man or woman. Several of the deceased's noroukuru-mates gather around the corpse, and after the noroukuru's sinapo-specialist has gained rapport with the ghosts of former wealthy noroukuru members through the ghost of the deceased, she (the sinapo specialist is usually an old woman [49]) prays to all these ghosts to help bring wealth to their living noroukuru-mates. The prayer invokes the ghosts by name and urges them to increase their descendants' property in pigs and shell money.

The particular procedure of the Legs-apart sub-sib's wealth-magic utilizes physical remains of the former members whose ghosts are invoked. Some of their fingernail parings are kept by the specialist in a coconut-shell bowl. When the rite is carried out, the specialist mixes red ocher with the parings and places the bowl by the hand of the deceased. She then puts an areca nut in the deceased's hand for a moment, removes it, and holds it in her own hand close to the bowl of nail parings and ocher. After this she holds in her other hand a pig's long-bone wrapped around with strips of high-value shell money,[50] and recites the prayer: "Immaruto, Pitaino, Kaŋku, etc. (that is, the names of deceased, wealthy members of the Legs-apart sub-sib), all you Ground-thudders (that is, persons of importance), let this money increase a hundredfold." (And so on, repeating the names of the ghosts and calling them by various flattering metaphoric titles.)

In carrying out the wealth-magic ritual of one Komma sub-sib, high-value shell money is wrapped around the arm of the deceased after the money has been steamed over a pot of boiling opossum meat. Since the opossum meat is later eaten by living sub-sib members and its essence by the ghost of the deceased, the rite is both sacrifice and communion and acts to induce the deceased, and through him (or her) the ghosts of all former wealthy sub-sib members, to give assistance to their living matrilineal descendants. The use of shell money in the ritual signifies specifically what the nature of the assistance should be.

Other noroukurus employ the more ordinary ritual gesture of head-rounding [51] as a sacrificial means of invoking supernatural aid.

The close connection between pigs and prosperity is indicated in the following ritual: When a man takes leave of a valuable pig before sending it away to be sold and eaten, he places a basket of high-value shell money nearby, circles the beast's head with a half-ripe coconut, and shakes the coconut near its head while saying: "I shake this coconut for you.[52] Let your ghost attach itself to the next pig I own so that the animal may become as big as you." This ritual is also called wealth-magic (sinapo).

The Siuai know and use a large number of devices for *protecting* property. These vary from simple "keep off" notices to spirit-sanctioned, death-dealing taboos.

*Kopuru* and *tanoto* are simple ownership marks placed on such items as knives, clusters of areca nuts, and trees left standing but intended by the owner for his own eventual use.

*Kokoua* are various kinds of signs used, among other purposes, to discourage trespassing. For example, a kokoua sign in the form of a bush bent across a path indicates that the owner does not want visitors; it is placed in pathways leading to a hamlet in which a death has recently taken place, serving as a sign that the residents do not want people other than closest relatives to attend the cremation.[53] A kokoua sign may also be placed on a path leading to a stream to indicate that the owner does not want outsiders fishing there. Other uses of kokoua include these: if two friends start out on a journey with one going ahead, the latter when arriving at a fork in the road will place a kokoua across the path he does not take; or, if a man goes to visit another at his hamlet house and finds no one there he will leave a kokoua sign to indicate to the owner the friendly intent of his visit.

*Haraka* is another type of taboo which has no magical implications. It usually consists of a length of coconut frond tied around a coconut or areca palm which the owner particularly wants left alone. In addition, a haraka may be left tied to a palm by some kinsman or friend of the owner as a sign to the latter of having taken some of its fruit; thus, when the owner sees that some of his fruit has been taken he will know that it has been borrowed rather than stolen.

Magical protection devices are also numerous. First, there are several that involve the use of intrinsically dangerous poisons,[54] including stinging nettles and poisonous insects, which are smeared onto the items requiring protection. Anyone contacting such poisons becomes afflicted with ailments of various kinds. *Koŋara* and *asiaru* are two of these poisons; they were both introduced from Terei and both of them cause boils to break out all over the body and eventually bring about death. *Rohku* is even more vicious, ultimately causing leprosy.[55]

A more deadly type of device is that known by the general name of *kuh*; it involves the use of spirit-consecrated poisons[56] and anyone who happens to go near an object tabooed with such poison is smitten by the associated spirits whether or not the hapless victim means to steal or to trespass. Many stories are told of owners smitten by their own kuh because of having gone near places and objects which they had earlier tabooed and forgotten about. Certain areas of hunting land and certain stretches of creeks have become permanently tabooed to hunting or fishing because their owners placed them under the protection of kuh and then died before removing the spells. The most widely used kuh poisons in northeast Siuai are *miro*, *kehere*, and *uratu*; uratu is typical of the workings of all these.

Men who use uratu cut a joint of consecrated povata cane and place it in the hand of a dead man. They command:

> We have placed this povata in your hand; you will guard it well. You will destroy the soul of any person who trespasses or steals: all those who steal coconuts or areca nuts from our palms, or fish from our streams, or opossums

from our forests. The souls of all such trespassers and thieves you will destroy with the aid of this cane.

Uratu is privately owned by some dozen or so men in northeast Siuai; it was originally bought from a Terei native and then sold by one owner to the next. Anyone can purchase the knowledge of how to prepare the poison, but the price for such knowledge (some fifty to one hundred mauai) is quite high so that most individuals who want to use it pay an expert to consecrate the povata cane for them (paying from ten to thirty spans of mauai for the service); they of course cannot then sell the materials to others. Anyone who walks near land or objects protected by uratu will die a very painful death: "His face will swell to enormous size, and he will plead to be done away with."

People who handle intrinsically dangerous or spirit-consecrated poisons are themselves endangered, and after using the poisons they have to perform a neutralizing rite (*hura*) to avoid being smitten.[57] There are also magical antidotes to many of these devices; most of these involve the use of finger-joint popping or head-rounding,[58] and are known to and practiced by the individual owners of the devices, but they are effective only if utilized shortly after the dangerous contact has taken place.

A few protection devices involve the use of homicidal spirit-familiars,[59] including club-house demons. The masters of these familiars induce them by sacrifice to guard over specifically named places and objects; then when the time comes to use the tabooed place or object, the familiar has to be called off by means of another magical rite.[60]

When a magically tabooed object has been stolen or destroyed, the owner need only keep his eye out for ailments among his neighbors, and if the telltale affliction strikes someone, then it is generally assumed that the victim is guilty of theft or unwitting trespass. And having already been punished for his deed, usually no other measures are taken to penalize him. But, if some object not under the protection of magic happens to be stolen or destroyed, the aggrieved owner may seek to learn the identity of the culprit by divination, utilizing ordinary divination techniques[61] or combining divination and vengeance in a single magical act. Among the latter techniques is *tukuveroro*, whereby the practitioner induces his spirit-familiar to capture the soul of the culprit and place it inside a small house-like structure where it can be identified and destroyed. Still other rites are intended to bring about the destruction of the culprit without necessarily discovering his identity. For example, the chips of flesh cut out of the ears of domestic pigs are not intended to be ownership "brands" but are rather used in avenging the theft of the pig if it should occur. The animal's owner keeps the ear chips hidden in the roofing of his house, then if his pig disappears under suspicious circumstances he will throw the chips into a stream or marsh known to be inhabited by an eel-demon (*kamaŋu*). The demon then devours the chips and ultimately brings about the death of the thief, whose soul is believed to be attached to the ear chips because of his having handled the pig from which the chips came.

It is noteworthy of all these magical devices for protecting property that their use is regarded as legitimate no matter what the outcome may be. Natives do not attempt to be secretive about their efforts to protect their property or avenge infringements. Even if the victim of some taboo device should die through having innocently touched the tabooed object, his survivors have no redress. In fact, I knew of several afflicted persons — some with hideous sores and some with infestations of boils — who were conceded to have been stricken through unwitting trespass, and not one of them appeared to bear grudges against the owners of the tabooed places or objects.

The Siuai do not depend entirely — or even predominantly — on magic for satisfying losses brought about through theft or property damage. In neighborhoods where a high-ranking leader holds sway, the plaintiff brings his complaint to that individual, who will usually either advise against action or, if guilt can be "established," suggest a suitable indemnity. Elsewhere the plaintiff places his charge before his official headman and a lengthy litigation takes place, which usually culminates in a decision by the Patrol Officer and involves either indemnity or fine or imprisonment.

Yet even with this imposing array of property protection measures, magical and legal, one must not imagine that all Siuai owners guard their property jealously against all kinds of incursions. With all their apparatus for safekeeping their possessions, these natives nevertheless honor bounteousness. Property owners have a variety of protective instruments at their disposal, but they must use them sparingly if they wish to be popular. Owners who are forever tabooing their land and trees are classed along with misers: "Stone hearts have tabooed their land to hide their scabby wives"; or "Hey there! such-and-such a group has walled itself in again."

CHAPTER 10

# Acquiring Renown

## WEALTH AND PRESTIGE

Possession of a large supply of capital (manunu) is instrumental but by no means indispensable to becoming a leader. Contrary to the native generalization, *potu* — the kind of renown which identifies the leader — is *not* directly correlated with possession of manunu. This I ascertained by comparing the results of a property survey with the census of leaders. Most leaders own more than an average amount of capital — or have done so at one time or another; but not all wealthy men are leaders.[1]

For example, the wealthiest Siuai native, Petuino of Korikunu district, owns 22,000 mauai units in shell money currency alone, but is not a leader, nor, in the opinion of some natives, is he even a mumi. He inherited much of his wealth and increased it by industrious pig-raising and shrewd trading but he very rarely gives feasts. Most natives term him a miser (*momina*); and although he is not deeply disliked, other men are somewhat contemptuous of his stinginess. They say of him, as they say of other misers: "spinach smokes it,"[2] meaning, "his shell money rests on the rack over his hearth and is begrimed with smoke from fires which cook wild greens rather than pork."

The attitude towards the miser is more explicable in terms of the general attitude towards selfishness and parsimony. Selfishness in a spouse is grounds for divorce,[3] and the tight-fisted man who does not rally to aid his kinsmen or neighbors in times of need is a "stone-heart."[4] Of such a man it is said: "He holds onto his capital and uses none of it to help men in need. His heart is of stone; he does not show sorrow when people die; he contributes nothing to their funerals."

Some misers may command respect because of their autocratic ways, or they may be feared for their secretiveness and suspected of sorcery, but they are rarely liked by their neighbors and could not become leaders.

Conversely, a generous man, a "person of soft heart,"[5] is universally liked. Such a man is Misam of Mataras who is quick to lend sympathy and capital to relatives and neighbors when need arises. It is said of Misam that he was once very wealthy but used up all of his wealth by lending it to neighbors who have since died, and by contributing pigs for their funerals. He is an easy mark for a loan, and a complaisant creditor — too complaisant for his own good, informants add. Generosity alone, however, does not engender renown (potu) and may not even generate respect. Some soft-hearted men, like Misam, although liked by their fellows, are regarded as too easy-going and pliable and exercise little or no influence over community affairs.

Renown comes from generosity manifested in frequent feast-giving and not from prodigality or mere largess. Moreover, such feasts must be well-attended to be effective; pork-hungry as they are, most Siuai men will stay away from feasts whose hosts they do not respect. Such a host is Kummai, who was appointed a village headman because of his knowledge of pidgin; he is heartily disliked by his neighbors on account of his selfishness and vindictiveness but feared because of his Administration-backed authority.[6] Kummai possesses a driving ambition to acquire renown, and through tireless industry has managed to accumulate a fairly large amount of capital. He has staged two club-house-raising feasts, one involving eight very large pigs and the other eleven — respectable numbers under most circumstances. In both cases, however, he was snubbed by all but his closest kinsmen and neighbors, and even these latter did not assist him in the preparation; and although his neighbors were most generously banqueted, some of them afterwards expressed contempt for the whole effort.

The fact that some of the leaders with most renown did not, at the time of my survey, possess conspicuous amounts of capital, received a ready explanation from nearly all informants queried on this point: "Such leaders," they agreed, "have spent their wealth giving feasts." As one leader commented to me: "What is the use of accumulating capital only to hoard it? When the owner dies, it will all be dispersed and the only memory of him will be that of his funeral. Far better to use the capital to keep the slit gongs sounding in his club-house."

But even this explanation did not fit the cases of a few leaders, including Soŋi, the most renowned of northeast Siuai. Long inquiries brought out that these individuals had never at any one time owned outright any large quantities of pigs and shell money. They had, it is true, given many bountiful feasts and distributed thousands of mauai, but they had accomplished these things by drawing on the services and resources of kinsmen and neighbors — by skillful manipulation of ties of kinship and friendship on their own behalf. Most people are well aware of these circumstances, and some of them grumble about unpaid debts and overworked loyalties, but no one denies that these leaders have great renown.

Hence, renown is more than accumulating and giving away wealth. Renown comes from utilizing capital in such a way that loyalties are mobilized, obligations created, prestige enhanced, and authority exercised *in traditionally acceptable ways* — above all, in the staging of special kinds of feasts.

## FOOD IN SIUAI LIFE

Everyday eating is a household affair in all its ramifications. For the most part the household produces, prepares, and consumes its own food independently of other social units. Here and there members of neighboring households may coöperate during some stages of food production — in clearing land for gardening, in hunting and collecting, in sago-processing, etc.; moreover in some instances separate households of the same hamlet may cook together. Everyday eating, however, is nearly always done in the privacy of the household. It is no wonder, then, that food and eating acquire associations of intimate social relationships.[7] Food-getting is the main preoccupation of the household, and the principal meal — the climax of each day's activities — is something of a domestic ceremony, the material as well as the ritual exemplification of rights and duties among members of the household.[8]

Food also occupies the central position in rituals formalizing kinship relations and life crisis episodes. Baptism is celebrated with a feast among relatives, and food items, along with ritual eating, are prominent components of the actual ceremony. The same can be said for other debut rites, for weddings, and for acts marking the end of mourning.[9] Similarly, "betel-chewing" — involving the ritual sharing and chewing of betel mixture, with or without the eating of food — is the standard act for formalizing greetings, cementing taovu-partnerships, concluding negotiations, and restoring peace after controversy and conflict.

Some of the most binding injunctions are expressed in terms of food taboos, for example, restrictions on eating certain foods are an accompaniment of immaturity and magical vulnerability; avoidance between a man and his mother-in-law is manifested in the prohibition against food-sharing; and the supreme injunction inherent in sib membership is the canon against eating the totem — even violations of that other sib canon, the incest taboo, is described as "*eating* the totem."

There are many other metaphorical usages which emphasize the importance of food as a symbol of relationships. "They fed me when I was a child," or "I drank milk from her breast" are expressions used by an adult to explain his obligation to care for aged parents. "He brought home delicacies every day" is the dirge of the sorrowing widow, her way of summarizing all the virtues of her deceased spouse. "We eat together" is the phrase used by a man to describe his friendly relationship with a male from a distant village, meaning that even though they are not neighbors and kinsmen they trust one another to refrain from practicing sorcery in connection with a shared meal.

Food is singled out for enshrinement in myths. Food-Maker and Orphan, two of the three most important kupunas, share honors for the discovery and creation of the major food plants; and the tales describing their gastronomic adventures are among the most widespread and oft-repeated of the genesis myths.[10]

Foodstuffs also occupy prominent positions in magical practices. Some divination rites are carried out by means of the meat and oil of coconut or the belly-fat of pig. Both curative medicines and destructive poisons are administered with comestibles; the souls of sorcery victims are entrapped by food leavings or are lured to their doom by means of food delicacies.

The Siuai are not a hungry, underfed people — there are nearly always enough of the staples to fill their bellies and leave them satisfied. Nor are they given to gluttony, even when surpluses are available. Nevertheless, food is ever present in their "thoughts," if one may so judge from their talk, and this preoccupation of theirs is that of the gourmet who seldom can indulge his appreciation of delicacies.

Food delicacies include puddings, fish, eel, opossum, and — above all — pork. Baked or steamed taro is favored fare for the everyday meal, much more so than sago or sweet potatoes. Natives are quite content to eat taro at their domestic meals; I have never heard a native complain of eating taro every day, provided of course it is balanced with a little greens, coconut oil, and, now and then, a sliver of fish or meat. And even though they yearn for their fill of delicacies, it would not occur to them to prepare large quantities of delicacies for home consumption. Such food is reserved for feasts, even though many households can afford more lavish fare. There is, in fact, little variation in menu between rich and poor households.[11] Just how invariable the domestic menu is — from household to household and from day to day — was ascertained from records of food consumption collected from a number of households over long periods of time. Although natives are content with this sameness for their everyday fare, they look forward with keen delight to a feast, the only kind of occasion on which it is possible, that is, conventionally permissible, to indulge their appetites for the food delicacies they so dearly love. As stated above, there is no physical reason why some households should not prepare and eat a pudding occasionally — the ingredients are usually at hand — nor is there any physical reason why some favored households should not occasionally butcher a pig and enjoy a hearty pork banquet. The reasons must be sought elsewhere: fine foods go with feasting, and feasting is not a household affair.

## FEASTS

The Siuai distinguish among several types of feasts, and menus differ accordingly. Rituals celebrating life crises — christenings, introductions, weddings, terminations of mournings, etc. — are attended by relatives and friends who are usually given cuts of uncooked pork together with steamed or uncooked taro; the guests then carry these foods home for cooking and eating. On all such occasions the ritual is the main feature, the food being in the nature of a supplement — like "refreshments" after a meeting in

America. Strips of pork are hung on a wooden frame to keep them out of reach of frantic dogs, and are handed out to the guests quite unceremoniously, along with small platters of uncooked or steamed vegetables.

Another type of feast is given to repay unsolicited favors: to mourners at a funeral, to friends who help one during illnesses or who "bring one out of mourning,"[12] etc. It is also customary for a father to feast the men who introduce his son to the technique of fighting.[13] At such feasts as these the distribution of pigs is the principal event; guests quickly disperse, carrying the food home for cooking and eating. A few warlike dances may be carried out to enliven these occasions but the presentation of pigs is the climax and the event is quickly over.

Feasts given to reward men for solicited service are much more elaborate affairs. It is in this manner that men are recompensed for their aid in building, repairing, or cleaning club-houses and in making or carrying slit gongs. For such occasions puddings are usually prepared and these along with steamed or roast pork are usually consumed by the guests on the spot. These may be all-night celebrations with singing, dancing, panpiping, and the performing of masques.

A fourth kind of feast is the *muminai* (literally: "mumi-pointing-out") or mumi-honoring celebration, in which an ambitious man singles out a real or potential rival and showers gifts of pork and shell money upon him to "honor" him but also to test his capacity to reciprocate. The mumi-honoring is crucially important in the competition for renown and deserves close attention, but we shall return to this topic later, after describing some of the other aspects of feasting and the steps which lead up to that climactic event.

In any feast involving more than four or five pigs, the task of assembling the animals is a formidable one. Few individuals have enough pigs of their own for the occasion, and even if they had, they would not wish to deplete their own herds — nor in many cases would they care to butcher animals looked upon as pets. Consequently givers of large feasts must begin months ahead to plan and negotiate for pigs.

The ambitious feast-giver must first of all construct a pen. There are three kinds of these: *huhu, tumutumu,* and *ko'sapakupaku*. Huhu and tumutumu are constructed alike, the only difference being that huhu poles are made of carefully selected trees cut to uniform size and stripped of bark.

After construction of the pen, the owner must reward the builders with a pork banquet. Then he is ready to begin accumulating pigs.

First of all he will collect medium-sized animals from several of his aŋurara-men.[14] These he will use mainly in trade for larger pigs. Then he will begin to make overtures to his taovu partners. If he is a very high-ranking man he will send couriers to make arrangements; if not, he will visit each taovu personally and negotiate prices. In either case he will send along a small pig, called "betel-chewing," it being customary for friends to chew betel together when they meet. No important feast is complete without a few very large tuskers, and it is generally only from a taovu that one can hope to purchase such a prized animal. In purchasing a tusker, "betel-chewing," is regarded as partial down-payment. A large tusker is valued at 100 spans of mauai; but when the purchaser makes payment he generally sends along some 20 to 30 spans over the 100 — this in addition to the "betel-chewing" down-payment he has already made. The seller then gathers together his followers or friends and they carry to the purchaser not only the tusker but two other pigs as well. One of these will be worth 30 spans, and is called "fastened-to-the-pig's-leg" (signifying that it is thrown in with the principal pig, for good measure). A second pig equivalent in value to the "betel-chewing" is taken along and presented to the purchaser, who in turn butchers and cooks and distributes it among the seller's kinsmen and neighbors who carried the three pigs. This process is repeated with every large tusker purchased.

Meanwhile the feast-giver seeks out other prospective sellers and bargains with them; it is during this phase of the preparations that he must be most enterprising. A shrewd buyer will exploit kin and friend. He might, for example, make this kind of proposal to a friend:

> Your young daughter will soon be of marriageable age. When her wedding is celebrated I will contribute a 60-span pig to the feast. But in the meantime, you can repay my [future] "gift" by exchanging that 60-span sow of yours for that tusker of your father-in-law's and by giving me the tusker for my feast. After all, he's your father-in-law and will not be a hard bargainer with you, whereas he and I are mere acquaintances.

When the hopeful purchaser first approaches a prospective seller, the latter usually fastens up the desired animal so that it will not run away before the sale can take place. During this period, which may last for several days, the animal is usually not fed. "Why waste food on another man's pig?" the seller argues. Naturally, the pig, especially if it is a small one, will weaken from starvation. If the seller perceives this to be the case, he will attempt to prolong the pig's life by knotting a grass stalk (mitoi, "tying up its life"). Then after the weakened animal has been safely delivered and paid for, the seller will untie the grass stalk knot; for "after that it's the new owner's responsibility!"

Delivering a large tusker pig to its purchaser is an occasion for celebration. The carriers — kinsmen and neighbors of the seller — construct a stretcher out of poles and rattan, and fasten the pig onto it; then over the animal they build a shelter to which they attach bright-colored calico streamers. They sing and shout as they walk along carrying the loaded stretcher, and are preceded by other natives blowing on conch shells. It is a lively and colorful procession as the natives push along singing *urugeŋke* — "pig-carrying songs" — borrowed from the neighboring Terei people. On arrival at their destination they dump the animal into the pen and cluster around excitedly, watching it charge against the posts and comparing its size with pigs already penned-up. Shortly afterward, the carriers have to be rewarded for their efforts with a small feast.

Penned-up pigs awaiting distribution at a feast are never fed, and after a few days of desperate ground-rooting in search of food the animals settle down into starved apathy. Smaller ones might die after a week; large tuskers sometimes actually survive for a month or so. Once a pig has been set aside for a feast the native owner regards feeding it uneconomical and quite silly. It was surprising to observe that the beasts could survive for so long, but I was amazed that natives allowed them to starve at all, having become so accustomed to seeing them treated as pets. Of course, starved pigs sometimes die before the feast takes place; in that case, their death is usually said to be due to sorcery practiced by an envious rival feast-giver.

The preparation of puddings also requires careful planning and supervision. The two best-liked puddings are sago-almond (*anitapu*, or *takupas*) and taro-coconut (*kihanu*). The former is made by mixing together sago flour, ground almonds, and water in a mortar, and by stone-baking the mixture in a leaf-lined wooden frame. For the other, steamed taro is ground into a mash to which is added coconut shreds and oil, and the whole thing likewise stone-baked. For these operations the wooden baking frame, about four feet long by eight inches wide and six inches deep, must be constructed by a specialist since it should be decorated with carved and painted designs. The ground oven consists of a hole about five feet square and four deep, heated by a layer of hot ash and stones; fully a day is required to bring it to proper temperature. After the puddings are mixed — and this process may take a whole day — they are poured into the leaf-lined frames, wrapped around with additional banana leaves, placed in the oven, covered with more leaves and ashes, and left to bake for five or six hours. Seldom are fewer than ten or twelve men engaged in these preparations, and their efforts require synchronization and a distinct division of labor. Extraordinary care and close timing must be observed in preparing a pudding; if it is burned or its flavor or texture wrong, that is a sign that the host is Near-death.[15]

Acquiring the ingredients of these puddings also requires long-range planning and negotiation. No man is able to produce enough taro from his own gardens to feed the guests at a large feast — it will be recalled that taro spoils quickly and no household's gardens are extensive enough to produce a sufficiently large simultaneous harvest. Consequently, a man planning a big feast contracts to purchase taro from kinsmen and neighbors over four months in advance so that he can be assured of an adequate supply at the right time. Similarly, he must arrange for plenty of almonds, and this involves negotiations with neighbors or taovus before the almond season preceding his feast. But even longer foresight must be exercised to assure a plentiful supply of coconuts; many hundreds of nuts are required for the puddings and for the thirsty dancers. The feast-giver will have to taboo his own grove for a year or more and rely on his closest supporters to do likewise. (Such a restriction imposes great hardships on the natives — comparable to a severe rationing of fats in a western household.) To make doubly sure that the taboo on his own grove will be maintained, the feast-giver ritually exhorts his club-house demon (horomorun), if he has one, to guard the coconuts against thieves; just before the feast this taboo is removed with another ritual.

Whether puddings are provided or not, at most feasts guests are given basket platters filled with chunks of steamed taro and sweet potatoes, slivers of opossum meat, cooked edible greens, and one or two drinking coconuts.

All these viands are placed upon a platform a day or two before the feast. The platform may be a tower-like scaffolding (*raoku*) or a long shelf (*pata*).[16] After the food has been placed on the platform, the host invokes his club-house demon to guard it; then, when the time arrives for distributing the food, the demon is called off, to permit people to mount the platform without danger.

The slit gongs in the host's club-house are beaten at each important stage of these preparations. Familiar signals announce to the surrounding countryside the moment at which each new pig is delivered to the corral, when puddings are poured into the frames, when food is carried up to the platform, etc., so that people for miles around can follow the progress with growing anticipation of the great event itself. Then on the eve of the feast, *pig-counting* takes place in the host's club-house: all gongs join in to signal the number and value of all pigs destined for distribution. Pigs that are thus "counted" — in fact, any pigs butchered at a club house — are thereby rendered inedible for females and children; one native explanation for this restriction is that such pigs are sanctified by the club-house demon and hence magically dangerous to all but men; another is that women would be ashamed to eat food that had been seen and discussed by so many men.

Early in the period of preparations the host assigns some talented musician the task of composing a eulogy to be sung and piped at the feast. The specialist is promised a small pig or a few spans of shell money, and is given a clue concerning the kind of song desired. After he has thought out a new verse, or found an old one just as suitable, he adapts it to lyrics for a panpipe of three, five, or ten reeds, according to his fancy. Then he cuts reeds in lengths to suit the required tones and binds them together. The model is passed around among the host's associates and copied by all of them who are able to play. Practice is held every evening at the host's club-house, or — if the melody is to be kept a secret — in some distant forest clearing.[17] Meanwhile, prospective guests to the feast select and practice their own songs for rendition there. Among the men of northeast Siuai, songs from nearby Terei are especially favored although most Siuai men find the ten-reed Terei panpipes very difficult to master. The Nagovisi three-note compositions are also popular; in both cases the Siuai take pleasure in singing the exotic words, whose meanings many of them cannot understand.

While musical preparations are taking place dances are also practiced. The technique is simple. A few strong-winded and loud-voiced individuals stand in the center giving the signals and all the others hop-dance around them counterclockwise — singing, piping, or merely dancing. The dancing consists of a loping gait, a succession of a few quick flat-footed steps ending in a heavyfooted jump, with each jump forward accompanied by a blast on the pipes. In fact, the dance movement appears to be controlled by the piping, by the need to get the whole body behind the puff blown into the pipes. The dancers inhale as they waddle ahead, then blow out vigorously on the jump, jerking their heads forward in the act. The same refrain is repeated for ten minutes or so — it is violent exercise and cannot be kept up for long at a stretch — then the song-leaders break it off, and the piping and dancing males stop with a series of yells — like the barking of flying-foxes. Performers congratulate themselves with shouts of: "Hey! That was good!" and there is a short interval for resting, then the song-leaders start them off again.

The song-leaders play on small *uraura* ("Spirit-voice"?) pipes; the others play whatever pipes they have along, either great wooden trumpets or three-, five-, or ten-reed panpipes of varying lengths and diameters. Despite the differences in note and tone, a large number of men playing together manage to produce a pleasing and even thrilling volume of sound.

Large feasts involving whole men's societies are usually commenced with a martial "attack" dance. As each group of visitors arrives, its members charge in single file at the host's club house, brandishing spears and finally falling into step in a threatening hop-dance. This "attack" dance (*runoto*) is modeled after a fighting tactic, and it is also performed at the funeral of an aged man who has been a noted warrior or leader.

Many large feasts are accompanied by a *tati*, a ceremonial speech of presentation usually performed by chief supporters of the host and the guest-of-honor. The tone of such speeches tends to be self-depreciatory, the donor usually belittling the quantity of valuables he presents and the receiver expressing amazement and chagrin at the huge size of the "gift." Though carried out with serious formality, these speeches are so obviously and probably purposefully hypocritical that natives have also dubbed them "joking-speeches." One typical tati I witnessed took place on the occasion of a feast given by a leader in honor of a taovu-partner who had previously presented him with a quantity of shell-money to terminate his mourning for a deceased son. The speech exchange went like this:

Host's spokesman: I want to tell you something.
Guest's spokesman: I listen to what you have to say.

Host's spokesman: You made me very happy when you ended my mourning. You overwhelmed me with the huge feast you prepared for me, and with the great sums of shell-money you gave me.

Guest's spokesman: Actually, I was very ashamed of the pitifully small feast and the bagatelle of a gift.

Host's spokesman: Now I am ashamed by the pitifully small gift which I must give you in return. Alas, there have been many deaths among my relatives, and all my resources have gone into providing cremations.

Guest's spokesman: But that small feast I gave to you was little enough for me to give to such a leader as you; such a taovu-partner as you. And now you shame me by the size of the feast you give to me in return. Et cetera.

The spokesmen stand at opposite ends of the dancing ground in front of the club-house and shout their speeches back and forth at the top of their voices, interspersing their sentiments with many eloquent graces, such as, "I who am lower than you," "You who tower over the rest of us like a giant tree," "This wretched little gift of mine," etc.

Some feasts feature the performance of masques (*nunuke*), with several neighbors and friends participating. Some masques are planned in advance; others are extemporaneous. They consist of burlesques in pantomime, usually ridiculing some unpopular neighbor. For example, one I witnessed reconstructed a recent seduction attempt made by a notoriously hypocritical native catechist. Another was a cruel take-off on the Patrol Officer and the most officious of the native officials. Ingenious props and costumes are devised for these affairs, and there is no mistaking the identity of the victims, who sometimes quit the feast in angry humiliation.

A guessing-game is also played at some feasts. Men appear before the club-house disguised in leaves, bark-cloth and trade-store blankets. To the men who guess their identity they must give a small prize consisting of areca nuts, tobacco, or the like.

Most men go to feasts in their best calico loincloths, and decorated with feathers, leaves, shell-money ornaments and paint. Red ocher is the color for feasting and it is generously applied to face and torso. When a men's society goes as a unit to a feast — as they frequently do — one of the members usually carries a long carved wooden standard (*koke*) decorated with paint and feathers; natives inaccurately liken these to the white man's flag. When dancing is going on, men usually remain near their own standard, but otherwise I could learn of no other meaning possessed by these objects; their designs are not identified with the group in question, and they are not handled with any special kind of care.[18]

An earlier mention was made of "praising,"[19] wherein natives flatter one another's children and receive token payments (*pavaru*) in return. This form of flattery also takes place among adults at feasts. If one or two of the participants at a feast happen to be ornamented and painted with especially lavish care, their companions may hoist them on their shoulders and carry them in a parade around the dancing ground. For this compliment the objects of flattery are expected to give their flatterers token payments (pavaru) consisting of a few shell money discs to each.

Magic turns up at many points during a feast. When the food is being prepared the host mixes in *Satiability* magic (*hapo*), a compound of leaves, insects, etc., which causes people who eat the food to become quickly satiated and hence able to eat very small quantities of delicacies. Sometimes Satiability is buried under the center posts of a club-house when it is being constructed; this affects all food subsequently prepared at that club-house. The purpose of these acts is, of course, to make the food go further and to embarrass guests by providing more food than they can eat.[20] But guests also have their magic; by chewing *Insatiability* (*ora*) with betel mixture before arriving at the feast, they are consequently able to consume all the food quickly and thereby humiliate the host!

Some men also chew magical substances to make themselves able to play pipes louder and longer — piping is exhausting, and the strong-lunged player is acclaimed. As for the great wooden trumpet (*marao*), no man can even produce notes from it until he has chewed the appropriate magic.

Feasts provide unexcelled opportunities for the practice of sorcery: so many men — so many potential sorcerers and victims — are together in close assembly, and in the surge and excitement defenses are likely to be relaxed and suspicious gestures unnoticed. To guard themselves from some kinds of sorcery most men acquire protective kuna (*sininno*) from a specialist, mix it with coconut oil and rub it all over their bodies. "Dirt" sorcery (*pukutu*) is more difficult to guard against, and some men will not attend feasts for this reason — or if they do attend they refrain from eating or chewing betel there in order to frustrate any sorcerer from obtaining food leavings and other exuviae. At many feasts attended by men from widely separated hamlets guests carry home all the food given them and consume it in the safety of their own club-houses; informants assert that the reason for this lies in the fear of sorcery.

As a further defense against sorcery the host buries magically treated lime in all the paths leading to his club-house and this has the effect of making visible all sorcery substances carried by guests. Finally, there is the protection to the host provided by his own club-house demon. But even with all these measures, some hosts of wide renown — and hence the objects of malicious envy — will not put in an appearance at their own feasts; such a leader will supervise the preparations and then retire to his house after deputizing a principal supporter to greet the guests.

In a sense most kinds of feasts reflect credit upon the host, and the ambitious man will utilize every legitimate occasion to stage a banquet. Occasionally, a man will repay a number of favors and services at a single feast; some very prominent mumis now and then resort to this device to clear up old obligations, but it is less effective as a renown-winner than is the giving of separate feasts. In any case, before a man can embark on an active feast-giving career he must provide himself with a club-house.

## CLUB-HOUSES

Most club-houses are larger and better-built than ordinary dwellings, and although club-houses are fundamentally alike in form they vary considerably in size and detail. Natives take special pains with roofing and lashings. The sheets of thatch are laid very close together so that they overlap all but three or four inches, thus making an unusually thick roof (thatch sheets on ordinary dwellings have much narrower overlaps). Moreover this roof thickness is made to look even thicker than it is by inserting short lengths of sago sheeting between the functional sheets of thatching at the exposed ends of the roof. The lashings do not attain the artistry of many Polynesian structures but are much neater than ordinary Siuai bindings, which often consist of rough granny knots and loose uneven ends.

Some club-houses are completely open-ended while others have an apse over one or both ends to expand their size and keep out driving rain. No club-houses are walled in but some are enclosed with low fences to keep out pigs. A few are decorated with wood carvings and painted designs. The most prominent decorations are the carved wooden likeness of hornbills which extend three to four feet from the front-end of the club-house. Informants stated that some club-houses formerly had carved posts consisting of high-relief human figures (*poripai*). The designs painted on the exposed ends of roof plates (*mouhe*) in a few club-houses follow conventionalized patterns.

All club-houses contain a number of wooden slit gongs, one to three hearths, one or more smoke-racks suspended over the hearths from the ridgepole, and a few benches. On the smoke-racks are to be found various sizes of cooking pots, basketry platters, and coils of rope. Long bamboo water containers rest against the side, and in the thatch are thrust bows and arrows, spears, and an ax or knife or two. Ranged along the lowest roof sheets, at the place where human skulls formerly were kept, are numbers of pig mandibles.

A less noticeable feature of many club-houses is the small wooden peg driven into the inside surface of the front pillar. This is the *sapu*, the place where sacrifices are left for the horomorun, the demon of the club-house. Horomoruns are the largest demons; their heads are enormous and sometimes covered with red matted fur. They are fierce beyond imagination and usually wander around settled areas — never in the forest — planning and carrying out malicious deeds. Usually, they are invisible but sometimes transform themselves into visible haŋoro snakes.[21] Ordinarily, haŋoro snakes are not at all dangerous; but when a haŋoro is seen in the vicinity of a club-house it is known to be a horomorun, and if it appears to anyone but the club-house owner or a mikai-magician, that person knows he is doomed to die. When such a person finally dies — whenever or however that happens to be — his death will be explained thus: "He saw a snake-horomorun."

Horomoruns survive only if they are fed continually, and they depend solely upon the essence (rumaruma) of pigs' blood. Consequently, horomoruns reside in club-houses where feasts are continually being held and pigs' blood always available. Before, however, a horomorun can take up residence in a club-house it must attain rapport with the owner of the club-house.

A wandering, homeless horomorun is careful to seek rapport only with a man of renown, with one whose reputation as a feast-giver is already established, or with a younger man whom the horomorun judges to be a potential leader. (How the horomorun is able to judge that, my informants could not say very explicitly. "The horomorun merely looks at a man and *knows* that he will be a mumi.") In order to attain rapport the horomorun frightens away the soul of his victim, who then sickens. First of all the victim's kinsmen try simple household remedies or engage the services of the local general practitioner. Then if these measures fail they send for a mikai who diagnoses the true cause of the illness and announces that the patient has been honored: "A horomorun has sought him out to establish rapport." The mikai goes on to explain that the horomorun wishes to eat the blood-essence of such-and-such a number of pigs in return for which it will reside in the patient's club-house and help him increase his renown. Then, he adds, if the patient *does not* accede to the horomorun's request the sickness might prove fatal.

Of course, the patient provides the pigs — either his own or his relatives' — and has them placed near his club-house. Then outside his dwelling is placed a large pole to which taro and coconuts are fastened, and the horomorun is invited to sit astride. A score or more men carry the pole to the club-house; others assist the patient to follow along. The pigs are slaughtered and their blood smeared on the forward pole of the club-house; while this is taking place a mikai laves the patient with water and repeats:

Strength (Let strength return).
Unavere did this (Unavere used to perform this ritual effectively, so I do likewise).
Makumi did this, Konukura did this, Makuna did this (etc.).
(Let) strength (return).
Tonoposi did this, Koronoruhi did this (etc.).
(Let) strength (return).
Thou (horomorun) who art angry with this man must go to the place of ghosts and allow his soul to return here from the north.

Thereupon the horomorun replaces the victim's soul in his body, partakes of the pigs' blood-essence, and begins residence in the club-house. And, of course, the victim recovers his vitality and prepares for renewed social-climbing. By dwelling in the club-house the horomorun makes it doubly untenantable for females. To be sure, females are barred from entering any clubhouse — whether it be horomorun-haunted or not; but the presence of a horomorun there adds to the danger. A frequent cause for a female's death is given as: "she walked too close to the club-house and the horomorun killed her." The horomorun also makes the club-house unsafe for any person who happens to be evilly disposed towards the owner.

It behooves people to speak respectfully of a mumi who entertains a horomorun in his club-house. A horomorun might become so jealous of the renown and safety of his mumi that it becomes unsafe for lesser persons to refer to the mumi by his personal name. Rather must one say: "the mumi did so-and-so," or even: "the horomorun (= mumi) did so-and-so."

The horomorun's resting place is on the largest slit gong or along the ridgepole of the club-house. Its shrine (sapu) is made by driving a peg into the front pole, and on this bits of pork are placed whenever a pig is slaughtered in the club-house. The owner does this quickly — as soon as the pig is slaughtered. Otherwise, the horomorun will smell the pork being cooked and will kill the mumi out of anger. Thus, although the horomorun is a constant source of pride for the mumi it is also a continuous threat, a dangerous responsibility. If pork meals are not forthcoming frequently enough, the horomorun might go in search of the mumi and cause him to sicken again. More pigs have to be slaughtered to induce the obstreperous demon to return to the club-house. This kind of placation must be continually resorted to, for the horomorun must be kept away from dwelling houses at all costs. Otherwise, it will visit the mumi with all sorts of illnesses, or it will play outlandish pranks on youngsters, or it will assume human form and copulate with women and thus bring about their deaths.

Under some circumstances, thunder and lightning accompanied by rain are perfectly normal occurrences; also, there are human rain-makers who can produce thunder and lightning. At other times Thunder-and-lightning (one entity) is regarded as a demon; it strikes trees and houses and causes devastation. Sometimes a hunger-angry horomorun transforms itself into Thunder-and-lightning (unaccompanied by rain), strikes down a large ficus tree and roars out a warning for food.

Horomoruns enter into the everyday lives of their mumis; a concrete example will help to illustrate. During November 1938, Mousi — a mumi of Hiunnai village — became ill, and it was suspected that his unfriendly brothers had poisoned him. But before he died, Mousi explained what had actually happened: he had quarreled with his brothers and had vowed by his horomorun never to enter their houses again. Later on, he forgot his vow and ate food with them in their houses. His horomorun became incensed and killed him. His brothers — he emphatically stated — had had nothing to do with his death.

Horomoruns are sometimes called "the mumis of all demons." They carry on much the same kind of existences as human mumis; for example, there is a tale about a horomorun that raises fish in the same way that a human mumi raises pigs. This demon placed *koriŋi* fish (a perch, *Dulces rupestris*) in a deep pool and called it "penning-up my pigs." Afterwards, men came along and killed the fish and ate them. Soon one of their number who was a mumi died; the koriŋi-eating was the horomorun's "mumi-honoring" feast to which the unfortunate mumi had made no equivalent return — and consequently died.

The most striking of all correspondences between horomorun and mumi is the belief that for every human follower of the mumi there is a lesser demon-adherent of his horomorun. It is even said that whenever a male is born in a village whose mumi entertains a horomorun, then there is also a demon born; and whenever one of the mumi's adherents dies, then one of his horomorun's demons also expires. As far as I could discover there is no rapport established between a human-adherent and his corresponding demon-adherent; the latter are said merely to "assist the horomorun in looking out for the interests of its mumi."

Backed up by its demon-satellites, the horomorun can aid the mumi in various concrete ways. One of the most important of these is to protect his coconut palms. There is not much thievery in Siuai, but the temptation to quench thirst with cool, tangy coconut water frequently leads one native to take nuts from another's palm. This state of affairs constitutes a serious disadvantage for a mumi who must keep his supplies intact in order to provide delicacies for his feasts. Accordingly, the mumi instructs his horomorun — by means of a simple rite — to guard his palms. The demon and its satellites carry out the instructions all too well. It is told of one mumi that he himself thoughtlessly took nuts from a palm he had tabooed in this manner, without first having released the taboo with proper ceremony. The horomorun was thoroughly literal-minded and its mumi died a miserable, writhing death.

A horomorun can become an effective instrument to enforce its mumi's wishes, and the more renown a mumi has, the fiercer becomes his horomorun. Within the framework of Siuai belief this constitutes a logical parallel. The more feasts a mumi gives, the more vitality-giving pigs' blood-essence there will be for the horomorun. Horomoruns have been known to become weak, wraithlike, and ineffective for lack of nourishment; sometimes they expire, but not without first having slain their mediocre-become host. If the horomorun is still vigorous after the death of its mumi, then it wanders around in search of another host; by preference it seeks rapport with a son or maternal nephew of its former host.

The club-house has an extremely important place in Siuai life. In view of the seclusion of hamlet residences, and the conventions against strangers or mere acquaintances visiting even line villages, club-houses remain the only sheltered spots where numbers of males can congregate.

The contrast between hamlet and club-house — or more broadly, between domestic life and public life — is pointed up by the owner's desire that his club-house be located along the most traveled paths. For example, when a former Patrol Officer required the Siuai to construct new and straighter trails, there was much oppositon from men whose club-houses were to be bypassed, and when the new trails were completed some men moved their club-houses alongside them. Just prior to my visit, Soŋi, the leader at Turuŋom, successfully used his influence to block the completion of a new Administration path that would have bypassed his club-house.

But even with all their accessibility, club-houses also provide quiet places for daytime naps and havens of refuge away from shrill-tongued wives and bawling children. Since they are usually situated along main paths, travelers can stop in them to rest and exchange gossip. I have already mentioned the fact that club-houses are the centers for feasting and other activities connected with men's societies. They also serve as courthouses and meeting places for men who wish to sell, buy, or negotiate.

The talk that goes on in the club-house exercises exceedingly strong influence on people's actions. If, say, a man commits an act of incest, an inevitable consequence is that his neighbors will sit in the local club-house and discuss it. They will either laugh at the offender or speak about him with shocked disapproval. Under such circumstances most Siuai males will be too ashamed to frequent the club-houses and will thereby be cut off from normal social intercourse for a while. I can solidly attest to the effectiveness of this kind of exile, having known several men so affected. One of them, Uŋkiro of Novei, still avoided going to club-houses some five years after he allegedly seduced a sib *sister*; he had become a bitter and taciturn man who remained all the time in his isolated hamlet house and garden. Others ashamed to go to the local club-houses have been known to move to distant communities or to sign on for plantation work for three years. Still others are said to turn sorcerer and seek to do away with all the persons who ridicule them.

The club-house's sanction also affects women, even though they are barred from going to a club-house in any case. Mention of a woman's name among strangers in the club-house is indelicate enough; but for her to be discussed there in a sexual context is a grave impropriety. If the talk about her is irresponsible, her kinsmen, and particularly her brothers and matrilineage *brothers*, may be expected to lodge a formal complaint against the slanderer or even try to injure him physically or magically. But if the talk is true the woman's near kinsmen will themselves keep away from the clubhouses until the case recedes from public interest; and as for the woman herself, she may suffer these consequences in shamed silence, or she may run away if she has any sympathetic relatives to go to, or she may even attempt suicide.

Even the thickest-skinned old sinners, along with the brashest and most insolent youths just returned from working and traveling abroad, do not remain indifferent to the sanction of the club-house. One of the latter I knew appeared to ignore criticism of his conduct until several men began to imitate his swagger one day at a nearby club-house. At first he threatened them with litigation but eventually subsided and sulked at his hamlet house for a few days until the incident was more or less forgotten. Again, I was visited one day by a loud-mouthed old liar who came to protest against some talk I had just heard about his character. "I don't mind how people malign me on the line (that is, line village); they are merely jealous of my renown. But," he added, "when they talk thus in the club-houses, that requires pay (i.e., is grounds for a suit for slander)."

All club-houses are named; here are the names given to a few of the larger ones:

Pakuropo — "for whom shall we wait?" (to kill).
Irisia — name of a hawk.
Kaopiri — the mythical lake of blood reserved for ghosts of the improperly mourned dead.
Rampa — pidgin for "hurricane lantern."
Uraivo — crocodile.
Tantanu — one of the principal kupunas.

Some club-houses possess special features in the form of restrictions: for example, one man will permit no weapons to be carried into his; another requires that all food cooked at the club-house be actually eaten there; still another demands the right to appropriate all knives and axes carried into the club-house. When imposing such a restriction the owner calls upon his club-house demon to enforce it — which occasionally produces some unforeseen results, as in the case of the owner who has to leave his own ax in his club-house because of his forgetfulness in taking it there one day.

Because of the connection between club-houses and feasting, no man can proceed far along the way towards acquiring renown until he owns a club-house. Actually, merely owning a club-house does not significantly enhance a man's renown; there is an average of one club-house to every eight adult males in northeast Siuai, and not every owner is even a mumi, much less a leader. Several men own club-houses through having inherited them from father or maternal uncle; but unless one of these inherited buildings is the scene of frequent feasting it does not enhance its owner's renown. In fact, to derive most credit from club-house ownership a man must construct his own, so that others will not say of him: "He is *high* (*koto*) only because of his father." From the standpoint of acquiring renown, the most effective way to erect a club-house is to assemble as many men as possible to do the construction, draw out the work as long as reasonable, and compensate the workers with so bountiful a feast that they will ever afterwards recall with pleasure both the occasion and the club-house. In this connection, it is the size of the reward rather than the size of the club-house which counts with most natives. I recall one occasion, sitting in a club-house with the owner, when a deputation from northwest Siuai arrived and invited the owner and his supporters to attend a club-house raising. My host, the owner, declined the invitation, later telling me: "The last time we built a club-house in that village we broke our backs and bruised our hands with so much work. And what did we get? A pig as thin as a dry old woman and as tough as a palm tree."

I was able to observe the construction of only one club-house during my visit; it was the unusually large one built for Kuiaka of Kapana village. Kuiaka provided the thatching (purchased by him from several neighboring hamlets), but commissioned the leader at Panakei village to do the actual construction. The latter assembled nearly all able-bodied males of his village, along with men from six other neighboring villages, and worked at the job somewhat desultorily over a period of twenty days. Some men assisted with the construction while the rest supplied them with materials. All told, some 85 youths and men had a hand in the construction, working a total of about 3600 man hours (not including the making of thatch, which I was unable to observe). While the construction went on, Kuiaka kept all the men supplied with drinking coconuts and, on three occasions, with pork and steamed taro. To compensate the workers Kuiaka held a feast for them four weeks later. In all, he spent on the construction: 18 pigs (total value, 1100 mauai), taro worth 50 mauai, thatching worth 200 mauai, and an estimated 2000 drinking coconuts.

Formerly, the Siuai used to consecrate a new club-house by waylaying and killing a man from an enemy community and placing his skull there. Until this was done the owner would not permit a fire to be made on the hearth.

Once a club-house has been built it has to be properly maintained in order to reflect continuing credit upon its owner. For example, when its thatch weathers thin it should be re-roofed — and not by the owner working alone but by a large number of men, preferably from neighboring hamlets, who receive a feast for their labors. Some owners go so far as to call in outsiders to sweep their club-houses, in return for a banquet of pork.

In all these instances it is not the cleanliness or the fine state of repair which adds luster to the owner's renown, but rather the adequately compensated labor that went into the building's upkeep. It is the shrewd and ambitious owner's way of insuring that people will continue to recall his club-house with pleasurable associations of lively activity and delicious food.

# ACQUIRING RENOWN

Proper "maintenance" of a club-house, then, means giving feasts for it and in it. After a number of occasions like these, men from neighboring settlements will begin to say of the owner: "He is a true mumi; he gives large feasts." And when they stroll about they will say more and more often: "Let us go to so-and-so's club-house; there's usually something going on there." They are at pains to ingratiate themselves with the feast-giver, to defer to his judgment, to fetch coconuts for him, and to laugh at his sallies of wit. In this manner the owner maintains the popularity of his club-house and increases his reputation as a good host. And, it will be recalled, there is a supernatural parallel to this process: the more feasts the owner gives, the more nourishment is provided for his club-house demon, which waxes in size, in ferocity, and in loyal and protective adherence to the owner's person as well as property.

## WOODEN SLIT GONGS

No club-house is complete without a full complement of wooden slit gongs — usually nine in number and ranging in size from three feet long and one foot in diameter to fifteen feet long and five feet in diameter. Gongs are made by felling a *moiķui* tree of desired diameter, cutting out a piece of the log to desired length, and hollowing the interior through a narrow longitudinal slit. The ends of the gong are chopped nearly flat and the bark is stripped away, otherwise the surface is not rounded or smoothed. Hollowing the log requires considerable skill since the slit opening has to be kept narrow. Nowadays steel trade-adzes are used for this operation, but many gongs are still in use that were hollowed out with stone adzes. Hollowing out in former days must have been a delicate and lengthy process since some of these old gongs have walls only two inches thick, thinner in fact than most of the modern steel-made products. Throughout northeast Siuai there are only a dozen or so men capable of making first-class gongs. In making a gong the log is shaped and hollowed out in the forest at the place where the tree is felled, being carried to the club-house only after it is ready for use.

The ideal arrangement of slit gongs in a club-house is shown in Figure 26, although there is some variation in this according to the number of gongs present. Gongs are placed and labeled according to size, the largest one being *The Big-one* (*ho ķou*), the next *His-younger-brother* (*paramoŋ*), then *Their-younger-brother* (*perimoŋ*), *Muvomiŋ*,[22] *Fifth-one* (*aŋumuķaŋ*), *Sixth-one* (*no'oriķi naraŋu*), *Seventh-one* (*ķi'iriķe naraŋu*), *Tapivo*,[23] and *Ragoi*,[24] the smallest gong. Also, the seven larger gongs are sometimes called *The-Body* (*mumu*) to differentiate them from Ragoi and Tapivo; and individual gongs are sometimes given specific names, such as "The-Thunderer" or "The-Killer." Many club-houses possess more than nine gongs; in such cases the intermediate ones are grouped with those of nearest size and are named accordingly.

Gongs rest on small wooden sleepers (*kupekupe*) with the slit up, and are beaten with the butt-end of a four-foot long stick [25] struck sharply against the center of the lip of the slit. Tones vary with the size and hollowness of the gong, although the tonal intervals between the gongs in any clubhouse are by no means regular (in fact, the Siuai have no concept of regularity in tone interval in their panpiping or in their gong-beating).

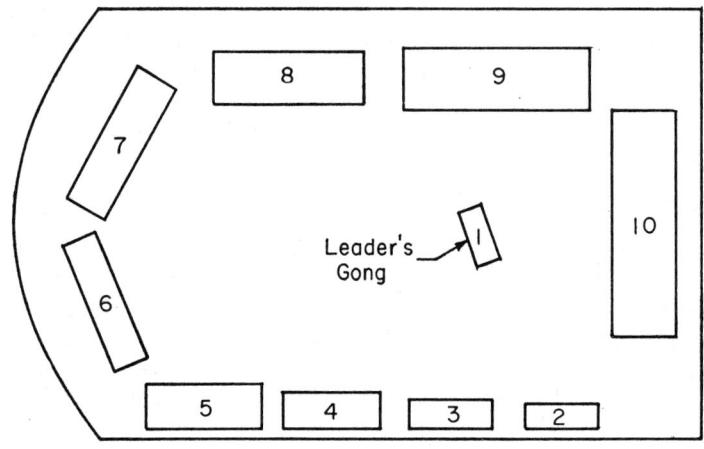

Figure 26

Gongs are beaten on a number of occasions, and although there is no systematic code, alphabetic or otherwise, the drum pattern of each kind of signal is universally well known and various patterns can be put together so that they describe a varying sequence of events. The following signals are beaten on only one gong, usually on Their-younger-brother:

*Kuŋkuŋkuŋ* — a call to assemble, usually sounded by a leader or Hat-man to call together his supporters or subordinates for some work project.

*Antara* — an announcement, usually made in the evening, alerting supporters or subordinates that there will be a kuŋkuŋkuŋ on the following morning.

*Akarumiŋmiŋno* — sounded at intervals during the preparation of a special pudding for a feast.

*Kavoero* — an announcement that the pudding is completed.

*Kuroto* — an announcement that someone of consequence (for example, a Patrol Officer or a visiting leader) is approaching.

*Enopi* — a signal beaten by the club-house owner to announce that he is angry — for example, when he has discovered that his garden fence has been broken through by a hungry pig, or when he has learned that someone has slandered him or tried to seduce his wife.

## ACQUIRING RENOWN

On other occasions *The Big-one* alone is sounded:

*Aokoto* — an announcement that a renowned leader or his wife has died, or that a large tusker pig has been penned up for a feast.

*Eruoto* — a signal that used to be beaten to announce that a man had been killed in fighting.

*Ekueku* — an announcement of the cremation of a man who has met his death by falling from a tree. On hearing this signal all other adult males keep away from the funeral in order to avoid similar fates.

*Takiruoto* — a signal that used to be beaten to summon warriors for a raiding expedition.

On the occasion of a large feast all the gongs in a club-house are beaten in unison at various stages of the preparations. The climax of these events is reached the night preceding the feast, at which time "pig-counting" (*hurehure*) takes place. The host's supporters assemble at his club-house after dark and take up their posts, one beater for each gong. The most expert beater sounds the small ragoi lead gong, while the strongest man present sounds Big-one; both of these posts are coveted, for though there is no special honor attached to them the Siuai nevertheless take great pleasure in sounding the deep-voiced Big-one or in leading their fellows on Ragoi. The host usually assigns these two key posts, while the other beaters pick their own places; there will always be more beaters than gongs so that the beating is done in relays. When everyone is ready the Ragoi beater sounds his gong, beginning with *Vitality-getting*, a quick warm-up signal. He first plays the signal twice through, then as he begins it for the third time Tapivo joins in. These two smallest gongs beat the signal through in unison and then as they start it again Seventh-one joins in, and so on until all the gongs are being beaten in unison. After three or four repetitions of the signal with all gongs beaten together, Ragoi sounds a quick series of terminal beats and leaves off beating. Following this, Tapivo does likewise, and so on around the oval until finally only The Big-one is beating; and then Big-one stops. Following this the beaters pause for a minute or two and congratulate themselves over their fine performance, then Ragoi sounds off on another signal. The initial *Vitality-getting* is followed by *Shell-Ornaments*, the general name for a large number of gong calls beaten for pleasure rather than for signaling specific information. The expert lead man may have as many as forty or fifty of these in his repertoire, and he takes great pride in his ability to lead for several hours at a stretch without repeating. Shell-ornaments vary greatly in length and complexity. Some are very simple, like *One-at-a-time* (*no'no'-ori*), a series of ten moderately slow beats evenly spaced and without variation in accent. Others are meant to describe real or imagined events, such as the lament for the *kouakoua* bird which has become separated from its mate: "As I, the kouakoua bird, was warming my eggs on the bank of the stream the water suddenly arose and washed me away downstream. And now I search for my mate."

This lament is known to nearly every Siuai, and as the Ragoi beater sounds it he reproduces each word in terms of its syllables and accents so that all hearers recognize the little poem on which it is based. A shorter example of Shell-ornaments will illustrate the technique:

| Morokiŋ | pupu | neuitoŋ | neuitoŋ |
|---|---|---|---|
| The flying-fox | sap-of-wild-banana | it-is-drinking | it-is-drinking |

When spoken, the line carries these accents:

Mórokiŋ púpú néuitoŋ néuitoŋ

And this is reproduced on the gongs by accent of beat and by tempo.

Some Shell-ornaments are humorous and evoke laughter, such as the plaint of the faithful wife who tells how her husband always dreams of seeing her fornicating with strangers and, believing his dreams to be true, beats her every morning upon awaking. Others are solemn, such as the sorrow of the man who has been driven out of his hamlet on the untrue accusation of sorcery. A number of them describe little events which are always occurring: "The frog is caught in the fish trap"; "The eel swims down the stream bed"; "Pigs have eaten my taro"; and so on. Many of them are direct borrowings from the neighboring Rugara. Siuai natives take great pleasure in performing Shell-ornaments, one of the few activities in which they coördinate their efforts willingly and effectively for hours at a time.

When the repertoire of Shell-ornaments runs out, after hours of drumming, the lead man pauses for a few minutes and then introduces the climactic *Pig-counting* signal with a few repetitions of *Man-killing*, the gong phrase that formerly was sounded to announce the killing of an enemy. When Man-killing thunders through the night, people for miles around strain their ears and tell one another: "Now it is coming. Now they will make the host's renown." Whereupon the whole gong chorus beats out in unison the value, in units of mauai shell money, of each pig destined to be given away at the forthcoming feast. Natives two and three miles away will waken one another to listen to these meaningful sounds, and to many hosts and prospective guests *this* event is the high point of the feast.

So explicitly does gong-beating signalize specific events that no knowing person would beat a gong without legitimate cause. If a sane man were to beat a gong signal for no good reason, he would risk losing his power of speech. The demented [26] Kea is the only man in northeast Siuai who ignores this convention, and even his otherwise tolerant neighbors drive him away when he approaches a club-house intent on "sounding his renown." Associated with those club-houses with horomoruns is the additional danger that the resident demon will afflict any man who beats the gongs there without permission of the owner.

Small boys play at gong-beating as avidly as American youngsters imitate their current cowboy heroes, but usually they have to be satisfied with beating on logs and house timbers. Before a big feast, however, the grown-ups sometimes indulge the small fry by depositing a small gong at one of the hamlets and allowing them to beat it to their hearts' content. Even little girls join in this play, much to the amusement of their elders, who accuse them of "wanting to own a penis."[27] There is no mystery associated with gongs and gong-beating, and by the time boys begin to frequent the club-houses they are well acquainted with the patterns and meanings of many of the signals; nevertheless it is considered improper and dangerous for them to play with real gongs without cause — except on the occasion just described. (One of the most serious criticisms leveled at the Methodist mission is that lads who attend the Mission school at the coastal station of Kihili are allowed to beat real gongs in play.)

The serious intent of gong-beating is also shown by the injunctions on use following a death. Mourning is considered an improper time for acquiring renown, and a sorrowing man will usually declare a temporary taboo upon the beating of his gongs. To restore them to use — in other words, to terminate the period of mourning — it is necessary to provide a feast for neighbors and kinsmen, and at this time the taboo is removed by beating on Big-one with a green coconut, part of its liquid being afterwards drunk by the club-house owner and part offered as a sacrifice to the demon guarding the club-house. In former days to terminate the mourning for a great war-leader it was necessary to secure a human victim and use his severed head as a beater in order to restore the deceased's gongs to use.

Whether or not a man inherits any slit gongs, he must obtain a few of his own if he wishes to acquire renown. For one thing, people will speak disparagingly of a man who possesses mostly inherited gongs; and in addition, obtaining new gongs provides the ambitious man with excellent opportunities for building up his own renown — provided, of course, they are obtained in the proper manner. Any able-bodied man can cut down a tree, hollow it out enough to make a passable sound, and drag it to his place with the aid of two or three helpers; some individuals actually do this, especially Christian catechists who need gongs to place in front of their chapels to call together their congregations for services. But this is not the way of the ambitious man. For him a gong is both a means and an end. He acquires renown in obtaining it, and then it serves as a continuing symbol of that renown. When such a man wants a new gong he commissions the leader of a neighboring community to fashion one for him, and then rewards him for his service with a pork feast. In this case the contractee usually furnishes a suitable tree from his own forest preserve and pays an expert to fashion the gong; and the reward he receives from the contractor usually exceeds his costs — a circumstance which reflects even greater credit upon the contractor.

The next step is to transport the new gong to the owner's club-house, and this may cost the owner as little or as much as he cares to invest in the enterprise. Usually he will commission the leader of another nearby community to transport it, afterwards rewarding the latter and his supporters with a feast. Depending upon his ambition, he may cause the transporting to be carried out easily and quickly or he may attach practical and magical impediments to the job. Practically, he may build around the gong a carrying frame made of such large timbers that the whole burden will weigh several times the weight of the gong itself. Or, magically, he may increase the difficulty of carrying the gong by "tying" the essence of its weight to various places along the trail to the club-house. This he accomplishes by use of *pukerai* magic, which, it will be recalled, is also employed to prolong life.[28] In the case of a gong its owner gathers some of the chips hollowed out of the gong and ties them with bespelled leaves (kuna) into a small bundle, thereby capturing the essence of the gong's weight. Then he hides the bundle at the spot in the trail where he desires the gong to become too heavy for its carriers to bear. He must guard against encumbering the load beyond the patience of the carriers; and, even more important, he must be prepared to reward them with a feast commensurate with their labors — for woe to the reputation of the man who causes people from other communities to waste their efforts in unrecompensed work. With all this in mind the shrewd owner will recover the gong's weight-essence from its hiding place, and running ahead of the carriers, will hide it further along the trail.

Meanwhile the carriers will know fairly well the intent and the ability of the owner to reward their efforts, and they will play along with his maneuvers accordingly. If, for example, they are dubious about the prospect of recompense, one of the mikai-magicians among them will sit astride the gong and cause his spirit-familiar to sever the link between the gong and its tied heaviness.

Another technique for increasing the weight of a gong is for the owner to induce his club-house demon to sit astride it. In this case, the weight can be decreased only through having one of the carriers cause *his* club-house demon to unseat the owner's; and this can come about only if the second demon is larger and stronger than the first, that is, if the master of the second demon has more renown than the master of the first. This technique is not often employed because it represents a too naked and direct comparison of affluence between host and guest, and may result in unnecessary ill feeling.

Most gong-carrying events last only a few hours, but some take up to three and four days; and while it would seem that the owner, having a given number of pigs to distribute among the carriers, would derive more

# ACQUIRING RENOWN

credit by rewarding them with extreme liberality for what was an easy task, it actually transpires that *more* credit is derived from rewarding them merely adequately for a more difficult and time-consuming job. As one articulate informant put it:

> When a gong is heavy many men will struggle day after day to carry it to the club-house. And all the while they are struggling they will think about the owner and the heaviness of his gong. Throughout Siuai people will ask: "Where are all the big men? We have not seen them about for days." And others will answer: "They are all carrying so-and-so's gong. It is very heavy and they seem never to get it far along the road." Thus will the owner's name and his renown spread, so that people will be obliged to hear and think about him.

Gong-carrying is one of the Siuai's most spectacular activities. One occasion I witnessed involved some two hundred men; and a twenty-five-foot-wide trail had to be cut through the forest and grove to get the gong to the club-house. Many coconut palms had to be cut to clear the trail — a most painful expedient for these thrifty, property-minded natives.

Although not immediately relevant, it should be noted that the carrying on this occasion, as on other occasions I witnessed, was done with extraordinary lack of effective coördination. Men shouted and groaned far more than they lifted, and the air was thick with recriminations hurled at the more obvious laggards.

As this motley crowd of swearing, shouting, perspiring natives staggered along the trail carrying the gong, boys walked ahead, blowing on conches. When they reached the clearing in front of the club-house some of the host's supporters began beating the gongs there in the kuroto tattoo.[29] Then, after the carriers dumped their burden in front of the club-house, they rushed over to a pile of drinking coconuts prepared for them by the host, and as they quenched their thirst began to congratulate themselves on their strength and coördination in having transported such a monster of a gong such a long, long way. Meanwhile some of the host's men rolled and levered the new gong into place in the club-house, and took turns at beating signals on it. After a few minutes of this, the carriers began drifting off homewards, and the host began conferring with the carriers' leaders to set a time for the feast of reward.

Unlike the host just mentioned, many owners of a new slit-gong make a separate special occasion of its first beating. In such cases the owner commissions another leader to bring his supporters and help try out the new instrument, and of course these too must be rewarded with a pork banquet. Meanwhile, between the time the gong is completed and the time it is ceremonially beaten, no person may beat on it lest the owner's club-house demon take away the premature beater's voice. (There were two such mutes in northeast Siuai at the time of my visit; informants believed their affliction to be temporary.)

Still other owners, who either cannot or will not require the gong to be manufactured, carried, and beaten as three separate operations, commission one neighboring leader to perform all three; or they may call on their own supporters to do the whole job. But in any event it is essential that a feast be provided for the laborers, for unless some pigs are killed and their blood-essence offered to the club-house demon, the latter will cause the gong to crack open and become useless. And if the club-house in question has no demon of its own, other local demons will inflict this punishment.[30]

It sometimes becomes necessary to move slit gongs from one club-house to another, if, for example, an old club-house is abandoned for a new one; or if a man inherits some of the gongs but not the club-house of a deceased kinsman. These gongs must also be formally carried and installed in the new club-house, and a feast provided for those who assist.

Finally, after a gong has been installed in the club-house, and after the laborers have been rewarded with a pork banquet for their efforts, the gong remains a symbol of the owner's renown. When natives hear the familiar gong sound thundering through the night, they recall with pleasure the festival and the food which accompanied its installation, and they regard with respect the man who made these things possible. Whatever the origin of the metaphor may have been, there is no present difficulty in understanding why the Siuai now identify metaphorically the making of a man's renown with the beating of his slit gongs. And when natives evaluate the blessings bestowed upon them by Orphan, his invention of the slit gong [31] ranks near the top of their list.

## COMPETITIVE "GIVING"

The principal episode in the muminai feast is a property transaction, in this case a *competitive gift.* The important element during the early stages of a man's social climbing is the non-solicited support of kinsmen and friends, but later on the crucial factor in a man's rise to high rank is his own ability to arrange transactions to his own advantage.

To begin with, the promising young man on the way to becoming a mumi receives support from close kinsmen in the form of material goods; there is of course an element of *sharing* in this support, and some of it must be considered nonreciprocable giving. A man cannot go far towards mumihood without possessing qualities which evoke benevolence from his kinsmen. For example, close kinsmen often give him shoats which kinswomen fatten for him, without any expectation of tangible returns that I could discover.

As the young climber extends his activities beyond his hamlet, other kinds of transactions come into play. He may *lend* small sows to distant kinsmen or to friends in neighboring hamlets with the expectation that they will repay with three or four shoats when each sow litters. Then, later on he will farm out pigs among neighbors and distant kinsmen, who thereby become his aŋurara-men.[32] Meanwhile these supporters will consume some of the food distributed at the young man's club-house, but they will also have devoted large amounts of their time and energy to collecting and preparing this food.

What induces these distant kinsmen and neighbors to support the promising young man? Except for the few situations involving nonreciprocable giving among close relatives, Suiai natives are not accustomed to transfer material goods, or contribute services without fairly explicit expectation of receiving at least an equivalent return, and yet at first glimpse it would appear that the returns they make to a mumi as his lenders, aŋurara-men, and feast-helpers far exceed the values they receive. In the Siuai view, however, these apparent discrepancies are offset in two ways. First of all, there is the privilege of eating delicacies fairly frequently, privileges which can only be enjoyed by associates of an active feast-giver. And secondly, as contributors to a mumi's rise they bask in his reflected renown.

It usually happens that as a mumi gives larger and larger feasts his demands on supporters become greater and greater and their tangible returns less and less. It even transpires that a leader's supporters may have to forego eating their due portions of feast pork and puddings in order to accommodate unexpected guests. Nevertheless, in the Siuai view all these contributions and deprivations are balanced by the supporters' share of the increasing renown of their leader.

Now, in actual fact, this situation presents a wide margin for controversy: both leaders and their supporters complain about not receiving equivalent returns. Leaders often harangue their supporters about lack of adequate support, sometimes even adding that "the hard work I put into preparing feasts is, after all, done to bring renown to our place." For their part, supporters are frequently heard grumbling about their meager portions of the rewards, but so long as a mumi continues to increase or maintain his renown these discontents remain inconsequential. (But just let the mumi's splendor begin to fade, then one or two of his erstwhile supporters may translate their discontent into formal claims for tangible restitution.)

All the above takes place within the men's society of kinsmen and neighbors which grows up around a feast-giving mumi. From this group the mumi derives his main support and within it he exercises a kind of authority.[33] Unless a mumi happens to be a Hat-man, backed by Administration power, he does not exercise authority beyond the neighborhood from which his club-house society draws its membership; but his rank in the tribal hierarchy of mumis depends upon his renown *beyond* the borders of his neighborhood, and within that wider social setting the mumi's property transactions must follow a different pattern.

We have already spoken of the taovu relationship.[34] Between taovu partners transactions are of the *exchange* (ootu)[35] type, which, it will be recalled, is a combination of sale or barter and coercive giving. In Siuai theory taovu partners should be about equal in rank, with their reciprocal exchanges being tangibles roughly equivalent in actual monetary value — that is, material commodity for material commodity and not material commodity for reflected renown. Taovu partners, then, should be regarded as allies in the the struggle for renown, and many actual partnerships are maintained on that basis, some being fairly quiescent, others very active. In addition to exchanging material commodities on a more or less rational commercial basis, most taovu partners also characteristically exchange goods in the manner of coercive giving; for example, when a man languishes too long in self-imposed mourning, one of his taovu partners usually "brings him out of mourning" by means of a mourning termination gift (*ruhoto*).[36] Or, when a boy is formally shown the ocean for the first time (*haraŋitutu*)[37] one of his father's taovu partners usually finances and stages a mock battle against the boy's companions, a distinctive way of honoring the lad and through him his father. These and similar gestures of esteem serve to embellish the ordinary commercial character of the taovu relationship, and they should of course be carried out with reciprocity more or less balanced over a long period of time.

Now and then a taovu partnership may be terminated altogether or transformed into another kind of relationship. If, for example, one of the partners is too dilatory in his repayments the other may decide to end the relationship. Or again, if one of them attempts to step up the values and frequency of the exchange beyond the other's wishes or capabilities, the latter may call off the pact. In other cases, if the partners live in neighboring hamlets, one of them may eventually become absorbed, as it were, in the other's expanded club-house society, thereby becoming a subordinate. And finally, a taovu partnership may develop into an active competition for higher rank, with *exchange* being transformed into competitive gift-giving. This kind of development may result from pique arising out of deteriorating taovu-ship, or it may occur because the two partners reach the point in their respective careers when feast-giving competition between them is normal and inevitable.

A man may acquire good and loyal friends outside his circle of close kinsmen and his local community by means of the taovu relationship, and this serves to widen his sphere of influence; on the other hand, this kind of influence is not to be equated wholly with *renown*. Widening influence accompanies increasing renown, but renown itself is acquired most directly by means of *competitive giving*. Within the context of competitive giving one man gives material goods to another with hope and expectation that the receiver will be unable to return material goods of equivalent value. Instead, the giver acquires renown theoretically equivalent in value to the unrequited gift. To acquire renown for a donor, an unrequited gift must of course be publicly known and talked about.

There is one other aspect of competitive giving to be mentioned. The donee who is incapable of reciprocating equivalently is thereby caused to feel humiliation (*maio*), and in the opinion of the general public his rank becomes lower (*koho*) than that of his victorious donor. Unlike the creditor in a simple exchange or in a taovu relationship, the donor of a competitive gift does not complain and attempt to force his debtor into repaying by means of a "shame device";[38] instead, he boasts of his victory in this contest — or, in the case of the more skillful and subtle leaders, he gives the cue to his supporters, who do the boasting for him.

Between bald-faced competitive giving at one extreme and the kinds of transactions that take place between a man and his close kinsmen, supporters, and taovu partners, there are some other kinds of property transactions initiated by a social climber in the interests of maintaining or even increasing his renown. Some of these might best be labeled *ceremonial exchange*. For example, when one leader is traveling and happens to visit another one who is neither kinsman nor taovu, the host usually prepares a special meal for the visitor and his companions and may even contribute a small pig for the occasion. There is an element of coercive giving about this hospitality, it being assumed that the guest will reciprocate if the occasion arises; on the other hand it would be extremely bad taste for an unrequited host to assert any claim against his former guest. Moreover, it is essential that a ceremonial exchange avoid all appearance of competitive giving: that is, the hospitality feast should be adequate and tasty but not lavish.

A man may also increase his renown by contributing to the life-crises feasts staged by acquaintances from other communities who are not taovu partners and who may or may not be rivals. When, for example, a bereaved parent prepares the funeral feast, some prominent acquaintance may send along a token of condolence, a pig or a few spans of shell money, the gift being publicized in such a way that it adds to or helps to maintain the donor's renown. This is a coercive gift: the donee is honor bound to reciprocate either in goods or services, although no donor should offend the canons of good taste by making an issue of this kind of unpaid debt.

By gestures of hospitality and assistance like these a man may maintain his renown without actually engaging others in competitive gift rivalries; in fact, such gestures may even serve somewhat to increase a man's renown, although major advances in rank come only through competitive giving.

A man usually begins his career of competitive giving by utilizing situations of sale or barter, exchange, and coercive giving.

Consider the opportunity provided by a commercial sale. If one leader sends thirty spans to another for the purpose of purchasing a pig for a feast, the latter will usually hand over a pig worth about forty spans — between men of high rank most of their commercial transactions should conform more or less to the taovu pattern whether or not they are taovu partners. On the other hand, if the vendor wishes to enter into an active rivalry with the purchaser he has merely to send along a pig worth about sixty or more spans. It is then up to the purchaser either to accept the challenge or return the difference in money to the vendor and thereby confess his inability to compete. If circumstances permit, most purchasers placed in this situation react promptly by sending along to the vendor a "gift" of two or three hundred spans of money, which will either chasten the vendor and discourage him from further tests of strength or cause him to retaliate with a competitive feast (*muminai*).

Similarly, one of the partners in an exchange relationship may purposefully transform it into competition with an excessive repayment. Or, a man may bestow upon another a gift of condolence or assistance of such unusually high value that this kind of coercive giving becomes transformed into a challenge to active competition.[39]

The donor of any large unrequited gift acquires increased renown, and this is a positive factor in competitive giving. But also implicit in competitive giving is the expectation that the donee will experience public humiliation if he is unable to retaliate, and some men utilize a competitive gift primarily as a means of humiliating an enemy or an upstart who cannot conceivably be considered a worthy rival — that is, under circumstances wherein the donor stands to gain little or no renown. Humiliating another with unfillable obligations significantly enhances a man's renown only when the victim is of the same or higher rank.

The muminai feast can best be understood, then, as an elaborately institutionalized device for gaining renown: (1) by dispensing hospitality (i.e., coercive gifts) to numerous individual guests, who repay the host in the currency of renown-making praise; (2) by giving to the guest-of-honor a large competive gift which, if not repaid, directly enhances the host's renown; and (3) by publicly humiliating the guest-of-honor, a socio-political rival, thereby reducing him to a rank below that of the host.

## THE COMPETITIVE FEAST

Large muminai feasts are comparatively rare events; only eleven of them took place in northeast Siuai during my visit. One of these was given by the most active feast-giver and the highest ranking leader in the area; it was the tenth muminai given by him since he began competitive feasting some twenty-five years previously. Other high-ranking mumis were described as having given from ten to fifteen muminais spread out over periods of fifteen to thirty years.

Preparations for a muminai differ from preparations for other kinds of large feasts only in being more elaborate and lavish, but spice is added because of the feast's nature as a challenge and because of the preliminary mystery surrounding the identity of the guest of honor.

The major work of preparation is carried out by the host's own supporters, the members of his men's society; and these attend the feast as co-hosts. In addition, the host singles out some allied leader, usually a taovu partner from a nearby place, to attend the feast with all his supporters and close allies in the role of "Resident-defenders" (*urinopo*). The designation of principal Defender is made many days before the feast and is in itself an important episode, formalized by presentation of an invitation-pig (*haramete*) which is divided among all men expected to attend the feast as defenders. The aim is to mobilize as many defenders as possible, the number being more or less prescribed by the amount of pork to be made available at the feast to feed them. Thus when the host invites an ally to serve as Defender he indicates how many pigs will be presented to the latter to be distributed among his co-defenders, and the Defender issues invitations accordingly. Except for the invitation-pig, these animals are regarded not as a gift but rather as payment for services rendered to the host, the Defender not being expected to reciprocate.[40] Sometimes co-defenders assist the host with his feast preparations; for this they are provided with everyday food.

The designation of a Guest-of-Honor is not a perfunctory affair. It is a climax unsurpassed in dramatic interest by the feast itself; this comes about as follows: Everyone knows the number and value of the pigs corralled and waiting to be distributed, this information having been publicized as the animals were being delivered to the corrals. Also, everyone knows the proportion of these pigs promised to the Defender. But no one knows who is to be given the remaining animals until the host makes known the identity of the Guest-of-Honor after most preparations have been made. The invitation, say the Siuai, must be in the form of a *surprise-attack*: "When the invitation is sent the news spreads that this or that place will be devastated, that such and such a mumi will be rendered Near-death (mohkoru)." Consequently, before any large muminai feast Siuai is rife with speculation concerning the identity of the Guest-of-Honor; and it is said that the most likely candidates manifest some nervousness at the prospect of being so "honored."

Informants explained that the host chooses a Guest whose social humiliation will have most positive effect upon increasing his own renown — after weighing carefully, of course, that Guest's capacity to retaliate, and making as sure as possible that the gift surpasses that capacity. The choice of Guest would thus seem to be based on rational calculations. At the same time, however, many hosts consult divination to determine the identity of the Guest-of-Honor — or rather *victim*, since the divination ritual used for this purpose is the one formerly used to fix upon the identities of victims to be killed in warfare (*tupunamu*).[41]

Tupunamu is carried out in this manner: a rare variety of red coconut is husked on a broken spear and its meat thrown onto a small fire in the host's club-house. Formerly war-magicians looked into the fire and saw there the souls of the victims; today it is usually the host himself, if he is a mikai, who takes the part of the war-magician — "so that there will be no mistake." According to some informants this rite is being discarded; in fact many of them regard it as a mere ruse intended to lend the appearance of supernatural backing to the host's rational choice.

The invitation (*haramete*) to the Guest-of-Honor is also in the form of a large pig; if the selected individual accepts the invitation he butchers the invitation-pig and sends strips to all his allies whom he wishes to accompany him to the feast as co-guests, or, in Siuai terms, as "Attackers" (*hikunopo*). These allies then distribute morsels of the pork to all their supporters so that in the end every Attacker going to the feast will, like every Defender, receive a taste of invitation-pig.

After the invitation has been sent and accepted the host decides upon a specific date for the feast and announces it by sending a second pig, a "date-marker" (*mitamita*) to the Guest-of-Honor; this animal is distributed the same way as the invitation-pig. (Later, when the Guest-of-Honor arrives to attend the feast he repays these gifts by presenting the host with two pigs, called *donou*, and equal to them in value.)

Throughout the night before the feast, gongs are sounded in the host's club-house. First of all the *Vitality-getting* signal is sounded, then numerous *Shell-ornaments* — lasting sometimes for hours, then *Man-killing*, and finally *Pig-counting* (*hurehure*) itself. Even though the number and value of all the pigs collected for the feast are usually common knowledge, *Pig-counting* is a dramatic episode, climaxing the months of planning and working, and publicizing with huge pride the actual weight of the host's armament in his fight for higher rank. No wonder that the Siuai call this "sounding renown."

On the following morning Resident-defenders arrive, carrying with them a donou pig to repay the host for the invitation-pig previously sent to them. Carrying their weapons and decorated in full war regalia, they form a line in front of the club-house — "to defend the host." Then a few hours later the Guest-attackers sweep in, shouting and brandishing their weapons as they execute a mock attack against the defenders. After the first rush is over both groups settle down to the business of dancing, piping, and singing the songs composed for the occasion.

More cautious natives try to keep the two groups well separated in order to avoid incidents, for the heightened excitement sometimes produces open clashes and bloodshed. Now and then individuals fall fainting to the ground (from fatigue and overexcitement?), an accident which is invariably attributed to sorcery caused by members of the rival group. All these factors — the warlike actions and paraphernalia, the aroused tempers, the fears and evidences of sorcery — tend to reveal more than anything else the deadly earnestness of rivalry implicit in the muminai feast. The host, above everyone else, remains apprehensive throughout the proceedings; not even the satisfaction he feels at having wrought all this splendor can cancel his fears of being harmed by the sorcery of envious guests.

After an hour or more of dancing and piping the host sends some of his supporters to the food platform from which they remove and spread on the ground all the food delicacies, after exorcising the horomorun demon which has been guarding it. Other supporters bring the pigs from the pens and stake them out on the ground in front of the club-house. After everything is assembled and with everyone waiting expectantly, the host indicates to the Guest-of-Honor his share of pigs, shell money, and delicacies. Sometimes this presentation is made with only a word or two; on other occasions the host or one of his chief supporters makes an elaborate speech (*tati*) in which the size of the "gift" is deprecated and shame is expressed at the modesty of the whole affair. (For example: "I am humiliated to offer you such a poor morsel, and would have honored you appropriately, with many more pigs, had it not been for the deaths of so many of my relatives, necessitating the expenditure of all my resources.") In his reply, the Guest-of-Honor or his spokesman acknowledges great humility before such largess and predicts that he will never be able to repay his host for singling him out for such honor and bounteousness.

During this exchange supporters of the Guest-of-Honor record the size of the gift on palm frond tallies and truss up the pigs which they carry home. At some muminai feasts Attackers set-to and eat the cooked food and coconuts on the spot; in connection with others the Attackers carry their shares home for eating because of sorcery fears. Finally, the Resident-defender carries away his share of the pigs for distributing among his co-defenders, thereby leaving only a pig or two to be consumed by the host's supporters in the now quiet club-house.

Back at his own club-house the Guest-of-Honor distributes the pigs he has received among the leaders of his fellow Attackers, and these take their shares to their club-houses for cooking and distributing among their supporters. This pork need not be repaid to the Guest-of-Honor; it is their reward for attending the feast as his co-Attackers.

Long before he has eaten the small portion of pork remaining to him the Guest-of-Honor has begun to concern himself with plans to repay the feast, for unless he can honor his erstwhile host with a feast of equivalent or more than equivalent value he loses in renown and, in the minds of fellow Siuai, becomes ranked lower in the social-political scale than his victorious rival. There is no specified limit placed on the Guest's time of repayment but it is generally recognized that a man who does not repay within about two annual almond cycles has neither the intent nor the capability of doing so.

If the debtor-guest can marshal only enough resources to repay his rival with a feast of approximately equal value, then further competition between the two is tacitly called off and they remain thenceforth as taovu partners. On the other hand, if the debtor-guest retaliates with a significantly larger feast, then it is up to the original host to balance the account with another feast, or to surpass it with a still larger one and thus move the competition into another round. Sometimes two closely matched rivals will compete several times back and forth, until one of them impoverishes and tires out himself and all his supporters. After that the victor may retire from active feast-giving, or he may take the measure of a more worthy rival. There would appear to be no limit to this expansion, but actually no men I knew of had ambitions to extend their renown beyond the Siuai tribal boundaries. At the time of my visit four individuals had reached the pinnacles in their own areas and two of them were beginning to compete for highest Siuai rank.

What happens to the man bested in competitive feasting?

Among the residents of northeast Siuai past forty or so years old, more than a score of defeated feast-givers were pointed out to me and their reactions to defeat are varied. Most of them rationalize their positions with characteristic Siuai logic: "their ambitions (*haokom*) are not as large as those of their successful rivals." Several of these more philosophical losers have become loyal and enthusiastic allies of former rivals; others seem to have lost interest in this aspect of Siuai life. Certainly none of this majority appears to be socially blighted; each one seems to live a full life and to have lost little or no esteem from most kinsmen and friends. Few of their erstwhile supporters pressed claims for unpaid debts, or deserted to other leaders.

Only a few of the defeated feast-givers appear to bear the stigma of defeat with resentment. (These I knew well; natives with grudges inevitably lay their woes before the ethnographer.) These individuals blame their defeats on rivals' unfair practices. ("He gives away his supporters' pigs which he has not paid for." "He makes excessive demands on his supporters, ignoring their welfare." "He selfishly hoards all his resources for muminai feasts, whereas I have dispersed my wealth to help kinsmen and provide funeral feasts for them when they die.") Without exception these men have sought power in other spheres; one of them became a mission catechist, the others became Hat-men. One of these latter also became a feared sorcerer, thereby supplementing his bullying Hat-man officiousness with threats of supernatural consequences.

Also among the older men of northeast Siuai there are several others who had started out on social-climbing careers but dropped out of the struggle before they reached the point of competitive feasting. They did not bear the stigma of defeat since they had not even reached the point of engaging in active and explicit competitions with specific rivals. Some of these men nevertheless are the ranking mumis of their own neighborhoods; but most of them have become the chief supporters (mouhe) of higher-ranking leaders, and what renown they possess is largely reflected from others.

## ACQUIRING RENOWN

Among the younger men of northeast Siuai there are numerous ones of ambition who are still in the earlier stages of social-climbing, few having reached the point of competitive feasting. They constitute no threat to the positions gained by their higher-ranking elders; in fact many of them are the protégés of the latter.

Summarizing, the *social* implications of defeat in competitive feasting concern mainly a man's rank in the social-political system outside his own neighborhood. Unless he becomes superseded by a member of his own men's society, his status in his own neighborhood remains essentially unchanged — except insofar as his frustration leads him to seek power from other sources. But what about the *supernatural* implications of defeat?

In Siuai belief the defeated feast-giver is rendered Near-death (mohkoru); this comes about in the following manner. A spirit-familiar associated with the host accompanies the gift given to the Guest-of-Honor, and if the latter does not reciprocate the gift the spirit tears out his soul.[42] Throughout western Siuai it is said to be one of the host's noroukuru ghosts that executes this task, but in northeast Siuai informants now believe it to be the host's clubhouse demon (horomorun). ("After all, the muminai is not an affair of the noroukuru.")

I did not succeed in fathoming the true effectiveness of this belief. The individuals I knew who were near-death from this cause certainly did not appear fearful of an untimely demise, but whether this apparent indifference was based on stoicism or on skepticism, I could not determine. A few of the older natives do actually assert that the term "near-death" is metaphorical in this context; on the other hand, others, including many young ex-plantation sophisticates, seem to place full credence in the belief, and one frequently hears that the death of some ancient has been brought about by this kind of Near-death. He may have incurred his fateful indebtedness decades previously, but "it caught up with him in the end."

CHAPTER 11

# The Rewards and Burdens of Leadership

## BELIEFS ABOUT A LEADER'S PERSONALITY

The possessor of renown is singled out among his fellows by means of special beliefs about his personality and destiny, constant praise of his attainments, and respect for his name and person. In addition, he exercises some authority in local affairs and some influence over affairs outside his own neighborhood. On the other hand, leadership in a men's society carries with it many burdens.

To begin with, the Siuai believe that the high-ranking leader possesses to very marked degrees the personal attributes of ambition, skill, industriousness, and goodness.

Ambition (haokom) is considered by many Siuai to be an inborn trait of some males, although not necessarily derived from either parent. Many men believe themselves capable of identifying this trait in lads of six and seven by means of such criteria as solemn mien, lack of timidity and whining, desire to remain with men rather than to play with other children, and quick obedience to elders. My informants agreed with near unanimity upon the identity of their neighbors' sons considered to possess ambition, and the criteria just listed seemed to fit these boys quite faithfully.

There are believed to be many kinds of technical skills (tana) — skill in craftsmanship, in gardening, in magical practices, in musical performance, etc. As previously stated,[1] skill consists of technical knowledge plus practice in using it. Skill is not inborn; technical knowledge is acquired by purchase or gift, but this knowledge has to be applied through much practice before a skill is perfected. The ability to accumulate capital is also regarded as a special skill, and without it no man can acquire renown.

Industriousness is claimed to be an attribute common to all leaders, although not peculiar to them. It is said of a leader: "When he sits down he works and thinks about pigs and money; whereas when we [non-leaders] sit down we sleep."

# REWARDS AND BURDENS OF LEADERSHIP

Some informants confided that they could not become leaders even had they possessed the requisite ambition and skill, "the work of becoming a leader is too difficult — never any rest from planning, negotiating, working, and supervising."

Another attribute believed to be indispensable to successful leadership is the complex of traits I have termed "goodness." The Siuai term for "goodness" includes "generosity," "coöperativeness," "geniality," and "decency," all closely interrelated aspects of the same attribute. As previously stated,[2] an individual cannot be deficient in one of these aspects without being deficient in all of them.

"Generosity" is not entirely synonymous with nonreciprocable giving; the Siuai also consider the coercive giver to be generous provided he gives frequently enough and does not weigh returns too exactly. The miser, who hoards his wealth; the stone-heart, who does not aid his relatives and friends; the petty-minded man who treats all transactions like barter between strangers — all these are opposites of the "generous man" (*nommai rakuraku*) and could not acquire renown no matter how great their ambitions, skills, and industriousness.

"Coöperativeness" is nearly synonymous with "generosity" but includes in addition a genuine liking for working with others. Privacy is commonly desired and respected in many phases of living, but the man who insists on working always independently and apart from his neighbors is regarded with distrust and suspicion, and could never acquire renown.

"Geniality" does not demand continual cheerfulness — there are times when solemnity or anger are called for, but the leader should be one who is slow to anger and is usually friendly and responsive. "Decency" or "trustworthiness" refers mainly to behavior in connection with property transactions. The decent, trustworthy man does not misrepresent his wares or claim property that does not belong to him. He gives full measure in purchase and barter transactions and does not claim excessive indemnities in suits for damage.

All these attributes — ambition for renown, skill in accumulating property, industriousness, and goodness — are believed to be essential for leadership. Deficiency in any one of them can frustrate progress towards acquiring renown. Noteworthy, however, is the fact that only one of these attributes, ambition, is believed to be inborn — and even that need not be genetically derived; how all these attributes come to reside in an individual no one bothers to speculate about — Siuai etiology has not concerned itself with such matters.

In tracing the rise of individual leaders, the important roles played by assisting kinsmen become apparent; but when generalizing about any one leader, informants nearly always stress his personal attributes, largely ascribing his success to his own individual efforts. In this connection it is noteworthy to recall that the Siuai's favorite culture hero is Panaŋa, the Orphan kupuna, who overcomes obstacles and establishes his supremacy through his own efforts.

A leader's effectiveness is ascribed to his possession of these specific attributes and not to any general mana-like supernatural quality. Moreover, effectiveness in acquiring renown does not automatically connote effectiveness in other activities. The leader is not necessarily a successful craftsman or magician. What effectiveness the leader has, *qua* leader, in the realm of the supernatural comes about through his mastery over a club-house demon. On the other hand, the beliefs held by the Siuai about the *destiny* of a leader could be interpreted as reflecting a notion of special inherent supernatural qualities. One of these beliefs concerns the leader's soul just before death, the other after death.

In the case of most adults on the point of dying, the soul leaves its body and assumes the form of a ball of fire (*ripo*, swamp phosphorescence?) and wanders about the neighborhood wilting banana trees with its heat. Finally it returns to the house where its owner is sleeping and moves from one side of the roof to the other, letting people know of the imminent fate of the person inside.[3] In the case of a leader this episode is far more spectacular; his soul assumes the form of a very large ball of fire (*umiai*, a bolide), hovers for a while in its club-house, then rushes through the air with a whistling sound, "*sisisisisi*——," which everyone hears. It flies to its nearest matrilineage shrine and alights on a tree there, whereupon the chief matrilineage ghost or demon of that place interrogates it concerning all the important things its owner has accomplished: how many feasts he has held, how many fights he has backed, how many men he has killed, how much shell money he has accumulated, how many gongs he has had constructed and carried, how many club-houses he has built, how many settlements he has devastated in warfare, how much cultivated land he has laid waste. Having answered all these questions,[4] the leader's umiai-soul falls from his tree-perch to the ground with a loud crash.[5] Upon hearing this crash all the people nearby speculate about the identity of the doomed leader, saying, for example, "Since the umiai fell on a Tree-rat shrine, a Tree-rat leader will die — possibly so-and-so, who is very old and frail."

After death, the leader's ghost has a better chance of reaching Paradise (Lake *Ru'no'no'*) than has the ordinary individual's because, presumably, more pigs are killed for a leader's funeral feast. Moreover, even if some leader's funeral feast is not a large one, it is said that Hoŋiŋ, chief demon of the afterworld, takes into account the dead leader's previous feast-giving record and grants him entry into Paradise.[6]

Again, the ghost of a leader is likelier than an ordinary individual's ghost to be invoked in wealth-magic rites (sinapo),[7] as well as in other kinds of magical rites based on rapport with ghosts possessing special technical skills; leaders do not possess a monopoly of special skills but in aggregate they possess more than would be found among a comparable number of

# REWARDS AND BURDENS OF LEADERSHIP

non-leaders picked at random. However, neither this circumstance nor the one described in the preceding paragraph betokens any special supernatural qualities of the leader *qua* leader. In another respect, though, there are situations which would seem to assume such qualities. Only the ghosts of leaders may become powerful eel-demons (kamaŋu) and club-house demons — few actually do so, but then I recorded no instances of the ghosts of non-leaders being thus characterized. Having been *dangerous* men in life, leaders continue to be so after death.

## PRAISE OF A LEADER'S ATTAINMENTS

The successful feast-giver is abundantly recompensed with that most desirable kind of Siuai reward, *praise*; or, rather, having high rank *means* having renown, that is, *being praised*. "Renown" is not merely a technical term used to designate a leader's rank; as a man rises in the socio-political scale he has the satisfaction of knowing that people are actually discussing his attainments with wonder and admiration. When addressing him people usually call him "mumi," drawing out the syllables and weighting the sounds with heavy affect. When lounging with him in his club-house, adherents and visitors alike discuss his superiority quite baldly and effusively — perhaps with the intent of currying favor but also because this is a favorite topic of conversation. But in addition to this general setting of flattery in which the leader basks he also receives special expressions of praise.

Occasionally the members of a men's society visit a neighboring leader at his club-house and serenade him by piping and singing songs that extol his character and attainments; for example:

Thunderer, Earth-shaker,
Maker of many feasts,
How empty of gong sounds will all the places be when you leave us.

Warrior, Handsome Flower,
Killer of men and pigs,
Who will bring renown to our places when you leave us?

A service like this must of course be recompensed, and the serenaders are usually feasted on the spot with pork or taro.[8]

Concrete expressions of praise are also voiced in the dirges sung over dead leaders, as we have seen.[9]

## RESPECT FOR A LEADER'S NAME AND PERSON

The respect accorded a leader's name shows up in several ways. First of all, others do not address him by name; instead they use a kinship term or, more frequently, call him "mumi." (Kinship terms are most often employed towards leaders by distant kinsmen seeking favors or snobbishly attempting to publicize a relationship.) Sometimes a leader's personal name is avoided in reference; on such occasions he may be referred to by the name of his club-house, his club-house demon, or even by the name of one of his henchmen. On the other hand, people often refer to places and people by calling them such-and-such a leader's adherents (*pokonopo*), or such-and-such a leader's place (*uri*).

We saw above [10] how residents of a place tacitly possess certain provisional rights to all the land identified with their neighborhood, and how these rights vary in strength directly with the activity of the men's society of that neighborhood. We also recorded the assertion of informants that "mumis own large tracts of land." [11] Both these generalizations have a bearing on the matter now being discussed. Consider for example the case of Kope, leader of important Unanai village and the most renowned man of central Siuai.[12]

Kope is almost landless. His matrilineage is centered in northwest Siuai, but he never goes there, and supposes, "there would probably be no land left there for me to garden on." While still a young man he left his own home and moved to his present place. Since then he has attained higher rank than all his neighbors, and commands obedience in his own district and enormous respect elsewhere, but he still dwells and gardens on land to which he is a mere *Attacher*.[13] Kope himself jokes about his paradoxical situation.

Consider, on the other hand, the cases of Kepina of Turuŋum village, Nonroki of Jeku, and Piria of Novei — all of them sole survivors of their respective matrilineages and thereby holding full or residual title to the extensive tracts owned by these matrilineages. Yet none of these men possesses renown. Much of the same thing is true of Peuru. He is a "nothing-man" of low rank, but his land (Mi'kahna-Parupa),[14] in which he owns an important controlling interest, is extensive and fertile and centrally located.

The above cases are extreme, but even after excluding them I was not able to find any significant correlation between an individual's rank and the quantity of land in which he possesses full ownership or important residual ownership rights. Suppose, though, we consider "tacit" ownership, the sort of relationship between members of an active men's society and the land on which they live and work. In this sense there is a very real direct correlation between rank and land ownership.

The leader, as the highest ranking member of the local men's society, is frequently personally identified with *all* the land associated with his neighborhood. For example, the land between the Honoro and Miraka creeks is sometimes spoken of as the land of the Turuŋum leader, Soŋi. Once during preparations for a feast Soŋi complained to his followers that he was planning to leave Turuŋum and to live near his matrilineage shrine at Rukarui: "You no not coöperate with me. I labor continually to increase the renown of us Turuŋum people, yet you remain in your houses and sleep with your wives when you should be helping me. I shall leave Turuŋom and go to live near my shrine."

His adherents pleaded with him to remain: "You cannot leave Turuŋom; it is *your* place; the land is *yours*."

And again, even though the leader and Paramount Chief Kope is a mere Attacher in his hamlet at Unanai, his adherents and other natives refer to Unanai and its surrounding areas as "Kope's place," "the land belonging to the mumi, Kope." This is partly in accord with the practice of referring to property by giving the name of the highest ranking co-owner; I learned to expect this euphemism whenever I went mapping with several natives. But the imputation is more than that — it is bound up with the concept of *tuhia*.

In a metaphoric sense the coercive or competitive giving of pigs takes on territorial significance. The packet of twigs retained by a creditor when he makes a loan is called his *tuhia*; for example, a packet of fifty twigs stands for a pig worth fifty spans of shell money. (The transaction usually takes place before witnesses, who are therefore in a position, if necessary, to attest to the authenticity of the tuhia.) In a slightly different meaning, every person to whom one frequently gives pigs is one's *tuhia*; and the man who makes frequent distributions to a great many persons has, of course, a large number of tuhias. The meaning of the term has been extended to signify also the region lived in by one's tuhias, so that it is said of a high-ranking feast-giver that such and such a region is his tuhia. Of course, an individual can become the tuhia of just as many feast-givers as invite him to their feasts, and it therefore follows that territorial tuhias must overlap. It is customary, however, to refer to a certain region as constituting the tuhia of the highest ranking feast-giver in that region. It is in this sense that a mission manual [15] translates the term as "kingdom."

That deference is shown for a high-ranking leader's *person* is unmistakable to any observer. Leaders are usually spared menial jobs; others fetch water for them, and climb palms to get coconuts and areca nuts for their refreshment. Boisterous talk usually becomes quieter when a leader approaches, and boys leave off roughhousing. In fact, one of the sternest lessons impressed upon a child is to stay away from a leader, or else remain quiet in his presence. ("Never play when a mumi is nearby; you might disturb him or hit him with your toys.") Females, especially, appear awed near the great men, often looking shyly to the ground. Men usually wait for a leader to open conversations, and take their cues from him concerning when to laugh, to commend, or to decry.

No supernaturally sanctioned taboos surround a leader's person in order to insulate him from plain physical contact with other natives, but few people would assume enough familiarity with him to place a friendly hand on his shoulder — a common gesture among equals. What protection from harm a leader enjoys derives from intervention of his club-house demon, or from specific magical devices available to anyone with the means of purchasing them.

When a leader is in mourning it behooves all his supporters to avoid unseemly activities, such as special work projects or celebrations; frequently even a leader's distant taovu partners respect his mourning in this way. Then, one of his allies or rivals usually presents him with a special gift (ruhoto) [16] to terminate his mourning.

The respect shown a leader's name and person does not end with his death. His demise is announced by the beating of the solemn aokoto signal [17] on the largest gong in his club-house, and after that all gongs in the neighborhood remain quiet until a taboo-lifting ceremony is performed some weeks later. Scores of persons, including allies, rivals, and their supporters, attend his cremation. If a leader dies in his prime the assembled throng keeps up a pandemonium of real and simulated grief throughout the whole duration of the cremation. Loyal supporters join family survivors in crowding as near as humanly possible to the blazing pyre; and even casual curiosity-seekers standing in the outer circle of mourners do not drift away to smoke or doze so long as the fire continues to burn. If, on the other hand, the dead mumi were already senile and past his social-political prime then the cremation assumes some of the character of a festivity, with singing, dancing, and distribution of pork.[18]

The equipment of a leader's cremation is more elaborate than that of an ordinary native. The pyre is larger, better constructed, and festooned with many new loincloths (like the stretcher used for carrying a very large pig!). A railing is attached to the sides of the pyre to enable the chief mourners to stand on the structure until forced back by the heat. Large quantities of complete taro plants are hung onto the fence frame surrounding the pyre, and larger quantities of the deceased's matrilineage heirloom money are thrown into the blaze. Also, at least one of the deceased's slit gongs is burnt at his club-house.

A day or two after the funeral of a leader his family and matrilineage survivors sponsor a *tapi* ceremony on his behalf. They invite one of the deceased's allies to bring his supporters and engage in an exhibition of spear-throwing as a memorial service. A wooden pile is set upright in the ground and men rush at it in attack formation throwing their spears as they run; no man can retrieve his own spear, so that the action has something of the quality of a sacrifice to the deceased's ghost.[19] The participants are recompensed with pork. (Formerly the tapi ceremony had the added character of a ritualistic display of anger, a preliminary and symbolic killing of the sorcerer assumed to have brought about the death of the leader.)

Following the death of a leader mourning is more stringently enforced than is normally the case. One of the only overt and premeditated acts of violence I witnessed in Siuai came about when a man prematurely resumed garden work after the death of his local leader. The deceased's kinsmen broke down a portion of the culprit's garden fence and uprooted some of his taro;

and the victim was so shamed by the episode that he followed an otherwise unheard of course and made no claim for damages!

A previous chapter described how land is *set-aside* to commemorate the death of a native.[20] This *setting-aside* varies according to the age, sex, and rank of the deceased. For example, on the occasion of the death of Turie, an orphan lad with no influential kinsmen, a small handful of people attended the perfunctory cremation given his remains. Afterward his sister *set-aside* the corner of a garden which she was harvesting and refrained from taking taro from it for four weeks. Such was little Turie's memorial. By contrast, when Kapika, the Mataras leader, died, over two hundred people attended his cremation. All garden work by his fellow villagers was suspended for a week. The entire northern half of Rinsa was *set-aside* in February 1938, and was still taboo when I finally left this area twenty months later.

In some instances very large and economically useful areas are *set-aside* for many years, thus depriving the residents of valuable resources and keeping fresh in their minds the memories of the leaders who, when living, also dominated their lives. Cultivable land is not the only kind of area *set-aside*. There are also large forests tabooed to all hunting; and east of Moronei village a long stretch of the Mivo River is tabooed to all fishing. The river at that point used to belong to the leader, Moki;[21] and when he died (about 1933) his heirs declared it *set-aside*. It was only during our visit, some five years later, that it was restored to use. Moki's surviving kinsmen and adherents constructed a large dam and carried out a fish drive at the tabooed place. The first few fish to be caught were thrown away as a sacrifice to the ghosts of all former fishing specialists who had consecrated this ritual. These words were uttered: "We threw away this fish for you, mara; see to it that we have a big catch." After this brief ritual the drive began. The catch was cooked and eaten at a feast, and the river thus restored to fishing activity.

In the case of a leader, it is assumed that sorcery is at least partly responsible for his death. Consequently, when a leader dies divination is usually carried out to determine the identity of the sorcerer. Nowadays, after relatives and adherents of the deceased leader have discovered the sorcerer's identity they have to content themselves with counter-sorcery. Formerly they would have organized a reprisal raid on the settlement of the accused sorcerer, and might even have taken possession of the land identified with that place.

The deferential behavior accorded a leader applies in some degree to members of his family. No sane man would make improper advances to a mumi's wife (*mumih kuina*), and children are cautioned against hurting or antagonizing his children. His daughters are more carefully chaperoned than other girls; their betrothals and weddings are carried out with more care and formality. The ordinary debut rites of his children are celebrated with larger feasts, and such special debut rites as ocean-seeing, club-house entering, and pig-pen-viewing [22] are held only for the offspring of high-ranking leaders. At death, also, a leader's wife and offspring receive special homage in the form of more mourners, more stringent mourning taboos, and larger distributions of pork. A leader's wife may even be acclaimed in death as no woman and few men are honored in life: her demise, like her spouse's renown and his demise, is publicized by the sounding of a club-house gong.

## AUTHORITY IN LOCAL AFFAIRS

Within his own neighborhood the leader also receives rewards of a more substantial nature, including strong protection for his own property and some degree of command over his adherents' actions and resources.

Any man with resources can acquire specialized and specific magical property-protection devices but it is only the leader or high-ranking sub-leader who commands the services of a club-house demon to safeguard all his possessions. In this instance belief effectively guides action; most natives simply will not court supernatural disaster by infringing on a leader's property rights.

Stratification in the men's societies was described in an earlier chapter,[23] both as idealized by native theorists and as constructed from my direct observations of hierarchically ordered behavior. We saw how the adherents of the leader of an active men's society may be called supporters (mouhe), messengers (turaturana), or legs (moŋo), according to the functions they perform, and that these functions may change with circumstances. From a hierarchical point of view it was found more useful to plot the positions of members of a men's society according to interaction criteria, and in this sense we found that each active society consisted of the following kind of hierarchy:

Class I. At the top, a leader who, in events having to do with activities of the society, only originates orders.

Class II. Immediately below the leader, one or more sub-leaders, men of some renown, who receive orders only from the leader but who originate them to all other members of the society.

Class III. The majority of the society's membership, who receive orders from Classes I and II and occasionally originate orders to each other and to Class IV.

Class IV. One or more members who usually only receive orders, very rarely originating them.[24]

In native terms, the leader is always called a mumi, while all other members of the men's society are sometimes referred to as the leader's kitoria (children) or pokonopo (his-friends or his-companions). The sub-leaders are also frequently known as mumi, and are usually referred to as mouhe (supporters). Any member of the society who acts as a messenger for the leader may be called turaturana. Finally, those members who carry out the most menial assignments are usually designated moŋo (legs), and they are generally to be found in Class IV.[25]

We have also described the kinds of activities participated in by members of a men's society and some of the kinds of services performed by adherents for their leader, hence will not repeat these observations here. At present it is sufficient to restate that a leader has, by definition, some degree of command over his adherents' services in connection with men's society activities. The next question is: does a leader's authority, *qua* leader, extend to other members of his neighborhood and to activities not directly concerned with feast-giving?

According to my observations, in those neighborhoods with active men's societies the authority of the leader extends to all persons directly and indirectly. Indirectly, a leader's demands on his adherents' services also affect other members of the latters' households. An adherent required, say, to produce pigs for feasts has to make greater demands on the services of his wife and children — that is inevitable. But more directly, a well-established leader may, for example, also be seen sending a neighbor's children on errands, or berating some young woman found walking alone on a public trail.[26] Other older men in the neighborhood may try to exert authority, but it is only the leader or the respected sub-leader — and in addition certain Hat-men — whose authority is effective among neighbors unrelated to him by close ties of kinship. As likely as not, a child will ignore an order from any other non-kin neighbor, or he might complain to his father who would then remind the neighbor to make his own children do his work; or, the young woman might invite her unwanted counselor to "insert his advice along with his penis into his own wife, where both are plainly needed." Not so, if the order or admonishment comes from the local leader; child and woman would do as told and their parents would voice no resentment.[27]

Leaders vary greatly in the *domain* of their authority — that is, in the extent to which they assert authority beyond the activities of feast-giving. Some are so preoccupied with their own social-climbing careers that they have neither the time nor, apparently, the desire to control other neighborhood affairs or to dominate neighbors' lives. Other leaders push their advice and instructions into every crevice of neighborhood life — supervising work teams; setting times for ceremonies; approving betrothals, etc.; and adjudicating quarrels. Factors of personality enter here, and persons who are not leaders also attempt to control the affairs of others around them, but it is only the leader or the high-ranking sub-leader whose intervention is accepted even though it lacks the moral sanction of a kinship tie or the physical coercion of a Hat-man.

If not physical force, then what kind of sanctions support a leader's authority in local affairs?

Supernatural sanctions safeguard his material possessions and person but do not help enforce his commands; I know of no instance wherein a leader ordered his club-house demon to punish an unruly or disobedient person.[28]

A leader's adherents support and obey him for a variety of reasons, including his control over such valued things as feast-giving and reflected renown; but of all such reasons the leader's influence over public opinion probably provides his authority with its most effective sanction.

Commendation from their leader is for many Siuai males the sweetest of all rewards. Some men will work for days on end, turn over their prize animals, reduce their consumption of coconuts, and then even forego eating the banquet made possible by their efforts and deprivations — all in return for commendation from their leader. Every men's society I knew contained a few individuals of this nature, but they constitute only the loyal core of adherents. A much wider circle of adherents is reached by the leader's capacity to focus disapprobation and anger.

Any form of disparagement rests uncomfortably on most Siuai, but coming from the leader of one's own men's society is almost unsupportable, for the great man's ridicule or condemnation will always be taken up by his adherents and their households. Even suicides result from such pressures. Moving to another settlement is of course possible but in addition to its physical hardships there are other difficulties involved. Some of the atmosphere of the former neighborhood invariably accompanies the refugee, and he must expect to be called a *deserter*: "like an adze-blade attached to the wrong kind of shaft, he has left his friends and now walks about with strangers." Even if his new neighborhood is antagonistic to his former one, the refugee is not allowed to forget his desertion.

A leader's "anger" (iro) is said to be "hotter" than other men's; and although most natives recognize this to be metaphoric, they point out that the leader whose anger is aroused does in fact have more resources than other men for translating his emotion into action. He can, for example, humiliate fractious subjects or enemies by giving them competitive gifts,[29] or he can purchase the collusion of diviners to point the finger of guilt at them. Or, he may even utilize his resources for commissioning sorcerers to destroy his foes.

Tangible evidence of a leader's authority is his ability to impose fines (rakai) [30] upon adherents. A leader may impose a fine if an adherent fails without good cause to assist in some episode of feast preparations, or if he does not show proper deference — for example, if he is overheard disparaging his leader's accomplishments or complaining about his excessive demands. Fines average about five or ten spans of shell money; some leaders make a practice of refunding the amount of the fine, but there are others who do not, thus leading to the allegation that their ostensible sensitivity to slight is based on more practical considerations.

In Administration practice the officially appointed Hat-men — paramounts, village headmen, and interpreters — are the proper persons to arbitrate cases tacitly within the jurisdiction of native "courts," but in many villages where leader and headman are different individuals it is the former who is in fact the principal judge, arbitrator, and sometimes even prosecutor, leaving to the bypassed headman only those cases involving violations of such Administration regulations as failure to do road work and failure to maintain a "line" house in good repair. It is true that the leader, unlike the headsman, has no physical force to back him up; nevertheless his decisions and assessments are usually executed.

It is perhaps significant that fewer cases of open litigation occur in neighborhoods dominated by a high-ranking leader. This may be partly accounted for by the greater amount of coöperativeness to be found in such communities; but it is also evident that in such places troubles are resolved informally before reaching the stage of formal litigation — resolved either by the leader or by the principals themselves acting on their knowledge of the leader's opinions about such matters.

Here in property-minded Siuai a leader appears to exercise more command over his people's services than over their material goods; for example, he does not have the authority of confiscation. On the other hand, he does enjoy certain other material advantages by virtue of his high rank.

Whenever a pig is butchered for local consumption the leader is always given the best cut, "strip-with-the-ear" (*ruŋ tuha*).[31] After large-scale hunting and fishing expeditions a choice portion of the bag is given him whether he participated or not.

We saw earlier [32] how in some cases residents enjoy "tacit" provisional rights of ownership in land otherwise owned by other members of their neighborhood. In a closely knit community all residents share such rights, but those of the leader may be said to outweigh all others. The leader has no difficulty in utilizing the choicest garden sites; in fact, adherents usually regard it as a privilege to have him share their land, with no question of rent.

Paying rental on land (*muhni ukom*, "of the landowner") is not a general usage. Persons of more or less equal rank rarely pay it to each other, nor does a leader customarily pay it to an adherent. In fact, it is usually paid only by adherents to their leader when they garden on the latter's land; and in such instances the rental consists of about one-tenth of the garden's produce.[33] As such, then, land rent can be regarded as a prerogative of leadership. In actual fact, however, it is a prerogative rarely exercised. A native still in the process of social-climbing, still trying to ingratiate himself with his neighbors, would be chary of asking tenants for rent. Also, some well-established leaders, exemplifying the principle of *noblesse oblige*, do not demand rent from their tenants.

## INFLUENCE BEYOND THE NEIGHBORHOOD

How does a leader stand outside his own neighborhood?

First of all, it is easily observable that when he travels to other places he is usually greeted with exceptional politeness and bountiful hospitality. When he needs new sources of goods or money he experiences less difficulty than other men in finding lenders or establishing exchange partnerships. He also possesses an advantage in purchase transactions: for example, when he sends his messengers out to buy a pig they have less trouble locating a willing vendor, and it is customary for the vendor to supply an animal worth somewhat more than the money paid him.[34]

A leader also enjoys free access to land outside his own neighborhood provided the land in question constitutes part of his tuhia; and in the case of the highest ranking leaders, they might be said to exercise a "tacit suzerainty" over all the areas constituting their tuhias, with very broad privileges of moving about and settling where they will. As the leader of Noronai community said to Soŋi, his highest-ranking ally: "Cultivate on our soil, honor our poor crops with your presence, for our land is your land."

Because of the "heat" of his "anger," the sting of his criticism, and the effects of his competitive-giving, a leader is also in a position to exercise considerable influence on affairs outside his own neighborhood. It is not unusual, for example, for a high-ranking leader to be requested to arbitrate disputes between leaders of neighboring settlements. On the other hand, he exercises little or no control over the services of persons outside his own neighborhood.[35] Some men voluntarily associate themselves with men's societies in other neighborhoods and become loyal adherents of the leaders holding sway there. Otherwise, no matter how high his rank, if a leader issues an order to an outsider, he is very likely to be told: "Do it yourself. I'm not *your* fool (*hunu*)." [36]

### THE BURDENS OF LEADERSHIP

"Becoming a leader is difficult; remaining one is dangerous. It requires ambition stronger than mine." So in effect asserted many natives in explanation of their apparent lack of desire for high rank.

To begin with, during the early stages of feast-giving it is indispensable for a man to possess numbers of close kinsmen capable of starting him off on his career, and he must conduct his relations with these kinsmen in such a manner that they will in fact support him. This calls for scrupulous regard for kinship obligations on his part: deference to his elders, careful maintenance of kinship taboos and avoidances, readiness to help relatives in times of crises, etc. A man who lives far apart from his relatives, or who is cynical and careless about his kin responsibilities, will not be likely to obtain the kind of start required for a successful social-climbing career.[37]

Once having become a leader, it is probably correct to say that a man's principal social duty is to *maintain* his high rank so as to provide his adherents with reflected renown, which is their main recompense for having supported him with their goods and services. Maintaining high rank is burdensome for any man, and becomes increasingly so with advancing age. It involves continuous hard work, constant planning and scheming. Allies have to be kept friendly, potential rivals checked.

The leader also suffers deprivations which the ordinary man would be unwilling to bear with. While it is true that he receives choice meats when they become available, he often goes without coconuts and almonds for months at a time in order to conserve resources for feasts. Almonds are a luxury food, but coconuts are a staple without which the everyday Siuai meal remains, to the natives, dry and nearly tasteless — like butterless bread. Even the occasional opossum bagged by the leader or given him by his adherents is usually smoked and put aside for the next feast. And if he is fortunate enough to spear a wild pig he cannot enjoy the luxury of a private domestic banquet but should make it the occasion for a small public feast.[38]

Achieving and maintaining high rank also involves dangers. There is of course the long-range prospect of being rendered NEAR-DEATH by rivals; but there is also the constant threat of magical attack by envious enemies. While no leader I knew showed evidence of being anxiety-ridden for this cause, most of them did take precautions regarded as onerous. Some of them refused to eat in the presence of strangers, and most of them are reluctant to travel because of the additional dangers involved. It is true that some special protection is afforded a leader by his club-house demon; on the other hand that demon can itself become a liability and a danger if its master does not maintain his rank. It will be recalled [39] that a club-house demon must be fed frequently on essence of pig-blood in order to remain "domesticated"; in other words, its master must keep on slaughtering pigs in his club-house. For, if the demon is not adequately fed it becomes wraith-like and angry, captures its master's soul, and abandons the club-house in search of a more worthy master.

The leader has to forego sex-adventuring to a degree which most natives would find too inhibitory. No woman having a rendezvous with a leader can be expected to remain discreet, with the result that her kinsmen and spouse or fiancé will either join the ranks of the leader's enemies or extort an unusually high indemnity from him. Also, such episodes are utilized to the fullest by his detractors to make him appear ridiculously hypocritical or worse. For example, the Siuai are still chuckling over the discomfiture of the leader, Konsei, on one such occasion.

Shortly after Konsei was appointed a Paramount Chief [40] he tried to impress an inspecting Patrol Officer by staging a clean-up of all native practices thought to be disapproved by the Administration. Among other things, he brought a charge of promiscuity against a handsome young woman. At this point the Patrol Officer stepped in and asked her to indicate all the men she had given her favors to. When she pointed to Konsei the latter at first blustered out a denial, whereupon the woman ingenuously described in detail and with most expressive gestures each meeting she had had with Konsei, adding that his payments had been meager and his body odor anything but fragrant! This episode and the pantomime constructed from it became political capital in the hands of his rivals and enemies.

Scrupulous trustworthiness is also expected of a leader, and any dishonesty on his part is sure to be deeply resented by his victims and widely publicized by his enemies as evidence of the shaky foundations of his renown. Coöperativeness and geniality on the leader's part are of course essential to the conduct of successful social-climbing; without them an ambitious man would experience difficulty in winning willing and loyal adherents. Above all, the leader must exhibit generosity — not only the formalized and calculated munificence of feast-giving but everyday open-handedness as well. The leader must be willing to assist his adherents when crises occur in their lives, and he should allow them access to his possessions except when these are under special taboo. In normal times natives do not hesitate to take coconuts or areca nuts from their leader's groves, asserting that, "We are his kitoria (children)." In walking about a mumi's groves one frequently sees half a coconut shell tied to a palm; this is a *haraka*. When a native takes nuts or bananas from another's trees he leaves a haraka nearby so that the owner will realize that it is not theft and hence will not become angry. In this and in other respects, the demands of *noblesse oblige* make deeper inroads on a leader's possessions than on those of an ordinary man.

In one other important way leadership is onerous. No high-ranking leader can escape being cast in the role of adjudicator and arbitrator, and although this circumstance can be regarded as evidence of his influence it should also be kept in mind that his decisions inevitably make enemies for him — the Siuai have no concept of a wholly *impartial* judge, and more enemies means more danger of being politically or magically injured. Partly for this reason no leader can be continually and consistently impartial even if he wished to be so; if he is to retain his most useful social-political ties he must shape his decisions accordingly. I recorded no evidence of any leader suffering qualms of conscience from such circumstances; however, the constant alertness and caution involved in making relatively safe and expedient decisions must be regarded as burdensome to natives most of whom would rather doze and observe than risk active implication in the troubles of others.

In summary, the burdens of leadership would seem to balance the prizes — or at least that is the rationalization given by some natives for their apparent indifference to becoming renowned. And when discussing this matter natives invariably hark back to the former days of warfare, when the onus — so they say — was far outweighed by the rewards.

CHAPTER 12

# *Leadership and Warfare*

"In the olden times there were greater mumi than there are today. Then, they were fierce and relentless war leaders. They laid waste to the countryside, and their club-houses were lined with the skulls of people they had slain. Today, we are mere children. We fight weakly, with our mouths; and men of no consequence can talk loud and slanderously against their mumis without fear of punishment. The olden times were better."

Thus spoke a Siuai man in the fifteenth year of the Pax Britannica — and the voice was not that of an old heathen, harking back to the days of his vitality, but that of a Christianized young Hat-man recently returned home after four years of work and travel in white man's civilization.

During my stay in Siuai not a spear was tossed in anger — if that had occurred, the furore and the resulting litigation would have been immense! — and yet blood and destruction engrossed these cautious moderns whenever their talk drifted to the glories of the past. The initial impression I formed of pre-European Siuai was of a society divided into innumerable little armed camps, all mutually hostile and constantly alert. Or so it seemed until I began to inquire into the actual extent of warfare in terms of specifically remembered hostilities and of known casualties. Many kinds of evidence convinced me that the Siuai area of two decades previously consisted of some six or seven regions of internal peacefulness — excepting, of course, the occasional outbreaks of individual feuds — and that inter-group warfare, between elements of separate regions, was far from frequent. Drawing on the memories of some of my older informants, it transpires that most of them can recall having taken part in only two or three organized wars: all of which is interesting and not altogether unreliable history. But there is another kind of "history" that is of interest to the ethnographer, and that is the kind of "memory" of the past that looms large in the utterances of people of the present. Of course, what my Siuai neighbors really "thought" about the past was not accessible to my shallow probings, but when they talked about the past spontaneously or in answer to my queries they spoke of an epic age of eager warriors serving under powerful and aggressive mumis. It is this kind of "history" about which I now write — "history" which may contain some elements of that other history, for all I know, but which would be ethnographically significant even if it did not.

## ORGANIZED WARFARE

The Siuai distinguish sharply between organized warfare (*kori*) and inter-personal fighting. In connection with the latter, two men may have had a quarrel which ended in violence with one or both of them being wounded or killed, or a sorrowing widower may have ambushed and killed the sorcerer suspected of killing his wife; but unless these or similar episodes led to organized retaliation they were of little consequence to the rest of the neighborhood. Nor did inter-personal blood-letting necessarily mobilize all near relatives for revenge, in the manner of blood-feuding of, say, Northern Luzon. Siuai warfare, natives claim, developed only out of the anger (*iro*) of mumis. Unless a commoner's cause was backed by a mumi it remained a familial or matrilineage affair. On the other hand, one measure of a mumi's stature was his willingness and ability to back the cause of a supporter. A true mumi, it seems, was quick to take revenge for any harm done to a supporter by an outsider. Some of these causes were petty enough: it is said of one mumi that he laid waste a whole hamlet when one of its residents was observed poaching in his stream. Other wars had more substantial beginnings: it is related that four men from Mokakaru were traveling through Jeku one day delivering a pig to a purchaser in central Siuai, and they peered over a garden fence at a woman leaning over to plant taro. One of the travelers shouted out, "Ho, just look at that female's vagina wide open and waiting for someone. I'll oblige her on our return home." The woman reported the episode to her husband, who rounded up a few of his neighbors, waylaid the travelers on their return journey and killed them all. When news of this reached Kupiraki, the leading mumi of Mokakaru, he sent all his followers to Jeku and devastated the place, killing all they could lay hands on and burning the dwellings.

One of the most frequently remembered wars took place between Moki, the mumi of Moronei, and the men of Ruhuvaku (southeast Siuai). On one occasion several men from Moronei traveled to Ruhuaku carrying almonds to exchange for lime and metal adzes. One of the visitors was Korerua, whose mother's brother was a man of some consequence in Ruhuaku. The trading went on amicably and the visitors were about to return home, when suddenly Korerua's uncle pulled him to the ground and held him while his companions killed the members of Korerua's party. When the uncle released Korerua he said to him, "Now, nephew, let's see what kind of a man you are. Let's see if you have enough of the makings of a mumi in you to revenge your friends." Korerua returned home and reported the calamity to Moki, who decided to accept the challenge. Moki then scraped together seven hundred spans of mauai and sent one hundred each to neighboring mumis, requesting them to join him in a mass attack on Ruhuaku. On the appointed day scores of men assembled in Moronei and they all prepared for the coming battle by adorning themselves and by feasting, spear rattling, and licentiousness. There was nothing secretive about the preparations, and Ruhuaku knew to the hour when the attack would take place. At a signal from Moki the northerners set out, and when they reached the gardens and groves of the southerners they began laying waste to the countryside, breaking down fences, pulling up taro, hacking down palms, and burning dwellings. Everyone they caught they killed — women, infants, and aged alike. Arriving at the club-house of the Ruhuaku mumi they cleared a large area of trees and waited for the southerners to retaliate. A pitched battle followed which ended with the vanquished southerners fleeing, having lost five men to the northerners' two. After this the northerners returned home and prepared for another raid. During the next year and a half the northerners invaded the southern area four or five times, until the Ruhuaku mumi finally sued for peace and acknowledged Moki's superiority in arms. To the reparations paid by the vanquished, Moki added more shell money of his own and distributed it among the neighboring mumis who had fought for him. This ended for all time the superiority of the southerners, who previously had been contemptuous of the northern "Hill-men" and had made forays into the north with impunity.[1]

For all cases of warfare remembered by my informants three kinds of precipitating causes stand out: revenge by a mumi for bodily harm inflicted on or believed to have been inflicted on one of his supporters; gestures of disrespect shown by one mumi towards another; and rivalry for renown. In connection with the third, there were cases reported of one mumi sending his followers to fight against another simply to test the latter's power; when these conflicts ended in a draw it was not unusual for the two rivals to become friendly taovu, with no serious residue of ill-feeling — except, perhaps, among bereaved relatives of warriors slain in the fighting, which was of course of little political consequence. Warfare, then, was a mumi's affair; but the picture of a stout-hearted mumi leading his followers into battle is quite inaccurate. Mumis organized and financed wars; they did not always fight in them. It may be that they risked their fortunes and their reputations, but they did not often risk their lives; I recorded only one remembered instance of a mumi pushing the fight to the extent of slaying his principal rival.[2]

Most mumis intent on waging war had first to secure allies; few of them had followings large enough to risk going it alone. They sent emissaries with shell money to friendly neighboring mumis, about 100 spans to each. If accepted, this token (*korekuvoto*, "war-announcing") bound each ally to mobilize all his able-bodied followers to fight. Each ally added money of his own to the "war-announcing" and distributed the total among his own followers, about five spans for each commoner and ten to twenty for each principal *supporter* (mouhe). In some instances the original war-maker would present a lump sum to one prominent ally and the latter would subcontract for warriors among neighboring mumis. The pay received by the actual warriors was called *hoitevare*; no Siuai would have fought for a mumi not his own without first receiving this fee. If casualties occurred during the fighting, it was the original war-making mumi who was held responsible for paying indemnities to the wounded or to the families of the slain. It was reported to me that these latter made no claims and entertained no rancor against their battle rivals, but held only the war-making mumi on their side accountable and liable for indemnities, and this was particularly the case if the war-maker had precipitated the hostilities. Even during my visit, fifteen years after all warfare had been outlawed, there remained a number of litigations involving unpaid indemnities, kept alive by kinsmen of men slain in old battles. One of the few surviving war-making mumis, a testy old man in his sixties, suffered such losses in prestige through having so many unsatisfied war claims lodged against him that he no longer enjoys a following, and hence is not a *leader* in the contemporary meaning of the word. Some victorious war-makers were able to collect reparations from their vanquished rivals, and used this money to help finance their war costs, but reparations were never sufficient to cover all costs of securing, preparing, and indemnifying warriors, so that warfare was a costly enterprise for both of the principals.

Preparations for battle were lengthy and elaborate. Warriors arrived at the war-maker's club-house two or three days prior to battle carrying with them their spears, clubs, bows and arrows, battle decorations, and magical accouterments. Among these latter were *Invisibility*, *Invulnerability*, and *Killing-stuff*.

*Invisibility* (*uramina*)[3] consists of kuna mixed with red paint (*ukura*) and carried in the hand or stuck in the arm-band. It enables a man to slip unobserved into the enemies' ranks. Invisibility is, however, a dangerous magic and may only be carried by a man of full vitality; it would inhibit the growth of a youth or hasten the death of a senile man — and of course contact with it would be fatal for any female. (Invisibility is used nowadays by a murderer to enable him to approach his victim unseen.)

*Invulnerability* (*mororo*) consists of consecrated kuna worn in the owner's arm-band or mixed with red paint and daubed on his face and arms. Such a man cannot be wounded or slain in battle. When his enemies see his Invulnerability they become paralyzed and cannot lift their weapons to strike him. This ghost-consecrated magic has to be obtained from someone already in possession of it, and it is usually purchased. It can only be obtained at the time some adult dies. Buyer and seller squat beside the deceased, with the buyer's hand placed in the hand of the deceased. The seller puts some Invulnerability into the buyer's hand, performs "head-rounding" (*ki'isaku*)[4]

— cracking open an areca nut and addressing the ghost of the deceased. He commands the ghost, "Hey, you ura, guard over this man here who is holding you. If someone tries to harm him you will render that person powerless, paralyzing him as if he were stone."

*Killing-stuff* consists of kuna consecrated, like Invulnerability, to a ghost and placed in a large cowrie shell worn on the forehead. If during a battle an enemy looks fixedly at the man thus armed, drawing sight on him to spear him or shoot an arrow at him, the sight of the magic-laden cowrie will render him near-death. The man wearing Killing-stuff is not altogether invulnerable, but at least his enemies are smitten.

*Rakana* magic [5] was also used for warfare. Warriors used to place some of it on their weapons to make them more effective.

In addition to using such magical devices as these, warriors preparing for battle also decorated themselves with feathers and leaves, and painted frightening designs on their faces and torsos with white paint.[6] They practiced grimaces and menacing gestures for hours at a time and boasted of the deeds they would perform. Their host, the war-making mumi, supplied them with pork and other delicacies and the whole atmosphere was one of festivity and tense expectation. Some mumis even supplied women for the warriors, and not only prostitutes. Here is the way one old informant described those exciting times:

> The periods of fighting were wonderful ones in our lives. That was the time when men were really strong. When we prepared for battles we felt ten times stronger than usual. Our chests swelled and we felt exceedingly virile. We desired women all the time. When a mumi told us to fight for him there was no question of continence.[7] On the contrary, if the mumi didn't furnish us with women we were angry. Moki (the Moronei mumi) used to assemble all the firm-breasted women in his place to copulate with the warriors before and after a battle. We were insatiable for women, and tireless. All night long we could copulate and still want more.[8] It was the same with eating. The clubhouse used to be filled with food, and we ate and ate and never had enough. Those were wonderful times. Our war with Ruhuaku lasted for a year and a half, and it was the best time of our lives.

Before every battle a divination ritual was held to learn which of the enemies were to be killed. Having this information the warriors were then able to concentrate upon the pre-ordained victims. A war-magician (*roma*) first obtained a coconut with a whitish husk (*kakoni*) and husked it in the usual way, by jabbing it against a pointed stick driven into the ground to break away chunks of the fiber; informants explained that this process resembled jabbing at a man with a spear. (This ritual gesture might be interpreted as having the effect of pre-killing the victims, although informants were not explicit on this point.) The stick (*pusu*) used in this husking may not be used for ordinary coconut husking.[9] After the coconut had been husked, oil was pressed from its meat and this was mixed with white paint and heated in a small pot. Then the war-magician exhorted the ghosts of former war-magicians, *romanopo*, with this war-magic (*kana*) formula:

> War-magic. Childless ones.
> Warfare. Honiŋ the Killer. War-magic.
> Ariku used to perform this war-magic.
> Tupa used to perform this war-magic.
> Mamisa used to perform this war-magic.
>
> Oh, all you who used to perform this war-magic, protect me from morning until night and from night until morning.
> Protect me, you Ariku and Tupa and Mamisa. War-magic.
>
> Mintu used to perform this war-magic.
> Siroma used to perform this war-magic.
> Teva'a used to perform this war-magic.
> Protect me, all of you, from morning until night and from night until morning.
>
> Let the arrows shot at me fly in another direction.
> You, Montoro and Mojo, who used to perform this war-magic, let the arrows shot at me fly in another direction.
>
> Suruma used to perform this war-magic.
> Teva used to perform this war-magic.
> Mapa used to perform this war-magic.
> All of you, make me as invulnerable as the vine and the palm which the two orphaned brothers were not able to hit with their arrows as they walked about having a shooting contest.[10]

Thereupon the ghosts of the former war-magicians went to the hamlets of the enemy and captured several souls and brought them back to the club-house, where the living war-magician was able to identify them by peering into the pot. The war-magician then extracted from the pot some little shreds which resembled — in fact, actually *were* — hairs from the heads of the captured enemies. (That these hairs were what the magician reported them to be was obvious, because there were gray ones for the older men captured and black ones for the younger!) These hairs along with the brew of coconut and white paint were given to the ghosts, who consumed them and thereby pre-killed the specified enemies.[11]

On the day of battle gongs were beaten in the war-maker's club-house and the warriors set out for the enemy's territory early in the morning. Everyone, including the enemy, knew their progress and their destination, for they shouted and blew on conches as they proceeded. If potential opposition were known to be weak the attackers moved slowly, laying waste to enemy territory as they went. But if they expected a stiff battle they proceeded quickly to an appointed battleground, a space cleared by the defenders for the occasion. There the opposing sides lined up facing one another about one hundred yards apart — a critical moment for the timid, one gathers, since informants say that many men present shook at the sight of their fiercely painted opponents and had to be restrained from running away. Usually, however, there were a few brave men among the attackers, and these led off the fight by rushing at the defenders one at a time, stopping halfway, hurling a spear, and returning to their line.[12] If this show of ferocity did not break the spirits of the defenders and send them running, a few of their heroes returned the attention. All this usually had the effect of encouraging both sides, and more and more men rushed forward until there was a general melee [13] which continued for a few minutes until one side broke and quit the battlefield leaving its dead and the wounded to be decapitated. The victors then returned to the club-house of their war-sponsoring mumi, who rewarded them with food and commendation.

Each war party eventually recovered what was left of its own dead and took the remains home for cremation; the war-making mumi not only paid an indemnity to the mumi of each slain warrior (which was passed on to the latter's family) but also contributed a pig for each funeral. The heads of all slain enemies were placed in the war-maker's club-house; they were arranged so that they faced towards their homes and this had the magical effect of discouraging their kinsmen from trying to revenge them. Also, a part of the ears of all slain enemies was cut off and cooked near the club-house altar, its essence going to feed the local war-magicians' ghosts.

The ghosts of all people slain in warfare went to Irinoru, the Lake of Blood in the northern mountains; many of these ghosts subsequently returned to Siuai where they participated in the affairs of the living.[14]

During periods of warfare natives did not scruple against killing females as well as males, of all ages; they reasoned, "This female may some time give birth to a male who could become a mumi and make war upon us." Sometimes, however, attackers spared young women and took them back to the war-maker who would either distribute them among his followers as wives or attach them to his own household as prostitutes.[15]

During a state of war, battles occurred every few weeks or months, with both sides organizing attacks. And in addition to the large-scale pitched battles, smaller parties from each side used to raid the other's territory, striking surreptitiously and escaping quickly. This situation called for alertness and measures of defense. Natives used to dig holes in the trails leading up to their dwellings and place upright bamboo splinters in them to cripple the feet of the enemy. In fighting times, also, dwellings used to be walled in solidly with wood, rather than sago thatch, to stop spears and arrows from penetrating. (Some informants state that defense was the primary reason for building the curious tree-dwellings (*kakanoni*),[16] but others dispute this and say that they were — and continue to be — built merely for show.) During such times of danger gardens were located nearer the settlements, and men usually accompanied their womenfolk to the gardens to protect them from sneak attack. If the war were protracted it even had the effect of causing householders to build their new dwellings closer together — but never to the extent now seen in line villages; and it appears that the hamlets tended to scatter again when the danger was past.

Sometimes supernatural warning was given of a raid: for example, when rain fell while the sun shone [17] that was a sign of an enemy's approach, and this touched off defensive preparations, including the brandishing of spears in the direction of the enemy's territory.

Sooner or later the vanquished mumi would sue for peace, usually by sending a span of high-value shell money to the victor. Then a peace ceremony would be arranged and reparations (*nori*)[18] agreed upon. The vanquished mumi along with his unarmed followers would go to the club-house of his victor and the two principals would chew betel mixture together, taking lime out of each other's hands. Whereupon, reparations consisting of several hundred spans of shell money would be paid and the war declared officially over. In some instances a truce, leading up to peace, was more difficult to arrange. For example, in the war between the northerners and southerners, Moki, the sponsoring mumi of the victorious northerners, was unwilling to end hostilities — the spoils were too attractive; and besides, the southerners had started the affair. He let it be known that he would slay any peace emissary sent to him by the southerners. Instead, the mumi of the southerners secretly sent an emissary to Nammito, one of Moki's chief supporters, and bribed him to induce Moki to call off the fighting. Nammito went about his task subtly, urging Moki, "Let's have done with this fighting. We've really fought enough, and our people have little time left for gardening." After a few days of this kind of reasoning Moki agreed to a truce and eventually went through with the peace ceremony. Only then did the news about Nammito's bribe leak out, and although Moki was very angry he could not reopen hostilities.[19]

Warfare, then, was an affair between mumis. Lesser men could not afford to engage in such an expensive enterprise. Lesser men had their inter-personal feuds but in their fighting for mumis they behaved like mercenaries. One informant described the impersonality in these terms:

> If friends and kinsmen from Turuŋum and Rennu (two neighboring settlements) were sitting together in a club-house, and an emissary from Kope appeared and asked the Rennu men to fight against Moki, and an emissary from Moki appeared and asked the Turuŋum men to fight against Kope, there would have been no difficulty. The kinsmen and friends from Turuŋum and Rennu would have fought against one another, and when the war was over they would again have been friendly as ever. If a Rennu man had been killed during the fighting, the other Rennu men would have been angry with Kope but not with their Turuŋum friends.

Other informants pointed out that, "Older brothers fought against younger brothers" if they lived in opposing settlements. It is unlikely that alliances and ties of loyalty were quite so fluid as these examples would indicate, for there seem to have been traditional alliances among several of the settlements — alliances based on personal kinship ties of mumi, buttressed by similar ties among their followers. Nevertheless, it does appear that close kinsmen did fight against one another.

In terms of prestige, mumis were the ones to gain — and lose — most from warfare. The title of *warrior-hero* (*hikum*) was given a war-making mumi whether or not he himself joined in combat. Lesser men could acquire the label *sisikei* after killing a foe in combat, and many non-mumis were known and feared as belligerent and dangerous fighters, but renown (potu) belonged only to the organizer and financer of successful wars.

## WAR LEADERS

How did men become mumis in the old days? Several stock answers were given by informants: a man became a mumi only if his father was a mumi and his mother the daughter of a mumi; a man became a mumi only if his noroukuru was rich and strong in fighting men; only fierce warriors could become mumis; mumis were men who used all their resources in fighting their enemies and the enemies of their neighbors; mumis were also wealthy feast-givers.

It would be profitless to speculate about the relative importance of these factors; it is probably correct to say that all of them were contributory. Genealogies indicate, for example, that membership in a large and land-rich matrilineage was useful — but so was descent from a prominent father. Aggressiveness, if not courage, must also have been essential, and along with it many of the same kinds of dispositions and skills required of the contemporary feast-giving leader.

However men became mumis in the olden days — and we shall never know that for certain — the rewards of the office are said to have been richer.

Every neighborhood seems to have had one leading mumi who combined in his office the various rights now divided between leader and Hat-men. Like the contemporary leader, the former one also had a number of adherents, including several lieutenants or chief supporters (mouhe) who were also called mumi. Moreover, each principal mumi is said to have had several "couriers" and "legs" who were in fact slaves, either captured in battle or bound to service through having sought asylum with him. These slaves lived nearby and carried out all the menial men's work of the mumi's household — working in his garden, cutting wood, repairing fences, guarding women of the mumi's household, etc. It is said that a master was privileged to beat or kill his slave without restraint of any kind. A few men are pointed out today as having once been slaves, and some of these remain loyal adherents of their former masters, although to all appearances they now lead normal lives, dwelling in their own households with wife and offspring and maintaining their own gardens.

Informants also tell that most mumis used to have attached to their households one or two female slaves, captured in warfare. Although called prostitutes (*nunnapoku*), the term now applied to women whose chief function is just that,[20] the female slaves of former days had a number of other functions. They worked as servants to the mumis' wives and daughters, but only occasionally did they act as concubines to their masters. Instead, their sexual services were sold by their masters to other men for strictly economic purposes; or, they performed gratis for their masters' warriors during periods of active fighting.[21]

We may suppose that the everyday life of pre-European Siuai did not differ markedly from that of the present, and that most events between mumi and adherents were not unlike those of today. On the other hand, if the accounts of informants can be trusted, the character of the relationship between mumi and adherent must have been significantly colored by the coercive powers behind the mumi's authority. All informants agree that the mumi had the power to wound or kill disobedient subordinates, and numerous cases are cited as evidence. On closer questioning, however, it would appear that such power was far from absolute except in the case of slaves (and even slaves could and did find refuge elsewhere). Now, slaves were usually men far removed from their kinsmen — for, as natives explain, "if a man has many kinsmen nearby they would not permit anyone to enslave or mistreat him."

As for the other prerogatives of mumis, their standard of living seems not to have been significantly better than other men's. Nor are they reported to have possessed such rights as eminent domain, sexual access, etc. Aided sometimes by slaves, they produced their own food and traded for other goods just as ordinary mortals did.

In the preceding chapter [22] it was described how the tuhia concept has been extended to include some of the elements of suzerainty. In the olden days it appears that a mumi's tuhia included all those settlements whose warriors fought as his mercenaries in large-scale warfare. While it seems to have been true that war-making tuhias overlapped just as feast-making tuhias do today, it also appears that for certain periods of time many neighboring settlements fought together so consistently that there emerged a pattern of war-making *regions*, each more or less internally peaceful and each containing one outstanding mumi whose war activities provided internal social cohesion. There were six or seven of these regions in Siuai during the decade just prior to European control; before that there may have been more, or fewer, for regional boundaries must have changed as wars were won or lost and new mumis emerged and faded.

In any case it would appear that the leading war-making mumi of a region exercised great influence and probably even some coercive authority over the whole population of his region. My evidence on this point is weak, but in at least four recorded instances a principal mumi is remembered as having killed a disobedient native residing in his region but in a neighborhood other than his own. It seems to have been more normal, however, for the principal mumi to leave the disciplining of individuals in the hands of their own local mumis.

Respect for the former war-making mumis received most dramatic expression on the occasion of their deaths. Mourning is said to have been exceedingly strict and was usually terminated only with the killing of a man. It is reported that grieving subjects sometimes ate only wild foods and drank water from toilet-creeks. Vengeance raids were invariably carried out and sometimes whole settlements were devastated if suspected of harboring the guilty sorcerer.

By piecing together many accounts of former days it would seem that the death of a particularly powerful mumi usually led to the breakup of his "realm," whose cohesiveness depended strongly on him. Some breakups were violent and involved uncontrollable internecine strife. In other instances whole neighborhoods are reported as having dispersed in order to escape the evil magic assumed to have brought about the mumi's death.

All the foregoing is "history" only in the sense that it represents the "past" as described by men who lived in it. As already noted, warfare was outlawed some fifteen years prior to my field work and that is a long time for retaining accurate recall. It is true that hundreds of Siuai are still alive who participated fully in the events we have just been describing; but that is no guarantee of accurate reporting, nor even of conscious objectivity. More "civilized" peoples than the Siuai have constructed myths out of their recent pasts.[23]

CHAPTER 13

# *A Leader in Action*[1]

Now, to exemplify the general statements of the preceding chapters, there will be presented an account of the career of a high-ranking leader, Soŋj, of Turuŋom village. Soŋi's career began before warfare was outlawed, and reached a peak during our stay in Siuai. It was our good fortune to reside in Turuŋom village during the very months when Soŋi's feast-giving activities were most intensive, when he carried out plans for consolidating his position as the most renowned man of Siuai. Soŋi's case is necessarily somewhat atypical — only one man at a time can rise to the very top; but it nevertheless indicates how one exceptional individual makes effective use of his culture's means to achieve nearly universally desired cultural goals.

## HISTORICAL SETTING [2]

The northern three-quarters of northeast Siuai is known throughout Siuai as the region of the *Rataiku*, "Hill-men." When used by outsiders "hill-man" has a derogatory meaning, connoting the scorn of the lowlander for the more isolated and conservative highlander. Nevertheless, the latter have accepted the term and now apply it to themselves and their region. Rataiku is bordered on the east and north by miles of uninhabited rain forest; its western borders are also marked by long stretches of forest. On the other hand, its southern border, abutting the region known as Mokakaru, is marked by social and political boundaries.

Judging by genealogies and myths, Rataiku has long been numerically dominated by members of the Tree-rat, Hornbill, and Kingfisher sibs, with only small enclaves of Parrots and Cranes and a scattering of natives belonging to other sibs. It is claimed that the Tree-rats (Left-behinds subdivision) also formerly dominated the present inhabited part of Mokakaru but were superseded there by fairly recent intrusions of Eagles (from Ruhuaku region) and of Cockatoos and Iguanas (from Terei).[3]

At the present time Tree-rats, Hornbills, and Kingfishers are scattered throughout Rataiku in numerous matrilineages which own most of the land. Of these three, Tree-rats are most numerous, most extensively subdivided, and wealthiest in land and shell money. It is impossible to determine who were the *original* residents of specific places — even myths conflict here; the farthest our evidence will carry us is five or six generations beyond the oldest persons now living.

Reliable political history is equally shallow but we can describe with some confidence the circumstances as they were three decades ago. At that time Hiniŋ, a Tree-rat man (Rukaruinai subdivision) of Maisua, was highest-ranking mumi of all the northern part of Rataiku; Moki, a Tree-rat (Hanoŋnai subdivision) of Moronei, ranked highest among the southeastern Rataiku; and Tokura, a Kingfisher (Legs-apart subdivision) of Jeku, ranked highest among the southwestern Rataiku. Some fighting took place among these three mumis but they eventually banded together against the Mokakaruans and Ruhuakuans to the south. This was also the situation later on when Australian control was becoming established.

It has already been reported how the Mokakaru mumi, Konsei, induced the Australian authorities to punish the Rataiku for alleged feuding.[4] In the process, the mumi Tokura was arrested and soon died in jail. Hiniŋ's adherents were scattered and he too died shortly thereafter. Only Moki, the Moronei mumi, survived this onslaught, living until about 1934. This left the Paramount Chief, Konsei, officially in charge of Mokakaru and most of Rataiku until his death in 1936. Konsei, however, was never able to win the support of the Rataiku.

Meanwhile, with fighting outlawed and new concepts of authority being introduced by the Australians, the traditional type of political authority underwent far-reaching change.[5] Native-style leaders lost their powers of physical coercion to the new Administrative-appointed Hat-men. Some of the former, it is true, became officials in the new regime, but even in these instances the new-style force was dependent upon outside powers and not entirely upon the personal effectiveness of the mumis themselves. The mumi, Moki, seems to have adjusted to the new circumstances without much loss of authority or influence — his having been a renowned war-maker added to his luster as a feast-giver. However, among the new generation of ambitious men renown had to be founded on feast-giving alone. Foremost among this emerging new generation was Soŋi of Turuŋom.

## THE RISE OF SOŊI

Soŋi was born around 1893 in Turuŋom; his mother was a Rukaruinai Tree-rat, his father a Whistler Kingfisher; both parents were also born in Turuŋom and their marriage conformed to a long-standing local tradition of "straight" cross-cousin intermarriage between local Rukaruinais and Whistlers. Soŋi was orphaned during early childhood, and for the next few years he was cared for by his own maternal uncle. Later on one of Soŋi's own paternal uncles took over the job of sponsoring Soŋi's rise to mumi-hood — the young man having begun to show promise at an early age. Meanwhile Soŋi slept about in the houses of several kinsmen and was provided with food by a matrilineage *sister* of his deceased father.

In terms of material possessions the young Soŋi was comparatively well off. His own matrilineage, the Turuŋonai branch of Rukaruinai Tree-rats, had settled in Turuŋom several generations previously and acquired much land in the course of time; it also possesed a large hoard of heirlooms. In addition, Soŋi had access to the resources of his father's matrilineage, much of whose property had become practically combined with his own matrilineage's through the many cross-cousin marriages that had taken place between members of the two units. Moreover, enough inheritance was left over from his father's private capital (pure) to start his accumulation of pigs. Soŋi purchased a few small pigs and turned them over to his sponsoring paternal uncle to fatten for sale. The uncle also solicited the aid of neighboring kinsmen, telling them: "Let us all help this boy Soŋi become a mumi. He has the ambition and industriousness but is an orphan and hence cannot depend on his father for help. Let us all make pots and sell them, then give (?) the money to Soŋi for buying pigs." Several men did as the uncle suggested, even fattening the pigs that were purchased with the money earned for Soŋi.

Then, when Soŋi was about fifteen, his uncle mobilized all the men in Turuŋom to help build a small club-house for the boy, and thus he was launched on his feast-giving career. It should be mentioned that the paternal uncle had a son of his own about Soŋi's age, but that individual showed no promise of becoming a mumi and hence received no special assistance from his father or others. This man later moved to a neighboring settlement and although he appears to harbor no resentment against Soŋi, neither has he assisted him in any way.

Another event cleared the way for Soŋi's continued advance. The maternal uncle who cared for Soŋi during the latter's early childhood was then the most prominent man in Turuŋom itself. The latter's son, Koŋkoma, was several years older than Soŋi, showed fair promise, and was beginning to be pushed ahead by his father until an interruption occurred. A resident of nearby Hiuannai died and divination singled out a Turuŋom native, Ham, as responsible for the death. The Hiuannai mumi then paid Koŋkoma's father to kill Ham, which he did. The only thing wrong with this action was that Ham happened to be a kinsman of the great Jeku mumi, Tokura, and when Tokura heard of the murder he set out with a few followers to kill Koŋkoma's father. The latter received ample warning and escaped with Koŋkoma to a distant settlement where kinsmen provided haven for them until Tokura died many years later. This episode left the field open for Soŋi's advance, there having been no other young man in Turuŋom with comparable promise or support. (Later, when Koŋkoma returned to Turuŋom Soŋi was already firmly established as highest-ranking leader there. Koŋkoma was jealous and angered by what he considered to be Soŋi's usurpation, but could do nothing about it. On one occasion when Soŋi had just completed a new club-house, Koŋkoma cleared a new path so as to make a wide detour around the club-house, hoping thus to deflect some of the traffic. This tactic backfired, causing Koŋkoma much embarrassment; Soŋi called the new path "empty-stomach trail," signifying that people who traveled along Koŋkoma's pathway would miss being fed at Soŋi's frequent club-house feasts. Eventually Koŋkoma contracted what appears to be tuberculosis, and now is a frail old widower dependent upon relatives for food and shelter.)

Soŋi consolidated his preëminence in Turuŋom by building, successively, two large club-houses and filling them with gongs, thereby keeping his neighbors actively working on his behalf and rewarding them with numerous pork banquets — pork, it should be added, which they themselves helped to fatten for him. Natives still tell of Soŋi's readiness, during that period, to contribute generously at the baptisms of their children and the funerals of their kinsmen. When the Patrol Officer wished to appoint a Headman for Turuŋom Soŋi was offered the position, but he would have no truck with the new regime and arranged for the Hat to be given to his elder matrilineage mate, Siham.

Soŋi has reportedly given scores of feasts but his adherents single out fourteen of these as having been especially large and significant for his sociopolitical career. The first seven of these were given to reward leaders of neighboring settlements for their assistance in building Soŋi's club-houses and carrying slit gongs. For the seventh, Soŋi had intended asking his rival, Konsei, the Paramount Chief, to assist in carrying his largest gong from an old club-house to a new one, but Konsei rejected the bid, terming it insolent. ("That Turuŋom is a place of no consequence. If they want me to honor them with my presence they will have to pay me in shell money.") On hearing this Soŋi redoubled his efforts and prepared a huge feast to which he invited all of Rataiku and none of Mokakaru. This episode served to publicize Soŋi's name throughout Siuai and caused him to be identified with Rataiku sentiment against the hated Konsei.

The four subsequent feasts were mumi-honoring affairs (muminai) given for neighboring Rataiku leaders. Two of these leaders reciprocated, while making it clear that they did not wish to compete further. The two others did not even attempt to repay and accepted defeat philosophically. Thanks to Soŋi's tact, all four of these erstwhile rivals became Soŋi's faithful allies. Later, on the death of Moki, the last of the great war-making mumis, Soŋi became tacitly recognized as highest-ranking leader of Rataiku and he began to prepare to extend his activities beyond Rataiku.

Mokakaru was the logical place to begin, but after Konsei's death there was no one left in Mokakaru to offer suitable competition. Soŋi disposed of Konsei's Chief Interpreter, the opportunistic U'ta [6] (who, by the way, is, like Soŋi, a Rukaruinai Tree-rat), with a feast which U'ta could never hope to repay; but Soŋi did this more as an amusement than as a serious social-climbing tactic. U'ta is universally disliked on account of his conceit and officiousness, and Rataikuans make a great joke of him by imitating his exaggerated salutes and his insistence upon giving orders in pidgin English. They dub him "the *kou*," in reference to a long-necked, supercilious looking bird,[7] which is described in a folk tale as acting as if all feasts it attended were being given in its honor. Nor was young Tomo, Konsei's successor as Paramount Chief, a suitable rival for Soŋi to compete with;[8] hence Soŋi turned towards central Siuai for the next stage of his career. It was at this point that we moved to his village and were thus on hand to witness his most ambitious enterprise.

## TURUŊOM VILLAGE

The consolidated line village of Turuŋom is fairly typical though slightly larger than the average Siuai line village.[9] It is divided into two lines: Turuŋom proper, the larger, and Ohinnai. Hamlet houses of Turuŋom villagers are scattered around the surrounding countryside in the following hamlets (households are identified by the names of their heads):

>   Mitapukori and West Ohinnai: Haiju, Opisa
>   Kupariri: Soŋi
>   North Turuŋom: Koura, Kepina
>   South Turuŋom: To'osi
>   West Pirui: Asinara, Tahiŋ, Tamaŋ, Siham
>   East Pirui: Naru, Tanari, Nakao, Pana
>   East Ohinnai: Pitaino, Koiri
>   Noveina: Ho'oma, Ronsa, Tampa

Among other Turuŋom household heads, Kukerei, Orim, and Maria do not possess hamlet houses; while Asinara and Tanari do not have line houses of their own. One resident, Pinako, has his hamlet house near Jeku village, his wife's home. Finally, there are two old men, Koŋkoma[10] and Kanasai, who live with kinsmen, having no houses of their own.

Turuŋom is located between two creeks, the Miraka and the Reraka.[11] The land verbally identified with Turuŋom does not ordinarily extend beyond these creeks even though various groups of Turuŋom residents own tracts outside that area. Several generations ago this Turuŋom area was "owned" by four matrilineages: a Komma matrilineage (subdivision of Kingfisher) in the north, a Left-behind matrilineage (Tree-rats) in the west, a Belly-fat matrilineage (Tree-rats) in the east, and a Legs-apart matrilineage (Kingfishers) in the south. Presumably, some members of these matrilineages resided here. Since then some land titles have passed to members of other matrilineages and now the Turuŋonai (Rukaruinai Belly-fats) are the biggest landholders.

The present residents of Turuŋom fall into the following extended families:

1. The senile Kanasai, his sons (Opisa, Haiju), his daughters (including Apavo, wife of Maria), and their spouses and offspring reside in Ohinnai on Kanasai's matrilineage land.

2. The most prominent extended family consists of members of the Turuŋonai [12] including Soŋi, Siham, Arapa, and their spouses, offspring, offspring's spouses, and the latter's children. They are descended from sisters who moved to Turuŋom after marrying Turuŋom men. The hamlet houses of these natives are somewhat scattered but their village houses are all together at the northern end of the line. All the women and children of this group are frequently together, either sitting under one of their houses, gossiping and nursing their infants, or trooping off to the gardens, or down to the spring. Sometimes they pool their food resources and cook in the same pot. When their menfolk are in the village they likewise join in. These Turuŋonai are an exclusive lot; other villagers almost never loiter near their houses. Other children may wander up to take part in some game, but the little Northenders nearly always send the small Southenders home crying.

3. Several generations ago some Komma men married Whistler women and took them to Turuŋom to live. The matrilineal descendants of these women are Pana, Pitaino, Koiri, Tanari, Nakao, Ho'oma, Pinako, and Koura; they and their spouses and offspring comprise the largest extended family in Turuŋom. Their hamlet and line houses are somewhat scattered and they are not as well-knit a unit as the preceding ones.

4. Ronsa, his brother's son, Tampa, and their dependents constitute an impoverished extended-family of refugees, Ronsa having left his home farther east and sought haven in Turuŋom during fighting times.

Koŋkoma, now sick and old, lives alone in Koura's village house; the latter resides entirely in his hamlet house. Kepina, Kukerei, and Tahiŋ live more or less separate domestic lives, having no close extended-family affiliations in Turuŋom. Orim, whose real home is Hanuŋ village, resides in Ohinnai by virtue of being the Methodist catechist there; also he is married to Siham's daughter. To'osi, also an outsider, is married to one of the Rukaruinai women and has become a member of that extended-family.

Many kinship ties form links between these families, and in addition most residents have close kinship ties with natives scattered throughout Rataiku.

Ohinnai residents are Methodist; the catechist, Orim, holds daily services there. Most adults in Turuŋom proper have been "converted" to Catholicism, but there is no chapel in the village and few bother to attend services elsewhere. Soŋi himself has remained aloof from the missions and this helps account for his neighbors' indifference.

Soŋi's matrilineage mate, Siham, is village Headman and sees to it that the villagers remain "straight," leaving Soŋi free to concentrate upon his political career. Opisa makes a loud but rather ineffectual Interpreter, Pitaino a completely useless medical orderly.

Five Turuŋom men own club-houses (Soŋi, Koura, Pana, Opisa, Ho'oma) but Soŋi's is the center of activity. All Turuŋom men except ailing Koŋkoma and senile Kanasai coöperate actively in Soŋi's feast-giving enterprises; in terms of interaction criteria they were arranged in the following hierarchy at the beginning of our residence there: I. Soŋi; II. Siham; III. Opisa, Koura, Maimoi,[13] Pana, Pitaino, Haiju, To'osi, Asinara, Tahiŋ, Naru, Ho'oma, Tampa, Orim, Koiri; IV. Tamaŋ, Ronsa, Pinoko, Siha, Tanari, Nakao, and Hooma's two sons, Koiai and Minsipi.

### SOṆI THE MAN

And now for Soŋi himself. He is about forty-five years old, of medium height and slender. He usually wears a conical fiber hat (ohkuna) and a dirty, ragged calico loincloth, seldom troubling to bathe — in fact, he is rather contemptuous of the fastidiousness of his Methodist neighbors. His manner is usually solemn, without appearing unfriendly, and his rare smiles are benign and infectious. His voice is high-pitched but he seldom speaks loudly. Occasionally his anger flares up, but manifests itself in masterfully worded sarcasm rather than in shouts or threats.

Soŋi has no intimate friends. Aside from his quest for renown the joy of his life is his two young sons by his first wife. This wife died in childbirth when the younger son was still an infant and Soŋi has lavished care and affection on the two little boys, explaining that he pities them because they have no mother. Soŋi's third wife also died in childbirth during our stay there, leaving only his second wife, with her young son and infant daughter. Because of the nature of the deaths of these two wives, Soŋi appears convinced that some envious man has carried out tao sorcery,[14] and often speaks of moving away from Turuŋom in order to escape this evil and thus be able to sire more children without risking their mothers' lives. It is often suggested to Soŋi that he take measures to divine the identity of the tao sorcerer, but he refuses, saying that his enemies would have him jailed if they learned of it, and that even if he learned the man's identity the Australian regime would not permit him to punish him.

While other men gad about visiting kinsmen or attending ceremonies and court hearings, Soŋi remains in his club-house or pottery shed, restringing shell money or making pottery. Now and then he disappears to his hamlet house and remains secluded there with his wife and children for days at a time. Few people visit him at his village house and even fewer venture near his hamlet house.

Soŋi is a mikai-magician and states candidly that he practices mainly in order to earn money. A few years back his services were in considerable demand but when his failures multiplied, clients dropped away. Now, Koura is considered a more skillful mikai than Soŋi by his Turuŋom neighbors.

Soŋi's spirit-familiar is the ghost of his younger brother (and only sibling), Mokekui, who died in infancy. Mokekui's ghost walks around with Soŋi and is given regular food offerings. Soŋi asserts that Mokekui's tender age may account for his run of failures as a mikai, and talks of acquiring a more effective familiar. Soŋi's club-house demon is said to have resided in the Turuŋom area for a long time, but prior to Soŋi it was unattached to any individual for as far back as informants can recall. This demon spends most of its time in Soŋi's club-house but occasionally appears (to Soŋi) at the latter's village house demanding food. Soŋi usually prevails upon the demon to return to the club-house by staging there a small pork feast for his adherents, with the essence of the pig's blood going to the demon. (It is, of course, a danger to women and children for the demon to lurk near the place where they stay.)

## SOŊI'S MUMINAI FEAST

The first overt action signalizing the preparations for Soŋi's new muminai feast occurred when he tabooed his coconut trees. This event took place in February 1938, and was described to us by a Turuŋom resident: "Soŋi slaughtered a pig, placed some of the pork in a pot along with a banana leaf and cooked them. When the stew was done he removed the leaf and fastened it around the trunk of one of his coconut palms, saying: 'Hey, there, you horomorun. Smell this food I offer you and look out for my coconuts. If a thief steals any of them, kill him.'"

After this, Soŋi began to formulate plans for financing the feast and obtaining a record number of pigs. First of all, in late October, he mobilized his Hand-money men (aŋuraranopo), telling Tamaŋ, Maimoi, Asinara, Pitaino, Koiri, Tampa, Ronsa, Tahiŋ, and To'osi to pen up the pigs he had farmed out to them and hold them ready for the feast. "The hand-money payment," he told them, "will come later." (Afterwards Maimoi told me: "The only hand-money we ever get is the smell of the cooking pig.")

Farming out pigs was one of the simplest methods used by Soŋi to accumulate animals for his feast. Some of his transactions were far more complex, as illustrated by the following example.

In May 1938, Soŋi said to Koura: "I am going to single you out as one of my principal mouhes (supporters) at the next feast. So you give to me now the pig which you would eventually give when I honor you." Koura went to Opisa and asked him to repay a pig lent to him months previously. Koura then gave this pig to Soŋi, who in turn presented it to Pitaino for slaughtering on the occasion of the baptism ceremony of Pitaino's infant daughter. Pitaino owned a fine tusker pig which Soŋi coveted. When Soŋi began to collect pigs for his own feast he turned to Pitaino and asked for the tusker in return for his earlier (coercive) gift. This tusker was then sent to Kaopa, leader of Noronai village, to induce him to lend Soŋi several hundred spans of shell money. Here is the actual record of these negotiations with Kaopa.

November 21: Soŋi sent for Siham and Opisa and took them along with him to see Kaopa. Soŋi and Siham waited in Kaopa's club-house while Opisa went to find Kaopa. After about two hours Kaopa arrived — he had been in his hamlet house. They all joined together in chewing betel-nut, then Soŋi told Kaopa that he wanted to give him a large pig and make him principal *Defender* [15] at his big feast. He also told him that he would like to borrow 500 spans of shell money. Kaopa thought this over for a while and went to find three of his followers. They conferred, and Kaopa told Soŋi that he probably could raise it. More betel-nut, and the Turuŋom natives returned home.

November 26: Today Soŋi sent Siham, To'osi, Tamaŋ, Tampa, Pitaino, and Ho'oma to Noronai. With them they carried the pig (the one given to Soŋi by Pitaino), which Soŋi gave to Kaopa, who in turn presented Soŋi with a small pig — "betel-nut" he called it, "to pay for your trip" — together with 400 of the 500 spans of shell money requested by Soŋi. Soŋi and his company returned home but I remained in Noronai and learned how Kaopa had raised the money: Kaopa had ordered several of his adherents to repay sums owed to him, and by this method he collected 350 spans; Kaopa himself added the other 50.

Later on, Soŋi officially named Kaopa principal Resident-defender for the feast.

Soŋi also sent messages to his taovu partners throughout Siuai that he wished to buy their largest pigs, some of which had already been promised him. (One noteworthy aspect of all these events was that no transactions took place with the residents of nearby Mataras village, the place where Soŋi's arch enemy, Konsei, used to reside.) In one instance negotiations led to the temporary dissolution of a taovu partnership. Soŋi had long had his heart set on obtaining a prize tusker pig belonging to his taovu, Maosiŋ, of Rapauru village, but when the time came to collect it Maosiŋ put the price at 200 spans. Soŋi refused to pay this, saying that no pig is worth so much, and announcing that he and Maosiŋ were no longer taovu: "Maosiŋ does not know how great mumis should act towards one another." Later, Maosiŋ relented and offered to sell the pig for 100, and the two met, exchanged expressions of mutual esteem, and resumed their partnership.

Most of the pigs and shell money needed for his feast Soŋi was able to procure from his own adherents, either from their own resources or by sending them out to canvass their friends and kinsmen. The methods he employed were quite direct, as the following diary entries indicate.

Today (November 2) Soŋi sent Siham and Opisa to round up all the male villagers. After an hour they began to straggle into the club-house; everyone

## A LEADER IN ACTION

came except Koŋkoma, who is ill. Soŋi asked Maimoi and Ho'oma for the loan of some shell money with which to buy pigs. And he told Pana, Pitaino, Opisa, and Haiju to pay back in pigs the equivalent of money he had previously lent them. Then he sent Koiri and Tamaŋ to round up his (Soŋi's) own pigs and put them in a pen. Then Soŋi left and went to his house. Maimoi grumbled a bit and told Ho'oma that he would be a rich man if Soŋi paid him back all the money he had lent him. Ho'oma replied that a mumi's ways are not like those of other men.

As far as Opisa was concerned, this was a surprise move. A few days later he told me about his experiences in trying to comply with Soŋi's order.

November 20: This morning Opisa told me that he had had a lot of trouble over the pig Soŋi wanted. He said, that it was true — he did owe Soŋi money, but he had made no plans for repayment. But finally Soŋi had transferred the debt to Pinoko, whereupon Pinoko began to pester him (Opisa) for a pig, much to Opisa's embarrassment. The latter said: "Soŋi shamed me by causing a menial (moŋo) like Pinoko to demand payment. My heart became hot and I went to my mother's brother in Hanoŋ to try and induce him and his son to lend me a pig so that I could repay Pinoko and finish with the whole matter." But in Hanoŋ he also had difficulties; in fact, it had caused a row in his uncle's family. The uncle's son had wanted to sell the pig for 50 spans of mauai. He wanted to use this money to make a final bride-payment to his fiancée's father. When Opisa's uncle finally overruled his son and gave the pig to Opisa, the son became very angry and left home. "He has gone to the coast to work on a plantation. He says he will never come back," said Opisa. "The boy's mother gave her husband and me a good tongue lashing and said that we thought more of Soŋi than we did of our own relatives. Her anger surprised us. She's always been a hot-tempered woman and used to rail at her son all the time; but she had never flared up at her husband before. He would have beaten her if she had!"

Widespread ramifications like these were common features of Siuai feast preparations.

Among all Soŋi's adherents, Koura was most heavily indebted to him for past loans, and Soŋi asked him to repay his debt of five pigs so that they could be used at the big feast. Koura, who is one of Soŋi's most ambitious adherents, decided to make the loan repayment into something of a renown-winning occasion. He invited residents of several neighboring hamlets to attend a feast and help him transfer a fine old gong from his old abandoned club-house to his new one. This feast was held in January, only a few days before the big feast, and Soŋi was requested to attend and receive his pigs. The other guests received four small pigs for their help in carrying the gong. Soŋi expressed mixed feelings about this affair of Koura's. On the one hand, he was somewhat annoyed at Koura for using up pigs which might have been saved for the big feast to come. On the other hand, he was pleased to have an adherent of his put on a feast and thereby increase both the adherent's and, indirectly, his own renown — but in this connection Soŋi complained that the four pigs distributed among the guests were inadequate and did not reflect enough renown upon Turuŋom.

After Soŋi had made initial preparations for collecting pigs he decided to go hunting opossums. He sent word to every able-bodied adult male in the village and set a date for starting out.

On the preceding night Siha-the-Cripple dreamt that a man fell from a tree. He told several villagers of his dream and warned them not to go opossum-hunting. Opisa, Pitaino, and Tamaŋ were sitting in the club-house discussing the advisability of hunting in the face of Siha's warning, when Soŋi arrived and said, very angrily: "You are a crowd of women, all of you. True, Siha is a dream prophet but who cares about his dreams? If I dream, that's different, that's something real." That night they all set out as scheduled, with Siha included.

As soon as they had arrived in the forest, Ho'oma went off alone in the direction of the Mivo River; he was armed with hunting spears and took his dogs with him. "He wants to taste pork," I was told. "He's a real bush demon, that one; and he will surely bring back a wild pig." Sure enough, three days later after all the men had returned loaded down with opossums, Ho'oma stalked in with the carcass of a wild pig slung across his back.

"Now," he said, "I'm going to have *my* feast." Whereupon he sent Ronsa, Pitaino, and Tampa off to get firewood, Siha and To'osi to get cooking pots, and Koiai to take out some taro from his garden. Meanwhile, he singed and butchered the pig, and joked about himself: "I've become a mumi now, a mumi with one pig!"

When everyone had returned, Ho'oma supervised the cooking. For my benefit he swaggered around in imitation of an officious Administration appointee, and enjoyed his joke immensely. Then he invited all men in the village to come and eat. When a crowd had gathered he distributed the pork — it was a typically thin wild pig, and didn't go far — and jokingly told his guests: "Just try and surpass my feast!"

When the materials were being assembled for his feast Soŋi commissioned a talented musician from Mokorino village to compose a eulogy to be sung and piped at the feast by the hosts and defenders. Soŋi provided the theme, a lament which he himself had earlier composed in the form of a complaint against an ulcer which had malformed one of his feet; in substance:

> You sore, demon, if you were a man I would rise and slay you and place your skull in the club-house. But alas, you are only a sore, and I can only look at you and weep from pain. (Meaning: I am a powerful warrior and a club-

house owner and can work my will on mortal men, but against a little sore I too am powerless.)

The composer elaborated somewhat on the theme and adapted it to music. He chose a panpipe of five reeds, cutting them in lengths to suit the required tones. Then he passed around his master panpipe for copying by Soŋi's adherents and Kaopa's co-defenders.

Prior to this, in mid-October, preparations for the feast were temporarily interrupted when Soŋi's third wife died in childbirth. Soŋi was visibly and probably sincerely grieved by her death, but he was also annoyed by its untimeliness and resolved not to allow it to interfere with his feast preparations.[16] As he said: "People here are always dying and causing me to use up my resources on funeral feasts. That's why my other feasts were not as large as I wanted them to be." He did, however, taboo sounding the gongs in his club-house for a while. Then, in mid-December, he held a *tureko* feast to celebrate the re-beating of his gongs, and to this feast he invited the male residents from all his tuhias, asking them to bring along their panpipes to practice singing and dancing the song intended for the big feast. He butchered seven small pigs and distributed baskets containing stone-baked pork, taro, sweet potatoes, and cooked greens among all the guests, giving one large basket to the leader of each contingent. After the food had been consumed two of the mikai magicians present removed the taboo by beating each gong with coconuts, which were then broken open and eaten. Then hosts and guests joined together in panpipe practice.

After this, practice sessions were held at several club-houses. The Siuai show tireless enthusiasm when actually performing at a feast, but become very bored and tired when learning and practicing, as the following incident illustrates:

December 4: At about nine in the evening while the village was quiet, Soŋi stalked in, evidently very angry, and cried: "Hey, you good-for-nothings. This is no way to prepare for a feast. You should all be in the club-house so that you could hear what work I've planned for you tomorrow. The time is short now, and all of you do nothing. You slip away to your houses and sleep with your wives when you should be all together in the club-house where men belong. You should be singing or playing on your pipes."

Two or three men crept out of their houses and turned toward the club-house. A few minutes later Pitaino began to blow on the conch shell and there was a little singing and playing, but this lapsed after a while. Tamaŋ walked around in the dancing ground feeling very sorry for himself and trying to rouse somebody to sing; Soŋi sat in the club-house by the small fire and shouted out for someone to sing.

Siha the Cripple joined Tamaŋ, as did Peuru,[17] and they began to sing Terei songs. They were cold, miserable, tired, and not in the least humor for singing; but were afraid to displease Soŋi. Peuru was the only spirited one there.

I left after an hour of this miserable business. All night, at infrequent intervals, the singing would break out again and continue for half an hour. During the early morning a small group from Morokaimoro and Maisua joined in and swelled the noise somewhat. The whole performance was as pathetic as could be imagined. No one wanted to sing. Least of all did they want to stay up all night after a hard day's work, and with the prospects of another day's work on Saturday.

Next, the time arrived for preparing puddings, but before this could be done Soŋi had to remove the taboo placed earlier on his coconut palms. He secured a live opossum for a scapegoat, and forced it to climb into one of the palms. Then he called out to his club-house demon: "Go away now." The opossum was then recaptured, killed, and cooked, and its essence was offered to the club-house demon. In explanation of this event an informant stated: "The club-house demon seized the soul of the opossum, and perceiving that it is no longer necessary to guard the palms, the demon called off all his demon followers."

It was decided to make *anitapu* (sago and almond) and *kihanu* (taro and coconut) puddings for the big feast. First of all, sago had to be secured.

During the second week of December Soŋi sent for Ronsa and Maimoi to arrange for cutting sago palms. Ronsa, it transpired, had none ripe enough, so Soŋi "bought" two from Maimoi, and promised to pay later. Then Soŋi set a date for the tree-felling and sent To'osi and Opisa to get some helpers. To'osi engaged the "shredders," while Opisa engaged the "washers." Maimoi — they were his palms and his job to fell them — asked Tampa, Siha, Ho'oma, and Ronsa to assist him with the felling. When the palms had been felled, Maimoi reported to Soŋi, who passed the word on to the "shredders." Early the following morning the "shredders" removed the bark from one side of the palms and began to chop away the pith. Soŋi sent Ho'oma to beat a gong to summon the "washers." Soon they all appeared with Opisa, and when the shredders gave them a signal they set about washing the shredded sago pith. When the "washers" had finished the job they called out to several "packers," who joined them and compressed the starch into leaf packages. When they had finished with this, Soŋi directed them to store the packages in the club-house and in their own houses.

Even though the adult males of the village were busily employed preparing food for the feast, the ordinary affairs of everyday life had to drone on, but with this difference: women had to perform much of the work ordinarily done by men. Such differences were evident in many families and resulted in some temporary changes in the relationships among family members. The case of Ho'oma is informative.

Ho'oma is a faithful subject of Soŋi's and at the same time is generally regarded as a good family man. He usually works very hard in the garden, even assisting his wife with planting and weeding, a task which most men consider undignified. His wife, Pirume, is a regular Xanthippe, but she was once overheard telling a group of women that her husband, Ho'oma, is a good husband: "He is unselfish; he divides his pork among us all."

The men of Turuŋom like Ho'oma — they always laugh at his buffoonery — but they do not have much respect for him. Younger men would not hesitate to send him on errands, and Ho'oma — anxious to please — generally does as he is told. As one would expect, Soŋi began to depend more and more upon him when preparing for his feast. By December 7, Soŋi was referring directly to Ho'oma whenever he wanted some important task done. He started conferring with Siham and Ho'oma preliminary to starting a job and left much of the business of preparation to them; consequently, Ho'oma began to give orders to other natives. At the same time he slept more often at the club-house and returned to his own home only for meals.

This behavior obviously annoyed Pirume because she railed at Ho'oma whenever he appeared, screaming to him to "try sounding wood (cutting down trees) in his garden rather than waste time sounding wood (beating wooden gongs) in Soŋi's club-house." After one of these squabbles Ho'oma stayed away from home for a week, during which time Pirume forced her lazy sons, Koiai and Minsipi, to do more work than was their custom.[18]

In spite of the redoubled efforts of men like Ho'oma, in mid-December it became obvious to the Turuŋom natives that there were not enough local laborers to carry out all the work of food preparation. Thereupon Soŋi acted as he had on many previous occasions and sent word to Tukem, leader of Rennu village to assist. Hitherto Soŋi and Tukem used to meet in each other's club-house and make arrangements for exchanging pigs or money. Each treated the other with greatest deference, addressing each other as "friend" (ŋonosim) and sharing betel nut. Tukem and his Rennu villagers stood in the same relationship to Soŋi and Turuŋom villagers as Kaopa and his Noronai adherents, and many other leaders and their adherents. When Soŋi, acting in his capacity as the leader of Turuŋom village, wanted outside assistance, he went directly to the leader of another village. Not even in his most expansive mood had he seriously attempted to usurp authority in another village. This situation is aptly illustrated by an incident that occurred in Rennu.

One of Tukem's old followers has, as a result of an old feud, borne a grudge against Soŋi since boyhood and he has always resented Soŋi's visits to Rennu. Once while Soŋi was there, he addressed the old fellow and his son and jokingly asked them to contribute a pig for the coming feast. The old man remained stolidly silent, not even bothering to look in Soŋi's direction. After Soŋi left, Tukem asked the ancient why he had not spoken to

Soŋi, and the old man replied: "I'm not his fool. One mumi's enough for me." Later Tukem suggested to Soŋi: "I will ask the ancient stone-heart for a pig, perhaps he will give it to me." Soŋi replied: "Never mind, if I had really wanted his pig, I would have asked you in the first place." And there the matter rested.

After Soŋi had received Tukem's assurance that Rennu villagers would assist in the food preparations, he turned to Siham and asked him to supervise. Siham is the most knowledgeable cook in Turuŋom. Besides knowing all the recipes, he controls a large number of magical techniques which insure successful baking and boiling. The cooking lasted for six days. During this time nearly every adult male from the two villages was on hand, even decrepit Kanasai and Koŋkoma. Only the bitter old man of Rennu remained at home, sulking.

Finally the time came for making sago-almond pudding. Siham set various individuals to do certain things, and the work proceeded apace. Stone-heaters called out to sago- and almond-grinders when the oven was prepared. Grinders, working with mortar and pestle, reduced, mixed, and thinned the ingredients, and passed on the mash to packers. Packers poured it into leaf-lined frames; then placed the pudding in the oven. Meanwhile Siham supervised nearly every step, regulating the speed and pointing out deficiencies. Soŋi also hovered around, and on several occasions sent numbers of Turuŋom and Rennu men to get more firewood and to refill the bamboos with water. This change in relations surprised me but, apparently, not the Rennu villagers. Having become so accustomed to the formality and restraint between Soŋi and those natives, I was not prepared to see the former order the Rennu villagers about as if they were his own adherents.

From this time on, Rennu villagers frequented Soŋi's club-house and aided Turuŋom natives with all their communal tasks.[19]

The first striking evidence of the "political" merger of Rennu with Turuŋom occurred just before the social-climbing feast, when Soŋi deputized Ho'oma to direct the construction of a display platform. Tukem complained that he had expected to supervise that job himself; and spent the rest of the day at his hamlet house, disappointed and sulky.[20]

But Tukem or no Tukem, the display platform was finished under Ho'oma's direction, and was decorated with food. The completion of these events was a signal for the feast invitation to be sent.

As early as September it was rumored about that "all the big leaders in Siuai are nervous over Soŋi's choice of a guest of honor for his feast; they would all be shamed by so much generosity." Soŋi appeared to enjoy the suspense he was creating, then, one day just after the display platform had been decorated with coconuts, he announced that he had made his choice, and without recourse to divination. This was the news the Siuai had been waiting for.

"Siham," ordered Soŋi, "collect as many men as you need and carry invitation pigs to Sipisoŋ of Kinirui."

This was a great surprise to the curious natives; that is, until they realized the significance of the gesture. Earlier, while Soŋi was making arrangements to collect pigs for his feast, he had a bitter quarrel with this Sipisoŋ, an Administration appointee of little renown. Soŋi had been frustrated in his effort to secure one of Sipisoŋ's great tuskers and obviously wished to humiliate him. Soŋi knew that to refuse an invitation to a muminai is to suffer contempt, but to accept without hope of reciprocating is to court even worse disaster. His move was successful. Siham returned with the invitation pigs and recounted how humiliated Sipisoŋ had been: "He felt so much shame that he vowed he would never again set foot in Turuŋom." (Nor did he — until the feast, which he attended and seemed to enjoy thoroughly!)

After having rebuked Sipisoŋ, Soŋi conducted divination and sent the invitation pigs to Kope, most influential leader and Paramount Chief of central Siuai. Wiseacres claimed they knew that he was going to be the choice from the beginning. Kope accepted and they agreed on a date. Messages passed to and fro, with Soŋi begging Kope's pardon for the presumption shown by inviting such a great man to so modest a repast; and with Kope expressing gratitude that a mumi as big as Soŋi would deign to notice him, and prophesying that he would never be able to reciprocate such a bountiful gift.

Kope slaughtered the invitation pigs sent to him by Soŋi, cut them in strips, and sent the strips around to all the leaders of central, southern, and western Siuai, as well as to a few leaders from the neighboring ethnic areas of Banoni and Nagovisi. They were invited to attend the feast with Kope, who designated them as his *allies* and urged them to join in the *attack* on Turuŋom.

While this was going on, Soŋi sent out other invitation pigs to Kaopa of Noronai and some other Rataiku natives designated to be his defenders. Kaopa, in turn, invited many other leaders to attend with their adherents as his co-defenders. He invited all Siuai leaders and Hat-men not directly asked by Soŋi or Kope, including Moŋko of Kupiŋku, the Paramount Chief and highest-ranking leader of northwest Siuai; Tomo, the Paramount Chief of northeast Siuai; and even some leaders from Terei.

In other words, this was to be not only a whole tribal affair and probably the first such ever given, but was also intended to reach out beyond the borders of Siuai.

Now there remained only one decision to make. Should or should not Soŋi appear at the feast and be seen by his guests? Hitherto on several occasions he had made all preparations for his feasts and then retired to his hamlet house in order to hide from envious sorcerers. The matter was not decided until Kope himself sent a message saying that "he would only come to the feast — Turuŋom is so far away! — provided he could be assured of seeing his renowned host." Soŋi decided to remain and he was assured that every device known to his followers would be used to protect him.

All was in readiness. The curious and excited Defenders strolled in hours before dawn on January 10, 1939, and took part in the final *pig-counting*. Koura claimed he saw Soŋi's horomorun dancing along the ridgepole, vastly pleased with the noise and the smell of food. Women huddled together around minute fires in the village and discussed the great event with animation; some of the bolder ones actually stole up to the edge of the dancing ground and peered through the reeds at the drummers.

The morning was spent by all the men applying cosmetics and decorating weapons, preparing themselves as if they were making ready for war. Spears were oiled and bows restrung and polished. Faces and torsos were painted both with powdered lime, sign of invulnerability in battle, and with red ochre, sign of warfare and festivity. Protective charms were distributed about the body to guard against sorcery.

By noon all the Defenders had massed around the front of the club-house and were straining to hear the faraway shouts that announced the approach of the Attackers. While some of the tardier ones quickly applied ocher and lime there was a last minute consultation to reconsider whether Soŋi should remain or hide. He remained, and sat upon his largest wooden gong alongside the spot believed to be occupied by his horomorun.

Then, like a shot, a single spearman rushed into the clearing, ran up to the front of the club-house, threatened the natives lined up there, and retired. A second followed suit, then a third, and so on until scores of howling natives had rushed in brandishing their spears and axes and twanging arrows against bowstrings. More men entered at a run carrying pigs, for the guest must reciprocate the invitation pigs previously sent to him.

The rush then slackened off and the Attackers began to mill around the southern end of the dancing ground, while the Defenders formed a revolving circle nearer the club-house. Then the piping began. Every native performed so strenuously that he could not hear the rival melody above the din of his own. The Turuŋom natives discovered that their song, the lament for Soŋi's sore, now seemed too complicated and slow, so after halting along with it for a while they abandoned it for a more spirited tune.

The music went on for an hour before the guests began to move gradually in the direction of the club-house. As they pressed forward the Defenders thinned out in order to give the guests a chance to see their host. Soŋi reluctantly slid down from his perch and stood upright while his guests stared at him.

Then, at a signal from Soŋi, some of his men rushed to the pens and dragged in the squealing pigs. Others climbed the display platform, whisked away with bundles of leaves the demons guarding it, and began to hand down baskets of food.

## A LEADER IN ACTION

After the pigs and puddings had been lined up on the ground, Soŋi motioned to Kope to accept them. This was the signal for a stampede. Puddings were ripped into, drinking nuts broken open. Meanwhile Kope recorded on a fern frond tally the value of the pigs, and distributed them among his allies. The pigs were quickly strangled and tied to poles, and the whole company of Attackers and Defenders moved off. The exit was as sudden and dramatic as the entry. The whole affair had lasted only two hours.

Some 1100 natives attended the feast and received 32 pigs, distributed as follows: 17 pigs worth a total of 1070 spans of mauai to Kope; 7 pigs worth a total of 450 spans to Kaopa;[21] 4 pigs worth a total of 220 spans to those Rataiku leaders who were directly invited; 3 pigs worth 160 spans given directly to Soŋi's principal taovu partners; and one pig worth 20 spans given to the Australian Patrol Officer, whom Soŋi invited in order to show him "how *Siuai* leaders act."

Every Turuŋom native seemed to sense the depression of anticlimax. A few of them strolled around the dancing ground, now red with betel juice. Some of them kept up a disconsolate piping. No pudding remained for them — "We shall eat Soŋi's renown for a day or two" — so the only thing left to them was talk about the feast, particularly about the number of guests who had been present. And of course by nightfall these numbers had been exaggerated to legendary proportions, as had accounts of everything else concerned with the feast.

"Now we shall rest," To'osi told me hopefully. "Now we can attend our gardens." I agreed with him, just as hopefully, and went away to sleep.

Yet early the next morning the wooden gongs boomed out again and they seemed louder than ever, probably because the noise was so unexpected. A few sleepy natives strolled in the direction of the club-house and heard Soŋi storm out:

> Hiding in your houses again; copulating day and night while there's work to be done! Why, if it were left up to you, you would spend the rest of your lives smelling yesterday's pig. But I tell you, yesterday's feast was nothing. The next one will be really big. Siham, I want you to arrange with Konnu for his largest pig; and you, Maimoi, go to Mokakaru and find a pig for Uremu; and — etc.

Opisa turned to me and whispered: "*That's* the fashion of a mumi!"

CHAPTER 14

# Analysis of Leadership and Its Effects

Here are some of the features of Siuai culture and history that provide at least a background for understanding the present leadership institution:

1. The existence of numerous small but economically fairly self-sufficient households.
2. The geographic pattern of Siuai settlements and the flexibility of rules of residence. (Both of these features favor social fission and spatial scattering, and discourage the development of large, actively functioning residence-kin groups having consistent patterns of social organization and opportunities for development of kinship roles characterized by strong authority.) [1]
3. The absence of other native nonpolitical forms of association that might conceivably have provided opportunities for development of powerful authority roles.
4. The occurrence of certain technological changes within recent decades, and attendant changes in social relations and social opportunities. (Chief among these have been the introduction of steel tools, providing men with more time away from subsistence activities; the increase in the number and size of pigs; and the increase in the quantity of circulating shell money.)
5. The *tradition* of mumihood. (While much of the pre-European form of mumihood may have been destroyed with the outlawing of warfare and native-controlled physical coercion, there remain certain attitudes about leadership which help to account for the modern institution. The *living tradition* of mumihood may not be historically founded — it could conceivably be a perpetual myth — nevertheless it is a cultural reality.) [2]

Other factors have been contributory but these are probably the main ones.

## ESSENTIALS FOR LEADERSHIP [3]

We are now in a position to list the principal requisites for exercising leadership, basing our generalizations on actual observations of natives' behavior rather than on natives' unsubstantiated assertions.

To begin with, to attain leadership a man must have many kinsmen capable of giving him substantial support. It is not true, as some informants assert, that an individual must have a high-ranking father to become successful, or that having a high-ranking father assures an individual of success. Case histories show that many kinds of kinsmen have played sponsors' roles to actual leaders: real and classificatory *fathers*, maternal *uncles*, *grandfathers*, older *siblings*, *cousins*, in-laws; and even classificatory *sons*. Probably, a man's matrilineage is the most crucial element; it is rare to find a leader living in a place where his matrilineage is not wealthy and numerically strong.

Also, a native must himself be intensely ambitious for high rank in order to achieve it. Numerous cases were recorded wherein ambitious fathers or maternal uncles have wasted their resources and efforts to push forward young men who while intelligent and industrious yet lacked the constant driving ambition essential for successful feast-giving.

Next, a would-be leader must have the ability to mobilize the support of a wide circle of kinsmen and neighbors; no matter how ambitious he is he cannot attain high rank by sitting back and allowing his sponsors to push him ahead. This capacity consists of several traits:

*Intelligence:* knowledge of his society and culture, and capacity to make long-range plans of action. (In Siuai the more important action plans formulated within a man's society are made by the leader himself rather than by council.)

*Industriousness:* continuous application to the difficult job of giving feasts. (This also calls for good health.)

*Charisma:* ability to win adherents; in Siuai this presupposes: a local reputation for being morally "good"; and a special type of personality, including a capacity to initiate and dominate in interaction.

*Executive ability:* a facility for delegating work and an adroitness in distributing rewards and credible promises of rewards.

*Mastery in the use of non-physical coercion:* this consists mainly of the effectiveness with which an individual can focus public opinion upon an adversary so that the latter feels embarrassment or shame. (Threats of sorcery do not win adherence; and only a Hat-man can nowadays apply effectively the threat of physical coercion.)

*Diplomacy:* tact in dealing with persons outside one's own men's society community; acumen in arranging and maintaining useful alliances.

## LEADERSHIP AND SOCIAL RELATIONS

The activities of leaders result in the formation and intensification of social relationships inside their own neighborhoods. This becomes evident when comparing neighborhoods with and without active leaders. In the former, men's societies are always to be found, and relationships among members of a men's society are characteristically patterned in a hierarchic manner and marked by fairly frequent interaction. Men's societies are also sometimes found in neighborhoods having no active leader, but in such cases there is little evidence of organization of activity, and interaction among members is not often focused on men's society activities as such, being more in the nature of gossip and lounging clubs. The presence of an active leader in a neighborhood also has the effect of increasing interaction among residents even outside the context of men's society activities. For example, interaction connected with production and exchange is increased, and along with it there is more everyday friendly visiting and conversation among all members of the neighborhood.

Active leaders also bring about the creation and intensification of social relations between neighborhoods, as manifested in political alliances or rivalries, commercial relationships, and attendance at feasts. Not only are separate neighborhoods bound closer together in this manner, but social relationships become extended even to neighborhoods in other language areas.

The leader also functions as an important instrument of social control.[4]

For every social relationship among the Siuai there is a normative code[5] which defines, among other things, the oughts and ought-nots of social actions; for example, children should obey their parents, matrilineage mates should avoid sexual intercourse with one another, neighbors should respect one another's property rights, etc.; in defining social relationships we have *ipso facto* described such norms and the sanctions supporting them.[6] For present purposes, then, social control may be regarded as the mechanisms for maintaining a proper degree of congruence between social behavior and social norms. Let us review, first of all, social control in connection with the family.

Some of the basic oughts and ought-nots among family-household members are: maintenance of a proper division of labor, and sharing of many items of property; sexual fidelity of spouses; obedience to parents and display of a certain amount of filial piety; some deference to elder siblings; avoidance of sexual intercourse between siblings and between parents and children; noninfringement of certain individual property rights; obligation to provide proper funerals for fellow members; etc. These norms are inculcated through education in childhood and through widely voiced maxims. They are mostly maintained by common cultural usages and moral values; but organized social control also operates in most families, particularly in those with infants or children, since parents usually have some authority — that is, they can maintain the threat to use force by means of applying such sanctions as withholding food, or in some extreme cases, actual physical coercion.

As we have seen, deviations from family-household norms are numerous and occur much more frequently than generalizing informants would have us believe. Incest is rare but laziness and selfishness are all too common, as are infidelity, disobedience, and disrespect. These are resolved — when they are resolved — mainly by such measures as divorce, fines, or blows, most of which actions (except for divorce) take place only within the group in question, although adverse *public* opinion also operates as a sanction in many instances. Adverse public opinion often is a factor in the resolution of such deviations, but active measures to resolve them are normally taken only within the family-household group itself. Such intra-family matters do not ordinarily become the concern of other persons or groups except, as we shall see, when the family-household in question happens to be located in a community dominated by an active leader or an officious Hat-man.[7]

The social norms of matrilineages (incest taboo, totem-eating taboo, mutual aid and responsibility, etc.) are likewise inculcated through education, maxim, myth, etc.; and they are chiefly maintained through common moral and ritual values, with even less *organized* social control than occurs in the case of the family-household. Some deviations from matrilineage norms (for example, incest, totem eating, wastage of tomui) are resolved by public censure and, theoretically, by application of supernatural sanctions. Clashes of interest among matrilineage mates (e.g., disputes over matrilineage property) are also known to occur, and these are normally resolved within the matrilineage itself — when they are resolved at all.

If necessary we could similarly enumerate for all kinds of group and pair relationships their social norms, their mechanisms of social control, the deviations and clashes of interest that occur characteristically with each of them, and their manners of resolution. On the other hand, most of these data have already been presented, and the point I am now attempting to establish is simply this: of all the indigenous groupings in any neighborhood only the men's society tends to widen the effectiveness of its social control mechanisms to include the whole neighborhood.[8] It is a matter of observation that in those communities possessing active, high-ranking leaders there is much less troublesome behavior in "the frictional area of clashing interests and dangerous deviations from the norms of the group."[9] Social control among members of an active men's society is effectively maintained through the common experiences and aspirations of the members and through the leader's own command over public opinion and his ability to apply certain sanctions.[10] But in addition, the presence of a high-ranking leader reduces the number of clashes and deviations associated with other kinds of groupings in the neighborhood, and he often steps in to resolve them when they occur. Consider, for example, a situation involving family relations. If a leader learns that some man in his neighborhood is considering marrying a girl from elsewhere who is known to be wanton, being fearful of the trouble she will cause he may dissuade his adherent from going through with the marriage even though he is not a close kinsman of the man. Or, if the wife of one of his adherents begins to cause trouble in the neighborhood, the leader may step in and persuade the husband to get rid of her, in order to head off other troubles. Moreover, the leader's direct intervention may not be required; fearing his anger and censure his neighbors are inclined to avoid deviations and to resolve conflicts of interest before they explode. In this sense most leaders tend, purposefully or unwittingly, to extend the scope and domain of their authority throughout and beyond their own neighborhoods and into many phases of Siuai life. And by and large, in most cases we were able to observe, the effects of leaders' actions were to increase adherence to social norms.

## LEADERSHIP AND RELIGION

Siuai religious behavior consists of innumerable beliefs and practices that are not explicitly systematized. Members of each sib and sib subdivision share certain beliefs and practices, and each matrilineage may be said to have a common and more or less systematic body of beliefs and practices, along with an official practitioner or two. Otherwise the Siuai possess no active supreme Being or unified set of Superior Beings capable of commanding society-wide loyalties or of lending certainty to beliefs and actions. The so-called Universal Beings (Orphan, Maker, Honin, Food-maker) are either otiose or unconcerned with human affairs in a positive sense, and most other spirits are more dangerous than otherwise. Even the ghosts of deceased relatives are fickle; only certain of them are associated with human affairs, and these only in highly specific ways. Spirit-familiars lend effectiveness to the actions of some individuals, and presumably are a source of some comfort to their human associates; but even such spirits as these are liable to become dangerous to their human associates if they are not continually appeased with offerings of food.

Nor do the Siuai practice many daily, monthly, or annually *repetitious* ritual acts by which they could reassure themselves that they, having done *their* parts, might reasonably expect the supernatural to do the rest. They possess countless magical devices for effecting desired ends and for testing whether intended actions are good-omened, but it was our observation that many of even these are performed with an air of some skepticism, which is probably not entirely attributable to the inroads of Christianity alone. Evidence of this common attitude towards their large and diversified inventory of magic can be seen in the alacrity with which they acquire and test new magical devices.

Lacking a literally memorized system of religious myths to fix belief into unchanging dogma, and not having an institutionalized tribal priesthood exercising a vested interest in maintaining fixed beliefs and practices, Siuai religious beliefs and practices are continually changing and, as in many nonliterate cultures of this kind, are unusually co-variable with other institutions which themselves undergo continual change. It is against this background that we have to consider the religious aspect of leadership.

To what extent does the leader exercise control over the supernatural?

In some respects the leader himself possesses peculiar supernatural attributes. While he does not have a mana-like quality during his life, his soul does assume a special form just before death; and after death his ghost is more likely than other men's to become an especially dangerous demon.[11] But this is a pale semblance of the godliness associated with political authority in many Oceanic cultures. Any religious significance that the Siuai leader may have derives mainly from his control of a club-house demon.

It will be recalled [12] that every high-ranking leader is associated with a fierce demon (horomorun) which inhabits his club-house and helps protect his property and person. Now, other natives have spirit-familiars with similar duties, but the significant point is that the club-house demon of a neighborhood's highest-ranking leader is believed to be the most powerful demon in that neighborhood, having its own following of smaller counterpart horomoruns equal in number to the leader's adherents.[13] Now, the map of Siuai can be divided into numerous subdivisions on the basis of the territorial "jurisdictions" of various local demons; [14] and in many instances these territories correspond with areas identified with hamlets, so that social and supernatural boundaries coincide. But when we search for the supernatural boundaries of those larger multi-hamlet "neighborhoods" we have isolated we discover that each one contains several supernatural territories, each having its own principal local demon. Moreover, since the residents of a neighborhood invariably belong to several distinct sibs and sib subdivisions, different ones focus their religious allegiances and fears upon different sets of supernaturals. If, however, there is a high-ranking leader in their neighborhood, his club-house demon provides a common and distinctive supernatural focus for all members of the neighborhood, the only one extant. As such these beliefs provide a symbol of the social unity and organization developed in the neighborhood by the leader, but they do little beyond that. The principal club-house demon remains essentially a familiar of the leader himself, and there have not yet developed any churchly rituals expressive of neighborhood-wide allegiance or fear. The modern politically organized Siuai neighborhood has not yet deified itself.

There is one other aspect of leadership which might be called religious. It is difficult to document this kind of generalization but it was nevertheless our impression that neighborhoods having active high-ranking leaders possess more *esprit de corps* and better morale than most others. As evidence we might cite their greater number of communal undertakings and the fewer number of factional quarrels and litigations. Some of these phenomena can be observed in a neighborhood like Moronei, which has no active high-ranking leader but does engage in much coöperative gardening.[15] But the neighborhood with a high-ranking leader has something additional. One has only to listen to the enthusiasm and reverence with which an adherent discusses his leader to realize that the latter constitutes for his neighbors an element of certainty and security which no other role of authority or set of beliefs has adequately provided. Moreover, he is an example of conduct on which many of his people try to base their lives. It is probably not too much to say that it has been the mumi institution, above all others, that has preserved the Siuai's pride in their culture, thus countering those forces of acculturation that in many aboriginal societies lead to anomie.

## LEADERSHIP AND ECONOMICS

Throughout this account there have been repeated references to the virtual independence of each household with respect to most of its own economic needs. Regional and individual specialization, and the needs expressed for items from such sources, have led to the development of some trade; but in general, the supplying of everyday needs does not encourage the production of a surplus or the development of a large-scale trade. The quest for high rank, however, does stimulate both production and trade, and consumption as well.

First of all, the rank quest stimulates agricultural production, leading natives to make larger coconut groves, and larger gardens of vegetables, for feeding pigs and for direct consumption at feasts. (Almonds are also required for feasts but we found no evidence that natives actually plant almond trees to satisfy specific socio-political needs; such planning would require foresight even beyond that of a potential or actual leader.)

The quest for high rank serves also to stimulate the raising of pigs to a very important degree. Of course, it might be objected that what we have termed a *surplus* of taro, sweet potatoes, and pigs is surplus only to observed everyday household consumption, and that if these seemingly extra goods were not needed for feast-giving they would be absorbed by the households without any change in total production. Replying to such an objection, it can be reliably stated that Siuai natives have all the root crops they can eat and their culture places no emphasis on conspicuous waste. Also, while it is true that they would like to eat much more pork at their daily meals, there is no tradition that they have ever done so nor much likelihood that they would do so even if present supplies were more plentiful. Pigs are feast food; and on historical and functional grounds it appears probable that the increase in feast-giving is chiefly responsible for any present increase in pig production.

The food requirements of the rank quest may encourage opossum hunting to a slight degree, but do not discernibly increase fishing activities.

Directly and indirectly, the quest for high rank stimulates the building of structures and the manufacture of tradable items, and encourages men to become money-earning specialists. It cannot account for all specialist activity but many men state explicitly that they work at their trades or professions in order to earn the money needed to participate somehow in the quest for renown.

## LEADERSHIP AND ITS EFFECTS

The quest for high rank undeniably encourages the procuring of shell money. While there are individuals who earn and then hoard large quantities of shell money, seemingly little interested in using their capital for acquiring renown, these are in the minority and their actions draw criticism from their fellow Siuai.

The circulation of goods is also materially increased by the quest for high rank. Several sections of this book are given over to accounts of the numerous kinds of exchange transactions directly or indirectly linked with the mumi institution. The accumulation of wealth and the preparation of feasts involve countless exchanges of goods, services, and credit. Life crises and other ceremonially celebrated occasions account for some circulation, as does the normal commerce associated with everyday life, but the complex and active network of exchange transactions which prevails throughout Siuai is largely the result of the activities of leaders or would-be leaders.

In this connection, it is worth noting that leaders tend to exercise a stabilizing influence on exchange valuations. When a high-ranking man makes a pronouncement on the valuation of an item it is usually accepted for purposes of that transaction and is afterwards referred to as a precedent. Such circumstances might appear to provide opportunists with chances for setting valuations to their own advantage, and some would-be leaders do try this game; but most high-ranking leaders are more mindful of their moral obligations for fair dealing and adhere to traditional valuations.

Finally, the quest for renown has marked effects on consumption of material goods. In one respect its influence is to decrease consumption: ambitious men often deprive themselves and their families in order to accumulate resources for feasts. For example, many men put aside their entire almond crop for feasts, or exchange the crop for money and pigs to be used in feast-giving. In other instances men place taboos on their coconut groves for months in advance of their feasts, thereby placing a severe restriction on their household's everyday consumption.

On balance, however, the total effect of the quest for high rank is to increase significantly the use and consumption of many goods, particularly money, pigs, and coconuts, as the preceding chapters have abundantly indicated.

There are many other respects in which the leadership institution, including the activities directly or indirectly associated with feast-giving and other actions of leaders, affects other aspects of Siuai culture and society. In connection with the arts, for example, feast-giving serves to stimulate composition and performance of music and drama; club-house construction encourages fine craftsmanship and artistic design; and feast-attendance increases men's interest in bodily grooming and adornment. Nor should the entertainment value of feasting be overlooked, especially in this society where other forms of organized diversion are so scarce. Other effects of the leadership institution will occur to the reader and need not be exhaustively enumerated here. Only one further point should be made about leadership before closing this summary account. In many respects leaders appear as influences for conservatism, helping to maintain cultural traits and patterns of the past. But in other ways they appear as innovators, creating new traits and patterns, or, by lending the weight of their influence, securing popular acceptance for cultural items from elsewhere.

# IV

GENERALIZATIONS, CONJECTURES,
AND QUESTIONS

CHAPTER 15

# *Integration*

With enough data and with better analytical techniques I believe (as an act of "faith") that it would be possible to construct a rigorously inductive, fully comprehensive, and faithfully balanced synthesis of the whole of Siuai culture.[1] As a beginning in this direction, I have indicated in several places throughout the text what I construe to be the premises underlying many Siuai thought and action patterns; however, I do not have sufficient data to compile an exhaustive inventory of patterns. Nor do I possess the techniques with which I could construct from such patterns, inductively and systematically, a synthesis embracing the whole culture. But even if my field notes and analytical techniques were adequate, the resulting synthesis would probably fall far short of the aesthetically gratifying models of perfect integration reported of some cultures. Actually, I suspect that even the most homogeneous of cultures embrace some inconsistencies and contradictions — and as for Siuai, these are especially numerous; here incongruence shows up not only between specific norms and related modes of actual behavior,[2] but between different sets of norms as well. In fact, with respect to the culture (or cultures?) exemplified by the behavior of persons who speak Motuna, who at the same time are members of a more or less bounded society, it is possible to distinguish *four* great systems of cultural tradition, four major assemblages of typical *normative* thought and action patterns between whose premises, goals, etc., occur many important inconsistencies and contradictions. Since a great deal, though by no means all, of the Siuai's behavior is explicable in terms of one or more of these four assemblages or systems of norms, which for shorthand purposes I call *Kinship* ideology, *Rank* ideology, *Administration* ideology, and *Mission* ideology, I propose in this chapter to summarize what I consider to be the most important *contrastable* characteristics of these four ideologies for the purpose of indicating similarities and contradictions among them.[3]

At this point the reader may well ask: What is the basis for differentiating these so-called ideologies?

There is a *historical* as well as what might be called a *functional* basis for this differentiation.

Historically, it is quite clear that the major assemblage of thought and action patterns termed *Administration* represents a particular kind of alien cultural tradition and native interpretations of that tradition, which originated at a particular source and began reaching Siuai at a particular time. The same thing can be said of the assemblage or ideological system termed *Mission* — although for purposes of more detailed analysis it would be useful to speak of two overlapping sub-ideologies, Catholic and Methodist. There is less reliable historical evidence for differentiating between *Kinship* and *Rank* ideologies. I do believe, however, that many patterns associated with the modern process of renown-seeking are direct, interrelated, and fairly recent adaptations to the situation created by the outlawing of warfare and use of physical coercion by native mumis. On the other hand, it is my belief that the core traits and patterns of the assemblage labeled *Kinship* ideology represent a way of life which has persisted in Siuai for a very long time.

What can be said of the functional basis for differentiating these four ideologies?

The Functionalists' truism, that changes wrought in one part of a relatively homogeneous culture ultimately bring about changes in all other parts, undoubtedly applies to Siuai. But it is possible to detect in Siuai — as indeed may be the case in all other cultures — particular areas or *systems* of relatively closer interdependence, of more responsive co-variability. For example, it is likely that if an epidemic were to destroy all Siuai pigs the repercussion would be most immediate and most far-reaching in the *Rank* ideological system. Or, if the Australian officials were to remit all taxes and provide native officials with resources for giving generous feasts in return for work on public projects, far-reaching effects would soon appear in the native *Rank* ideology system but would probably become more immediately evident in thought and action patterns associated with the *Administration* ideological system.

All these generalizations and conjectures about ideologies are rather impressionistic and imprecise, and as the reader will doubtless perceive, the characterization of each ideology, which will now be presented, falls far short of the ideal of systematic induction. Part of this is due to a desire to spare the reader a long and painful step-by-step recapitulation, and part to my ignorance of how otherwise to proceed. In any case, there is probably enough data in the foregoing chapters to permit the reader to construct his own synthesis if he does not find this one to his liking.

## KINSHIP IDEOLOGY

All Siuai occupy statuses and play active roles in the Kinship system. The *goals* motivating most behavior referable to this system are: adequate subsistence and maintenance of a suitable standard of living; stable marriage; prolific reproduction; and physical and spiritual welfare. *Activities* carried out in pursuit of these goals include: a major portion of the work of gardening and collecting; more than half of the work of shelter-construction; about half of the work of pig-raising and manufacturing, but a smaller portion of the work of hunting and trading; a major portion of sex activity; the physical nurture of children; the celebration of rites of passage; the protection and restoration of physical-spiritual welfare; and a major portion of acts carried out to revenge injuries to physical-spiritual welfare.

Let us review some of the *circumstances* surrounding these activties and list some of the basic *premises* associated with them.

## I

The physical environment of Siuai, though deficient in certain respects, must be considered highly favorable for the growth of plants, which provide nearly all things these natives subsist on. Moreover, the Siuai possess tools and techniques which enable them to exercise effective control over their supply of food staples, with the result that they are fairly well fed and seldom if ever anxious about future supplies. Also, the forests provide plentifully most of the other subsistence items they need. Reflecting these and other circumstances are the following Siuai premises:

1. Plants and animals are being continually replenished by natural processes of reproduction and growth, and man can help along these processes by means of such rational measures as planting, cultivating, and protecting plants from natural pests; or he can obtain most other things he needs for subsistence by industrious collecting. Spirits seldom intervene to inhibit natural processes, and only occasionally is it necessary to utilize supernatural powers to stimulate them or insure success in collecting.

2. From the above it follows that getting a living depends more upon work and widely known techniques than upon specialized or spirit-manipulating skills; hence destitution results more often from indolence than from other causes.

3. Economically productive land is the most important kind of property.

## II

The family-household is the social unit of subsistence economy, producing nearly all the things its members need to subsist on. All households enjoy about the same standard of living, that is, they eat the same kinds and relatively the same amounts of food, live in the same type of house, use the same kind of tools, etc. In addition, most households produce goods in excess of subsistence needs. Some of this surplus is required for contracting marriages, for celebrating rites of passage, and for trading to obtain the few domestic consumption goods which the household may be unable to produce. Reflecting these conditions, the Siuai hold that: Ability to satisfy domestic and other requirements associated with the Kinship system is easily within the capacity of all households, and every householder should insure that his household lives well and carries out its kinship obligations.

### III

Sexual relations are difficult and hazardous outside marriage. Also, the conventional division of labor puts an economic premium upon marriage. These circumstances, along with a favorable sex ratio and the fairly close ages of most spouses, make it possible and probable that nearly every adult will marry; and monogamy is the modal form of marriage. After an initial period of instability most marriages remain fairly stable, and it is an observable fact that monogamous families are more harmonious than polygynous ones. Underlying many of the thought and action patterns associated with marriage are these premises:[4]

1. Every adult ought to marry and marriage should be harmonious.
2. One wife is better than many.

### IV

Disease is generally rife among the Siuai and life spans are relatively short; moreover, infancy is a particularly hazardous period. Miscarriages and stillbirths are frequent, and the mortality rate of infants and parturient mothers is high. Many marriages are without issue, and even with fruitful unions an average of only two or three offspring survive into childhood. Premises reflecting these circumstances include the following:

1. Life itself, as distinct from the resources of subsistence, is precarious on account of capricious attacks by the innumerable indifferent or malicious spirits which comprise most of the spirit-universe. Disease and death are caused mainly by these spirits; relatives should not harm one another and do so only in the case of jilted lovers.
2. The times of pregnancy, childbirth, and infancy are particularly dangerous, and elaborate measures are required to protect the mother and infant from malicious spirits.
3. If an old person finishes out his time, death is brought about more through natural processes than through direct intervention of spirits.

The above premises find ritual expression in the proliferation of religious rites having to do with birth, infancy, and the death of non-senile persons.

### V

Turning now to social relationships within the Kinship system, we can summarize the premises underlying relationship *norms* as follows:

1. Mankind consists of relatives and strangers. Relatives are usually interlinked by both blood and marital ties; most of them live nearby, and persons

who live nearby are all relatives. Relatives should interact quite frequently and at least in times of crises and on the occasion of one another's rites of passage. Transactions among them should be carried out in a spirit devoid of commerciality — preferably consisting of sharing, nonreciprocable giving, and bequeathing, among closest relatives, or of lending, among more distantly related ones. Among themselves relatives should feel and express emotions of affection or at least amity — colored, when appropriate, by expression of deference, or polite constraint, and of sex avoidance.

Except for a few very distantly related sib-mates, persons who live far away are not relatives and can only be enemies. Most of their customs are unsuitable for the Siuai, but a few of their goods and techniques are desirable. One interacts with them only to sell or buy — utilizing hard bargaining and deceit to make as much profit from such transactions as possible. Such persons are usually intent upon theft, so it is necessary to protect one's women and goods from them at all times. Many troubles are due to their indiscriminate use of harmful magic, so it is perfectly permissible to practice such magic openly against them.

2. One's relatives are divided into own sib-mates, and all others (including father, spouse, and their sib-mates). However, since each person is the product of both mother and father, and since marriage must take place between sibs, the division between one's own sib-mates and all other relatives is continually being bridged by familial ties, which are particularly close. Nevertheless, the relationship among sib-mates is unique. The family-like blood tie between sib-mates, which carries about the same rights and obligations, is reinforced by ties of mystical identity which are supernaturally ordained. Since these ties are matrilineally perpetuated it is highly important that a marriage produce daughters.

3. Men are stronger than women and the things which men excel in doing and producing are superior to women's preoccupations and material products, hence men should be shown deference by their female relatives. However, women are not chattels; they are skillful in their own essential activities and their male relatives ought not to require too much deference from them.

4. By and large, younger persons should show deference towards their older relatives, because of the latters' age and greater skills.

5. The good of the kinship unit (family, matrilineage, sib, etc.) outweighs the good of the individual member; and the ownership of kinship-unit property should not be individualized. In fact, individuals ought to contribute their own acquisitions and property creations to their kinship units.

6. To be an ideal relative one must be "good" to one's relatives (i.e., unselfish, coöperative, rule-abiding, congenial, trustworthy). Normally intelligent relatives are born with a disposition towards "goodness," and usually become "wicked" only through pique, through association with other wicked

persons, or through magic — either actuated by malicious persons or contacted accidentally. Strangers, on the other hand, are innately wicked.

7. Among the large and varied population of the spirit world the only ones benignly disposed towards the living are a few who are relatives — sib ancestresses, totemic archetypes, and ghosts of some of the recently deceased; and the continued benignity of these few depends upon one's conformance to sib norms or upon occasional sacrifices of food.

## RANK IDEOLOGY

Most adult male Siuai occupy statuses in the socio-political Rank system. The principal *goals* motivating behavior referable to this system are renown and the power that accompanies it, and the most important *activities* carried out directly in pursuit of these goals are: acquisition of negotiable capital in excess of amounts required for subsistence and other Kinship system purposes; construction and maintenance of club-houses, and manufacture of wooden slit gongs; and that part of feast-giving specifically related to acquiring renown.

The *premise* which is probably basic to all thought and action patterns associated with these activities is as follows:

1. The most praiseworthy thing a man can do is to exceed the transactional requirements of ordinary trade and kin relationships by paying *generously* (in goods) for all goods and services he receives, by giving goods to persons to whom he is not directly obligated, and by doing these things after the manner of the leaders of the past.[5] From this it follows that:

2. The man who excels in these transactions deserves most praise and deference.

Having described in some detail the Rank system and the whole process of renown-achieving, we need not review it again. Instead, it will be useful to list some of its associated circumstances which differ from those associated with the Kinship system, and indicate how these have led to the development of normative thought and action patterns which contrast or conflict with those of Kinship ideology.[6]

I

Unlike the resources required for subsistence and for carrying out ordinary kinship obligations — items which can usually be obtained without great difficulty by an average monogamously based household — the resources required for renown-achieving are relatively scarce and can be accumulated only by *extra* effort. Moreover, since most of the pigs and negotiable shell money inherited by a Siuai should be and usually are spent on funeral feasts for his parents, the initial acquisition of substantial amounts of these items depends largely on the efforts of the man himself and his household. Being particularly scarce, and obtainable only by extra effort, these items are the subject of competition, and supplies of them are greatly affected by humanly and naturally produced vicissitudes, as manifested in frauds, thefts, and increased concern with obtaining and keeping them. Reflecting these circumstances are the following premises:

1. Important as land is for subsistence, pigs and negotiable shell money are the marks of real wealth.

2. Anyone can produce the necessities for subsistence and for kinship transactions, but ambition and special skills are required to obtain real wealth.

3. Also, special supernatural aids are needed to obtain this wealth, and special measures — practical and magical — are required to protect it from damage or loss.

## II

In the household of the active renown-seeker members must work very hard to accumulate wealth, and they have to forego many of the food tidbits which enrich living in other households. Also, the active renown-seeker often falls down on his kinship obligations by trying to conserve resources for feast-giving. Reflecting these circumstances, some hold that: Renown is better than leisure or a full stomach; and to be closely related to a leader brings reflected renown.

## III

Under conditions of unusually hard work one woman can carry out the garden work necessary to feed her household and about five or six grown pigs. If a man wishes to keep more pigs he has to obtain the services of more women, and the only normal way to do this is to acquire more wives. Reflecting these circumstances, some Siuai hold that: Having more than one wife at a time produces strife in the household, but it is the price which has to be paid for renown.

## IV

The competitiveness which accompanies renown-seeking breeds envy and covetousness, which materialize in numerous instances of sorcery and in measures for defense against man-made troubles. Accordingly, however senile he may be, when a man of high rank dies, some of his relatives and friends seek a human killer and attempt to avenge his death. Underlying these thought and action patterns is this premise: Men of high rank are in constant danger of attack by envious persons, even including envious kinsmen.

This premise finds expression in the wave of interpersonal recrimination and death-dealing sorcery which is stirred up by the death of a high-ranking man.

## V

From the standpoint of men actively engaged in renown-seeking, the premises underlying social relationship norms differ from and sometimes clash with those of the Kinship ideological system. Here are some of the more important comparable premises of Rank ideology:

1. Members of a men's society should behave towards one another like closest relatives, regardless of actual kinship ties; and if any relative outside one's men's society happens to be a potential or actual rival for high rank then it is permissible to treat with him on terms of rivalry rather than of kinship. Moreover, ties of trade-partnership and political alliance do not depend upon kinship and spatial proximity.

2. Regardless of the nature of the kinship tie, one's relatives are divided into those who assist one in acquiring renown, and all others. (With the prevalence of patrilocality this means that patrilateral relatives are often closer than actual sib-mates are in terms of interaction, sharing, etc.) Also, from the standpoint of perpetuating renown a son is preferable to a daughter.

3. The events that take place in club-houses are important, and women are not fit to participate. Women should concern themselves only with subsistence and kinship matters.

4. Deference should be shown to persons of higher rank regardless of relative age.

5. To achieve high rank it is necessary to own and distribute property *individually* and not only as the member of a social unit.

6. To become a high-ranking leader it is necessary to be "good" to all one's neighbors but not necessarily to all one's far-flung relatives; moreover, it is necessary to be "ambitious" and "skillful."

7. Club-house demons, more so than the ghosts of relatives, provide assistance in the struggle for high rank, and the aid of these demons has to be won and maintained by frequent sacrifices.

## ADMINISTRATION IDEOLOGY

All Siuai natives are subject to the absolute authority of the Australian Government, which actually controls several aspects of their lives. The result of this contact has been the development in Siuai of a distinct system of actions, relationships, and premises. The explicitly stated official *goals* associated with this system are the well-known aims of colonial trusteeship,[7] including such general objectives as order, public health, and culture change — subject, of course, to the varying definitions given to these words by different policy formulators and executors. Particularly are these objectives subject to special interpretation by whatever Patrol Officer happens to be in charge of the southern Bougainville administrative area.

In addition to these official goals, which are largely alien in origin and understood imperfectly, if at all, by the Siuai, some natives recognize in this system opportunities to gain influence and power.

*Activities* carried out in pursuit of all these goals include: annual line-village assemblies for census and tax-collection; court hearings and trials conducted by native officials and, occasionally, by the Patrol Officer; payment of fines and serving of jail sentences; treatment of physical ailments by native medical orderlies and, occasionally, by European medical officials; construction and maintenance of line villages, trails, and bridges; occasional porterage of European travelers' cargo.

The carrying out of all these activities is enforced, ultimately, by the sanction of physical coercion which resides in the Administration. From the point of view of the Administration the general premise implicitly underlying all these actions is, presumably, that European culture is superior to that of the Siuai in most respects, hence it is right and inevitable that Siuai culture should conform or adapt to European ways. Some native officials may partly share this view, but underlying the actions of many native officials is the general premise that social power is desirable whatever its source.

Let us list some of the more specific aspects of the Administration ideology to indicate points of similarity and conflict with those just listed for Kinship and Rank.

I

One resource required for carrying out their obligations in the Administration system is labor. Able-bodied adult males must work many hours every week or fortnight on Administration public-work projects, usually without compensation of any sort. Underlying this *corvée* is the alien officials' premise regarding obligations of *citizenship*; most Siuai object strenuously to this corvée, holding that (1) services performed for anyone but the closest of relatives require equivalent returns; and that (2) services performed by the Administration (maintenance of "order," etc.) are without value.

Natives also state that the corvée takes away time which should be devoted to food production, but this complaint is not based on fact, nor, I suspect, is it actually believed by many natives.

The other item required for carrying out obligations in the Administration system is Australian currency, for paying the annual head-tax. In other words, whereas land is the most important material resource according to Kinship ideology, and pigs and negotiable shell money according to Rank ideology, many adult males must in addition own a supply of shillings in order to avoid penal sanctions. Natives hold these premises about Australian currency: (1) Spirits have nothing to do with the accumulation of shillings; (2) Any male who is willing to work on European plantations can earn shillings, no ambition or special skills being required; (3) Shillings may be essential for keeping one out of trouble with the Administration but it is not proper to use them in the more ceremonialized transactions connected with Rank or Kinship.

## II

Native catechists and some native officials receive small annual salaries but most other natives needing shillings have to earn them by leaving home and working on European plantations. Now, some youths are keen for adventure, while still others work on plantations specifically to earn tax money, holding that: Sanctions controlled by the Administration are more frustrating than those traditionally supporting ties of kinship and rank.

## III

The Administration exempts from taxation any man who has four or more living children by one wife. The alien premise underlying this measure presumably recognizes the desirability of stable marriage and many offspring, and as such reinforces similar premises associated with Kinship ideology. Administration officials also over-support stable marriage by penalizing adulterers and, in some instances, by requiring errant natives to return to their spouses.

## IV

The general premise underlying Administration policy towards disease and death is, of course, that of modern science. Consequently, officials carrying out this policy come into sharp conflict with native thought and action patterns in several kinds of situations. For example, official policy rules that sickness should be treated medically rather than magically; that birth practices (seclusion, dietary taboos, etc.) should be ignored if they endanger health; that sorcery, while actually ineffective, is illegal no matter whom it is directed against — but that any unsupported accusation of sorcery is also illegal; et cetera. On the other hand, it should be stated that Administration policy, insofar as it is formulated and executed by on-the-spot European officials, does not scoff at or condemn wholesale all native religious beliefs and practices — although some *native* officials claim to do so, hoping to curry favor with their white superiors.

## V

Here is a list of some of the premises which appear in underlie the actions and assertions of European officials regarding social relationships and which differ from comparable premises associated with Kinship or Rank ideologies:

1. An illegal act is wrong no matter whom it is committed against — whether close relative, neighbor, stranger, friend, or enemy.

2. Paternal ties are more important than maternal ones.

3. Men are more important than women, but it is not absolutely essential that the sexes be segregated on public occasions.

4. Deference should be shown to Administration officials, European and native.

5. The individual, the line village, and the Administrative district are more important social units than are matrilineages, hamlets, and men's societies.

6. To be an ideal native one must obey Administration laws and acquire some of the marks of westernization, including cleanliness and knowledge of pidgin English.

7. European officials do not foster any beliefs in supernaturalism, but for many natives the high officials at Kieta, Rabaul, and "Sinni" (Sydney, Australia) — along with the "King," who is occasionally invoked — occupy near-supernatural statuses and constitute the ultimate source of Administration norms.

These are not the only instances wherein norms associated with the Administration system differ from those of the Kinship and Rank systems; for example, the official insistence upon residence in line villages conflicts with native residence patterns. Also, by permitting and encouraging wider travel, trade, and other contacts with the outside world, the imposition of Administration control has led indirectly to the development of some new thinking which differs markedly from older native thinking, including, for example, the development of a sense of Siuai tribal unity, or, in the case of some Siuai men who have traveled widely, the creation of an attitude of cynicism about many fundamental native beliefs and practices. (The surprising thing, however, is that there is not more of this cynicism — a circumstance which is likely due to the continued vitality of Rank ideology.)

## *MISSION IDEOLOGY*

Nearly all Siuai natives are nominally Christian and many of them participate in mission *activities*, which include: daily or weekly attendance at local chapel service, and — in the case of Catholic converts — occasional attendance at services conducted by a European priest; in the case of children, sporadic attendance at local "schools" conducted by native catechists; in the case of a few children, month-long residence and training at schools conducted by European missionaries at mission headquarters; and in the case of some Catholic converts, occasional participation in rites of passage conducted by priests.

Behind all these activities are the *goals* of missionaries: to convert natives to the "true" faith and thereby save them from limbo or worse, to instill in them Christian norms of morality; and to improve their physical welfare along western lines. These goals have been partially implanted in some converts, but in addition many converts participate actively in mission activities for recreation. Also, some natives become catechists in order to acquire influence and the kind of social power provided by the backing of European missionaries.[8] When the missions were actively proselytizing, it is probable that many natives joined because of social pressures to conform to a new, prestige-laden movement; but with most natives now nominally converted this factor is no longer influential.

The sanction which serves principally to enforce conformance to mission norms is the disapproval of the European missionaries. Fear of supernatural punishment is effective with only a few; and I could detect little sense of shame and no feelings of guilt among natives over violation of norms *distinctively* associated with the Mission system.[9]

Reviewed below are some of the main points of similarity and conflict between Mission ideology[10] and those of the Kinship, Rank, and Administration systems.

I

Native converts are not required to pay for mission membership, but they are encouraged to attend services regularly, to build and maintain chapels, and — in some instances — to contribute food and handicraft for support of mission activities. In general there is little or no hardship involved in carrying out these informal obligations, and few natives voice objections to them.

On the negative side, mission doctrine — at least as it is promulgated by native catechists — condemns the use of native magic for producing and protecting material resources, the "wasting" of resources in heathen rituals, and excessive preoccupation with property accumulation — rather should "treasure be stored up in heaven."

The missions also teach that charity should be extended to the destitute, whereas natives hold that destitution comes about mainly from indolence, and that the indolent deserve to be hungry — that is, except for one's closest relatives.

Many catechists teach that crop failure and the like are punishments for *sin*, whereas native beliefs attribute most such misfortunes either to undeserved maliciousness on the part of spirits or human enemies or to more rational causes.

II

The Mission system impinges on household economy and men's society activities mainly in connection with the Sabbath work taboo imposed upon Methodists and with the absences from home of youths attending mission schools.

## III

Missions condemn not only polygyny but all extramarital sexual intercourse as well.

## IV

Mission doctrine towards disease and death, at least as it is explained to Siuai congregations by their native catechists, serves to substitute — or, as it actually works out in practice, to supplement — one set of supernatural powers for another, and this probably helps to account for the ease with which natives appear to accept many mission-taught beliefs. Also, many mission rites of passage closely resemble native ones in a superficial way, the chief exception being the Methodists' encouragement of interment in place of cremation.

One mission-taught belief which natives appear neither to accept nor to comprehend is that which rejects sorcery and "accidental" magic as a cause for most disease and death, and substitutes for it explanations based either on natural causes or on God's punishment for sin. By condemning the practice of sorcery and many other forms of magic the missions do succeed in impressing upon some natives the immorality of such practices, but actually this only serves to reinforce many natives' beliefs in their efficacy.

## V

Judging from the assertions and actions of native catechists, who do not necessarily reflect the views of their white superiors, here are some of the catechists' premises regarding social relationships:

1. People are born neither good nor wicked. They become good through conversion and obedience to mission rules; they become wicked through refusing conversion and through breaking mission rules. One should not have enemies, but even with enemies one should be amicable and honest in transactions.
2. Family ties are all-important, and sib ties have no supernatural basis.
3. The sexes are about equal "in the sight of God."
4. Deference should be shown to parents and to mission officials.
5. The individual, the family, and the denomination are the most important social units.
6. To be an ideal native one must believe mission tenets and obey mission rules. Also, one should obey Administration rules provided these do not conflict with mission rules, and one should acquire some knowledge of reading, writing, and pidgin English. In addition (this applies particularly to Methodists), one should bathe often and wear clean clothes whenever possible.

7. The theologies of Methodists and Catholics differ of course in several details, but they differ alike from indigenous beliefs in that the Christian divinities are fewer in number, more powerful, and more directly concerned with human affairs — being actively benign towards those who obey mission rules and fiercely vengeful towards unrepentant breakers of those rules.

## OTHER CHARACTERISTICS OF SIUAI CULTURAL SYSTEMS

Other examples could be cited to point up differences between the four systems. Consider, for example, the matter of men's dress. The characteristic everyday costume of many men of high rank is a dirty, tattered, calico loincloth and a native conical hat (ohkuna). Many catechists and other mission stalwarts, on the other hand, like to wear spotless white loincloths and cotton singlets; while the more officious Hat-men wear khaki loincloths — like the Patrol Officer's native constables — whenever they can get them, and are rarely seen without their official caps. Some catechists — especially Methodist ones — may often be heard expressing disgust at other natives' slovenliness, calling them "bush kanakas."[11] The latter reciprocate by ridiculing mission-influenced fastidiousness, and they are even more contemptuous of the Hat-men who always wear their caps. In fact, one method used by some Hat-men to demonstrate their opposition to unpopular Administration rulings is to leave off their official caps and wear ohkunas on official occasions.

Gong-beating is a practice more or less reserved for occasions connected with the Rank system: gongs are for "sounding renown" and should not be "beaten for nothing." In the event of death the announcement should be made by gong-beating only if the deceased was a person of high rank (or the wife of such a person). Women should never beat gongs, and children may do so only as a special treat when their older male relatives are preparing a club-house feast. It is all right for a catechist to beat a single gong to summon his congregation to services, and it is also permissible for a Hat-man to beat a gong to assemble natives for public work; but excessive use of gongs for Mission or Administration purposes evokes charges of pretentiousness.

Such examples could be multiplied — the text contains many of them — but for present purposes of summarization it will be sufficient to refer to only one more point of comparison, albeit a very important one, that of *time orientation*. We have considered elsewhere the ways in which the Siuai cut up time into meaningful units and cycles: the time context of activities referable to the Kinship system being days and life cycles, that of the Rank system being the annual almond cycle, that of the Mission system being weeks and other periods of the Christian year, and that of the Administration system being weekly or fortnightly labor corvées and the annual visits of tax-collecting officials. But there is another aspect of time orientation which deserves comment, namely: What relative emphasis do the Siuai place on past, present, or future? Or, as one author [12] phrases the problem: "What is the direction in time of the action process?"

I believe it is justifiable to state that Siuai natives mainly preoccupied with kinship activities are concerned partly with the present, partly with the past — insofar as the past provides rationale for the present — and hardly at all with the future. Men preoccupied with renown-seeking, however, are mainly concerned with a future realizable here among the living, their interest in the past being largely nostalgic. Administration zealots are also oriented towards a future, on earth, when everything will be done according to white man's laws. And, of course, mission devotees at least assert their interest in a life after death; and like some other admirers of western ways, they reject the past as being a time of ignorance and crudity.

## COHERENCE?

If, say, the Rank ideological system represented in most respects an extension and elaboration of the goals, premises, etc., associated with kinship, we might expect that the hypertrophy of renown-seeking activities would serve to reinforce the relationships, values, etc., of the Kinship system, as conceivably occurs in some cultures. But it is obvious from all the foregoing that this is not the case; and the many instances of inconsistency and contradiction become socially and psychologically manifest: in conflicts between individuals [13] and in conflicts "within" individuals.

To begin with, authority statuses in the four systems are rarely interlinked, and this leads to irreconcilable conflicts between, say, a leader and a matrilineage First-born, a leader and a Hat-man, and a Hat-man and a catechist. Secondly, many individuals are often troubled by irreconcilable role conflicts, as, for example, the case of the fairly devout young Catholic who after long soul-searching reluctantly disobeyed the priest's admonitions and acquired additional wives in order to advance in the Rank system.[14] To record what is admittedly a poorly founded impression, I suggest that the reasons why Siuai men are in general more uneasy and unpoised in their social relationships than are women may be sought not only in the anxieties engendered by renown-seeking but also in the circumstance that women are usually involved only in the Kinship system whereas men often become deeply involved in other systems as well and hence are subject to more numerous and more serious role conflicts.[15]

Of course, all is not contradiction and conflict: in fact, from some perspectives the culture traits exemplified in the behavior of speakers of Motuna appear remarkably coherent; for example, some mission doctrines and practices serve to supplement and reinforce rather than replace indigenous ones. And socially, the increased number of transactions between an active renown-seeker and his supporting kinsmen signifies in itself a strengthening of kinship ties. Moreover, in those cases where statuses in two or more social systems do happen to be interlinked, a high degree of coherence can be said to be achieved. Also, there are hosts of thought and action patterns which are not directly referable to any one ideology and action system — including many aspects of knowledge and technology; and there are numerous others which, though referable to one particular system, have no analogies and hence no points of identity or conflict with others. Among these latter might be included such patterns as mourning, women's dancing, and many aspects of child care. Nevertheless, contradictions among ideologies do exist, at many points, and many individuals are often placed in positions of having to decide between two or more alternative and mutually irreconcilable courses of action. If enough evidence were available concerning choices made in such situations over a period of time it should be possible to make an accurate statement about the direction of culture change.[16] Even without much systematic evidence of this nature, it appeared to me during the course of field work that the trend was away from other systems towards a more elaborate, a more time-occupying, and a more potent decision-influencing Rank system.

CHAPTER 16

# *Explanation*

How did Siuai culture get to be what it is?
There are probably few direct explanations for particular culture traits and patterns, and interpreters who ignore this circumstance construct such patently improbable theses that almost every attempt to *explain* cultures has become unfashionable. Unfashionable or not, however, I claim the privilege of setting down some of my opinions on these matters; and if any reader regards unhappily all such exercises he can safely pass on to the final chapter without further grimaces.

## ENVIRONMENTAL

The *physical environment* of southern Bougainville imposes few absolute limits. There is no readily available ore for making metal tools and there is not sufficient game to support a large hunting and collecting population, but otherwise the environment is favorable enough to permit wide choice of ways of living. Parts of Java having no better climate and soil than here support rural farming populations about thirty times as dense. But let us not dwell on what Siuai is *not*; it will be more profitable to recapitulate how the Siuai have responded positively to certain cues provided by their physical environment.

First of all, they have responded to this ideal plant-growing setting by becoming dependent upon plants for nearly everything they consume and use.

They have ready access to the sea, but no longer having the objective of interisland trade to keep them on their beaches they live and work far inland. Some negative factors probably behind this are the plagues of mosquitoes on the beaches and the exposure of their shores to full wind and wave action, making boating and fishing extremely hazardous.

The physical environment also shows through in connection with specialization and the resulting trade — pottery being made in the clay-rich northeast, lime in the south, etc. It also shows through in the contrast between northern and southern garden layouts.[1] (On the other hand, the well-known hazards of flooding have not discouraged some natives from building their houses directly on the banks of large streams.)

Another positive way in which the environment affects Siuai life is through the local diseases, which shorten lives and reduce energies to a considerable degree.

Certain aspects of their *location* have had immense effect upon the Siuai.

Southern Bougainville is isolated by some 2000 miles from the nearest places where native peoples made their own metal tools and were in more or less direct touch with centers of high civilization. Moreover, the intervening area is populated by native peoples who are technologically just about as undeveloped as the Siuai.

The location of the Siuai has also had certain positive effects upon their culture. Through contact with neighboring peoples several traits that we know definitely about — including high-value shell money, raoku display platforms, many magical techniques, and myth themes — have been added, and a comparative study would doubtless reveal many more. The contact with the neighboring Terei and Banoni has been especially close, and until recently direct contact was maintained with natives of Alu and Mono. One result of the relations with Alu and Mono islanders may have been an increase in warfare and in the number of its associated thought and action patterns.

In recent times Siuai's location has been an important factor in determining the nature and intensity of culture changes derived from Europeans. Some western traits have been introduced directly through the medium of Administration law and through personal intervention of white missionaries; but in many respects the distance of Siuai from the settlements of Europeans has permitted natives to be more selective in what they take over from the West. For example, many western traits reach Siuai only after profound reinterpretation by *native* carriers; and the distance from western markets has discouraged development of a new cash crop economy.

## CO-VARIABLE

It is also possible to offer partial "explanation" for certain specific culture traits by referring to other equally specific ones — quite apart from the more general explanations in structural terms. For example, the dependence upon taro and continuous gardening probably help to explain the general indifference to seasonality and to natural cyclical events such as weather changes. Also, the methods of pig-husbandry undoubtedly favor living in hamlets as against large stockaded villages, and add greatly to the labor of gardening by necessitating the construction of strong pig-proof garden fences.

Here are a few more partial "explanations." I suggest that the relative simplicity of most Siuai technology and the unimportance of esoteric knowledge have much to do with the lack of emphasis on age as a differentiating factor. Nor do subsistence techniques *require* large scale coördinated action, hence there is no *necessity* for large, highly organized work groups on this score. It also seems likely that women's work habits and the practices associated with confinement are responsible for some of the high death rates of mothers and infants, which, in turn, help to account for the intense ritualization of birth, infancy, and early childhood.

While in a speculating mood, we should not overlook the parts played by individual natives in inventing or actively disseminating new traits or trait combinations. I have indicated at several places throughout the text how receptive the Siuai have been to certain kinds of alien traits, and it is my impression that receptivity increases markedly if the new trait is introduced by a man of high rank. The very fact that Siuai culture differs in many respects from neighboring cultures implies inventiveness and distinctive reinterpretation on the part of past generations of Siuai natives, but there is also some concrete evidence of "inventions" having been made by recent individuals. For example, a native now living in Moronei is *credited* with discovery of the idea that certain demons can be attracted by whistling, and another one in Mokorino with invention of a larger size carrying-pouch for men.[2] Probably, more important in this connection has been the influence of certain individuals in adding *emphasis* to some activities. For example, I feel that the growing importance of the spirit-familiar type of magic technique is due in large measure to the personal influence of a few living mikai-magicians; and I am almost certain that the generally increasing preoccupation with competitive feasting in northeast Siuai has been brought about to an important degree through the activities of three or four individuals, notably Soŋi, the leader at Turuŋom. In fact, I believe it would be possible to account for wide segments of Siuai culture change in terms of the routes to social power chosen by certain individuals from among the several possibilities offered by the culture.[3]

We could continue with these conjectures, citing numerous examples to "explain" how Siuai culture came to be what it is, but it may be more useful to place them in a chronological sequence. Here, then, is my conception of the more important changes that have been taking place in Siuai culture in recent decades and of the principal factors behind these changes.

## HISTORICAL

I envisage the Siuai of 1850 as having consisted of a number of small scattered hamlets whose men and women worked continually and just about equally in their gardens. The slow progress involved in clearing land with stone adzes did not allow production beyond the subsistence level, nor did the staple crop, taro, permit the production of preservable surpluses. Moreover, the character of the native pig did not encourage natives to grow and "bank" vegetable surpluses by feeding them to the pigs. In other words, I picture an almost totally subsistence-type economy, where men worked at it as hard as women and where internal trade was narrowly limited by paucity of surpluses and, perhaps, by the restraints of feuding. There may have been some coastal trade with Alu and Mono islanders, but this cannot have been very lively inasmuch as the Siuai had few material surpluses to offer in exchange and inasmuch as the islanders did not to my knowledge offer a large market for slaves.

My picture of the society of those times is of a number of smaller endogamous areas, each one made up largely of two intermarrying matrilineages and characterized by more frequent matrilocality, land having been the most important form of wealth. I also envisage there having been a higher status for women, and a closer identity between political leadership and matrilineage seniority. In matters relating to the supernatural I surmise that there was more emphasis on growth and welfare magic and on relations with sib and matrilineage spirits.

Briefly, I suggest that in the middle of the past century Siuai culture resembled very closely the assemblage of thought and action patterns which I summarized in the last chapter under the heading of "Kinship Ideology." Now, it is interesting to note that my reconstruction bears many similarities to the present-day culture of the neighboring Nagovisi people, which I have described elsewhere;[4] and it is tempting to speculate that the marked differences between present-day Nagovisi and Siuai may have developed mainly as a consequence of Siuai's location and terrain. Being closer to the coast, Siuai has experienced more intense contact with alien influences; and having more level terrain, the Siuai have been better able than the Nagovisi to increase communications made possible by the outlawing of warfare and to take advantage of food production opportunities made possible by the introduction of metal tools.

To my mind, the first major changes in the way of life just pictured came about as the result of the introduction of metal axes and adzes, which probably began to reach this area about 1870. The immediate effect of this innovation was to provide men with the means to speed up their end of garden work and allow them time for other activities. Meanwhile, the increasing world demand for copra prompted Mono and Alu islanders to set up trading settlements along the Siuai coast; and some Siuai males, relieved of continuous preoccupation with subsistence work, turned to active trade with the islanders, exchanging copra and weapons for iron and shell money. In this manner shell necklaces assumed importance as currency whereas formerly they had served mainly as decoration and matrilineage heirlooms.

Another major innovation was the introduction of European pigs, brought home by some of the first Siuai natives to work on plantations owned by whites. Noting how these new pigs responded to increased feeding, the Siuai used their metal axes and adzes to expand their gardens and fed the surpluses to their pigs, which were then used to increase feasting, trading, and probably fighting. Pigs and shell currency assumed greater importance as wealth, partly replacing land; and as men were the active economic agents in this new form of wealth acquisition and ownership, patrilocality also increased, and women, whose gardening tools remained unchanged, spent relatively longer hours in their gardens.

Later on, the Administration's prohibition of warfare and interisland trade served to widen and increase internal trade and to place more emphasis on feasting, which became a substitute for fighting. This culminated in the present institution of social-climbing and its wide ramifications, and accompanying these developments were a widening of endogamous areas, an increase in virilocality, and speedier matrilineage fission. All this, aided by Mission and Administration ideologies which tend, respectively, to devalue sib incest taboos and matriliny, has served to undermine the beliefs and practices associated with sib affiliation. Club-house demons and black magic tend to replace sib kupunas and growth magic as religious preoccupations.

While the values associated with kinship and warfare have been undergoing partial supplementation and supplantation by those of the modern institution of rank, some individuals have made attempts to acquire social power by entirely alien means, for example, by acquiring authority statuses in the Mission and Administration hierarchies, or by trying to deflate native currency in relation to the Australian money they earned on plantations. Thus it was that power-hungry men like Kummai,[5] Poroni,[6] and U'ta,[7] unable to acquire high places in the native *rank* hierarchy, have sought power in competing kinds of hierarchies. Also, the history of the Methodist mission in northeast Siuai can only be understood in these terms. It gained a foothold not because of recognized moral superiority over native or previously established Catholic institutions, but because it gave certain ambitious natives opportunities to gain superior statuses denied them in other social systems. Despite these competing alien ideologies, however, the ideology associated with the rank system appeared to be gaining ground in 1939.

## PSYCHOLOGICAL

To what extent can we explain adult Siuai behavior by socialization processes?

There is probably no branch of cultural anthropology now being enriched with so many theoretical inventions as is the study of culture and personality, including research on "national character." And it is with deep regret that I have to recognize the limitations of my Siuai data in this respect. However, it is best to be candid: when I went to Bougainville I was not interested in this relatively new field of research and I did not focus observation and inquiry in this direction — for example, I conducted no psychological tests, made no systematic observations of socialization processes, and probed only superficially into individual life histories. Now, years later, after having read the standard works in this field, I believe I can discern some suggestive causal relationships between adult behavior and what little I saw of socialization processes, but, knowing how faulty memory can be, I do not feel justified in indulging in this kind of retroactive insight. Also, there is a certain aesthetic consideration involved. I find myself now and then annoyed by the practice of some ethnographers to punctuate their descriptions with tautological "psychological" explanations based, not on the use of special techniques of inquiry but merely on rephrasing of sociological generalizations already made. For example I feel that it is not only redundant but somewhat affrontive to the reader to elaborate such an obvious conclusion as, say, that the continuing viability of the modern Siuai institution of rank is to be partly explained by the following aspects of socialization: use of *verbal* rewards and punishments; emphasis on achievement rather than on age grading and formal initiation rites; lack of physically competitive games; use of cultural instruments for aggression in place of direct physical combat; absence of strong authority statuses in household and matrilineage organization. Surely, there is no necessity for the ethnographer to point out explicitly the rather obvious connections between these factors and, for example, the cultural emphasis on *verbal* manifestations of *renown* and *shame*, and on the expression of rivalry in competitive feasting and sorcery rather than in direct contests of physical strength. On the other hand, because of my failure to probe deeper into the histories and psychologies of individuals I cannot explain even to my own satisfaction why some individuals utilize the instruments provided by their culture to rise to positions of leadership, while others are content to follow.

CHAPTER 17

# *Evaluation*[1]

There are at least three "general" points of view from which to evaluate any culture: (1) the continuity of the society (or societies) constituted by the persons bearing the culture; (2) the satisfaction of the needs of the persons bearing the culture;[2] and (3) the utilization of the potentialities of the persons bearing the culture.

There are also several special points of view from which to evaluate a culture: for example, the One-World protagonist would wish to learn the extent to which various cultures contain premises that perpetuate inter-societal conflict; and the political strategist would wish to learn the degree to which certain cultures contain goals and organizational norms that promote wars of conquest. Both of these approaches to evaluation are legitimate and in fact highly essential in the world of today, but they will be left for analysts having these special objectives.

## *SOCIETAL CONTINUITY*

This topic can be put in the form of a question: How effectively and efficiently does the culture, viewed as an instrument, ensure the continuity of the comprehensive social structure interrelating the persons bearing the culture?

We can address ourselves to this question without agreeing with the premise, apparently held by some writers concerned with this matter, that the continuity of this or that social system is necessarily a "good thing." In fact, it can probably be shown that many societies are structured in such a manner that, from the standpoint of, say, the satisfaction of individual needs, they are grossly deficient and requiring of change.

Many social scientists have concerned themselves with listing the necessities for societal continuity, but the most comprehensive and systematic statement I have seen on this matter is the one titled "The Functional Prerequisites of a Society";[3] the criteria set forth in this paper form the basis for the present evaluation. Before proceeding with this evaluation it behooves us to bring our own definition of *society* into line with that given by the authors, namely, "A society is a group [4] of human beings sharing a self-sufficient system of action which is capable of existing longer than the life span of an individual, the group being recruited at least in part by the sexual reproduction of its members." [5] The authors are careful to distinguish between "society" and "culture," and between "society" and the individuals who participate in it.[6] By "system of action" they refer to the Parsonian theory of action,[7] and they exemplify "self-sufficient" in the following terms: ". . . the United States is a society. While imports and exports are necessary to its maintenance, arrangements for foreign trade are part of its self-sufficient structure of action. It is this, and not the group of individuals, that is self-sufficient." ". . . A group of American Indians governed by the United States for a sufficient length of time may lack the crucial structures necessary for continued existence as an independent entity and therefore be considered part of American society, in spite of an important cultural variation. An American town does not constitute a society because of its thorough participation in American political, economic, value, and other structures." [8]

The authors then go on to list the four conditions terminating the existence of a society as:

"The biological extinction or dispersion of the members."

"Apathy of the members. — Apathy means the cessation of individual motivation."

"The war of all against all."

"The absorption of the society into another society." [9]

We shall take as our "society" the most extensive unit possible, that is, the three Administrative Districts whose outer boundaries coincide almost exactly with those of the Motuna language and the other characteristics of Siuai culture described in this book. As we have seen, kinship, trade, and socio-political ties bind these Districts together into a fairly compact social unit. And although this "society" is continually changing and will eventually become a different "society" from what it is today, this change is now proceeding at a relatively slow rate.[10] Even so, contemporary Siuai "society" cannot be considered a "whole" society, since the use of physical coercion as a control measure now rests ultimately in white officials' hands, and this has the effect of making Siuai "society" a part of the larger society of New Guinea — or, for that matter, of world society, in view of its inclusion in the League of Nations and the British Commonwealth. Nevertheless, Siuai "society" remains more or less autonomous in a number of important respects, so that I believe we are justified in evaluating it according to the criteria formulated by Aberle *et al.*

Here then is a brief evaluation of Siuai culture in terms of the above author's nine "functional prerequisites" of a society. According to the logic employed in formulating this scheme, "The performance of a given function is prerequisite to a society if in its absence one or more of the four conditions dissolving a society results."[11]

1. "Provision for adequate relationship to the environment and for sexual recruitment. — This includes modes of adapting to, manipulating, and altering the environment in such a way as (a) to maintain a sufficient number and kind of members of the society at an adequate level of functioning; (b) to deal with the existence of other societies in a manner which permits the persistence of the system of action; and (c) to pattern heterosexual relationships to insure opportunities and motivation for a sufficient rate of reproduction."[12]

Let us consider these points in the order listed.

There can be no doubt as to the instrumental effectiveness of Siuai culture with respect to Point 1 (a).[13] In the first place there is no evidence of any significant change in the numbers, ages, or sex ratios having taken place during the last two decades. The temporary absences of youths, attending mission schools or working on plantations, results in some disturbances in relationships and some reapportionment of work loads, but probably does not seriously affect the birth rate or the total production of subsistence items. Moreover, writing as of 1939, there are no visible signs of increase in such absences or in emigration. Almost without exception Siuai youths hurry home after work or training abroad. Also, the physical resources of Southern Bougainville are so extensive, natural cataclysms are so improbable, and the technology, though crude, is so generally well adapted, that there is no apparent danger of a lessening food supply in the future. The only conceivable threat to the population is in the form of a plant-destroying pest or an epidemic introduced from outside.[14]

Siuai "society" is of course no longer able to deal with outsiders in a manner that would ensure its own continuity. On the other hand there is no evidence to suggest that there will be any serious decline in the birth rate.

2. "Role differentiation and role assignment." This criterion is put in the form of two questions: How explicitly are *roles* differentiated and assigned, thereby avoiding indecision concerning who *does* what? and How explicitly is *property* allocated, thereby avoiding conflict concerning who *gets* what?[15]

In connection with subsistence activities and with the performance of other obligations arising from kinship I have the impression that roles are well enough defined and assigned so that necessary things get done without undue duplication of effort and without waste of time through indecision. Moreover, these things are accomplished by means of a method of role allocation which lacks the rigidity of some other Oceanic cultures.

When we turn to larger-scale coöperative activities the impression is not so favorable. Anyone who has watched coastal Melanesian-speakers conduct fish drives or ceremonies would probably conclude, as I do, that the Siuai are exceedingly uncoördinated. In such enterprises as club-house construction and gong-carrying they waste prodigious amounts of time and effort through indecision, duplication, querulous complaints, and lack of effective direction.

The Siuai display a picayune concern about property rights and in most of their transactions they are inclined to pettifogging. Along with all this there are wide areas of ambiguous allocation, with the result that much time is consumed and many hostilities aroused in quarrels over conflicting claims.

3. "Communication." ("No society, however simple, can exist without shared, learned symbolic modes of communication . . .")[16]

Motuna is not split into dialects; there are a few local lexical variations from place to place but even these are well understood, and joked about. Also, Motuna appears to be a perfectly adequate medium for comprehensible face-to-face communication. At least, I found no evidence of serious misunderstandings which could be blamed directly on the language — that is, I recorded no *public* quarrels or litigations based on mistaken meanings. But my evidence has only limited value since I was not privy to most of the kinds of conversation where such misunderstandings are more likely to occur.

Beyond having this oral, face-to-face communication, however, the Siuai are strictly limited. Gongs serve certain signaling purposes, and a few mission-trained natives exchange laboriously penned letters as a stunt; otherwise, indirect communication leaves much to be desired. The so-called "coconut-wireless" is anything but trustworthy. I have known natives to miss appointments by days, to assemble for wholly imaginary visits by officials, and to break off old friendships on the basis of misreported hearsay.

4. "Shared cognitive orientations." In this respect Siuai culture is an effective instrument. It provides the natives with enough common knowledge to adapt satisfactorily to their environment, and with enough common definitions "to make stable, meaningful, and predictable [most of] the social situations in which they are engaged."[17] Of course, as Aberle and his associates point out, in any society the unexpected happens, and Siuai is no exception. Here, however, there are innumerable ready-made explanations for understanding, and devices for dealing with, such occurrences, with the result that the Siuai are a long way removed from the common picture of the frightened savage trembling on the threshold of the unknown. Anxieties are aroused not by what they cannot explain but rather by what they believe to be the intentions and powers of *known* adversaries.

5. "A shared, articulated set of goals." In Chapter 15, "Integration," were listed the principal goals associated with each of the ideological systems, and the opinion was voiced that all Siuai natives are alike in seeking after the goals associated with kinship. We have also seen how many adult males are alike in striving for power and influence — expressed mainly in terms of rank in the native socio-political system, but with alternatives provided by opportunities for status-achieving in the Administration and Mission hierarchies. On the surface these goals would not appear to be incompatible, but when

one examines the thought and action patterns associated with achieving them they are seen to involve serious inconsistencies and incompatibilities, leading to many instances of inter-personal and role conflict — but not so serious as to result in a quick restructuring of Siuai society.

6. "The normative regulation of means." The Siuai agree with near unanimity on the means for attaining most goals. There are some local differences of opinion concerning the ethics of how to accumulate property for giving renown feasts, but these differences seem slight and unimportant when compared with the amount of agreement in this area of culture. Perhaps disagreement about means is most far-reaching and significant in the area of magic, and while this leads to much skepticism and experimenting, it does not appear to approach a condition of *anomie*.

7. "The regulation of affective expression." As the authors imply,[18] this criterion may be applied in the form of three questions:

First, to what extent does Siuai culture serve to regulate the expression of those emotions which must be suppressed if the society is to survive in its present form? In this respect Siuai occupies an extreme position. For example, incest taboos are strict and quite effective, rape is practically nonexistent, and anger is rarely allowed expression in physical violence, being tidily channeled into less destructive activities such as formal litigation, competitive gift-giving, and sorcery.

Second, how clear and communicable are the cues which permit mutually appropriate "responses in affectively charged situations"?[19] As previously noted, the Motuna language is rather deficient in this respect, and among men there is little manifestation of "emotion" by means of gestures. This does not, however, apply to women, nor to women vis-à-vis men. Moreover, by means of property transactions men manage to communicate their socially significant "emotions" to other men with entire comprehensibility.

Third, to what extent does Siuai culture serve to produce the affects appropriate to those relationships which contribute the central framework of Siuai society? In Siuai mutual affection between spouses is not as indispensable as it is, say, in the United States; nor is deference for the aged as essential for societal continuity as it is, for example, among the Murngin.[20] On the other hand, Siuai society in its present form depends heavily upon the maintenance of *avoidance* between certain relatives, of *amity* between co-wives and between siblings, and of *deference* towards men of higher rank. If mission influences were to increase substantially there would probably be some weakening of *avoidance*, especially between distant sib-mates. And if Administration policies became more acceptable native officials would undoubtedly capture some of the deference now shown to men of high rank. However, neither of these possible trends is gaining much momentum at present.

8. "Socialization." (How effectively does Siuai culture ensure that every individual will acquire "a working knowledge of the behavior and attitudes

relevant to his various roles" along with sufficient identity with those attitudes?)[21]

With respect to subsistence techniques and to norms referable to relationships within the family of orientation, the matrilineage, and the father's family of orientation, it is my impression that Siuai methods of socialization are quite effective, being indelibly inscribed during the infant's and child's long years of almost exclusive interaction with this narrow circle of relatives learning and doing "practical" things. Induction into married life and its consequent relationships is also moderately effective in those cases where the bride spends part of her betrothal period in her fiancé's household. In other cases, however, the transition to marriage appears to be inadequately prepared for, as witnessed by the instability of many such marriages. Nor does the culture provide for effective socialization with respect to behavior and attitudes relating to outer circles of kin. Adherence to such "utopian" ideals as affection and nonreciprocable giving towards *all* relatives remains a pious adage which is not very energetically pressed by training or by active measures of initiation.

Although there is little formal initiation for entry into men's society activities,[22] such as exists in many Oceanic societies, the gradual way in which boys begin to participate in these activities probably ensures as much if not more effective socialization for the roles they eventually play. Also, attention has been called to some other aspects of enculturation which help to prepare males for such roles; these include the use of *verbal* rewards and punishments, the emphasis on achievement, etc.[23] Yet, despite all this training, I retain the strong impression that few Siuai men are comfortably "at home" in the social milieu of interpersonal rivalry for renown. They plan and execute their campaigns in deadly earnest and with much skill and industry, but show little of the exuberance in direct social combat which marks comparable enterprise elsewhere. This may be due in some measure to the long childhood experience in the social setting consisting almost exclusively of a few close relatives, where physically competitive games are largely lacking and where protection against the wider world is almost complete.

9. "The effective control of disruptive forms of behavior."[24] Generally speaking, the Siuai manage to deal quite effectively with most disruptive violations of norms through public opinion alone, but public opinion is not adequate for all situations, and the fact that use of physical coercion is reserved for white officials means of course that Siuai society is no longer autonomous.

## SATISFACTION OF THE INDIVIDUAL'S NEEDS

At the outset it will be useful to restate the conventional distinction between *physiological* needs and all other needs and wants, including so-called psychological needs and more or less universal "situational" needs — i.e.,

## EVALUATION 479

needs engendered by the coexistence of the two sexes, the helplessness of infants and senile persons, etc. Of course it is not a simple matter to extricate physiological from other types of needs; consider, for example, the Siuai's need for land, which is intimately connected with their basic physiological need for food.

Land is primarily required for taro garden sites. Taro is the staple crop. The average annual consumption of an individual is 640 corms — a total of 950 pounds.[25]

Garden sites are laid out in plots (nopu) two spans wide by nine spans long (10 by 45 feet). In each plot is an average of 102 plants — a total of 151 pounds of edible taro. In other words, each typical household (comprising four members: the mode for Siuai) would require a minimum of .26 acre (11,250 square feet) annually planted in taro. I say "minimum" because pathways have to be left free inside garden fences along the borders of the plots, comprising about 15 per cent of the garden enclosure. This would bring the total required to .3 acre a year. But this figure must be further qualified. It will be remembered that land from which taro has been harvested is allowed to be idle for approximately 68 months; six years after the previous planting the family can return to the site and begin again. Their need for land, then, is 1.8 acres, or six times the annual area cultivated. The total need for taro garden land by all the persons in northeast Siuai (east and north of Mopiai River) would be about 450 acres (equals .7 square mile).[26]

Bananas and yams also are important food crops, but their production involves no need for land in addition to that required for taro; bananas are planted interspersed among taro plants, and yams and the like are trained along fence uprights.

Sweet potatoes, on the other hand, do require separate cultivations. They cannot be interspersed among taro plants; whole plots have to be given over to them. What's more, it would be foolhardy to plant sweet potatoes in taro enclosures, which frequently are in the vicinity of settlements. No ordinary fence could resist a hungry pig that smells sweet potatoes,[27] natives claim. Accordingly, potato gardens are located far away from settlements. Natives like to plant them in flood plain valleys. There, out of reach of domestic pigs, there is little danger from marauding; and if the gardener wishes to take the extra precaution of a fence, he has only to build on the landward side of a bend. Furthermore, the natives claim that the alluvial soil in flood plain valleys is better suited to the cultivation of sweet potatoes. The requirements of sweet potato cultivation, then, constitute a need for about 80 acres of a specific kind of land — a need, moreover, which is increasing.

The area of land needed for growing coconut palms is difficult to determine. During the course of the property inventory which I carried out for the whole of northeast Siuai, I recorded the number of palms. The average for each family was 22 palms; total for all northeast Siuai was about 5500 palms.[28] Had the older method of planting palms in a circle around the settlements persisted, there would be little more than academic interest in the area of land required. But latterly this method is being superseded by grove planting with adequate spacing between palms. Moreover, there is a very noticeable tendency to increase the number of palms,[29] so much so that coconut plantations will probably become important factors in land use. At the present, any attempt to describe precisely the amount of land required for groves, made on the basis of number of palms recorded, would inject a semblance of accuracy which the data do not warrant. One can merely estimate such an area; this I did, basing my estimate on grove area mapped precisely in two sample village regions, from which it could be reckoned that roughly thirteen acres are required to support the present stand of palms in northeast Siuai.

Land is also needed for growing sago and areca nut palms and for canarium almond trees, but the strictures applying to estimating size of area required for coconut palms apply even more so here. Sago palms grow in marshy terrain which is unsuited for ordinary crops. I recorded an average of 15 palms per family — which would bring the total to around 3750 palms for northeast Siuai. According to a very rough estimate, only about eight acres would be required to maintain the present stand of sago palms in this area.

Canarium almond trees grow scattered about the whole region — sometimes in gardens, sometimes on the edge of virgin forest. There is no attempt made to concentrate them in one place, nor to set aside from gardening those spots where they grow, so there is no way of estimating the area required for them.[30]

One very obvious need for land is for places on which to erect *village* dwellings. That in itself is not a very extensive need in Siuai because of the disposition of houses — in Turuŋom village 16 dwellings accommodating 65 persons are crowded together in an area 400 by 100 feet.

But when we consider *hamlet* dwellings there enters a complicating factor. As described above, the natives have been prevailed upon to consolidate — for part of the time, at least — into line villages, yet maintain their older settlements, small hamlets, off by themselves. Unquestionably, pig-raising has something to do with this. Natives claim that it is impossible to keep pigs domesticated if one lives in a line village all the time. Small pigs in particular have to be tenderly cared for; this cannot be done at the line dwellings, since according to Administration sanitation regulations pigs are not allowed inside the village fence. Then, too, natives insist that there must be a range of uncultivated land around the hamlet house so that pigs can forage there and not be tempted to run wild in search of food.

In addition to the prepared food pigs are fed, the animals are everlastingly foraging, and probably secure the larger proportion of their food in this way. Translated into spatial needs, this means that a certain amount of land is required — even if not consciously set aside — for pig forage. The reality of this need becomes clear when one speculates about what would happen if there were no forage land available near the dwellings. In that case natives would have to augment their garden lands in order to provide enough food for pigs; moreover, they would probably have to strengthen their garden fences or pen up the pigs altogether.

Thus, although one cannot state how much land is required for pig-foraging, it is a factor which must be reckoned with when considering need for land.

In many cultures needs for such estovers as firewood, building materials, and thatching materials require that tracts of land be set aside. That is not the case to any great extent in Siuai. Firewood and building timbers are obtained from gardens, and thatch from sago palms. Only rattan, and similar materials required for fastenings, has to be obtained from regions of primary or secondary growth.

Finally, there is the need for hunting and fishing territory. There are only very indirect clues to the kind and amount of land and water areas needed. Virgin forest is certainly the main reservoir for wild pig and opossum; very rarely does a wild animal wander near settlements or gardens. One hunting expedition which I observed spent two days and nights in the forest north of Mokorino village. It covered, roughly, a three-square-mile area, drained it of animals, they said, and brought back a bag of 48 opossums. According to my records of food consumption, an average household would eat 48 opossums in 18 months. That is the nearest indication of hunting land requirements that I can give, and even such a rough indication as this would be completely vitiated by such considerations as: How long would it take the land to become restocked? How many opossums are consumed at feasts?, etc. Complications of much the same sort invalidate any attempt to determine the amount of stream areas required to fulfill fishing and prawn-collecting needs. These problems are mentioned because it is believed that they are of importance for a discussion of the economic aspects of land use; the lack of precision of my own data constitutes a gap, but not so serious a gap as it would be were the Siuai more dependent upon hunting and fishing for their food supply.

In addition to the more basic economic needs for land, there are certain other socially conditioned wants not directly connected with the physical maintenance of life. I know of no method to estimate the extent of these wants; I can only guess that they nearly always exceed available land resources.

One of these wants is best defined as a desire for "elbow room." It is exemplified by the jealousy with which natives guard the privacy of their hamlets. Of necessity village houses have to be crowded closely together. Not so with hamlet houses, which stand isolated in woods, or at most in sight of a few houses of relatives. Most natives are willing to put up with the press of villages provided they can retire now and then to their hamlet houses.

Any person setting out to change Siuai land use would have to reckon with this desire for privacy which is translated into a "want" for land.

We have already seen that the Siuai place little or no value on taro for purposes of display, such as is the case with *taytu* in the Trobriands.[31] As a matter of fact, most Siuai take pride in their ability to estimate their immediate consumption needs, and to produce just enough taro to satisfy them. Nevertheless, consumption needs vary considerably: there is a lot of difference between the amount of taro consumed by an ordinary man with his one or two pigs, and an ambitious feast-giver with his larger herd. The latter has to cultivate more and more land in order to feed his increasing number of pigs and to provide vegetable food for distribution among guests at his feasts.[32]

The want for more and more arable land, growing out of the desire for bigger and better feasts, is certainly far removed from the economic needs described earlier. Nevertheless, that want is quite concrete and was in fact inferred by observing feast-givers augment their garden territories.

Sometimes, a want can become as important a cultural factor as a basic physiological need. "Lots of land" has become a symbol of political ascendancy. The want to increase landholdings goes far beyond needing and wanting land on which to grow taro. Land aggrandizement goes hand in hand with a desire for renown; in fact "acquiring land" and "winning prestige" are often used as metaphoric equivalents. It is mainly this desire for land-prestige which leads many natives to continue to make nori-purchases of land long after they have acquired sufficient for even the maximum requirements of gardening.

What is the relationship between needs and wants for land, on the one hand, and available territorial resources? To what extent is there a "population problem" among natives residing in northeast Siuai?

With respect to wants for land as an equivalent of prestige, one might probably answer in the tradition of economic theory, and state that there is not and never could be enough land. And in support of this observation one could point to the frequency and bitterness of land litigations, and to the social-climbing activities which characterize so much of Siuai's behavior. Yet, if that theory is accepted how can there be explained the cases of some individuals who consistently act out their claims that they wish no more land than is required for food-production? Use the easy way out and call them "deviants"? Or resort to guessing and say that they express another side of native character? The question will have to be left open since there is no way of measuring the wants of the avaricious social-climber, nor of testing the sincerity of the complacent "deviants."

Turning to the more concrete *needs* for land for specific nutrition and residential requirements, the problem becomes soluble. There is certainly enough land to fulfill all those requirements of the whole population. The map (Figure 27) illustrates that.

## EVALUATION 483

Even allowing for such limitations to land-use as swamps (sago will grow there), stream gullies and hillsides (sweet potatoes will grow there), *setting-aside* of land after death (generally only a temporary withdrawal), the designation of land as sacred places, etc., it is quite evident that land is plentiful.

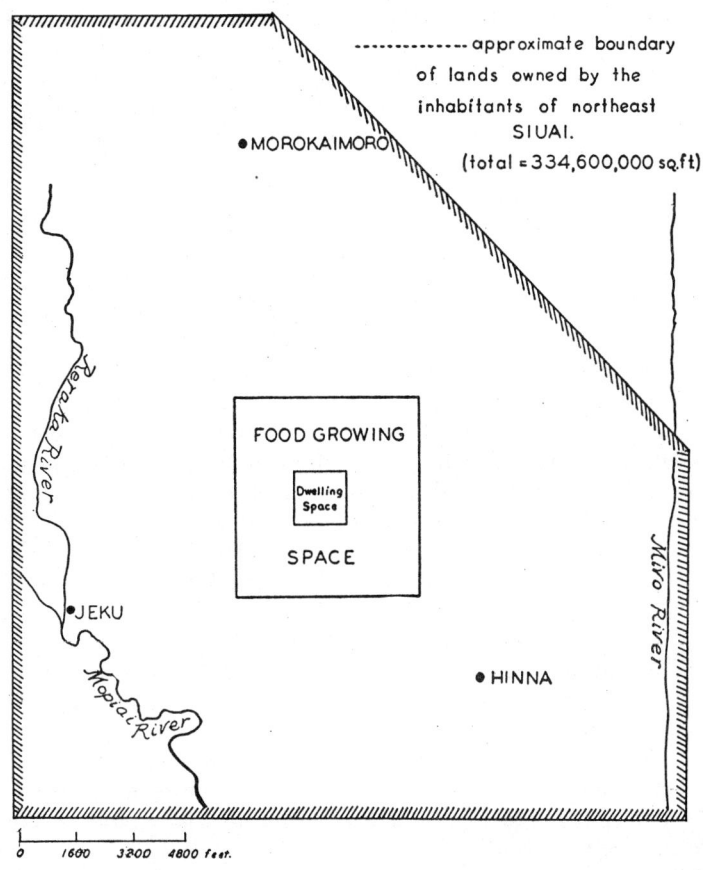

FIGURE 27

Also even where we make liberal allowances for additional, less well-defined needs and wants for pig forage, "elbow room," garden space for feast-givers, etc., there appears to be no land shortage in northeast Siuai: such at least is the case if we consider total population needs against a background of all the land — undifferentiated into separately owned tracts.

But what if we refer to another kind of map, one on which tenure boundaries have been drawn and each tract referred to its full or *residual* owners? Does everyone still own enough land to satisfy concrete needs? Most natives do. There are of course inequalities in distribution but few natives are entirely landless. Somewhere in the area there will be tracts toward which he can assert full or residual ownership claims. But even if he lives far away from his own tracts, he can always garden on land belonging more specifically to nearby relatives and other neighbors. In fact, the ease of access to others' land, coupled with the desire of most Siuai to garden near their dwellings even if this involves gardening on others' land, is demonstrated by the circumstance, which has already been reported, that two out of five households garden on land in which they do not possess full or residual title.[33]

To summarize, there is enough land to go around to satisfy all physiological food needs as well as most other kinds of land-based needs and wants — except the wants of the more avaricious.

In connection with the latter, Siuai is like all other cultures in the sense that its bearers' wants will inevitably outrun available resources. By using ethnographic data from several societies it should be possible to compare the degree to which various cultures provide satisfaction for their respective populations' definable wants. In such a study it would probably be found that in *achieving* societies like Siuai the gaps between certain kinds of wants and their satisfactions are wider than in societies where more roles are *assigned*. However, since this is not a comparative study I shall leave that exercise to others and go on to note the *degree* to which Siuai culture aids or retards the satisfaction of its bearers' *basic physiological needs*;[34] the *manner* in which the culture does or does not satisfy its bearers' physiological needs has already been spelled out in detail.

*Food.* Returning again to the problem of the need for food to sustain life, it can be said that Siuai culture serves instrumentally to ensure physical survival of its bearers, although from the point of view of the nutritional standards defined by modern dietary science, the food habits of the Siuai leave much to be desired. There is reason to believe that many of the diseases which sap the energies and shorten the lives of these natives are at least exacerbated by dietary deficiencies.[35]

*Water.* There is a plentiful and easily available supply of water for drinking purposes, and there are no cultural patterns that inhibit the necessary consumption of water.

*Air.* I have no conclusive evidence on this subject, but it may well be that the smoke-saturated interiors of their houses, in which the Siuai sleep every night, contribute to the high incidence of respiratory diseases among them.

*Evacuation.* The conventions which surround urination and defecation are only mildly inhibitory.

*Avoidance of extreme heat and cold.* While no Siuai burns to death,[36] the practice of working in the midday sun without adequate protection does lead

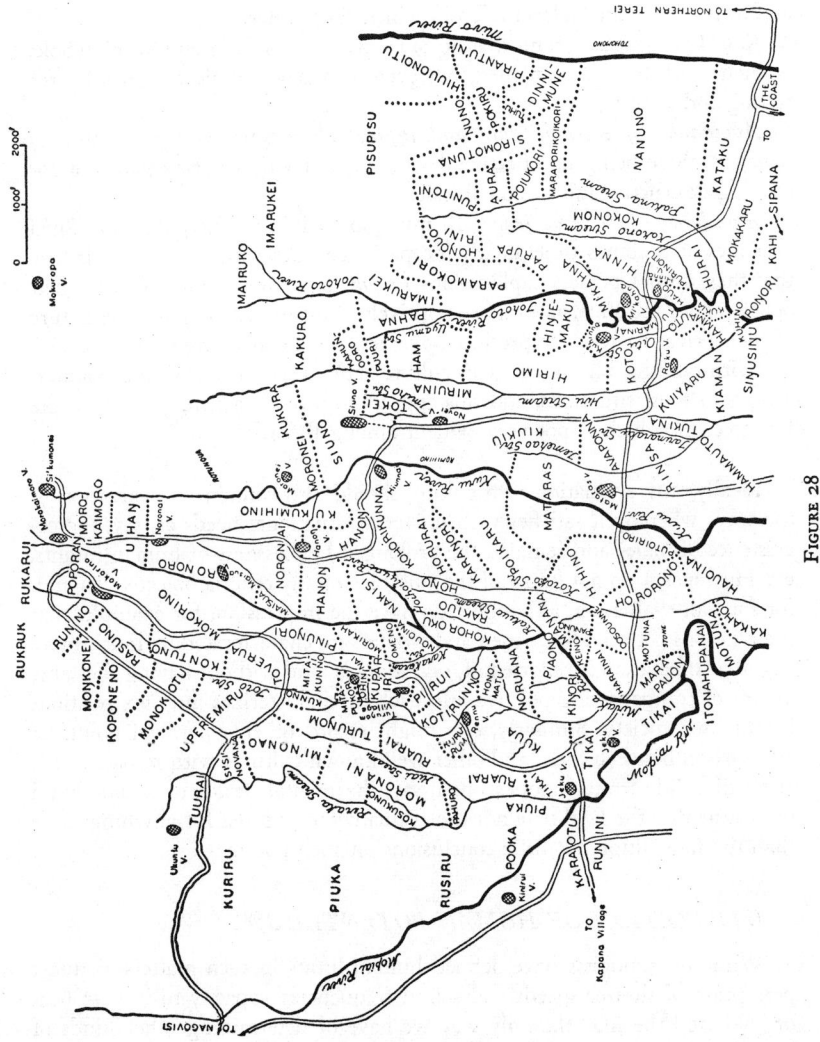

FIGURE 28

to occasional sunstroke and sore skins. No one freezes to death, either, but drafty pile-dwellings, damp clothing, and inadequate protection from chilling rains probably contribute to the high incidence of respiratory diseases and to the frequent malaria relapses which they suffer.

*Rest.* I am just as certain that no Siuai ever dies of fatigue! On the whole, women work harder than men, but even they have ample opportunity for resting and sleeping.

*Avoidance of extreme pain and injury.* Here Siuai culture is entirely deficient, there being no effective devices for relieving extreme pain nor for treating destructive injuries or illnesses.

*Avoidance of extreme fear.*[37] In my opinion it is unlikely that any Siuai ever dies or becomes functionally incapacitated on account of fear. It is true that they do not possess explanations for *all* happenings, and some of their beliefs about the supernatural are positively fear-productive. Also, the nature of men's rivalries tends to produce anxieties, and the men are great brooders. Notwithstanding all these, their culture empowers them to take counteractions in most situations, and this appears to provide a defensive substitute for stoicism, which is not very evident among them.[38]

Ideally, any evaluation of a culture should also contain an evaluation of the ways whereby it satisfies such universal situational needs as, say, the coexistence of males and females, the prolonged helplessness of human infants, etc. However, I do not know of the existence of any criteria objective enough for such an evaluation, although I do have the impression, for example, that the relations between Siuai men and women are characterized by much more negative affect than is reported of, say, Manu'a, and without having the same degree of compensating positive affect which characterizes inter-sex relations in our own society. Similarly, one might record other superficial points of comparison between Siuai and other well-known cultures with respect to the effect of child-care techniques upon, say, the mental health of adults, but I possess neither the field data nor the evaluative techniques for anything more than the most impressionistic conclusions on such points.

## UTILIZATION OF HUMAN POTENTIALS [39]

While physiologists have defined human limits in such matters as direct perception of shutter speeds and sound frequencies, capacity to survive heat or cold, and the like, the only way we have of determining other kinds of human potentialities is by pointing to the great historical achievements in the fields of pure and applied science, social relations, aesthetics, etc. Obviously, though, the individuals credited with these achievements have possessed enormous initial advantages over, say, the Siuai gardener or song composer, through membership in societies whose cultures were (or are) immensely more highly developed than Siuai is in most of these fields. But

# EVALUATION

Siuai culture has developed almost wholly isolated from the major centers of post-neolithic civilizations, and short of making a wide comparative study — which I am not prepared to do — it would be unfair and rather pointless to try and evaluate Siuai achievements in all these fields. There are however some more equitable and relevant general criteria [40] which may be applied to Siuai culture and which come within the scope of this limited inquiry. These may be put in the form of questions.

First of all, to what extent does Siuai culture serve to free its bearers from such noncreative, time- and energy-consuming things as subsistence activities, physical and mental disabilities, social tensions and conflicts?

Secondly, to what extent does Siuai culture promote interpersonal communication?

Answers to these questions have already been given, implicitly, throughout the text, and there is not much point in extending this account further by reviewing all of these answers here. However, there is one more question which relates to one of the most important problems of our times and which deserves more explicit restatement:

To what extent does Siuai culture promote realization of the supreme worth and complete moral responsibility of each individual? [41]

The most fruitful way I know of to formulate an answer to this question is to apply the seven criteria suggested by Gorer,[42] who states in the form of hypotheses that "The concept of the supreme worth and moral responsibility of the individual is positively correlated with":

1. "The cultural phrasing of social goals (success) as attainable by the great majority of the population."

2. "The higher proportion of socially eligible people who participate" in [the] responsibility of "controlling the counter-social behavior of people in the society and of planning for the prosperity of the total society or portions of it."

3. The number of achieved [as against ascribed] statuses.

4. The degree to which social rights and duties are not separated.

5. "The extent to which women and children are given socially significant, responsible, and esteemed roles in the life of the community."

6. Lack of "contrasts in accessibility of property"; and, finally,

7. "The accessibility of knowledge considered socially significant."

I shall close this account by inviting the reader to decide for himself how well Siuai culture meets the tests implied by these hypotheses.[43]

488  A SOLOMON ISLAND SOCIETY

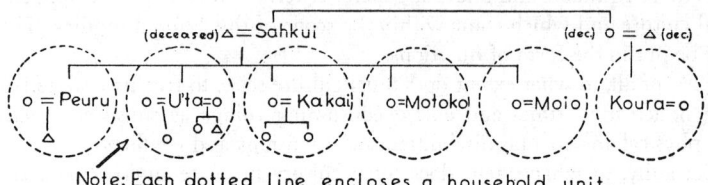

Note: Each dotted line encloses a household unit.

Figure 29

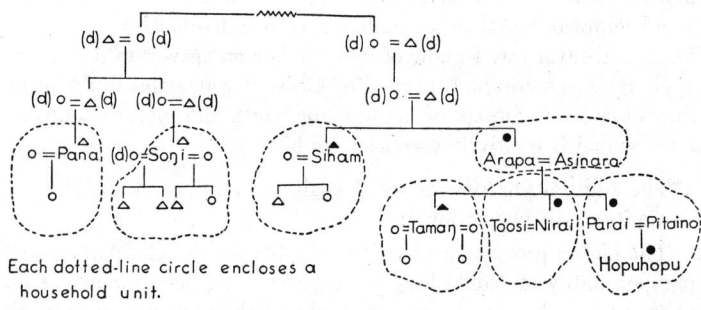

Each dotted-line circle encloses a household unit.

Figure 30

# NOTES

# NOTES

## Introduction

1. *Siuai* is usually written "Siwai" on maps, etc., and native pronunciation of the middle phoneme varies between the vowel *u*, the semi-vowel *w*, and the bilabial spirantal stop *v*. I use the form *Siuai* because it is the most common one spoken in northeast Siuai, where I did most of my work.

2. The present tense will be used throughout this account to refer to the period of field work, 1938–39. Since then, southern Bougainville has been the scene of long military occupation and fierce fighting. What if anything remains of the Siuai culture I am here describing, I do not know.

3. I suspect that one reason why so little progress has been made in the comparative study of the political institutions of nonliterate peoples lies in the lack of some generally acceptable set of definitions such as those now applicable to the study of kinship and religion. The simplest and most useful terminology I have seen, and the one adopted in the writing of this book, is that developed by Robert Bierstedt ("An Analysis of Social Power," *American Sociological Review*, vol. 15, no. 6, Dec. 1950). This author proposes the following definitions:

*Force*: the application of sanctions.

*Sanctions*: the limitation of alternatives to social action.

*Power*: the predisposition or prior capacity which makes the application of force possible; i.e., latent force.

*Authority*: institutionalized power.

*Prestige*: "Knowledge, skill, competence, ability, and eminence — all these are components of, sources of, or synonymous of prestige, but they may be quite unaccompanied by power."

*Influence*: is persuasive; power is coercive.

*Dominance*: is a psychological concept; power a sociological one. Power appears in the statuses which people occupy; dominance is a function of personality or of temperament.

4. Not "fifty," as was erroneously reported in my "Studies in the Anthropology of Bougainville, Solomon Islands," *Papers of the Peabody Museum of American Archaeology and Ethnology*, vol. 29, no. 1 (Cambridge, Mass., 1949).

5. I do, however, plan to publish grammatical notes on what I have collected.

## Chapter 1

1. H. S. Ladd, "Geology of Vitilevu, Fiji," Bernice P. Bishop Museum *Bulletin 119* (Honolulu, 1934), p. 51.

2. The word *Buin* is also applied to the Terei natives and their territory (see Figure 1, page 4) by many whites, but throughout this account it will be used in the sense indicated above.

3. Also shown on the map in fig. 2 are Baitsi, an area of mixed *Motuna* and *Sibbe* speech, and *Piva*, a strongly Papuanized dialect of *Banoni*. The southern part of this map is fairly accurate but further exploration will probably require that major changes be made in the interior northern and eastern parts.

4. Beatrice Blackwood, *Both Sides of Buka Passage* (Oxford, 1935).

5. See works by Richard and Hilde Thurnwald. My article on "The Peabody Museum Expedition to Bougainville, Solomon Islands, 1938–39," *Papers of the Peabody Museum of American Archaeology and Ethnology*, vol. 29, no. 1, contains an anthropological bibliography of the Island.

6. On Bougainville we made measurements and morphological observations on some 2000 males, representing nearly every language area.

7. I am indebted to the Reverend J. B. Poncelet of the Marist Mission for nearly all identifications of Bougainville fauna.

8. High temperature extremes were recorded during April and May, when the temperature rose to 96 degrees Fahrenheit on several midafternoons. The lowest reading we recorded was 64 degrees at 5 A.M. during October.

9. The rainfall in Siuai is probably not greatly different from that of Kieta, where the annual average precipitation recorded for twelve years was 133.87 inches. We had no rain gauge in Siuai, but noted that the heaviest continuous rainfall occurred during September and October; at one period there was a downpour which lasted for thirteen days except for a few half-hour letups.

10. Former Administration officials used the estimated age of fourteen as the threshold between "childhood" and "adulthood," hence I use it here for purposes of comparison. In many cases I was able to arrive at the true ages of young people by reference to datable events in the past, but I may have erred in several other cases so that this breakdown may not be entirely reliable.

11. For two line villages this interval was 22 months, for all the rest it was about 12 months.

12. That is, distinguishable by western criteria; for distinctions made by the Siuai, see Chap. 2.

13. That is, 25 years prior to the period of field work (1938–1940). See n. 2 of the *Introduction*, p. 491.

14. Carl Ribbe. *Zwei Jahre unter den Kannibalen der Salomoinseln* (Dresden-Blasewitz, 1903). Henry B. Guppy, *The Solomon Islands and Their Natives* (London, 1887). R. Parkenson, *Dreissig Jahre in der Südsee* (Stuttgart, 1907).

15. Mission membership also has some effect on grooming habits. See p. 315.

16. The *Motuna* word for Choiseul Island, where these bracelets are said to have been made.

17. Said to be obtained from the south.

18. Burning used to be the main technique, whereas scarification by cutting is said to have been popularized by men returned from working on plantations.

19. It may be that taro stalks could be planted closer together; I do not know what effect, if any, this might have on growth. The Siuai offered no rationalization for the conventional spacing.

20. I listed over fifty, distinguished according to size, color, flavor, texture, etc.

21. Northeast Siuai contains about twenty-two palms per nuclear family.

22. For a more detailed account of foods eaten by natives in South Bougainville and adjacent islands, see H. B. Guppy, *The Solomon Islands and Their Natives*.

23. *Sinu* ("wild" sago) differs from the sago ordinarily used, in having a more fibrous pith which is so rough to handle that natives tread out its starch with their feet.

24. *Mijo* salt is produced from the ashes of the base of branches of the sago palm,

choice *moŋke* salt from burnt coconut hulls or the inner bark of the areca palm, a third kind of salt from the woodier parts of the *hoŋona* vine.

*Chapter 2*

1. The reader should bear in mind that the materials in this chapter relate to *indigenous* beliefs. Many Siuai also hold beliefs which are derived from such alien sources as missionaries and administrative officials; these will be described in later chapters. Of course, not all the assumptions and beliefs described in this chapter are peculiar to the Siuai, but it is unlikely that the totality of them could be matched in any other culture.

2. B. L. Whorf, "The Relation of Habitual Thought and Behavior to Language," *Language, Culture, and Personality* (Menasha, Wis., 1941), p. 75.

3. See p. xxi.

4. Myths undoubtedly have several "functions" in any society, as numerous anthropologists like to point out; and some of these will be touched upon in due course. At present, however, I am concerned only with reproducing them as documentation for the way Siuai natives look upon their universe.

5. *Kupuna* is the singular form of this word, *kupunaŋarum* the plural; however, for the convenience of the reader I have Anglicized the plurals of this and of other native words when it becomes necessary to use them in this book.

6. The Siuai do not speculate about the universe prior to this era of creation and discovery. In fact, they appear to have little curiosity about such remote matters. The creation myths contain many suggestions, explicit and implicit, about that primeval landscape but these fragments do not piece together into a comprehensive picture. Rather than list these fragments here, out of context, it seems preferable to reproduce them within the bodies of the myths, where they actually occur in the telling.

7. The word *kupuna* may possibly be etymologically linked with the one for stone, *kupuri*.

8. See especially G. C. Wheeler, *Mono-Alu Folklore* (London, 1926).

9. See p. 74.

10. It does however have significance when viewed as an aspect of culture change, i.e., the readiness of the Siuai to invent and accept new ideas, etc.

11. See p. 52.

12. There is no literal translation for *Hoŋing*.

13. Natives give this as explanation for the fact that most trees growing along the south Bougainville coast grow bent toward the west — the real cause being the continuous blowing of the southeast trades during many months of the year.

14. See p. 8.

15. The Siuai are not troubled by the inconsistency, i.e., that it was Maker and not Food-maker who originated cultivated food plants.

16. Natives do not collect this food to eat — it is too sacred (*mikisa*) for direct eating; but if their own gardens are not producing satisfactorily they occasionally attempt to encourage growth by obtaining a plant or two from the place Siuai for replanting in their own gardens. Also, the place Siuai is a hunter's paradise; there are many opossums there, also put there by Maker.

17. Wheeler, *Mono-Alu Folklore*.

18. See p. 29.

19. There is a small branch of Tree-rat-people living in this vicinity today and calling itself the Mokakarui.

20. Note how this episode identifies Orphan with a single sib.

21. I am indebted to Miss R. B. Inman and Mr. J. C. Greenway, of the Harvard University Museum of Comparative Zoölogy, for providing me with the common names of these birds.

22. Another version identifies Kohka with the Pakoram demon, and calls the women who escaped merely kupunas.

23. Compare with Hornbill's version of invention of Climbing, p. 50.

24. See Origin of the Parrot-people, p. 52.

25. There are two principal versions of this genesis myth. Version A is current in western Siuai, where most of the Eagle-people live today; Version B is known by only a few men in north central Siuai.

26. See n. 21.

27. On the basis of both linguistic and nonlinguistic behavior I am convinced that the Siuai do in fact regard the universe as being made up largely of separate entities, of clearly distinguishable *things*. I feel certain that they do not conceive of the whole universe as consisting of diffuse substances which are merely *contained* in numerous forms. To them, redness or hardness or supernatural dangerousness, for example, are not diffuse realities in themselves; they are qualities of specific things. (Generalizations like these deserve more than footnote mention, but for reasons given in the Introduction I will not attempt to document them in terms of Motuna language forms, and hence am not justified in giving them more prominence.)

28. Ethnographers realize of course that mankind's beliefs are in actuality always changing, and the Siuai can be no exception; but the Siuai belief system is static to this extent: many of the novelties and changes which become widely accepted are eventually credited to the kupunas. The Christian missions' translation of "God" as Maker (Tantanu) has served to strengthen this kind of logic.

29. There may be more; forty are all I can identify with confidence.

30. However, five (*aŋumuka*), ten (*naram*), and multiples of ten remain constant in most instances.

31. The items listed are a partial and, I trust, suggestive list of those belonging in each class.

32. For example, in calling out to someone climbing a coconut palm, it would be customary to say, "Throw down one-round-object to me," instead of "Throw down one-round-object coconut to me."

33. See, for example, the analysis of Trobriand logic made by Dorothy Lee using Malinowski's data. (D. D. Lee, "A Primitive System of Values," *Philosophy of Science*, vol. 7, no. 3, July 1940.)

34. Again it should be emphasized that these are my categories; the Siuai themselves do not explicitly make such classifications.

35. Throughout this book the term "spirit" will be used when referring generally to supernatural beings.

36. Sometimes the Turuŋum konopia is frustrated, as happened when she attempted to seduce Miheru, a native of Hanoŋ. See below, p. 86.

37. Nor are there many Eagle-people in this area.

## CHAPTER 2     495

38. That is, generally acceptable to informants residing in the territories designated; informants from, say, Jeku village, would know very little about the local spirits around Moronei, five miles away.

39. I believe there is firm ground, linguistic and otherwise, for my use of the word "cause" here and elsewhere in connection with Siuai beliefs. In this sense, Siuai "thought" contrasts markedly with Trobriand "thought" as interpreted by D. D. Lee, "A Primitive System of Values." Full linguistic documentation for my view is lacking, but it should be mentioned that causality is unequivocally expressed by means of the Motuna suffixed particle -*ko* (or *ŋo*) and by verbal infixes.

40. In another version Koko is sent by its master, Hoŋing, to the house of a person already having Near-death. Koko secures a sapling of the kind of tree used in the construction of cremation biers, and throws it at the house of the Near-death person. Next day, when people see the sapling they exclaim: "Look there! Koko has been here; so-and-so will soon die."

41. See Introduction.

42. Some natives assert that Hoŋing's younger brothers, Komarara and Komakiki, are in charge at Kaopiri.

43. Blood-place is ruled over by the kupuna Hokeru, another brother of Hoŋing.

44. Except in the case of the soul of an infant who dies while in "hiding." See p. 176.

45. Perhaps this is correlated with the circumstance that most Siuai activities do not require the high degree of specialized knowledge and facility which ordinarily comes only with age and experience, such as is the case with, say, Australian aborigines.

46. In recent years such factors as *position* in Administration units and in Christian mission congregations have further differentiated social behavior, but those factors will be discussed in a later chapter.

47. The Siuai use this term *noroukuru* for sib as well as for any recognizable segment of a sib. Throughout this book I shall use the terms *sib*, *sub-sib*, and *matrilineage* when the reference is clear, reserving *noroukuru* for instances where more precise reference is not possible.

48. Some exception is to be found in those residential groups characterized by successive generations of patrilocality.

49. This web also overlaps the boundaries of neighboring tribes.

50. In reality, of course, "distant" (stranger) and "nearby" (neighbor) have sociological implications and are not entirely a matter of spatial distance.

51. This is the Anglicized plural, the singular being *mumi*, the plural *mumariŋom*.

52. In Motuna, the plural for *moŋo* is *moŋonom*.

53. Cf. W. Lloyd Warner, *A Black Civilization* (New York and London, 1937), p. 245.

54. I hold this opinion as a result of many inquiries. In response to my question: "What kills the taboo-breaker?" a few natives replied that it is probably the kupunas who do so, a few others said that it is the ancestral matrilineal ghosts. In neither case, however, could it be explained how these supernaturals apply their sanctions beyond the general explanation that they "inflict" Near-death. In fact, the manner in which the replies were given and the lack of spontaneous supporting data convince me that little or no previous thought had been given to this matter.

55. Climbings are held every three or four years in northeast Siuai; none occurred during my visit.

56. There are specialists who actually practice sorcery. In numerous instances misfortunes are erroneously attributed to sorcery — erroneously not only from the viewpoint of modern science but also from the circumstance that sorcery was not actually performed in connection with the case in question. On the other hand many Siuai do in fact practice the black art either openly or surreptitiously, according to whether the victim is a common (and usually distant) enemy or some neighbor against whom the sorcerer bears a personal grudge.

57. In this case it is said that the sun's rays (i.e., heat) carry the essence of the poison. This technique is reported to be very popular among magicians in the neighboring Nagovisi region. Siuai natives say that when they visit friends in Nagovisi the latter caution them against walking about in the early morning or late afternoon when the long shadows would make them easy marks for "shadow" sorcerers.

58. Presumably these ghosts eventually lose their powers, because the Ash-places have to be replenished with new ashes from time to time in order to remain effective.

59. In some situations *mirina* magic also can be made to avenge a death by sorcery.

60. By "scarce goods" I mean *scarce* means for purposive maximization of satisfactions.

61. The phrase in quotes is from the definition of property given by E. A. Hoebel in his *Men in the Primitive World* (N. Y., 1949), 329. In my attempts to formulate Siuai principles of property I have also been influenced by A. I. Hallowell's essay on "The Nature and Function of Property as a Social Institution," *Journal of Legal and Political Sociology*, I, 115–138; by Ward H. Goodenough's interesting analysis of Trukese property ("Property, Kin, and Community of Truk," *Yale University Publication in Anthropology*, no. 46, 1951); and by lessons learned in the writing of my "Land Tenure in Northeast Siuai," *Peabody Museum Papers*, vol. 29, no. 4 (Cambridge, Mass., 1949).

62. *Ownership* being "a total complex of reciprocal relationships with respect to the enjoyment and use of something as property." Goodenough, p. 33. *Type of Ownership* "refers to the social composition of the holders of a title, e.g., an individual, a partnership, a clan, a corporation, a state." G. P. Murdock *et al.*, *Outline of Cultural Materials*, 3rd Rev. Ed., p. 51. *Title* is the "constellation of rights, privileges, and duties devolving on one party as owner in such a complex of relationships." Goodenough, p. 33.

63. See Chap. 3 for definitions of *group* and *aggregate*.

64. *Webster's Collegiate Dictionary* (Fifth Ed., 1947), definition of *corporation*, "Any group of persons treated by the law as an individual or unity having rights or liabilities, or both, distinct from those of the persons composing it," is satisfactory for our purposes provided "group" is taken to mean "Social unit" and "law," "custom."

65. For example, male speaking:

| | |
|---|---|
| naramoŋ = my-younger-brother | noniramoŋ = our-younger-brother (excl.) |
| | neramoŋ = our-younger-brother (incl.) |
| raramoŋ = thy-younger-brother | rerimoŋ = your-younger-brother |
| paramoŋ = his-(her-, its-) younger-brother | perimoŋ = their-younger-brother |

66. Natives believe that the new moon pierces green coconuts, thus allowing their meat-forming fluid to run out.

67. See p. 37.

68. Actual matrilateral relationship is assumed to be the basis of co-membership

in all matrilineal social units (sibs, sub-sibs, matrilineages) but in connection with sib and sub-sib membership the ties among co-members are *explained* by common totems, taboos, and traditions rather than by "actual" genealogical ties. In this respect the Siuai lineage system stands in sharp contrast with the polysegmentary lineage system of the Tallensi and the Nuer.

69. See p. 62.

*Chapter 3*

1. This definition is paraphrased from George Homans, *The Human Group* (N. Y., 1950), and from E. D. Chapple and C. S. Coon, *Principles of Anthropology* (N. Y., 1942).

2. To be entirely consistent it might be advisable to classify as a *group* each individual's kindred, or *ramage* of kin, that comes together on occasion to celebrate that individual's life crisis events. However, only siblings of same mother and father have kindreds containing the identical persons, and as a matter of fact the composition of these units tends to expand and contract according to the cultural importance attached to the event, hence I feel that such units should best be described as consisting of gatherings of two or more groups along with other assorted relatives.

3. In other words, not only is the Siuai leader in a position to apply sanctions if his orders are disobeyed, but in actual fact his orders are usually *obeyed*.

4. As defined by western standards.

5. Formerly there were two.

6. Chap. 2, pp. 46 ff.

7. "When the members of a consanguineal kin group [read *unit*] acknowledge a traditional bond of common descent in the paternal or maternal line, but are unable always to trace the actual genealogical connections between individuals, the group is called a *sib*." G. P. Murdock, *Social Structure* (N. Y., 1949), p. 47.

8. Murdock, *Social Structure*, p. 47.

9. "A consanguineal kin group produced by either rule of unilineal descent is technically known as a *lineage* when it includes only persons who can actually trace their common relationship through a specific series of remembered genealogical links in the prevailing line of descent." Murdock, p. 46.

10. There are some other Rukaruinais dwelling in this neighborhood who are not members of the Turuŋonai matrilineage.

11. See Chap. 2, p. 59.

12. This diagram does not illustrate segmentation throughout the whole Siuai Tree-rat sib, which consists of more than a score of sub-sub-sibs.

13. Chap. 2, p. 57.

14. See above, note 9.

15. Also, they own land corporately, etc.

16. Except for some marriage prohibitions. See below, pp. 117–118.

17. Compare with the Tallensi. (M. Fortes, *Dynamics of Clanship among the Tallensi*, Oxford, 1945.)

18. Murdock, p. 47.

19. Cf. Chap. 2, p. 55.

20. Chap. 2, p. 56.

## Chapter 4

1. See p. 32.
2. For details on distribution see Chaps. 5 and 9.
3. For the sake of clarity, I call a fenced-in unit of a taro garden, a *patch*; a *patch-sequence* consists of those patches associated in the same crop chain, while *adjoining* patches are those physically contiguous but associated with separate crop chains (see pp. 22–26).
4. Nonfunctional in the sense that they are not required to keep out pigs, the usual rationale given by the Siuai for building fences.
5. Based on records kept of the daily activities of several households.
6. See pp. 134–135.
7. See note 62 of Chap. 2, p. 496.
8. This belief, which is not widespread in Siuai or rigid, is the only trait I recorded analogous to the complex of beliefs and practices of some New Guinea cultures — viz., the Arapesh — concerning the magical incompatibility of sex and gardening.
9. See p. 344.
10. The same principles of magic are employed for the protection and growth of sweet potatoes, coconuts, sago, almonds, and breadfruit — although such devices are not used as frequently as for taro.
11. Two hundred seventy-three households, comprising 910 persons, or about 90 per cent of the total population of northeast Siuai, were surveyed; and of these, 23 households possessed only hamlet houses, 213 possessed both hamlet house and village house, and 37 only village houses.

## Chapter 5

1. Lacking the training required for probing more than superficially into individuals' reasons for getting married, I had to rely upon general observations and informants' rationalizations. It is not unlikely, for example, that the principal, though unexpressed, reason why some restless young women want to marry is to escape from the strict surveillance of their bad-tempered fathers. Again, a club-footed young neighbor of ours may have wanted to get a husband quickly in order to spite her prettier companions. Without minimizing the importance of such individual and, to me, often inaccessible reasons for getting married, I list here only the widely acknowledged, more readily discernible, incentives for marriage; none of these operate alone, in fact they usually buttress one another.
2. What little sodomy there is in Siuai was introduced by youths who learned about it while working on plantations. The practice appears so bizarre to most Siuai that they describe its inception with almost clinical interest. It was first introduced to Bougainville natives, it is said, by a Buka Island native who learned it from white sailors aboard a warship and who later on worked at an east coast plantation and taught others about it. Subsequently, the Siuai say, the "redskins" of New Guinea and Rabaul have kept the practice alive. My informants describe the practice — from secondhand knowledge, they insist — as being superior to copulation because of the smaller and tighter aperture. Nevertheless, they consider it reprehensible and speak contemptuously of the one native in northeast Siuai who practiced it a few times, and who because of

it was brought by his neighbors before the Patrol Officer and jailed. (In due course this native married and is said to have given up his habit.) Bestiality is just as rare in Siuai, but it is laughed off as an utterly ridiculous practice. Natives tell with ribald embellishments about the man who experimented with a dog and couldn't extricate his penis so had to carry the animal around wherever he went.

3. Throughout this monograph, English words denoting kinship will be unitalicized only when used descriptively; when a classificatory meaning is intended, the word will be italicized.

4. However, phallic symbolism and coitus figure prominently in decorative art, which is mainly men's work.

5. Even discounting for the circumstance that such statements come from male informants, they seem to me to be credibly consistent with other aspects of Siuai life.

6. One skeptical informant believed this saw to be nothing but female propaganda, perpetrated by them to prolong their sexual pleasure!

7. Named after this mythical incident: a man, Suivoru, once obtained some *kiruhko* grass and placed it at the top of an almond tree. A pigeon in the act of eating almonds also swallowed the grass, flew straightaway to Suivoru's house and remained there, unable to leave and unable to digest the *kiruhko*.

8. *Paheo* is a magical ingredient obtained from bark scrapings and operates similarly to Pigeon-can't-eat-it.

9. Even some women believe that if a single man leaves one village and goes to live in another for no apparent reason, it is because some woman at his new place has lured him there with love magic.

10. Is this evidence of infrequency of female orgasm?

11. Vaivai is made by crushing fragrant flowers and putting them in coconut oil.

12. See p. 70.

13. Ten years is my estimate based on individual cases pointed out to me.

14. At Turuŋum village Poroporo finally gave up sleeping alone in the medical orderly's storehouse after he had received several midnight visits there from an importunate niece of the local leader; Poroporo was not averse to marriage but lacked resources for acquiring such a highly placed wife and did not want to risk the uncle's anger by dallying with the girl.

15. The Siuai have a term for maidenhead (*taritari*) and apparently realize that copulation punctures it. However, there is no notice taken of its presence or absence; and although men say they know if and when they puncture it, and hence realize the meaning of that, no significance is attached to it.

16. See pp. 117–121.

17. See p. 118.

18. See p. 256.

19. I recorded a few instances of pre-pubescent girls living in their prospective fiancé's households even before formal betrothal, but these came about through special circumstances: e.g., the girl was either an orphan or a cross-cousin (see below).

20. The only other kind of instance that I recorded of a betrothal shading into marriage concerned a motherless girl whose father and only brother died while she was dwelling at her fiancé's household. No payment was made, no protests were voiced, and the couple began married life as soon as a separate dwelling had been built for them.

21. See p. 59.

22. See p. 285.

23. Although to the best of my knowledge no such case occurred in northeast Siuai while we were there, natives said that occasionally a betrothed girl may be ceremonially carried to the residence of her in-laws at the beginning of her pre-marriage stay there. She is carried by a delegation of her fiancé's relatives and friends, for whom the girl's father provides a pork feast. The pigs consumed at this feast (*kurai*) are eventually reciprocated by the fiancé's family.

24. At least one of these venal men has been caught in his machinations: a native Police Constable forced him to return the payment in toto when his daughter was divorced by her husband.

25. The question was asked of informants when I was collecting census and genealogical data of the residents of northeast Siuai. I asked the question concerning the primary unions of all living adult males, and because of some cross-checking feel a fair degree of confidence in the data.

26. Later sections will describe subsequent residential shifts which occur in the lives of many Siuai, pointing out, for example, that numbers of men leave their birthplaces upon death of their fathers and move with their wives and children to places associated with their matrilineages.

27. See p. 175.

28. In some instances men even resort to love-magic to win back an estranged wife.

29. Of the 900 existing or genealogically recorded nuclear families which I listed for Siuai, 220 were childless — or at least had produced only children who did not survive past infancy. For the remaining 680 fruitful families an average of 2.3 children survived past infancy.

30. There are many tales about the miseries of barren women and about their efforts to obtain offspring. One favorite tale describes the sad case of the childless woman and the demon's child:

"Once a demon left her infant on a path while she went searching for areca nuts. While she was away a woman walked by and saw the infant. She was very happy at finding it and carried it home, announcing to everyone that she had at last found a child. Her relatives realized that it was a demon-child, but the woman's happiness was so great that they could not bring themselves to tell her. She carried it around everywhere she went and fed it tidbits. But one day the demon-child's mother took it away, leaving the woman to weep and weep and finally to hang herself in grief."

31. Magic is employed to prevent conception, the roots of any one of several reed-like plants (*kutapaka, kimam, rumai*) being used. The woman scrapes off some of the root's bark and chews it with betel; the rest of the root is smoked dry and hidden in her house roof for safekeeping — as long as it remains intact she will not conceive. Later on, when she wishes to conceive she destroys the root by burying it in the ground, where termites eat it.

32. See pp. 69–70.

33. See p. 70.

34. See p. 46.

35. As far as we could ascertain, natives do not consciously speed up weaning just for this reason.

36. See pp. 91–92.

37. Informants did not volunteer information on caul births and we neglected to make specific inquiries about it.

38. Informants agreed that twins are occasionally born, and some say that one of them is killed — "the weaker one," whatever its sex. However, I could not probe any deeper into this subject — not, I believe, because of natives' reluctance to discuss the subject but rather because of a general lack of significance attributed to the happening.

39. I distinguish here between *medical* and *magical* because the Siuai themselves do so, regarding some measures as having direct natural effects not associated with supernatural beings or forces.

40. Henceforth, in the interest of brevity, the native term *kuna* will be used, signifying any kind of substance which has *intrinsically* potent magic qualities.

41. Formerly, natives say, the women assisting in childbirth used to smother to death, and then bury secretly, any child born with serious deformation, such as an extra digit or a webbed foot; and the same fate awaited the infant who did not cry within a short time after birth (i.e., "it had no soul"). Informants assert that these practices are no longer carried out ("it is against Government and mission law") but we discovered no reliable evidence on this one way or another.

42. We were unable to obtain a rationalization for this belief.

43. The effect of this regimen, added to the rigors of childbirth, was plainly evident in the appearance of the women we saw after "hiding" was over: they were emaciated and weak to an alarming degree.

44. There are several variants to this ritual sequence, and no great pains are taken to ensure absolute standardization of performance.

45. However, this bond is not institutionalized in terms of transactions.

46. This is the only explicit reference we discovered concerning a concept of "growing power" separate from physical growth, soul, vitality, or strength.

47. One might surmise that a more general canon is involved here: anything associated (by contact) with childbirth is inherently dangerous to everyone (because of the imminence of death and death agents) and men are especially susceptible to these dangers when they are so close to death, i.e., when they are climbing dangerously high trees.

48. But see the myth of the Hornbills, in which the infant Crocodile is hacked to pieces by its father. P. 49.

49. Another reason for this reticence is the natives' experience that white Administration officials become disturbed and make unwelcome investigations when many deaths are reported in any one village.

50. What happens to this soul if its mother bears no more children? When we asked natives this they were at a loss for an answer, apparently not having formulated beliefs to cover this contingency.

51. The only other Siuai death situation comparable to this is the fearsome awe manifested by men in connection with the death of a man who has fallen from a tree.

52. This is a *koija* associated with members of the Tree-rat sib; Tuhuhroru is one of the places (in Terei) through which the Tree-rat kupunas are said to have passed on their way to Siuai. See p. 46.

53. See p. 92.

54. This is the formula of the Tree-rats; it differs only slightly from the pile scattering formulae of other sibs.

55. "We come to sing and dance to celebrate the baptism of an infant."

56. See p. 71.

57. Like the vague belief in the incompatibility of sexual intercourse and gardening

(see above, page 132), this belief may be another facet to a more general premise concerning incompatibility of sex and growth, such as is found among the Arapesh.

58. After the death of its mother, an infant's soul attaches itself to its new foster mother, whoever that may be.

59. See p. 55.

60. See p. 59.

61. This lacuna in our field observations shows up all too glaringly when comparisons are made with such excellent ethnographic reports as those of Margaret Mead, *Growing Up in New Guinea*, etc. (N. Y., 1930), John Whiting, *Becoming a Kwoma* (London, 1941), and Cora Dubois, *People of Alor* (Minneapolis, 1944).

62. The subject of *socialization* is of the utmost importance to the student of cultures but it is full of pitfalls for the nonspecialist — including the writer. The ethnographer occupied in piecing together a pictorial map of a culture cannot, and indeed need not, observe and question every adult participant; if the representativeness and reliability of informants can be satisfactorily established and if the findings appear reasonably consistent, it is fairly safe to make certain assumptions about the individuals not questioned, and the practices not actually observed. However, unless the investigator has devoted long and methodical attention to this subject, assumptions about *socialization* cannot be made with the same degree of assurance, no matter how *consistently* they would appear to be deduced from the usual picture of the culture.

63. See pp. 143–144.

64. This of course is a marked overstatement, for not only is there considerable conflict between fathers and sons during the latters' adolescence, but there is some evidence of such occurrences during the latters' childhood.

65. See p. 47.

66. See pp. 43–44.

67. See p. 72.

68. A pidgin phrase denoting the country hick of the unwesternized back areas.

69. I am compelled to use vague terms like "most," "some," "frequently," etc., because I unfortunately neglected to count these and similar kinds of social data and must consequently record impressions gained from limited samples. This kind of gap convinces me that ethnographers need to have a fair outline of a culture before they can begin to ask meaningful questions about important areas of social organization. In other words, ideally the investigator should return to the field after he has had an opportunity to digest his first findings — but before the culture has had time to change significantly, which is patently impossible in the case of this Siuai study.

70. See note 2, Chap. 5, pp. 498–499.

71. See p. 157.

72. I could not discover how frequently spouses have sexual relations so cannot state that they become less frequent; informants merely said of an older couple that "her vagina becomes too large for pleasure." Nor could I learn very much about the timing and effects of menopause; all those I questioned about it were rather surprised that I should show interest in such a totally commonplace and unheeded event. See p. 73.

73. See p. 75.

74. Except in the case of death of a Hidden-One, a newborn infant still in "hiding"; for description of this see p. 176.

75. See p. 75.

76. For descriptions of dirges see pp. 275–282.

77. However, this diet austerity does not apply to children, who are not expected to give up their normal eating.

78. Elsewhere in Siuai, we came across many other unused tracts of land labeled "set-aside," their original names forgotten along with the circumstances of the setting-aside.

79. Except that whole taro plants are not used to decorate the pyre — because, reason the Siuai, "the old-one has already used up all his taro."

80. See pp. 402–403.

81. The vengeance rites carried out at the cremations of sorcery victims were described on p. 91.

82. According to the household census figures for northeast Siuai, there were four households consisting of widows with or without offspring, and six consisting of widows, married offspring, and grandchildren.

83. See pp. 43–46.

84. See p. 162.

85. See p. 153.

86. Murdock, *Social Structure*, p. 29.

87. See p. 221.

88. *Papers of the Peabody Museum of American Archaeology and Ethnology*, vol. 29, no. 3.

89. See pp. 221–222.

90. See p. 218.

91. In the case of persons being interrelated in more than one social unit (e.g., being members of the same matrilineage *and* men's society) it becomes necessary, for analytical purposes, to factorize the data referable to membership in each unit. Whenever the word "relationship" is used in this text it should be clear, from general context or from specific qualification, which social unit is referred to.

92. My usage of this dimension is adapted from E. D. Chapple, and C. M. Arensburg, "Measuring Human Relations," *Genetic Psychology Monographs*, vol. 22 (1940).

93. See note 60, Chap. 2, p. 496.

94. My usage of the term "emotion" corresponds in part to the behavior called "sentiment" and "expressive behavior" by Raymond Firth in *We, The Tikopia* (London, 1936), p. 160, and George Homans in *The Human Group* (N.Y., 1950), pp. 241 ff.; but I also signify social etiquette, e.g., the behavior designed to express the actor's "inferiority" to his betters, or his "distance" from mere acquaintances, etc.

95. In a sense all the behavior now under consideration is ritualistic, hence *symbolic* (see E. R. Leach, "The Structural Implications of Matrilateral Cross-cousin Marriage," *J.R.A.I.*, vol. 81, parts 1 and 2); but in the interest of specificity I prefer to use the word "symbolic" in the sense given above.

96. In his definition of "communication structures" Claude Lévi-Strauss speaks of communication operating on three different "levels" — "communication of women, communication of goods and services, and communication of messages" ("Social Structure," *Anthropology Today*, ed. by A. L. Kroeber, Chicago, 1952, p. 536). Although Prof. Lévi-Strauss's formulation is exceedingly interesting and, for the purposes designed, highly useful, I have found the three-dimensional approach just presented more useful in analyzing the Siuai data. In the first place, "women" are not "communicated" in Siuai — only *functions* of women (e.g., sexual services and food-producing services); as a matter of fact I suspect that this is the situation in most other cultures as

well. (See Meyer Fortes, "Analysis and Description in Social Anthropology," *The Advancement of Science*, no. 38, London, 1953.) Secondly, I feel that these functions of women that are "communicated" are scarce goods no less than are all the other kinds of culturally defined scarce "means" (including Lévi-Strauss's "goods and services") which I place in this category. (E. R. Leach makes a somewhat similar point in his brilliant essay, "The Structural Implications of Matrilateral Cross-cousin Marriage," *Journal of the Royal Anthropological Institute*, vol. LXXXI, parts 1 and 2, p. 52, when he speaks of "prestations.") Furthermore, "messages" ofttimes involve the exchange of scarce *valuable* information (i.e., scarce goods), as well as communicating what I have termed *emotion*; but probably most everyday conversation, which makes up the bulk of "messages," is ritualistic interaction almost entirely unaccompanied by goods-exchange and quite low in affect.

The principal advantage of this three-dimensional analytic technique is that it sets up more inclusive definitions of "scarce goods" and "transactions" and thus places one in a position to construct a more comprehensive model of a society's "economic" structure.

97. In describing these categories I have drawn heavily on the ideas and terminology presented by Ward Goodenough in his outstanding monograph already cited (see above, p. 496). Also, the reader will observe that in this connection I am indebted to the writings of Marcel Mauss, Bronislaw Malinowski, Claude Lévi-Strauss, and E. R. Leach. In formulating these ideas I have also profited from conversations with John M. Roberts.

98. See p. 95 for definition.

99. Perhaps this strong emphasis on unobstructed usufruct of land leading eventually to full ownership may be partly accounted for by the availability of much unused (but not unowned) land in Siuai. There is little economic pressure on owners to assert continously their title to distant territories.

100. Margaret Mead ("The Mountain Arapesh." Part III. Socio-economic Life, vol. 40: Part 3. *Anthropological Papers of the American Museum of Natural History*, New York, 1947) defines coöperation in the following sense: the act of working together, of pooling services, to achieve common possession of a common goal.

101. Some informants classified a man's present to his mistress in this category, but others called it a *gift* (*o*).

102. For a discussion of what constitutes "equivalence," see below.

103. Both coercive and competitive giving also contain the implication of *purchase* of praise, for they have the general effect of increasing the renown of the donor.

104. This poses something of a problem of definition. For example, some informants assert that fathers *ought* to give tidbits frequently to their sons, thereby reducing this transaction to a matter of normal division of labor, hence *sharing*, as herein defined. Other informants disagreed with this and stated that fathers were not required to give tidbits frequently to their sons.

Siuai nonreciprocal giving corresponds to D. D. Lee's interpretation of the Trobriand concept of *giving* as being a "futile" disparate act ("A Primitive System of Values," *Philosophy of Science*, vol. 7, no. 3, 1940). In this connection, however, I suspect that the Trobriand culture, like Siuai, includes several kinds of "giving," and that all Trobriand gift-transactions are not to be reduced to the single category of "futile," "disparate" acts.

105. Inheritance being "the transference of a deceased person's rights in property to certain of his or her survivors." E. A. Hoebel, *Man in the Primitive World*, p. 354.

106. This does not apply to the matrilineage's sacred heirlooms (*tomui*), which are so exclusively identified with the matrilineage as to be nontransferable; when the matrilineage faces extinction informants said that the guardian of its heirlooms ought to bury them.

107. Obviously, if female members had surviving offspring the question of matrilineage extinction would not arise.

108. See above, pp. 215–217 for an account of this contribution (*nori*).

109. The former practice of capturing humans for sale or for personal use belongs in this category.

110. Or behavior which is *designed* to express an "internal state," such as the etiquette manifested in the behavior of a low-ranking man to his leader.

111. Compare this with the fine distinctions that can be expressed in the Samoans' kava ritual.

112. "Adequately" to me, in terms of the kinds of generalizations I am attempting to make.

113. My basis for grouping the various patterns of emotional behavior into assemblages is as follows: First I noted how certain persons behave toward or with respect to certain other persons. Then I grouped together those behavior patterns which occur consistently between specific persons, and gave labels to the assemblages thus constituted.

The reader's apologies are begged for introducing another set of definitions; in any case, the labels given to the assemblages connote meanings not too far removed from their ordinary dictionary definitions, so that memories will not be unreasonably burdened. This tack involves, of course, the danger that the reader will translate these labels too literally — forgetting, for example, that the behavior patterns which constitute the assemblage labeled *affection* include such actions as de-lousing and hand-holding but not some of the more ardent expressions of emotion which many Americans would include under the term.

114. Under *affection* should also be included special voice inflection and various other manifestations not greatly unlike the milder expressions of fondness in American society; however, I did not observe these manifestations carefully or systematically and so cannot write with confidence about them.

115. See n. 114.

116. At this point the reader might well ask: why should not nonreciprocable giving be classed as a pattern of emotion-expressing behavior, a component of the assemblage called *affection* rather than as a property transaction pattern? And why should not competitive giving be classed as an expression of *enmity* and hence placed under the rubric of "expressive behavior"? Why not indeed! Presumably any transaction may be *expressive* of some internal state or other, and with respect to such a transaction as nonreciprocable giving we may assume with reasonable assurance what that internal state happens to be. The only defensible basis for maintaining these somewhat arbitrary distinctions between various "dimensions" of behavior patterns is the matter of emphasis. No irreparable harm will be done if the reader keeps in mind that *interaction*, *transaction*, and *emotion* are simply different dimensions of "communication events."

117. Adapted from *Webster's Collegiate Dictionary*.

118. For details see pp. 141–151.

119. This repudiation may be signalized rather dramatically, as in the case of the man who seduces his brother's wife in vengeance for that brother's seduction of his.

120. See Chap. 2.

121. For example, if a son is not properly *deferential* to his father, the latter may withhold the shell money necessary for the former to contract a marriage. If a youth were to have sexual intercourse with his sister or his mother, he and she would automatically die. Etc.

122. In this writer's opinion there are two principal ways to generalize about social structure. First, one may start with *symbols*; discover what certain persons are called with respect to one another (e.g., father:son, clanmates, *gam:lam*, neighbors, enemies, foreman:worker, etc.); observe how such symbolically linked persons behave toward or with respect to one another; discover what they own in common, how they rationalize their relationship, etc. Or, the analyst may take as his starting point the ownership of property: finding out, for example, which persons are associated in the corporate ownership of land, and then going on to observe what they call one another, how they behave toward or with respect to one another, etc.

The second principal way to generalize about social structure involves starting with what is called herein a "dimension" of behavior. For example, one may start with the dimension of *interaction* and isolate all kinds of interaction units observable in the society under study, and then go on to describe the relations of such interacting persons in terms of the other dimensions (transaction, emotion), and in terms of the more explicitly symbolic aspects of relatedness mentioned above. Alternatively, one may start with one of the other behavior dimensions, say, transaction: discover the kinds of transactions implicit in the behavior of the persons constituting the society; learn by observation which dyads are characterized by particular kinds of transactions, or combinations of transactions; then find out how often, etc., such persons interact, what they call one another, and so on.

Either one of these methods should produce approximately the same end picture of any society's social structure. In this book I have used them in complementary fashion, depending upon the first method for isolating, and generalizing about, aggregates and institutionalized dyads outside of groups; and upon the second for isolating, and generalizing about, groups.

*Chapter 6*

1. This useful term is from H. I. Hogbin and C. H. Wedgwood, "Local Grouping in Melanesia," *Oceania*, vol. 22, no. 4, p. 242, who define it as "residence of a married couple in the hamlet, ward, or village of the husband's male matrilineal relatives."

2. In my paper on "Land Tenure in Northeast Siuai" I stated that these relationships *are* hypostasized, and gave as evidence the fact that "in a few communities children taboo the totem of their father as well as that of their mother"; and added that in "Moronei, Manrai's children were christened with their father's *maru*" (p. 45). On reconsideration, it seems to me that such evidence is not decisive; all First-borns respect their father's totem as well as their mother's, and not all the cases of paternal totem observance by *all* of a man's offspring occur among members of patrilineally aligned corporations. Moreover, although baptism should be carried out with one's matrilineage or sib *maru*, other *maru* is occasionally used — and not only by members of a patrilineal corporation.

On the other hand, if Siuai society had continued to develop in the directions I suggested by trends discernible in 1938–39, these patrilineal corporations might in time have become full-fledged patrilineage groups, bearing many of the characteristics of matrilineages.

3. As a rule only adults are labeled *Attachers*, the name not being applied to children or young people who reside in a settlement because of adoption.

4. See p. 237.

5. See pp. 166–167.

6. See pp. 129, 132.

7. Nevertheless, he still has the obligation to pay *something* toward a mortuary feast, in order to ensure his father's after-life bliss.

8. See pp. 153–154.

*Chapter 7*

1. That is, actual and imputed.

2. It is assumed that the reader realizes that any kinship system is a matrix, that behavior between any pair of relatives is influenced by all the other relationships by which they are indirectly linked. To keep this outline as brief as possible I have had to perform the somewhat artificial operation of factoring out and describing only the direct pair relationships, but with these building blocks the reader should be able to piece together something comparable to the whole kin relationship system.

3. For an elaboration of this thesis, see George Homans, *The Human Group*.

4. By "intensity" I mean here the conscientiousness with which the members of the pair observe, or believe they should observe, reciprocal obligations. A method comparable to the scale analysis employed by Goodenough in "Property, Kin, and Community of Truk," forms the basis for my grading of kinship distance, although I must add that the Truk behavior patterns appear to lend themselves to this kind of precise and systematic formulation much more readily than do those of Siuai. See also Chap. 5, "Family Structure," concerning the lack of gradations in expressive behavior patterns.

5. Actually, if we were intent on making a more detailed analysis of kinship behavior patterns we should distinguish between "Utopian," compulsory, alternative, and other kinds of norms. (See Clyde Kluckhohn, "Patterning as Exemplified in Navaho Culture," *Language, Culture, and Personality*, Menasha, Wis., 1941; "Covert Culture and Administrative Problems," *American Anthropologist*, vol. 45, no. 2, 1943; and "The Concept of Culture," *The Policy Sciences*, eds., D. Lerner and H. D. Lasswell, Stanford, 1951.) For example, a few Siuai moralists express "Utopian" norms when they assert that *all* relatives should interact a lot and that their interaction should always be characterized by nonreciprocable giving and affection. In the following outline, however, I shall describe only the more "typically" held norms regarding kinship behavior. Again, in my description of *rank* in the socio-political order, given elsewhere in this book, I have found it necessary to distinguish native reports concerning "actual" behavior from my own observations of that behavior; but since in connection with kinship behavior I found the discrepancies between these two kinds of data slight and probably not very significant, I have combined them in working out the scales of "behavioral gradations."

6. This shorthand means that a mother calls her son *nuri*; a son calls his mother *nuka*. Also, a kinship term which can refer to either sex is printed in full caps when the referent is male. *Nuka* means "my-mother," *nuri*, "my-son," there being no general

word for "mother" (or "son," or any other kinship term). The paradigm for "-mother" is given below.

*Singular*

| | |
|---|---|
| nuka, my mother | nonnikuku, our (exclusive) mother |
| | nekuku, our (inclusive) mother |
| roku, thy mother | rekuku, your (dual or plural) mother |
| poku, his, her, its mother | pekuku, their mother |

*Dual*

| | |
|---|---|
| nukakuruko, my two mothers | nonnikuruko, our (exclusive) two mothers |
| | nekuruko, our (inclusive) two mothers |
| rokuruko, thy two mothers | rekuruko, your (dual or plural) two mothers |
| pokuruko, his, her, its two mothers | pekuruko, their two mothers |

*Plural*

| | |
|---|---|
| nukakuri, my mothers | nonnikukuri, our (exclusive) mothers |
| | nekukuri, our (inclusive) mothers |
| rokuri, thy mothers | rekukuri, your (dual or plural) mothers |
| pokuri, his, her, its mothers | pekukuri, their mothers |

Suffixes denoting dual or plural vary considerably from one kinship term to another, but the pronominal possessive prefixes are fairly regular for all kinship terms (except for first person singular), and conform to the following paradigm:

| | | |
|---|---|---|
| | nonni- | — our (exclusive) |
| | ne- | — our (inclusive) |
| ro-, ra- — thy | re- | — your (dual or plural) |
| p-, (po-, pa-) — his, hers, its | pe- | — their |

7. Other than own father, obviously. In all these tabulations lower-ranking subclasses do not include statuses already listed in higher ones.

8. It would lengthen this account unduly to document each gradation of every kinship pair relation, so only a few points of wider sociological significance will be mentioned. Admittedly, in doing so, much of the flesh and blood of Siuai kinship relations will be sacrificed and the resulting picture of Siuai culture will be incomplete, but that is the inevitable outcome of any attempt to portray a culture within a single volume. The facts about residence, already noted, provide clues on how much various relatives interact, and a later section will show how emotion becomes conventionalized and expressed in dirges.

9. See p. 216.

10. This important relationship, the axial one of Siuai sibship, deserves much closer scrutiny than I gave it.

11. Provided, of course, this anyone is not more closely related through some other channel.

12. See Chap. 6.

13. It will be recalled that sibship segmentation follows the lines of differentiation between sisters.

14. See p. 47.

15. It should be recorded, however, that my data on this relationship category are not adequate.

## CHAPTER 7  509

16. As previously noted, in the case of native kinship terms which can denote persons of either sex, the term is printed in caps when the referent is male.

17. This manner of categorizing kin is followed only for convenience in presentation; it does not correspond to any distinctive behavioral denominators shared by all the classes of kin thus included and comparable, say, to the Type I or Type II kinfolk of the Arapesh, as differentiated by Dr. Mead in "The Mountain Arapesh."

18. For some conjectures about the history of Siuai kinship see Chap. 16.

19. See p. 237.

20. A man ordinarily uses the term *papa* only for those distant male sibmates who are known or thought to be in his mother's generation; all others are usually called *tata* (older brother).

21. See also pp. 119–120.

22. However, this constraint is not as strict nor as institutionalized as in the case of such natives as the Tallensi, whose customs serve to keep discrete the woman's conflicting roles of wife and daughter. Meyer Fortes, *The Web of Kinship among the Tallensi* (London, 1949), p. 124.

23. See p. 158.

24. Perhaps the virtual absence of the "purchase" element in most property exchanges connected with betrothal and wedding may account for some of this, the father usually having no important financial stake in maintaining the marriage; but there are also other factors involved, including the strong ties of affection between most fathers and their daughters. As the "purchase" element begins to creep into the concept of wedding exchanges, which it seems to be doing (Chap. 5, p. 162), it is reasonable to expect that the above picture will also change.

25. See pp. 245–246.

26. The element of constraint in the relationship between brothers-in-law can undoubtedly be rationalized in terms of "structural tensions," but its occurrence in Siuai cannot be explained away, as it can in some societies, by reference to any explicit conflicting rights in the wife-sister, namely, a husband's rights over her domestic and sexual services versus her brother's rights over her procreative capacity. The Siuai do not appear to regard a woman's offspring as one of the "resources" of her matrilineage.

27. Another interesting problem which is insoluble on the basis of my field notes is this: To the extent that the cross-cousin relationship is similar to the brother-in-law relationship, is this similarity based on the "anticipation" of cross-cousins becoming brothers-in-law, or is it based on the fact that the fathers of the cross-cousin pair are brothers-in-law, with some aspects of their relationship being carried over into the next generation? Perhaps, in keeping with the "logic" of the Siuai kinship system (see later) both explanations are admissible.

28. Chap. 5.

29. See p. 247.

30. For an interesting sociological explanation of this aspect of the relationship between alternate generations, see George Homans, *The Human Group*, p. 251.

31. That is, disparate acts, which, however, should not be confused with direct "reciprocity."

32. Compare this with the degree to which some Australian aborigines have elaborated this structural principle by combining alternate generations into important social units with ritual and marital functions.

33. See pp. 220–222.

34. See pp. 211–212.

35. This is the pidgin term for hospital or infirmary. The Australian Administration set up one at Ku'hinna to service all eastern Siuai. It is under the supervision of a well-trained native medical orderly or "rokuta" (doctor) who is authorized to dispense first aid and treat minor ailments.

36. A sapling too weak and small for fence construction hence thrown away or used only for training yam vines.

37. This dirge goes back to fighting times, when it was unsafe for people to attend cremations during nighttime in distant places. Hence relatives from distant places used to wait until dawn to start out for the cremation site.

38. *Raisiku* is the alternative name for *Sikurai*. For nearly every place name there are one or more alternate names, which are used in poetic expression, like this one, or which are used in everyday speech by individuals who are prohibited from using the ordinary name because of a name-calling taboo. The etymologies of these substitute terms differ. For example, *Raisiku* is merely a reversal of the syllables in *Sikurai*. Another example, *Si'ieiras*, one alternative for *Mataras*, was originated by a woman who had a son-in-law named Masanu, hence could not utter the syllable *mata*, because of its similarity to *masa-*. Now, *masa* is also the general name for certain kinds of insects, one of which is the *si'iei*; the woman merely used *si'iei* for all *masa*, and extended this usage to *Mataras*, which became *Si'ieiras*.

39. To throw them onto the local ossuary: this being a duty reserved for the closest kin of the deceased.

40. *Kainoru* is a mat made by sewing together about 100 spans of *mauai* (shell money).

41. A span of high-value shell money worth 50 ordinary spans.

42. I collected eighty-six distinctively different ones, and many more that differed only slightly from these in length and in order of phrase.

43. See pp. 76–77.

44. A male *Old-one* will also have occasion to represent his hamlet in dealings with the Hat-men of the territorially based line-village to which his hamlet is officially attached.

45. All these generalizations apply also to sub-matrilineages.

46. See p. 216.

47. See p. 115.

48. See pp. 162, 198–199.

49. For exceptions see descriptions of the growing modern tendency on the part of some guardians to retain the brideprice for themselves (p. 162).

50. See pp. 158–163.

51. See p. 220.

52. See pp. 156–157.

53. This point has been brilliantly developed by Lévi-Strauss, "Social Structure," and Leach, "Structural Implications of Matrilateral Cross-cousin Marriage."

54. As previously stated (p. 171), I interpret the *numehu* paid by a man to the brother of his wife on the occasion of the latter's pregnancy as a kind of indemnity directly related to the incest taboo. I feel that it is quite incorrect to rationalize it in terms of any "superiority" of the woman's brother over her husband, and just as in-

# CHAPTER 7   511

correct to interpret it as a payment by the husband for the wife's sexual services for the anticipated child (who will be a member of the wife's brother's matrilineage).

55. Secondary marriages differ from primary ones in several details, but the basic premises underlying the transactions could be held to be the same.

56. Leach, p. 52. This important analysis of inter-group relations has provided many insights useful to me in formulating my hypothesis regarding Siuai marriage transactions.

57. See p. 244.

58. See p. 247.

59. A Siuai does not, however, strive for consistency throughout his kinship system, e.g., if a distant kinswoman he calls *apu* marries a distant kinsman he calls *tata* he will continue to call them *apu* and *tata* respectively, undisturbed by the terminological inconsistency of having a *father's sister* married to an *older brother*.

60. For the exception see p. 264.

61. See note 5, Chap. 7, p. 507.

62. The fact that ego's father's sister's daughter (*mama*) is terminologically "older" than his mother's brother's daughter (*naramana*) may be "explained" by the fact that the former, as a member of his father's matrilineage, theoretically has some voice in determining whether ego inherits any of the land belonging to his father's matrilineage. However, just as plausible, or perhaps more so, is the "explanation" previously suggested, namely, that ego's father's sister's daughter does tend to be biologically older than his mother's brother's daughter (cf. p. 269). Whatever the explanation may be — and it is unlikely that the true one could ever be discovered — the fact remains that the contemporary terminological practice does reflect the circumstances just mentioned regarding property and relative biological age.

63. See p. 286.

64. For example, the assertion of kinship with a person as distant as father's sister's husband usually takes place only when there is need for getting a loan from him. For another example of how natives try to utilize distant kinship ties for practical purposes, see my "Land Tenure in Northeast Siuai."

65. The case of To'osi of Turuŋum village exemplifies this (Fig. 30, p. 488). He moved to Turuŋum from Jeku when he married Nirai. When recording the kinship system of this 25-year-old man I learned that he is a distant *mother's father* to 45-year-old Soŋi, and they sometimes call one another by kinship terms (To'osi:Soŋi, *mother's father:daughter's son*). More often, however, To'osi calls Soŋi "leader" (*mumi*), and is a loyal and obedient subordinate to Soŋi in every respect. Similarly, To'osi calls other Turuŋum residents by kinship terms which appear to have little or no congruence with his actual behavior toward them. On the other hand, when To'osi travels on pig-purchasing missions for Soŋi he seeks out *fathers, brothers-in-law*, etc., in distant settlements and behaves more or less appropriately toward them.

66. Such as, for example, the Tallensi custom of prohibiting sexual intercourse between man and wife in the house of the latter's father. See Meyer Fortes, *Web of Kinship among the Tallensi*, pp. 123–126.

67. See p. 260.

68. For a method of comparing the degree of authority centralization in different societies, see D. L. Oliver and W. B. Miller, "Suggestions for a More Systematic Method of Comparing Political Units," *American Anthropologist*, n.s., vol. 57, pp. 118–120.

69. This circumstance brings Siuai into sharp contrast with many other Oceanic societies, where, in the words of one writer, there is a "dependence upon kinship

patterns for politico-economic forms . . ." Margaret Mead, "The Mountain Arapesh. Part III. Socio-economic Life," p. 204.

*Chapter 8*

1. H. B. Guppy, *The Solomon Islands and Their Natives*; Carl Ribbe, *Zwei Jahre unter den Kannibalen der Salomoinseln*.
2. G. C. Wheeler, *Mono-Alu Folklore*.
3. The last of the coast dwellers moved three miles inland in 1939 and built a new hamlet at Flying-fox creek (Morokentu).
4. See later for data on exchange value.
5. See p. 230.
6. By "lots" I mean separate transactions.
7. For this latter kind of classification see Chap. 2.
8. See p. 299.
9. See pp. 173-174.
10. To the best of my knowledge this rite was performed in northeast Siuai only twice during my stay, both times by the same life-prolonger. Unfortunately I was not able to talk with the patients and learn their reactions to the rite. It would have been interesting indeed to discover how they felt about untying the knots!
11. See p. 89.
12. In some cases a *kuna* specialist buys his mixture ready-made and does not collect it — often not even knowing its ingredients; under these circumstances he will replenish his stock by merely adding red clay from time to time.
13. In other cases the specialist himself rubs the *kuna* onto the patient's fontanelle, ear opening, upper lip, stomach, and nipples.
14. See pp. 91-92.
15. See pp. 87-92.
16. See pp. 87-88.
17. See p. 105.
18. See pp. 171-173.
19. See p. 172.
20. See p. 89.
21. See pp. 91-92.
22. For example, see p. 315.
23. See p. 172.
24. For a comprehensive interpretation of *debt*, see E. E. Evans-Pritchard, *Social Anthropology* (London, 1951), pp. 107-108, which is based partly on C. M. Arensberg, *The Irish Countryman* (New York, 1937).
25. See p. 229.
26. A very tall tree with few limbs; anyone climbing it would be completely exposed to public view.
27. See pp. 213-214.
28. See pp. 29, 434.
29. Finer distinctions could be drawn to classify converts into several categories, according to scope of knowledge of church doctrine, adherence to mission rules, participation in rituals, etc.; but these distinctions are not significant enough sociologically to warrant giving more space to them in this general monograph.

30. E. W. P. Chinnery, *Territory of New Guinea Anthropological Report No. 5* (Canberra), p. 87.

31. See pp. 110–111.

32. The only instance of general inter-sect rivalry that occurred during my visit to Siuai took place when native evangelists of both sects organized a contest ("race") between their best-informed members, to see who possessed better knowledge of biblical history. The "race" took place in the dancing ground in front of a club-house and was attended by scores of partisan onlookers. First of all two blackboards were set up to see which evangelists could write better. Then questions were hurled back and forth in the manner of a spelling-bee. Out of this demonstration of learning came, among other jewels, the following explanation of the origins of Methodism, produced by a Methodist evangelist:

"The Popis were first, but their customs were not good since they kept all the news about Maker out of reach of blackmen by hiding it in a Bible written in the Roma language. Then later on the Methodists came up, the first of them being a man named John Wesley, who put the Bible into English. This caused a mumi named King Herod to become angry, so he cut off John Wesley's head. King Herod's place was Gariri, but I don't know whether he was a Popi or not."

33. See p. 309.

34. This is according to native reports, which might be exaggerated.

35. The two Novei kinsmen of Poroni who did not become stanch Methodists have retained their amicable relations with other Moronei villagers; for example, they participate in the Moronei gardening team previously described (see p. 309).

36. This account is based entirely on natives' reports; I was not able to check their explanations with official records.

37. This continues to be the case. The last decade of numerous contacts between Siuai and whites has not resulted in a uniform attitude towards all whites. The latter are all called by the pidgin term "master" but to the Siuai this by no means carries the full English meaning. Some "masters," such as the District Officer in Kieta, are held in great awe and are feared because of their seeming omnipotence. Others are feared and hated; still others are held in utter contempt; while a few are even liked and respected! No one who has listened to Siuai natives discuss known white personalities in their own language would long entertain any illusions about the attitudes of these people towards their so-called superiors.

38. From the whites' point of view this kind of incident was not as unreasoning and ruthless as it here appears. It was merely a standard technique for establishing the authority of the Australian Administration, it having been considered (I imagine) to be the most practical and effective way to introduce the natives to the new regime and the western civilization it represented.

39. See p. 58.

40. See p. 115. Informants say that the northern part of Mokakaru used to be dominated by Left-behinds (Tree-rat's sub-sib).

41. The hamlets now forming the line villages of Turuŋom and Jeku were excluded from Konsei's jurisdiction, and consequently added to Kope's, at Konsei's own behest. According to residents of those two villages, their hatred of Konsei was so bitter because of the punitive raid he had perpetrated that Konsei was afraid to have direct contact with them because of their sorcery.

42. See p. 15.

43. *Kukerai* is the pidgin word used throughout the Kieta District of the Territory of New Guinea to mean village headman; elsewhere in the Territory the headman is called either *kukerai* or *luluai*.

44. *Tultul* is taken from the Blanche Bay (New Britain) language, and originally meant "chief's messenger."

45. The Native Administration Regulations specify as follows (Part III, 120): "(1) The Director of District Services and Native Affairs shall appoint such luluais and kukerais as are necessary for the control and good order of tribes and villages, having due regard to the hereditary and customary chieftainship."

"(2) The Director of District Services and Native Affairs may appoint luluais and kukerais of specified portions of a district, and such luluais and kukerais shall have the chief authority in such specified portions of a district."

"(4) District Officers shall appoint such natives as they think proper to be tul-tuls of the tribes and villages."

46. See below, p. 425.

47. Native Administration Regulation. Part III. 120 (3).

48. In reality, however, many native officials *do* conduct "courts" and render decisions more or less tacitly approved by their superiors. (See below.)

49. The village book is a useful record for Patrol Officers but often an anathema to some natives; on his annual tour the Patrol Officer records in each village book the cases he has adjudicated, along with remarks about the more unsavory characters in the village. Successive Patrol Officers can therefore profit by the experiences of their predecessors, and this makes it more difficult for natives to perpetrate their favorite frauds, such as reopening old litigation, registering complaints against enemies, and claiming hardship tax exemptions.

50. See, for example, p. 156.

51. Overlooking its irony, it continually amused me to see a crowd of natives walking single file down a beautifully finished road 12 to 15 feet wide.

52. Including Constabulary pensioners.

53. See p. 206.

54. See p. 317 for the exceptions.

55. Many Hat-men like Kummai use their authority to induce women to copulate with them, some going so far as to threaten jail sentences if the women do not comply. These measures usually backfire inasmuch as the female victims invariably publicize the episodes in trysting songs (*jiŋje*) ridiculing their unwanted suitors. Medical orderlies are particularly notorious for the tricks they play; some trysting songs describe in vivid detail how certain orderlies "examine" women in search of symptoms, and how they "cure" slight ailments by copulating with the patient — claiming this to be part of white man's medical science.

56. See pp. 105–106.

57. See p. 326.

58. See pp. 201–203.

59. The definition herein used for "community" is "the maximal group of persons who normally reside together in face-to-face association." G. P. Murdock, *Social Structure*, p. 79.

60. See pp. 309–310.

61. See pp. 110–111.

62. See pp. 78, 82.

## Chapter 9

1. It should be kept in mind, however, that *manunu* does not correspond in all respects to the usual English dictionary definition of *capital*.
2. It has, however, begun to be used by some individuals to purchase pottery, lime, and even foodstuffs. In such cases, the vendor usually accepts it, instead of shell money, in order to raise money to purchase western goods or to pay his head-tax. The shilling is also coming into use as "payment" for a mistress' sexual favors.
3. See p. 361.
4. See p. 362.
5. See pp. 165–166.
6. See p. 78.
7. Of such a man it is said: *pesi ru'kori reura*, "Shell money in-earning he-excels."
8. See, for example, pp. 178–182.
9. See p. 59.
10. For a useful definition of "money" see M. J. Herskovits, *Economic Anthropology* (New York, 1952), pp. 238 ff.
11. See H. I. Hogbin, *Experiments in Civilization*, pp. 61 ff., for an account of the manufacture and trading of this shell money in the Central Solomons; much of that now in use in Siuai probably came originally from there. There is also the possibility that some of it originated as far away as New Britain and New Guinea.
12. A span-long string of *mauai* may occasionally be cut into fractions of the span (see page 99) for the purpose of buying certain inexpensive items.
13. A few individuals store their shell money in small storage huts (*nu'ukuunapa*).
14. This difference in valuation might be accounted for on the basis of the relative scarcity of raw materials for manufacturing the red discs, which are made from the lip portion of the red-lipped spondylus; this explanation would apply directly, however, only to the original manufacturers.
15. See p. 46.
16. See p. 53 for another account of its mythical discovery.
17. In addition, the Siuai possess bead "blankets" made by sewing together strings of shells into one- to two-foot squares to which are attached various other shell trinkets. A blanket made of *mauai* is called a *kainoru*, one of white *koso* a *kia*, one of red discs a *pihpino*, etc. All these are matrilineage heirlooms, and while they may be evaluated in terms of *mauai* units, I have never heard of one leaving the possession of its matrilineage owners. My query as to whether anyone ever broke one up to use as money was denied vehemently and, I believe, honestly.
18. Certain high-yielding varieties of taro are more expensive, to cover the cost of the special magical properties involved. (See p. 299.)
19. See p. 410.
20. See pp. 215–217.
21. See p. 110.
22. For details of survey see note 1, Chap. 10, p. 517.
23. See p. 212.
24. Natives are exhorted not to waste this heritage, but such occasionally happens, as attested by the complaints sometimes heard to the effect that "formerly we were wealthy, but our First-born used all our capital."

25. See p. 215.
26. See note 1, Chap. 10, p. 517.
27. See p. 28.
28. See p. 298.
29. *Manoa horova.*
30. See pp. 298–299.
31. See p. 224.
32. At one divorce case I witnessed, the wife-plaintiff testified: "My husband is miserly and will not buy a pig for me to feed, so that other women taunt me and I am continually ashamed."
33. See pp. 30–31.
34. One with a girth of *tusinni* is worth 20 mauai; *ku'kurua*, 30; *mukonna*, 40; *morokeŋkuho*, 50; *monikoŋ hoŋoma-kuruho*, 60; *ho'rorimeruho*, 70; *hoŋomirumiruruho*, 80; *kumoputoruho*, 90. For meanings and lengths of these span fractions see p. 99.
35. I have no data on the situation that would result if a provisional owner of a pig, the *aŋurara*-man, were to dispose of a pig to someone or for some purpose other than to or for the residual owner. In fact, I doubt if such things occur.
36. See Peabody Museum Papers, vol. 29, no. 3.
37. *Ibid.*
38. See p. 328.
39. See p. 305.
40. See p. 304.
41. See pp. 302–303.
42. This is an impression which I was unable to document, most *mikai* being rather secretive about their earnings — probably to avoid unfavorable comparison with professional rivals.
43. See pp. 307–308.
44. See pp. 134–135.
45. See p. 165.
46. See pp. 177–182.
47. In some cases this applies to sibs, in others to sub-sibs or to even finer subdivisions, depending upon the degree to which the *noroukuru* has become segmented for symbolic purposes. In this connection it should be noted that the *sinapo* rite is even more exclusively identified with the *noroukuru* than is *maru*; it is permissible, though not desirable, for *maru* identified with one *noroukuru* to be used on behalf of a member of a different *noroukuru*.
48. For other occasions when many of the elements of *sinapo* ritual are performed see Chap. 2.
49. The sinapo-specialist is not necessarily wealthy in her (or his) own name; the office being passed from mother to daughter or mother's brother to sister's son. This office is separate from that of the First-born, although one individual may hold both offices.
50. In some instances this shell money is part of the heirloom of the deceased's matrilineage; in others it is merely borrowed from one of the onlookers for the occasion. Logically, since wealth-magic is designed mainly to increase the supply of currency rather than matrilineage heirlooms, it would seem more appropriate to use

currency in the ritual. Perhaps the occasional use of heirlooms points to a time when most objects of wealth were, in fact, property of the matrilineage.

51. See p. 92.
52. A sacrifice to the pig, the essence of the coconut meat and milk being intended as a meal for the pig's soul.
53. An economy measure, to avoid having to distribute large quantities of pork at the funeral feast. (See pp. 209-210.)
54. See pp. 87-88.
55. See p. 87.
56. See p. 88.
57. See p. 90.
58. See p. 92.
59. See p. 88.
60. See p. 92.
61. See pp. 89-90.

*Chapter 10*

1. I carried out a property inventory throughout all fifteen line villages of northeast Siuai, recording each household's possessions in terms of shell currency, pigs, producing coconut and sago palms, and almond trees; for the rest of Siuai I attempted to record only shell money. For northeast Siuai I believe my data to be fairly reliable; but for the rest of Siuai I am convinced that many individuals held back information because of suspicions of my motives; and for computing purposes I have included data only from those line villages about which I feel reasonably safe, that is, from 18 out of 43. Using this sample, then, two out of five households reportedly possess either no shell currency at all or at most only a few spans. Among the remaining households, possessing 20 spans or more, the average for all Siuai is 634 spans. However, this figure by no means represents a normal distribution curve, as the following indicates:

| Amount of shell currency (spans) | Number of households |
|---|---|
| 20-100 | 37 |
| 100-199 | 58 |
| 200-299 | 50 |
| 300-399 | 29 |
| 400-499 | 19 |
| 500-599 | 15 |
| 600-699 | 12 |
| 700-799 | 5 |
| 800-899 | 10 |
| 900-999 | 6 |
| 1000-9999 | 28 |
| over 10,000 | 1 |

2. *Rohorahki paru.*
3. See p. 166.
4. *Muuking kupuri.*

5. *Nomai rakuraku.*

6. See p. 327.

7. A living native's *ura* can visit most spirits with impunity (i.e., it does not become Near-death) unless it eats with them.

8. See pp. 135–137.

9. See pp. 212–215.

10. See pp. 41–46.

11. What menu differences there are depend upon other factors.

12. See p. 213.

13. *Haraŋitutu.* See p. 189.

14. See p. 351.

15. See p. 74.

16. The *raoku* is described by natives as having been introduced from Terei, the *pata* from Nagovisi.

17. After the feast these pipes will be destroyed. This is not done in order to make a mystery of them — it is merely that they have served the unique purpose for which they were made; the song itself may be recalled and sung by individuals whenever they are moved to music but thenceforth no host would again feature it at a feast. Siuai panpipes do not form part of the cult paraphernalia of men's societies as is the case in Sepik River cultures; they are not deified or hidden from females, etc.

18. Siuais say that these *koka* used to be carried only when men played panpipes made in Ruparu.

19. See pp. 193–194.

20. Another device is to use a special bivalve, a satiation-maker (*hapokisi'ha*), for peeling the taro used in the puddings.

21. *Boiga irregularis.*

22. I know of no other meaning for this word.

23. I know of no other meaning for this word.

24. A term taken over from the neighboring Terei language and having no other meaning in Motuna.

25. Drumsticks (*aŋuaŋu*) are made out of a very hard wood (*raŋu,* or *rumai*), and are sometimes carved in the form of an elongated hornbill.

26. See p. 233.

27. Alas! this is the only overt expression of "penis envy" I observed in Siuai — and it is in direct opposition to the oft-heard admonition hurled at little tom-boys: "Stop that! Or you'll grow a penis."

28. See pp. 301–302.

29. See p. 380.

30. Informants stated that formerly all war-leaders used to consecrate a new gong by dismembering a man, stuffing the parts of his body into the hollow, and using his head to beat the first signal.

31. See p. 43.

32. See p. 351.

33. See note 3, Introduction, p. 491.

34. See p. 297.

35. See p. 230.

36. See p. 213.

37. See p. 189.
38. See pp. 307–308.

39. Until I grasped these principles in the field I was sorely puzzled when natives appeared more chagrined than pleased to accept good bargains and what appeared to be generous gifts from acquaintances in other communities.

40. Sometimes a Defender will add some pigs of his own to the host's in order to mobilize more co-defenders. By doing this he makes a *coercive gift* to the host of the services provided by the extra co-defenders, and thereby adds to his own renown. This action does not, however, serve to increase the host's renown as well, since everyone knows the part played by the Defender in mobilizing the extra-large force of co-defenders.

41. See pp. 415–416.

42. Here enters an inconsistency: the recipient must redistribute the gifts he has received among his co-attackers, and they promptly consume them; consequently the recipient cannot simply hoard the gift intact and later on give it back to the donor. He must repay an equivalent amount but he may not repay it with the actual pigs and shell money received. On the other hand, the donor's spirit-familiar accompanying the gift is said to guard over it to see that it is eventually returned. This inconsistency does not trouble the Siuai; informants simply shrug it off.

*Chapter 11*

1. See p. 78.
2. See p. 78.
3. See p. 74.
4. This colloquy (*tati*) has no direct consequences; the supernatural guardian of the shrine takes no action whether the *Near-death*'s *umiai* acknowledges few or many accomplishments.
5. This obviously refers to a bolide's explosion, which the Siuai have either heard or heard about.
6. See p. 76.
7. See pp. 356–357.
8. Compare this trait with the paying of *pavaru* in return for flattery. See pp. 370–371.
9. See p. 227.
10. See pp. 333–334.
11. See p. xviii.
12. See pp. 328–329.
13. See p. 239.
14. See pp. 110–112.
15. *Solomon Islands School Exercises: English-Motuna.*
16. See p. 213.
17. See p. 381.
18. See p. 214.
19. A variant on the *tapi* ceremony is the *suke* ritual, consisting of spears thrown one at a time.
20. See pp. 213–214.
21. See p. 309.
22. See p. 189.

23. See pp. 330–332.

24. It should be emphasized that this hierarchic arrangement is based only on interaction events having to do with activities of the men's society. In other social contexts the interaction order may be reversed; for example, in connection with affairs of a matrilineage it is not unusual to find a sub-leader, in the position of First-born, originating orders to his men's society leader, who happens to be a younger member of the matrilineage.

25. Formerly, a few Siuai natives owned the services of prostitutes (*nunupoku*) but this was not the prerogative of leaders alone.

26. Not because of any moral issue but rather because of the troubles that attend promiscuity.

27. There are however, definite limits to a leader's authority over women's actions; for example, he possesses sexual use-rights over only his own spouse.

28. Men often warn women and children not to go near club-houses because of the demons there but this is in the nature of a reminder of a well-known state of affairs.

29. See pp. 229, 386–390.

30. See p. 230.

31. See p. 33.

32. See pp. 333–334.

33. See p. 344.

34. See p. 350.

35. Except, of course, over those relatives who are subordinate to him in other respects.

36. The term *hunu* is also heard in another kind of situation: when one man speaks harshly or imperiously to another, a bystander might ask, "Is that his fool, that he can talk so abusively to him?"

37. One possible exception to this may be the leader Kope (see above, p. 328), whose career I did not investigate very closely, however.

38. In connection with this description of the drawbacks of leadership I should again record the opinion of some informants regarding the misfortunes of polygyny. These cynics point out that a man is almost required to have more than one woman in his household if he wants to produce enough food to feed the pigs needed for a feast-giving career. And if it could be avoided, what man in his right mind would imperil his domestic tranquility by having more than one wife!

39. See p. 375.

40. See p. 319.

## Chapter 12

1. Informants stated that several Solomon Islanders had settled down among the southerners, and that these had been responsible for the aggressiveness of the southerners.

2. This killer was Kupiraki, of Mokakaru. (See p. 412.)

3. A Rugara term, "soul-hiding," the Siuai having acquired this trait from Terei.

4. See p. 92.

5. See p. 90.

6. White paint (*hiku*), made from clay, is a symbol of death; people wear it only when mourning or when preparing for a fight.

7. This was said in response to my explaining that in some places men had to avoid sexual intercourse before fighting.

8. In all my inquiries I learned of no other kind of occasion characterized by such sexual license.

9. I saw one such stick, some twenty years old, hidden away in the thatch of a clubhouse; the local Methodist catechist had tried in vain to get the owner to destroy it because of its evil associations and persistent magical potency.

10. This *kana* formula lists the names of men who formerly performed the ritual and explicitly exhorts them to protect the war-magician and his associates during battle. And implicitly, by calling the names of those former romanopo, it solicits their aid in "pre-killing" the doomed enemies.

This *kana* ritual is believed to have been created by Orphan, who passed it on to another kupuna, Ikaipakai, who in turn passed it on to Ariku, and so on down the list. When the current performer dies his name will also be added to the list.

The shooting contest (*suke*) mentioned alludes to an episode in a myth about two brothers who walked about the countryside with their bows and arrows, shooting at objects as a gesture of mourning for their deceased parents. (See p. 402.)

11. So powerful, however, is Invulnerability magic that its wearer will not be slain even if pre-killed in this manner.

12. The tactic known as *runoto*, now used at *muminai* feasts (see p. 369).

13. Spears, bows and arrows, clubs, and trade ax-adzes were used in warfare, and all my informants were agreed that the bow was the most effective weapon, spears and clubs having been more for show. Evidently, these fierce warriors did not care for close-in fighting! I could extract no evidence of disciplined combat; after the first few challenging spear-runs fighting seems to have been a free-for-all.

14. See p. 76.
15. See p. 154.
16. See p. 126.
17. A phenomenon known as *kikiriva*.
18. See p. 230.
19. Inter-personal feuding, unlike wars, sometimes continued for generations; both a man's son and his sister's son would carry on his grievances against his adversary's son or matrilineage.
20. See p. 149.
21. See p. 415.
22. See p. 408.

23. Before leaving this subject of warfare it needs to be recalled that some of its elements have survived in the tamer institutions of the present day. The human skulls that once adorned club-houses are now replaced by pigs' mandibles, but competitive feasting possesses many of the traits of fighting: for example, the host and his followers and allies are "Defenders," the guests "Attackers"; the arrival of the latter dramatizes in dance the challenging attack-opener of battle; the competitively successful host "kills" his vanquished guest; and so on in various ways that the reader will doubtless already have noted. Moreover, certain aspects of warfare have also survived in present-day litigation: Invulnerability and Killing-stuff are often used by the principals, and the successful litigant speaks of "slaying'" his opponent. But these are all pallid reminders of the times when men fought with weapons rather than with words and pigs.

## Chapter 13

1. To any reader interested only in the general account of rank-acquiring, this chapter may be passed over without risk of loss of continuity.

2. Some readers may object to the use of the word "history" in this context since there is no written documentation behind it. In defense it can only be said that the "history" presented covers a relatively recent time span and that the events in question were independently described by several informants. Moreover, even if this "history" were not "true" it nevertheless possesses ethnographic significance (see Chap. 12, pp. 411–412).

3. See p. 319.

4. See p. 319.

5. For the cultural anthropologist some more detailed information about this period of uncertainty and change would be of great interest, but unfortunately such information is not available.

6. See p. 328.

7. Identity unknown.

8. See p. 328.

9. The average size of 64 Siuai line villages was 70 in 1938; the average size of Turuŋom during 1938–39 was 95.

10. See pp. 424–425.

11. Reraka, and not the Ronoro creek, as was erroneously reported in my "Land Tenure in Northeast Siuai," p. 62.

12. See p. 111.

13. Maimoi was a loyal adherent of Soŋi's although a resident of Rennu village.

14. See p. 171.

15. See p. 391.

16. Because of the nature of death in childbirth it cannot be postponed by "life-tying." (See p. 89.)

17. A visitor from Mi'kahna village.

18. After the feast, when there was no need for his full-time services at the club-house, Ho'oma slipped back into his usual routine; slept at home and worked industriously in his garden. He no longer directed fellow villagers as they worked at their more prosaic tasks; and his two sons resumed their customary roles as the village laggards.

19. By October 1939, the social merger of the two villages had become so complete that the Australian Patrol Officer officially recognized it and persuaded Soŋi to become Headman (*kukerai*) of both villages. This merger was not a mere verbal political alliance, it was effected by the closer associations among natives of the two villages and by the direct authority which Soŋi began to exercise over all of them — an authority, moreover, which did not refer through Tukem. At first Tukem did not behave as though he objected to being supplanted. He appeared to share in the renewed *esprit de corps* just as all the other natives did, with one exception.

The exception was Soŋi's old enemy in Rennu, who used to sit alone in Tukem's club-house while his friends flocked to Turuŋom. He even forbade his wife and daughter to attend a memorial feast given on behalf of Soŋi's deceased wife. Later on, he moved out of Rennu in disgust and returned to his birthplace at Mataras.

20. Tukem's authority was weakened so considerably by this merger that he later became involved in an argument with one of his former adherents and was threatened with an ax. He became so resentful that he expressed his intention of returning — along with the old man — to Mataras.

21. The principal Defender.

*Chapter 14*

1. Compared with kin-group authority role-holders in many nonliterate societies, Siuai First-borns and Old-ones have only weak traditional powers behind them.

2. Any attempt to explain living Siuais' deference for mumis in terms of universal psychological factors (e.g., the "impulse to surrender" of C. E. Merriam, *Political Power*, New York, 1934, pp. 231–246) seems to me to be wholly unacceptable. Siuai natives behave deferentially towards mumis because they are culturally conditioned to do so.

3. I have already described the present-day institution of leadership in some detail, so in order not to lengthen this account even more I shall not attempt to summarize in formal terms the organization of men's societies or the mode of operation of leaders. There exist numerous systems of terminology applicable to this sort of analysis, and particularly for comparative studies; but in a descriptive monograph like the present one it seems to the writer that the reader's understanding of these phenomena would not be significantly increased by paraphrasing the materials in terms of some other writer's formal systematics.

4. In formulating the following I have been influenced chiefly by the writings of Georges Gurvitch, *Sociology of Law* (New York, 1942); "Social Control" in *Twentieth Century Sociology* (New York, 1945); E. Adamson Hoebel, "Fundamental Legal Concepts as Applied in the Study of Primitive Law," *Yale Law Journal*, vol. 51, no. 6 (1942); "Law and Anthropology," *Virginia Law Review*, vol. 32, no. 4 (1946); *Man in the Primitive World* (New York, 1949); (with K. N. Llewellyn) *The Cheyenne Way* (Norman, Oklahoma, 1941); and George Homans, *The Human Group* (New York, 1950). I have also profited by reading the various published works of Bronislaw Malinowski and A. R. Radcliffe-Brown on this subject. However, in a descriptive work like this one it seems best to avoid terminological dilemmas and leave it up to the reader, utilizing his own favored terminology, to decide whether an action is a "private delict" or a "crime," whether a control measure is a "custom" or a "law," etc. Hence the following analysis will be couched in general terms.

5. See p. 227.

6. As Homans states: "the understanding of social control comes from looking *differentially* at the relations of mutual dependence in the social system," *The Human Group*, p. 292.

7. Divorce is also an exception to this generalization; other relatives of an injured spouse sometimes intervene and take the steps which culminate in divorce.

8. Authority role-holders in Congregations and Administrative groups also attempt to extend their effectiveness throughout all phases of life, but these are not indigenous institutions.

9. E. A. Hoebel, *Man in the Primitive World*.

10. This is of course a redundancy, since by calling a men's society *active*, we are also expressing the idea that its social control mechanisms are effective.

11. See p. 399.
12. See pp. 372–375.
13. Unfortunately I did not inquire about the fate of the Rennu *horomorun* after Rennu's men's society became consolidated with Turuŋom's. See p. 436.
14. See p. 68.
15. See pp. 309–310.

*Chapter 15*

1. This belief is based on the encouraging progress already made in this direction by Clyde Kluckhohn (for a summation of his views and for references to earlier writings, see his paper "The Concept of Culture" in *The Policy Sciences*, Eds., D. Lerner and H. D. Lasswell, Stamford, 1951); by D. D. Lee, "A Primitive System of Values"; by B. L. Whorf, "The Relation of Habitual Thought and Behavior to Language"; by Harry Hoijer, "Cultural Implications of Some Navaho Linguistic Categories," *Language*, vol. 27 (1951); by Ward Goodenough, "Property, Kin, and Community of Truk"; and by Margaret Mead, in many of her ethnographic writings. For some other interesting but more apperceptive and less inductive methods of analysis the reader is referred to the works of Ruth Benedict, Gregory Bateson, Morris Opler, and J. J. Honigmann.
2. Including imperfect congruity between linguistic patterns and "thought."
3. There are of course several other conceivable ways of indicating the degree of "integration" of a culture (or of the sub-cultures associated with members of a single society), but the one utilized here seems to me to be at least as fundamental as any other method of analysis.
4. There are of course several other premises underlying the patterns which go to make up the marriage institution — including those relating to choice of spouse and exchange of valuables, but these will not be recapitulated here since our present concern is with *comparable* premises of the four systems.
5. Underlying this last point are some even more basic premises — e.g., "old customs are best," etc. — which, however, underly many of the premises specifically associated with Kinship as well.
6. Comparable generalizations are grouped under identical roman numerals to permit the reader to compare similar or contrasting aspects of the four systems.
7. Being those of the League of Nations Mandate system, which prevailed at the time of this field work.
8. Catechists receive small annual salaries and in addition are tax exempt, but I do not believe that these incentives are influential in determining a native's decision to become a catechist.
9. In situations where Mission norms happen to be identical with those of the Kinships system — e.g., rules against incest among family siblings — shame or guilt may however accompany violations.
10. For a more detailed summary it would be necessary to distinguish between Catholic and Methodist sub-systems.
11. Pidgin English derogatory term for country bumpkin.
12. Florence Kluckhohn, "Dominant and Substitute Profiles of Cultural Orientations: Their Significance for the Analysis of Social Stratification," *Social Forces*, vol. 28, no. 4 (May 1950).

13. I do not mean to imply by this that norms of social behavior analytically referable to a single ideology are entirely congruent. Recall, for example, the case of social relationships within men's societies. There is inevitably some conflict of opinion between followers and leaders concerning the relative valuations of the scarce goods transacted (i.e., services, etc., for reflected renown). In this sense norms regarding the "economy" of intrafamily transactions are more explicitly "balanced" — although in actual practice there are frequent breakdowns in "economy," leading to social conflict among members.

14. See p. 225.

15. Role conflict may be "bad" from the standpoint of personality integration, and social conflict may be "bad" if it consumes energies needed, say, for physical survival in a difficult environment, but otherwise I do not wish to imply that I believe a high degree of ideological integration is necessarily a "good" thing. As a matter of fact, the existence of alternative goals and behavioral norms can be considered "good" in terms of providing better conditioning for adaptation to environmental change and in terms of producing fewer socially penalized deviant persons — provided the role and social conflicts thereby engendered are not "too" serious. (Judgment concerning the point at which conflicts become "too" serious depends of course upon the evaluation criteria applied. See Chap. 17.)

16. It is clearly evident to me that all the field work which went into the formulation of these generalizations should be regarded as merely preliminary, a plotting out of the outlines of the culture. Really significant findings could only follow from another period of field work devoted to following clues such as this one about the direction of culture change. Unfortunately, Siuai culture was so buffeted about by World War II that a second study based on the present formulations is no longer feasible.

*Chapter 16*

1. See p. 24.
2. Naturally, I cannot vouch for the originality of these "inventions."
3. In this connection it is interesting to point out that the Siuai had not succumbed to "Cargo-cultism" up to the time of our departure.
4. "The Horomorun Concepts of Southern Bougainville," in *Peabody Museum Papers*, vol. 20 (Cambridge, Mass., 1943).
5. See p. 327.
6. See p. 317.
7. See p. 328.

*Chapter 17*

1. From what follows the reader may correctly infer that I consider it both legitimate and essential for anthropologists to evaluate the cultures they study. My position in this matter closely resembles that of David Bidney as stated in his "Concept of Value in Modern Anthropology" (in A. L. Kroeber and others, *Anthropology Today*, Chicago, 1952), hence need not be expounded here in detail.

2. These first and second vantage points from which to evaluate cultures have become more or less identified with anthropological "schools": the first with A. R. Rad-

cliffe-Brown and some of his students; the second with Bronislaw Malinowski and some of his.

3. By D. F. Aberle, A. K. Cohen, A. K. Davis, M. J. Levy, Jr., and F. X. Sutton. This paper appears in *Ethics*, vol. LX, No. 2 (Jan. 1950). The authors of this paper modestly acknowledge that their list of "functional prerequisites" may not be definitive, stating, "It is subject to revision with the growth of general theory and with experience in its application to concrete situations," p. 100.

4. These authors' use of the term "group" corresponds to my use of the terms "group" and "aggregate." See above, pp. 102–103.

5. Aberle, *et al.*, "The Functional Prerequisites of a Society," p. 101.

6. "There may be a complete turnover of individuals, but the society may survive." "Functional Prerequisites," p. 101.

7. "Our theory of action uses the concept of an actor whose orientation to his situation is threefold: cognitive, affective, and goal-directed. The actor is an abstraction from the total human being. Many of the qualities of the human being constitute part of the situation, the set of means and conditions, within which the actor operates." "Functional Prerequisites," p. 100. See also, Talcott Parsons, *Essays in Sociological Theory: Pure and Applied* (Glencoe, Ill., 1949).

8. "Functional Prerequisites," p. 102.

9. Op. cit., pp. 103–104.

10. The reader will bear in mind that these statements are written in terms of conditions existing in 1938–39, and do not take into account the disasters which soon afterwards befell.

11. "Functional Prerequisites," p. 104. If we were engaged in evaluating any one trait or complex, etc., from the point of view of societal continuity, it would only be necessary to inquire concerning the extent to which it assists or blocks realization of one or more of these functional prerequisites. See Chap. 14.

12. Op. cit., p. 104.

13. If we were to ask how effective an instrument Siuai culture provides for adapting to and exploiting the physical environment in terms of the potentialities suggested by modern western science then we would of course have to give it a low score in most respects. As for the Motuna language, however, it is probably not much more defective than some western ones as a frame for comprehending and expressing the logic of western science.

14. Or a war of near-extermination!

15. Op. cit., pp. 105–106.

16. Op. cit., p. 106.

17. Op. cit., p. 107.

18. Op. cit., p. 108.

19. Op. cit., p. 108.

20. W. L. Warner, *A Black Civilization*.

21. "Functional Prerequisites," p. 109.

22. An exception is to be found in the case of the sons of some leaders. See p. 403.

23. See Chap. 5.

24. "Functional Prerequisites," p. 110.

25. These and the following figures are based on systematic observations of consumption in several sample families in various villages.

26. This figure does not represent an estimate such as might be made by an expert

agronomist using modern methods of soil analyses, crop rotation, etc. It is rather an estimate based on Siuai gardening techniques, and takes into consideration their aesthetic requirements of "orderly, directional gardening." (See above, pp. 22–26.)

27. See p. 27.

28. This figure is certainly not absolutely correct, but is very near to being so because I covered the region intensively while mapping it, and would have been aware of major discrepancies.

29. Stimulated partly by the Administration prescript that ten palms be planted for every newborn child; and partly by the example of ex-indentured laborers just returned from plantations.

30. The same is true of areca palms and breadfruit trees.

31. See the writings of Bronislaw Malinowski.

32. These differences in consumption needs were taken into consideration when estimating the extent of land in taro.

33. See pp. 132–133.

34. For advice and information on physiological needs I am indebted to J. W. M. Whiting.

35. Which are mainly of cultural origin.

36. It is not beyond the realm of possibility, however, that some natives might be cremated before they have actually expired. In one instance I witnessed, a young girl who was only unconscious was considered dead, and active preparations were under way for her cremation. Fortunately she revived before being placed on the pyre.

37. The tentative proposal of this "need" is based on some findings announced by Gregory Pincus and Hudson Hoagland in *American Journal of Psychiatry*, vol. 106, No. 9 (March 1950), "Adrenal Cortical Responses to Stress in Normal Men and in those with Personality Disorders": "It is possible that faulty potassium metabolism in the face of the repeated stresses of daily life may be an important cumulative factor in the development of a psychosis." Pp. 649–650.

38. For readers who are disturbed by exclusion of *sex* from this list, I should explain that I regard sex as a *drive*, but not as a physiological *need*. Of course, no society can continue without reproduction, but most individuals can survive without sexual satisfaction.

39. Main stimulus for this section came from discussions recorded in *Science, Philosophy and Religion: A Symposium*, Second Symposium of the Conference on Science, Philosophy and Religion in their Relation to the Democratic Way of Life, Inc. (New York, 1942). Specifically, the ideas are based on the paper by Margaret Mead, "The Comparative Study of Culture and the Purposive Cultivation of Democratic Values," and on comments on this paper by Clyde Kluckhohn and Geoffrey Gorer.

40. That is, *equitable* and *relevant* from the standpoint of this writer's personal value system, which, admittedly has little or nothing to do with Siuai values.

41. Again, the value involved in this question is not a Siuai value.

42. Op. cit.

43. The author is of course aware that, logically, "evaluation" is meaningful only with reference to some other culture or cultures. However, in writing this chapter it has been left to the readers to supply their own references, from knowledge of other cultures, including their own.

# SUBJECT INDEX

Abnormalities, physical and mental, 78, 151–2, 189, 382
Abortion, 171
Acculturation, 201–3, 295–6, 318–9, 458–9. *See also* Administration, Missions
Administration, xvii–xviii, 106–7, 125, 128, 304, 307–8, 312, 318–29, 406–7, 409, 458–61, 471
Adolescence, 72, 201
Adoption. *See* Orphans
Adultery, 167–8, 170, 186, 197, 234, 265–6
Adulthood, 72–3
Affection, definition, 234
Aged, the, 72–5, 208–9
Age-grades, 73, 77, 99
Aggregates (social), definition, 102–3. *See also* Sibs, Tribe
Agriculture, 17–9, 22–30, 98, 129–35, 309–11, 352, 446, 479–84. *See also* Almonds, Bananas, Breadfruit, Coconuts, Sago, Sweet potatoes, Yams
Agricultural magic, 131, 134–5, 301
Almonds, 28–9, 37–8, 43, 96, 298, 311, 347–8, 480
Amity, definition, 234
Anatomy (human), beliefs about, 69–70
Ancestors, 80–1
Animals, principal species, 9; use of, 11–2, 30–1; beliefs about, 46–62; 65–9, 84, 453. *See also* Chickens, Dogs, Hunting, Pets, Pigs
Animal husbandry. *See* Chickens, Pigs
Annual cycle, 37–8, 96, 329
Architecture, 19–21, 35, 125–7, 372
Areca nut, 480
Artists, 306, 355
Arts, 35–7, 447, 499. *See also* Dancing, Music, Ornamentation, Poetry, Woodcarving
Astronomy, 68–9
Authority, definition, 491; general, 465; in hamlets, 238–9; in households, 228, 235; in matrilineages, 111; in men's societies, 387, 435–6; in neighborhoods, 388, 405–7, 441–4; in villages and districts, xvii–xviii, 407–8; pre-European (political), 419–21
Avoidance, definition, 234; 265–6

Bachelors, 138
Bananas, 26, 479
Baptism, 45, 176–82
Barrenness, 500
Basketry, 14, 35

Beauty, ideals of, 150
Betel chewing, 35, 234, 328, 363, 366. *See also* Areca nut, Lime
Betrothal, 154–8, 499
Beverages, 322. *See also* Coconuts, Water
Birth, 173–4, 454, 501
Birth order, 82, 111, 195–6. *See also* Family structure
Blood, beliefs about, 81. *See also* Menstruation
Boats. *See* Rafts
Body, beliefs about, 69–76
Borrowing and Lending, 229, 344, 356, 407. *See also* Credit
Breadfruit, 28
Breath, beliefs about, 69
Bride price, 154–8, 161–3, 284–8
Burial, 322. *See also* Cemeteries
Buying and Selling, 229, 340–4, 350–1, 365–7, 389–90, 429–32. *See also* Money, Trade partners

Calendar. *See* Time
Capital, definition, 337–8
Captives, 149, 154, 296
Cardinal points, 100
Cemeteries, 76, 212
Ceramics. *See* Pottery
Ceremonies. *See* Baptism, Birth, Funerals, Weddings, etc.
Chastity, 141, 152
Chickens, 34
Chiefs. *See* Administration, Authority (village and district)
Childbirth. *See* Birth
Childhood, beliefs about, 72
Children, 169, 187–97; activities of, 141, 189–91, 383; education of, 141, 191–4; discipline, 194–5; rituals for, 188–9, 214–5. *See also* Orphans, Illegitimacy
Christianity. *See* Missions
Churches. *See* Congregations, Missions
Cleanliness, 150–1, 204
Climate, 9, 19, 37–8, 492
Clothing, 12, 21, 161, 464, 322
Clubs. *See* Men's societies, Weapons
Club-houses, 86, 372–80
Coconuts, 14, 27–8, 347, 479–80, 492
Collecting, economic, 12, 30
Colonial administration. *See* Administration
Community. *See* Neighborhoods
Composers, 306, 355, 368–9, 432–3

# SUBJECT INDEX

Conception, 69–70, 80, 169–70, 500
Condiments. See Food, Salt
Confinement, 174–8. See also Birth, Pregnancy
Congregations, 313–8. See also Missions
Containers, 13–5, 35
Continence, 170–1, 182, 186
Contraception, 170
Conversation, styles, 232–3
Cooking, 14, 34–5, 44
Corporation, definition, 496
Cosmology and Cosmogony, 39–69
Courts and Trials, 322–3, 325–6, 410. See also Litigation
Courtship, 144–6, 156. See also Marriage negotiations, Sexual behavior
Creation, of mankind, 39–62; of culture traits, 39–62, 79; of property, 228
Credit, 307–9, 430–2
Cremation. See Funerals
Crime. See Law
Culture heroes. See Universal spirits

Dancing, 36, 178, 369
Daughter. See Family (nuclear)
Day. See Diurnal cycle
Death, 52, 74–7, 176–7, 209–20, 398–9, 402–4, 421, 454. See also Suicide
Defecation, 15, 69, 183, 185, 192
Deference, definition, 234
Defloration, 499
Deformation. See Abnormalities, Mutilation
Deities. See Spirits
Demography. See Population, Birth, Disease
Demons, definition, 67–9. See also Spirits
Descent, 80–1, 107 ff., 239–40, 284, 291–2
Diet, 484. See also Food, Eating
Diffusion, 79–80, 295–6, 468
Dirges, 275–82
Discipline. See Children
Disease, attitudes about, 70, 72, 188, 454; prevention of, 88; treatment, 22, 90–1; occurrence, 10–1, 468. See also Death, Magic and Magicians
Districts (political), 319–21, 328–9
Diurnal cycle, 37–8, 96–8, 135–8
Divination and Diviners, 89–90, 171–2, 304–5, 355, 391–2, 403, 415–6, 437
Division of labor. See Social structure
Divorce, 198–200
Dogs, 30–1, 34
Dominance, definition, 491
Drama, 36, 370, 447
Dreams, 69, 145, 207, 432
Dwellings. See Housing
Dyads (social), definition, 103, 107; kinship dyads, 249–75; specialist-client, 301. See also Artists, Composers, Credit, Family structure, Magic and Magicians, Trade partners
Dyes, 14, 35

Eating, 34–5, 37–8, 69, 129, 135–8, 363–4. See also Diet, Food
Education. See Children, Schools
Elopement, 154
Emigration, 475
Emotion, definition, 227, 231–4
Endogamy (local), 153–4, 222, 246
Enmity, definition, 234
Environment. See Geography
Equality, definition, 234
Ethnocentrism, 79–80
Exchange, definition, 229
Exogamy, 108, 117–21, 246
Exorcism. See Therapy and Therapists

Familiars (spirit), definition, 68; general, 218, 305–6, 338, 372–5, 401–2, 428–9, 445
Family (composite). See Hamlets
Family (nuclear), 140–235; activities, see Households; terminology, 157, 161, 222, 226. Social structure: general, 60, 151, 155–8, 164, 166–9, 215–20, 222–35, 431, 435; mother-child, 182–5, 196, 206–7; father-child, 194–6, 199–200, 205–7; husband-wife, 186–7, 197–200, 223–6, 285–6; siblings, 196, 207–8. See also Divorce, Households, Orphans, Polygamy
Famine, 30
Fashions, 14, 304–6
Fasting. See Mourning
Father. See Family (nuclear)
Fauna, 9, 492, 494
Feasts, 364–72, 390–5, 425–6, 429–39. See also Baptism, Weddings, etc.
Fecundity, 173
Fertility (human), 173, 500
Feuds. See War
Finance, 335–56, 429–32
Fines. See Indemnity
Fire, 13, 322
Fishing, 12, 31–2, 43, 311, 481
Flora, 8–9. See also Plants
Flutes, 36, 368–9, 518
Food, 34–5, 136–7, 363–4, 367–8, 434, 484, 492; beliefs about origin of, 41–3. See also Agriculture, Diet, Eating, Feasts
Force, definition, 491
Friendship, 153, 332–3
Fuel, 23, 481
Funerals, 76, 209–12, 214–5, 402, 404
Furniture, 126–7, 163–4, 372

Games. See Play
Genealogy, 98–9, 111. See also Matrilineages, Sibs
Genitalia, 43–4, 144
Geography, 3–4, 8–9, 467–8

## SUBJECT INDEX 531

Ghosts, definition, 68, 76–7. *See also* Spirits
Gifts, definition, 229–30, 386–90
Gods (Christian), 314, 494. *See also* Missions
Gongs. *See* Slit-gongs
Gourds, 14, 26
Government. *See* Authority, Administration
Groups, definition, 103. *See* Congregations, Hamlets, Households, Matrilineages, Men's societies, Production teams, Villages, Districts
Growth, beliefs about, 70–4, 77–8, 175–6, 188–9. *See also* Baptism, Childhood, Infancy, Initiation.
Growth magic, 171, 175–6
Guardian spirits. *See* Familiars (spirit)
Guests, 389, 391–5, 436–7

Hair, 11–2, 21–2
Hamlets, 105, 236–46; composition, 236–7; activities, 238; social structure, 238–46. *See also* Dyads (kinship)
Heaven and Hell, 42–3, 74, 76–7, 398, 422–6, 495
History, 98–9, 411–21, 451–2, 469–71, 491. *See also* Administration, Missions, Trade
Hoarding, 361
Holidays (religious), 38
Homicide. *See* Sorcery and Sorcerers
Homonyms, 175
Homosexuality, 202, 498–9
Hospitality. *See* Feasts, Guests
Households, 104–5, 125–38; composition, 138–9, 218–9; activities, 127–39, 163–6; property, 125–6, 129, 132, 163–4. *See also* Family (nuclear)
Housing, 16–7, 19–21, 125–9
Humor, 43, 143–4, 168. *See also* Drama
Hunger, 364, 484
Hunting, 12, 30–1, 43, 311–2, 349, 432, 446, 481
Husband. *See* Family (nuclear)

Illegitimacy, 142–3
Immortality, 80. *See also* Heaven and Hell
Implements. *See* Tools
Incest, 108, 117–21, 150–3
Indemnity, definition, 230; general, 406
Infancy, 70–2, 182–7, 454
Infanticide, 501
Influence, definition, 491
Inheritance, 215–8, 226, 230, 342–3, 345
Initiation, 183, 189, 403–4. *See also* Baptism
Insanity. *See* Abnormalities
Interaction, definition, 227
Invention, 448, 469

Jealousy (sexual), 151, 167–8, 197
Justice, 76, 82, 398, 410

Kin aggregates and groups. *See* Family, Hamlets, Households, Matrilineages, Phratries, Sibs
Kinship, 78, 80–1, 247–94, 408; scope, 247–8; system, 288–94, 452–6; terminology, 288–91, 511. *See also* Dyads (kinship), Social structure, etc.
Knowledge, 62–9

Labor, 133, 352, 354
Landlords. *See* Borrowing and Lending
Land tenure, 112–7, 132–4, 199, 216–8, 243–6, 311–3, 400–1, 407–8, 420, 483–4
Land transactions. *See* Inheritance, Borrowing and Lending
Land value, 342–5
Land use, 479–84. *See also* Agriculture, Settlements, etc.
Language, xxi–xxii, 6–7, 39, 62–4, 96, 99–101, 104, 185, 192–3, 493–6, 508, 510. *See also* Kinship terminology, Slit-gongs, etc.
Law (colonial), 322–3
Leadership, definition, 106
Learning. *See* Children (education), Schools
Leasing. *See* Borrowing and Lending
Legends. *See* Myths
Lending. *See* Borrowing and Lending
Levirate, 220–1
Lime, 297–8
Lineage. *See* Matrilineages
Literacy, 314, 316
Litigation, 326, 351, 387. *See also* Courts and Trials
Local groups. *See* Districts, Congregations, Hamlets, Households, Neighborhoods, Villages
Love magic, 144–5, 500
Lunar cycle, 37–8, 96

Magic and Magicians, 83–94; general practitioners, 304–5, 355, 428–9. *See also* Divination and Diviners, Sorcery and Sorcerers, Therapy and Therapists, and under other subject headings, e.g., Agricultural magic, Feasts, Initiation, War, Familiars (spirit), etc.
Marriage, 140–1, 150–1, 220–6; regulation, 81, 108, 117–21, 151–4, 220–1, 225, 245–6, 286; negotiations, 154–8, 221, 284–5. *See also* Weddings
Matrilineages, 111–7, 237, 239, 283, 286–7, 345, 441. *See also* Sibs
Measurement, of distance, 99–100; of time, 37–8; of pig size, 342, 350
Medicine, 11. *See also* Magic and Magicians, Therapy and Therapists
Menopause, 73, 502

## SUBJECT INDEX

Men's societies, 105–6, 329–32, 387, 404, 458. *See also* Rank
Menstruation, 47, 69, 72, 96, 154–5, 201–4
Miscarriage, 70, 170–1, 173. *See also* Sorcery and Sorcerers
Missions, xvii, 38, 47, 107, 304, 313–8, 355, 383, 461–4, 471, 513. *See also* Congregations, Holidays (religious), Gods (Christion)
Money, native, 36, 48, 53, 59, 84, 111–2, 203, 337, 339–45, 361, 457; Australian, 202–3, 338. *See also* Taxation, Capital
Monogamy, 138, 223, 454, 460, 463
Moon, 60, 64, 68, 96, 183, 203–4, 496. *See also* Lunar cycle
Morality, definition, 78–9, 191
Mourning, 212–5, 402–4. *See also* Dirges, Funerals
Murder. *See* Sorcery and Sorcerers
Music, 36, 368–9, 432–4, 447. *See also* Composers, Dirges, Flutes, Singing, Slit-gongs
Mutilation, 22, 183, 188. *See also* Scarification
Mythology, 39–62

Naming, 175
Neighborhoods, 311–13, 333–4
Netting, 14
Numeration, 62–3, 100–1
Nursing, 184

Oaths, 374–5
Obstetrics, 173–4. *See also* Birth
Ochre, 21, 178, 298
Omens, xviii, 74–5, 418, 432. *See also* Death
Oratory, 369–70
Orientation. *See* Cardinal points
Ornamentation, 21–2, 35, 370–1, 447
Opossums, 30–1, 178–80. *See also* Hunting, Food
Orphans, 219, 499. *See also* Universal spirits
Ownership, definition, 496

Pain, 183–4, 188
Painting, 36
Parent. *See* Family (nuclear)
Partnerships. *See* Trade partners
Paternity, 240. *See also* Conception, Family (nuclear), Kinship
Personality, concept of, 70, 78–9, 396–9
Pets, 34, 349
Phallic symbolism, 499
Phratries, 117
Physiology. *See* Body
Pigs, 30–4, 127–8, 136–7, 140, 164–6, 221, 337, 348–54, 357, 359–60, 365–7, 446, 457, 471, 480–1
Plaintains, 26

Plants, ideas about, 453, 493; uses of, 11. *See also* Flora
Play, 36, 190–1, 383
Poetry, 146–9
Political organization. *See* Administration, Men's societies
Polygyny, 220–6, 242–3, 352–3, 457, 463
Population statistics, 4–7, 9–10, 16, 475
Pottery, 13–4, 297, 346
Power, definition, 491
Praise, 193–4, 370–1, 390, 399
Prayer. *See* Magic and Magicians
Pregnancy, 169–73, 454; taboos, 170–1; magic, 171
Prestige, definition, 491; general, 362, 388–90, 399, 419, 456
Production teams, 105, 309–13
Property, definition, 94–6, 215–6, 227, 496; statistics, 353–4, 517; protection, 357–60, 375, 429; increase and destruction magic, 351, 356–7
Prostitution, 149–50, 296, 420
Puberty, 71–2, 201, 203–4

Race, 7–8, 492
Rafts, 295
Raids. *See* War
Rain and rain-making, 60, 65. *See also* Climate
Rank, 82–3, 121, 213, 283–4, 396–410, 456–8, 466
Rape, 82, 145, 477
Recreation, 36–7. *See also* Dancing, Feasts, Play, etc.
Reincarnation, 176
Relatives. *See* Kinship
Religion, 444–6. *See also* Magic and Magicians, Mythology, Spirits, etc.
Rent. *See* Borrowing and Lending
Reproduction, 69–70, 169–70
Repudiation, definition, 234
Residence, 163, 215–20, 236–7, 239–46
Ridicule, 144, 148–9, 151, 192, 194, 307–8, 370, 377, 409, 436–7
Rites of passage. *See* Birth, Weddings, Funerals, Initiation, etc.
Routine, daily. *See* Diurnal cycle

Sacrifice (human), 378, 383, 518
Sago, 29–30, 43, 311, 346–7, 434, 480
Salt, 30, 492–3
Sanctions, definition, 491; general, 442–4. *See also* Social structure
Scarification, 22, 492
Schools, 314
Science, 39
Seasonal activities. *See* Annual cycle
Seclusion, at childbirth, 173–7; menstruation, 204; mourning, 213

# SUBJECT INDEX 533

Seizure, definition, 231
Selling. See Buying and Selling
Semen, beliefs about, 69–70
Senility, 72–5, 208–9, 214
Servants, 149, 331, 404–5, 420
Settlement patterns, 15–9, 125, 481–2
Sexual behavior, 43–4, 69–70, 77, 82, 141–52, 167–8, 201, 501–2
Sexuality, definition, 234
Sharing, definition, 229
Shrines, 60
Sibs, 46–60, 66–8, 81, 83–5, 107–21, 422–3
Sib-spirits, definition, 46–60, 67–8
Sib magic and magicians, 356–7. See also Birth, Weddings, etc.
Siblings. See Family (nuclear), Kinship
Sickness. See Disease
Signaling, 368, 380–3
Sin, 314–5
Singing, 36, 178–9, 186–7, 366, 399, 432–4. See also Dirges
Slavery, 419–20
Sleep, 126, 129, 137
Slit-gongs, 36, 43, 368, 379–86, 464
Social units. See Aggregates, Dyads, Groups
Social structure, 227, 282–8, 313–8, 391–3, 506. See also Emotion, Interaction, Transaction, Social units, etc.
Sodomy. See Homosexuality
Soil, 11
Sorcery and Sorcerers, 87–93, 171–3, 241–2, 303–5, 322, 371, 403, 496. See also Property destruction magic
Sororate, 159, 222
Soul, 54, 69–70, 73–7, 182–3, 398–9, 501, 502
Specialization (labor), 297–9, 301–7, 346, 354–5
Speech, 36–7; learning of, 185, 192
Spirits, classification, 66–9; general, 79–93, 444–6. See also Familiars, Ghosts, Sib spirits, Souls, Territorial spirits, Universal spirits, etc.
Stars, 68
Sterility, 173
Stillbirth, 171, 173
Stone (tools), 11
Succession, xix, 328, 441
Suicide, 67, 167, 197
Sun, 96–7. See also Diurnal cycle
Sweet potatoes, 27, 131–2, 479

Tales, 60–2. See also Mythology
Talking. See Speech, Oratory
Taro, 22–6, 129–31, 298–9, 348, 479, 492
Taxation, 319, 325
Territorial spirits, definition, 68
Textiles, 14
Theft, 89, 91, 351–2

Theology. See Mythology, Missions
Therapy and Therapists, 301–3, 354–5
Time, 37–8, 96–9, 464–5. See also Annual cycle, Lunar cycle, Diurnal cycle, Week
Tobacco, 26, 35
Tools, 11–2, 14
Torts. See Administration, Law
Totemism. See Mythology, Sibs
Toys, 36
Trade, 17, 295–301, 346–8, 447
Trade partners, 296–301, 350–1, 388, 430
Trails, 19, 324
Transaction, definition, 227–31
Tribe, 103–4
Twins, 50, 501

Umbilical cord, 175–6
Unconstraint, definition, 234
Universal spirits, definition, 64; general, 39–46, 219
Universe, beliefs about, 61–6. See also Magic and Magicians, Mythology, Spirits, etc.
Usufruct (concept), 95, 129, 132. See also Land tenure
Utensils, 13

Value (economic), 339–45
Vengeance, 172. See also Sorcery and Sorcerers, War
Villages, 106–7, 326–8. See also Administration
Virginity, 152
Visiting, 166–7, 227, 241–3, 257, 271

Wages, 202, 325, 354–5
Walking, learning, 186
War and Feuds, 45, 52, 296, 313–4, 319, 403, 411–21
Water, 11, 484
Wealth, 361–2
Weaning, 171, 184, 187
Weapons, 30–1, 35, 521
Weather. See Climate
Weaving, 35
Weddings, 158–63
Week, 38, 96
Widows and Widowers, 138–9, 153, 215, 221–6. See also Funerals, Mourning, Dirges
Wife. See Family structure
Wood, work in, 35–6
Work. See Labor
Work teams. See Production teams
Writing. See Literacy

Yams, 26, 479
Year. See Annual cycle
Youth, 201–8

# AUTHOR INDEX

Aberle, D. F., 474–8, 526
Arensburg, C. M., 503, 512

Bateson, G., 524
Benedict, R., 524
Bidney, D., 525
Bierstedt, R., 491
Blackwood, B., 492

Chapple, E. D., 497, 503
Chinnery, E. W. P., 513
Cohen, A. K., 474–8, 526
Coon, C. S., 497

Davis, A. K., 474–8, 526
Du Bois, C., 502

Evans-Pritchard, E. E., vii, 512

Firth, R., 503
Fortes, M., vii, 497, 504, 509, 511
Fortune, R., 241

Goodenough, W. H., 496, 504, 507, 524
Gorer, G., 487, 527
Greenway, J. C., 494
Guppy, H. B., 492, 512
Gurvitch, G., 523

Hallowell, A. I., 496
Herskovits, M. J., 515
Hoagland, H., 527
Hoebel, E. A., 496, 505, 523
Hogbin, H. I., 506, 515
Hoijer, H., 524
Homans, G., 497, 503, 507, 509, 523
Honigmann, J. J., 524

Inman, R. B., 494

Kluckhohn, C., 507, 524, 527

Kluckhohn, F., 524

Ladd, H. S., 491
Leach, E. R., 503–4, 510–1
Lee, D. D., 494–5, 504, 524
Lévi-Strauss, C., 284, 503–4, 510
Levy, M. J., 474–8, 526
Llewellyn, K. N., 523

Malinowski, B., 482, 494, 504, 523, 526, 527
Mauss, M., 504
Mead, M., 486, 502, 504, 509, 511–2, 524, 527
Merriam, C. E., 523
Miller, W. B., 511
Murdock, G. P., 108–9, 496, 497, 503, 514

Oliver, D. L., 491–2, 496, 503, 506, 511, 516, 525
Opler, M., 524

Parkenson, R., 492
Parsons, T., 474, 526
Pincus, G., 527
Poncelet, Rev. J. B., 492

Radcliffe-Brown, A. R., 523, 525–6
Ribbe, C., 492, 512
Roberts, J. M., 504

Sutton, F. X., 474–8, 526

Thurnwald, R. and H., 492

Warner, W. L., 495, 526
*Webster's Collegiate Dictionary*, 496, 505
Wedgwood, C. H., 506
Wheeler, G. C., 493, 512
Whiting, J. W. M., 502, 527
Whorf, B. L., 493, 524